Hellenistic Sculpture II

PUBLICATION OF THIS VOLUME HAS BEEN MADE POSSIBLE IN
LARGE PART THROUGH THE GENEROUS SUPPORT AND
ENDURING VISION OF WARREN G. MOON.

Hellenistic Sculpture II

The Styles of ca. 200–100 B.C.

Brunilde Sismondo Ridgway

THE UNIVERSITY OF WISCONSIN PRESS

The University of Wisconsin Press
1930 Monroe Street, 3rd Floor
Madison, Wisconsin 53711-2059

3 Henrietta Street
London WC2E 8LU, England

5   4   3   2

Library of Congress has catalogued volume I as follows
Ridgway, Brunilde Sismondo, 1929–
    Hellenistic sculpture I: the styles of ca. 331–200 B.C. /
Brunilde Sismondo Ridgway.
    pp.   cm.—(Wisconsin studies in classics)
    ISBN 0-299-11820-7
    1. Sculpture, Hellenistic.   I. Title.   II. Title: Hellenistic
sculpture I.   III. Title: Hellenistic sculpture one.   IV. Series.
NB94.R535   1989
733.3—dc20   89-40266
    ISBN 0-299-16710-0 (volume II, cloth)
    ISBN 978-0-299-16714-1 (volume II, paper)

To Dr. Paul Bookman,
my dentist

Contents

Plates

Plates

Plates

Plates

Illustrations

Preface

With this book, I have completed the penultimate volume in my survey of Greek sculpture. One last effort shall review the century before Christ, from approximately 100 to 31 B.C., the date of the Battle of Actium, when the last of the Hellenistic monarchies came to an end. I hope to be able to accomplish the task and finish my series.

Hellenistic Sculpture II is entirely the product of my retirement years, yet it was not conceived entirely away from the classroom. As early as the Spring Semester of 1990–1991, I had given a Graduate Seminar on second-century sculpture attended by the following students: Thomas Brogan, Jane Francis, Angeliki Kosmopoulou, Geralyn Lederman, Danielle Newland, and Jamie Terry, of Bryn Mawr College. Two graduate students from the Archaeology program at the University of Pennsylvania—Christofilis Maggidis and Paul Scotton—also attended and actively participated with reports and discussion. Individual contributions have been acknowledged in my pages wherever pertinent, but all members of the seminar should here be thanked for their stimulating input.

My own ideas found more concrete expression in a series of six lectures on the second century, which I was privileged to give as Visiting Professor at the Institute of Classical Archaeology at Aarhus University, Denmark, during the period from October 22 to November 12, 1995. The program was expanded by visits (with all the graduate students) to the Classical Collection of the Ny Carlsberg Glyptotek and the Museum of Casts in Copenhagen. I am most grateful to the faculty of the Aarhus Institute, especially Professors Pia Guldager Bilde and Niels and Lise Hannestad, not only for the invitation itself and for generous and outstanding hospitality, but also for their ideas and fruitful discussions on scholarly topics. At the Ny Carlsberg, Dr. Mette Moltesen greatly added to our "symposion" in both tangible and intangible ways. The excitement generated by these friendly exchanges has continued across the Atlantic, and I now feel a real intellectual link with my Danish colleagues. The students who attended my lectures provided much welcome feedback and made particularly per-

Preface

tinent comments on many occasions. I was especially gratified that Professor Jacob Isager came from the University of Odense to hear my last lecture, on the Sperlonga sculptures and the Laokoon, and gave me the benefit of his opinions on Pliny and on the monuments under discussion.

One more chance to refine my thinking and to sample that of other prominent scholars was given to me by my appointment as Langford Family Eminent Scholar in the Department of Classics at the Florida State University at Tallahassee, for the period January 6–April 25, 1997. As the organizer of the Fourth Langford Conference, I was free to choose a topic within my own interests. I selected "Sperlonga and the Pergamon Altar" and invited papers from (in alphabetical order) Nancy de Grummond, Peter Green, Erich Gruen, Stephan Steingräber, Andrew Stewart, Mary Sturgeon, and Ann Weis. The Conference, held on February 21–22, proved so rewarding and attracted so much discussion from the numerous participants that it was decided to publish the various contributions. The resultant volume, with additions, is at present being published by the University of California Press, and I was able to edit the written versions, thus being able to cite them here in my various chapters. I am most grateful to the Langford Family and to the Florida State University for having given me this unusual opportunity.

Yet this Conference was not the only benefit that accrued from my Florida stage. Two more, and equally important, were the opportunities to give a graduate seminar on topics related to the conference theme and to take a group of graduate students and faculty to Berlin for a direct examination of the sculptures from the Pergamon Altar. This memorable trip took place from March 12 to March 17 and allowed me to study again that spectacular monument, at a remove of almost thirty years from my first visit to the Staatliche Museen. I want to thank here Dr. Huberta Heres, who welcomed us to the Pergamon Museum and allowed us lecturing privileges in front of the displays, and Professor Hans-Friedrich Mueller of FSU, who chaperoned us through the intricacies of the Berlin subway and the city's amenities.

This is also the place to thank the graduate students who attended my Florida seminar: Lara Atkins, Sophia Chaknis, Alexis Christensen, Jillian Curry, Melissa Eaby, Michael Mozina, Stephen Sarles, Sarah Stinson, and Shelley Whiddon in Classics, and Robert Bowman, Christine Morton, and Amy Wright in Art History. I could not have asked for more enthusiastic and friendly students. Also outstanding was the general atmosphere within my host department. Professor Nancy de Grummond has now become a close friend, generous with her positive criticism and ideas, and I feel a great sense of gratitude toward my other colleagues, especially Christopher Pfaff and Daniel Pullen, with whom I have "Greece" in common.

Back at Bryn Mawr, I began writing this book in September 1997, and I finished what I consider a final draft at the beginning of October 1998. I am glad to acknowledge here, first and foremost and most gratefully, the constant and patient help provided by Eileen Markson, Head Librarian for Art and Archaeology at the College,

Preface

and by her various assistants. In the process of writing, I asked for critical advice and received much information from generous friends and scholars. All such debts will be acknowledged throughout my pages, where pertinent, but some deserve special mention. At Bryn Mawr College, Professor Corey Brennan read the historical survey of the first chapter and suggested many useful additions. Chapters 1 through 4 were distributed to the graduate students of Professor Stella Miller-Collett's seminar, for discussion, but the first version of Chapter 2 (on the Pergamon Altar as a whole and the Gigantomachy) had already been seen and critiqued by Professor Andrew Stewart of the University of California at Berkeley, and the section on the Telephos Frieze had been submitted to Dr. Huberta Heres in Berlin for her kind review. Professor Miller-Collett saved me from several errors on the Aemilius Paullus Monument, thanks to her expertise on things Macedonian. I am deeply indebted to all three scholars for their help, although they should not be held responsible for the points in which I have maintained my own theories against theirs. Professor Carol C. Mattusch, of George Mason University, read the section on the bronze herms and the Mahdia wreck in Chapter 7, and those on the Villa of the Papyri and the Hellenistic Ruler in Chapter 9. Professor G. Roger Edwards carefully perused my entire text as it was being written. One final friendly reader, Dr. Pamela Webb, made many helpful and insightful comments throughout. Several scholars answered my queries and gave me advance copies of their or others' writings; here I should single out Carmen Arnold-Biucchi, who helped with numismatic matters and bibliography in connection with Damophon of Messene; Jim McCredie, who sped to me a copy of *Samothrace 1998*; Olga Palagia, who provided me with several offprints, publications, and references; and Brian Rose, who kept me abreast of his campaigns at Troy. To all these individuals go my sincerest thanks.

In a book of this scope, so many monuments are mentioned that it would be impossible to illustrate them all. I have attempted to show some that make specific points and some that are little known, especially those in the United States, although I am sure my readers will regret the omission of many others. I have, however, given references to published illustrations of each sculpture, even when a figure has been included, because different reproductions and viewpoints often permit additional insights. For help in providing photographs, I am deeply indebted to the following: Thomas Brogan, Carol W. Campbell, Maria Conelli, Colette Czapski, Robert Fleischer, Mark Fullerton, David Greenewalt, Kurt Gschwantler, Niels Hannestad, Kim Hartswick, Wolf-Dieter Heilmeyer, Angeliki Kosmopoulou, Sandra Knudsen, Barbara Labate, Ilknur Özgen, Caskun Özgünel, Michael Padgett, Carlos A. Picón, Daniel Pullen, Giovanna-Luisa Ravagnan, Despoina Tsiafakis, and Pamela Webb.

Like my previous books, *Hellenistic Sculpture II* contains its inconsistencies and idiosyncrasies. I still waver in my transliteration of Greek words and geographic names, but I increasingly tend to approximate the spelling of the original language, with results that, in some cases, may seem awkward and distasteful to the general reader. Yet the rationale behind my approach is correct (it avoids the Latinized and then the Anglicized transliteration), and this style is becoming more widely accepted in scholarly writings, including the authoritative *Lexicon Iconographicum Mythologiae Classicae.* It is not meant as an affectation, but simply as a way of determining etymologies and (especially for an Italian native) of avoiding misspellings.

I continue to use A.C. for dates within the current era. When no specification is added, all chronological mentions should be understood as B.C. The word "classical" in lower case refers to the entire Graeco-Roman culture, in upper case, to the fifth and fourth centuries down to 331.

In this volume, I have confined all references to the lengthy Bibliography, except for works I could not consult (in which case, I have added "*non vidi*"), abstracts of papers, occasional field reports, and book reviews unless article-like in length and nature. Using author's name and year of publication emphasizes the chronological sequence in which ideas were expressed, simultaneously clarifying the trends of the times. I have constantly referred to accessible sources of illustrations, especially the handbooks and the *LIMC,* keeping in mind the students who do not have at their disposal the excellent resources of the Art and Archaeology Library at Bryn Mawr College. For the same reason, I have made my endnotes as extensive and explicit as I could, perhaps excessively so. Yet I know that students might not have the leisure to read as widely as I have on any given topic. At the same time, I wanted to provide leads for future research. In many cases, I have used the endnotes to mention additional monuments that could not coherently be included in the main text, or to express personal opinions. To my mind, the endnotes of each chapter carry almost as much weight as the chapter itself. I attach great importance also to the many cross-references among chapters, which should point out to students connections and similarities across topics. Some repetition may seem redundant, but I know that few will read this book from cover to cover.

As already mentioned, I was fortunate to have access to several works in advance of publication. I have announced them as "forthcoming," trying to give as complete a reference as I could. In one case, the book edited by Olga Palagia and William Coulson, *Regional Schools in Hellenistic Sculpture* (Oxbow Monograph 90, 1998), reached me too late for me to take into account the various theories there expressed, although I have cited by title some of the items most obviously related to my topic. Conversely, in several instances I have had to refer to works already discussed in my previous writings, if different dates for them have been proposed. I apologize for the unintentional overlapping, but I also have welcomed the opportunity to update the literature and to revise or clarify my thinking. Scholarship is a continuous process, and theories must be kept flexible, to be changed as new evidence becomes available or greater insight develops. I trust none of my pronouncements will be taken for dogma, but simply as temporary expressions of opinion, to be considered and challenged as the case may be.

Preface

Finally, I must admit that my survey has not produced a clear understanding of second-century sculpture. Although I might have acquired a certain "sense" of whether individual works do or do not belong to that span of time, that sense is based on intangibles and is incapable of proof unless external evidence is available. Despite my efforts to remain objective, I too am influenced by the shadow of the Pergamon Altar, unconsciously using it as a touchstone for other monuments. The complexity of the period, the extent of its geographic reach, and the perpetuation of its formulas into advanced Imperial times render the picture hard to read. It is up to future generations of students to throw a stronger light upon it.

I cannot close without recording my pleasure of having had, once again, Jane Barry as my excellent editor. Adam Mehring at the University of Wisconsin Press provided invaluable help with all the artwork and illustrations. I also gratefully acknowledge the continuous support of my understanding husband and, among the children, the cheerful and ingenious diversions provided by Christopher and the occasional escape to the sea made possible by Conrad's cottage at the New Jersey shore. Such breaks have made my work all the more pleasurable.

Brunilde Sismondo Ridgway

February 12, 1999

Hellenistic Sculpture II

CHAPTER 1

Hellenistic Sculpture in the Second Century B.C.

"Why are we looking at the same things we looked at fifty years ago and coming up with completely different conclusions?" This question was asked by A. E. Samuel at the Symposium on Hellenistic History and Culture held at the University of Texas at Austin on October 20–22, 1988; it was addressed in particular to M. Robertson's paper, "What Is 'Hellenistic' about Hellenistic Art?" and to the response by J. J. Pollitt. Samuel's question was answered by Pollitt in a tentative manner: new evidence coming to light, new attitudes toward works of art and literature, different interests of different generations, may all contribute to the current re-evaluations of what was once thought to be established knowledge.[1] Whatever the reasons behind these revisions, however, the phenomenon is welcome—indeed essential. Yet old theories die hard and are often invested with emotional overtones that make open discussion difficult if not impossible.

Less than a decade ago, it would have been considered foolish to study Hellenistic sculpture by centuries, accepting chronological round figures (200–100) rather than the traditional intermediate dates postulated on the basis of hypothetical shifts in stylistic currents, in their turn tenuously anchored to possibly influential historical events. A typical tripartite division of the Hellenistic phase recognized an early period (The Age of the Diadochoi) ca. 323–275, a middle period (The Age of the Hellenistic Kingdoms) ca. 275–150, and a final one (The Graeco-Roman Phase) ca. 150–31.[2] More significantly, the entire span was generally seen as a time of reaction to the Classical styles, or at least as one of great innovations, partly caused by the influx of Oriental cultures commingling with the Greek. Now, elements of continuity with the past are emphasized instead, as well as stylistic breaks and revivalist trends in the art of the preceding phase, the fourth century; at the same time, actual changes in institutional policies and private practices are noted around 200 and throughout the second century into the first.[3] It is obvious that the general picture is still far from clear, thus justifying our own division in purely chronological terms, from ca. 200 to ca. 100.

At the same time, we must acknowledge that a great deal of effort is being expended at present in trying to clarify that very picture from all sorts of aspects—historical, sociological, artistic, and religious. Congresses, symposia, and exhibitions on different manifestations of Hellenistic art and culture have multiplied in recent years, and the resultant publications offer much food for new thought. Besides the already-mentioned Austin symposium, another was held at the University of California at Berkeley, on "Images and Ideologies: Self-Definition in the Hellenistic World" (April 7–9, 1988), and the entire XIII International Congress for Classical Archaeology, held in Berlin on July 24–30, 1988, was focused on the Hellenistic period. All these papers have since been published.[4] More recently and more narrowly defined, a symposium at the J. Paul Getty Museum in Malibu (April 22–25, 1993) discussed the contribution(s) of Alexandria in Egypt to the period, and a Conference at the American School for Classical Studies at Athens (March 15–17, 1996) was devoted to "Regional Schools in Hellenistic Sculpture."

Although these events also have produced important publications,[5] to some extent they have simply added to the rapidly growing number of books on Hellenistic topics, which are too many to be listed here and will be cited throughout my chapters where appropriate; the University of California Press alone has established an entire series devoted to "Hellenistic Culture and Society," which at the time of writing encompasses approximately 30 volumes. What has, however, created more of an impact on the general consciousness are the exhibitions of Hellenistic objects and monuments, which have attracted hordes of visitors and confirmed that Hellenistic art is worthy of attention. The stigmas of decadence and excess that used to adhere to it are now being removed, as the variety and power of Hellenistic production strike a responsive chord in contemporary viewers. I shall here mention only two such exhibitions whose success I have witnessed personally: "From Alexander to Cleopatra: Greek Art of the Hellenistic Age" (Nov. 20, 1988–Jan. 29, 1989) at the Walters Art Gallery in Baltimore, and "Pergamon: The Telephos Frieze from the Great Altar," which was shown at the Metropolitan Museum of Art in New York (Jan. 16–April 14, 1996) and at the California Palace of the Legion of Honor in San Francisco (May 4–Sept. 8, 1996). The essays accompanying both catalogues, while addressed to the general public, have much to offer to the specialist and the scholar in terms of new theories and insights.[6]

THE HISTORICAL SITUATION

This virtual rehabilitation of Hellenistic art is nonetheless made difficult by several factors, primary among them the complexity of the historical events that took place between 200 and 100 and the consequences we tend to attribute to them. The previous century had seen the establishment of strong monarchies that competed with one other to assert their rule over vast territories. By 200, although such struggles had not abated and boundary lines continued to shift, a certain definition had been achieved and the major Hellenistic centers of power, by our understanding, had consolidated their core areas of control. Yet, approximately a hundred years later, all apparent balance was long lost, to be replaced by the ever-expanding presence of Rome. This drastic rearrangement is bound to have profoundly affected art and culture in all the countries involved. But is this picture true?

To take a simplified time-line across the ancient world at 200: **Athens** had lost its political voice and was a virtual "has-been" on the international scene; Attika was being repeatedly raided by the Macedonians and had to be "rescued" by the Pergamenes.[7] **Sparta** was also weakened and, after King Nabis' clash with Rome in 195, lost its independence and was included in the Achaian League. The balance of power, in Greece, had shifted to the northern areas and to Aitolia, with the **Aitolian League** (which, however, was not without internal dissension), and the efforts of the more central **Achaian League. Macedonia** (which, to some extent, also influenced Greece and parts of Asia Minor) was under one of the last of the Antigonids, Philip V (reigned 221–179), who had just emerged from the so-called First Macedonian War (215–205) and, in his second attempt to join forces with the Seleukid king, was to be defeated by Rome at Kynoskephalai in 197. **Egypt** was ruled by the fifth in a steady line of rulers who took the name of the founder (Ptolemy I Soter, one of the Diadochoi) almost as if an official title equivalent to the Egyptian "Pharaoh." Yet Egypt's power was in decline: a young Ptolemy V Epiphanes (204–180) was enduring native uprising and, in 195, saw his territory curtailed by the loss of Palestine to **Syria,** at that time under the rule of Antiochos III the Great (223–187), one of the major figures in the Seleukid line. Antiochos too, however, was soon to be defeated by Rome in 191–190.

Connected with the Seleukids through marriage, but less powerful and significant —certainly less well known to us—the kings of **Pontus** were represented by Mithradates III (220–185). Equally little is known at this time of the minor kingdoms of **Bithynia** (under Prousias I, ca. 230–182) and **Cappadocia** (under Ariarathes IV Eusebes, ca. 220–162). We do know, however, that both Pontus and Bithynia were shortly to create problems for the last and newest line of Hellenistic monarchs, the Attalids of **Pergamon.** Yet, around 200, the Pergamenes were far more visible, acquiring increasing prominence under Attalos I (241–197, soon to be succeeded by one of his four sons, Eumenes II), and about to enter their period of greatest prosperity. **Rhodes,** "the strongest of the second-rank Hellenistic powers,"[8] was an independent republic, important for its economic and diplomatic role throughout the Mediterranean, and its police work against the pirates, but in 201 it saw its holdings on the Asian coast (the "peraia") threatened by Philip V and was forced to ally itself with Attalos I and to call for Roman help, with the consequences outlined above. The other major island with a Greek contingent, **Sicily,** and specifically Syracuse, which under Hieron II (269–215) had enjoyed a Hellenistic splendor comparable to that of the great monarchies, by 210 was wholly part of the Roman Republic (the western part of the island had been a Roman province since 241), and thus unable to play a role in the struggles within the Mediterranean basin. The Greek colonies of **South Italy,** especially Taras, had long since come under Rome's sway. **Rome** itself had just emerged from the Second Punic War (218–201), and its presence had not yet been threateningly felt in the Aegean area.[9]

By approximately 100 the picture is entirely changed. The line of the **Attalids** had ended in 133, with the last ruler (Attalos III, 138–133) bequeathing his kingdom to Rome; a revolt by a presumed Attalid (the illegitimate son of Eumenes II?), Aristonikos, had brought about a massive Roman intervention and ended in failure. The Romans then organized "Asia" (i.e., western Asia Minor) as a province in the years 129–126. **Egypt** was in a state of internal unrest, with two contending brothers, Ptolemy IX and X, taking turns on the throne while trying to retain their hold on Cyprus. **Macedonia,** under her last king, Perseus, had been defeated by Rome in 168, divided into four districts, and, after the revolt of another alleged royal son, the adventurer Andriskos (149/8), reduced to a Roman province (146); these events spelled also the end of the **Aitolian League.** **Syria,** too, was at the virtual end of the steady Seleukid line, with Antiochos VIII Grypos (126–96) struggling against his half-brother, who in turn could not cope with the dynastic quarrels among Antiochos' five sons. **Corinth,** as well as the power of the **Achaian League,** had been destroyed by L. Mummius in 146, the same year that saw the end of the Third Punic War with the equally thorough destruction of **Carthage. Rhodes** had lost some of its economic dealings to **Delos,** which in 166 had passed under Athenian control and, with Roman support, had been granted free-port status. Although **Cappadocia** (Ariarathes IX, ca. 100–88) and **Bithynia** (Nikomedes III, ca. 127–94) were still ruled by their own line of monarchs, only the **Pontic kingdom** was gathering strength in the face of Roman expansion, which Mithradates VI Eupator (120–63) would challenge, ultimately unsuccessfully. Finally, even the fight against the pirates was taken up by Rome, through the new province of Cilicia set up by the Senate in 101 specifically for that purpose.[10] The Mediterranean, which around 200 was basically under Hellenistic-Greek control, by ca. 100 could already be considered a Roman pond.

Yet, paradoxically, this century of upheavals and monarchical struggles carried out under the pervasive and expanding shadow of Roman power is not reflected in the economic strength and the healthy civic life of the individual cities during the second century. Scholars who tend to attribute excessive importance to specific wars and diplomatic intrigues lose sight of the many positive signs that occur at the level of the masses, or rather of the bourgeois citizens away from the splendors of the royal courts. The various Hellenistic monarchies, under renewed scholarly scrutiny, are now increasingly seen as encapsulated nuclei of power that left largely undisturbed the bureaucratic structures of the conquered territories. Even Rome, which had seemed interested in annexing Greece, had surprised the assembled visitors at the Isthmian Games of 196 (after Kynoskephalai) by having T. Quinctius Flamininus announce dramatically that the Senate was restoring to the Greeks "eleutheria, auto-nomia, demokratia," the same terms traditionally used by Hellenistic rulers.[11] And the *poleis*, once presumed dead or at least insignificant in terms of civic autonomy, appear to have been far more alive and active in a variety of ways. Gymnasia and theaters—the great civic institutions—were built or renovated in many of them, and in Athens the philosophical schools were thriving.

The case of Egypt is typical, especially for the second and first centuries, quite dif-ferent from the third. Upper (i.e., southern) Egypt was never fully part of the Ptole-maic empire and often revolted. The Battle of Raphia (217, against the Seleukids) had seen the integration of natives into the Greek army, and when the influx of Greek troops (and future veterans) into Egypt was no longer needed and stopped, the villages (nomes) increased their autonomy, or rather paid tribute to their immediate land-owners, the temples, and not to the court, in a religious/administrative dependence that ended only (much later) under the Romans.[12] The Greeks preferred mostly to live in cities, where they continued to produce art of high quality, regardless of the mon-archs' problems. And this state of affairs is also true of the cities of Asia Minor and the islands, even less disrupted by the presence of alien populations except as immigrant merchants and artisans, and where increased emphasis was put on the benefactions by citizens, who were correspondingly honored with official statues or grave monu-ments.

To be sure, the Hellenistic monarchs continued to make donations to cities and sanctuaries, but the emphasis seems to have shifted—from a desire to ensure political loyalty through gifts reminding recipients of their military might to a sort of com-petition to beautify the cities through actual structures.[13] In this field, the Attalids may have made the greatest contribution in terms of personal propaganda and with respect to their own city as well as Athens, Delphi, and Delos—indeed, the second century can be considered the Hellenistic period of greatest building activity. But the cities themselves competed in terms of individual monuments. It could, in fact, be said that the most distinctive manifestation of the Hellenistic period is the honorary statue; yet many were in bronze and are now known only through their empty bases. Others, of marble, have survived in fragments, often divorced from their pedestals and identifying inscriptions, although many more went to feed the lime kilns. Even when complete images remain, their quality is not outstanding and their iconography is formulaic, based on a few stock types. It is difficult to judge Hellenistic sculpture from this evidence, although an attempt at a survey will be made in a later chapter.

STYLISTIC EVIDENCE: FIXED POINTS

The long-held theory of a linear, regular development of sculptural style has already been exploded with regard to the fourth century, and even more for the Hellenistic period, when increased skill in all techniques allowed for a variety of forms expressed in correspondingly varied styles, including retrospective ones. Baroque, which used to be considered a typical manifestation of the second century, is now acknowledged to have started as early as the late fourth, whereas "Classicizing," which was formerly seen as the deliberate revival of a "dead" style brought back toward the end of our span as the nostalgic evocation of a golden age, is now recognized as a continuously available stylistic option.[14] Yet the resultant mixture makes it even harder than usual to date works on stylistic grounds, especially when such works are only known through Roman replicas and simply correspond to our approximate understanding of what Hellenistic sculpture should look like.

To overcome this impasse, scholars have tried to establish a series of fixed points —monuments for which firm dates can be claimed—thereby hoping to derive from them some firm criteria on which to evaluate Hellenistic sculptural styles. Yet the danger of this method is that often the monuments selected have been assigned a date on the basis of their presumed relationship to historical events, once again forcing the external warp and weft of wars and kings to provide the fabric on which the art is embroidered.[15]

To be sure, some works of sculpture commemorate historical events, as attested by inscriptions; but even such cases are not always clear-cut, and they are, at any rate, very few and far apart. Gaps have been filled with assumptions that are often presented as facts—the dating of the Nike of Samothrake being a typical example, as will be discussed in a future chapter—with the result that no two scholars' lists of presumed fixed points coincide. To mention only the opinions of two influential writers in the field of Hellenistic art, Pollitt (1986, 267–68) is a minimalist, with only 10 entries for the entire second century, several of them cautiously qualified, whereas Andreae (1989, 241–42) is more expansive, with 28 entries for the same span of time, some of them comprising multiple groups attributed largely on stylistic grounds. Yet, on a rigorous check, only five of Andreae's selections seem certain; another seven are probable but of debatable date, three are uncertain, and as many as 13 are unprovable or uncertainly identified in Roman copies (e.g., the Antisthenes and the Asklepios by Phyromachos).

There is no point, in this chapter, in debating specific dates and attributions. I shall discuss each monument per se, according to my various categories, and eventually will provide my own list, but simply in terms of probability rather than certainty, and concentrating on Greek originals rather than Roman copies, or—to be precise—works sculptured during the time of Roman political supremacy, which basically means the Roman Imperial period. Such works can occasionally provide valuable information on lost Greek originals, but a growing awareness of the endless variations possible in creating sculpture only vaguely inspired by Greek prototypes has made us properly cautious in accepting "Hellenistic" style at face value.[16] Yet something even more revolutionary has now penetrated our stylistic consciousness.

Firmly basing her observations on technical evidence and procedures, Carol Mattusch has recently alerted us to the fact that each ancient bronze statue, while having the potential of being a unique creation, was also probably cast from one or more master models, with minor adaptations demanded by subject, circumstances, and a desire for apparent differentiation. The basic model could, and often was, extensively altered by artistic touches provided only on the wax layer, which, by being melted away during the casting process, caused the permanent loss of the "original." Yet the fact that a master model was used ensured a basic repetition of forms that need not be substantially modified. The Riace Warriors, so similar that they are traditionally grouped together, yet so dissimilar that a 30-year interval is occasionally advocated between them, may exemplify the issue. The entire concept of original versus copy—with all its implications of creativity versus uninspired repetition—is thus demolished at one stroke. Any such assessment is made more precarious by the recognition that Classical works, through the taking of molds from a finished product, could be recast in later times, either exactly or approximately, with variations introduced solely in "external" details, such as a new head or different attributes. In such cases, stylistic analysis of what has survived (often in fragments) is therefore irrelevant and even positively misleading.[17]

Despite this new awareness, the issue of "copies" will not go away—witness the still-heated debate on the epic groups from the Sperlonga grotto in Italy, which some would take back to specific second-century prototypes whereas others affirm ad hoc creation only vaguely inspired by Hellenistic precedents, perhaps in the two-dimensional arts. This topic too will be discussed under its appropriate rubric. Here I shall only mention the new attention being paid to the problem of replication and copying, to which a symposium, a session, and a seminar, to name just three events under American sponsorship, were dedicated in recent years. The symposium was held in 1985 at the National Gallery in Washington, D.C.; the session was part of the annual College Art Association meetings in 1988; and the seminar—this last concentrating on ancient art—was financed by the National Endowment for the Humanities and took place at the American Academy in Rome in 1994. As one of the participants in the Washington symposium commented, "Something, clearly, is in the wind."[18]

It is perhaps significant that this conceptual problem should concern the art historians of later periods, with their relatively abundant documentation, as well as the art historians of ancient art, with their virtually non-existent hard evidence. In this context, I shall only stress that students of Hellenistic sculpture should take into account this more discriminating approach in using such otherwise valuable books as Bieber (1961) and, to some extent, even more recent publications such as Smith (1991) and Moreno (1994).

ANCIENT SOURCES, MASTERS, SCHOOLS
Traditional wisdom on the use of copies to visualize lost Classical masterpieces held that the *opera nobilia* of the past would never have been allowed to die, and that it was only our lack of diligence in investigating their reproductions which prevented us

from recovering them. Yet even this belief was primarily concerned with the oeuvres of the great Classical masters, whose names had been handed down to us by literary sources.[19] This seems not to be the case for the Hellenistic period. Although many names of Hellenistic sculptors have survived, either through mention in Pliny and other literary sources or through actual inscriptions, very few of them have attracted attention, either in antiquity or in the present. We therefore have the impression that the entire Hellenistic phase is devoid of major artistic personalities—just at the time when sculptors' status may seem to have changed, after a fourth century that gave us not only the major triad of Praxiteles, Skopas, and Lysippos, but also anecdotes about them that invested them with a personality beyond their actual works.

It is well to realize that such anecdotes are probably later fabrications; nonetheless, the very fact that they could be fabricated implies a consciousness of the artist as a unique individual worth speculating about. Since silence appears to surround Hellenistic masters, it would be easy to draw the conclusion that none of them had sufficient skills to be glorified. Yet this is certainly not the case, as witnessed by some of the *original* monuments that have come down to us. We shall later discuss as many such known masters as possible; here, however, we should investigate what has promoted this state of affairs.

Perhaps primary responsibility falls on the literary sources, foremost among them Pliny's *Natural History*, on which we have come to rely so heavily in our assessment of Greek art. With a peculiar expression, the Roman writer asserts (*NH* 34.52) that during the 121st Olympiad (therefore ca. 296–293) art ended (the famous saying: *cessauit deinde ars*), to revive (*ac rursus reuixit*) only during the 156th Olympiad (ca. 156–153), approximately a century and a half later. This pronouncement is eventually followed (*NH* 34.85–90) by a list of names of Hellenistic artists who are distinguished by their limited ability (*aequalitate celebrati artifices, sed nullis operum suorum praecipui*) and of masters who worked within set categories (*eos qui eiusdem generis opera fecerunt*), such as statues of athletes or philosophers. But very few of their creations are actually described by more than two or three words, and are thus almost impossible to visualize, let alone recognize among extant sculptures.

What Pliny meant by his famous statement is a vexed question that has found different answers.[20] One could assume that Pliny simply did not like Hellenistic style and was therefore dismissive of its practitioners. Some scholars have suggested accordingly that the "revival of art" coincided with the advent of the Classicizing style, which used to be dated to the Late Hellenistic phase. As mentioned above, however, we now know that Classicizing trends occur much earlier, thus invalidating the suggestion. We also acknowledge that Pliny seems to have liked Hellenistic sculpture well enough,[21] if he could declare the Laokoon superior to all other works of (bronze?) sculpture and painting (*NH* 36.37); whatever the actual carving date of that complex group and whether its status is that of a Roman creation, adaptation, or outright copy, there is no question that its formal language is Hellenistic and indeed typical of the period during which, for Pliny, art had ended.

Hellenistic Sculpture in the Second Century B.C.

This apparent contradiction can be explained if we assume that Pliny's statement applies only to the art of bronze statuary and not to the totality of sculpture, specifically that in marble.[22] But even this solution is not supported by Pliny's positive references (*NH* 34.84) to undoubted bronze works made to commemorate Attalid victories, which therefore fall within the period of alleged artistic penury. To counter that Pliny here used another source, and that his first one, Xenokrates (a third-century artist and writer), had stopped at Lysippos, thus prompting Pliny to stop his own account, would still not explain the drastic assertion that not information but art itself had ceased.[23]

A solution has now been proposed that would satisfy all objections. Ancient theories on the development of art were clearly patterned after similar theories on rhetoric, which in turn were dependent on historical events. The time of Alexander and the Diadochoi was seen as a period of stability, during which rhetoric and art could flourish. When such political freedom ended, so did rhetoric, and therefore so did art, to revive only when Rome began to take over the Greek states, thus creating a fairly stable international climate and sparking a revival of artistic production through the opening of a vast new market.[24] This is obviously an artificial construct that need not reflect actual situations, as shown by the truly important monuments, such as the Pergamon Altar, that were created during the period of supposed stagnation. Yet the theoretical principles that informed the ancient views of events have percolated into our own times, sponsoring a similar, unverified, connection between historical and artistic manifestations.

If, however, even for Pliny, art "revived" approximately mid-way through our selected span of time, why are we not better informed about artists from ca. 150 onward? The answer may lie in another peculiar Roman viewpoint that values the monument for what it commemorates—not because of its maker, but rather because of its sponsor. Most Roman sculpture is in fact anonymous, including the historical reliefs that, however, play such an important role in communicating the Emperor's messages. Should this be the case, even in retrospect, Pliny's silence or diminished attention to masters may be explained by the change in monarchic policies outlined above. One scholar goes so far as to suggest that no monument, during the second century, was set up to commemorate a specific military achievement in the "old-fashioned" way.[25] What this phenomenon means for us, however, is to underscore the excessive reliance we place on the Roman sources, since our knowledge of the Classical masters depends almost entirely on them, not on greater availability of monumental or epigraphic evidence.

The scholarly answer to this state of affairs, in modern times, had been to concentrate not on masters but on regional schools, in the belief that certain artistic trends were specific to certain areas: thus, illusionism, sfumato techniques, and genre topics were considered characteristics of the Alexandrian school, Baroque was earmarked for Pergamon, Rococo for Rhodes, Classicizing for Athens and the Attic school on Delos. A typical example of this approach is a book by Dickins (1920), influential in its time, when relatively little was written on Hellenistic sculpture, although many of the monuments there listed under each region were not found in their alleged place of origin and were mostly known through Roman copies. A more discriminating but still comparable division was followed by Bieber (1961). Yet more recent studies have started to challenge these theoretical positions: first Isager (1995) and now Pollitt (forthcoming) have questioned the existence of a Rhodian school; Stewart (1996b) has done the same for the Alexandrian style, isolating themes of interest (such as symbolism and allegory) rather than formal trends. Even Attic Classicizing is being redefined chronologically and ideologically.[26]

THE PURPOSE OF THIS BOOK: PITFALLS AND METHODOLOGY

Given the situation described above, a book on the styles of ca. 200–100 would seem not simply impossible but even dangerous, producing apparent answers when none could or should be given. Yet, as for the previous century, specific monuments existed, and they can be examined and discussed, at least in terms of their eligibility for a second-century dating. If no stylistic "development" will be revealed by the process, at least some traditional attributions hitherto taken for granted will be exposed for all their pitfalls and uncertainty while others will be confirmed and taken at their own face value. I had followed this same procedure in my earlier book on Hellenistic sculpture (Ridgway 1990), analyzing in order to exclude from the third century works that had been so dated but seemed instead to belong to later times. If some of these sculptures fall within the second century, they shall be revisited here, but mostly to refer to my earlier treatment, simply updating present information and bibliography on them.

In dealing with second-century monuments, I shall not follow a strictly chronological order but will discuss Hellenistic originals by types and broad categories, roughly proceeding from the more to the less securely dated. Architectural sculpture, because of its connection with buildings that may provide additional evidence, will be treated first, but I shall begin with an unusual structure, the so-called Pergamon Altar, because of the enormous impact it has had on our conception of Hellenistic styles. In general, I shall deal with statuary known solely through works of the Roman period only when these have been deemed of fundamental importance in reconstructing alleged prototypes, but I want to state at once my basic distrust of this type of evidence. My bias may force me into minimalist positions of excessive skepticism, but I prefer risking this criticism to the dangers of perpetuating phantoms with no reliable substance in the Greek past. Even with strict adherence to original material, whether securely found in pre-Roman stratified contexts or attested by Hellenistic epigraphic, literary, and numismatic sources, the pitfalls are numerous. Some have already been mentioned; a few more can be cited here.

We are aware, for instance, that a certain amount of repairs and reworking took place at different times, so that monuments, although untouched by Renaissance or modern restorers, may no longer preserve their original appearance even as they come out of the ground. An inscription from Delphi tells us that Eumenes II sent money and men to the sanctuary to repair the theater, dedications, and furniture, as needed. The Attalids also sent masters to copy paintings and masterpieces, so that we might not be sure, in stylistic terms, whether we are looking at a Hellenistic original creation with Classicizing traits or at a copy of a Classical work betraying its Hellenistic date of carving—the replica of the Pheidian Athena Parthenos at Pergamon will stand as the typical example. In addition, we are familiar with the Greek practice of refurbishing earlier monuments to rededicate them when the occasion demanded—as best epitomized by the so-called Monument of Agrippa in Athens, which was previously a Pergamene chariot-group.[27]

Booty and homonymy present additional problems: a series of bases found in Pergamon carries the inscribed names of famous sculptors—Myron, Praxiteles, and others —and may have supported sculptures by the Classical masters "collected" by the kings of Pergamon. Yet a mid-second-century Myron is known to have existed, and a late fourth/early third-century inscription from Olympia attests to another. In one family of sculptors the names Polykles and Timarchides alternated for several generations, and the Greek tradition of naming a son after one's own father ensured that such repetitions were common. On the basis of our scant evidence, it is often impossible to tell which master is involved, from what generation.[28]

Evidence from Hellenistic coins may also prove misleading. It has been suggested that images of poets began to appear on coins only after 150, yet undoubtedly some of the statues they depict were erected earlier. This numismatic phenomenon is perhaps revealing from a sociological point of view, yet it does not help our sculptural reconstructions. Epigrams and poetry occasionally describe objects so vividly that the writer seems to have been standing in front of his subject; yet often nothing tells us whether the description refers to a large-scale statue or to a small terracotta or metal figurine. We should also constantly remember that poetry and literature have their own validity, without necessarily finding a correspondent in real life—an author can use his imagination more readily than his physical eyes.[29]

In recent years, a new technique—underwater archaeology—has offered the promise of more precise chronology, or at least clearer *termini ante quos*, as the contents of wrecks are being excavated rather than just salvaged, with all the concomitant information (type of ship, furnishings, cooking pottery, etc.) that such a procedure can recover. One of the most influential events of this last decade has been the reassessment (as well as the restoration and re-examination) of all the materials from the Mahdia shipwreck—not just the sculpture alone, or just some of the finds, as previous publications had done. The resulting two volumes (Hellenkemper Salies et al. 1994) have had a major impact on our thinking about Greek and Roman art, the creation of Neo-Attic and Classicizing works, even the subject matter preferred at certain times. Yet the problem with a shipwreck, even under the best of circumstances, is that its cargo can contain contemporary works as well as heirlooms, objects picked up at random for ballast as well as selectively looted from sanctuaries or dilapidated buildings—in brief a congeries of pieces unrelated in time and provenience that forces archaeologists to fall back on our dangerous stylistic analysis.[30]

Bibliography in recent years, as already stated, has expanded enormously, and not even computer systems like Dyabola can keep pace with the most recent publications. I want to make special mention, nonetheless, of the helpful compilations devoted exclusively to Hellenistic sculpture by Mary-Anne Zagdoun (1988, 1991, 1995), which include short summaries and comments. In writing my own chapters, I shall take all new information, as much as possible, into consideration, and I shall also rely heavily, for general accounts and illustrations, on four basic works: Pollitt 1986, Stewart 1990, Smith 1991, and Moreno 1994. The slant of the discussion and the burden of final opinion, however, will be my own.

NOTES

1. See Robertson 1993, Pollitt 1993, and following discussion in Green 1993, 103–105. Pollitt's answer to Samuel states: "I doubt that this question is really answerable in a rigorous way." See also the more extensive reply by P. Green in his "Introduction" to the volume, pp. 1–11.

Equally important is the point, albeit not raised by the speakers at the Austin symposium, that wide-ranging surveys of Greek art (whether of the entire span or limited to the Hellenistic period) tend to repeat the accepted viewpoints, whereas specific questions in a more critical context make their authors admit to different answers: note both Robertson's and Pollitt's statements in the same volume.

2. I am giving here the schema promoted by Pollitt 1986, because his book has been so influential in scholarly circles; other divisions are possible and are mentioned in Ridgway 1990, 3–6. Add Moreno 1994, who uses Classical Manner (323–301), Hellenistic Baroque (301–168), and Roman Restoration (164–31). Ridgway 1990, 10–11, offers a justification for a survey by centuries

3. For continuity with the Classical past, see Robertson 1993 and Pollitt 1993. Note also M. M. Austin's review of *CAH*[2], vol. 7 (*The Hellenistic World*) in *JHS* 107 (1987) 229–30. For revivalist styles in the 4th c., see Ridgway 1997b, 366 and passim. A break in style around 380, which introduces many Hellenistic elements, is advocated for the votive terracottas from Akrokorinthos by G. S. Merker in her forthcoming catalogue. Overlapping and continuity in pottery are noted by Edwards 1975, 2 and n. 4. Changes around 200: several essays in Wörrle and Zanker 1995, esp. Gauthier; cf. the review of the volume, by G. L. Reger, *AJA* 101 (1997) 418–19. See also Webb 1996, 4–5.

4. Austin symposium: Green 1993; Berkeley symposium: Bulloch et al., 1993; Berlin congress: *Akten XIII*, 1990, and the related publication on Hermogenes: Hoepfner and Schwandner 1990.

5. Alexandria symposium: Hamma 1996; American School in Athens symposium: Palagia and Coulson 1998. Note also Wörrle and Zanker 1995, after a colloquium in Munich, June 24–

26, 1993. I am not citing here gatherings and publications that discussed primarily philosophical or historical issues.

6. Baltimore exhibition: Reeder 1988. Telephos Frieze: *Pergamon 1*, 1996, and *Pergamon 2*, 1997; this exhibition traveled also in Europe, and the essays accompanying the catalogue have been translated into other languages.

7. For Athens during the 2nd c., see Habicht 1997, chs. 8–12, pp. 194–296 (esp. pp. 287–96 for "conditions at home" by the end of that timespan).

8. This statement is made by Berthold 1984, 80; although it occurs in the context of Rhodes' political position after 304, it also applies to the time around 200, considered the island's "period of greatest prosperity and power" (p. 101). For the vicissitudes of the island's navy, see also Gabrielsen 1997.

9. To be sure, the first known official contacts between Rome and a Greek state date back to 306, when trade discussions were held with Rhodes (Berthold 1984, 80). But in terms of a presence that could influence artistic modes, we have to wait until the 2nd c. As previously stated (Ridgway 1990, 373), "the third century would therefore appear as the last truly Greek time." For Roman "philhellenism" and the contrasting official policy, see Gruen 1984, 250–72.

10. For the purpose of establishing Cilicia, see Crawford 1996, 231–70, no. 12 (*Lex de provinciis praetoriis*), esp. 239, Knidos copy, col. III, lines 28–37 (with Latin trans. on p. 249, and English trans. on p. 254). For the date, see p. 236. For this reference and much historical help, I am deeply indebted to T. C. Brennan.

11. Cf. Gruen 1984, 132–57, esp. 145–46 for Roman intentions.

12. Many of my comments on 2nd–1st c. Egypt are derived from a lecture delivered by J. G. Manning at Bryn Mawr College on February 3, 1995 ("Ptolemies, Peasants, and Local Power in Hellenistic Egypt"). See also Samuel 1993, 174–80; and Robertson 1993, 73: "Alexandria [was] a political and cultural enclave in a virtually unchanged country." In this respect, note our general reassessment of the minimal influence of non-Greek art on the development of Hellenistic forms, in contrast to previously held assumptions. Particularly significant, although focusing on architecture, are the comments by L. Bongrani in her review of P. Pensabene, *Elementi architettonici di Alessandria e di altri siti egiziani* (Repertorio d'arte dell'Egitto greco-romano, Ser. C, vol. 3, Rome 1993), in *BollArch* 19–21 (1993) 277–80, esp. 279–80.

13. See, e.g., Gauthier 1985, Schaaf 1992, Umholtz 1994, Bringmann and von Steuben 1995, and, more synthetically, Bringmann 1995, esp. 94–95. This last author attributes the shift in approach to the increasing supremacy of Rome, which made wars among rulers virtually obsolete as a theme of dynastic fame and allowed only for civic benefactions (the financing and dedications of non-religious buildings and of festivals) to count toward their reputation (cf. also p. 97, for a statement on the reasons for kings' benefactions). Bringmann focuses on cities rather than sanctuaries, for which other considerations may apply. The phenomenon of sponsored construction appears to cease after ca. 150–140.

14. For a defense of this position, see Ridgway 1990 and 1997b; Robertson 1993; Smith 1991, 17–18. In a brilliant public lecture delivered at Bryn Mawr College on April 20, 1994 ("Dates versus Chronology: Style and Periodization in Hellenistic Sculpture"), M. D. Fullerton made a similar point with respect not only to the Hellenistic period but also to all previous phases of Greek sculpture. Given the availability of all trends (Baroque, realistic, Classicizing, etc.) at any given time, he then argued that even the establishment of absolute dates for certain datable

monuments (the so-called fixed points, on which see infra) served only to date those monuments alone, not others existing at the same time, and could therefore not produce a stylistic chronology. I am indebted to Prof. Fullerton, who made the text of his lecture available to me before publication.

15. A typical example of this procedure, despite a lengthy discussion of various methodological approaches, is Moreno 1994. Cf. p. 9: "A questo punto [after all philological, sociological, and artistic considerations] si è cercato di ridisporre gli oggetti entro la griglia dei luoghi e del tempo, scandita da alcune aree di produzione o centri meglio attestati [examples] e da episodi salienti [battles]; ovvero da avvenimenti di portata locale [more battles, earthquakes, and kings]." Although the Italian scholar obviously plans an objective treatment of each monument, he seems definitely influenced by his belief that important events result in important artistic manifestations; he thus even suggests (p. 250) that the Amazonomachy of the Artemision at Magnesia is "among the first figural complexes commemorating the Roman and Pergamene victory over Antiochos the Great of Syria" in 190/89. This monument will be discussed infra in ch. 2, but the quotation is here introduced to illustrate Moreno's method. For more extensive comments, see my review of Moreno's book, *AJA* 100 (1996) 426–27.

Note also that Robertson 1993, 85, urges us "to remind ourselves how artificial and distorting our division of art into periods is. We can only study art through the imposition of such a framework, but art when it's happening isn't really like that. Conquest or revolution has a violent and immediate effect on everyday living . . . but its effect on art is much less calculable."

16. On this point, see the judicious comments by Smith 1991, 14–17; other important statements by Fullerton 1997.

17. Mattusch 1996, 37; see esp. 62–67 on the Riace Warriors (dated 5th c.); and 206–16 on the torso from Vani (Georgia), from a 2nd- or 1st-c. context but in early 5th-c. style. Her book is reviewed and intelligently critiqued, against a wider theoretical background, by Hurwit 1997, 589–90.

Conclusions similar to Mattusch's have been reached on specific bronzes outside the English-speaking world: cf. Moser von Filseck 1990, and, more tentatively, Gogräfe 1996. I continue to believe that the Riace Warriors may be much later than the 5th c. (1st c.?), and Mattusch's insights on reproduction may actually confirm my opinion.

18. The quotation is from Rosalind E. Krauss' introduction to the published papers of the Washington symposium: *Retaining the Original* (1989) 7. The publication of the papers from the NEH seminar, "The Roman Art of Emulation," edited by E. Gazda and A. Haeckl, is forthcoming. On the issue of copies, see also infra, Ch. 8 with additional refs.

19. This sentiment is expressed by Dörig 1977, ix, and reads, in its entirety: "the conviction that neither avarice nor neglect have the power wholly to obliterate the masterpieces of the past, and that we ourselves are to blame for not perceiving them through the forms in which they still continue to exist among us." Although I can agree in part with this position, I fear that it is also responsible for our looking at every piece of sculpture solely as an implicit reflection of a Greek prototype, thus denying it any originality of its own. Equally dangerous is the concept of "masterpiece," based on our modern understanding of artistic genius rather than on the factors that may have made a work important for the ancient viewers.

20. I briefly touched on this issue in Ridgway 1990, 4. I bring up the subject again because a plausible solution to the riddle has been found. See infra, n. 24.

21. To be sure, our second major source on ancient art, Pausanias, omits Hellenistic monuments almost entirely from his account of Greece—because of his own antiquarian interests, however, not because of a dislike for them. On Pausanias' approach to the art and architecture of his times, see Arafat 1996, 36–42.

22. This solution is advocated in an important book on Pliny: Isager 1991, 98; cf. his n. 324 for references to others' opinions, including supporters of Pliny's negative reaction to non-Classical styles.

23. This second solution seems implicitly accepted by Isager 1991, 102, who notes the contradiction of the Attalid monuments. For an account of various opinions on the subject, see also Pollitt 1974, 26–28, with bibl. in n. 40 on p. 95.

24. Expressed so synthetically, the argument may not seem too convincing, especially in view of the very relative freedom and stability we might think existed under the Diadochoi. Yet when the argument is developed in full, on theoretical grounds, the equation applies. This important theory is properly formulated by Donohue 1995, 341–44, who points out a clear analogy in Winckelmann's own thinking and his conception of liberty; see also her more concise statement in her review of Isager 1995, in *Bryn Mawr Classical Review* 3.3 (1992) 192–97, esp. 195. Donohue's article is significant not only for her illumination of the ancient sources, but also for the light she throws on modern art histories that have, consciously or unconsciously, been influenced by the classical writers.

25. Bringmann 1995, 95; he suggests that the Pergamon Altar and the Smaller Attalid Dedications (which he attributes to the sponsorship of Attalos II) are exceptions in that they reflect the spirit of the previous century. Other explanations could be given for these monuments, as I shall discuss in a later chapter.

26. Rhodian attributions had already been undermined by Merker 1973, and the ethnicity of the sculptors by Goodlett 1991. Pollitt (forthcoming) revises somewhat the position he took in his 1986 book (pp. 113–18). By contrast, Moreno 1994, 127–46, 359–413, 605–46, is a firm supporter of a Rhodian school. Stewart 1996b and Isager 1995 provide a review of the literature that led to the modern belief in the respective regional schools. Attic redefinition: Themelis 1996; Fullerton 1998a. For comments on the illusory existence of regional schools, see also Smith 1991, 17. By contrast, the 1996 congress held in Athens seems, judging by its theme, to have implicitly accepted the existence of geographic distinctions, although individual papers reach opposite conclusions.

27. Delphic inscription: Pouilloux 1960, 51–63, esp. 57; Bringmann and von Steuben 1995, 148–51, cat. 93 [E1–E2], dated 160/59. On ancient repairs and recuttings, see, e.g., Hannestad 1994, 13–14 with bibl. in ns. 1–6, although his main emphasis is on Roman monuments.

On Attalid copying, see Hansen 1971, 367–68 and n. 392 with refs. The copying of paintings is attested by inscriptional evidence; that of sculptures is less definite, since some of the statues originally thought to be copies are now better seen as Classicizing creations; they will be discussed in a later chapter. Yet the intent to reproduce the Athena Parthenos, even if in a modernized version, is undoubted. Cf. Hansen 1971, 353–56.

Rededication of earlier monuments: Blanck 1969. Monument of Agrippa: Travlos 1971, fig. 622 on p. 493, and bibl. on p. 483; the chariot of Eumenes II, erected in 178, was replaced by the chariot of Agrippa.

28. Pergamon inscribed bases: *IvP* nos. 135–44; cf. Hansen 1971, 317; Pollitt 1986, 166–67

and n. 13 on p. 311; Stewart 1990, 63 and bibl. (for ch. 5) on p. 338 . On later Myrones, see also Ridgway 1990, 347 n. 37 with various references. For a possible stemma of Polykles and Timarchides, see Pollitt 1986, 313 n. 12; cf. Stewart 1990, 304–305, and esp. infra, Ch. 7. See also the discussion of various sculptors named Skopas, in Ridgway 1997b, 251–53, and cf. Mielsch 1995.

29. Coins: cf. Schefold 1997, 68–69, who seems to attribute the occurrence of poets' images on coins to the Romans' control of the Mediterranean. On the fictional element in poetry, see his pp. 455–56, where the invention in the epigrams is compared to the invention in the portraits of men who lived centuries earlier. On a slightly different level, to cite just one example of many, see the comments by Levi 1993 about Theokritos' poems, esp. 116 and n. 20, and the remarks by D. M. Halperin in Green 1993, 131, and (in discussion)133.

30. Hellenkemper Salies et al. 1994: see my review (Ridgway 1995b) with additional bibl. on discoveries made after the exhibition volumes had been published (and cf. Hellenkemper Salies 1996). On the *terminus post quem* that the cargo of the Mahdia wreck seems to provide for epic sculpture, see Himmelmann 1994, but note my cautionary comments (1995b, pp. 346–47).

The Shadow of the Pergamon Altar

The so-called Pergamon Altar[1] is not only arguably the most important structure extant from the second century; it has also become for us the defining monument of the entire Hellenistic period. Virtually the best-preserved and largest complex of both Hellenistic sculpture and architecture, from the moment of its discovery[2] it was hailed as the representative of a new and powerful stylistic trend, the so-called Baroque, and thus comparable only to the Athenian Parthenon, in turn thought to have marked the inception of the true Classical style. Both buildings soon came to function as the touchstones against which every other artistic manifestation was tested and, to use another metaphor, entire chronologies were built on their watersheds—any undated piece of sculpture that came to light thereafter was classified as either earlier or later than the Parthenon, before or after the Pergamon Altar, with the consequence that the true nature of both the fourth and the third centuries was left in a somewhat nebulous state, as if in limbo, and the production of the rest of the Hellenistic period was seen either as imitation of or as reaction to the Pergamene style. There is no denying the vast significance of both Parthenon and Altar, and the impact they must have had on their own times; yet their enormous shadow has colored our understanding of ancient sculpture and iconography beyond all reasonable limits, influencing our approach to the art of all other areas and times. We need not discuss the Parthenon in this context,[3] but we should keep it in mind in reviewing the evidence on the Pergamon Altar, especially given the intentional connection between the two.

The Pergamon monument was until recently considered one of the most reliable fixed points in Hellenistic chronology. The subjects of its reliefs—the colossal Gigantomachy Frieze of the podium and the pictorial Telephos Frieze in the inner courtyard—were identified beyond doubt; their reconstruction was reasonably certain; their message, and a partially preserved dedicatory inscription, provided a date for the complex, based on historical data, around 180–160. The general appearance of the Altar was also considered an established fact, with many architectural elements surviving from the whole and the entire gridlike substructure extant in situ. A third- or fourth-century Roman source, Lucius Ampelius (*Liber Memorialis* 8.14), mentioning a great altar (*ara*) at Pergamon with colossal sculptures and a Gigantomachy, apparently provided a definition for the building; and a bronze coin of the Severan period may have suggested its appearance. This was the scholarly position when Margarete Bieber published her major compendium of Hellenistic sculpture (1961).[4]

Approximately forty years later, the situation has drastically changed. Although location, general appearance of the whole, and subject matter of the friezes are still established facts, now the purpose of the monument, reconstruction of the inner sacrificial table, location and meaning of the many figures in the round, reading of the dedicatory inscription, and, above all, date have been called into question.[5] The literature on the subject has grown enormously, especially, as mentioned in Chapter 1, because of the recent restoration and re-examination of the Telephos Frieze and the traveling exhibition that exposed it to a much wider public than before. I shall not attempt to describe the Altar in detail and to summarize all the various scholarly theories that have been advanced.[6] I shall rather focus on individual issues, from my personal point of view.

THE ALTAR AS A WHOLE

The Impact of the Discovery
Historiographic analysis has shown that the overwhelming importance attributed to the Altar was partly due to its acquisition (in the 1880s) by the Berlin Museum, which, in the wake of its establishment within the new capital of the young German Empire, was trying to "enhance Berlin's cultural legitimacy," in unstated competition with Paris and Rome.[7] The many excavational activities sponsored by the prestigious German Archaeological Institute meant that subsequent discoveries of comparable monuments were influenced by the Pergamene precedent and produced reconstructions largely based on the conception of the Pergamon Altar current at the time. Attributions of sculptures previously known through Roman copies were made on comparison with the Baroque style of the Gigantomachy Frieze, while quantities of inscriptions and statues continued to be uncovered in Pergamon itself and provided the first image of what a Hellenistic capital was like in its heyday. Alexandria and Antioch were virtually lost; Pella had not yet been excavated, and nobody in those days expected much from a Macedonian capital. Pergamon therefore became the epitome of a Hellenistic royal seat, the splendor of which had hitherto been glimpsed only through literary sources. In terms of immediate impact, its one viable comparison, *mutatis mutandis,* is with the tomb of Tutankhamen, which, having been found unplundered, hinted at the riches that were once probably contained within the pillaged graves of more important pharaohs like Tuthmosis III or Ramesses II. Public excitement in both instances can also be compared.

The Shadow of the Pergamon Altar

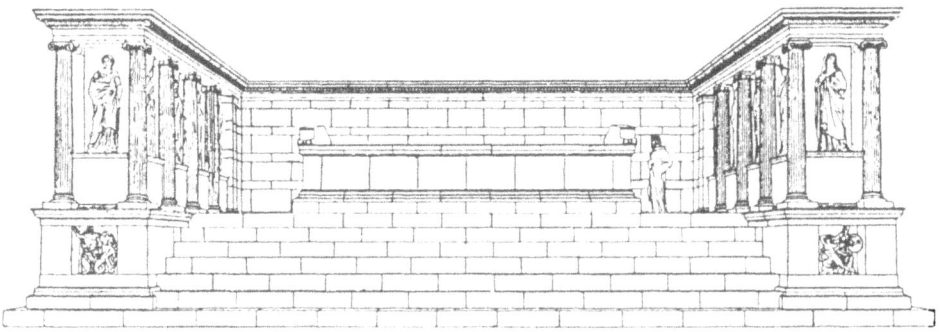

Ill. 1. Superseded reconstruction of the Altar of Athena at Priene, incorporating the coffers from the Athenaion (drawing by F. Krischen). [After M. Schede, *Die Ruinen von Priene* (Berlin 1934) 36 fig. 44]

Within scholarly circles, the influence of the Altar can be exemplified by the official reconstruction produced for the altar of Athena at Priene—on a high podium decorated with relief panels illustrating a Gigantomachy (Ill. 1). Joseph Carter has now convincingly shown that the original monument was much lower and that the reliefs belong to the peristyle coffers of the temple itself. Another altar originally visualized along the lines of the Pergamene example was that of the Artemision at Magnesia, but new studies have lowered its height and questioned the distribution of its decoration. I can finally mention the Tarentine reliefs in soft stone, from funerary structures, that used to be dated according to their lesser or greater Baroque elements, whereas an analysis of the pottery from the burials has now raised their date to a phase preceding the Pergamon Gigantomachy, thus convincingly proving that the style existed before the Altar.[8]

The Date

Pottery comes again into play in the current debate over the date of the Pergamon Altar. At the time of the first excavations, little or no attention was paid to sherds from the foundations of the structure. The entire complex was dated on its style, on the fact that Eumenes II was said (Strabo, 13.4.2, C 624) to have raised Pergamon to its level of magnificence, on the fragmentary inscription mentioning a queen (taken to be Apollonis, Eumenes II's mother), on the Gigantomachy as a theme of victory over barbaric forces—the Gauls, and perhaps also the Bithynians and even the Seleukids—and on the use within the Royal Palace (Building V) of some architectural members originally intended for the Altar. An inception date ca. 180 was extended to ca. 160 for the Telephos Frieze, not only on stylistic and contextual grounds but also because parts of both the architecture and the courtyard reliefs were left unfinished. Eumenes' death in 159 would have been responsible for the interruption; alternatively, the attack by Prousias II of Bithynia, in 156, may have caused it.

Collection of pottery sherds was, however, standard archaeological procedure when renewed excavation took place within the foundation grid of the Altar in 1961. Callaghan was the first to raise the possibility that this evidence lowered the inception of construction to ca. 165, a date even better in keeping with Eumenes II's victories over rebellious Gauls in 167–166. Renewed excavation and analysis by German archaeologists have not yet settled this issue. As far as I can tell, within a field where I can claim no expertise, the situation is as follows. Relief fragments of so-called long-petal bowls have been found within the foundations, whereas no sherds of Pergamene appliqué ware (supposedly starting around 170) have come to light there. On comparison with dated pottery deposits from Athens and Corinth, long-petal bowls seem not to occur before the advanced second quarter of the second century. Gerhild Hübner, who has most recently studied the Pergamene pottery from various contexts, and especially from the Asklepieion, has argued instead that the sherds from the Altar foundations are not of the typical form, but rather represent an unusual version without parallels. That such a version is, however, earlier than the traditional one may be an assumption, and the absence of appliqué ware could have a different explanation. A recent German report from Pergamon seems to support a compromise date for both pottery and Altar, but one gets the impression that the Altar itself is being used to date the pottery, rather than vice versa. Other suggestions on how the sherds might have infiltrated the foundations, thus accounting for their lower chronology, seem unconvincing.[9]

Although ceramic dating often provides only relative (not absolute) chronology, based on principles of style and decoration, pottery evidence is traditionally counted as objective. Much more subjective is any kind of dating based on alleged pro- or anti-Roman sentiments expressed by details of the Gigantomachy and the Telepheia, anti-Macedonian feelings conveyed by giving a starburst shield to one of the Giants (Pl. 1), identification of the free-standing images (Pl. 2) as personifications of cities controlled by Pergamon after the Peace of Apameia (in 188), and other similar suggestions. On such grounds, it must be admitted, no reliable conclusion can be reached. I would personally tend to accept an inception date just before Eumenes II's death (159), when Attalos II was co-regent, and a lack of completion caused by the succession problems and the death of Attalos III (138–133), but I would justify my position with arguments that are no less disputable than all others. On the other hand, I want to emphasize that a purely stylistic analysis should definitely be considered inadequate, especially in view of the alleged difference between the two contemporary friezes on the Altar itself.[10]

Plate 1
Plate 2

The Inscription
Both date and definition would be made much easier had the votive inscription of the building been preserved in its entirety. At present, only two fragments from the inscribed architrave remain: the letters $\Sigma I\ I\Sigma\Sigma$ appear on one, and $\Sigma\ A\Gamma A\Theta$ on the

other.[11] Various ways of completing the formula have been proposed, but all center on the first fragment, which is read as *BA*] *ΣI* [*Λ*] *IΣΣ* [*HΣ* ("of Queen") and considered the matronymic of Eumenes II—the king would be acknowledging both his parents, Attalos I and Queen Apollonis, in establishing his identity as the dedicator of the monument. The second fragment would be referring to good events, or good gods, or other such words connected with the adjective "good."

Eumenes II and Attalos II had the same parents; the formula, even if completed as suggested, would not privilege one brother over the other. Indeed, the Stoa of Attalos in Athens carried a dedication by the younger brother with a similar mention of both mother and father.[12] Attalos I was in turn the son of another Attalos (albeit not a king) and his wife Antiochis, and one more Attalos, the future third king by that name, was born by 168 to Eumenes II and Queen Stratonike. In Athens, it could be argued, Attalos II felt the need to avoid any possible confusion about his identity, especially in a city that was already acquainted with the donations of Attalos I. Yet the same reasoning could be applied to Pergamon. The use of both patronymic and matronymic in dedicatory inscriptions is in fact rather rare. When employed by the Ptolemies, it can usually be explained by the fact that both parents shared a title, for instance, "soteres," "theoi adelphoi," "theoi euergetes," which makes the double mention somewhat different in purpose. The Attalids seem to have been devoted to their mothers, but their legitimacy did not rest on matrilinear descent, and the frequent shifts from the direct line of succession may have made the extra identification mandatory. Eumenes II, however, could have used his patronymic alone, different from that of his homonymous predecessor (Eumenes I, son of Eumenes, reigned 263–241), in order to establish his claim. Thus the inscriptional evidence from the Altar, on strictly logical grounds, would seem to favor Attalos II over Eumenes II. The use of Roman numerals to indicate successive kings is a convention unknown in classical antiquity, and epithets (as routinely adopted by the Ptolemies) seem not to have been in vogue for the Attalids.[13]

On the other hand, the word "queen" could refer to one of the queens of heaven, and the major role played by female divinities in the Gigantomachy might even suggest that the Altar was dedicated to one of them. The votive formula on the Temple of Hera in Pergamon seems to have called Hera "the Queen" (or at least "royal"), and Auge, Telephos' mother, was the queen of King Teuthras, according to one version of the legend.[14] This is not to say that I advocate a mythological solution over others, but I simply wish to highlight the inadequacy of the preserved inscription.

The Location

Much has been made of the siting of the Altar in trying to connect it with the Temple of Athena on the terrace just above it. Yet the temple is oriented almost due north–south, whereas the Altar complex was probably entered from the west to reach a sacrificial platform that would have made the priest face east.[15] Had the cult image been meant to benefit from the offerings at the Altar, a more direct correlation between the two would perhaps have been adopted. On a plan, the west wall of the temple seems aligned with the west edge of the Altar platform,[16] but in situ the difference in level between the two respective terraces makes the alignment unnoticeable; the situation might even have been worse in antiquity, when other buildings intervened between the two levels.

To be sure, the Athenaion does not seem to have had its own altar, and the Altar is not connected to a temple. Yet an ash altar for Athena would have been possible, especially given the relative antiquity of her shrine as compared with all other buildings in Pergamon.[17] As for the Altar, the name begs the question: can we be sure that this is what the structure was? I see its location as determined, not by a temple on a higher level, but by a desire to place all monuments, no matter on which terrace, as close as possible to the edge of the theater, so as to make them visible from the city below and from as far as the Asklepieion. All visitors, even today, as they leave the sanctuary of the healing god, are invited to stand on the marble-paved, colonnaded Roman road facing the citadel, to view the spectacular sight of the precipitous cavea of the theater, crowned, as it were, by the various terraces each with its own individual monument, in a truly scenic display. Even the peculiar orientation of the Athenaion could be explained in landscaping and compositional terms, given that the slope of the rock predated all structures and its potential for city-planning must always have been apparent.

Although the Altar terrace might have been reshaped to house the grandiose monument, it was certainly not created for the occasion, since the Altar foundations rest on earlier structures that were demolished for the new project. Blocks from the destroyed buildings were used as fill in the many "chambers" that form the grid of the Altar foundations. Not all of them have been properly examined, but some remains are considered habitations, and it seems that Byzantine construction, after the Altar was taken down, may also have altered the layout. In some areas within the foundations, the natural bedrock rises to the level of the grid, so that the Altar must have extended over ground previously unoccupied, as far as we can tell. One specific feature, however, has attracted particular attention.[18]

It is an apsidal structure, now preserved only as a few courses of andesite blocks, which appears intentionally enclosed within the Altar foundations; its destruction may be due not only to later building activity but also to the early excavations; at any rate, the present remains do not seem to allow a sensible reconstruction. It has even been questioned whether houses preceded the apsidal building and were partly destroyed by it, or whether they existed simultaneously and were all replaced by the Altar. Niches in the apsis have suggested identification as a nymphaion, but there are also windows, which may imply a different purpose.[19] That the apsidal wall seems too flimsy to have supported a roof may not, of itself, be sufficient argument against identifying it as a heroon, since other examples of such hypaethral shrines are known, and the presence of houses nearby would not automatically invalidate a sacred function.

The Shadow of the Pergamon Altar

As the Heroon of Telephos, this apsidal building, if correctly identified, could establish the Altar as its more grandiose replacement and thus provide its true definition.[20] As cenotaph or heroon, moreover, the Altar need not be connected with any specific historical event, thus eliminating the many suggestions for its date of inception.

The Structure

Some details may remain unclear, but the basic features of the Altar seem established: a *Π*-shaped high podium, resting on three or more steps, was decorated all around with a high-relief frieze depicting a Gigantomachy and, above a dentilled cornice, was crowned by an Ionic colonnade. A steep staircase between the projecting wings of the podium brought the visitor to the level of the columns and of a central courtyard delimited by a wall (of the same shape as the podium) inside the outer colonnade; an inner colonnade (small double half-columns on tall pedestals) around the courtyard and across the entrance may or may not have been completed (Ills. 2–3). The inner face of the courtyard wall, above a dado, was decorated in low relief by the Telephos Frieze (Ill. 4).[21] A roof over inner and outer colonnade protected this frieze and supported numerous akroterial figures, including at least 11 horses (cf. Pls. 26–27). The center of the courtyard would have housed the sacrificial table, although nothing of it was found in situ. Entablature blocks attributed to such a table have been reconstructed in two different ways, but the following sequence seems certain (Ill. 5, Pl. 3): Plate 3 a two-fasciaed architrave topped by various carved moldings, an anthemion frieze below dentils, and a rinceau sima with unpierced (therefore non-functional) lion-head waterspouts, which on its top surface retains shallow beddings and cuttings for metal fastenings, probably for added ornaments, perhaps set up in more than one installment.[22]

A recent discussion (Linfert 1995) of so-called luxury altars as civic manifestations has pointed out that the Pergamon Altar is simply a more elaborate, greatly magnified, and thus typically royal, version of third-century predecessors. The basic elements—a relatively low podium with steps, surrounded by a *Π*-shaped colonnaded wall with relief sculpture—were already adopted at Priene, Magnesia, Teos, Klaros, and other sites. These, in turn, were influenced by such structures as the altar of the Artemision at Ephesos or the so-called Altar Court at Samothrake. The concept of an outer enclosure for the sacrificial table was therefore well established, and it would not have been surprising for Pergamon to want simply a bigger and better rendering of the traditional formula.

On the other hand, as Linfert has stressed, in several instances the erection of such decorated altars was prompted by the establishment of a new festival or the conferring of the right of asylum, or even by an oracle and an apparition of the main deity, as was probably the case at Magnesia. The altar could then precede the erection of a new temple, and replace a simpler and smaller structure along the same general lines. Other altars, apparently not prompted by similar motivations, were simply imitations

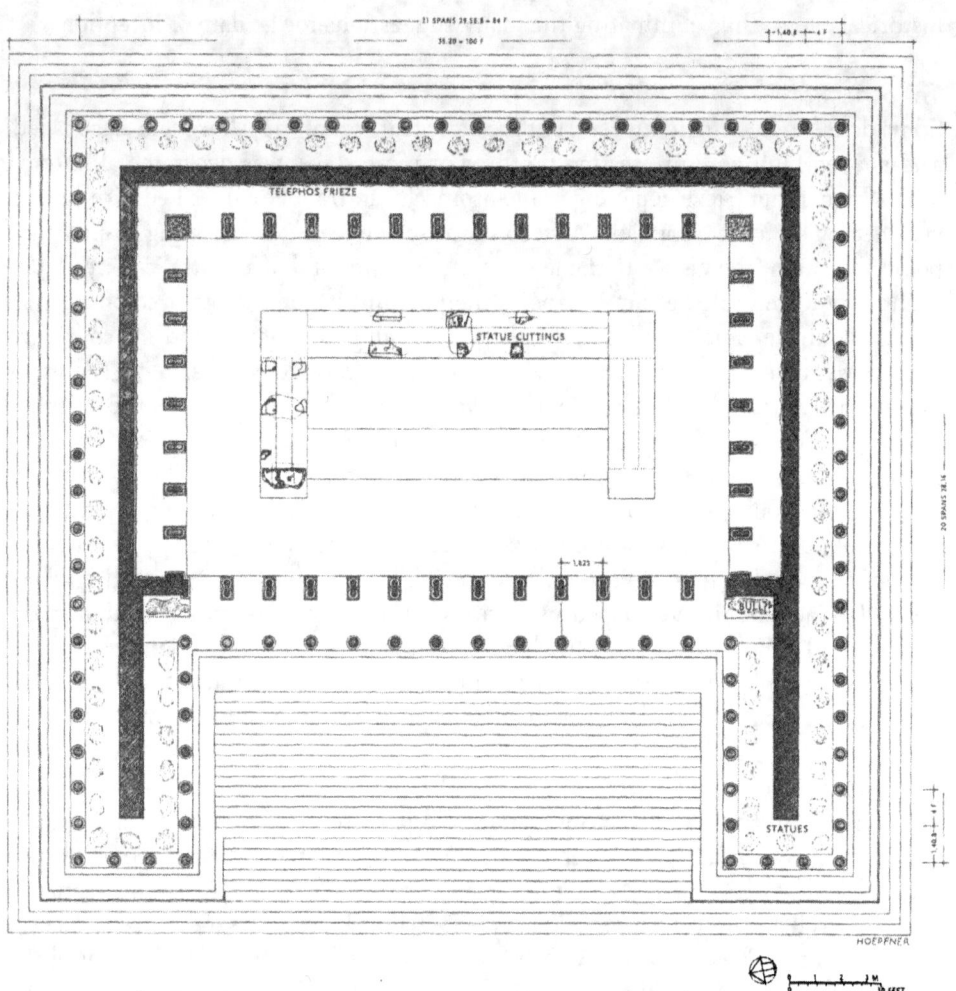

Ill. 2. Plan of the Pergamon Altar and sacrificial table, by W. Hoepfner. [After *Pergamon 2*, 1997, 54 fig. 27]

of what was becoming an accepted formula. But no right of asylum was connected with the Pergamon monument, no immediate association with a temple existed, and the elaborate form and decoration postulated for the sacrificial table made it a "luxury altar" in itself, within an outer luxury altar.[23]

Despite this accumulated and updated evidence, I am not comfortable in calling the

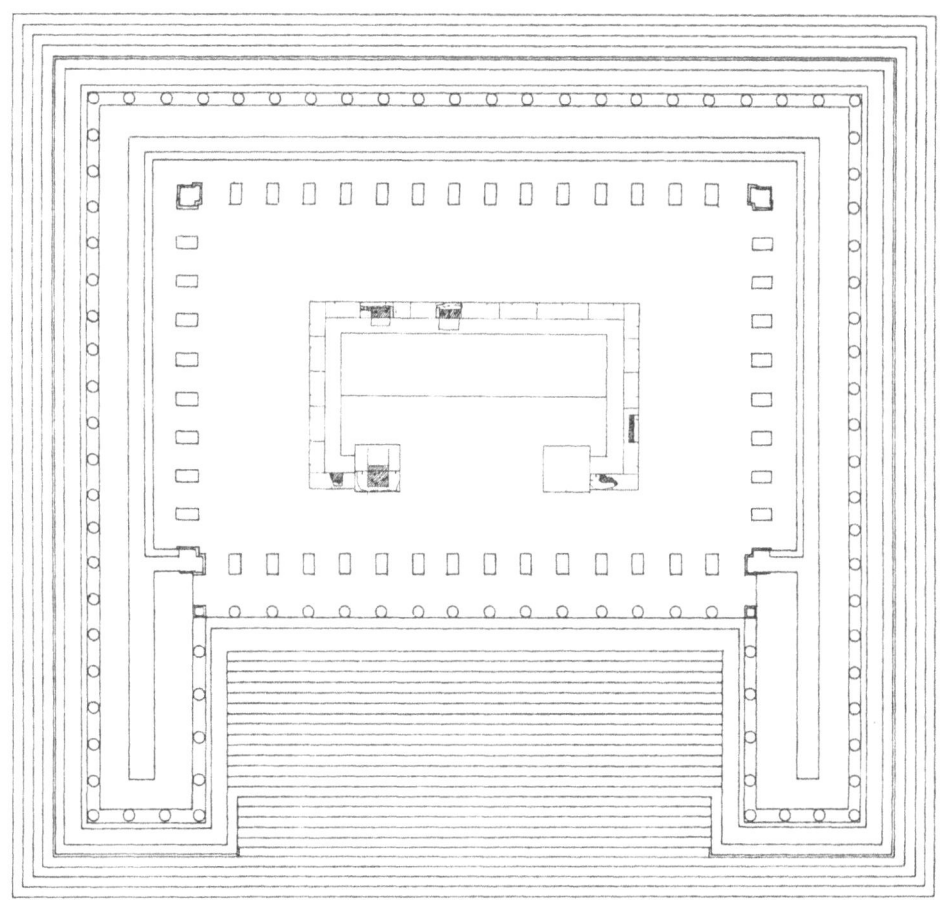

Ill. 3. Plan of the Pergamon Altar and sacrificial table, by V. Kästner. [After *Pergamon 2*, 1997, combining fig. 1 on p. 71 and fig. 8 on p. 81]

Pergamon monument an altar. To be sure, others have pointed out, with greater or lesser emphasis, that the building carried numerous connotations. Its Gigantomachy Frieze, and perhaps some of the free-standing statuary that adorned it, emphasized a theme of triumph over hostile forces and turned it into a victory monument. The Telephos Frieze glorified the heroic/divine descent of the founding hero, thus of the

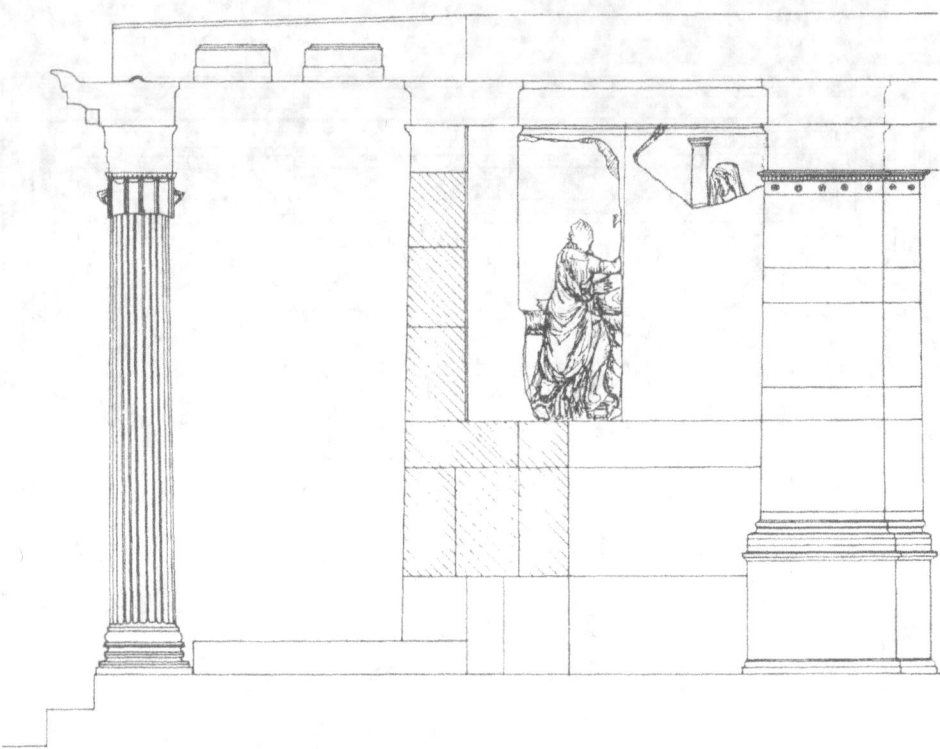

Ill. 4. Pergamon Altar, section of the south wall, showing the Telephos Frieze (drawing by V. Kästner). [After *Pergamon 2*, 1997, 76 fig. 6]

ruling dynasty, and its location and setting may have paralleled the decoration of the andron in the royal palaces.[24] Attributed akroterial figures—horses, centaurs, tritons, griffins, lions (cf. Ill. 9, Pls. 26–28)—carried funerary meaning that recalled monumental graves and especially the most famous tomb of all, the Halikarnassos Maussolleion. The projecting wings and the grand stairway would have reminded the visitor of the Athenian Propylaia, and so would the many Parthenonian allusions in the style and iconography of the Gigantomachy Frieze.[25] This many-layered message is typical of ancient monuments and it should not be doubted, even if few viewers would have perceived it in its entirety. My questions center on the alleged presence of an interior sacrificial table, for a variety of reasons.

1. The cornice blocks attributed to such a table (cf. Pl. 3) were not found in situ but scattered on the Altar terrace (Ill. 6). Admittedly, this was true for many other elements from the Altar, but findspot alone can therefore neither prove nor disprove

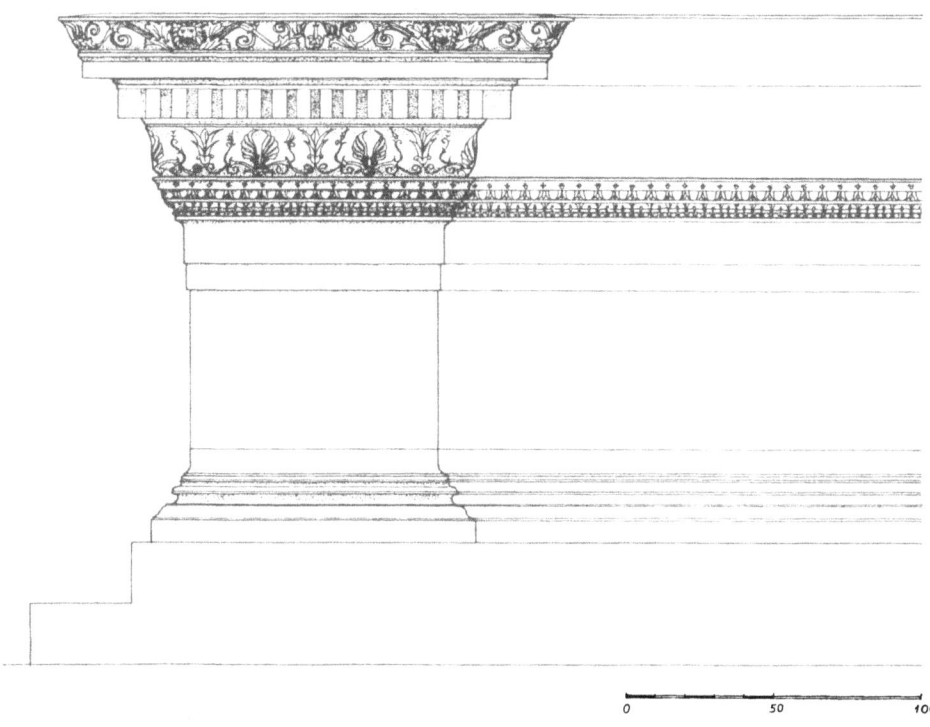

Ill. 5. Pergamon Altar, sacrificial table, detail of elevation (drawing by V. Kästner). [After *Pergamon 2*, 1997, 79 fig. 7]

their connection with the monument, especially if the blocks indeed belonged to another architectural structure within the same terrace. Their roof-like appearance is unparalleled among other inner altars, especially the inclusion of waterspouts, even if they are considered purely decorative. The anthemion ornaments are not echoed by corresponding elements in the architecture of the Altar itself.[26]

2. The extant paving of the inner courtyard shows no traces of a central construction. This may not be surprising, given the dilapidated state of the remains, but the presence of the table is therefore argued on analogy and assumption, not on positive evidence.

3. The Severan coin traditionally used to confirm the presence of an inner altar within the colonnade, in my opinion, does not show the Pergamon Altar. The sacrificial table on the coin has slightly concave sides, perhaps implying a round shape, and its top surface retains what may be considered burnt offerings. The baldacchino

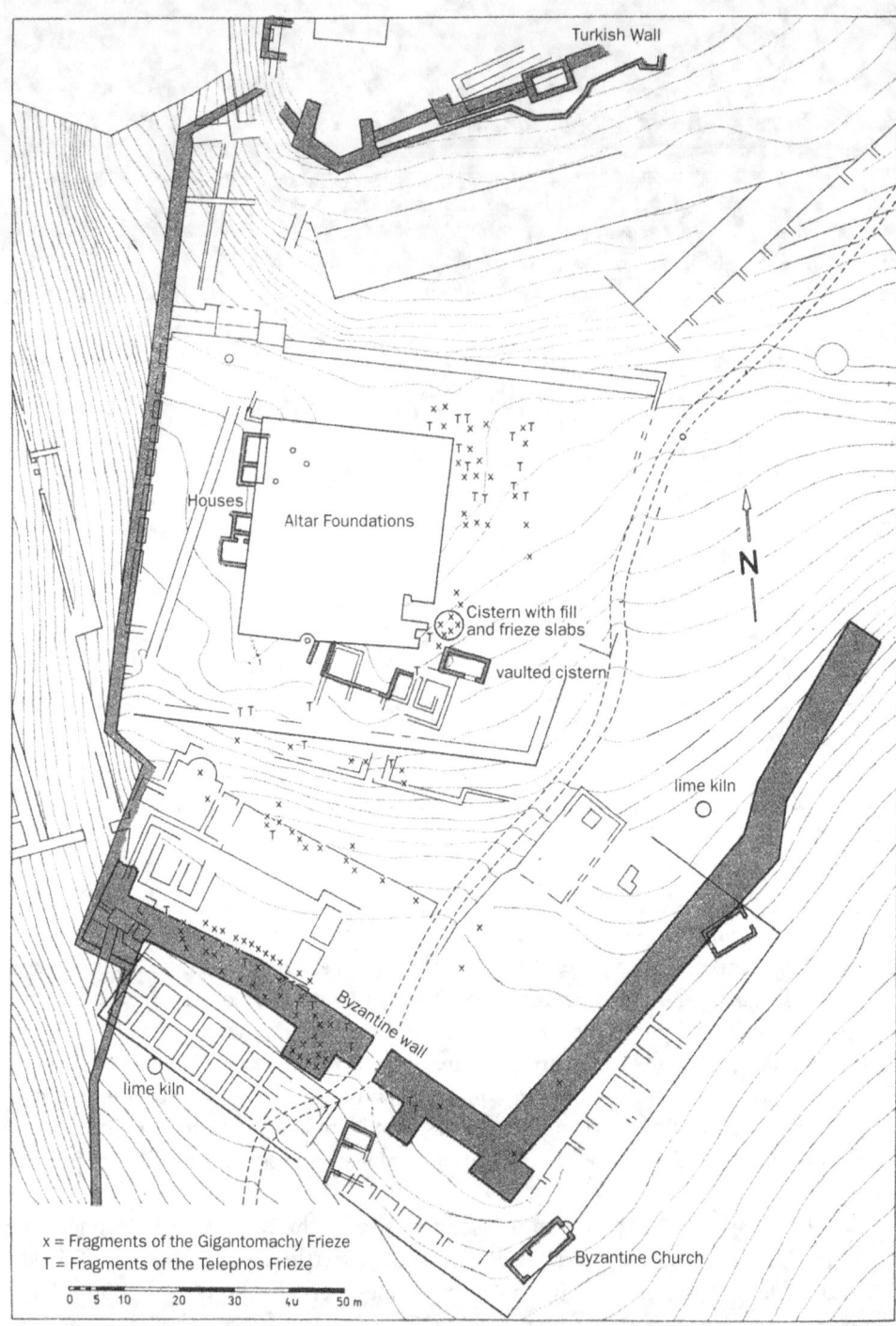

Ill. 6. Plan of post-classical constructions on the Pergamene akropolis (Altar Terrace and Upper Market) showing findspots of frieze slabs from the Great Altar. [Adapted from Kunze 1986, 12]

is not of concern, since it could have been added in Roman times, but the colonnades on either side of the sacrificial structure may as easily refer to flanking stoas (like those of the Trajaneum?) as to the enclosure of the Pergamon Altar, since they do not recur *behind* the sacrificial table. The bulls on bases before the colonnades are sculptures apparently flanking the sacrificial altar, although coin-engravers' conventions may make them appear in front of the colonnades. Those who see the Pergamon Altar on the coin assume that the bull statues hide the podium with its distinctive Gigantomachy and once stood on the space before the structure.[27]

4. A sacrificial table with barriers supporting additional figures or embellishment is, on current knowledge, unprecedented. Smoke and soot from burnt offerings would have damaged this decoration.[28] Only non-burnt offerings could therefore be postulated for such an inner altar (as, indeed, advocated by Hoepfner 1993 and 1997, despite the sacrificial implications of the bull statues he restores at the antae), making its dedication to major Olympian divinities unlikely.

5. The very steep and long staircase, which even humans do not negotiate with ease in the Berlin Museum, would have prevented large sacrificial animals from reaching the courtyard. Only victims small enough to be carried could have been brought to the inner altar. All other altars with a comparable format have far fewer and shallower steps. Yet a shorter staircase (even with the addition of landings) is made impossible at Pergamon by the assured height of the podium.[29]

6. A hypaethral courtyard without a central sacrificial table is quite conceivable if the total Pergamene monument is not an altar. Perhaps one or more colossal statues of the Attalids (or of Telephos and his mother) stood in the open area, with an arrangement somewhat comparable to the Belevi Mausoleum or, to a lesser extent, the Ptolemaion at Limyra.[30]

The blocks currently attributed to the inner sacrificial table could belong to a different monument. Since the Altar terrace seems to have had its own entrance, perhaps these fragments adorned the upper entablature of its propylon, on analogy with the one for the Temenos of Athena on the next terrace; yet the non-functional nature of the waterspouts is problematic. Perhaps, like the Altar, the propylon was never completed. Three fragmentary reliefs (Pls. 4–6) were traditionally assigned to the Plates 4–6 balustrade of the Athena propylon; a recent proposal (Hoepfner 1996c, 1997) would place them instead at the upper level of the peristyle for Andron V, as part of the royal palace. If, however, they were to be given to the propylon of the Altar terrace, their subject would clearly anticipate the sculptural message of the main monument. One slab shows a Gigantomachy—a god, most likely Zeus, stepping on a Giant, faces a second, snaky-legged opponent while Athena, her aigis on her left arm, fights next to him on the left. The ends of two adjacent slabs preserve the construction of the Trojan Horse, with human figures around and inside the device, under Athena's supervision—perhaps an allusion to the eponymous hero Pergamos, who allegedly came from Troy, and to Telephos' dealings with the Greeks searching for the Trojan site. One more slab depicts a seated female next to a shield, probably Athena, in conversation with a muscular bearded man, his foot raised on a rock, perhaps Telephos.[31]

THE GIGANTOMACHY FRIEZE

Masters

Tradition has not preserved the name of the architect responsible for the Altar. One suggestion—that he was Menekrates, supposedly from Rhodes, cited by Varro as one of seven famous architects—is based on inconclusive evidence; another—that he was Hermogenes or one of his students—does not seem better founded.[32] No single name of a mastermind for the entire iconographic program (like that of Pheidias traditionally, albeit perhaps erroneously, connected with the Parthenon) can be cited, perhaps because, as in Imperial Rome, the fame of the sponsor took precedence over that of the executors.[33] Yet some sculptors' names have come down to us, inscribed on the base molding below the frieze slabs, and clearly distinguished from those naming the Giants, on the same architectural element,[34] by their lower level and the added verbs, ethnics, and patronymics, when preserved. The gods' names, in turn, were engraved on the cavetto molding above the dentils, or, in the case of Ge, on the background next to her head.[35]

Regrettably, only a few names survive for the many sculptors who must have worked on the frieze: fragments of 15, possibly 16, signatures are preserved, whereas three times as many may have originally existed. No fewer than four double signatures are extant, implying either collaboration or workshop ownership, and unnamed apprentices might have contributed minor figures or details throughout. From all the inscriptions, only five ethnics can be derived: three men were Pergamene, one was an Athenian, and one double signature has been restored as [Trall]ianoi, men from Tralleis, near Magnesia. Yet it is generally stated that sculptors were recruited from everywhere, given the magnitude of the enterprise; this may stand to reason, but it is an assumption, not a fact. We should keep in mind that two other major projects—the Artemision at Ephesos and the Didymaion near Miletos—were probably still under construction; other temples of the area (the Artemision at Magnesia, the Smintheion in the Troad, even the fourth-century Athenaion at Priene) saw continuous activity through the second century.[36] In brief, marble workshops were probably busy over a vast part of Anatolia.

On the other hand, what the Altar needed was sculptors, not simply marble carvers, and previous activity at Pergamon seems to have involved monuments in bronze rather than in stone. Where was the needed workforce recruited? We have already mentioned the lack of evidence that Menekrates was from Rhodes, and in general the Rhodian connection of the Altar's sculptors has been postulated on elements of style, not on preserved inscriptions.[37] We may note that, according to Goodlett's charts, sculptural activity on Rhodes seems to have plunged between 200–150 and 150–100, to peak again in 100–50. Although her diagram is based on signed bases on Rhodes, primarily for (mostly bronze) honorary statues, rather than on total (uninscribed) monuments, one could conjecture that the low-activity span corresponds to the time when many of the masters usually working on the island, whether native or foreign, had gathered at Pergamon to satisfy the demands of the Altar. This, however, is simply another assumption.[38]

However few ethnics are preserved, it is nonetheless clear that many hands worked on the Gigantomachy, and it is impressive that the results could be as coherent as they appear, even in their present fragmentary state. Scholars' opinions vary, some seeing great differences in style, others stressing the unity of the whole. Yet diversity was obviously desirable, and styles were meant to conform to subjects; thus unity seems to me the truly relevant feature. Whether a scale model of the frieze was made is hard to tell. Cartoons might have been inadequate, given the extremely high relief of the figures, on which some details are carved entirely in the round, free from the background. Here comparison with the Parthenon frieze is certainly invalid,[39] because the low projection of the Athenian composition would have allowed outlines to be sketched directly on the slabs, to be carved in position on the building. Yet no agreement exists on whether the Gigantomachy blocks were sculptured in situ or in the workshop. I cannot imagine how the crawling Giants of the risalits could be executed in position without damaging the steps on which they rested, and would advocate carving in the workshop; but then a model becomes almost inevitable, even if only approximate in detail.[40]

One name frequently mentioned in connection with the Altar Gigantomachy is that of **Krates of Mallos,** thought to have been the director of the Library under Eumenes II, or to have simply worked there at the time. The Stoic thinker and grammarian would have been responsible for providing the information on the many divinities, Titans, and Giants that fill the enormous length of the frieze, drawing it from various literary sources. The complexity of the iconographic enterprise is demonstrated by the fact that, where names or distinctive attributes are not preserved, we cannot identify individual figures from all three categories. Some of the preserved names have come as a surprise, since the Titans are fighting on the side of the Olympians, although mythology made them, at some point, their adversaries as well. The theory that Hesiod's *Theogony* provided the guideline for the victorious party (Simon 1975) can be accepted in general, although disputed in some details. That local scholars provided information for the frieze is, however, undoubted—a heterogeneous (or even homogeneous) group of sculptors would not have had the knowledge required to supply over one hundred named figures and their appropriate familiars.[41]

This is not the place to argue for or against specific names. We should rather focus on the point that so much inscriptional aid was provided, so that the viewer would have "read" the Great Frieze like a text. The complexity of the rendering perhaps required that all combatants be identified, but the fact is nonetheless striking. It may seem to hark back to such early monuments as the Siphnian friezes at Delphi (ca. 525), with their engraved and painted labels for all participants; yet those Archaic narratives, closely paralleled by contemporary vase paintings, existed at a time of budding literacy, Homeric recitals, and incipient theater with its emphasis on epic scenes and characters. The practice in sculpture ceased, however, after a few decades at the most, to resume only, as far as we know, over three centuries later. At Pergamon, it was perhaps the connection with literary works that prompted its resumption—as seems to be the case with the so-called Homeric bowls—but the phenomenon appears typical of the late second–first century, as observable on the "Apotheosis of Homer" relief, the Tabulae Iliacae, the Zoilos Frieze at Aphrodisias,[42] and, I would add, probably the Ara Pacis. It could be explained by the increased intellectualism of the era, and the scholarly approach to the visual arts, yet the Homeric poems had always been popular. I wonder, rather, whether the mixture of peoples, and specifically the Roman influx, could have determined this need for extra clarity, especially since all the monuments just mentioned had a Roman component.[43]

A different explanation must, however, be sought for the sculptors' signatures. Attribution of slabs to workshops for practical purposes (such as payment due) could have been accomplished with masons' marks or other symbols; the inscriptions, moreover, were not only highly accessible but also permanent, beyond the requirements of installation and remuneration.[44] If fame had been the purpose, it is remarkable that none of the names preserved is well known or mentioned in later sources. Perhaps execution was more important than conception, if a master model was indeed available, and a desire to advertise may explain the apparent increase in the popularity of sculptors' signatures during the second and first centuries, despite the apparent lack of emphasis on major artists. The contrast with the literary sources could not be more obvious, and should make us reconsider their limitations.

Iconography and Meaning

So much has been written on the Pergamon Gigantomachy that only personal comments will be offered, some of them relegated to the notes to avoid breaking up my text excessively.

The tradition of anguiped Giants existed well before the Hellenistic period, not only on vases, but also, as it seems assured, on the coffers of the Athenaion at Priene, now seen to predate the Altar. It should here be stressed that many elements attested at Priene recur at Pergamon: Ge rising from the ground, a goddess (Kybele) riding sidesaddle on a lion, another lion (probably with Dionysos) biting a Giant on the shoulder, Athena's opponent with snaky legs but also with wings.[45] A set repertoire, therefore, may have already existed, to some extent, within Asia Minor workshops. Yet the Altar's sculptors were clearly inspired by the Parthenon in creating some of their figures. It has been frequently mentioned that the Athena and the Zeus at Pergamon imitate the Athena and the Poseidon from the west pediment at Athens, as we shall examine in more detail in the section on style. But other citations are also possible.

Artemis   Leto   Apollo

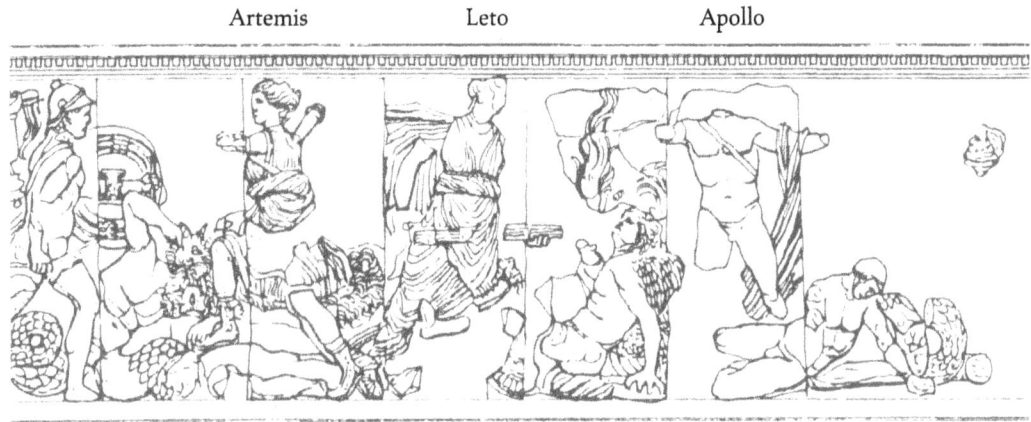

Ill. 7. Section of the Pergamon Gigantomachy, east side, showing Artemis, Leto, and Apollo (drawing by M. Heilmeyer). [Excerpted from *Pergamon 2*, 1997, folding pl.]

It is often stated that the Apollo from the east side of the Altar (Ill. 7) is "quoted" on the Hekateion at Lagina, as part of the west frieze showing the Gigantomachy. It is also supposed that both images are patterned after the so-called Belvedere Apollo, traditionally attributed to the fourth-century master Leochares. I believe, however, that the Pergamene Apollo may have been meant to recall another, and more public, image of the god: the central figure on the west pediment of the Temple of Zeus at Olympia.[46] The distinctive feature of the Belvedere Apollo type (whatever its actual date—and I believe it is Roman) is its split motion: the god moves to his right while looking and gesturing toward his left, in diagonal movement. The Pergamon Apollo is strictly frontal, his median line (*linea alba*) vertical, his body spread-eagled against the background despite the fact that he is standing *in front* of a fallen Giant. This frontality could be expected at Lagina, where it is shared by several other figures, but not at Pergamon, where profile, diagonal, and back-view poses predominate. To be sure, the Olympia Apollo is a mirror-image of the Pergamene one, but the emphatic gesture of the raised arm is what attracts attention in both, whether with or without added mantle. Olympia was certainly well known to both Greeks and Romans in the second century, and an influential site in its own right. Such a quotation would be well in keeping with the panhellenism of the Attalids.[47]

My hypothesis could be strengthened were the head of the Pergamon Apollo preserved; the Belvedere Apollo has a distinctive bow-knot coiffure that, to my knowledge, does not recur on any of the Altar figures (not even on Artemis or Aphrodite, where it could have been expected), despite the fact that the hairstyle was used since the late fourth century. A head occasionally, albeit tentatively, attributed to Apollo is the so-called Alexander in Istanbul, clearly Pergamene in style, and appropriate in size. Recognized (Radt 1981) as belonging to a relief because of a peculiar projection in the back and the asymmetry of its features, it was cautiously proposed as an Alexander within the Gigantomachy, although the presence of *two* mortals fighting with the gods (only one, Herakles, was required for victory) would have been unusual propaganda. To be sure, at least one of the Dioskouroi, probably present on the frieze, was also mortal, and other humans have at times been suggested. In Athens, the peplos of Athena had once included in its woven Gigantomachy the figures of Demetrios Poliorketes and his father, Antigonos, although with disastrous results. But I am convinced that the Istanbul head is neither Alexander nor Apollo or another god: he is one of the Giants, since the supposed *anastole* in his hairstyle—the distinctive central part with locks rising on either side—recurs in several unmistakable opponents of the gods on the Altar.[48]

The wide range in representations of the Giants on the Altar has always been emphasized. Many have non-human features, such as snaky legs or wings, but three are distinctly animal-like: a bull-giant, a lion-giant, and a bird-giant—unprecedented renderings that may have been inspired by Near Eastern monsters but may also have
Plate 7
had specific connotation. The bull-giant (Pl. 7), in fact, much like a wilder Acheloos, has been identified as Brychon (= the Bellower), a river at Pallene, an area in the Chalkidike peninsula, where the Giants were supposedly born. At the same time, the location of the river may have alluded to one of the enemies of Pergamon.[49]

Similar allusions can be read into many other opponents of the gods. A griffin-crested helmet appearing on the groundline, between the legs of a (now headless)
Plate 8
figure seen from the back (Pl. 8, Ill. 8), is of the so-called Thrako-Phrygian type, used in Macedonia by kings like Alexander, Philip V, and Perseus. The Giant with a starburst shield (cf. Pl. 1), supposedly carries Macedonian connotations, since that shield device seems to have been reserved for Macedonian kings. It may also be significant that this defensive weapon is held by the figure fallen under Hera's quadriga: her four winged horses are said to be an allegory for Queen Apollonis' four sons, given the queen's supposed identification with Hera. Yet the starburst is not the typical Macedonian one with rays of alternating lengths, and stars as shield devices for Giants seem to be common since earlier times, at least in Etruscan art.[50]

Other such weapon decorations are puzzling. The rim of the shield held by a cuirassed Giant on the north side, behind Nyx/Persephone (according to different inter-
Plates 9a–b
pretations), has a design of stars alternating with winged thunderbolts (Pl. 9a–b). The rim is partly broken, partly hidden by the shield of the Giant's divine opponent, as the two clash against each other, but the motif would have been enhanced by paint, and it is, at any rate, still clearly visible to one facing the sculpture in its museum setting. Why give Zeus' thunderbolt—a motif that recurs on one of the Ionic capitals from the Altar—to a Giant?[51]

Another peculiar iconographic element occurs on the shield-strap (*porpax*) of Artemis' opponent, probably Otos. This young Giant is entirely human, indeed even handsome, and stares at his future killer with such an intense gaze that one is reminded of the fateful glance between Achilles and Penthesileia, here made ironic by

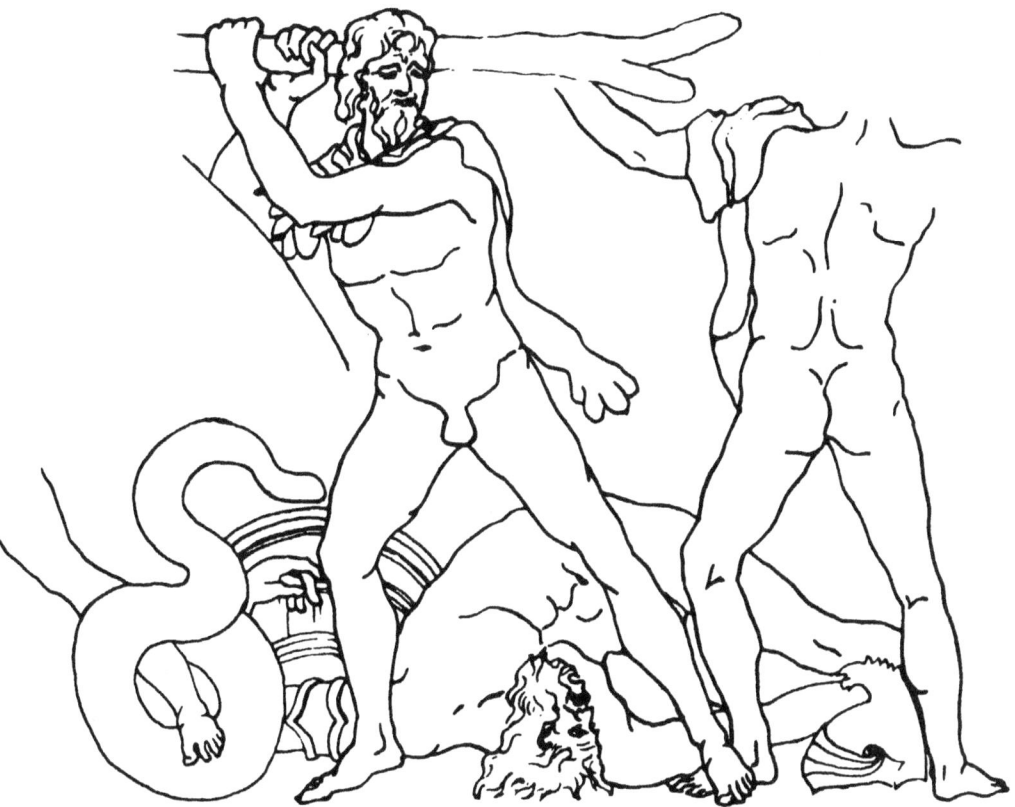

Ill. 8. Reconstruction of the section of the Pergamon Gigantomachy Frieze incorporating the Fawley Court Giant. [After Haynes 1972, 741 fig. 10]

the fact that the female will destroy the male, rather than vice versa. The Giant's porpax is decorated not simply with a gorgoneion, but with a gorgoneion against an aigis, both typical attributes of Athena (Pl. 10). Once again, why give the protective symbols of a major divinity to an opponent of the gods—especially one representing unruly and rebellious forces? The allusion here could be to the golden aigis with gorgoneion dedicated by one of the Seleukids, either Antiochos III or IV, on the Akropolis in Athens, where it hung on the south wall, above the Theater of Dionysos.[52] The Gigantomachy would then truly be an allegory for all the enemies of the Attalids and, indirectly, of stability and order—a total victory monument, as advocated by Hoepfner and others, not just a commemoration of Gaulish victories.

Plate 10

If Seleukids and Macedonians are included among such enemies, it would explain the diversity in the rendering of the Giants: the Pergamenes would not symbolize other Greeks like themselves in the guise of monstrous creatures. Although the hoplite Giant was iconographically known since the time of the Siphnian Treasury, it would acquire special meaning on the Altar, where the more barbaric Gauls would be represented by the Mischwesen with snaky legs or wings.[53] As often mentioned, the Pergamon relief is a multilingual text, whose various layers of meaning would be "read" by viewers according to their personal knowledge and perspective. But a few basic principles were certainly observed. (1) The Gigantomachy was primarily a recollection of Athens and its own Panathenaic festival celebrating Athena's defeat of her Giant, which was duplicated by the Pergamenes with their own Panathenaia—hence the specific allusion to Parthenonian iconography, with Nike crowning Athena

Plate 11   at the moment of victory (Pl. 11). Pergamon was seen as the Athens of the East.[54] (2) Diversity was needed because of the great number of figures and the extent of the frieze, unprecedented in previous depictions of the Gigantomachy—hence the various imaginative renderings, such as the fins and seaweed patterns of the Giants fighting the divinities of the sea on the northwest risalit, and the fishskin boots worn by Doris

Plate 12   on the same side (Pl. 12). In general, the marvelously elaborate footwear depicted on the participants in the Gigantomachy demonstrates clear attention to details and clues to identification that may escape us.[55] But these identifications were primarily mythological, and we should not assume that historical hints—if such they truly were—took precedence over traditional iconographic overtones. The first and primary level of meaning of the subject was, and had to remain, religious.

That the line between historical and mythological can be thin indeed is demonstrated by the apparently contemporary armor worn by the "hoplite" Giants: not only helmets and shields but also cuirasses with flaps (*pteryges*; cf. Pl. 9), as depicted in battle scenes on the Alexander Sarcophagus and the Alexander Mosaic. Three helmeted heads had been tentatively attributed to the Altar because similar to others still in place; a recent examination of the two in Germany has shown that they cannot be placed on the frieze, but should perhaps be attributed to a large Pergamene victory monument of the first half of the second century that stood either in the Nikephorion or elsewhere outside the city.[56] One more head from the Asklepieion area, somewhat larger in size and with its back peculiarly hollowed out—the so-called Wild Man—has been given to the Zeus of the east side. Were the connection confirmed, it would show that fragments from the Altar could migrate far from their place of origin; but the suggestion is controversial. That some pieces even found their way to Europe is, however, a proven fact.[57]

Among such pieces, the so-called Fawley Court Giant (from its British home) has shown us the face of death: the unnatural pose betokens a broken neck, and the eyes are closed (cf. Ill. 8). Other Giants can be presumed dead, as they lie on the ground, but their faces are usually hidden. It has been noted that "one or two gods seem to be losing." But it has not been pointed out how ineffectual the Giants' offensive usually is: snake-legs bite shields or folds of garments but mostly threaten rather than attack;

Plate 13   fingers probe animals' eyes and grab furry skin (Pl. 13), but seldom do Giants grasp
Plate 14   their divine opponent's arm (Pl. 14; cf. Pl. 11); even boulders are clutched for support

more often than hurled, despite their being traditional Giants' weapons even among fighters in armor.[58]

Two more iconographic comments must conclude this section, potentially endless given the richness of the frieze. The first concerns the famous scene of Athena, her opponent, and Ge, on the east side (cf. Pl. 11). It is usually stated that the Giant is Alkyoneus, a son of Ge who derived immortality from contact with Mother Earth. At first glance, it looks in fact as if Athena is trying to break his hold on his mother's arm by interposing her thigh between the two and by lifting him by the hair; yet several peculiarities remain. First of all, it is surprising that a Giant who needed such earthly contact should be given not single but double wings, as if for powerful flight. In addition, the Giant is still in touch with the ground (and even with Ge), at least with both feet, although Athena's snake is inflicting the fatal wound. It has been noted that "paradoxically, it is in the air, domain of immortality, that A. will find death, killed by a serpent, which elsewhere on the frieze (Hesperides, N frieze) appears as guardian of life."[59] Paradoxes, of course, can be quite intentional. The snake, as Athena's familiar, is an excellent, almost Dantesque *contrapposto* for the serpentine legs of most Giants. Moreover, the goddess herself is covered with snakes: one for her scaly belt, others for the fringes of her feathered aigis, and a few more around the gorgoneion in its center—fighting fire with fire. The Giant's wings can also be explained as needed balance for Nike's, who is crowning Athena, as in Parthenon metope E 4. But Ge's rendering is peculiar on all counts. Her expression is one of deep sorrow, and her raised right hand is begging Athena for mercy, but her left hand (enormous) appears, palm out, at the bottom edge of the slab, supporting an undisturbed, overflowing cornucopia that seems incongruous, even ironic, as symbol of her bounty and fertility, an unnecessary attribute given her clear iconography and engraved label.

The second peculiar detail occurs on the west face of the south wing and can be fully appreciated only in situ and from the side, not in photographs. Dionysos is accompanied by two small satyrs, but one is so completely overlapped by the other that only his head and neck, in low relief against the background, are visible, his throat characterized by a caprine gland that stresses his animal qualities. Yet his companion in the foreground does not have a hairy body or wear a goatskin, but rather sports a satyr's *costume*—furry shorts—as if he were an actor and not a true creature of nature. Dionysos' fluttering mantle all but hides this surprising detail.[60]

Style

That the style of the Pergamon Gigantomachy is "Baroque" is taken for granted; yet it is not clear what is meant, in an ancient context, by a term that usually refers to a much later period in European art (ca. 1600 to 1750) and applies to various manifestations, such as painting and architecture. In antiquity, to our knowledge, the style manifests itself primarily in sculpture and is largely considered typical of Asia Minor, although it has now been observed at Taras and other areas of the Greek world. Its features have been described as "exaggeratedly massive, tension-filled bodily forms and pathetic facial expressions that seem to echo the masks of tragic drama . . . used to convey a sense of dramatic crisis in such diverse monuments as portraits . . . , architectural sculpture . . . , and propagandistic victory monuments."[61] Another study has focused on ancient Baroque as a medium of sculptural narrative, and has listed its characteristics as "grandiloquence, theatricality, emotionalism, energy, floridity, obsessions with extreme contrasts, penchant for surprises, and passion for novelty." On this basis, the sculptural manifestations of Hellenistic Asia Minor have been linked with rhetorical "Asianism" but without the disapproval inherent in such a comparison because of their efficacy as a narrative device.[62] From a purely formal point of view, however, I prefer Rhys Carpenter's definition of Baroque: "Useful or emotional purposes of devices which are no longer functional," where, by devices, such drapery patterns as modeling or motion lines are meant, or anatomical renderings like the abdominal partitions that revert to being used as mosaic pieces, and other features that only give the appearance of reality without being faithful to nature.[63]

Modeling and motion lines were typical discoveries of the Athenian fifth century, as best exemplified on the Parthenon, and their exaggerated use led to the quasi-Baroque (if I may coin a term) of Paionios' Nike and the Nike Balustrade. It seems therefore more useful to examine elements of the Pergamon Gigantomachy against these stylistic precedents than to describe them per se, since such descriptions already exist, most of them excellent.[64]

We can begin, paradoxically, with figures that display very few, if any, Baroque traits. I have already suggested that the Apollo from the east side (cf. Ill. 7) recalls the same god from the Olympia pediment; another comparison can be made with the Lapith fighting a centaur on Parthenon metope S 27. Actually, the Parthenonian figure exhibits more motion, and has a greater intake of breath and expansion of his ribcage, but his youthful build, the linear definition of his hip muscles, his abdominal partitions, and even his arm attachment bear some similarity to the Pergamene god. All resemblance, however, disappears in the treatment of the respective mantles: heavy and majestic, like a theater curtain, in Athens; twisted and tortured, of finer texture, at Pergamon. Apollo's opponent finds a possible parallel in the "Ilissos" from the Parthenon west pediment; not only the physique, but also the pose is comparable, although the Giant's is more torsional, since his right arm crosses the chest and his head bends down.[65]

The Lapith from metope S 27 can also be profitably compared with Alkyoneus (cf. Pl. 11), and with three figures on the north side: Dione's opponent, "Heoos" (albeit more torsional), and, to a lesser extent, the snake-legged Giant next to the Thrako-Phrygian helmet mentioned above, who, with his pronounced musculature and tendons, seems more definitely Baroque. All four, however, show that peculiar dislocation of the abdominal area which separates it into two superimposed sections at different levels, and which I have defined as an intake of breath. In Alkyoneus, the rendering is partly justified by his position; in the others this is less so, but the feature recurs elsewhere in the Gigantomachy. The mannerism recalls not only several of the Parthenon Lapiths, but also torso H from the west pediment and some naked fighters from the east frieze of the Hephaisteion; it is therefore a typical rendering of the fifth century.[66] Similar horizontal accents accompanied by wrinkles above the navel can be found on Pergamene Giants and on Hephaisteion figures, as well as on Lapiths on the Parthenon south metopes.[67]

Amphitrite's opponent, on the front of the northwest wing, exhibits a more dramatic rendering of musculature, yet even he finds an echo on the Parthenon north frieze: the marshal standing frontally between galloping chariots has a similar rounded abdomen marked by a curve that parallels the groin, pronounced hip muscles, and distended ribcage; his sternum and the apparent rib attachment between the pectorals correspond to those of several Giants on the Altar (cf. Pl. 9a).[68] Finally, even the most powerful, hence the most Baroque, of all Altar torsos, that of Zeus on the east side, resembles in amplitude and pattern the Poseidon from the Parthenon west pediment. To be sure, the Zeus has a more emphatic modeling of the digitations (the *serratus magnus*), and the entire surface is more chiaroscural than on the Poseidon, but the diamond-shape catch at the sternum and the peculiarly mannered curves of the clavicles in both are very close. In prosaic terms, the Zeus looks like the Poseidon after intensive weight training, but the resultant effect is more impressionistic than realistic, for all its apparent imitation of nature: the torso suggests strength, yet each muscle is a separate, disconnected feature with its own unnatural linear contour.[69]

Drapery is more uniformly "Baroque," yet a similar progression can be traced, from more to less "Classical" renderings, and therefore to a more distinctive manifestation of second-century styles. The rolled mantles at waist level, with their drilled slashes (cf. Pls. 13–14), had existed since the fourth century, with some precedents even in the fifth—now they are simply more voluminous, more twisted. The deep carving of cloth along bodily contours, which in the fifth century had produced an effect of transparent drapery, in the fourth had been turned into a way of recovering the human forms hidden under heavy cloth; on the Altar, the device is exploited for the same reasons as well as for strong effects of light and shadow. Many Classical formulas—the railroad-track folds, the sanguisuga wavelets (Pls. 15–16), the nicks and bends of inflated tubular swags, the omega- or curved maeander-patterns at hems of garments, the S-curves denoting motion, the effects of transparency over the abdomen (cf. Pl. 12)—all of these can be paralleled on the Altar.[70] It is amazing how closely the formal vocabulary of the Gigantomachy corresponds to Classical idioms.

Plates 15–16

The way in which the surface of a primary fold is covered with smaller ridges to convey the effect of a thin cloth is not new to the Altar: we had seen it earlier on the Parthenon pediments and on the Nike Balustrade. Press folds appear on the Gigantomachy costumes and on fourth-century sculptures. Even poses are not unique to the Pergamon frieze: the similarity of some Giants to some Lapiths on the Parthenon

Plate 17

metopes or some warriors on the Hephaisteion east frieze has already been noted, and now other comparisons can be added. The Aphrodite of the north side (Pl. 17), bending over to retrieve a weapon from the chest of a fallen Giant, recalls a Nike from the Balustrade; Klymene from the south moves like Figure G from the Parthenon east pediment.[71] If compositional patterns are usually less obvious, it is because of the extensive overlapping of images that blurs contours, and because of the extremely high relief and undercutting that turn the Gigantomachy figures into virtual sculptures in the round. Struts are in fact unobtrusively used between wings, for instance, or to secure projecting limbs to bodies and snake coils to the background; a certain amount of piecing is also apparent.[72]

What is new, therefore, about this style? Should all of it be understood as an exasperated elaboration of pre-existing motifs, as an acquired language shouted rather than spoken in a normal tone of voice? In some cases even previous formal achievements seem forgotten, as in the Helios on the south side, where the motion lines slash across the body, virtually neutralizing it under the drapery; or in the god's horse, too short in the back, whose length equals that of the neck, in turn too full of plastic wrinkles that destroy the beautiful echoing curves of the Parthenonian steeds. Leto's garments (her mantle, her skirt) seem to pull away from her body, and the relentlessly oblique lines of figure and folds in Asterie conceal the position of the raised left thigh.[73]

Yet some traits are novel, or at least used in an effective new way within the context. Among the distinctive features, I would count the use of arrow folds (cf. Pl. 14) that force the eye along prescribed paths rather than around a body, as in the fifth century. Drapery through drapery, incipient in the third century, is here rampant (cf. Pl. 15). Textures, as so often mentioned in all descriptions of the frieze, are superbly juxtaposed and differentiated (cf. Pl. 16). The drill is used not only to carve channels but also to punctuate the ends of grooves and to create eye-folds (cf. Pls. 13–14). It is also used, dramatically, to separate strands of hair, not only from each other but especially from the contour of the faces or to outline upper lids within eye-sockets

Plate 18

(Pl. 18). Hairstyles are in fact quite notable within the Gigantomachy. Goddesses and even some gods show thick, undifferentiated masses rolled up to the nape like twisted ropes, with only marginal separation from coil to coil; the Giants and their mother Ge have clearly articulated and loose strands like twisting snakes in which the dark furrows play as much a part as the light ridges—a further manifestation of proper orderliness and composure versus unruly, unchecked nature.[74]

Faces deserve one more comment. Besides the often mentioned range from beautiful to monstrous, and the apparent serenity of the gods as opposed to the tortured Giants, we should note the plastic, almost pinched appearance of female faces, which

Plate 19

give the impression of being modeled in soft clay (Pl. 19). Not only are they fleshy and dimpled, they also have rounded chins, full lips—the upper articulated in two curves to form the so-called rosebud mouth typical of the Parthenon style—and wide open eyes.[75]

The Shadow of the Pergamon Altar

STATUARY IN THE ROUND

Very similar traits are found in the sculptures that were recovered on the Altar terrace and its vicinity and are now supposed to have stood just behind the colonnade above the podium (cf. Ill. 9, Pl. 2). Over thirty such figures, mostly female, have been re- covered—some seated, some standing, some with their head covered (Pls. 20–25). At- tributes were fastened separately and are often missing, but one majestic female (the so-called Tragoidia, Pl. 22) wears a sword strap and scabbard: together with the high soles of her shoes, interpreted as theatrical *kothornoi*, they have served to identify the figure as a personification of Tragedy. Yet high soles are not limited to actors' shoes during the Hellenistic period, it would seem. Nonetheless, current prevailing opin- ions would accept that all statues may have represented personifications or Muses, in some special form of the myth, standing around the Altar. A sculpture of Zeus Am- mon has also occasionally been grouped with these figures, though I would doubt it.[76] My concern here, however, is not so much with identification and location as with style and chronological assessment.

Plates 20–25

Those who place these statues around the Altar can support their argument with the fact that their backs are perfunctorily carved, that they stand on shallow plinths, and—most important—that their style is very close to that of the Gigantomachy. They display the same twisted mantle rolls forming strong horizontal accents at the waist or below; the same deep carving outlining legs under massed skirts; the same dense drapery that nonetheless can reveal the contrasting pattern of underlying folds. Faces, when preserved, have the same features as the goddesses of the Great Frieze, with perhaps an added tinge of pathos in the circumflex eyebrows of a woman seated on a round kista(?) with moldings at top and bottom. Another woman apparently sits on a rock.[77] Long comma-locks mark the cheeks, escaping from the ropy hair strands framing triangular foreheads (cf. Pl. 20). In some ways, they seem better carved than some Gigantomachy figures, but they exhibit extensive piecing, not only for arms, feet, and attributes, but even for heads, which may be surprising in ideal figures. Or are we dealing with workshop products, for which the better master carved the more expressive parts and the apprentices dealt with the rest?

These female figures are over-lifesize, the same scale as the goddesses in the Gigan- tomachy. If they stood behind the colonnade, they would have been in keeping with the podium, although they may have blocked the rhythm of light and shadow created by the (not too tall) columns. They certainly would have recalled such monuments as the Halikarnassos Maussolleion, with similar (probably ancestral) statues in a compa- rable position. It is surprising, however, that other sculptures attributed to the Altar should be considerably smaller in scale: horses, two griffins, one lion, two centaurs, two tritons, and five divine images, clearly under-lifesize. Again, I shall not debate the distribution of such pieces, which is highly controversial; I shall only venture a few comments.

The five human figures at small scale are thought to represent deities because one is clearly identifiable as Athena through her aigis with gorgoneion (Ill. 9). She is in

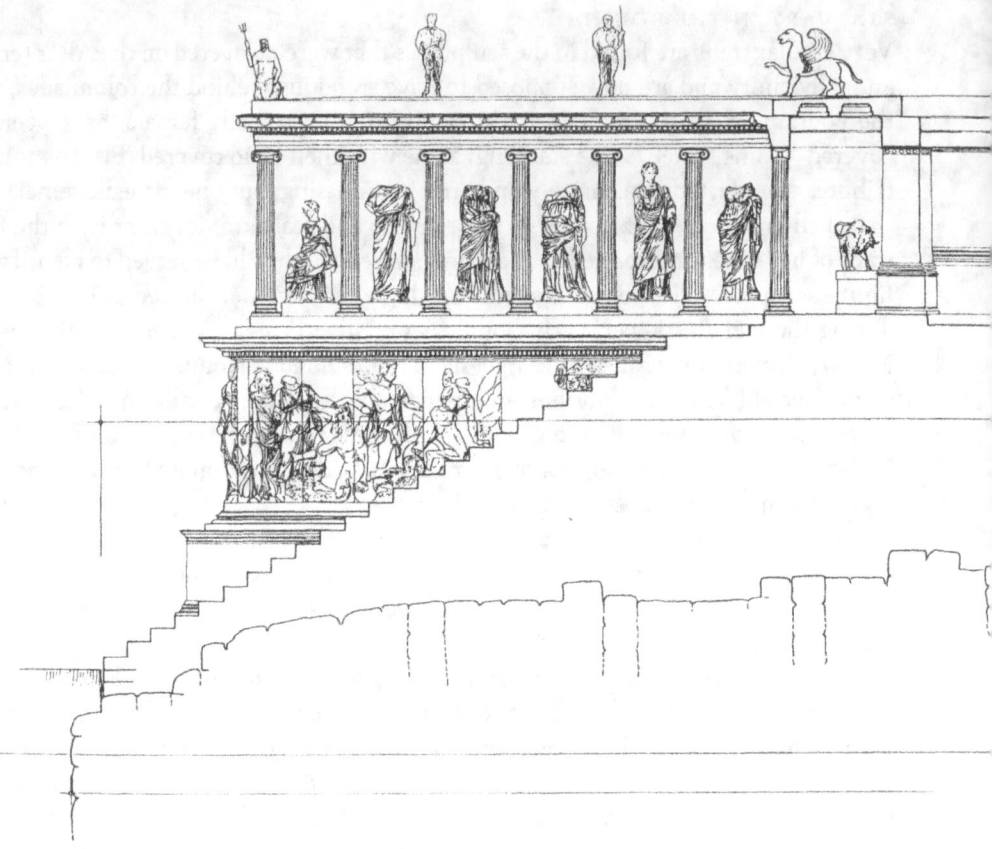

Ill. 9. New reconstruction of the Pergamon Altar and its free-standing sculptures, by W. Hoepfner, E–W section. [After *Pergamon 2*, 1997, foldout 4]

rapid motion to her right, as indicated by her skirt with the characteristic sweeping folds from right thigh to left ankle. Like the goddess in the Gigantomachy, she betrays the influence of Classical patterns—for instance, in the motif of opposed curves at her left knee—but her long apoptygma, her high waist, the deep carving along her left leg, and her press folds place her within the time of the Altar, albeit in a softened Baroque style. Another female figure, not better identified, is more dramatic in her rendering, despite the almost identical pose: her skirt folds are more numerous, deeper, with more pronounced shadows, nicks, and bends; her apoptygma flutters in a more lively way, and the mantle rolled under the breasts creates a strong horizontal accent. A male figure moving in the opposite direction is dressed only in a long chiton, but his similarity to the female statues is remarkable. He is thought to be Apollo. All these pieces are headless, with heads once inserted separately. Better preserved is a male believed to be Poseidon. His Baroque traits are unmistakable: stringy hair sepa-

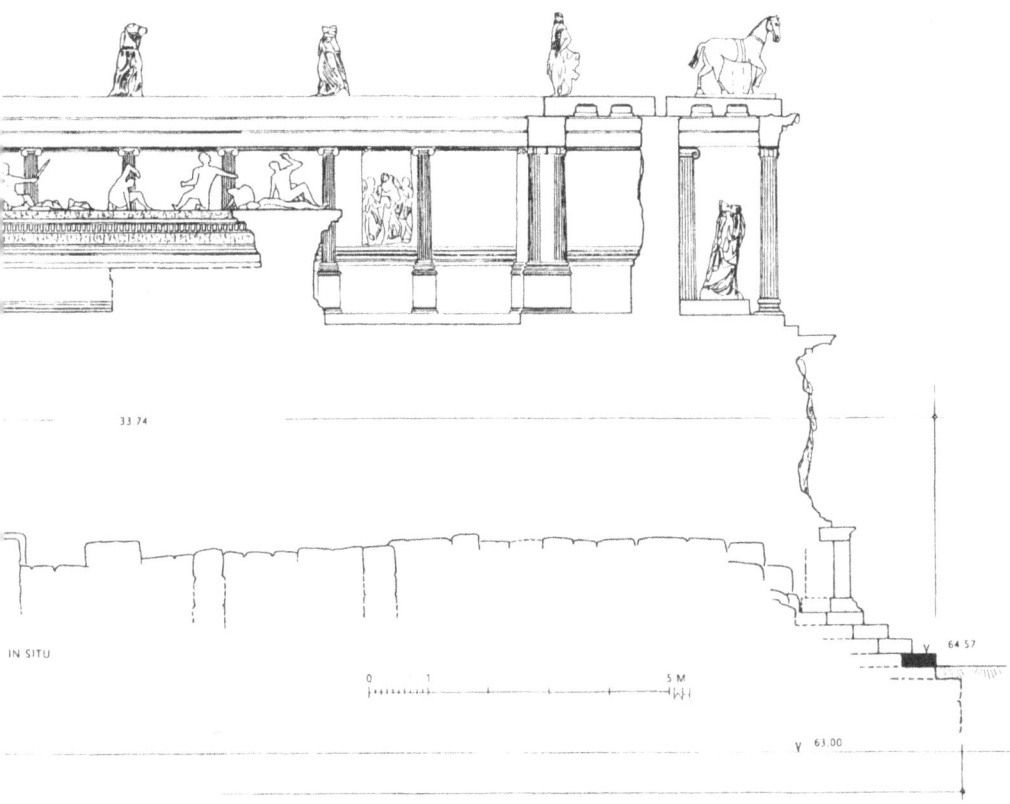

rated from the facial contour, "plastic" face, pronounced musculature, and mantle that clings to the body as if wet or diaphanous (note especially the folds at the crook of the left elbow and at the left knee). One more male figure, a torso, is probably Diony-sos.[78] Because all backs are perfunctorily finished, these human figures are presently assigned to the Altar roof, as if displayed against the skyline, although they had once been placed on the cornice of the sacrificial table. Other solutions—such as a setting against a backdrop—are possible.

The horses are the most numerous, as preserved: at least 11 (Pls. 26–27). Because of matching cuttings and dowels, they seem more assuredly placed on the roof over the colonnade, facing out: they are restored at present in a row of seven quadrigas along the east side, where they might echo the chariots of the Gigantomachy below, but theoretically they could go over the other sides as well.[79] No traces of chariots have been found, and only some horses have a neck harness, like the great steed from the Halikarnassos Maussolleion, and even a body strap. Other horses have only face harness, but carved rather than attached separately in metal.[80] The animals reveal ex-

Plates 26–27

45

tensive piecing (not only the top knots, but even some legs, tails, part of the rump) and were supported by struts under the stomach, toward the front legs. They seem to be standing quietly, heads down, and are much less modeled than the Gigantomachy horses, perhaps because they could not be observed at close quarters.

If chariots are allusions to royalty, heroes, and perhaps apotheosis, centaurs in this context may refer to Dionysos, since they too stand quietly, without hint of fight. The two tritons, then, could go with the Poseidon. But the present reconstruction places two centaurs at either end of the roof on the east side, framing, as it were, the seven quadrigas, and at the outer corners of the west wings; a triton is restored at each corner of the central opening, facing toward the inner courtyard. Other arrangements are also possible.[81] To be sure, the tritons in the round do not resemble their counterpart in the Gigantomachy: although the torso musculature is comparable, the heavy skirt of long pendant leaves (akanthos?) starting at the groin line of the statues is quite different from the fully animal body of the winged creature on the relief, only occasionally marked by vegetal elements.

Of the other animals, only one lion and two griffins remain. The former is crouching with one paw raised, in heraldic fashion; the latter seem to have been rampant, and have sickle-shaped wings characterized by long flight-feathers contrasting with ruffled, shorter feathers close to the chest (Pl. 28). Because the heads (once separately inserted, like the front legs) are missing, identification as lion-griffins is based on the hairy strip on the chest and comparison with the Alexander Sarcophagus. Given the phantasy of the Pergamene monsters, an eagle head would be just as plausible, or perhaps even a horse's or a sphinx's head, for a Pegasos or a funerary symbol.[82] The current model multiplies the animals and places at least four griffins on the roof over the entrance colonnade, facing outward toward the visitor; I have not been able to find the location of the lion on the model.

Plate 28

It is certainly a great advantage to have the benefit of a three-dimensional model and reconstruction drawings (cf. Ill. 9), and it is perhaps unfair to criticize them according to modern taste. I admit, however, that I find these reconstructions overcrowded, insufficiently documented, and obviously disputable and disputed in several details. On the principle of economy, all extant sculptures have been accommodated on the Altar, yet this distribution (and multiplication) is by no means ascertained. That each of these figures carries a symbolism appropriate to a funerary/commemorative/victory monument is no assurance that they indeed decorated it. Admittedly, the general style is in keeping with that of the Gigantomachy, and even with that of the Telephos Frieze, but this is to be expected from the workshops that carved the Altar and might then have been given commissions for additional dedications. The amount of piecing in the animals (and even the human figures) is remarkable, considering the virtuoso carving of the Gigantomachy and the apparent availability of large blocks of marble for the structure; alleged distance from the viewer seems inadequate justification for the patchwork. Particularly disturbing is the fact that some statues (especially the deities), as currently placed, would have had their perfunctory backs exposed and almost certainly visible from specific viewpoints, even if not accessible at close quarters. Akroterial narrative along an Indian file (as in a scene of the Birth of Athena) seems more typically Etruscan than Greek, and Roman influence cannot be claimed on this specific point. The reduced size of the sculptures assigned to the Altar roof may have enhanced the impression of height given by the monument— a comparable effect was indeed sought for, and produced by, the under-lifesize scale of the Nereids on the Nereid Monument at Xanthos—but at Pergamon the disproportion seems greater. The overcrowding of sculptures on the Halikarnassos Maussolleion (even in Hoepfner's less elaborate reconstruction) would have been mitigated by the considerable height of the podium; at Pergamon, the distance from the viewer seems insufficient to soften the effect. Yet we cannot expect to understand fully the principles and aims of Pergamene architectural sculpture. We can only point out that other buildings on the citadel appear remarkably sober by comparison, and even the carved balustrade of the stoas in the Athena precinct does not lead us to expect the riot of figural decoration attributed to the Altar.

The Telephos Frieze, with its own narrative, compositional requirements, and style, will be discussed in the next chapter, against the background not just of the Altar but also of other continuous-narrative sculpture elsewhere.

NOTES

1. For convenience' sake, I retain here the traditional appellation, but the true nature of the structure remains in question, as I shall discuss infra. I capitalize Altar when I refer to the main Pergamene structure, and use lower case for the alleged sacrificial table inside it and for any other altar.

I was able to study the Altar in detail during a visit to Berlin in March 1997.

2. Karl Humann (the railroad engineer responsible for the first finds in 1873) sent a telegram to the Berlin Museum in 1880, when regular excavations had started: "Wir haben eine ganze Kunstepoche gefunden!" Cf. Bieber 1961, 113. On the state of Hellenistic studies at the time and for details of the discovery, see Kunze 1986, 5–9 and esp. 10–15 (U. Kästner). With specific reference to the Telephos Frieze: Pergamon 1, 1996, 19–28 (U. Kästner).

3. On "the shadow of the Parthenon," see Ridgway 1981, 10, and, with somewhat different meaning and greater focus on style, Ridgway 1995a; my expression is actually taken from Green 1972, although that author means something different from what I have in mind.

4. Severan coin: see, e.g., Kästner 1997, fig. 2 on p. 73 (exemplar in Berlin) and discussion on p. 78. The coin, minted in Pergamon, is generally dated to the reign of Septimius Severus, 193–211 A.C. Details of the baldacchino above the altar, best seen in the Berlin exemplar, suggest that it was of a temporary nature, perhaps erected in Roman times. The incurving sides of the sacrificial altar are more clearly visible in the London exemplar: Rohde 1964, fig. 19 on p. 43. See also infra, ns. 22, 27.

Ampelius mentions an "ara," but that is what the building might have seemed to him in his time; if the baldacchino of the Severan coins stood in fact within the Altar, the added feature could justify Ampelius' description.

Bieber 1961, 120, believes that the Telephos Frieze was carved ca. 164–158; for a general span of 180–160, see her p. 113.

5. Cf. Ridgway 1988, 27–28. For the latest chronological discussion, see Andreae 1997; also *Pergamon* 2, 1997, passim. A very good summary of all elements that could help in dating, with a review of various theories, is Rumscheid 1994, vol. 1, 36–39, and cf. vol. 2, 56–57, cat. 208, where a date within the span 190/180–160/150 is accepted on stylistic grounds; he concludes that the ornament is insufficient to narrow this bracket further.

6. Detailed descriptions of the Gigantomachy and the Telephos Frieze, including new arrangements and recent additions, can be found in: Pollitt 1986, 97–110 (Gigantomachy), 198–205 (Telepheia); Stewart 1990, 210–13; Smith 1991, 157–66; Moreno 1994, 429–91; Webb 1996, 61–66. On the Telephos Frieze, besides *Pergamon* 1, 1996, and *Pergamon* 2, 1997, see also *LIMC* 7, s.v. Telephos, no. 1, pp. 857–62, figs. on pp. 858–59, pls. 590–94 (H. Heres). On the Gigantomachy, with variant identifications but excellent illustrations, see Simon 1975, but cf. Stewart 1993b, 153–58, and E. B. Harrison, *AJA* 82 (1978) 567–68, for criticism of some of her suggestions. See also Rumscheid 1994, vol. 1, 36–39, for debate over the possible iconographic allusions in the frieze.

7. The quotation is taken from a pamphlet, "The Pergamon Altar," distributed by the Pergamon Museum in Berlin and obtained March 1997. The entire passage reads: "Due to Prussia's military successes several years earlier, the German Empire had been proclaimed in 1871 and the new capital, Berlin, had begun to play a dominant role in the cultural life of Europe. These political developments led to the commencement of large excavation campaigns in different cities from Egypt to the Near East in order to acquire objects from the antique world that would enhance Berlin's cultural legitimacy." This view is in keeping with the recent tendency to criticize the "colonial" aspirations of European states and institutions around the turn into the 20th century. I am quoting this pamphlet, rather than a more permanent publication, because the former is being widely distributed to the general public, whereas the second might be read only by a restricted number of scholars and intellectuals.

A somewhat comparable situation occurred earlier in the century when Munich bought the pedimental statues from Aigina. Their presence on German soil had a vast impact on contemporary literature and psychology (perhaps even Hegelian aesthetics), out of proportion to their artistic value when compared, for instance, with the Olympia sculptures, also the fruit of a German excavation, yet not accessible to the German public because the finds remained in Greece. For important information about the impact of the Aiginetans I am indebted to A. A. Donohue.

8. For influence on altars' reconstructions in general, see Linfert 1995, initial comments. Priene altar and coffers: Carter 1983. Convenient summary of previous positions in Webb 1996, 99–100; see also 94–96, for Magnesia. Useful comparison of plans and reconstructions in Linfert 1995, esp. 134 n. 17 for his criticism of Hoepfner 1989. This altar will be mentioned also infra, Ch. 4. Tarentine Reliefs: Carter 1975; cf. Ridgway 1990, 180–85; the date of some reliefs has now been lowered by Lippolis 1996 (cf. infra, Ch. 4 n. 4), but the early inception of the style is not affected.

9. First alert on the Pergamene pottery: Callaghan 1981a and 1982. Chronological debate at the 13th International Congress in Berlin, 1988: Andreae et al. 1990, Appendix on Altar,

with contributions by M. Kunze and T.-M. Schmidt, 123–62. Publication of Pergamene wares and Altar chronology: Hübner 1993 (reviewed by S. I. Rotroff, *Gnomon* 68 [1996] 358–59) and 1994, esp. 290 (lack of close parallels) and 292 (lack of proof for foundation date). I am greatly indebted to Dr. N. Vogeikoff for bibl. and help on this subject. One of the latest campaign reports available (Radt 1996, 446–47 and 454) states that the results of the most recent ceramic analysis had not been made available in time for publication. The previous report (Radt 1995, 575–88) suggests that the pottery from the foundations is compatible with an inception date falling *within* the span ca. 185–ca. 160 (p. 588 and n. 20; my italics). "Selbst Fragen der relativen Chronologie einzelner Gefäss- und Dekorationstypen dürften durch die Altarfunde auf verläßlicher Basis geklärt werden" (p. 588) is, however, a statement that makes me wonder whether the alleged date of the Altar is being used to establish a ceramic chronology. Radt 1997, 423–25, besides listing the discovery of new architectural fragments from the Altar, announces that the manuscript on the pottery and the small finds from the foundations, by G. de Luca and W. Radt, was closed in October 1996 and is in press.

Moreno 1994, 478, suggests that the central portion of the Altar platform might have been left open until work on the Gigantomachy podium was completed, thus allowing sherds of later date to infiltrate the foundations, but this seems a structural impossibility.

10. A dating from ca. 165 to Attalos II's death in 138 is suggested by Webb 1996, 62–63, where other arguments are summarized, including the iconographic allusions in the Gigantomachy Frieze outlined above, with proper refs. See also Webb 1998, 250–51. I am deeply indebted to Dr. Webb for providing me with the text of her article in advance of publication. My own supposition is that Attalos II may have wanted to strengthen his position of loyalty toward his brother (after the mishap of Eumenes' supposed death at Delphi and Attalos' reaction to the news; cf. Webb 1996, 62) as well as that of his dynasty, but that the obvious end of the family line under Attalos III put an end to construction. The allusions on both friezes would therefore be to various (and generic) campaigns and enemies, not to single episodes or moments. In terms of construction time, consider that the Parthenon took 15 years to complete—yet it made use of a pre-existing platform and a great deal of material already quarried for its predecessor, the Older Parthenon, from a relatively proximate source, Mount Pentelikon. By comparison, a span of slightly over 20 years, perhaps with some interruptions, does not seem excessively long for the Pergamon Altar. Cf. Webb 1998, 251. Callaghan 1981a would prefer a span of only six years, which to me seems insufficient. Hoepfner 1996a, 116, believes that the Altar was *not* unfinished, but, at least for the Telephos Frieze, this statement can be challenged; therefore, would the interior colonnade have been erected while the sculptors were still carving the slabs *in situ*? The external waterspouts of the roof were left largely unworked, although one extant example suggests that they would have been shaped into lion heads. Many other architectural details apparently incomplete could also be mentioned.

11. For a recent photograph of the inscribed fragments, see *Pergamon* I, 1996, 102–103, cat. 35; for a drawing, see Smith 1991, fig. 194. Discussion and new proposals for the completion of the Altar dedication appear in Stewart's and Green's, forthcoming essays. Note that all reconstructions locate the dedicatory inscription on the E side (i.e., the back) of the building, whereas ancient practice would normally have it on the front. To be sure, the E side provided the first view of the Altar to visitors entering its terrace through its propylon, but access to the structure would still have required that they proceed to the opposite side.

12. *IG* II², 3171: *ΒΑΣΙΛΕΥΣ ΑΤΤΑ[ΛΟΣ] ΒΑΣΙΛ[ΕΩ]Σ [ΑΤ]ΤΑ[ΛΟΥ] ΚΑΙ ΒΑ[ΣΙ]ΛΙΣΣΗΣ ΑΠΟΛΛΩΝ[ΙΔΟΣ* . . . The restoration of the Athenian inscription is said (Thompson and Wycherley 1972, 106 n. 121) to be "very tentative" but the name Apollonis is largely preserved and therefore assured; the dedication is, however, fragmentary, and the drawing in Travlos 1971, 513 fig. 645, may give the wrong impression. Note that the name Attalos was even becoming popular for Athenian citizens, since it is now proved that the Attalos and Ariarathes who dedicated a statue to Karneades were not the royal homonymous individuals: Habicht 1990. In Pergamon, there was even a Consul Attalos (2nd or 3rd c. A.C.), as attested by an inscribed (albeit headless) herm found in a private house north of the lower agora, in the city proper: Hansen 1971, 252–53.

13. All my information on matronymics was provided by Dr. G. Umholtz, to whom I am greatly indebted. On practical grounds, she questioned whether a longer or a shorter dedication was conditioned by the space available on the building, the architrave of a stoa providing a much longer field than that of a temple. She also pointed out the Ptolemaic examples, and added (*per ep.*, Oct. 15, 1997) that special importance was attributed to the pairing, as made obvious by symbols and images on coins, gems, and other monuments extolling family unity and concord. For the Attalids, she suggested that mothers may have kept a greater degree of individuality, even when not of royal blood, but stressed that other extant epigraphic mentions cite dedications *in honor* or *on behalf* of mothers, rather than matronymics proper. I would add that both Ptolemies and Attalids, when (and because of) sharing the same name, needed extra identification through full parental mention, although the Ptolemies solved the problem through the systematic use of epithets, in accordance with the Egyptian Pharaonic tradition. Attalos II seems to have acquired the epithet "Philadelphos" primarily late in Eumenes' reign and in posterity: Hansen 1971, 127, with refs. in n. 188.

I believe that Attalos I (*not* Attalos II) was the Pergamene who dedicated the statues of Gauls, Giants, Amazons, and Persians on the Akropolis: see infra, Ch. 5 with ns. 45–46.

14. Hera Temple: Hansen 1971, 280; cf. *AM* 33 (1908) 402 no. 27, pl. 23.2; *AM* 37 (1912) 264: *ΒΑΣΙ]ΛΕΥΣ ΑΤΤΑΛΟ[Σ ΒΑΣΙΛΕΩΣ ΑΤΤ]ΑΛΟΥ ΗΡΑΙ Β[ΑΣΙΛΕΙΑΙ]*. Note that only the patronymic is included in this inscription—for lack of space, or because no confusion was possible in Pergamon by that time? The Pergamene emphasis on mother-son relationship, especially for mythical figures, is stressed by Webb 1998, 250, who argues that the Altar was the Heroon of Telephos. The structure could have been dedicated to both Telephos and his mother, Auge. The latter was either married by King Teuthras (Hekat., Apollod.), or adopted as his daughter (Hes., Hyg.): see *LIMC* 3, 45, s.v. Auge. The Telephos Frieze seems to show only the interrupted wedding of Telephos and Auge, but so much is missing from the narrative that we cannot be sure of the version it followed. See infra, Ch. 3.

For a different suggestion—that Apollonis may have been interred within the Altar podium sometime after her death—see Fehr 1997, 55; he strengthens this claim through a lemma in Suidas, s.v. *Apollonias limne*, stating that Attalos II buried his mother in the greatest *hieron* of Pergamon which "he had himself built." Fehr believes, however, that the Altar was begun in Eumenes' time in the 160s, although continued under his brother, thus explaining the later (mistaken) attribution of the structure to Attalos II. His position is rebutted by Stewart, forthcoming. For an advance copy of Fehr's article, I am greatly indebted to Dr. P. Guldager Bilde.

15. For uncertainty in the location of the flight of steps within the Altar, see, e.g., Webb 1996,

70 n. 77, with refs. The latest examination of the foundations does not seem to have altered the present reconstruction in this respect.

16. This is the alignment noted by Kähler 1948, 15 and plan pl. 65. Hoepfner 1990, 282, states that the alignment has been rechecked recently; he marks it (folding plate, Beil. 1) as going through the axis of the temple, along the edge of the Altar steps, down to a Hellenistic tumulus in the plain (Jigma Tepe). I do not question that such an alignment might have been intended; I question whether it would have been perceivable with the naked eye.

17. The Athena Temple is usually dated to the early 3rd c. See, e.g., Hoepfner 1997, 30, and ns. 44–46 with discussion of an earlier chronology (rejected). Hoepfner states that the temple faced south; yet it seems to have had a double cella, and therefore it is impossible to tell whether Athena was housed in the section toward the Altar. Since the entire precinct was in her honor, she is more likely to have been facing north, toward the central area and her own statue on the round pedestal. Hoepfner, at any rate (pp. 55–57), rejects the connection between the Athenaion and the Altar, on the grounds that the sacrificial table was perhaps not meant for religious ceremonies, although he would envision non-burnt offerings. For an early date for the theater, see Hoepfner 1997, 29–30.

It could also be pointed out that the Altar lies outside the inner circle of fortification walls that encompassed the Athenaion and the royal palaces, and that the road leading from the Altar to the gate of this inner circuit winds so that all visual connection between Altar and Athenaion would have been mentally lost by the time the visitor reached the temple.

18. The structure is mentioned in Hansen 1971, 239–40, with previous suggestions as to its function.

19. I have derived this information from Radt 1995, 585–86; see fig. 11 for the window in the south wall of the apsis, and fig. 1 on p. 576 for a plan of the foundations including the apsidal structure. The outside walls had traces of red plaster, the inner walls were coated with white plaster; there were drains on the rock floor to the north and south, but the annual report in M.-H. Gates, "Archaeology in Turkey," *AJA* 100 (1996) 323, states that they are unrelated to the apsidal structure (see the entire account, pp. 322–24 and figs. 36–38). No further information is given in Radt 1996. Another plan of the foundations is given by Hoepfner 1991, 190 fig. 1; cf. also Hoepfner 1993, 113–14, for the nymphaion identification—yet water supply would seem to create difficulties: cf. Hoepfner 1997, 30, on the pipeline built under Eumenes II and meant only for the royal precinct. Andrew Stewart points out to me that "flimsy walls" may not be able to support a vault, but could certainly have held a lighter roof.

20. Identification of the apsidal building and, in consequence, of the Altar as the Heroon of Telephos was particularly argued by Stähler 1978; it is now supported by Webb 1998, esp. 248–50, and other authors; it is rejected by Stewart, forthcoming.

21. For the position of the Telephos Frieze, see Kästner 1997, fig. 6 on p. 76. For the double half-columns of the courtyard, see, e.g., Hoepfner 1997, fig. 27 on p. 54; he argues (Hoepfner 1996a) that the inner colonnade was in fact erected.

22. For the most recent reconstructions of the Pergamon Altar, see *Pergamon* 2, 1997, 58–67 (W. Hoepfner) and 68–82 (V. Kästner). The two authors differ particularly in the reconstruction of the inner sacrificial table, which Hoepfner sees as having only a back and two side walls (his fig. 28 on p. 55), whereas Kästner (figs. 7–8 on pp. 79, 81) makes the side walls turn in toward the front and terminate in pier-shaped antae. See *Pergamon* 1, 1996, 100–102, cat. 34,

for discussion and photograph of one of these entablature blocks; Hoepfner 1996a, figs. 11–12 on pp. 126–27, and Hoepfner 1997, fig. 6 on p. 65, for drawings of the extant blocks. Hoepfner 1993, and 1997, foldout 4 (cf. also *Pergamon* 2, 65–67) would place the "Smaller Attalid Dedications" in the beddings of the sacrificial table (for a total of 25 reclining statues); this controversial proposal is refuted in some detail by Stewart, forthcoming, who offers his own reconstruction (captured weapons). Kunze 1990, 130, and Kästner 1997, 80–81, suggest that the cuttings are for a baldacchino added in Roman times, as seen on the Severan coin (supra, n. 4).

In a lecture delivered on March 1, 1996, at the Metropolitan Museum in New York, W. Radt stated that features of the Altar still uncertain included: the number of steps below the podium (four or five?), the exact dimensions (*not* 100 ft. in length, as restored at present), the coffers and beam spacings of the roof ceiling and the arrangement of akroterial figures, the height of the inner altar and the decoration of its top surface, the presence of statues between or behind the outer columns, and whether the monumental staircase was a straight flight of steps or included one or more landings. Note also that the platform now thought to have held statues in the round behind the outer peristyle was once reconstructed as a much narrower bench probably for trophies.

23. Linfert 1995, esp. 140, with conclusions articulated in three points. He calls the Pergamon Altar a "Prunkaltar" around a "Prunkaltar," built on its own terrace even if connected with the Athena Temple; the right of asylum was associated with the Nikephorion. He seems to prefer the higher chronology for the structure (p. 131).

On the Samothrake Altar Court, most recently, *Samothrace* 1998, 89–91, no. 14, fig. 37 (probably dedicated by Philip Arrhidaios), but see also infra, Ch. 5 n. 31.

24. This theory is advocated by Hoepfner 1996c, and repeated in Hoepfner 1997, 39–40. His attribution of narrative reliefs to the balustrade of the upper colonnade around the courtyard of Palace V (Hoepfner 1996c, 24, fig. 17; Hoepfner 1997, 40, fig. 15: four subjects, one per side) seems to me quite different from the arrangement of the Telephos Frieze (which was a true wall decoration, *behind* a colonnade) and much closer to the appearance of the stoas in the Temenos of Athena. To be sure, Hoepfner 1997, 55, states that the double columns of the Altar courtyard, comparable to those of a stoa, were meant to correspond to rows of windows in the royal andron of the palace, but even this reconstruction would not make the similarity greater. Note that Hoepfner calls "andron" the entire palatial complex of a central courtyard surrounded by rooms: cf. his labeled plan of Palace V, fig. 13 on p. 38. Figured reliefs have been found within Macedonian palaces; see Hamiaux 1998, 180–81, nos. 199–201 for three fragments from the round room at Vergina, but their original location is unclear.

For the Altar as a victory monument, see Hoepfner 1993 (also 1997). For similarity to other heroa, e.g., Webb 1998, who stresses (pp. 243–44) that the entire Athenaion terrace, with its inscribed propylon and its commemorative monuments, was rather the locus of victory celebration; see also Brogan 1998 on the same point. For comparison of the Altar with theaters, see Sturgeon, forthcoming.

25. That Athenian elements are present even in the architectural forms of the Altar is argued by Schädler 1991, esp. 317, with a suggested date after 165. See also Kästner 1997.

26. To be sure, Linfert 1995, 136–37 and fig. 9, tentatively attributes to the altar at Teos a sima with lion-head waterspouts that he saw in the vicinity and that he considers appropriate

for the structure in terms of date and scale; but he admits that the altar is not well published. I cannot tell from the photograph (and Linfert does not mention) whether the spouts are functional. I know of no other such arrangement for a monumental altar; two fragments of a thin (0.08m) table in black marble, decorated in front with floral motifs and an unpierced lion's head were found in the so-called Kultexedra of the Heroon of Leon at Kalydon (ca. 100), but the motifs recall the terracotta sima of the building: Dyggve et al. 1934, 67–68 figs. 66–67.

Rumscheid 1994, vol. 2, cat. 209 p. 57, dates the Pergamene blocks stylistically to the 2nd quarter of the 2nd c. but does not commit himself on reconstructions, although he calls it "sacrificial table."

27. See, however, Hoepfner 1989, fig. 27 (= *Pergamon* 2, 1997, 62 and fig. 5 on p. 63), who places bull statues in front of the returns of the courtyard wall atop the staircase, in imitation of the Severan coin, although he admits that the long low socles may have held equestrian images of the royal donors. See also supra, n. 4.

28. The postulated figures were, on present evidence, lined up for the entire length of the cornice blocks. They would therefore have been directly exposed to the smoke and the greasy soot of the offerings, and are thus quite different from the examples of statues allegedly connected with large altars (e.g., Artemis at Ephesos, Apollo at Halieis), which might have been brought out for special occasions and placed in a special area to the side, *not* directly above the flame. The bronze statuette permanently set into one corner of the square altar at Kalapodi does not overlook the sacrifice, and its scale (as well as that of the potential offerings) places it out of danger; its "altar" moreover may be a sacred trapeza, which was not used for burning. The akroteria (of whatever form: cf. infra, Ch. 4 and n. 57) on the antae of the Tenos altar were also reasonably far from the sacrificial fire.

29. That monumental staircases were not a typical Pergamene feature is argued by Hollinshead 1992, 90–91, against the background of other examples.

30. Colossal statues within Pergamon Altar: see, e.g., Sturgeon, forthcoming. Belevi Mausoleum: Webb 1996, 76–79, esp. 79 and n. 32; Ridgway 1990, 187–96. Limyra Ptolemaion: Webb 1996, 125–26; Ridgway 1990, 196.

31. For Hoepfner's theory, see supra, n. 24. By placing the narrative reliefs within Palace V, he would then restore weapon frieze slabs to the Athena propylon. Attribution of the cornice blocks to the propylon of the Altar terrace has already been suggested by Webb 1996, 62; for the narrative reliefs, see her pp. 60–61 (propylon to the Athena terrace); Hoepfner 1997, figs. 14a–c on p. 39. The reliefs were found rebuilt into Byzantine walls, together with many other elements from the Altar terrace, but some fragments are said to come from the NE slope below the Temenos of Athena. Although the panels with the Gigantomachy and with Athena and Telephos could be synoptic excerpts on single slabs standing for entire topics, the Trojan Horse requires at least two full slabs, which implies an extended, friezelike composition. How three different subjects could then be accommodated on a propylon is, admittedly, not clear.

A. Stewart warns me that the cornice blocks attributed to the sacrificial table (see supra, n. 22) could not belong to a propylon because they are not hollowed out behind the lion-head waterspouts, as they would be for a true sima. This is a very strong point; I could conjecture that the propylon, like the Altar, was never fully completed, but this is a weak explanation.

32. For the first suggestion see, most recently, Moreno 1994, 437; it is based on a sculptor's name inscribed on the Gigantomachy Frieze that ends in -*krates* and gives Menekrates

as patronymic. It is therefore assumed that father and son were working together at the same monument, albeit in different capacities. This possibility is undermined by Goodlett 1991, 673, who states that, since no ethnic is preserved, there is no reason to link -krates son of Menekrates with Rhodes. He signs, moreover, in collaboration with a Dionysiades who is not otherwise attested for the island. That Menekrates could also have been a Boiotian sculptor who signed some bases at Delphi is cited by Hansen 1971, 335. and n. 232. Varro's mention (*Ebdomades*) is known through Ausonius (4th c. A.C.), *Mos.* 307, but no building or ethnic is there assigned to the architect, and the transcription of his name may be erroneous: infra, Ch. 8 n. 18. Hoepfner 1997, 57, on stylistic details and on the alleged grid plan of the Altar, suggests that it was built by Hermogenes or by one of his students. But moldings can be repeated by masons' workshops without requiring a mastermind, grid plans existed since the 4th c., and the theory seems advocated primarily because such a major enterprise would have demanded a famous architect.

33. Andreae 1992 (and now 1997, 124) suggests that the Athenian sculptor Phyromachos, who is known to have worked for the Attalids, may have been that mastermind, but he seems to oscillate in this opinion, and Stewart (review of Andreae et al. 1990, in *Gnomon* 65 [1993] 710–16) objects on chronological grounds. See also Müller 1992 and infra, Ch. 7 n. 10.

34. On the walls of the podium flanking the stairs (the German *Risalit*—a term I am going to adopt here for brevity's sake and lack of an English correspondent), where the bottom molding was omitted, the sculptors' names were inscribed on the cornice, and the Giants' on the background of the frieze, between the figures. The sections carved by individual masters were delimited by vertical lines engraved on the base molding, and often coincided with the joins between frieze slabs. Cf., e.g., Hansen 1971, 334–35; Pollitt 1986, 101–102. Thimme 1946 calculated that ca. 40 units by different masters could be identified on the frieze, but some sections were carved by two sculptors, and therefore an exact total cannot be reached. For a division of the Altar by setting marks on the bottom molding (probably for the placing of the Giants), see Kästner 1994, 128 fig. 2, and cf. table on p. 134. Other setting marks appeared above the dentils, on the cornice, probably for the placing of the gods.

35. At current counts, 25 gods' names are preserved, although others can be conjectured; a drawing of the Gigantomachy slabs in Pollitt 1986, 96–97, distinguishes among degrees of certainty for the various divine identifications. Fehr 1997, 61 n. 13, mentions that the identification of 33 (= over 50 percent of the ca. 60 fighting deities) is assured or non-controversial. He further (p. 60 n. 6) breaks down the totals to 32 goddesses and 21 gods (cf. Simon 1975, who fills up the gaps and counts 38 goddesses and 24 gods).

To the 17 Giants' names listed by Smith 1991, 164, that of Porphyrion can now be safely added (Kästner 1994) on the basis of a new fragment joining a previously known one; it can be shown to belong to Zeus' opponent with hollow eyes, as previously hypothesized, although Simon 1975 had suggested Typhon: see her chart on rear of foldout pl. 1 (approx. p. 69).

36. That it was typical of Hellenistic (Asia Minor?) buildings not to be finished at once was brought out in the discussion following Kreeb 1990. See additional comments and refs. in Ridgway 1999, 191–92 and n. 16. For the ramifications of Pergamene style (in connection with a female head from the Letoon near Xanthos), see, e.g., infra, Ch. 7 and n. 31.

37. My numbers are derived from Thimme 1946, who, however, believes in a strong Rhodian connection, on stylistic grounds. So does Hansen 1971, 334–37, but see Goodlett 1991, 673, esp. her n. 25 for the frequency of the name "Menekrates" outside Rhodes. The well-known comparison with the Laokoon and his three Rhodian masters need not detain us here, since it

seems now established that those sculptors worked no earlier than ca. 40 B.C. and the location of their prototype (if such there was) cannot be determined with certainty. A Rhodian link has more recently been advocated by Heilmeyer 1994, on comparison with the Altar's groundplan and on the assumption that the structure was dedicated to all the gods. Moreno 1994, 436, who believes that the distribution of carving tasks on the Altar reveals a vast cultural *koiné*, adds masters from Ephesos, but does not state his source.

See Kästner 1994, p. 134, for the association of some Giants' names and masters' signatures along the Altar: the Athenian sculptor, named Orestes (perhaps son of Athenaios), worked on the north side, Dionysiades and [Mene]krates on the front of the south wing; Theorrhetos, a Pergamene, is not included in his placements, and neither is Melanippos, although their names are preserved; the former appears above the first Giant of the SW risalit, whose leg/snake has an open mouth being grasped by the claw of the corner eagle: cf. Simon 1975, pl. 30.1.

38. Goodlett 1991, fig. 1 on p. 674, diagrams sculptural production in Hellenistic Rhodes. However, while the numbers of total and independent works seem to drop sharply during the span mentioned, that of collaborative works remains approximately steady and actually increases somewhat, to peak again at 100–50. Perhaps workshops continued their activity on the islands, whereas independent masters were free to travel abroad.

39. Note that the Panathenaic frieze was 160 m long, and the Gigantomachy Frieze, ca. 120 m; the Parthenon frieze slabs are 1.06 m high, as against the 2.30 m of the Gigantomachy slabs. Up to 0.30 m of marble was carved away from the blocks to produce the very high-relief figures.

40. Smith 1991, 159–60, presents a good discussion of how he visualizes the planning and execution of the Gigantomachy. He advocates detailed scale drawings first, then layout of figures drawn on the blocks, with lowest parts carved before setting and uppermost parts carved in position because the lifting holes of the blocks have been partly or wholly obliterated by the carved figures. The cornice, however, would have been added when the sculptures were completed. See also Webb 1996, 65, with additional refs. It may be significant of working practices that the figures on the NW risalit seem to rest directly on the Altar steps, whereas those of the opposite, SW, risalit have low plinths below the points of contact: cf. Simon 1975, pls. 2 and 30.

41. On Krates of Mallos and his Stoic cosmogony, see Simon 1975, 56–57; cf. also Stewart 1993b, 153, and *OCD*[3], s.v. For arguments against some of Simon's identifications, see reviews of Simon 1975: Harrison (supra, n. 6); R. Wenning, *Gnomon* 51 (1979) 355–61; and cf. Stewart 1993b, 153–58. For a proposal with different identifications, see Pfanner 1979. *LIMC* 4, s.v. Gigantes, no. 24, pp. 204–205 (F. Vian), tabulates the names attributed to the various divine figures by seven authors (see also a drawing of the Gigantomachy frieze, pp. 202–203, with names in upper or lower case according to degree of certainty; inscribed names of gods and Giants are transcribed on p. 207). We shall not be concerned, here, with either disputing or supporting proposed identifications. Other literary sources that may have been consulted for the Altar are mentioned, e.g., by Pollitt 1986, 107, and by Moreno 1994, 433.

It is perhaps significant that some of the immortals included in the Gigantomachy received altars at the sanctuary of Demeter at Pergamon: Ge, Helios, the winds (Anemoi), Nyx, Selene. These dedications have been explained within the context of the Orphic mysteries at times associated with the Eleusinian cult: Guthrie 1935, 260; Ippel 1912, 288–93, no. 19. At any rate, this evidence may show that their presence on the Altar was not as exceptional as usually surmised.

42. This comment is made by Osada 1993, 83–84, who would include the Hekateion friezes

at Lagina among the examples of labeled compositions; there, however, the distance from the viewer may have made such labels illegible. That the figures of the Ara Pacis processional friezes were identified in writing has always seemed to me a distinct possibility, especially in view of the many foreign visitors for whom the message was intended; Prof. Gerhard Koeppel made the same point during a public lecture at Villanova University in 1994. Stewart 1993b, 159–60, stresses that the location of gods' versus Giants' names is a spatial metaphor: the former are "up," the latter "down."

43. This point, although in a somewhat different form, has now been made by Fehr 1997, who stresses, however, the procreational value of all the female divinities on the Altar—a concept/message that would appeal not only to the Romans but also to the other peoples living in Asia Minor. The interest of the iconographic program of the Altar for Mysians, Karians, Lydians, Phrygians, and other non-Greeks in Anatolian lands had already been mentioned by W. Neumer-Pfau, "Die kämpfenden Göttinnen vom großen Fries des Pergamonaltars," *Visible Religion* 2 (1983) 75–94 (*non vidi*).

44. A block of the Chariot Frieze from the Halikarnassos Maussolleion is inscribed *Apollo [. . .] epo[iei]*, a sculptor's signature. Whether the frieze ran around the base of the quadriga on the roof (Jeppesen 1992, 87, pl. 23.2), or the interior of the underground tomb chamber, as more recently suggested (Hoepfner 1996b), the inscription was certainly inaccessible to the casual viewer. The case is therefore different from that of the Altar, yet it may be indication of an incipient trend (see also infra, Ch. 3, on the Knidian altar). Stewart 1993b, 160–62, attributes the Altar's signatures to "a marked degree of originality" on the part of the sculptors; yet (p. 168) he also points out that such signatures are so uniform as to correspond to labels, mandated by Eumenes to signal the universal reach of his enterprise. I tend to believe that inscriptions were routinely cut by masons, not the figure-sculptors themselves, which could explain the uniformity of script and formulas. Personal signatures in our sense of the word probably did not exist in antiquity.

45. Priene coffers: Carter 1983, 44–180 (cat. 1–67 on pp. 103–80). Coffer with Ge: cat. 27; Kybele on lion: cat. 14 (comparable to Rhea/Magna Mater on the Altar: e.g., Moreno 1994, 456 fig. 577); Dionysos/lion biting Giant: cat. 37; Athena and opponent: cat. 31–32. Note also cat. 38–39 for Giants fighting with shield and helmet, cat. 46 for a cuirassed Giant or warrior; cat. 44 for a Giant's hand holding a boulder. For additional comments and bibl. on the Priene coffers, see Ridgway 1997b, 135–40. When the Priene reliefs were dated after the Altar, they were considered poor imitations of its iconography. Their redating has changed the sequence, but Carter (p. 97) has opted for emphasis on the coffers' 4th-c. traits, since he had to prove their precedence.

46. Pergamon Apollo: e.g., Moreno 1994, 465 fig. 588 and cf. p. 474 for comparison with the Belvedere Apollo; see also Stewart 1993b, 163 and fig. 58, who accepts that a version of the type existed at Synnaos in Phrygia, a Pergamene possession. Contra a Greek date for the Apollo type: Ridgway 1990, 93–94. Lagina Apollo: e.g., Webb 1996, fig. 82; Smith 1991, 207.1.

47. On this feature of Attalid propaganda, see Gruen, forthcoming.

48. Pergamon/Istanbul Alexander, as Apollo: Moreno 1994, 474–75. Stewart 1993a, 332–33, bibl. on p. 428, figs. 128–29, could accept a free-standing statue. Additional mortals on the Altar, e.g., Phaethon and Tithonos (the latter eventually made immortal): Simon 1975. Others have suggested Kephalos, also mortal, instead of Tithonos. Against attribution of the "Alex-

ander" to the Altar: Kreikenbom 1992, 117–18, cat. I.5. See also comments in Ridgway 1990, 143 n. 28, with ref. to further opposition on technical grounds, and to specific Altar Giants with anastole. Radt 1981 assigns the head to the E side on stylistic grounds and because of the lacunae there; Hermes and Herakles are also possible candidates, and the latter (epigraphically attested and surely located, although missing at present) might explain the allusion to the Macedonian. But he recognizes the similarity between the "Alexander" and several of the Giants; see his refs. to specific figures.

49. Bull-giant (thick neck, bull's horns and ears on human face; S side): Moreno 1994, fig. 578 and comments on p. 464. (For convenience' sake, I refer to Moreno 1994 and his illustrations, but excellent photographs can be found in a variety of publications on the Pergamon Altar.)

Lion-giant (snaky legs[?], mane, and animal face; S side): Moreno 1994, fig. 581. His divine opponent is identified as Ouranos because of a pattern understood as owl's eyes on his wings — allusion to the night sky. See also the fragment illustrated in *Pergamon* 1, 1996, 90–91, no. 25: to me the "terrifying eyes" said to form the pattern on the wing recall rather the front of a helmet with nose-guard.

Bird-giant (wings, claws for hands and feet; E side): Moreno 1994, fig. 588; he is Leto's opponent. Another Giant with some animal features is Phoebe's opponent (butterfly [fringed] wings, pointed ears, small horns; S side): Moreno 1994, fig. 582 and cf. comments on p. 470. Porphyrion, Zeus' opponent on the E side, has pointed ears (detail in Moreno 1994, fig. 561).

50. Thrako-Phrygian helmet, on N side: Moreno 1994, drawing fig. 552; better illustration in Simon 1975, pl. 8, which clearly shows the griffin-head finial with open mouth. The plain type is called "tiara-like" by Dintsis 1986, 23–56, who illustrates a detail of the Pergamene frieze on his pl. 21.3. The plain type has been found in Macedonian tombs, as well as over a wide area: Vokotopoulou 1982, esp. 518 for Macedonia. Even more significantly, Dintsis 1986, 45, shows that coins of Philip V and of Perseus depict the kings wearing the griffin-finial helmet (cf. his pl. 21.1–2). The griffin type ultimately goes back to a tetradrachm of Alexander the Great: Dintsis, cat. 47, foldout 2.47. It is perhaps meaningful that this helmet, on the Pergamon Altar, belongs to the single extant example of a dead Giant (the Fawley Court torso): see infra, n. 58. On the other hand, the widespread use of armament types among different peoples makes specific suggestions dangerous; for the range of shield and helmet forms and decorations, see, e.g., Polito 1998, 39–45 and 49–53 respectively.

Giant with starburst shield, on S side: Moreno 1994, drawing fig. 549 and comments on pp. 429–30 (read as allusion to Philip V); cf. Simon 1975, pl. 16. For the Macedonian shield types, see Liampi 1990, who considers the type a dynastic emblem. For Hera = Apollonis, see, e.g., Fehr 1997. For the star as a Giants' shield device in Etruria, see de Grummond, forthcoming. For additional allusion to Pergamon's enemies, see Moreno 1994, ad loc., and Webb 1996, 63.

51. For this detail, although barely visible, see, e.g., Simon 1975, pl. 7, where the Giant is identified as Aither's opponent, and the goddess next to him as Nyx. For identification as Persephone, see Pfanner 1979, on the basis of the pomegranate flower(?) at the end of Nyx' fillet, visible against the background. Moreno 1994, 451, identifies her instead as an Erinys. Ionic capital with thunderbolt: *Pergamon* 1, 1996, 96–97, cat. 31; cf. Kästner 1997, 70, capital Type C. But Zeus' thunderbolts on the Altar are not winged. Could the symbol allude to Roman legions?

52. Giant opposing Artemis: Moreno 1994, fig. 583. Unfortunately, the detail of the shield-strap is unclear in most photographs. It was pointed out to me first by Dr. Pia Guldager Bilde, of Aarhus University. Stephen Sarles, a graduate student in Classics and Archaeology at Florida State University in 1997, has called to my attention, as a possible parallel, the two shields on the Grand Camée de France (Gemma Tiberiana) that have aigis and gorgoneion as device: see, e.g., the large color illustration in Andreae 1977, col. pl. 57. Surprisingly, those shields are held by the barbarian prisoners in the exergue, a further example of a divine emblem used for enemies of the power sponsoring the artwork. But I cannot find a commentary explaining or identifying the barbarians who hold those shields; Sarles suggested that they are Cappadocians, who fought both the Pergamenes at the Battle of Magnesia (190, when Cappadocia was under Antiochos III) and Germanicus, ca. 200 years later.

For the golden aigis hanging on the Akropolis S wall, see Paus. 5.12.4 and 1.21.4. For a discussion identifying the Medusa Rondanini type as the gorgoneion on that monument, attributed to Antiochos IV (ca. 170; r. 175–164), see Belson 1980. Callaghan 1981b, argues for a dedication by Antiochos III (r. 223–187) but Bringmann 1995, 96 and n. 21, prefers Antiochos IV because of his other benefactions to Athens. If this connection with the Gigantomachy symbol could be proved, the lower chronology for the Altar could be supported.

53. I do not understand why Andreae 1997, 123, points out that allusion to the Gauls is made clear by the similarity in Greek between the name *Titanes,* the Titans, often in antiquity confused with the Giants, and *titanos,* the feminine noun for "plaster" with which the Kelts were known to coat their hair. To be sure, Kallimachos (4.173–87) compared the Gauls to Titans, but on the Altar the Titans are fighting on the side of the gods, not of the Giants. I also find it remarkable that not one of the Giants is given a torque, an ornament distinctive of the Gauls and easily applicable to the more humanoid figures on the Altar, and no beardless Giant sports a mustache, a fashion again typical of the Kelts.

54. On the true meaning of the Panathenaic festival in Athens (celebrating *not* Athena's birth, as traditionally stated, but Athena's victory, as explained by Aristotle) and on its connection with Pergamon, see Pinney 1988. For the Pergamene festival, see also Hansen 1971, 448 (Panathenaia mentioned in a letter by Eumenes I to the people of Pergamon).

55. Giants of the NW risalit: Moreno 1994, fig. 576. Details of Doris' footwear in Morrow 1985, pl. 122a–b and comments on p. 139; for additional comments on the footwear on the Pergamene Gigantomachy, see her pp. 108–109 (pls. 81–87), 123–25 (pls. 112–120), 136, 138–39, and concluding remarks on p. 141.

56. Heads attributed to the Gigantomachy: Brommer 1970 (two in Fulda, one in the Astarita Collection in Capri); the Fulda heads attributed to a different monument: Yfantidis 1993. Is the Nikephorion suggested as a possible locale because its unexcavated status makes the attribution unarguable? That these heads found their way to Europe is not an objection to their provenience, since several fragments have now been demonstrated to belong to the Altar and to have been taken abroad by early travelers. Interestingly, Yfantides notes that the Fulda heads wear Galatian helmets but are closer to some on the Altar frieze than to the Ludovisi Gaul, which I continue to consider a Roman creation (see infra, Ch. 5 and n. 46).

That the use of contemporary armor in mythological depictions need not carry historical allusions is perhaps shown by the "Lapiths" defeating the centaurs on the coffers of the Belevi Mausoleum (supra, n. 30; Ridgway 1990, pls. 90–94)—unless a connection with the armies of

The Shadow of the Pergamon Altar

the tomb owner is postulated. But we should beware of over-interpreting ancient representations of highly traditional themes.

57. Wild Man head from road to Asklepieion, Bergama Museum: e.g., Smith 1991, fig. 189 "(Marsyas?)." Tentative attribution to the Altar as Zeus: Jessen 1968; photomontage and arguments in support of connection: Meischner 1972. Against: Rohde 1976. The style is certainly in keeping with the Gigantomachy; why would a Marsyas in the round be hollowed out? Stewart 1990, 209, suggests that the huge figure might have been from a group like that within the temple at Lykosoura, hollowed out for weight reduction, and set against a wall. He states that the head has a pointed ear and could thus even be a centaur (Cheiron?). On the Altar, the scooping out of the cranium would be needed to make the head rise to the level of the dentils, above all others, as appropriate for the most important personage of the frieze. For pieces taken to Europe, see, e.g., the Worksop Torso and the Fawley Court Giant (Ridgway 1979, with refs. in ns. 11 and 13; see also infra, n. 58). Recent additions to the Gigantomachy frieze are helpfully listed, with commentary, by Zagdoun 1988, 132–34.

58. Fawley Court Giant: Haynes 1972, esp. 737–42; on p. 742, it is described as the only extant example of a dead figure on the Gigantomachy. For a drawing, see Simon 1975, fig. 3 on p. 27. See also supra, n. 50. Other possibly dead Giants: Giant under Hera's horses; Giant stepped on by Artemis; two Giants near Aphrodite (see Moreno, 1994, fig. 564, and note his striking comparison with two Sabine warriors on a Roman sarcophagus in Villa Mattei, his fig. 566). A "beautiful" Giant, unusually rendered with snake-legs, seems to be removing a weapon from his chest, behind the Giant with butterfly wings: Moreno 1994, fig. 582; Simon 1975, pl. 22.

Losing gods: the quotation is from Stewart 1993b, 163; the god struggling with the lion-giant has his left forearm scored by the claws of the lion's right paw (Moreno fig. 581; Simon pl. 23); one god is in the wrestling grasp of a snake-legged Giant who bites his left arm (Moreno fig. 567; Simon pl. 9); the Worksop torso, alone among the deities, is on his knees—his muscular torso seen from behind could cause him to be mistaken for one of the Giants (Moreno fig. 578; Simon pl. 26). The "biting scene" recalls similar motifs on the W pediment of the Temple of Zeus at Olympia and on the frieze of the Temple of Apollo at Bassai (centaur biting Lapith youth). If the bitten god is the mortal Dioskouros, as some advocate, and if the equation (attested by coins) Eumenes II/Attalos II = Dioskouroi holds, it seems remarkable that one of them should be shown in such a precarious situation—unless we have an allusion to the near-fatal ambush suffered by Eumenes II near Delphi in 172?

Snake-leg biting shield of Hekate, while snake-leg of Giant on opposite side bites her skirt: Moreno fig. 583; Simon pl. 19. The latter Giant, Artemis' opponent, tries to gouge her dog's eye (cf. Parthenon metope S9; youth jabbing finger in centaur's eye). Giant (opponent of Asterie) grabbing dog's fur: Moreno fig. 582, Simon pl. 22.

Giants grasping deities' arms: e.g., Alkyoneus, Athena's opponent; Doris' opponent on NW risalit (same pattern as Athena's). Giants clutching boulders: see, e.g., Simon pls. 3, 18. Giant hurling boulder (Hekate's opponent): Simon pl. 19. For Giants hurling boulders even among hoplites, see, once again, the Siphnian Treasury, N frieze.

59. The quotation (originally in French) is from *LIMC* 1, s.v. Alkyoneus, 564 no. 33 (R. Olmos/L. J. Balmaseda). Identification is provided by a fragmentary inscription, . . .]ΝΕΥΣ, that may belong to the scene. Harrison, in her review of Simon 1975 (supra, n. 6), points out that

Athena is pulling the Giant toward, rather than away from, his mother; that wings are unusual for Alkyoneus; and that Enkelados, "whose name evokes the sound of rushing winds," would be a better identification. Simon's argument (pp. 22, 44) that both Athena and Zeus are given the two "immortal" Giants as opponents, is rendered invalid by the recent integration of Porphyrion's name instead of Typhon's (supra, n. 35). Simon explains Alkyoneus' four wings as an indication that the goddess can overcome her opponent only in the air (p. 22). But the Greek name *alkyon* means kingfisher, the sea bird who might have inspired Alkyoneus' wings.

60. Cf. Simon 1975, pl. 28, and her n. 157 on p. 31: "Die beiden mit Schurzen bekleideten Satyrn . . ." She also discusses the small size of the satyrs, typical for the Hellenistic period, as emphasizing Dionysos' might.

61. See Pollitt 1986, 7; additional comments on p. 111, where other features are identified, especially "the formal devices by which . . . theatrical excitement is achieved—restless, undulating surfaces; agonized facial expressions; extreme contrasts of texture created by deep carving of the sculptural surface with resultant areas of highlight and dark shadow; and the use of 'open' forms which deny boundaries and tectonic balance." For Baroque architecture, see infra, Ch. 4 n. 80.

62. Stewart 1993b, 133–35; the quotation is from p. 134.

63. These comments were made by R. Carpenter at Bryn Mawr College, in the course of a graduate seminar on Hellenistic sculpture, on Feb. 24, 1955. Carpenter 1960, 208–209, writes about "a release of traditional devices to 'free emotive' use"; he sees the style as only a brief period in Hellenistic art, and believes it was found objectionable "not for its lack of restraint or its restless search for variety; its fault was that it contravened the innate Greek sense of sculpture as a revitalization of the human body without distortion of its physical reality." We now know that the Baroque style had a much longer currency and a greater acceptance than envisaged by Carpenter, but his comments are illuminating nonetheless.

64. For convenience, I shall refer to the plates in Simon 1975, more manageable and perhaps more readily available than the truly best illustrations in H. Winnefeld, *Die Friese des großen Altars* (*AvP* 3.2, Berlin 1910). As a result, I shall give the identifications with which Simon labels her figures, for quick recognition, although occasionally mentioning possible alternatives. The Parthenon illustrations are taken from Brommer 1963, 1967, and 1977. For the Nike Balustrade, I use Carpenter 1929; for other comparisons, Stewart 1990.

65. Pergamon Apollo and opponent: Simon 1975, pl. 18. Parthenon metope S 27: Brommer 1967, pls. 217–19 (it is important to look at the Lapith from various angles to appreciate his muscular rendering). "Ilissos" (Figure A) from Parthenon W pediment: Brommer 1963, pl. 81. In the Apollo, the muscles do not swell plastically from beneath the skin, but seem worked from the outside. The pose of Apollo's opponent has often been compared to that of the Capitoline Gaul, as part of the argument for the Pergamene origin of the latter monument, yet the same torsional rendering, although less pronounced, appears as early as the pediments of the Temple of Aphaia on Aigina (Stewart 1990, pls. 668, 245–46 respectively). That the allusion is not impossible is suggested by the fact that Attalos I bought the island in 210, taking away some of its monuments (Hansen 1971, 316). Howard 1983 discusses that situation, although he focuses on the "Dying Gaul" rather than on the Gigantomachy figures.

66. Simon 1975: pls. 14 (Alkyoneus), 10 (Dione's opponent), 9 ("Heoos" or Polydeukes, one of the Dioskouroi, according to other interpretations), 8 (Giant near Thrako-Phrygian helmet).

The Shadow of the Pergamon Altar

Intake of breath: Ridgway 1981, 25, 49, and cf. p. 86 for the Hephaisteion E frieze. Parthenon W pediment, torso H: Brommer 1963, pls. 91–92. Hephaisteion E frieze: Ridgway 1981, figs. 48, 51–52. Note the bumpy digitations of the man to the right of the kneeling prisoner, slab E 1, in fig. 48.

67. Cf. esp. the kneeling Giant in front of Heoos/Polydeukes, Simon 1975, pl. 9, and the kneeling prisoner on Hephaisteion E 1 (Ridgway 1981, fig. 48). See also the Lapiths on Parthenon metopes S 8 and S 30 (Brommer 1967, pls. 190–91 and 229–30 respectively).

68. E.g., Simon 1975, pls. 3 (Amphitrite's opponent), 2 (Doris' opponent), 10 (Dione's opponent). Cf. Parthenon frieze, N XVII.58 (Brommer 1977, pl. 73).

69. Pergamon Zeus: Simon 1975, pl. 15. Poseidon, Parthenon W pediment: Brommer 1963, pl. 103. To be sure, some of the more animal-like Giants have similar distorted, bombastic anatomy—e.g., the bird-giant opponent of Leto, pl. 18, with his bumpy digitations, or the bull-giant, pl. 23—as do some of the gods (e.g., Okeanos, pl. 2, and Triton, pl. 3), but the Zeus best exemplifies the use of pattern enhancement to create an emotional response.

Anatomical traits in the Gigantomachy are analyzed by Amberger-Lahrmann 1996, but her emphasis is on the physiognomic implications of the renderings. Her plates with comparisons to actual anatomical features are, however, very useful, and her conclusions (pp. 55–56) coincide with mine: a general return to Classical elements leads to forms characterized by the enhancement of details, "overdimensional muscles, overswelling modeling," for rhetorical emphasis beyond anatomical reality. She analyzes the Zeus (pp. 23–27) and the Giants around him (pp. 28–35), Alkyoneus (pp. 36–41), and a few other figures.

70. For a definition of the stylistic terms here used, see Ridgway 1981, xvii–xviii.

Rolled mantles, on Altar: e.g., Simon 1975, pls. 6 (1st Moira), 10 (Dione), 16 (Hera), 19 (Hekate, Artemis, Leto). *In 5th c.:* e.g., several of the standing male figures on the E frieze of the Parthenon (Brommer 1977, pls. 166, 183); on the Nike Balustrade (Carpenter 1929, pl. 20.1). *In 4th c.:* e.g., Muses on the Mantineia base; so-called Maussollos and Artemisia from Halikarnassos (Stewart 1990, pls. 494 and 535 respectively).

Deep carving along contours, on Altar: e.g., Simon 1975, pls. 2 (Doris), 3 (Amphitrite), 6 (2nd Moira), 7 (Nyx/Persephone), 14 (Nike). *In 5th c.:* e.g., Nike of Paionios, Bassai frieze Kentauromachy (Stewart, pls. 408, 451 respectively); Nike Balustrade (Carpenter 1929, pls. 8, 11). *In 4th c.:* e.g., W akroterial aura from Epidauros Asklepieion; Apollo "Patroos" (Stewart 1990, pls. 457, 512 respectively).

Railroad-track folds, on Altar: e.g., Simon 1975, pls. 7 (Nyx), 10 (Dione), 14 (Athena). *In 5th c.:* Nike of Paionios, Bassai metope (Stewart 1990, pls. 408, 454 respectively). *In 4th c.:* e.g., Nereids from Xanthos (Stewart, pls. 469–70).

Sanguisuga wavelet, on Altar: e.g., Simon 1975, pls. 5 (Keto), 7 (Nyx), 32 (Selene). *In 5th c.:* e.g., Nike Balustrade (Carpenter 1929, pls. 7, 13). In the 4th c. the pattern may disappear.

Nicks and bends, on Altar: e.g., Simon 1975, pls. 5 (Keto), 19 (Hekate). *In 5th c.:* e.g., Parthenon E frieze, seated gods (Brommer 1977, pl. 181 for details), Nike Balustrade (Master B: Carpenter 1929, pls. 7, 13). The pattern is not so common in the 4th c., but cf. the truly Baroque mantle on the lap of the seated woman in the so-called "telauges mnema," gravestele Athens NM 3716 (Stewart 1990, pl. 479).

Omega (butterfly) pattern, on Altar: e.g., Simon 1975, pls. 2 (Doris, overfold of peplos), 6 (1st Moira, kolpos), 7 (Nyx, veil). *In 5th c.:* e.g., incipient in the Parthenon (Brommer 1977, pl. 188,

E VIII, figures 57, 61), abundant in the Bassai frieze (Stewart 1990, pl. 449, Amazonomachy frieze). *In 4th c.:* e.g., Dexileos Stele (Stewart 1990, pl. 480).

Curved maeander pattern, on Altar: e.g., Simon 1975, pls. 2 (Doris, skirt hem), 10 (Aphrodite). *In 5th c.:* e.g., Parthenon E pediment, Figure K (apoptygma hem, Brommer 1963, pl. 46.2); Nike Balustrade (Carpenter 1929, pls. 5, 19).

S-curves to indicate motion, on Altar: e.g., Simon 1975, pls. 14 (Athena), 15 (Zeus), 22 (Phoibe). *In 5th c.:* e.g., Parthenon E pediment, Figure G (Brommer 1963, pl. 39); Nike Balustrade (Carpenter 1929, pl. 7, Master B).

Transparency over abdomen, on Altar: e.g., Simon 1975, pl. 2 (Doris; note indication of navel). *In 5th c.:* e.g., Parthenon, E pediment, Figure M; W pediment, Figure N (Brommer 1963, pls. 48 [detail], 111); Nike Balustrade (Sandalbinder, Carpenter 1929, pl. 27).

71. *Belaboring of primary folds to obtain crêpe effect,* on Altar: e.g., Simon 1975, pls. 10 (Aphrodite), 22 (Phoibe), 26 (Eos), 28 (Dionysos). *In 5th c.:* Parthenon E pediment, Figure E and Figure K, skirts below mantles (Brommer 1963, pls. 35 and 36.4; 46); Nike Balustrade (Carpenter 1929, pls. 5, 6.4).

Press folds, on Altar: e.g., Simon 1975, pls. 7 (Nyx), 15 (Zeus), 27 (Klymene). *In 4th c.:* Apollo Patroos, "Maussollos" (Stewart 1990, pls. 512, 535). Cf. also an Attic gravestone in the University of Pennsylvania Museum, Philadelphia: Ridgway 1997b, pl. 44. Although photographs may not show these details with clarity, I have verified all of them directly on the monuments.

For additional significant drapery patterns, cf. the ragged appearance of Ouranos' costume (Simon 1975, pl. 23) which seems to hang on his right thigh like a cobweb, and the motif behind the knee of the alighting Nike by Master E, on the Balustrade (Carpenter 1929, pl. 25); or the tension folds between the legs of the riding Eos (Simon, pls. 25–26), and Figure Q from the W pediment of the Parthenon (Brommer 1963, pls. 119, 121; to a lesser degree, also Figure F from the E pediment, pls. 35, 38).

Poses: Simon 1975, pl. 10 (Aphrodite)—cf. Carpenter 1929, pl. 5; pl. 27 (Klymene)—cf. Brommer 1963, pl. 39 (Figure G from E pediment) and pl. 41.1 (restored cast with mantle).

72. Note also that the penis was usually inserted separately on naked torsos; in the present state, all exposed genitals of the male figures appear as if they had been deliberately broken or hammered off.

73. Simon 1975: Helios and horse, pl. 25; Leto, pl. 19; Asterie, pl. 22.

74. Simon 1975, e.g., pls. 5, 6 (arrow folds: Keto, 1st Moira); 5, 7 (drapery through drapery: Keto, Nyx); 32 (textures: Selene); 6, 19 (drill punctuating folds: 1st Moira, Hekate); 27 (eye-folds: Klymene); 7, 9, 14 (hair separated from face contour: Nyx, "biter," Alkyoneus and Ge). Alkyoneus is the typical example also for the drill channels contouring the upper eyelid and the hair strands; for the "ropy" hairstyle of gods and goddesses, see, e.g., Aphrodite (pl. 10), Astraios (pl. 23), Selene (pl. 32). The best photos of the Aphrodite head are shown by Luschey 1961, pls. 1–7.

Great textural contrasts appear also in the Zeus panel (Simon, pl. 15): the god's aigis next to both his eagle and the animal skin used as shield by Porphyrion. The flaming thunderbolt piercing the Giant's thigh to the left of Zeus is reflected on the interior of his shield.

75. See esp. the face of Nyx (Simon 1975, pl. 7) and compare it with the Apollo from the E frieze of the Parthenon or the fragment Akr. 1222 (Brommer 1977, pls. 182.2 and 195.3 respectively). The so-called Beautiful Head (Schöner Kopf), which should belong to the Altar or

to one of the surrounding statues, is also a useful example: Pollitt 1986, fig. 111. In my analysis of faces I differ from Amberger-Lahrmann 1996, who finds Nyx' face basically flat, empty in expression, with barely defined lips (p. 53). She is, however, contrasting Nyx' face with a Giant's, thus stressing different characteristics. She equates female faces (oval) to panthers', male faces (quadrangular) to lions', according to established physiognomic beliefs of the time.

76. Tragedy/Tragoidia: e.g., Pollitt 1986, fig. 113; *LIMC* 8, s.v. Tragodia, no. 4 pl. 27. Morrow 1985, 122–23 and pl. 111, accepts the traditional interpretation for the figure, but note her own pls. 67–68, showing statues of women from Magnesia with comparably high soles and indentation after the big toe. For a thorough argument identifying the Pergamon statues as a local version of Muses, see Stewart, forthcoming. For a reconstruction of the Altar with the statues in place, see, e.g., Hoepfner 1997, foldouts 3–4; Moreno 1994, fig. 545. It seems surprising that Hoepfner (who in his 1996b article, pp. 106–110, had criticized K. Jeppesen's and G. Waywell's reconstructions of the Halikarnassos Maussolleion for postulating too many statues on too fragmentary evidence, and had suggested that at least the lifesize pieces were votive or honorary sculptures from the temenos) has no difficulty reconstructing (from just over 30) the wealth of statuary needed to fill the 73 spaces of the Altar colonnade, and all the various other positions on the roof of the peristyle and the top of the sacrificial table. Even the number of female statues is variously given, *Pergamon* 2, 1997, 60 (Hoepfner) stating that "28 or more" are extant.

Not all free-standing statues were found in the pit of the destruction deposit N of the Altar; a few had been incorporated in an early Byzantine wall in the market below, and others came from the theater precinct below the Altar terrace. Kunze 1990, 134, notes that some of them were uncovered on the slope between the Altar and the Athena temenos and may have fallen down from the upper terrace. He also points out that the intended viewpoint of the seated and standing figures is not from below (as would be required, had they been standing behind the colonnade) but from approximate eye-level; he therefore would position them on a 68-m-long podium on the N wall of the Altar terrace. Early suggestions that they belonged to the Altar had met with some opposition, on the grounds that the figures did not form a homogeneous group, and indeed some of them have a different treatment of the drapery. See also n. 77.

Zeus Ammon, Istanbul Arch. Mus. E 359: for attribution to the Altar colonnade, see refs. in Stewart, forthcoming. Yet the piece has been variously dated: cf. Niemeier 1985, 38; *LIMC* 1, s.v. Ammon, no. 6 pl. 670, even considers it Roman Imperial. Stylistic discussion: Niemeier, 38–41, 136–39, figs. 16–19 (Classicizing, but contemporary with the Altar, although no direct comparison can be found on it: p. 40); Lewerentz 1993, 114–15, 270 cat. V.3, fig. 24 (eclectic new creation of mid-2nd c. echoing 5th-c. works, esp. in bronze, but not specifically Classicizing). The statue (ht. 2.13 m without plinth) was found N of the Altar but findspot alone, as mentioned, is insufficient for attribution. Identification is based on the two cuttings on the head for the insertion of horns. I view the piece as far too stiff and mannered (overregular hairline and head contour, inserted nipples, flat musculature) to belong with the female figures.

77. For two of these statues, see Moreno 1994, fig. 607; three others are shown in *LIMC* 7, s.v. Mousa, Mousai, 1003, no. 261a–g and pl. 722, where they are said to belong to a cult area of the Muses to the N of the Altar. No. 261d would represent a kitharode Apollo. The cutting for a metal addition in the center of the head veil worn by the woman seated on rocky ground (261b) is said to have once held the feathers of the sirens (as trophy of the Muses' victory over them),

and to be the first attested instance of that attribute (cf. p. 1009). No. 261g, without traces of attributes and headless, is tentatively accepted within the group because of her resemblance to a common Muse type. Her drapery, however, differs somewhat from that of the other figures on display in the Berlin Museum, appearing thinner and more transparent. Given the variety in the Gigantomachy renderings, her connection with the group remains plausible. Muses, of course, were carved in relief around the altar of the Athenaion at Priene, probably datable to the 3rd c. (supra, n. 8). See also Stewart, forthcoming.

Koch 1994, 100–103, discusses five of the seated figures from Pergamon (her cat. 86, 88–91 on pp. 221–22—corresponding to Pergamon nos. 62, 65, 60, 63, 61 respectively). She dates them ca. 160 but cites the disparate dates once given to them by different authors. Although accepting their connection with the Altar (except for her no. 86 = Pergamon 62, considered honorary), Koch doubts that such a high number as postulated for all intercolumniations could represent mythological figures or city personifications, and opts for identification as priestesses of Athena (and Muses, she points out, sit on rocks).

78. Athena and Poseidon: *Pergamon 1*, 1996, 78–81, cat. 17–18 (illustrated in color); see also Moreno 1994, fig. 601 (female, Athena, Apollo); Kunze 1990, pls. 82.1–3 (Athena, Apollo, female) and 83.1 (Poseidon). The unidentified female could be Artemis because of her rolled mantle. At a public lecture in connection with the Telephos Frieze exhibition in San Francisco on Sept. 8, 1996, Dr. M. Kunze suggested that the Athena, the Apollo, and the second female formed a group depicting the Birth of Athena, but I find it difficult to visualize a narrative in linear form on the Altar roof, although possible for a dedication. Kunze 1990, 130, doubts that the "Dionysos" belongs with the other divine figures. See also infra, n. 81, for his theory on the Poseidon. In the trapezoidal shape of his visage and the separation of hair from face contour, the Pergamon Poseidon is remarkably similar to the Mounychia Asklepios and a torso from Nemi in Nottingham, to be discussed infra, Ch. 7 ns. 41–42.

79. The chariots of Hera and Ares frame, as it were, the main scene with Herakles, Athena, and Zeus on the E side; indeed, Moreno 1994 begins his description of the Gigantomachy with the NE half of the frieze, to pick up the SE section after completing the circuit of the Altar and a visit to the interior to view the Telephos Frieze. But no chariots appear on the southern half of the frieze; therefore the horses on the roof would have had no counterparts below. Another chariot (of Helios) is shown on the S side, but it would not have corresponded to the roof decoration.

The number of the roof horses is disputed: *Pergamon 2*, 1997, 67, mentions fragments of 16; Kunze 1990, 132, gives a total of 13, from which he subtracts two that he identifies (I believe correctly) as centaurs, although he thinks they too may have drawn a chariot (see infra, n. 81). The restoration of seven quadrigas, as on the model, would require 28 animals.

80. Halikarnassos horse, certainly from a quadriga, with its preserved metal harness: e.g., Stewart 1990, pl. 538. To be sure, the Pergamon horses turn their heads in opposite directions, as typical for animals harnessed to a chariot. The position of their struts, toward the front legs, may suggest that the rear legs were automatically strengthened by the chariot. I wonder whether the male in a long costume ("Apollo," supra, n. 78) could be a charioteer, rather than a god (or a chariot-riding god, like Helios), to go on one of the chariots.

81. At the lecture on Sept. 8, 1996 (supra, n. 78), Dr. Kunze suggested that the two centaurs should go with the Dionysos torso, the tritons with the Poseidon. For the latter theory (tri-

tons driving Poseidon's chariot), see also Kunze 1990, 131–32, pl. 83.1–3, with the comment that these figures were not meant to be seen from below, like the other akroterial statues, and were therefore an independent dedication. The current model of the Pergamon Altar renders the centaurs as rampant, using as a guideline those from the Asklepieion (on which see, e.g., Ridgway 1990, 302–303, 324–25; Smith 1991, fig. 192). But for the actual centaurs from the Altar, see Kunze 1990, pl. 85; their upper (human) torso was inserted separately, at a line just above the navel, and they seem to have had only one front leg raised. *Pergamon* 2, 1997, 66 fig. 9a–b, and n. 28 on p. 175, states that the centaurs in the illustration come from the Asklepieion, but are attributed to the Altar on the basis of size, material, and technique (the two large dowel holes where the two halves of the equine bodies are joined). Yet the "Wild Man" from the Asklepieion (supra, n. 57) was considered unsuitable for the Altar partly because of its provenience. Moreover, the two centaurs identified by Kunze (1990) differ from the Asklepieion ones, which are joined at a different spot, have a more active pose, wear animal skins tied around their neck, and have long tufts of hair at the spinal meeting point of human and equine body.

Pergamon tritons: beside Kunze 1990 (supra), see also Lattimore 1976, pl. 25 fig. 36; Webb 1996, fig. 27; *Pergamon* 2, 1997, fig. 8a–b and foldout 4. The two Mischwesen used to be restored, singly, at the four front corners of the two projecting wings, although only two of them are extant. This position would be appropriate for the NW wing, where the Gigantomachy shows the divinities of the sea, but not for the SW wing, with Dionysos and his relatives. Perhaps, rather than grouping centaurs and tritons with the gods, the two centaurs should be placed as the akroteria for the front of one wing, and the tritons for the front of the other (where the model now places single centaurs), especially since the sea creatures were found at the N rim of the Altar (*Pergamon* 2, 175 n. 27). We should not expect complete symmetry from Greek buildings, as shown by some of the akroterial terracotta Nikai from Olympia (Moustaka 1993, 65–74, pls. 52–59, Nikai F1, F3; cf. *LIMC* 6, s.v. Nike, nos. 29–30 and figs. on p. 855) and by the W lateral akroteria of the Epidaurian Asklepieion (Stewart 1990, pls. 457–58). For akroterial tritons on the Tenos altar(?), see infra, Ch. 4 and n. 57.

For the triton on the Gigantomachy frieze, with seaweed wings and sea-centaur body, see, e.g., Simon 1975, pl. 3. The long leaf adhering to his equine chest is quite different from either seaweed or the akanthos-like vegetation of the akroterial triton. One more finlike leaf grows from the point of attachment of his front right leg.

82. Admittedly, a sphinx's head, unless male, would require a more feminine body, to judge from the so-called Lykian Sarcophagus from Sidon (Stewart 1990, pl. 466), and the general evolution of the sphinx. Yet male sphinxes are known from Labraunda (Gunter 1995, 21–30, cat. 2–3), and Karian influence (the Maussolleion) has been postulated for the Altar. The griffins (one in Berlin, one in the Bergama Museum: cf. Kunze 1990, 133) are said to be summarily finished on one side, but, at least for the animal in Berlin, the effect could simply be due to weathering. Emphasis on one side, if verifiable, might imply, however, a matching animal at close quarters or a specific location, different from the present reconstruction on the model, where the griffins are widely spaced above the entrance colonnade.

The lion could be placed above the chimaira/lion near Keto, on the N side, or on the S, above Rhea's mount (Simon 1975, pls. 5, 27), but the heraldic pose would also presuppose a matching animal. For a purported discussion of the model see *Pergamon* 2, 1997, 58–67 (Hoepfner), but note that it differs from the three-dimensional reconstruction and accords rather with the drawings of foldouts 3–4. The two are at variance, esp. in the arrangement of the E side (model: paired centaurs at all four main corners, single centaurs facing toward the two risalits; drawing on foldout 3: only chariots on E side; section on foldout 4: triton on NW wing, facing toward stairs, centaurs, singly, along N side). The divine statues in the drawing are placed on the inner edge of the roof as if looking in onto the courtyard, toward the defeated Gauls that Hoepf-ner visualizes on the cornice of the sacrificial table, but they are omitted in the model. Kästner (supra, n. 22) obviously disagrees with this reconstruction, and so does M. Kunze. See also Stewart, forthcoming, for a critique of Hoepfner and additional suggestions. It is clear that the last word has yet to be spoken

The Telephos Frieze and Continuous Narrative

The Telephos Frieze is such an integral part of the Pergamon Altar that it seems arbitrary to discuss it under a separate heading. Yet its composition is sufficiently different to deserve independent treatment, within its own artistic genre. The spotlight thrown on this monument by its recent cleaning, restoration, and exhibition has prompted clarifications and reordering in the sequence of slabs and episodes. Yet many details remain unclear, especially since much of the frieze is missing, some parts of it remained unfinished in antiquity, and the story it illustrates is not only little known but also, probably, different from other accounts in a Pergamene retelling.

Two main treatments of the monument have appeared in recent years: the discussion (by H. Heres) in volume 7 of the *Lexikon Iconographicum Mythologiae Classicae* (1994) s.v. Telephos, with sequential drawings of the slabs and many cross-references to previous entries; and the various articles in the two volumes of the traveling exhibition, *Pergamon 1, 1996*, with catalogue of 16 panels and fragments, and *Pergamon 2, 1997*, with a new sequence of slabs, drawings, and photographs (Ill. 10). The position of the frieze within the building is now certain because panels with beveled edges (some revealed by the recent examination) prove the existence of four inner corners, thus demanding that the frieze be limited to the area of the courtyard rather than extending into the wings, as once thought. It is also known that the relief slabs rested on a projecting string course of blue-gray marble, in turn supported by orthostates of the same color above a wall base of white marble (cf. Ill. 4). This type of color contrast is attested at the Halikarnassos Maussolleion, but I am primarily reminded of a comparable arrangement (over white wall courses and orthostates, however) for the panel paintings in the Pinakotheke within the Athenian Propylaia, which, as noted in the previous chapter, may have provided inspiration.[1] The string course below the Pergamon carvings would thus have enhanced their pictorial effect.

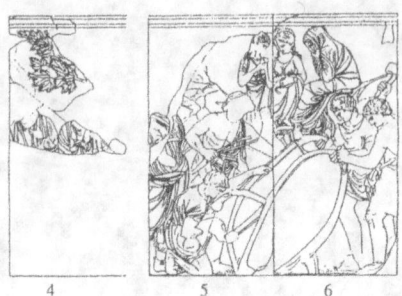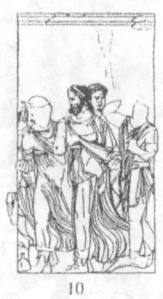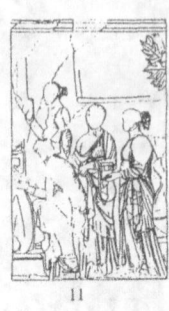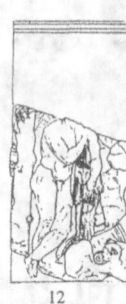

Ill. 10. New sequence of some slabs of the Telephos Frieze (drawing by M. Heilmeyer). [Excerpted from *Pergamon 2*, 1997, folding pl.]

The frieze was probably meant to be seen primarily from within the peristyle, whose columns would have supplied an effective scansion of the different episodes; yet enough room existed beyond the colonnade (cf. Ill. 2) for visitors to walk up to the reliefs and examine them at close quarters.[2] The composition therefore required some inner divisions to separate scene from scene and clarify the recurring presence of the same protagonists in different circumstances. These inner divisions were effected by columns, piers, trees, indoor versus outdoor backgrounds, and figures turning their backs to the preceding or following action. These compositional devices are the hall-mark of a continuous-narrative frieze, and although the subject has been discussed well and at length recently,[3] it demands a brief definition here.

In continuous narrative, actions develop through time, as if in a film-strip, rather than taking place simultaneously in a single timeless moment. In visual terms, however, the important point is that such diachronical scenes involving the same personages must appear *within a single frame*. The often cited example of the Deeds of Herakles in the metopes of the Temple of Zeus at Olympia, by such definition, cannot qualify, since each scene is separated from the other by a triglyph and can thus be read as an independent unit. To be sure, the main personage, Herakles, appears increasingly mature from metope to metope, and a person standing in front of either pronaos or opisthodomos could have perceived a sequence of six metopes at one glance. None-theless, each episode had validity in itself and did not need to be seen with the others to acquire its full meaning. By contrast, the compositional divisions within the Tele-phos Frieze are subordinate to both actions and actors and appear definitely subsumed to the undivided, uniform architectural frame provided by the string course on which the slabs rest and the crowning elements.

Recent publications have explored possible antecedents and consequents of the Telephos Frieze. Predecessors have usually been sought in vase painting, metalwork, and book illustrations, none of them entirely appropriate. The genre had been considered rare in the Greek world, but fully typical of the Roman, with its penchant for historical narrative and its panel paintings of military campaigns carried through the streets in triumphal processions. This Roman preference has recently been confirmed for the famous Odyssey Landscapes, often thought to copy a Greek prototype but now seen as an ad hoc creation for an Esquiline atrium later in date than traditionally assumed.[4] Knowledge of Roman practices may even have influenced our understanding of a possible predecessor to the Pergamene narrative: the Aemilius Paullus Monument in Delphi (ca. 168), to be discussed below. Yet a few examples exist within the purely Greek sphere that have not been mentioned in this context and may be briefly reviewed.

The first may also partake of a pictorial tradition exemplified by the modest painted pinakes set up as ex-votos in healing sanctuaries and now no longer preserved except in treasurers' accounts. It is a fourth-century marble relief, probably once mounted on a tall stone pier, that comes from the Sanctuary of Amphiaraos at Oropos, near Athens. Its dedicant is Archinos, who went to the hero's shrine seeking help, and obtained it. On the slab, he appears three times, in a sequence probably to be read from right to left: as an entering worshiper making a gesture of adoration; as a sleeper, reclining in center field while a snake touches his affected shoulder; and finally as a patient, standing near a taller male, presumably Amphiaraos, who is treating Archinos' damaged arm. The repeated presence of the donor within the single frame of the votive relief, and the temporal sequence of the actions, probably involving an overnight stay at the sanctuary for incubation, qualify Archinos' gift as continuous narrative.[5]

Such an early and unpretentious precedent can hardly have had an impact on the Telephos Frieze, but a structure closer to Pergamon, the Nereid Monument at Xanthos, in Lykia, albeit approximately contemporary with Archinos' relief, offers a more convincing example. The first of the two friezes crowning the tall podium of the monument shows various city sieges and battle scenes. The use of landscape elements to characterize the events, although formulaic and limited, is probably derived from Assyrian (and Egyptian?) renderings that could have supplied the narrative incentive as well. The west side in fact may depict, in temporal sequence from right to left, victory in battle, flight toward a city, and capitulation. The victorious Dynast appears twice within the same architectural frame: being crowned as he subdues an enemy, and receiving emissaries from the city while sitting under a parasol indicative of his rank. All episodes could have been read at a single glance.[6]

Finally, we should remember that luxury hangings and tapestry, although lost for us, probably represented a conspicuous medium for narrative and, unlike monumental paintings, could travel. In Euripides' *Ion* just such weavings are mentioned, not only by the women standing in front of the sculptural decoration of the Delphic temple and comparing it with their own work at home, but also as part of the textiles gathered by Ion to erect a vast banquet tent in front of the building. Among the hangings, we are told, he selected a depiction of naval battles and combats with monstrous creatures taken from the barbarians, as well as others given by Herakles and by the Athenians. The peplos given quadrennially to Athena at the Panathenaic festival in Athens showed the Gigantomachy, and although the various encounters between gods and Giants were conceived of as simultaneous, the complexity of the depiction suggests that true narrative was possible as well. Unfortunately, this tradition can no longer be attested through excavated evidence.[7]

One more object does not qualify as an example of continuous narrative, but should be included here because its use of landscape, especially rocky, mountainous ground, is comparable to that in some scenes of the Telephos Frieze: the bronze Derveni krater. It has been rightly noted that metal Phoenician bowls are unlikely sources of inspiration, given their much earlier and shorter currency. But Hellenistic, or even (as in the case of the Derveni Krater) late Classical, metalware may have contributed to the diffusion of styles and forms, especially in the wake of Alexander the Great. We should take note of their potential for textural contrasts, polychromy, and pictorial devices.[8]

THE TELEPHOS FRIEZE

The Storyline and Its Iconography

Aleos, king of Tegea, has been given a troublesome oracle that prompts him to consecrate his daughter Auge to Athena so that she will not bear children. When Herakles, visiting Aleos' court, sees Auge and makes love to her, the results of the amorous encounter must be neutralized: the baby Telephos is exposed on Mount Parthenion and Auge is placed in a boat and set adrift at sea. She reaches the coast of Mysia, where King Teuthras adopts her and where she establishes the cult of Athena. Meanwhile, Telephos has been suckled by a wild animal—at Pergamon, a lioness rather than the traditional hind—and thus recognized by an unsuspecting Herakles as his offspring (cf. Ill. 10). Given to local nymphs to be brought up, Telephos eventually sails to Mysia in search of his mother (Pl. 29), and successfully fights against Idas, King Teuthras' enemy. In recompense, he is offered Auge's hand (regardless of generational difference—echoes of the Oidipous myth?), but an omen (the apparition of a snake) prevents the wedding. Telephos then marries the Amazon-like Hiera, and they fight against the Greeks who have landed in Mysia in their quest for Troy. Telephos is wounded by Achilles at the Kaikos River because the offended Dionysos trips him with a vine. Hiera's death at the same battle brings about a pause in the hostilities, so that she can be buried. The Greeks eventually retreat, and Telephos, being told by an oracle that only the wounding agent can heal his wound, travels to Argos, where he is honorably received at the court of Agamemnon. To force Achilles to treat his wound, Telephos threatens the infant Orestes at an altar. He is finally cured by Achilles with scrapings from the spear that pierced his thigh, perhaps having agreed to lead the Greeks to Troy, but this part of the story is not recoverable from the extant

Plate 29

relief fragments. Other scenes from the frieze show the establishment of various cults at Pergamon, and eventually Telephos' heroization.

This storyline is partly derived from the frieze slabs themselves, since different versions of the Telephos myth existed in antiquity. The variant chosen by the Pergamenes is perhaps the most dignified and the one best able to stress the connections between mainland Greece and Mysia. Thus Herakles probably did not rape Auge while drunk (although the actual scene of their encounter is missing); Telephos was not put into the boat with his mother, so that he could grow up in Arkadia; and he did not leave it after killing his maternal uncles (as predicted by the oracle), but only in search of his still-living parent. His marriage to Hiera and her death at the battle of the Kaikos River, to our current knowledge, are mentioned at the earliest by a third-century A.C. source (Philostr. *Her.* 2.14–18), whereas previous versions have Telephos marry the Trojan Astyoche or the Mysian Argiope, Teuthras' daughter.[9] It is important to stress, however, that our understanding of the Pergamene narrative is conditioned by our interpretation of the various relief scenes—should some of them be reinterpreted, or be shifted from the present sequence, the storyline may change as well, and indeed some difficulties with the arrangement of the slabs still exist, as mentioned above.

One major revision occurred during the preparations for the traveling exhibition. Slab 1, supposedly representing Aleos receiving the oracle that warned him against Auge's future son, was shifted to a place after slab 31 (the Kaikos battle), and interpreted as showing Telephos consulting the oracle that sent him to Argos to have his wound healed. The change occurred because the bearded man next to the idol, under a laurel tree, wears a long-sleeved costume, as appropriate for a person living in Asia Minor but not for one living in Greece.[10] If this argument is correct, as I believe, questions also could be raised about slabs 2–3, where a man dressed in a long-sleeved chitoniskos and a chlamys stands near an enthroned lady. The scene supposedly represents the arrival of Herakles at Aleos' court and his reception by Queen Neaira, but neither the royal nor the Heraklean entourage would require Oriental attire. To be sure, slab 3 contains a shift of settings: from indoors, within the palace, to the outdoors, where Herakles (standing under an oak tree) is thought to be seeing Auge for the first time. Yet both scenes could be taking place in Mysia; thus the locale would change from Teuthras' court to a wooded area nearby. Herakles might have been shown here next to an oak tree to identify him as the son of Zeus (no other oak appears on the panels, to my knowledge), and as a pendant to Dionysos with his vine. The two deities and their vegetal attributes would then be framing the battle scene at the Kaikos River, Herakles watching over Telephos, Dionysos causing Telephos' wound. Yet, if the present architectural reconstruction of the frieze is correct, insufficient room on the east side prevents the shifting of these slabs.[11]

Given the abundance of labels for the Gigantomachy on the Altar podium, and the idiosyncratic version of the Telephos legend on the frieze, we would expect identifying names written above or near the figures, to ensure the correct reading of the scenes. To my knowledge no such inscription has been found, perhaps confirming the unfinished state of the monument. To be sure, the sculptors used as many iconographic devices as possible to provide the viewers with clues—besides long versus short sleeves, and distinctive weapons, also the use of different footwear for Greeks and Mysians, which characterizes Telephos and his entourage as people of Asia Minor.[12] Two more iconographic details should be mentioned in this context.

Plate 30

The first is the surprising rendering of the "slipping strap" or rather chiton that uncovers the shoulder and occasionally also the breast of female figures. This device suggestive of feminine allure and beauty had been introduced in the fifth century to identify Aphrodite or comparable deities.[13] On the Telephos Frieze, the motif recurs twice: on panel 11, presumably showing the establishment of Athena's cult in Pergamon (Pl. 30), and on panel 17, with Telephos' arming before his battle against Idas. In the first instance, both right breast and shoulder are revealed; the woman stands in the center of the slab, and although she is not the figure closest to the idol, she may be Auge. On panel 17, the more modestly slipping chiton occurs on the woman holding the crested helmet, who is usually identified as an attendant because she does not stand next to Telephos and is shorter than the adjacent figure, but I find this rendering surprising for a subsidiary personage.[14] One more figure, a kneeling female on panel 7, surprisingly has her entire upper torso bare, but her likely activity—the bathing of the infant Telephos—may explain her attire; perhaps it, too, is meant to identify her: as a nymph rather than a mortal woman.

The second detail is the suckling of the infant Telephos by a wild animal (panel 12; cf. Ill. 10). It has been repeatedly pointed out that the hind of the standard version has been here replaced by a lioness, and various reasons have been given for the change. The cave setting in which the scene takes place has been compared to Nymph reliefs, which may also have provided inspiration for some perspective arrangements, and the bucolic tenor of miraculous nursings of this kind has been associated with the Dionysiac mysteries. I wonder whether another possible connection may be with Asklepios, who, according to the Epidaurian version of his legend, was also abandoned on a mountain and suckled by a hind. Telephos seems in fact to have been considered a healing hero, perhaps because of his own successful treatment.[15]

Technique and Style

As repeatedly noted, the Telephos Frieze is unfinished. The most obvious evidence occurs on panel 11 (cf. Pl. 30), where a large rectangle of rough surface has been left over the heads of the women attending to the idol. The leaves of a plane tree have been carved in detail at the right edge of this area, with a good deal of undercutting and punctuations by the drill, and it does not look as if the uncarved portion was meant to receive additional elements of the same tree. If an independent image, like the bird on slab 49 or perhaps an architectural feature, had been planned for that area, no outline of it remains today, and perhaps the excessive surface would have been totally removed during the next working stage. Yet the regularity of the contours makes me suspect that a representational item would have been included.

This suspicion may be strengthened by the fact that other unfinished details of the frieze are limited to the figures themselves, not to background surfaces. One such example of incomplete work occurs on slabs 5–6, showing the making of Auge's boat. Chisel marks are evident on the arms of the workmen, their faces, and in general the lower portions of the reliefs, although the heads of the three women at the upper level retain "cushions" of stone, as if they had not yet been contoured free of the upper border. The frieze was obviously sculpted in situ, but the framing moldings at the top were probably executed before the slabs were put in position on the wall, thus providing a sort of guideline for the intended depth of the carving.[16]

It is important to remember that this frieze was meant to be seen virtually at eye level. Archaic and Classical friezes were usually placed on the entablature of buildings, which, even when of modest size, allowed only distant viewing. Wall friezes were rare until the Hellenistic period, when we find the marine cortege of the Hall of the Bulls at Delos or the external decoration of the altar of Athena at Priene. Yet the latter featured individual images framed by engaged columns and may have given the impression of statuary in the round placed in intercolumniations. Comparable in terms of levels, but different in conception and visual compass, are the sculptured column drums and pedestals of the late fourth-century Artemision at Ephesos.[17] We find closer parallels in non-Greek monuments of a funerary nature—not so much the decorated podia of the Halikarnassos Maussolleion and the Nereid Monument at Xanthos, but two other structures of more unusual design. All the interior wall-surfaces, plus the exterior ones on façade, of the open-air enclosure forming the Heroon at Gjölbaschi-Trysa (ca. 380–370) were covered with narrative reliefs, some of them with small figures so steeped in atmosphere as to form the only virtual antecedent to the Telephos Frieze. Somewhat comparable, though less pictorial, the two processional compositions on the sides of the Heroon of Perikle at Limyra (ca. 370–360) were also visible just above eye level.[18] Both structures are on Lykian territory, and Lykian influences are certainly attested on the Pergamon Altar, as we shall see presently. We have already mentioned (Chapter 2) Hoepfner's theory that sees the Telephos Frieze as an imitation of relief balustrades around the peristyle of Royal Palace V, but the location of those carvings on the upper story, if correctly reconstructed, would have placed them considerably higher than the Altar frieze, while the rhythm of the colonnade would have broken them into framed panels, thus altering the continuous-narrative sequence of the Telepheia.

Much has been written about the landscape elements of the Telephos Frieze, its perspective arrangements with figures placed at higher levels to indicate recession of planes, or arranged in a semicircle that violates the impression of parallelism to the background typical of other friezes. The major source for these devices has been seen not so much in monumental paintings as in book illustrations, despite arguments to the contrary, but votive and funerary reliefs (the so-called Funerary Banquet stelai, the Nymph reliefs) have also been cited.[19] Differences from the Gigantomachy on the podium have been so consistently emphasized that it seems useful, at this point, to stress possible similarities.

Plate 31

First of all, technical devices. The use of drill channels to outline figures against the background is inevitably more obvious on the Telephos Frieze because of its low relief (Pl. 31), but some traces of the same practice can be noted in some background elements of the Gigantomachy. The drill has also been used to punctuate the ends of folds and to carve drapery channels on the figures, as we have noted in the podium sculptures. Finally, the so-called disembodied heads that have attracted so much attention on the Telepheia, because they seem a Roman, even Flavian, technique, rather than a Greek one, recur at least once on the Pergamon Gigantomachy: if the farther faces and curtailed limbs of Hekate (cf. Pl. 13) do not qualify because of the peculiar iconography of this goddess, at least certainly one of the satyrs accompanying Dionysos does, appearing basically as a head trace on the background, and almost completely hidden by his companion, who in turn stands behind the god and his panther.[20]

Trees as a way of concealing (or of emphasizing) joins had already been used at the Trysa Heroon,[21] but those trees appear leafless and lifeless, incapable of conveying a sense of landscape. The trees of the Telepheia are much more naturalistic, even recognizable by species—plane, oak, and laurel—yet they serve as attributes and clues to locales rather than as true landscape, as scholars have noted. Worth emphasizing in this context is, however, the simultaneous presence of mythical personages to suggest physical or geographic features, with an animistic approach that recalls the Ge emerging from the ground in the Gigantomachy. At the forefront of the Kaikos battle, for instance (panels 27–29), two fragmentary figures with legs wrapped in their mantles recline peacefully facing each other, apparently undisturbed by the turmoil nearby; they have been identified as the two rivers of the region, the Kaikos and the Selinos, or comparable personifications. Two more reclining spectators in similar pose (the rivers Selinos and Ketios?) watch the erection of an altar in front of a naiskos, presumably at Pergamon (panels 49–50), and a mountain goddess (Arkadia?) from her rocky elevation supervises the bathing of baby Telephos (panels 7–8). Yet at times the line between an attributive and a participatory role seems too thin; how are we to interpret the two satyrs who sit on rocks in front of a mountainous background while surrounded by attendants and women (panels 44–46)? [22]

Stylistically, the "Baroque" of the Telephos Frieze has been judged as toned down, but this is only true when compared with the violent Gigantomachy. I find the same "pinched" and plastic faces (cf. Pl. 31), the same rosebud mouths of the podium frieze, the same arrowhead folds, the same nicks and bends to inflated pleats, the same omega patterns and transparent drapery typical of the divine figures of the larger composition. Textural contrasts are present also on the Telepheia—for instance, the differentiation between the hairy outside and the smooth inside of Herakles' *leonte* as he leans on his club to watch Telephos within the lioness' cave. A similar contrast, enhanced by metals of different colors, had been obtained earlier on the pelt worn by the elderly satyr on the Derveni Krater. Male figures have the same emphatic musculature as we see on the Gigantomachy without the exaggeration demanded by the epic topic—but note the sternal "ribs" of the seminude workman using his drill on Auge's boat on panel 5, and Telephos' pronounced thigh and hip muscles, his abdominal fold of flesh, as he sits on the altar threatening the baby Orestes (panel 42).[23]

Fifth-century devices and mannerisms already outlined for the Gigantomachy can be pointed out for most of the figures of the Telephos Frieze. In particular, I am struck by the movement in Auge's skirt as she sits on the high ground awaiting her fate (panel 6)—her pose is static, almost a hieroglyph for mourning, but her garment flutters with a life of its own, like that (albeit more textured) of the riding Eos in the Gigantomachy. More motivated but equally artificial is the motion pattern of the costumes on King Teuthras and his retinue as they hurry toward the shore (panel 10); even a reduced sanguisuga fold appears above the king's ankle, and the inflated tubes in his skirt form what I have called "the Lykian wavelet," with reference to the frequency of this motif on Lykian carvings.[24] The apparent incongruity of cloth that is thick and dense away from the body but becomes thin and transparent when overlying anatomical forms, even if double-layered, finds its best expression in King Teuthras, but is also typical of Lykian reliefs. Since they in turn were influenced by fifth-century Athens, it is legitimate to conclude that Lykian carvers may have contributed more than usually acknowledged to the making of *both* Pergamene friezes, thus helping to perpetuate those same Attic motifs that had become traditional in their repertoire.

One more feature seems, however, exclusive to the Telepheia: the use of Archaizing formulas. To those already pointed out—in furniture, helmet types, even actions, like sitting instead of reclining at banquet—I would add the matching zigzag folds in the mantle swags of several figures, specifically those engaged in ritual actions (panels 11, 17, 46). Although women on the Telephos Frieze wear the same rolled himatia and bordered chitons as the Gigantomachy goddesses, they also let the edges of their cloaks cascade in parallel waves that form decorative as well as functional patterns (cf. Pl. 30), suggesting the layered fullness of the garments. Some Pergamene sculptures in the round—the so-called Dancer from Palace V, probably a utilitarian piece, a *lyknouchos* (cf. Pl. 77a)—reveal the same motifs, in a comparable desire to remove them from the world of contemporary reality, qua statues. On the frieze, the intent was probably to place the action within the context of a remote if quasi-historical past, but some headgear and footwear details appear contemporary, or at least comparable to some on the Gigantomachy Frieze.[25]

Was the Telepheia carved simultaneously with, or several years after, the podium sculptures? I cannot detect a true development or change in style between the two. To put it in other words, all the differences between the larger and the smaller frieze seem to me explainable through height of relief and subject matter, yet practical, constructional considerations would demand that the inner carvings be considerably later than the outer ones, and their level of finish would support this assumption. One additional detail may be cited in favor of a later dating: whereas the beards of gods and Giants, where observable, seem to be full, undifferentiated masses, those on the Telephos Frieze often appear divided along a central part. This symmetrical arrangement is not a Classical formula, and I suspect it may represent a Hellenistic development, perhaps under Roman influence, unless its specific iconographic meaning presently escapes us.

THE AEMILIUS PAULLUS MONUMENT

It may seem strange to include in this chapter a frieze that is not architectural in the strict sense of the term, since it stood toward the top of a tall pillar meant to support a bronze equestrian group; the figured strip could indeed be viewed as nothing more than a decorated statue base. Yet several reasons exist for this inclusion: (1) the reliefs occur within the canonical entablature of an Attic-Ionic frieze—above a three-fasciaed architrave and below a dentilled cornice; (2) the short chronological span firmly established by the dedicatory inscription on the monument (after June 22, 168, when the Battle of Pydna took place, and before Nov. 29, 167, when Aemilius Paullus celebrated his triumph and therefore relinquished his title of *imperator*) makes it a possible contemporary or even an antecedent of the Telephos Frieze; (3) some scholars have viewed the scenes as an example of continuous narrative, primarily because of the Roman dedicant but also because the events seem to have a beginning, a middle, and an end, in temporal sequence, and the same personage may appear on more than one side; (4) the frieze has therefore acquired an importance beyond its actual artistic value, because it has been seen as representative of Roman historical traditions as against the symbolic depiction of historical events preferred by the Greeks—a Roman monument within a Greek context.[26]

The Factual Evidence

Recent discoveries at Delphi have, if not clarified, at least enriched the general picture. Three ancient sources refer to the Aemilius Paullus Monument: Polybios (30.10.2), Livy (45.27.7), and Plutarch (*Aem. Paul.* 28.2). The first author, who was sent to Rome as a consequence of the Battle of Pydna and became a friend of Aemilius Paullus' family, speaks of two columns (κίονας . . . ἀτελεῖς) set up at the sanctuary by Perseus but left unfinished and completed by the Roman winner, who placed on them his own images. Livy basically translates Polybios, but adds that the columns were *in vestibulo*, thus probably meaning that they were near the entrance to the Temple of Apollo rather than in its pronaos. Finally Plutarch, who spent part of his career at Delphi in an official capacity, and was therefore well acquainted with its monuments, refers to a single column, but his description makes it clear that it is a pier (κίονα μέγαν τετράγωνον ἐκ λίθων λευκῶν). Perhaps the second pillar was no longer standing in his day, or was considered less important and therefore disregarded. But it existed, since some blocks from it have now been found.[27]

This second pier is made of limestone, rather than marble, and its crowning block is missing; the size of the shaft, however, makes it unlikely that it supported another equestrian group. A single, over-lifesize standing image is suggested, or, at most, a figure being crowned by another, perhaps a personification like the Delphic people (*demos*) or the sacred council of the sanctuary, the Amphiktyony. The pier itself must have served as a monumental bulletin board for Macedonia propaganda, since its courses were inscribed with documents referring to Demetrios Poliorketes (ca. 302), yet its method of construction and its base moldings find their only parallels in the Perseus/Aemilius Paullus Pillar, which must therefore be contemporary. Perseus is known to have sent two hieromnemoi to the Amphiktyonic Council in 178, and to have visited Delphi in person in 174. The French scholars who published the monument thus believe that the king might have wanted, on that occasion, to remind the Delphians of the tradition of friendship existing between the sanctuary and the royal family by making a Macedonian presence tangibly felt there again after almost a century of absence. This was an important move, on the eve of the Third Macedonian War, in view of the defamatory campaign being waged by the Roman Senate against him, which had gained favor with the city of Delphi even though the Amphiktyony was numerically pro-Macedonian.[28]

One block from this Limestone Pier was found on the esplanade (the so-called Aire) in front of the Stoa of the Athenians, but it is assumed that the total monument stood near the Temple of Apollo with the other pillar dedications. Equal uncertainty exists about the location of the Aemilius Paullus Pier. A set of foundations at the southeast corner of the temple, albeit at a lower level, is tentatively assigned to it by some, while others would want it at the same level as the Pillar of Prousias, near the temple façade, as suggested by the Latin source (Ill. 11). If the first location is accepted, although somewhat tucked away into a corner, the reliefs atop the pillar could have been seen not only from the Sacred Way but also from the temple steps on the opposite side. If the second location is preferred, the frieze might have been somewhat less visible at close quarters but the height of the pillar might have seemed more impressive, in true competition with its predecessors.[29]

We also know that the equestrian group faced toward one of the short faces of the pillar, but since it rested on a separate two-block layer above the dentilled cornice, we cannot be sure about its original direction in relation to the figured scenes below: Kähler believes that the front of the monument corresponds to the short side comprising figures 11–15 (his scene II, Ill. 12), whereas Jacquemin and Laroche (1982, 212) assert that the front lies on the opposite side (Kähler's scene IV, comprising figures 24–29).[30] Compositional features are not sufficiently clear to provide a solution to the issue.

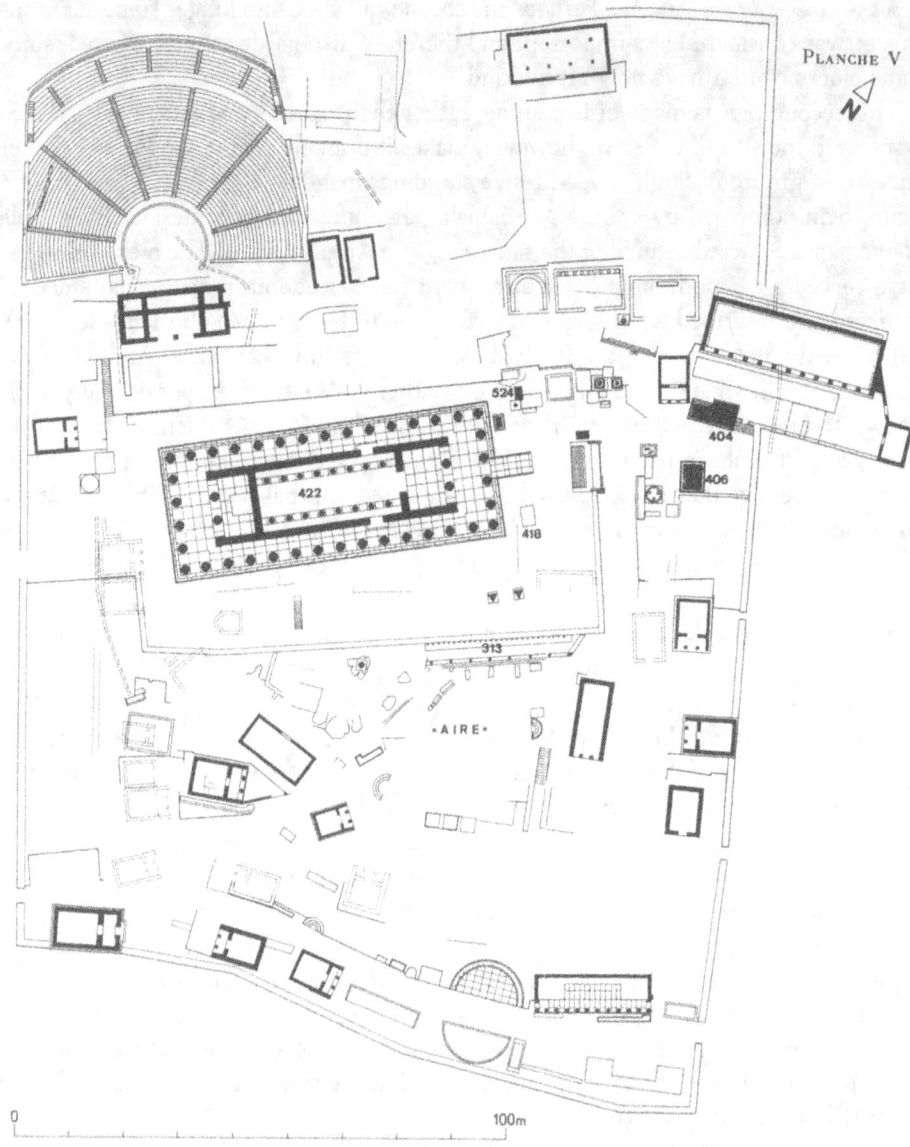

Ill. 11. Delphi, plan of Apollo Sanctuary. The Aemilius Paullus Monument is here located at no. 418, the Pillar of Prousias at no. 524, the Pillar of Eumenes II at no. 404, the Rhodian Chariot of the Sun at no. 406, the Stoa of the Athenians at no. 313, and the Temple of Apollo at no. 422. [After *GdDs* 1991, pl. 5]

The Telephos Frieze and Continuous Narrative

Somewhat different construction methods are observable on various sections of the monument. It has been noted that its lower part consists of a pedestal base between top and bottom moldings, in bluish marble, which used horizontal pouring channels to secure in place small dowels; in contrast, the shaft, in white marble, used vertical pouring channels for large dowels. It has therefore been assumed that Perseus intended to set up his statue simply on a tall base, which was then appropriated by Aemilius Paullus and turned into a pillar, thus explaining the different material, technique, and form of decoration. Yet a similar technique is said to have been used for the Limestone Pillar, which must have been intended as a companion piece and had a shaft of approximately eleven or twelve courses. Thus, each point made above could be given another motivation: the white marble may have been used to create an intentional color contrast with the bluish base, a different doweling method may have been required by the higher elevation, and the form of decoration, in my opinion, may be a sign of the times.[31] Increasing elaboration can be noted, in fact, on each successive Delphic pillar: the Rhodian monument (the alleged first example of the type) had a running-wave pattern perhaps suggested by the subject of its crowning sculpture, the Chariot of the Sun; the Pillar of Prousias carried an Ionic entablature with a frieze of boukrania, garlands, and mesomphalic phialai; and the Aemilius Paullus Pillar even added a course with carved rosettes below the architrave and the figured frieze.[32]

An important point concerns the dedicatory inscription carved on a short face of the socle: L. AIMILIUS L. F. INPERATOR DE REGE PERSE MACEDONIBUSQUE CEPET. It has been noted that it was placed over an effaced Greek inscription. Had the Greek text given the same information as the Latin one, there would have been no need to erase it, and the Latin wording could have simply been added above or below it. Should we then assume that the original dedication in Perseus' name had already been made? In which case, how far had the pillar been completed? The crucial issue for our purposes is whether the figured frieze was added on command from Aemilius Paullus or whether the Roman limited his takeover to placing his equestrian statue above the pier and replacing the Macedonian inscription with his own.[33]

The other pillar monuments at Delphi, characteristically, were erected not to commemorate victories, but simply to honor royal personages, given either by the king himself for personal profit, or by Greek bodies celebrating the king.[34] As the Limestone Pillar was meant to recall earlier Macedonian dealings, so the marble pillar with its figured frieze might have wanted to celebrate previous Macedonian campaigns against Rome and its allies—not a single event. On the other hand, if the encounter illustrated by the reliefs is the specific Battle of Pydna with its peculiar beginning, then the carvings could only have been commissioned after the fact, by the winner.

Erich Gruen has emphasized that if Aemilius Paullus ordered the frieze, he certainly did not remain at Delphi to supervise its execution. His visit to the sanctuary was part of a tour of Greece which the Roman commander undertook after Pydna, and which he continued afterward, meeting with Perseus at Apollonia, arranging for a grand festival at Amphipolis, pursuing further the devastation of Epiros, and eventually returning to Rome. Gruen also considers it fairly certain that no Italian artists had followed Aemilius Paullus to Greece, despite obvious similarities between the Delphic reliefs and a battle frieze from a tomb in Lecce, in southern Italy. Nor is it likely, I would add, that any sketches were made during the event itself. It is generally agreed that the pillar frieze uses patterns culled from the traditional battle repertoire of Greek art.[35] It is important, however, to determine whether we can consider the treatment as continuous narrative, according to the definition above. It is therefore time to turn to the reliefs themselves.

The Frieze

The four sides of the pillar strip have been read as a continuum, with a beginning, a middle, and an end, as already mentioned (Ill. 12). Yet we have also pointed out that scholars do not agree on the proper sequence for the reading, some privileging one short face over the other, and Moreno beginning the narrative in the middle of one long side and moving counterclockwise around the monument to end on that same long side, parallel to the Sacred Way.[36] Aemilius Paullus is also supposed to appear more than once on the monument, thus qualifying the frieze as continuous narrative—yet this distribution would create an effective separation from scene to scene, making it impossible for the visitor to perceive the repeated personage within the same visual frame. Indeed, were this looser formula to be accepted (within the same frieze, if not within the same *side* of the frieze), then the Nike Balustrade in Athens could already qualify as continuous narrative, since Athena appears on each side, as she receives the offerings brought by the Nikai and supervises their activities. Finally, scholars disagree in identifying Romans and Macedonians, let alone Aemilius Paullus himself amidst his men.[37]

The concept of a temporal sequence to the events, per se, cannot constitute continuous narrative. It may already have existed in the Classical period, if the painting of the Battle of Marathon in the Stoa Poikile at Athens did in fact progress from a fight on equal terms to the Persian flight to the ships, as Pausanias describes it.[38] Moreover, the scenes seem to be self-contained units, with an uninterrupted groundline beginning and ending at the edge of each side and no characterizing features of landscape. In addition, a certain symmetry of composition prevails within each scene, with matching poses and equivalent numbers of horses and hoplites. Only one side shows corpses (scene IV, figures 25 and 29), and of these two only one can be positively identified as Macedonian by his shield, thus suggesting that the other dead in "heroic nudity" may be from the opposing party.[39]

Two main reasons are therefore central to our reading of the frieze: the fact that it was part of a Roman monument, where historical depictions of events could be expected, and the peculiar rendering of a riderless horse that seems to correspond to ancient reports on the Battle of Pydna (scene I, figure 5).

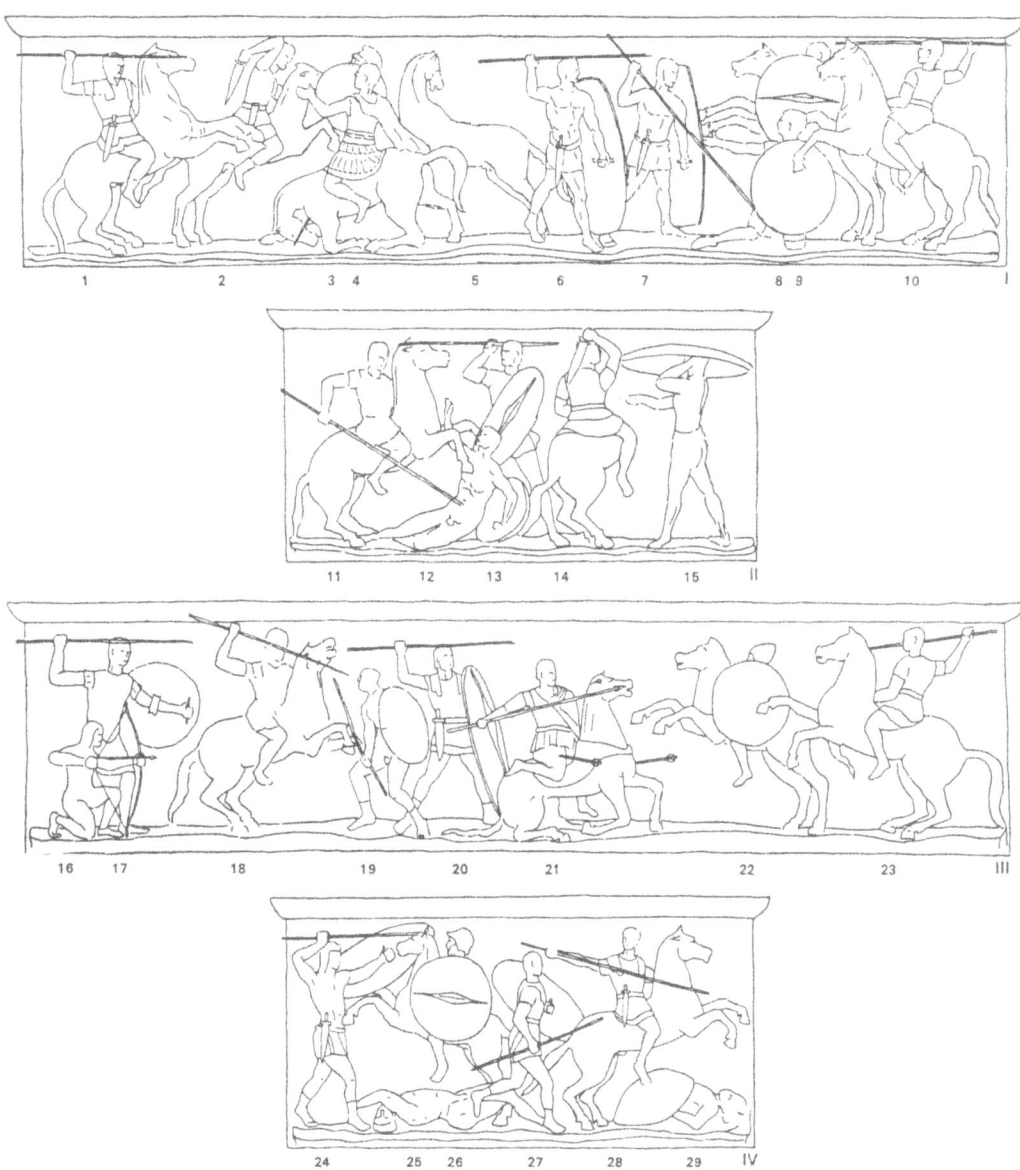

Ill. 12. Reconstruction of the frieze slabs on the Aemilius Paullus Pillar. Note that the drawing of side II does not take into account the newly added fragment (figure 13 should be fighting with a sword). [After Kähler 1965, 24]

We have two accounts of the event. Livy (44.40.4–10; 44.41.3–5) speaks of a Roman pack animal that escaped from his grooms and crossed to the other bank of the river, where the Macedonian army was waiting. When both sides tried to capture the runaway animal, the battle began. One of its phases involved the use of elephants by the Romans, which decimated the enemy, although the Macedonian cavalry escaped almost untouched. The second account, by Plutarch (*Aem. Paul.* 18.1) gives two versions of the inception of the fighting. According to some, the historian says, Aemilius Paullus, reluctant to move first in observance of an oracle, devised a stratagem (the Greek term used is τεχνάζειν) for making the enemy attack instead: he had a horse driven forth without a bridle, the pursuit of which started the battle. Others, however, state that Thrakians under Alexander tried to capture some beasts of burden that were bringing provisions to the Romans; these were defended by 700 Ligurians, and when reinforcements arrived for both sides, the full fight began. Plutarch does not choose between the two versions, but it seems significant that pack animals are mentioned by both Livy and Plutarch's second source of information. I wonder whether Plutarch's first source might not have been an anecdote generated by the Delphic relief itself, with its prominent riderless horse.

That animal is certainly not a beast of burden—it looks exactly like the other mounts on the frieze. It has been taken for the runaway horse because it turns its head to look in one direction while moving in another, thus conceptually joining both halves of the frieze, but a more logical explanation is that its rider has fallen off in the heat of battle, and the animal turns around to look for its master, a pictorial motif that recurs in other ancient sculptural compositions: not only the already-mentioned Lecce frieze, but also a block from the Smintheion in the Troad, and a still virtually unpublished **frieze from Veria** (Beroa), probably from a Macedonian tomb (Pl. 32). Far from being a signifier of the Pydna encounter, this turning horse would then be a common topos of ancient cavalry battles and chariot scenes.[40]

Plate 32

Another conventional pictorial motif is the horse seen from behind (scene II, figure 14). In the Alexander Mosaic, the animal is riderless, but in the great mural of the so-called tomb of Philip II at Vergina it carries a hunter, although not in identical position.[41] The rendering is striking enough that it has been taken as a device to focus attention on a main personage, identified by Kähler as Aemilius Paullus himself—an identification supported by Moreno through comparison with several portraits in the round. Yet the relief head is diminutive (ca. 5 cm), distinctive now through the close observation made possible by a museum display or modern photography but virtually indistinguishable once in position on the pillar; even the comparanda provide little confirmation, since they are unidentified in turn. A more devastating comment would see rider 14 as Macedonian, since his opponent (warrior 15, who holds a shield high over his head—another compositional motif) is a Roman.[42]

Von Vacano (1988, 379) identifies Aemilius Paullus in the tall warrior in full armor (scene III, figure 20) standing behind a wounded cuirassed rider on his kneeling horse (figure 21), whom he takes to be Perseus because of the animal-skin saddle of his mount. Yet, were the Battle of Pydna precisely illustrated, both depictions would be incorrect: Aemilius Paullus rode without helmet and cuirass, and Perseus, who had previously received a bruise on his leg from a horse's kick, used a pack horse and wore no breastplate. In the battle, he received a second injury from a glancing javelin that tore his tunic and left a red welt on his side for a long time (Plutarch, *Aem. Paul.* 19.2, as told by Poseidonios, a participant in the battle who wrote a *Life of Perseus*). Yet the rider on the saddled horse has an arrow piercing his thigh. Looking at the composition without preconceived ideas, it seems to me that both figure 20 and 21 should belong to the same party, the warrior on foot defending the endangered rider against two mounted horsemen charging from the right (figures 22–23).

Although some shields are distinctive enough to be identified as Macedonian or Roman, an almost intentional confusion of ethnic details has been introduced into all scenes, so that allegiances are hard to determine; there is even what has been reconstructed as a Skythian archer in Oriental attire, kneeling with his weapon cocked next to a standing Macedonian(?). Finally, some warriors are shown in ideal nudity, although at least one wears boots. The horseman galloping off the field in scene IV may suggest the retreat of the Macedonian cavalry, yet he is usually identified as a Roman and was probably meant (as Moreno suggests) to lead the eye around the corner to the next scene. In that case, however, scene IV cannot be considered the true end of the encounter, despite the presence of the two corpses. As Osada has noted, there is a tangible toning-down of violence on the entire frieze: no enemy being grabbed by the hair, no clear losing side, no very close encounter between warriors. He explains this "reduction of pathos" as the Greeks' reluctance to show themselves defeated by Romans, yet the Greeks of the time still thought of themselves as part of independent states, and some of them, notably the Pergamenes, fought on the Roman side.[43]

I am inclined to believe that the frieze had been carved *before* Aemilius Paullus appropriated the monument; it either showed previous (generic) Macedonian encounters, or it predicted the Battle of Pydna without, by necessity, depicting its outcome. This chronology would explain why the Greek dedication was erased and replaced by a Latin one. It may also explain why the distinctive sarissai of the Macedonian phalanx, which so frightened the Romans, were omitted, as were the equally distinctive elephants used by Aemilius Paullus.[44] I also wonder to what extent the bronze equestrian statue surmounting the pillar would have been a true portrait of the Roman general; presumably identification was based primarily on type of armor and inscribed label. Even this type of addition to the pillar would have required some time, but it is also logical to assume that no telegraphic connection existed between Rome and Delphi, to notify the sculptors that the title of *imperator* could no longer be used. The chronological bracket is simply useful in determining the span of time within which the commission was given and the pillar was inscribed.

In conclusion, we still have a sculptured frieze closely datable between 174 and 167, but I do not believe it represents Roman traditions, nor does it qualify as true continuous narrative. Its lack of Baroque elements cannot be interpreted as an Athenian expression of Classicism, nor its reduction of pathos as a reaction to the dramatics of the Pergamon Altar. Both Baroque style and pathos were mostly conveyed through drapery, anatomy, and facial features, which, given the subject matter, location, and size of the Delphic frieze, offered little scope for expression. Even the distance between fighters was probably meant to ensure readability, and the slight overhead space did not carry atmospheric connotations. Some mannerisms of Pergamene sculpture are present—for instance, the superimposition of figures, which thus appear curtailed, as "disembodied heads," without lower limbs, or without their mounts—but some are due to pictorial conventions that probably added entire details in paint. As a whole, the quality of the frieze is not outstanding, although, as in most Greek works, the workmanship is competent. In comparison with the epic Telepheia, it is obvious that the Aemilius Paullus frieze cannot have influenced its narrative form nor have provided its historical counterpart. It rather shows us what a standard workshop could produce with the aid of pattern books and pictorial models.

OTHER FRIEZES

Narration in successive chronological episodes may not have occurred on the Delphic pillar, but it seems attested from other areas, especially in Asia Minor, where the continuous (so-called Ionic) frieze may have staged a comeback after a relative absence during the third century. Perhaps the most extensively preserved example of continuous narrative is the entablature frieze from the **Temple of Apollo Smintheus at Chryse,** in the Troad, a pseudo-dipteral building (6 × 14) theoretically associated with the architect Hermogenes. The structure has not yet received final publication, but it is already clear from preliminary reports that it was one of the most highly decorated temples of the time, with carved column drums immediately below the Ionic capitals, and a continuous frieze at present described as showing scenes from the *Iliad* and the *Ilioupersis.* It is not clear how each scene was separated from the adjacent episodes, but no architectural framing is suggested, and no background division is apparent in the published photographs. It is significant, however, that some of the *columnae caelatae* may also have illustrated themes from the *Iliad,* which would have stood in some kind of chronological relation to the episodes on the frieze above.[45] The excavators would date the temple ca. 160–130, but perhaps on purely stylistic grounds, since probes in the foundations yielded no datable material. Even a tentative association with Hermogenes, based on plan and proportions, cannot pin down the construction, since the architect's chronology is still disputed.[46]

Because final publication has not yet appeared, only preliminary comments can be made about the style of the sculptures, especially in comparison with the Pergamon Altar. Many of the reliefs are badly effaced, and heads are almost entirely ruined or missing. Except for the scene of the sack of Troy, no true sense of space is conveyed by

The Telephos Frieze and Continuous Narrative

the slabs, and even that episode may seem steeped in atmosphere only because building elements are introduced. The staggered line of three cuirassed warriors behind an
altar recalls the city scene at Trysa and may reflect Anatolian conventions. We have
already mentioned the horse of a biga turning its head back, a device perhaps again
meant to differentiate two parallel animals with superimposed bodies. Quite effective
is the furious gallop of the horses probably dragging Hektor's body; Achilles in armor
stands on the quadriga with his back to the viewer while the charioteer, his long hair
falling in tresses on his shoulders, bends forward to control the animals. Archaizing
details are therefore apparent in the eniochos, whereas the double row of pteryges of
almost equal length in the cuirasses throughout is different from any rendering on
the Gigantomachy or the Telepheia.[47]

One fragment shows a frontal woman, tentatively identified as Andromache, with
a veil flying behind her on either side of her head (Pl. 33). The tubular folds and the
curling edges recall the similar veil of "Nyx" on the Pergamon Gigantomachy (cf. Pls.
15, 19), but here the effect is incongruous, since the woman's pose is static and the
double direction of the drapery appears impossible, unless a strong wind is blowing
on her back. Yet this is the best example of Baroque style from the Smintheion.[48] Figures from the carved drums are slightly better preserved, and their relative isolation
may be due to both position and curved background. We may note the same desire to
outline legs with long shadow channels that we have observed in some of the Pergamon sculptures, coupled here, however, with a drier rendering of drapery and less
pronounced contrast of textures. There is something mechanical in the parallelism of
folds and in the use of fifth-century devices to indicate knee bends and ankle gathers.[49]

The same double-tiered flaps on a cuirass appear on the fragmentary **"Iphigeneia"
Relief in Izmir,** said to be so similar to the Telephos Frieze that attribution to it was
considered, but precluded by dimensions. The relief is thought to come from Pergamon, perhaps simply on stylistic grounds, and to date shortly after the Telepheia. It
shows two youths dressed only in mantles that hang behind them like a curtain; one
stands frontally, the other in profile, but both have their hands being tied behind
their backs by two cuirassed warriors. The scene has been interpreted as Orestes and
Pylades in Tauris, perhaps in the presence of Iphigeneia, since remains of one more
personage in a long dress occur at the extreme right. The composition is very dense,
with figures overlapping and affording virtually no glimpse of background, but the
top of the slab is broken, and therefore no sense of the relationship of images to overhead space can be gained. The depth of the carvings is also greater than on the Telephos Frieze. The one Baroque element is perhaps provided by Orestes' musculature—
"Polykleitan," with a pronounced epigastric arch. The important point is, however,
that a narrative must have been involved, since the single scene would make little
sense. Regrettably, the relief cannot be attributed to a definite building.[50]

Dimensions also separate the Izmir fragment from **two limestone frieze slabs in
Termessos** with a similar subject. The two do not join, but belong together because

Plate 33

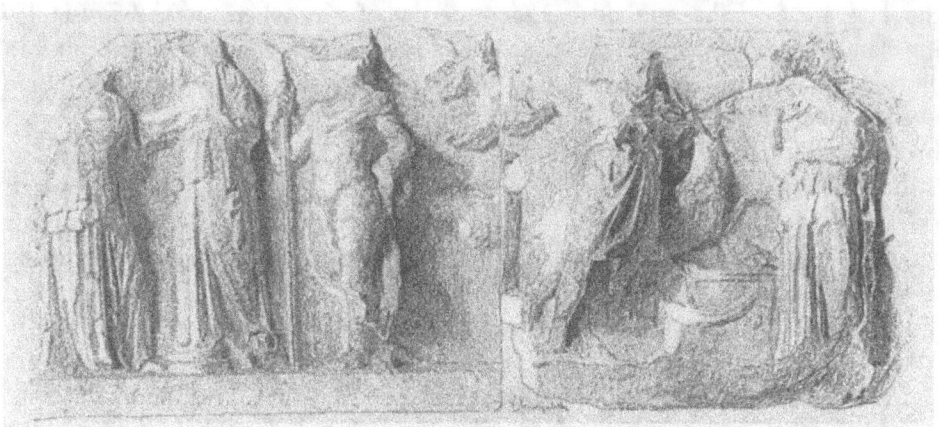

Ill. 13. Iphigeneia Frieze in Termessos, drawing. [After G. Niemann, E. Petersen, Ch. Lanckoronski, *Les Villes de la Pamphylie et de la Pisidie*, vol. 2 (1893) 49 fig. 5]

of size and findspot. Known at first through an early drawing (Ill. 13) and considered lost, they have now been identified at the site, lying close to a temple tentatively attributed to Artemis, to which they cannot belong because they are too large for its frieze area. Photographs show the reliefs badly weathered, so that little can be said about them. One slab has a female figure in a pensive pose (Iphigeneia) standing to the right of an altar to which a deer is being brought by a running female, probably Artemis. The scant remains of a third figure may belong to Chalkas, Agamemnon, or Achilles. A second slab depicts two females and a male leaning on a spear, his left arm bent and resting on his back; his attire (similar to that on the Izmir fragment) may suggest that he is Pylades (or Orestes). The central female stands on a low base, yet her costume and gesture belie identification as a divine idol; since she is goddess-like, she may be a priestess in the service of a goddess, therefore Iphigeneia, in Tauris. The scene does not correspond to the Euripidean version, but finds comparisons on South Italian vases. The remaining female on the slab would then be an attendant.[51]

The frieze has been stylistically dated not before 130 and its continuous narrative emphasized. How scenes were separated from each other remains uncertain, comprehension probably relying on the closed grouping of figures. In contrast to the Izmir relief, the main emphasis of the Termessos slabs has been said to be on the goddess Artemis, rather than on Orestes or Iphigeneia, but I am not sure that I see the point. I am struck, on the contrary, by the fact that continuous narration seems to occur in connection with temples and with epic/tragic subjects, and is therefore free from the propagandistic ancestral evocations of the Telephos frieze, for whose version no single literary source can be claimed at present. Other temple friezes, to be discussed in the next chapter, have more traditional (i.e., chronologically non-sequential) compositions as their subject. Both Kleiner and Stähler mention possible Pergamene influence

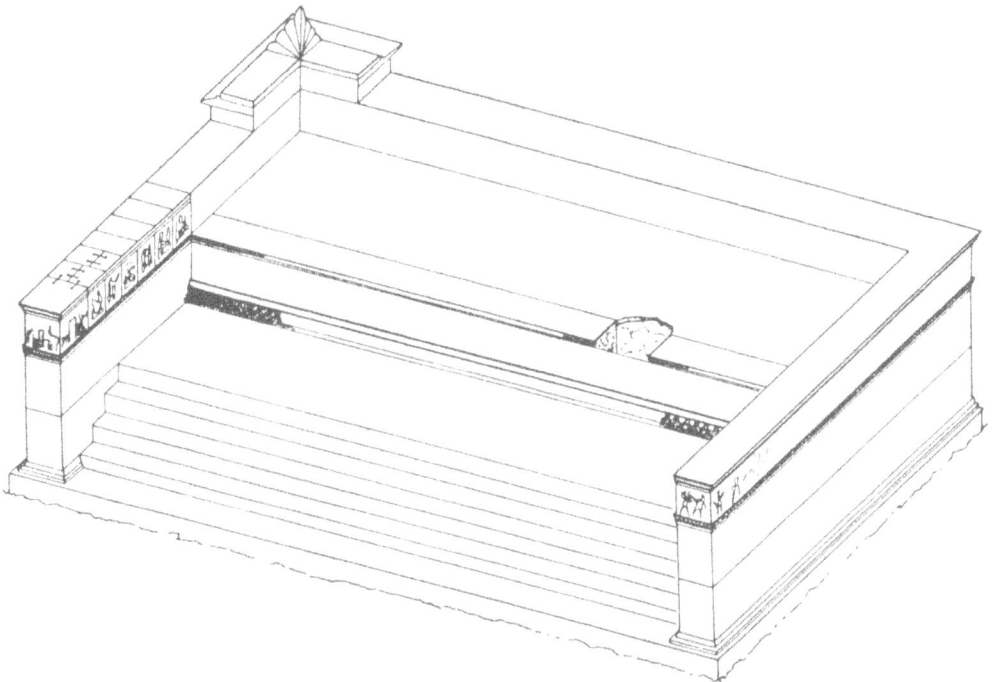

Ill. 14. Reconstruction of the Altar at Knidos (by N. C. Stampolidis). [After Webb 1996, fig. 95]

at Termessos, especially in view of **two frieze slabs with Gigantomachy** from the Temple of Zeus Solymeios that seem to echo the Great Altar, and of the stoa donated to that city by Attalos II. I know the reliefs only from a drawing and cannot judge. I would accept, however, that after the major commission of the Altar, many workmen spread throughout Asia Minor in search of new markets, as happened in Greece after completion of the Parthenon in Athens. They would have carried elements of the style with them.[52]

Two more monuments deserve to be mentioned because they are comparable to the Telephos Frieze in their treatment of space.

The frieze from an **Altar at Knidos** (Ills. 14–15) has recently received extensive discussion. From an originally much longer strip, only five relief blocks survive, one of them from a projecting wing/anta and therefore carved on three sides. The other four blocks do not join, and some of them were found reused in a nearby wall, so that their sequence is uncertain. They belonged to the exterior face of a *Π*-shaped barrier framing the few steps and a relatively low sacrificial table. The frieze zone was crowned by blocks articulated, from bottom to top, into a plain fascia, bead-and-reel and egg-and-dart moldings, and finally a horizontal garland of laurel leaves held together by a spiraling fillet. The base moldings consist of an unusual Lesbian leaf over a three-

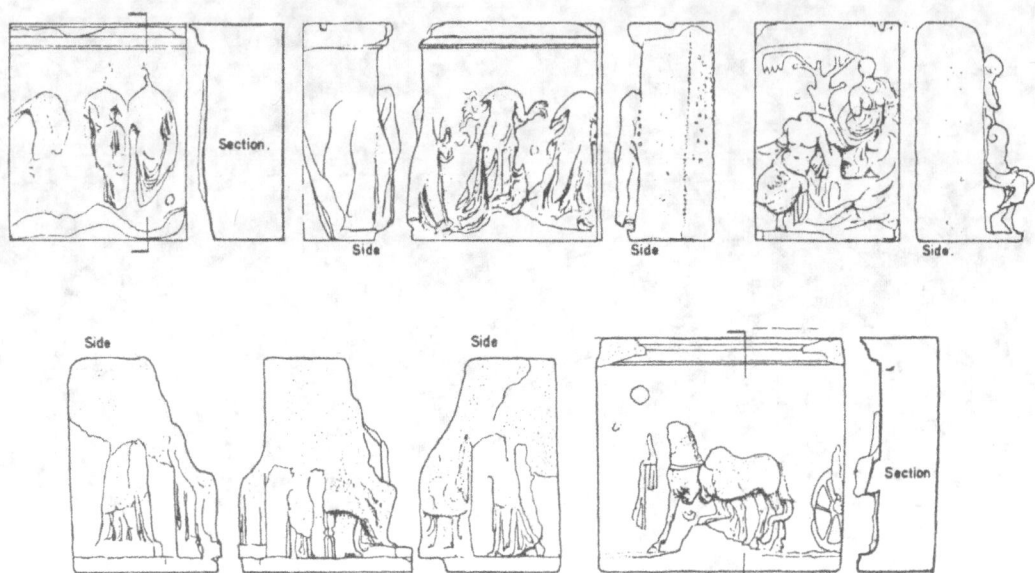

Ill. 15. Drawings of the frieze blocks from the Altar at Knidos (by Love 1973). [After Webb 1996, fig. 96]

strands guilloche with concave strands and convex eyes. The altar lies on a terrace below the round temple, in front of two rectangular structures identified as temples to Apollo. Two inscribed blocks from the altar's antae preserve an inscription ensuring its dedication to Apollo Karneios, and carrying the signatures of two sculptors—Theon of Antioch (in Cilicia) and Zenodotos, son of Menippos, from Knidos. With these signatures they were probably claiming responsibility for the entire structure, but they may have carved specific segments of the frieze, as we shall see below. Fragments of a colossal male statue, probably an Apollo Kitharoidos type because of the long back mantle, may belong to the cult image. But the presence of a spring in the general area and additional features of the landscape, as well as depictions in the frieze, support identification of the sanctuary as the Triopion, and therefore connection with a variety of other deities including the Nymphs.[53]

NYMΦAI is in fact the name inscribed on the empty background above a quadriga on one of the frieze slabs. It is surprising that the scene should correspond so little to what we visualize as a nymph-like environment, since no elements of landscape are included. A draped figure (Hermes?) stands in front of the horses but is too effaced to be identified with certainty. Another block is more in keeping: two figures sit on rocky ground, under a leafy tree; the one in the foreground is a river god, as indicated by the inscription *INΩΠOΣ* engraved below his left foot on the base molding of the slab. The other figure is female and reclines at a higher level, suggesting recession into space. One more tree may have appeared at the broken right edge. The spatial effect is enhanced by the ample overhead room above the figures, which, in conjunction with the natural setting, has prompted comparison with the Telephos Frieze, especially the scene with the making of Auge's boat. Other blocks from the Knidos frieze are less pictorial, but some of the long-robed females appearing against a plain background have Archaizing traits that recall the so-called Pergamon Dancer from Royal Palace V. Above one such scene with three women, the signature of one of the two sculptors recurs: *ΘΕΩΝ ΑΝΤΙΟΧΕΥΣ ΕΠΟΙΗΣΕ ΤΑ ΤΡΙΑ ΖΩΔΙΑ*. Theon had already signed on an anta front, but this second signature specifically claims authorship of the three small images on the slab. It is therefore to be assumed that other masters (including the Knidian Zenodotos, and perhaps workshop assistants) carved the adjacent reliefs, although their signatures are not preserved.[54]

This Knidian altar is therefore important for three main reasons, in relation to the Pergamon sculptures: it used elements of landscape, overhead atmosphere, and recession of figures into space to create pictorial effects similar to those of the Telepheia; it labeled images, and allowed for engraved sculptors' signatures, as in the Gigantomachy; finally, it used elements of style comparable not only to the Baroque renderings of the Pergamon Altar but also to the Archaizing tendencies of some contemporary sculpture in the round. The ethnic variety of the masters is also significant: a Knidian from a family of sculptors originally from Chios, and a Cilician who had been active on Rhodes, as attested by signatures from Lindos. Once again, we can assume that artists gathered and trained at the great practical school of the Pergamon Gigantomachy may have spread to other sites in Asia Minor, but we can also visualize certain styles and conventions as being current throughout the area, without direct association with Pergamon. Whether we can establish chronological differences on fine points of rendering is perhaps more dubious. Certainly the relief is higher than on the Telepheia, but the different size and level of the Knidian frieze and its exposure to direct sunlight, rather than to the shadows of a surrounding colonnade, may explain the choice. A date around 150 is suggested to indicate a time shortly after the Telephos Frieze.[55]

The final monument is an unpublished, fragmentary **votive relief in Aberdeen** that would not qualify for inclusion in this discussion, were it not for its use of space (Pl. 34).[56] Only the right end of the small slab is preserved, with a plain band at top Plate 34 that may have carried an additional molding and perhaps a crowning, separate block, as suggested by traces of a dowel hole on its roughly picked top surface. An anta terminates the scene on the right, the moldings of both its capital and base continuing along the side of the slab. Two warriors fight facing left. The first, seen from the back, wears a tunic or chitoniskos, belted and with a baldric supporting a scabbard; he holds a large oval shield and a lowered spear. The second warrior appears at a higher level, partly covered by his companion, yet his legs are also shown, his right in profile, his left frontal with an awkward foot seen from above. He wears an exomis that leaves his right shoulder and breast uncovered, carries a similar oval shield, and raises a short sword over his head in the Harmodios pose. Both men seem bareheaded, but their faces have been almost entirely effaced. Behind their legs, a third figure reclines, right arm along the body and left leg bent at the knee, visible in very low relief against the background; faint traces of wide folds along the arm suggest that he may also have worn some kind of garment, although what remains of his body is naked.

This modest relief would probably not attract attention, except for two features: it is unusual to have scenes of combat on votive reliefs, especially of the Hellenistic period; and the botched rendering of recession in space shows that the carver knew about such devices but was not fully capable of reproducing them. He therefore felt compelled to draw the legs of his farther figure in front and in between those (in much higher relief) of the warrior in the foreground, thus making this second man much taller than his companion. Yet the original "pattern," if such there was, probably meant to convey the staggering in depth of two warriors fighting side by side, of equal height, with the nearer man covering most of his companion. The very low relief of the corpse (in traditional iconography) adds one more level to a composition that should therefore be visualized as telescoping three separate planes regressing into the distance—an impression heightened by the ample overhead space.

Nothing is known about the provenience of this relief, but I find it useful to demonstrate that spatial effects could be attempted in a modest format, away from the epic or historical context of the Telepheia, the Aemilius Paullus Frieze, and the overvalued influence of Pergamene art. We shall return to the "shadow of the Pergamon Altar" in discussing sculpture in the round.

NOTES

1. Similarity to Propylaia: supra, Ch. 2 and n. 25.
Colors of the setting for the Telephos Frieze: Kästner 1997, 75–77, fig. 6 on p. 76; the relief panels are 1.58 m high, and from a possible total of 74, 47 are partly or fully preserved. Many fragments do not join and "numerous questions concerning details are still to be resolved" (p. 70). Some fragments previously included, and even joined, have been eliminated (cf., e.g., *Pergamon* 2, 1997, 134, fig. 2, panel 4; the numbering of the slabs/panels, which follows the order of the former placement, is retained in these recent publications although the sequence is altered). The drawings in Pollitt 1986, fig. 213 (= Smith 1991, fig. 197), and in Moreno 1994, figs. 589–98 (who follows Bauchhenss-Thüriedl 1971) are now obsolete.
Corner panels are nos. 2 (NW, beginning of N side), 8 (NE), 9 (E side, beginning), 35 (SE on E side), 36 (S side, beginning), 47 (SW, on S side), 48 (W return wall), followed by 43 as last slab (but see infra, n. 10). The string course below the relief panels is 0.25 m high; it ends below the frieze in a cavetto-like molding and projects ca. 0.10 m above blue-gray orthostates ca. 0.59 m high; the white marble base is 0.48 m high. The total length of the frieze was probably 55.50 m, as contrasted with the previously postulated 58 m (Heilmeyer 1997).
For the use of colored stone in the Athenian Propylaia and other buildings, see Ridgway 1999, 121–22, 128 and notes. The tradition of building with stones of contrasting colors goes

The Telephos Frieze and Continuous Narrative

back to Persia, and may have influenced the Halikarnassos Maussolleion, but both Pergamon and Halikarnassos absorbed a great deal of Athenian influence, and that derivation is therefore more likely than a Persian one. See also supra, Ch. 2 and n. 25.

2. Cf. Heilmeyer 1997, who calculates that the space between columns and relief wall was ca. 1.20–1.25 m wide. The colonnade did not rigidly frame the scenes, and some of them seem structured differently, to fit behind the square pilasters at the NE and SE corners. The author acknowledges, however, that some difficulties remain in the current arrangement and drawing of the panels, largely based on the theories by Bauchhenss-Thüriedl 1971, 40–74. Even the present display in Berlin, hampered by a space smaller than the original courtyard in Pergamon, differs somewhat from the published drawings in that slabs 37 and 43 are not exhibited, whereas slab 27 has been added. I shall mention below a few queries of my own.

3. In general, see Froning 1988; von Hesberg 1988; with specific ref. to the Telephos Frieze, see Osada 1993, 58–61, Stewart 1996a and his bibl. refs. in n. 1 on p. 115. The initial definition of continuous narrative goes back to F. Wickhoff, *Die Wiener Genesis* (1895).

4. Esquiline paintings: see Biering 1995, where the extensive modern modifications to the originals are revealed through ultraviolet photography, and the cycle is dated to the last years of the 1st c. B.C., thus to the middle of the Augustan period rather than to the Late Republican, as traditional, according to recent revisions of masonry chronology. For a review that brings out some controversial aspects of the book, see B. Bergman, *AJA* 101 (1997) 802–804.

A possible precedent for an Odyssean narration in continuous format may be found in the Tomba dell'Orco II at Tarquinia (1st half 4th c.): see de Grummond, forthcoming. The so-called Roman tradition could therefore go back to Etruscan practices.

5. Archinos relief, Athens NM 3369: *LIMC* 1, s.v. Amphiaraos, no. 63 pl. 564 (dated 1st half of the 4th c.); Ridgway 1997b, 195–96, pl. 49, and 220–21 n. 13 with further bibl. Osada 1993, 125–26 n. 207, would probably not consider this relief a precedent for the Telephos narrative, given the short span of time between the events depicted.

6. Nereid Monument at Xanthos: Ridgway 1997b, 81–82, ill. 10 on p. 80, pl. 17; Childs and Demargne 1989, 266–67 (dated ca. 380).

7. On these narrative textiles, which she calls "story-cloths," see Barber 1992 with additional refs.

8. Derveni Krater: e.g., Ridgway 1997b, 350–52, pls. 85a–b, with additional refs. For the Phoenician bowls, see Stewart 1996a, 45.

9. For Hiera, see *LIMC* 5, s.v., nos. 1–2, pp. 421–23 (E. Simon) where two slabs from the Telephos Frieze are provided as the only visual commentary; yet the Amazon-like torso (with one bared breast) of the rider shown there on pl. 298 has now been removed from the sequence of slabs 22–24 because of an impossible join: cf. Heilmeyer 1997, 128. That the fighter on horseback was, however, an Amazon is postulated on the basis of the weapon carved in low relief against the background, a typical Skythian axe with curved end—a "fossil" no longer in actual use in the Hellenistic period, as pointed out to me by Dr. H. Blinkenberg-Hastrup at Aarhus University. See also infra, n. 11. Intelligent comments on this and other interpretations of the Telephos Frieze appear in Rumscheid 1994, vol. 1, 36–39, who doubts political overtones in the iconography of the Telepheia.

Slab 51 (cat. 12) is currently placed between slabs 24 and 25 (the Kaikos battle) because Bauchhenss-Thüriedl 1971, 56–57, believes that the curly hair is typically female and an Amazonian fashion; the person lying in state is therefore not Telephos, as previously suggested. His death, moreover, could not have formed the closing episode of the narrative. I would agree that the deceased is a woman, but could she be Auge, who must eventually have died? This suggestion is also made by Heres 1997, 93–94, who points out that the two men at the head of the bed are in civilian clothes. To me, it seems even more significant that they are a Greek and a Mysian respectively, as indicated by their footwear (infra, n. 12). Hostilities might have been interrupted for Hiera's death, but would both parties have attended the lying in state? If the Pergamon Altar was indeed a cenotaph/heroon for both Telephos and his mother, moreover, Auge's death should have been included in the Telepheia. Yet the new drawings and current installation of the frieze follow Bauchhenss-Thüriedl's reconstruction. For remaining difficulties in the sequence of the slabs, see supra, n. 2.

10. Note that the drawings in *LIMC* 7 (858–59, commentary on pp. 857–62) still follow the original arrangement, with slab 1 at the beginning of the series. The new drawings in *Pergamon* 1 (pp. 16–17) and 2 (foldout plate added separately) show the revised sequence. Another shift from traditional arrangement and reading occurs with panels 13, 32, 33, 14 (cf. Heres 1997, 86, fig. 5a–c), now read as Telephos boarding a boat to travel to Mysia in search of his mother; the boat scene used to be interpreted as the Greeks fleeing to their ship from the battlefield at the Kaikos, after the fight between Telephos and Achilles (as still in *LIMC* 7; cf. also Webb 1996, 64). Bauchhenss-Thüriedl 1971, 71, makes the point that a change of locale from Mysia to Arkadia and vice versa is always indicated by ships. There is still debate as to whether panel 43 (a woman next to a column) should go with the episode of Telephos at the Argive court or at the very end of the frieze: Heres 1997, 96, and contrast Kästner 1997, 75.

11. My suggestion would place slabs 2–3 before slabs 28–31, but Dr. Huberta Heres kindly informed me (*per ep.*, Dec. 17, 1997) that the arrangement is made impossible by lack of space and by the fact that slab 2 belongs to a corner position, which can only be at the beginning of the N frieze. The man in a sleeved costume is currently believed to be one of Neaira's sons (Bauchhenss-Thüriedl 1971, 46) or a member of Aleos' retinue (Heres 1997, 84, fig. 1).

Admittedly (Heres 1997, 86), the exact sequence of events at the Kaikos battle (slabs 22–33) can no longer be reconstructed; cf. p. 88, fig. 9 (slabs 27–29) with additional fragments not included in the drawings. See also supra, n. 10, about slabs 32–33, moved in order to gain additional space, although thematically the previous sequence (after 30–31) seemed more meaningful.

The Skythian axe on slab 23 is indeed a typical Amazonian weapon, but (since the female torso has been removed: supra, n. 9) it could also serve to characterize the troops of the two Skythian warriors (Heloros and Aktaios, sons of Ister = the Danube) on panel 25 (*Pergamon* 1, 1996, 66–67, cat. 8), whose ethnic is similarly suggested by their distinctive gorytos. That the figure on panel 23 is fighting on horseback is no hindrance to this argument, since even the two brothers are shown over a fallen horse. A Greek warrior places his foot on the horse's flank (drawing on p. 17), which may further suggest that the animal was not harnessed to a chariot, as usually thought (Bauchhenss-Thüriedl 1971, 57; cf. cat. 8). Osada 1993, 123 (n. 199) describes the scene of panel 25 as static: a pile of corpses lying over their horses and being robbed of their weapons by the victors, *not* the action moment of bodies being thrown off their chariot.

I had also thought that slab 20 could not be interpreted as Teuthras leading Auge to Telephos for the future nuptials, because the king (characterized by his scepter) appears to wear a double-folded mantle over a short-sleeved tunic, instead of the long-sleeved costume typical of his first appearance on slab 10. Direct examination has now convinced me that the man is indeed wearing an Oriental costume, although the unfinished state of the relief makes it unclear. A few folds occur, however, along his right arm, and "cuffs" seem to circle both his wrists. One qualm remains: the large head at present joined to the male body is equally unfinished, but this alone would not account for its disproportion in respect to the rest of the figure; perhaps it does not belong with it.

12. Greeks wear "high-strapped *krepides* [sandals] with laces wrapped around the lower leg and heel tabs with high points," which, together with the short chlamys, suggest military attire: Morrow 1985, 110; cf. also 136–37. The easterners wear *embades* (low boots) over *piloi* (a form of sock; cf. Pl. 31). For the use of distinctive headgear, see Heres 1997, 96.

13. For a discussion of this rendering, see Ridgway 1981, 52 and passim; in greater detail, Delivorrias 1991, 135–50, for whom the trait "constitue l'expression codifiée de la provocation érotique par la beauté corporelle" (p. 147). The torso once joined to slab 23 does not qualify because her dress is not slipping but is rather unfastened, in Amazonian fashion. Another female, seen in rear view on panel 44, seems to have her right shoulder bare, but she may be wearing only a mantle, and the Dionysiac context (with Priapos: Bauchhenss-Thüriedl 1971, 67–68, pls. 8.2, 9) could explain the rendering.

14. Bauchhenss-Thüriedl 1971, 45–47, had already suggested that the woman with revealed breast on slab 11 is Auge, whom she sees next to an Athena statue different from the Hellenistic-costumed idol of slab 20, which is localized in Mysia. The scene of slab 11 would therefore be taking place at Tegea and would represent the first time that Herakles (on panel 3) sees Auge; the slipping chiton would be an allusion to future events, and the arrangement of the panels would be 2–3, 11. *Pergamon* 1, 17, retains, however, the traditional reading of slab 11 and does not include fragment 68 (which contains another image of Athena); Heres 1997, 84, rejects the sequence proposed in 1971 because Herakles stands under an oak, while the tree on slab 11 is a plane tree, indicative of a different locale. If, however, slabs 2–3 could go next to the Kaikos battle, the discrepancy would be eliminated, and another image of the hero gazing at Auge would have to be postulated.

The woman holding the helmet on slab 17 as an attendant: *LIMC* 7, 860, commentary on slabs 16–17; cf. *Pergamon* 2, 86 (Heres). Zanker 1993, 223 and n. 56, points out that, on East Greek gravestones, "a garment falling from the shoulder is a typical sign of a nurse's dedication" and "occurs often on little servant girls" (cf. Pl. 60). Perhaps semantic messages had changed or expanded by the 2nd c.

15. The lioness replacing the hind at Pergamon has been seen as an upgrading of the nursing animal in view of the wolf-suckled Romulus and Remus, and therefore as an anti-Roman statement: cf. Schmidt 1990, 147–50 (also Andreae 1997, 123: Telephos stronger than Romulus). But see the review by A. Stewart, *Gnomon* 65 (1993) 710–16, and Stewart 1996a, 39, who suggests that the deer was the sacred animal of the Kelts and therefore could not have been used in a monument commemorating victory over the Gauls. The lioness, as queen of animals, was also a better choice for a future king.

Nymph reliefs and cave setting: see, e.g., Ridgway 1997b, 197–99 (with bibl.), 200, pl. 53, for a relief with the infant Asklepios on Mount Titthion (Athens NM 1351): cf. *LIMC* 2, s.v. Asklepios, discussion of no. 5 on p. 868, for the Epidaurian version of his suckling by a hind. The Dionysiac connection is suggested by Bauchhenss-Thüriedl 1971, 72. Heres 1997, 98, notes that the frieze version of Telephos' infancy seems to have had no effect on subsequent representations, even on coins from Asia Minor, which traditionally show the baby suckled by a hind. That Telephos may have been worshiped at Pergamon near or in connection with the Asklepieion is pointed out by Stewart, forthcoming, on the basis of Paus. 3.26.10 and 5.13.3, but see also Webb 1998, 249–50.

16. I wonder whether background surfaces, roughing out of details, perhaps even drapery patterns, were left to the younger members of the workshops, with the final touches to the figures being reserved for the more experienced masters. As for the Gigantomachy Frieze, however, the work must have been apportioned by slabs and number of figures. As often noted, specific scenes are not delimited by the extent of the individual panels, since changes of locale and of episodes can occur in the middle of a block.

17. See, e.g., Ridgway 1990, 28–30 (Artemision), 164–67 (altar of Athenaion at Priene), 172–75 (Delian Hall of Bulls).

18. See, e.g., Ridgway 1997b, 88–94 (Heroon at Gjölbaschi-Trysa), 94–99 (Limyra Heroon).

19. For a lengthy discussion of both perspective arrangements and possible sources, see Osada 1993, 34–63. Against book illustrations as source see, e.g., Stewart 1996a, 47 (I would agree). Perspective arrangement of figures at different levels: e.g., panels 5–6 (building Auge's boat; *Pergamon* 1, 1996, 56–57, cat. 2–3 with perceptive comments), 7–8 (bathing the infant Telephos). Semicircular arrangement: panels 39–40 (banquet of the princes at Argos), and, less successfully, 44–46 (open-air sanctuary). Semicircular effects had been sought, presumably, since the time of the E Siphnian Frieze, improved by the E friezes of both Parthenon and Hephaisteion, and certainly achieved by the semicircular bases of Classical monuments in the round at Delphi and Olympia. Osada 1993, 48, usefully compares a (Hellenistic) funerary relief from Rhodes: Bieber 1961, fig. 490 (see infra, Ch. 4 n. 60). A good analysis of motifs derived from other contexts (e.g., the *dexiosis* of panel 18) is provided by Heres 1997, 98–101.

20. Disembodied heads on the Telephos Frieze: see esp. the facing young man on panel 10 (Teuthras rushing to the shore to view Auge), *Pergamon* 1, 1996, 58–59, cat. 4, who sports an *anastole* comparable to some Giants' hairstyles on the podium frieze. The slab offers also a good example of contouring drill channels, and of folds ending in drill holes on the figure at the extreme right. For the parallels on the Pergamon Gigantomachy, see Ch. 2. A somewhat similar treatment of background figures (or at least of figures whose bodies are not completely rendered) occurs already on the processional friezes of the Limyra Heroon and may be a local (Anatolian) trait.

21. See Ridgway 1997b, 92, 108 n. 32; Gschwantler 1993 sees the device as a Lykian masonry technique. Leafless trees also provide a sort of scansion within the small hunting frieze at the bottom of the Sarcophagus of the Mourning Women (mid-4th c.).

22. See Heres 1997, 88, fig. 9, for panels 27–29, since the first slab with the two personifications is not included in the available drawings, and cf. her comments on p. 89; see also 93 fig. 17, for panels 49–50, where she states that the presence of the river gods marks the importance of the shrine in front of which the altar is being erected. The satyrs of slabs 44–46 appear almost entirely human, but they have definite pointed ears (Heres 1997, 93 figs. 15–16); Bauchhenss-Thüriedl 1971, 63–64, believes that the scene takes place on Mount Parthenion, not at Pergamon. On these personifications, see also Stewart 1996a, 42.

23. Panel 42: see *Pergamon* 1, 1996, 72–73, cat. 11. The entry (and cf. Heres 1997, 96; Bauchhenss-Thüriedl 1971, 59) states that Telephos threatens Orestes with his clenched fist, but an

attachment hole near Agamemnon's staff, above Telephos' hand, might have held a metal blade, perhaps not a sword but a knife, as permissible at a banquet.

24. For reference to all these mannerisms in the Gigantomachy, see Ch. 2, ns. 70–71; for the "Lykian wavelet," see Ridgway 1997b, 87, n. 22 on pp. 105–106, and cf. pls. 17, 19. The Lykian connection has also been noted by Heres 1997, 104, who compares a detail from the Nereid Monument frieze (her fig. 25) although dating it to the late 5th c.

25. On the Pergamon "Dancer," most recently, Kunze 1996a, 117–18, fig. 5. See also infra, at n. 54, and Ch. 9 with ns. 42–43. For Classicizing and Archaizing details on the Telephos Frieze, see Heres 1997, 96 (Corinthian helmet), 99 (furniture). I wonder whether the column finial "with uncertain meaning" (p. 99) on panel 40 may have been meant as an Aiolic capital like those from Archaic Larisa, perhaps again to suggest a remote past. The lion on a column (panel 44) may be a similar archaism or a Lykian feature (cf. the Nereid Monument). I would much like to know the meaning of the ear(?) carved on the boat taking Telephos to Mysia (panel 14), in place of the traditional eye; the wing carved in the register below the ear has the two different layers of feathers already noted on the griffins in the round from the Altar (Ch. 2 n. 82).

The idol of Athena on panel 20 (*Pergamon* 1, 1996, 64–65, cat. 7) seems to wear the Archaizing peplos typical of Classical Hekate figures, which is meant to characterize it as a statue, but has the rounded, low-slung hips and narrow shoulders of a Hellenistic woman. For the distinction I make between Archaistic and Archaizing, see Ridgway 1993b, 445–46; also infra, Ch. 9 and n. 44.

26. The main publication of the Aemilius Paullus Monument remains Kähler 1965 (with additional bibl.), whose progressive numbering of the figures is here followed; since that book appeared, a new fragment has been added to figure 13 on side II (Jacquemin and Laroche 1982, 207–14, fig. 14), one more article (von Vacano 1988) has discussed in detail the possible identification of all combatants, and one more pillar at Delphi has been identified as Macedonian (Jacquemin, Laroche, and Lefèvre 1995). Important recent accounts within a more general context are: Pollitt 1986, 155–58, figs. 162–64; Osada 1993, 26–33; Moreno 1994, 538–41, 661–63, figs. 656–60, 790 (neither Pollitt nor Moreno includes the newly found fragment in his illustrations). Concise but important information about the monument also in *GdDs* 1991, 235 no. 418, and *GdDm* 1991, 124–26, fig. 92. The pillar-monument form, as a statue base, is discussed by Schmidt 1995, section XII, 155–68, with catalogue on pp. 512–27; only 15 examples of the type are listed (omitting the second Macedonian), beginning in the late 4th c. (a single example) and flourishing in the 2nd c. (the Aemilius Paullus Monument is cat. XII.10, pp. 521–23, figs. 183, 225). See also Webb 1996, 36, summarizing appendix II, pp. 533–52, from her 1989 Ph.D. dissertation, with her own identifications.

27. It is therefore possible that the Greek term κίων was used by Polybios to mean pillar and was simply mistranslated by Livy, who had not seen the monument. For the second pillar, see n. 26. That the Aemilius Paullus Pier stood at least until the 2nd c. A.C. is shown by Roman Imperial inscriptions engraved upon it: Jacquemin and Laroche 1982, 214.

28. Among the documents inscribed on the Limestone Pillar is a letter from Adeimantos (of Lampsakos) to Demetrios, which gives at least a date *post quem* of 302 for the monument; the French scholars suggest that Perseus may have arranged for the construction of his two piers after his visit to Delphi, in the late 170s.

29. The block of the Limestone Pillar from the Aire was the one with the most northerly

findspot; others were found much farther south: Jacquemin, Laroche, and Lefèvre 1995, 129. The location of the Aemilius Paullus Pier, at the SE corner of the temple, on Foundation 418 (cf. numbered plan on pl. 5), which lies ca. 4 m below the level of the terrain at the time, is tentatively suggested in *GdDs* 1991, 235; see also p. 168, fig. 70, for comparative drawings of other pillar monuments at Delphi, including that of Prousias II (180/79). Its location at the higher level is proposed by Jacquemin and Laroche 1982, app. pp. 215–18. If the suggestion about the Limestone Pillar is correct, the two Macedonian monuments would have stood in clear proximity to the temple entrance, as suggested by Livy.

30. Kähler's suggestion (1965, 18) is partly based on his identification of rider 14 as Aemilius Paullus (see infra, ns. 37 and 42). The frieze image would then have been directly under the front of the rampant horse of the equestrian group. The reliefs were carved on three equal blocks arranged side by side, so that each long relief scene comprised the central block, flanked on either side by the returns of the other two. In other words, each long side was formed by three headers, each short side by a stretcher face of the outer blocks. Cornice and statue base proper were each composed of only two blocks, and could thus be viewed as indication of different construction and perhaps later date; yet this may also be a way of securing the stability of the image in an area subject to frequent earthquakes.

31. Kähler 1965, 12, suggests that at least one of the frieze blocks was originally longer (his fig. c, top; because of clamp and dowel cuttings) and was probably reused, but he has no doubt that the frieze was carved after the pillar was appropriated by the Roman commander. Jacquemin and Laroche 1982, 208–209, state that the frieze blocks show no traces of having been remounted, and note the same system of construction and anathyrosis from the entablature to the bottom of the shaft; but they too are convinced that the frieze shows a Roman victory—if a Macedonian relief had existed, they assume that it would have been removed by Aemilius Paullus. They therefore advocate a "Roman" shaft and frieze added to a "Macedonian" pedestal. Chronological difference between pedestal and pier: see also *GdDs* 1991, 235, where the original form of the monument is assumed to have been similar to that of base no. 317 for an equestrian statue of Attalos II in front of the Stoa of the Athenians (p. 147, fig. 55, right; two plinths with moldings framing at top and bottom a high rectangular socle). Yet the Limestone Pillar (not yet known in 1991) definitely included a finished shaft over a pedestal. Prof. Christopher Pfaff, consulted at the Florida State University about the vertical pouring channels of the A.-P. shaft, found them most unusual—he knows of no other example. Plutarch speaks of a pillar of white stone, which might imply that the shaft had already been completed by Perseus, but his wording cannot be considered probative.

32. Pillar monuments with sculptural decoration occur also at **Priene,** but the carvings take the form of sofa capitals decorated with floral ornaments, probably influenced from Didyma: see Müller-Wiener 1982, where the most elaborate (capital II, on foundation F, figs. 7a–d on p. 699 and 8 on p. 700) is dated to the 1st half of the 2nd c. See also Rumscheid 1994, cat. 298–301 on pp. 72–73 and pls. 161–62.1; no. 300, capital III, is accepted as dating from the 1st half of the 2nd c. A **small frieze** from the short side of what is described as a pillar monument is **in Samos:** Horn 1972, 46–47, 206–208, cat. 172, pl. 79 (dated ca. 125); Osada 1993, 101–102, 154 no. DF 10 (dated end 3rd/beg. 2nd c.). It is decorated with Erotes carrying various objects (bow, club, fruits, perhaps an animal) toward a female in Archaistic dress and polos, who holds her skirt with her right hand, her left hand raised (with a painted scepter? [Horn]; in a karyatid gesture [Osada]). The piece is remarkable because it seems to derive its repertoire from relief

ware (the so-called Megarian bowls) and is a forerunner of the painted frieze in the House of the Vettii in Pompeii. Schmidt 1995 does not include this example among her catalogue entries, although she lists one item from Samos (525–26, cat. XII.14) ending in an Asiatic–Ionic anta capital.

I find it remarkable that pillar monuments occur only at Athens, Delos, Delphi, Priene, and Samos (Schmidt 1995, 157 and distribution map on fig. 293); even if the form is influenced from the East, we would expect some examples at Olympia, if visibility at major sanctuaries was the intent. Those in Athens are mostly Attalid dedications, yet no example is known from Pergamon itself, despite its terraced arrangement. Delos and Samos have level layouts.

33. For the statement on the inscription, see Jacquemin and Laroche 1982, 210. For comments on the possible meaning of this superimposition, I am indebted to Prof. Lise Hannestad of Aarhus University.

34. For instance, the Pillar of Prousias was given by the Aitolian League; that of Eumenes II, by the Delphic Amphiktyony. The only exception is the Chariot of the Sun, set up by the Rhodian democracy in honor of their patron god. The point is made by Schmidt 1995, 168. To be sure, the idea of illustrating one's achievements on the base of one's monument is not a purely Roman idea: Xenoph. *Hipp.* 1.1 mentions the hipparch Simon (late 5th–early 4th c.), who set up the statue of a horse in the Athenian Eleusinion, on a base that depicted his deeds in relief (for a discussion, see Krumeich 1997, 144–46, 240–41 cat. A45–46). For another possible commemorative base (the Galatian Battle Relief in Ephesos), see infra, Ch. 4 and n. 39.

35. Gruen 1992, 141–45, esp. 142–43 on the frieze being carved in the Roman's absence, by Greek artists. Gruen seems to accept that the reliefs depict "a Roman victory, a specific event, and perhaps even particulars of the battle." He sees, however, a special meaning in the Roman's use of a Greek medium and of Greek conventions "to display both Rome's participation in and its control of the cultural world of the eastern Mediterranean" (p. 145). Moreno 1994, 540–41, seems to leave all possibilities open, when he mentions that the philosopher/painter Metrodoros was taken by Aemilius Paullus to Italy to tutor his children, that the conventions of the frieze recall the 4th-c. painter Nikias' statement about "cavalry battles, where he could show many compositions for the horses—some galloping, for example, some being reined in, and some crouching down—as well as many men throwing spears and many others falling off their horses" (*apud* Demetrios, *On Style* 76, trans. J. J. Pollitt), and finally that Italian artists who happened to be part of the Roman army may have been urgently mobilized for the carving task. Lecce frieze, in Budapest: Kähler 1965, pl. 23b; cf. Ridgway 1990, 184, for a possible context and additional bibl. For a repertoire of stereotypes (a statement made by almost all scholars), cf. *GdDm* 1991, 126, although "incontestablement" the initial episode of the battle should be seen on one of the long sides of the frieze.

36. On the possible location of the pillar, see supra, n. 29. Moreno 1994, 538–39, compares this order of reading with the one he proposes for the Pergamon Altar (cf. supra, Ch. 2 n. 79); he sees the horse galloping off the frieze (figure 28 in scene IV) as leading the eye around the corner to the completion of the battle (figure 1 in scene I is in fact almost identical).

37. Aemilius Paullus is tentatively identified as follows by Webb 1989, 550 (and cf. Webb 1996, 36, where she repeats her opinion and points out that Herakles appears on each side of the Artemision frieze at Magnesia, certainly simultaneous Amazonomachy): scene I, rider figure 1; scene II, rider figure 11, although Kähler, Pollitt, and Moreno prefer the rider seen from the rear, figure 14 (see infra, n. 42); scene III, rider figure 18, although von Vacano prefers the

standing man figure 20, who seems to tower over the others; scene IV, rider figure 28. Moreno 1994 is not explicit about the possible presence of Aemilius Paullus other than in scene II.

38. Paus. 1.15.4. The painting of the Battle of Marathon was by the 5th-c. painters Mikon and Panainos. For a possible reconstruction based on representations on Roman sarcophagi and on the Nike Temple frieze, see Harrison 1972.

To some extent, even the Parthenon frieze could be said to show a temporal sequence, since the W side depicts scenes of preparation, the procession gets underway on the long N and S sides, and it culminates in the central scene of the E.

39. Groundline under each scene, interrupted at corners: Kähler 1965, 12, although only two corners are still preserved; the others are broken off, so that it is impossible to tell whether the groundline ended abruptly before the edge of the scene, as in the drawings. Since the battle took place near a river, a gap in the groundline could have conveyed that physical feature: cf., e.g., the Ilissos Frieze, slab D (Ridgway 1981, pl. 53). Osada 1993, 29–30, analyzes the inherent symmetry of all four compositions.

40. Osada 1993, 30 and cf. his n. 111 on p. 116 for an additional ref. He believes that the rider tossed by the horse is figure 8, and describes the "lesser" symmetry created by riders 1 and 2 against riders 3 and 4 on the left half of the scene, which is thus not endangered by an additional animal that provides instead a center to the composition. On the right half of the scene, another "lesser" symmetry is obtained through foot soldiers 6 and 7 confronting riders 9 and 10, with the dismounted rider 8 toward the center. The "greater" symmetry is produced by riders 1–2 and 9–10 bracketing the entire scene, as in the Battle side of the Alexander Sarcophagus; making allowance for the greater spacing of the Delphic scene, the analogy is compelling.

Lecce frieze: supra, n. 35. Smintheion frieze: e.g., Webb 1996, fig. 11 (Priam's chariot, departing to recover Hektor's body), p. 54 n. 22; the comparison had first been made by Weber 1966, 108–109. Veria frieze (racing bigae): *ArchDelt* 36 (1981) Chron. 326 (B. Allamani), pl. 219γ, announcing the finding of a second fragment (numbered 711) that belongs to the same monument as Veria Mus. inv. no. 292; Tancke 1990, 97, cat. 2, drawing fig. 3, and p. 102 for a possible early 3rd c. date; Osada 1993, 154, cat. DF8. To be sure, the horses turn their heads with less spatial penetration than the other examples, but the motif is the same. I owe the photograph of both sections of the Veria frieze to Prof. Niels Hannestad; Dr. Pia Guldager Bilde alerted me to the recurrence of the "turning-horse" motif.

41. See, e.g., Pollitt 1986, figs. 2 (Alexander Mosaic) and 205 (Vergina painting).

42. Kähler 1965, 17–18; Pollitt 1986, 157, fig. 164 (detail); Moreno 1994, 539–40, and figs. 790 (detail)–796—the supporting portraits are a marble head from Rome, another from Apollonia, and a bronze one recently recovered from the sea near Brindisi (the wreck of Punta del Serrone). None of these heads can be joined to a body, thus rendering identification questionable; for a computer composite of the bronze head atop a naked torso of the "Hellenistic Ruler" type, see *Fire of Hephaistos* 1996, 34, fig. 21, with bibl. in n. 56. The Macedonian ethnic of rider 14 is suggested by several scholars, including Jacquemin and Laroche 1982, 212, and von Vacano 1988. Kähler points out that rider 14 is a mature man (supposedly, Aemilius Paullus was approximately 60 years old at the time of Pydna), and that his features differ from those of other figures on the frieze; yet only four more heads are preserved, the others are all effaced, and even the Roman's age is uncertain.

43. On the wide distribution of shield types, see Polito 1998, 39–45, esp. 42 (B1A). Roman shields are usually considered to be the tall rectangular ones covering almost the entire body (e.g., scene I, figures 6–7), or the long oval shapes with central ridge and umbo (e.g., scene II, figure 13—but note the round and ridged shield of rider figure 26 on scene IV, thought to be Macedonian; similar oval shields appear, presumably, in the hands of Greeks during a naval encounter, on a gravestone from Asia Minor: *DOG* 1979, no. 1227 fig. 79 on p. 310; cf. Ill. 22). The Macedonian shields are recognizable through their decoration of concentric semicircles, but only three are clearly shown (scene I, figures 4 and 8; scene IV, corpse 29). The Oriental archer is figure 16 in scene III, but he is almost entirely reconstructed in the drawing from the presence of a long-sleeved arm in low position, probably holding a bow, and from the arrow wounds on figure 21 in the same scene. Yet the archer is shooting to the right, whereas the arrows have reached their mark from the opposite direction. Nude fighters: scene II, figure 12; scene III, figure 19 (with boots); scene IV, corpse 25. In scene I, figures 6 and 7 wear short skirts that leave the torso bare.

Horseman galloping off: scene IV, figure 28 (cf. supra, ns. 36–37). Osada 1993, 32: "Reduzierung des Pathos." He believes that the Delphic frieze cannot be considered the first example of Roman historical relief—it simply uses historical personages in an unrealistic setting (p. 31).

44. On the Macedonian sarissai, especially at Pydna, see Markle 1977, 331–33, and cf. Markle 1978, for additional comments. To be sure, most, although not all, of the weapons on the frieze were added in metal, and we cannot therefore judge the length of the lost spears; yet the sarissai were primarily used by footsoldiers, whereas on the frieze they appear mostly in the hands of the cavalry or of Roman infantry. The new fragment added to scene II shows that figure 13 probably used a sword rather than a spear, as restored in the drawing.

It is perhaps noteworthy that the only Macedonian victory monument attested epigraphically after Kynoskephalai (in 197) was dedicated by Perseus and the people of Amphipolis for the defeat of the Thrakian king Abroupolis: Bringmann 1995, 94–95 n. 11.

45. For a recent discussion and description of the sculptures on the Smintheion, see Webb 1996, 52–54, figs. 6–9 (column drums), 10–12 (frieze blocks). To Webb's bibl., add Rumscheid 1995, on the moldings, which he uses to reach a date in the 3rd quarter of the 2nd c., one generation after the Pergamon Altar (pp. 54–55); the grid foundations of the Smintheion (and other details) offer a parallel for those of the Pergamene structure. The original discussion of the then available frieze slabs is Weber 1966. Recent annual reports state that two fragmentary entablature blocks suggest the presence of three windows in the gables (*AJA* 100 [1996] 327; cf. Rumscheid 1995, 47–48 and addendum, p. 55), and that the 1995 season saw the finishing touches to the temple restoration (*AJA* 101 [1997] 294). Note that three of the seven extant sculptured drums are ornamented with garlands, phialai, and boukrania (boukephalia), in contrast to the other four, which seem to show scenes from book 1 of the *Iliad*. At present, the subjects of the frieze have been thought to derive from books 11, 17, 22, 24, and the *Ilioupersis* (by Polygnotos?), so that a temporal progression from columns to frieze would indeed exist. The Chryse frieze is, however, not included in *LIMC* 8, 650–57, s.v. Ilioupersis (M. Pipili).

46. Date: Bingöl 1990a; foundation material: Özgünel 1990. For the debate on Hermogenes, see the various papers in Hoepfner and Schwandner 1990; Webb 1996, 13–14. Dinsmoor 1950, 272–73, thought the Smintheion preceded Hermogenes, and Weber 1966 dated the sculptures

to the end of the 3rd c. Rumscheid 1995, 54, states that the architect of the Smintheion used elements employed three generations earlier by Hermogenes, thus clearly differentiating him from that master.

47. For illustrations of the Smintheion slabs mentioned, see, most conveniently, Webb 1996: figs. 12 (Ilioupersis), 11 (horse and chariot), 10 (Achilles, charioteer, quadriga). For the Trysa warriors, see, e.g., Ridgway 1997b, pl. 25c. The cuirasses with two rows of pteryges of almost equal length find their best comparison on some (not all) of the warriors on the Lagina N frieze: see, e.g., Webb 1996, fig. 88.

48. The Andromache identification was mentioned by C. Özgünel during a lecture at Bryn Mawr College in April 1990. I am deeply indebted to Prof. Özgünel for sending me a photograph of the fragment. The woman's neck seems to have pronounced Venus rings, and her head preserves the outline of either a high coiffure or a polos from which the veil descends. If the latter description is correct, the figure may represent a goddess, perhaps Kybele.

49. See, e.g., Webb 1996, fig. 7, running female at extreme left of picture (Artemis?), as well as the seated male and standing female (Zeus and Thetis?) on fig. 9, for these Classical conventions. The Artemis gives the impression of "wet drapery" because of the way in which the cloth clings to her legs; the triangular pattern between her legs looks artificial and almost divorced from the rest of the costume. The muscular torso of the standing Zeus on the same drum may also reveal some Baroque traits.

50. Frieze fragment, Izmir Arch. Museum 1002: Kleiner 1956, Beil. 113–14; Stähler 1968, passim; *LIMC* 5, s.v. Iphigeneia, no. 28 (scene uncertain; fragment said to be from Pergamon; dated 2nd/1st c.); Osada 1993, 147, cat. MF15. Kleiner compares the dimensions of the Izmir frieze to the Telepheia to point out how they differ, but assigns the fragment to a Pergamene master.

51. The main treatment, with photographs (figs. 2–3), is Stähler 1968; the early drawing (his fig. 1) is repeated in *LIMC* 5, s.v. Iphigeneia, no. 5, p. 711. See also Osada 1993, 148, cat. MF19. Stähler, p. 280, is against attribution of the slabs to the Temple of Artemis; p. 286, against Euripidean affinities. He suggests that Iphigeneia, in the slab with the altar and the replacement deer, is in the Pudicitia pose, but it seems to me, from the drawing, that she is rather in the so-called Medeia pose, as of a person contemplating a major deed.

52. Kleiner 1956; Stähler 1968, 288. Termessos Gigantomachy: *LIMC* 4, s.v. Gigantes, no. 29, drawing on p. 210. One slab shows Zeus about to throw a thunderbolt against an anguiped Giant, whom he grabs by the hair while the arm of another Giant appears in the field. A second slab shows Apollo, in profile to right, drawing an arrow from his quiver while stretching his bow against a similarly snake-legged Giant. Fluttering mantles on both deities and animal skin on Zeus' opponent would well agree with a Baroque assessment.

53. Knidos Altar: initial reports in Love 1972, 404, pl. 84.31–32; and Love 1973, 421–24, pl. 77.27–29 (reliefs), pl. 77.30 (view of altar remains in situ), pl. 77.33 (drawings of blocks) and 34 (plan of area), pl. 78.19, 23, 26 (frieze block in wall). For an extensive treatment of the sculptures, see Bruns-Özgan 1995, esp. 273–76 and figs. 17–20 for the colossal statue of Apollo (found built into a nearby wall) and attribution of the altar to that god; figs. 10–11 on p. 267 show the crowning blocks with laurel garland, figs. 13–14 on p. 269 show the base moldings (the Lesbian-leaf pattern uses three fleshy petals in place of the conventional dart). Elevation and other architectural details of the altar are given in Bankel 1997, 53–57, figs. 1, 9–12, and gen-

eral plan on p. 67, fig. 30 (where the altar is indicated with no. 6); the suggestion that the area is the Triopion, where the contests of the Karneia were held, is on p. 69. Stampolidis 1984 had already proposed this identification, attributing the altar to interrelated divinities: the Nymphs, Hermes, Demeter–Kore, Apollo, and perhaps even Poseidon. For the inscriptions, see Blümel 1992, 107–10, nos. 164–68; the dedication to Apollo (in honor of the Karneates Klearchos, son of Anaxiodoros, given by Timoxenos, son of Aristokles and Lyka Anaxippida, Klearchos' granddaughter) is no. 165. See also Rumscheid 1994, vol. 1, 21, vol. 2, 26–27, cat. 87, for the moldings ("firmly dated between 190 and 140"). Webb 1996, 121–22, figs. 95–96, shows drawings of the frieze blocks and reconstruction of the general shape of the altar. A brief mention in Osada 1993, 91, 147, cat. MF16.

54. The blocks mentioned, in Bruns-Özgan's 1995 numeration, are: block A9, with quadriga and inscription "Nymphai" (p. 244 fig. 5); block A6 with Inopos and landscape elements (p. 241, fig. 1); block A8, with Theon's signature (p. 243, fig. 4). Corner block A7 (p. 242, figs. 2–3) includes more draped figures in dancing(?) pose, lifting the skirt with the left hand, like the right-hand woman on A8. The anta block is A10 (p. 246, figs. 6–8) with carvings on three faces, the front one with a personage sitting on a throne with carved (Archaic?) legs, and, on the left face, one leaning on a pillar.

The point about Theon's signature being limited to the one block is stressed also by Stampolidis 1984, 124, who reports a comparable inscription on a marble (revetment?) plaque from Knidos of the mid-2nd c.: *ΒΟΥΛΙΣ ΠΑΡΙΟΣ ΕΠΟΙΗΣΕ ΑΠΟ ΤΟΥ ΕΡΩΤΑΣ ΕΣΤΕ ΤΟΥ ΗΕΡΑΚΛΕΥΣ* (Boulis the Parian made from the Eros to the Herakles); cf. Rubensohn 1935, 49–50, who suggests that the inscription is too small to belong to a temple frieze and comes perhaps from an altar. It confirms the practice for the Pergamon Altar. Zenodotos' name is only attested on the other anta of the Knidos altar, but he might have contributed and signed some of the now missing frieze slabs: see comments in Blümel 1992, 107, no. 164. Wherever visible, the looping folds, the many catenaries, the fluttering, scarflike mantles, the massing of folds along and in between the legs, are all traits that recur on the Pergamon Altar and the Pergamon Dancer (supra, n. 25; for comparison with the latter, see Bruns-Özgan 1995, 260, there dated to the 2nd quarter of the 2nd c.). The heads were in very high relief and are all lost or badly effaced, so that no stylistic conclusion can be derived from them.

55. This is the date suggested by Bruns-Özgan 1995, 265. Stampolidis 1984, 125–27, discusses a more precise date for Theon's activity, based on signatures from Lindos that suggest a span of activity ca. 180–148 (see also infra, Ch. 4 n. 62). He would place the Knidian altar ca. 160, and finds its style different from the "aulic" one of the Pergamon Altar as well as from the "provincial" one of the Kos and Teos friezes (on which see infra, Ch. 4 ns. 53 and 22 respectively). Bankel 1997 speaks more generally of the 1st half of the 2nd c.; cf. his p. 111, no. 171.6 for information on Zenodotos, who signed other works on Knidos (nos. 177, 187, and perhaps 113). He is the descendant of two sculptors who signed the base of an honorary statue as Chians (pp. 69–70, no. 112: "Zenodotos kai Menippos Chioi epoiesan"). The Sosibios honored by the statue was a minister of Ptolemy IV, thus yielding a date at the end of the 3rd c. for the portrait. See supra, n. 53, for Rumscheid's date of the altar. The height of the Knidian blocks is ca. 0.715 m as against the 1.58 m of the Telephos slabs. Two other architectural friezes exhibiting elements of landscape, albeit without implying recession in space, are definitely earlier than the Pergamon Altar: the Ilissos Frieze in Athens (5th c.; see, e.g., Krumme 1993 with bibl.), and

the clerestory frieze from the Monument of the Bulls in Delos, perhaps with a Trojan theme (end of 4th/early 3rd c.; Ridgway 1990, 172–75, pls. 80a–b; Osada 1993, 19–20, 144, cat. MF6).

56. The relief is exhibited at the Anthropology Museum of the University of Aberdeen, Marischal College, in the new town. I was able to examine it in November 1989, and owe a photograph of it to the courtesy of the Museum Director. The label in the case states: "Marble funerary relief with men in combat. Greece or Asia Minor. Hellenistic style, 400–200 B.C." I would tend to date the piece within the 2nd c., and to consider it votive. Its estimated height, on visual inspection, is around 0.35 m. I was unable to see the relief outside its case, and therefore to examine its rear and bottom surfaces.

CHAPTER 4

Architectural Sculpture

A Roundup

Theoretically, architectural sculpture should represent the best-dated evidence for the evolution or the survival of styles within a given span of time—in our case, the second century—because its chronological assessment rests not only on itself but on the various other elements that contribute to a permanent structure. Thus, the profile and decoration of moldings, the shape of the capitals, the proportions of the elevation in general and the entablature in particular, and finally the materials associated with the foundations can be brought to bear on the final dating to be given a frieze, a pedimental assemblage, or other forms of figural embellishment. Occasionally, historical events can be connected with the erection of a building, and inscriptions engraved on antae or other parts of it may provide *termini ante quos* for at least that particular feature. Yet, for the Hellenistic period, the situation is not as clear-cut as it might seem.

It is by now generally accepted that temples could remain under construction for long spans of time, regardless of their scale. Thus, not only the gigantic Didymaion, but also the Temple of Athena at Priene could receive attention from the late fourth century to the Roman period. We also know that additions were made, and even changes of orders: at the so-called Hieron in Samothrake, a whole colonnaded porch and façade extended the original format, and at Pergamon the Temple of Hermes and Herakles was initially Ionic but was changed to Corinthian during a later phase. Finally, extensive repairs of the Roman period could replace some elements of architectural sculpture: not only akroteria, so vulnerable because of their exposed position, but also a continuous frieze, perhaps in its entirety, as we know from Teos.[1] Two more problems can be added to this list.

The first is that Roman sculpture in Asia Minor can easily be mistaken for Hellenistic. This difficulty can readily be exemplified by many statues and reliefs of excellent quality from Aphrodisias that can be dated on other grounds, but it has now become a crucial issue in the case of the frieze of dancing women from Sagalassos, to be discussed below. The second problem is that several items of architectural sculpture, not simply akroteria but also friezes, have been found divorced from their structures and at some distance from their original context, so that no additional information is available about them. We have already mentioned some examples of this type in Chapter 3, and shall include some more below.

The results of our chronological uncertainty were made obvious in my previous book on Hellenistic sculpture (1990). Because the same structure had been variously dated to the third or the second century, I had to discuss it under the third-century rubric, even if only to reject it in the end. I shall here mention again all the buildings (and their sculptures) that I consider products of the span between 200 and 100, but I will focus on new evidence or new suggestions, referring the readers to my earlier publication for more extensive coverage.

In general terms, the second century seems to experience a revival of architectural sculpture, especially in Asia Minor. On closer analysis, however, this impression requires serious qualification. The predominant form of figural embellishment is the **continuous frieze,** which, however, can be of mediocre workmanship when sufficiently removed from close inspection. In some temples, distance from the ground level is so considerable that densely spaced figures may have produced simply the effect of a glorified molding. Better quality together with larger scale is occasionally found on altars, but even they are not exempt from shoddy carving. Funerary monuments adopt friezes, either in the interior or on the exterior, that seem appropriate for the specific owner, but heroa on the scale of the Belevi Mausoleum or the Ptolemaion at Limyra are no longer in vogue; one example at Messene, in the Peloponnesos, has carved rosettes "throughout the building," but its date (either third or second century) is uncertain, and so is its purpose.[2]

Other forms of traditional architectural sculpture are distinctly rarer. **Pedimental compositions** are almost totally absent, and toward the end of the period may consist of a bust on a shield or a round frame, set in the center of the tympanon.[3] **Carved metopes** are equally scarce, occurring primarily—in novel fashion—within house decoration, and figured coffers may have disappeared entirely (Ill. 16).[4] **Akroteria** are consistently used, but, when figural, can hardly be attributed if found out of context, and, except for the Pergamon Altar, show little variety, depicting primarily Nikai, whether in Asia Minor, Magna Graecia, or Greece proper, or "akanthos figures."[5] Yet many carved elements appear in unusual positions—as images within capitals, on simas, as crowning elements of screen walls and parapets, and in relief panels that do not belong to a proper entablature. Perhaps the most striking examples, albeit in terracotta, occur at Messene, where a raking sima is decorated with winged "akanthos figures" (Nikai?) reaching toward floral centerpieces, and a Corinthian capital has naked Nikai and Erotes emerging from the akanthos calyces and holding spiral stems.[6]

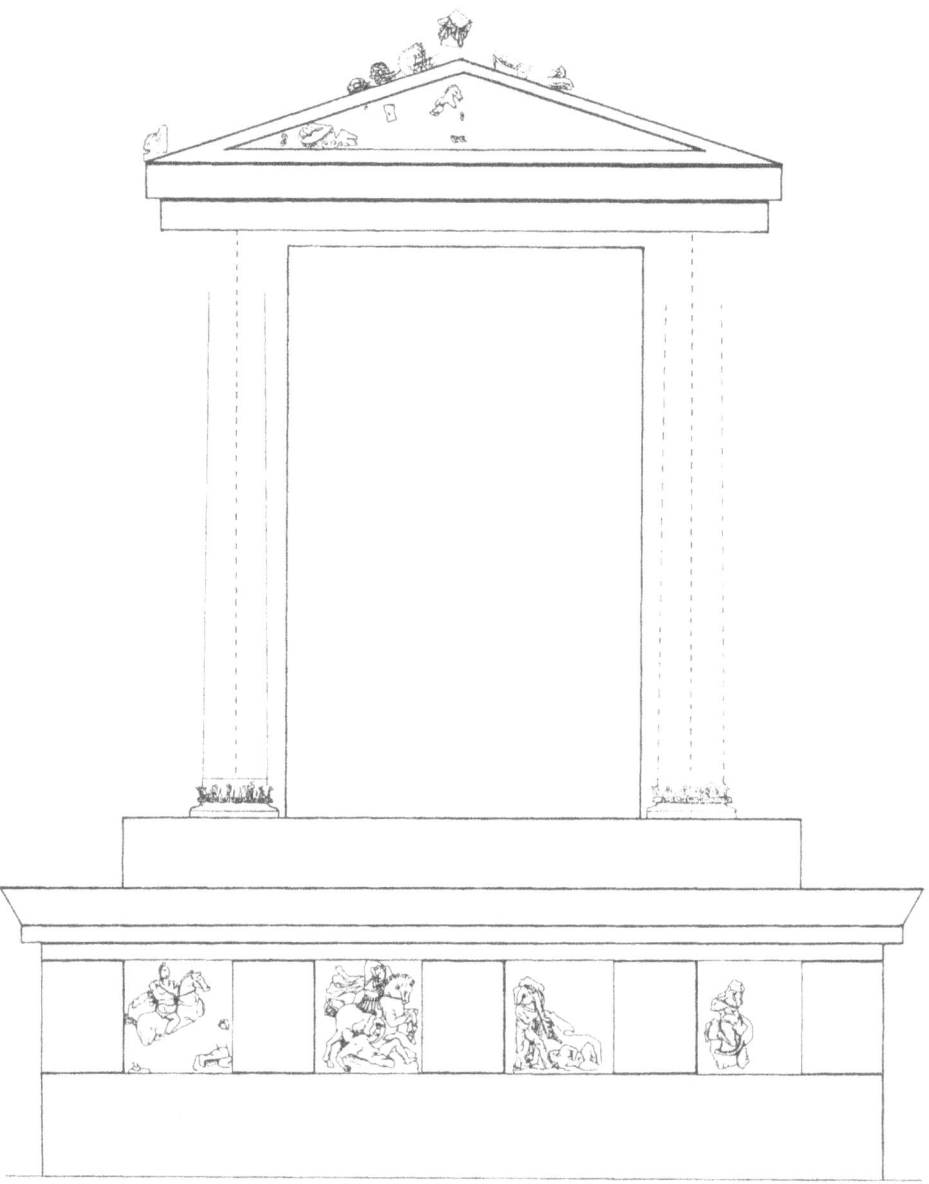

Ill. 16. New reconstruction of the Tarentine Heroon from Via Umbria (cf. n. 4). [After Lippolis 1996, 500]

At Reggio Calabria (therefore from Magna Graecia), the corner of a terracotta sima has a high-relief figure sitting on a rock, but the formula revives an Archaic tradition that was used at Paestum in the sixth century and may have originated in the East.[7]

It would therefore seem as if architectural sculpture in the second century, when not properly narrative, as in the cases examined in the previous chapters, increasingly turned to the decorative. This is not to say that motifs that may appear to us purely ornamental did not carry within them a deeper symbolic meaning. When deer heads replace boukrania at the Temple of Artemis at Magnesia, when "akanthos figures" make their epiphany amidst floral compositions, they obviously carry allusions to the main deity of the building and possible connotations of regeneration and life.[8] But the more traditional forms of architectural sculpture recur only when an intentional reference to the Archaic period (as to, perhaps, a golden age) may be the motivating factor. On the other hand, the presence of stucco friezes (whether Doric or Ionic) within houses, and the occasional bull's head decorating the columns of a Delian domestic peristyle, show that religious formulas are infiltrating the private domain, whether because their sacredness could apply also to that environment or because their original meaning was somehow reduced and fossilized. I believe that the trend may have been sparked by the Italian influences on the holy island, since similar private embellishment begins to be found in second-century Italy. Perhaps the most surprising are the terracotta Telamones from the unusually large atrium of a private house of the late second century at Fregellae, a site destroyed in 125 B.C.—this form of human supports had so far been known only from temples or theaters, which also carry a religious meaning.[9]

We shall now turn to specific buildings, from the more to the less safely ascribable to the span under review.

TEMPLES

One building that can be securely dated to the time of Eumenes II and his brother Attalos after their mother's death, thus in the second quarter of the second century, is the **Temple of Queen Apollonis at Kyzikos,** allegedly built in her honor and decorated with *stylopinakia.* Yet the information comes from a single literary source: 19 epigrams forming the third book of the *Anthologia Palatina* and datable to the fourth or the sixth century A.C., which describe the mythological scenes of this decoration.[10] They supposedly exemplified children's love toward parents, especially mothers, in keeping with Eumenes II and Attalos II's devotion to their own—for instance, the story of Kleobis and Biton, the punishment of Dirke, but also the suckling of Romulus and Remus by the she-wolf. Thus not all topics can be reconciled with the alleged message. Not only is there disagreement about the nature of these stylopinakia (which some would place as reliefs on the columns, whereas others visualize them elsewhere), but I find it hard to believe that a whole temple could be dedicated to a mortal and contemporary queen, albeit divinized, even if located at her birthplace. Perhaps a temple to Hera or other major goddess was in late Roman times ascribed to Apollonis because of the fame of its sponsors or the presumed theme of its embellishment. Alternatively, an elaborate heroon for Apollonis was later understood as a true temple. Yet it is equally possible that the epigrams are a purely literary construct with no correspondence in reality. Until archaeological evidence can be found, it is useless to speculate on this unprecedented form of architectural sculpture.

Among the examples attested architecturally, I am most comfortable attributing a second-century date to the Amazonomachy frieze of the **Temple of Artemis at Magnesia** (Pl. 35). Most recent discussion continues to place the inception of the structure at the end of the third century, yet at least one author argues for a date (and project) as early as just after 221. At any rate, and given the already-mentioned tendency to prolong completion over considerable spans of time, there should be no difficulty in placing the entablature frieze around 150 or later. Architectural details confirm a long building period with different phases of construction.[11]

Plate 35

The choice of an Amazonomachy may seem surprising on a temple to Artemis—the deity supposed to protect these warrior women, who had sought asylum at her altar in Ephesos and had allegedly founded that city (Paus. 7.2.4). The battle shown all around the large building is in fact that of Herakles, presumably at Themiskyra, when the hero was ultimately victorious and therefore the Amazons were implicitly defeated. Herakles is clearly depicted on the west, south, and north sides, and perhaps even on the east, as argued by Webb. Should this distribution be accepted, a quasi-temporal sequence of events could be construed, with the hero at first wearing his lionskin and progressively loosening it, finally to appear nude but still clearly recognizable because of his typical physiognomy—possibly the only bearded man among the Greeks—and his club.[12] A comparable arrangement, with an Athena on each side, had already appeared on the Balustrade of the Nike Temple in Athens, with the goddess receiving the offerings of the Nikai or supervising their work.

Because the Amazons mostly fight on horseback, they should have a certain advantage over the Greek foot soldiers; yet they are unmistakably losing. I could find only two that are unquestionably shown as dead (as contrasted with a single Greek, who may be still alive, although severely wounded), but many of them are in serious danger, being pulled off their horses by the hair (the most frequent pattern), or on their knees, or defending themselves strenuously. Hence, I find it difficult to believe that this subject was chosen to honor Artemis. On the other hand, I also doubt that it commemorates the victory of the *Romans* (albeit allied to the Pergamenes) over Antiochos, a Greek even if fighting with Syrian troops. I can only surmise that the Amazonomachy, with its imprecise number of participants and therefore its potential to stretch to fit the required space, was a perfect choice for a long continuous frieze that encircled the temple like an embroidered border or a woven ribbon. I suspect that all previous allusions of the subject to Athenians against Persians or Greeks victorious over "barbarians" were lost by that time, and that the myth was used simply as a popular and immediately recognizable topic, especially given the frieze's distance from the viewer.[13]

The "antiquity" of the myth by the second century may in fact be revealed by its apparent iconographic stratification. As already mentioned, the straight axe terminating in a curl at the non-functional end is a typical Skythian weapon of the sixth century, given to Amazons when they were thought to originate in the North. On the earlier Maussolleion at Halikarnassos, the women fight instead with the double axe, which was not only appropriate for a region that supposedly kept Hippolyta's weapon at its major sanctuary, Labraunda, but was also traditional by the mid-fourth century. Such a weapon is, however, absent on the Artemision, despite its geographic proximity to what should have been an influential precedent. At Magnesia we also see the archer Amazons in full Persian costume, with long sleeves and leggings, reflecting the evolving conception of their origin that eventually placed them in the East; at Halikarnassos, however, all Amazons, even the archers, wear Greek costume with flashing thighs and revealed torsos. One more Magnesian stratification, the last, shows some rider Amazons with a Boiotian helmet, the typical cavalry headgear of the Hellenistic period. Some Greeks, too, are in full lappet cuirass and pseudo-Attic helmets, therefore in contemporary battle dress. Like the *Iliad*, therefore, the frieze was composed for a contemporary audience although incorporating a number of elements from times past, in this case, specifically, the sixth and fifth centuries.[14]

This layered iconography bespeaks an accumulation of models in carvers' ateliers. Despite the variety of its in weapons and costumes and the apparent desire to differentiate gestures and poses—indeed, perhaps because of them—the Artemision frieze gives the impression of a workshop product, relying on pattern books and standard motifs. Horses stumble and their riders are violently pulled off, with schemata that go back to the fifth century and to the Bassai frieze, yet the more original riderless animals are absent, and the compositions are fairly traditional, close to sets of duels, at times appearing too static for a real battle. The occasional wind-blown skirt or even the appearance of the "Lykian wavelet" impart motion to immobile figures, but the rendering, together with the use of the so-called railroad tracks, seems almost a fossil, deprived of its original force.[15]

The lack of corpses noted above may be due to the height of the frieze from the ground, which would have prevented visitors from seeing the lower levels of the composition. Accordingly feet, hooves, and groundlines are often unfinished or approximately carved.[16] Yet some awkward renderings cannot be attributed to intentional shorthand or deliberate carelessness. Whereas some figures are completely detached from the background, with a great deal of undercutting, others are solidly anchored to their slabs with straight-back cutting that concentrates on contours and surface modeling rather than on volumes and three-dimensionality. Some Amazons on horseback look completely disproportioned, neckless, almost dwarfish; other Amazons, on foot, are oversized, with huge arms and hands, overlarge especially in comparison to some diminutive horses that seem almost like toys.[17] To be sure, such discrepancies are partly due to the desire for isokephaly, all figures reaching from top to bottom of the slabs regardless of their rank, whether infantry or cavalry. But some of them simply reveal incompetent carving.

In the best renderings, the latest stylistic developments are apparent. Garments show press folds and some texturing, anatomical features reflect the twisting poses, and sloping shoulders and high waistlines point toward the end of the century. In the worst cases, drapery is slashed and mannered, fluttering hems are turned into pure design; anatomy is disjointed and overemphasized, with epigastric arches assuming unprecedented prominence and sternal ribs marked. Back views, of which quite a few are extant, reveal muscular torsos with rippling surfaces that range from highly successful to mosaic-like effects. Few heads are preserved for proper analysis, but eyes are often deeply set in pathetic expressions and jaws seem unusually heavy. The drill is used sparingly in some coiffures, but is entirely absent in the majority of them.[18]

Finally, the most distinctive feature of the Magnesia frieze is the figures' parallelism to the background. Even those in violent torsion show little or no penetration into space, and most foot soldiers are depicted either entirely from the front or entirely from the back; horses and riders, to be sure, are in profile, but the animals are consistently lunging forward or even stumbling in one plane, without pronounced turning of heads and legs. Because of the relative height of the relief, the frieze from a distance looks almost like à-jour work, and we wonder what polychromy might have added to its appearance and comprehension. Since weapons and even horse trappings are carved in stone, metal attachments would not have played a part in the final effect.[19]

The Amazonomachy as a subject recurs on the frieze of the **Temple of Apollo Isotimos at Alabanda,** at least the fourth time that the topic was considered appropriate for that divinity. Yet we cannot detect a particular link between the subject and the god, although he was Artemis' brother and partner in some functions. Once again, myths may now be chosen more for their architectural suitability than for their implications—the times of political propaganda through mythological allusion may be over, as we shall see in the better-preserved Hekateion at Lagina.[20]

Little can be said about the Alabanda frieze, since the four extant slabs are now lost and were in poor condition even at the time of discovery. Only one is legible, and shows the unusual scene of a corpse (or a wounded man?) being carried by two companions while an Amazon with pelta attacks from the left—hence the deceased is a Greek. Recent publications stress the similarity between this frieze and that of the altar at Kos (on which see below), so strong as to warrant attribution to a single workshop. Since Vitruvius (3.2.6) attributes the Apollonion to Menesthes, a pupil of Hermogenes, a date within the second half of the second century seems inevitable, but the chronology could be as low as 130–100, or even down into the first century.[21]

Dionysiac themes are popular, even if the thiasos includes some unprecedented participants, such as centaurs. The **Temple of Dionysos at Teos** represents a case similar to the Magnesian Artemision in that it can be connected with Hermogenes and probably was started at the end of the third century; significantly, both structures added a *figured* frieze in entablature, perhaps the earliest *temples* in Asia Minor to accept a formula typical of Athens and the Greek Mainland. Like the Artemision, the Tean building was under construction for a long time, and therefore its frieze could be contemporary with that at Magnesia, but the situation is here complicated by the fact that the structure underwent two thorough repairs in the Imperial period. It has therefore been suggested that the frieze, either entirely or in part, is a Hadrianic "copy" of the original sculpture. If the whole entablature was renewed, even the pedimental sculptures (only two reclining male figures are preserved) could be a Roman addition, perhaps intended to suggest the antiquity of the cult.[22]

Given this possibility, the iconography of the frieze should be more important than its style, yet a few words could be said about it. The figures bear a certain similarity to those at Magnesia in that they fill the entire space and are somewhat squat with large heads. The presence of male and female centaurs playing musical instruments and peacefully mingling with maenads, satyrs, and other revelers in the presence of a bearded and fleshy Dionysos reclining in the lap of Ariadne(?) is a Hellenistic feature that becomes especially popular during Roman times, but the topos seems to occur much earlier in Greek literature, thus providing no definite clue for dating the frieze.[23] The emphatic use of the drill to separate drapery from torsos or to outline folds within garments is more in keeping with Imperial renderings, but its effect may be accentuated by the present weathered state of the reliefs. I find it interesting that the god is corpulent and bearded, in contrast to his long-limbed and youthful image on the Derveni Krater; the rejuvenating tendency of the fourth century is now giving place to deliberate archaism, perhaps to emphasize antiquity.

At present, the Dionysiac frieze is understood as surrounding the entire temple, like the Amazonomachy at Magnesia, but some unpublished fragments lying at the site may depict a Kentauromachy, with a "centaur rearing over a fallen opponent" and some human warriors.[24] If two aspects of the same creature were shown on a single temple—the bellicose side in the Kentauromachy and the "domesticated" side in the Bacchic revel—an intentional contrast may have been built between the former understanding of the wild, unruly centaur and his later change under the civilizing influence of Dionysos. This pattern of contrasts is also known from the Berthouville scyphi and seems typical of the moralizing tendencies of the Roman period.[25]

One more Dionysiac frieze slab that could almost belong to the Tean building in terms of subject matter and decoration comes from a possible **Temple of Dionysos on Knidos,** although it cannot be attributed to specific remains. The four figures extant have been identified as a semi-draped Dionysos leaning against a female (Ariadne or a maenad?) in motion to left, a satyr with crossed legs holding a thyrsos, and a maenad with a mantle spiraling around her body; a large krater in the center separates the two groups. The most recent mention of the slab dates it to the last quarter of the second century; the elongated proportions of the figures, especially the fourth, with her pronounced hip and small upper body, make me think that a date closer to the Lagina frieze, perhaps around 100, may be closer to the mark.[26] Both the Tean and the Knidian frieze are significant as part of temples, since a similar theme, as we shall see, recurs on the altar of Dionysos at Kos, but mingled with narrative elements. Whether a similar juxtaposition occurred on the temples is now impossible to tell, given the poor preservation, although the "Kentauromachy" slabs at Teos may suggest it.

The last temple for which a date still within the second century could tentatively be advocated is the **Hekateion at Lagina,** in Karia (Pl. 36). This building differs from the previous examples in that it is Corinthian rather than Ionic (albeit with an Ionic pronaos), and the only one among the other Hellenistic temples in this order to carry a figured frieze. Here, despite the smaller size of the structure in comparison with the others already discussed, the subject changed from side to side, and only the Gigantomachy on the west (rear) is clearly intelligible. More difficult is the interpretation of the other three sides, especially because Hekate is not a divinity associated with specific myths (except, perhaps, in the Eleusinian context), and because definite historical events might have been commemorated *not* by epic topics, as was probably traditional in the sixth and fifth centuries, but by personifications. Yet the importance attached to this frieze must have been considerable, since it is quite high in proportion to the very low (two-fasciaed) epistyle; perhaps labels might have helped in antiquity to elucidate some of the less distinctive figures. It should be stressed that the temple is one of the two major sanctuaries in Karia, an area not entirely Greek and certainly housing cults and divinities only approximately equivalent to the Greek Olympians. Moreover, several sections of the frieze are missing on each side, and the arrangement of the extant slabs can be debated, although all four corner blocks are preserved. Additional fragments of the sculptures have been found in the last few years. Recently, a number of publications have dealt with this monument, and I shall therefore try to summarize the main arguments, offering only a few comments of my own.[27]

Although the Gigantomachy on the *west side* of the Hekateion probably derived some inspiration from the Pergamon Altar (especially for the anthropomorphic and anguiped Giants), some features are its own—for instance the two Giants who are shown partly *in* the ground, as appropriate to Ge's children. Typical of this formula is also the fighting scheme by which the victorious god is represented directly behind the sunken enemy, with a vertical emphasis and a frontality that are distinctive traits throughout the four friezes.[28] In comparison with Pergamon, moreover, there is greater distance between figures, relatively little overlapping, more overt use of weapons, including boulders, and a definite presence of landscape elements, although the effect of a natural setting is more symbolic than realistic. Symbolic—of motion— seems also the circular or semicircular sweep of garments around figures, for instance the goddess in the center of slab 225A, or the one at the left edge of slab 226. Mantles, and occasionally a wavy hem, add movement to the lower part of figures whose upper

Plate 36

torso is completely static, or, vice versa, a vertical skirt anchors an upper body in torsion.

A special case is the so-called niche mantle of the central goddess on slab 228, probably Hekate. She stands immobile, without facing a clear opponent (the Giant to the right is being attacked by Artemis on slab 229), recalling the Athena Parthenos in her pose and attire, except for that billowing scarf that acts like a sail inflated by wind and flutters outward from her lowered arms.[29] The same effect, in profile, obtains on the *east side*, where the Birth of Zeus is plausibly represented. Hekate, with polos and long himation, moves rapidly to the right, carrying the stone wrapped in swaddling clothes to Kronos, who will devour it. This mantle rendering may therefore have been chosen in both cases to highlight the main deity of the temple. In this scene, as contrasted with those on the other three sides, a certain effect of depth is achieved by the Kouretes in the background, their legs hidden by Rhea reclining on her couch, which is in turn overlapped by an attendant in the foreground who hurries off to the left carrying away the real baby, Zeus. For all its apparent division into two horizontal levels, the composition suggests a circular arrangement. The "perspective" principle that would dictate a smaller scale for figures in the farther plane is here plausibly offset by the fact that attendants can be shown at smaller size, as on the Telephos Frieze, whereas the Kouretes may be heroic in height, comparable to the superhuman Hekate.[30]

The two-tiered composition of other sections of the east frieze is, however, unexplained except as a tendency of the time. The relief is very high, with a certain amount of undercutting that frees some limbs from the background, and figures in the foreground occasionally project much farther than the others, but they still look like statuary pushed against the (very uneven) background.[31] The ultimate expression of this stylistic formula will be achieved, almost three centuries later, in the continuous friezes of the Severan Arch at Lepcis Magna. Yet, for all the late-second-century originality of the east frieze, some use of patterns is evident: the semi-draped nymph sitting on a rock with her back to the viewer (slab 212) recalls not only Rhodian nymph sculptures, as mentioned by Osada, but also the Nereids riding sea monsters, popular in back view in the minor arts since the third century. The two mantled ladies at the right end of slab 211 are also typical of the "dancers" that, from the fourth century, infiltrate the Neo-Attic repertoire for over three hundred years.[32] Yet, for all their visual familiarity, these Lagina figures remain anonymous, perhaps understandable only as personifications of natural features and minor divinities present at the birth of Zeus.

Mythological characters, more or less securely identified, are attested for both façades. But the two long sides are much more problematic. In a re-examination of the *north frieze*, Junghölter has made several suggestions. He does not believe that the handshake scene of slab 223 represents the focal point of the entire composition; he sees instead several other elements within the same frieze as marking *caesurae* and establishing various groupings that eliminate a central emphasis.[33] He also notes a concentration of supernatural images and personifications on the eastern half of the frieze, while the remainder is occupied by military figures or by scenes that unite the two spheres—warlike and divine respectively. He then gives distinct identities to the military personages depicted: the Amazon-like figures, unusually shown in peaceful attitudes, would be the peoples of central and eastern Asia Minor who followed Mithradates VI; the naked warriors or those wearing the chitoniskos would represent the Greeks of western Asia Minor; finally, the cuirassed soldiers would be the Romans, and the handshake scene symbolizes the Peace of Dardanos in 85, thus demanding a date after the First Mithradatic War for the carving of at least that part of the decoration. Peaceful Amazons cannot be connected with any known myth; they must therefore be purely symbolic, and the whole frieze must show a historical event; if this is true for the north side, then the south side as well probably has an historical subject, and the temple sculpture must have been planned to show two mythological and two historical topics.

To see Mithradates' forces as Amazon-like requires special pleading for a Laginan iconography. It is also difficult to accept as Roman a type of cuirass that at Magnesia consistently characterized Greeks. Webb has emphasized this discrepancy, preferring to read the alliance scene as an Amazonian Dea Roma shaking hands with a Greek soldier who symbolizes Hellenistic Karia. As on the east side, she sees on the north an echo of the Hesiodic *Theogony*, where the goddess is conceived as bringing victory to warring men.[34] The other Amazons on the frieze are explained by Webb as representing the Federation of Zeus Karios, based in Mylasa and having its major sanctuary at Labraunda, where the double axe of Hyppolita was kept. Although this interpretation seems more plausible than Junghölter's, it would limit the Roman presence to the Dea Roma personification, and thus to a relatively minor role. If, however, the frieze symbolizes the right of asylum conferred on Lagina by a *senatus consultum* dated to the year 81 and inscribed on a wall of the temple itself, then the variety of the warriors' attires might allude to the different armies that might have sought refuge at the sanctuary through time (including the mythical days of the Amazons), since, as Rumscheid suggests, the Corinthian peristyle envelops an early Hellenistic Ionic temple in antis repaired and enlarged after 130 or even after 81.[35]

To be sure, a date within the first century cannot be excluded, but I should here state my own preference for placing the frieze within the late second century, probably 120–100, as advocated by Osada on the basis of close comparisons with Hellenistic gravestones. Admittedly, the latter are seldom dated on external grounds, but are numerous enough to be placed in a relative sequence that would confirm the date. Many details typical of this funerary and votive art find such close correspondence on the temple (including the leaf-shaped fans) that the same workshops might have produced both types of sculpture. In particular, the type of rendering that reduced an animal to a protome emerging from the background next to its leader, rather than representing a full animal behind the man, seems to me the type of process that began with the "disembodied heads" of the Telephos Frieze and found its full expression in the flattened compositions and attributive syntax of both funerary and architectural sculpture.[36]

Standard types may also have been used for some of the "divine" figures represented elsewhere on the north frieze. On slab 217, for instance, a sequence of three personages has been read as Poseidon, Ares, and Aphrodite, because the first male is in the pose and attire of the Poseidon of Melos and the female figure has been compared to the Aphrodite of Arles or, as I would say, to that of Melos, although neither parallel is exact. These sculptures may well have supplied inspiration, but they may also have been popular renderings that could be given different identities, like the so-called stock bodies. It has also been noted that the "Aphrodite" on the frieze is closer to male mantle figures in that a part of her himation covers her left shoulder and arm. Given the duplication of certain types (on the south frieze an Athena type appears twice, for instance—slabs 198 and 202), it is not even possible to assume that the Olympians are represented, rather than local Karian divinities.[37]

In contrast to Junghölter and others, on the eastern half of the north frieze Webb sees not just personifications and gods but human beings supervised by some deities during their celebration of the Hekatesia. She assumes a similar depiction of what she calls "civilians" on the fringes of the *south frieze* (slabs 205–208), framing a scene in which she finds another echo of Hesiod's *Theogony*. Slab 201 portrays an enthroned couple: a Zeus-like male and a female with four children, one of them an infant in her arms. She would be Styx with her progeny: Zelos, Nike, Kratos, and Bia, while the apparent consort should rather be considered Zeus in one of his Karian *personae:* as Karios, Chrysaoreus, or Panamaros. A difficulty here lies in the sex of the children, since the three shown standing in front of the seated personage are undoubtedly male, whereas at least Nike and Bia are clearly female names. Traditional explanations see the couple as Hekate and Zeus Karios with his three children Kar, Mysos, and Lydos, ancestors of the Karians, Mysians, and Lydians—but this interpretation omits the infant in the woman's lap; or the two would be Hera Teleia and Zeus Panamaros, with the children representing unnamed demes in the area of Stratonikeia where the couple had their main cult. It should be admitted that our knowledge is too imperfect to reach definite conclusions.

I therefore limit my comments to factual details of iconography and style. On the south side, as on the other three, some images are drawn from a standard repertoire: the seductive slipping of the neckline occurs on a female on slabs 199 and again on 206, in the latter in conjunction with a raised foot and a pose that recall the Melpomene Type; a seated male holding a staff looks like Alexander the Great (slab 204); the usual nymphs with bare upper torso (slabs 205, 206) sit on rocks, and one holds a leaf-shaped fan; and there are a surprising number of peplophoroi with apoptygma belted high under the breasts, like the Hekate of the west side.[38]

In summary, we could state that the Lagina friezes, in their own way, are as stylistically distinctive as the Pergamon Gigantomachy with its Baroque trends, the Telephos Frieze with its pictorialism, and the Aemilius Paullus Frieze with its Classical forms. The Magnesia frieze stands perhaps apart because of its location and workmanship, rarely at the level of any of the other monuments. I do not believe that a progression can be established from one style to another—indeed, the first three friezes are virtually contemporary, and all three use quotations from earlier sources, whether in sculpture or in painting. Even on the Hekateion, moreover, some faces show elements of pathos in their deeply set, angled eyes and eyebrows, while some retain Classical, almost expressionless features. Yet the Lagina reliefs—with their elongated figures, their frontality, their apparent immobility and "statuesque" character, their relative lack of emphasis on ponderation, and their symbolic (semiotic) approach to both the human body and its drapery—seem to stand in a chronological place of their own, if not exactly at the end of a phase. Inspiration from Hesiod's *Theogony* is in keeping with the learned trends of the second century, yet subject matter appears to have had little influence on the renderings. The undoubted presence of local personifications, however, and the relative obscurity of topics intended to allude *directly* to specific historical events are novel elements that may bespeak Roman input, as may the depictions of human participants in a ritual, if Webb's surmise is correct. The heavy use of the drill is a harbinger of Imperial carving practices.

Because of its alleged historical content and its possible Roman connection, I mention here another relief, although it surely did not belong to a temple: the so-called **Galatian Battle Relief from Ephesos,** now in Vienna. Only one pieced-together section survives in a reasonably readable state (Pls. 37–38), but many more fragments are extant, especially since some heads and limbs were carved entirely in the round and broke off easily. The frieze might have extended over at least three sides of a structure of uncertain form, perhaps a podium for a statuary group, but not a pillar, like the Aemilius Paullus Monument, since the relief seems meant for close viewing, even details at the lowest level being fully finished. The back of the slabs, originally roughly picked, was sawn off (in some spots to excessive thinness) and the cutting for a clamp on one fragment (cat. 2) suggests reuse. Although earlier mentions of the relief had considered it possibly Roman, the official publication, through a thorough comparison with other monuments, from Ephesos and elsewhere, has excluded an Imperial date or one within the first or the third century B.C. Considerable affinity with the Telephos Frieze has led to a dating around 160–150, which is then supported with historical evidence: the last Pergamene war against the Gauls after a wild insurrection in Galatia in 168. The commemorative relief must therefore have been made shortly after 167, and it depicts Gauls fighting Ionic Greeks, probably Ephesians. A later chronology would be made impossible by the fact that the Ionian cities, after that time, were no longer in a position to fight the Galatians, and no further encounters are reported. Yet other dates and interpretations have also been suggested, and some doubts may remain.[39]

Plates 37–38

The best-preserved section shows a battle between "barbarians" and cuirassed war-riors, both armies fighting on horseback and on foot; yet it is clear that the barbarians are being defeated—one is dead and lies on the ground with his legs bent under him, one kneels, and one falls off his mount headlong, so that only the top of his head is visible. Other horses stumble and overlap with great animation. The barbarians are depicted either entirely nude or wearing trousers, but not the tight-fitting leotards of the Oriental archers. They have beards and mustaches, and exhibit relatively long hair that in two instances is knotted over the brow in an unusual rendering for which no parallels have been found.[40] They are certainly not Greeks, but their Gaulish identifi-cation rests on one hexagonal shield with central ridge, which supposedly can only be Keltic, and their attire, which is not incompatible with Gauls, especially in compari-son with the so-called Smaller Attalid dedications. I remain uncertain. At least one barbarian (cat. 2) carries a small round shield, and other shapes occur throughout the frieze. The presence of both mustaches *and* beards is uncommon on original Greek statues of Gauls, like the colossal head from Gizah or the fighter in Delos, and the Roman works usually considered copies of the Smaller Attalid dedications cannot be accepted with confidence.[41] No torque or other distinctive feature serves to character-ize the barbarians, and two peculiar symbols, probably standards (one at the right edge of the recomposed section, another in the middle of it) cannot be paralleled exactly.[42] One wonders what the *Syrian* troops of Antiochos III might have looked like.

Another surprising feature is a possible trophy to the left of barbarian figure 4: it is a cuirass of the type worn by the other combatants, but it is larger in scale, it is not being worn, and a shield is placed just below it. If the barbarians are losing, why would they erect a trophy with the weapons of their opponents? And were the Gauls in the habit of erecting trophies, like their Greek allies/enemies? Moreover, the battle of 167, if this is what is shown, did not follow a special Galatian victory; nor did the encounter in 189, which certainly followed the defeat of Antiochos III. The trophy remains puzzling.[43]

The cuirassed fighters wear muscle corselets with two rows of pteryges over a chito-niskos, and Attic (or pseudo-Attic) helmets. This attire is used for undoubtedly Greek warriors, for instance, on the coffers of the Belevi Mausoleum, but it could also be worn by Romans, for instance, on the Gemma Augustea, the Column of Trajan, and the Ephesian Parthian Monument, as mentioned by Oberleitner. Chronology, there-fore, becomes of overriding importance. The campaign against the Gauls encamped at the foot of Mount Olympos was carried out as a form of punishment for their support of Antiochos III, and to satisfy the Greek cities that had suffered from Galatian sacks. But it was meant primarily to bring honor and glory to the Roman commander. The enormous booty mentioned by Polybios (21.40.2), who took part in the 189 battle, was taken to Ephesos, and part of it could have been used to erect a statue to the Ro-man victor. This frieze would therefore be "the first historical relief with Roman sub-ject known to us," or, even with the later dating, "one of the earliest fully historical monuments and the only one from Ephesos showing Gauls."[44]

Architectural Sculpture—A Roundup

If a date in the middle of the second century is acceptable, this relief with densely overlapping figures, a certain amount of overhead space, and some perspective effects would more closely resemble some sections of the Telephos Frieze than the Aemilius Paullus Monument or the Lagina friezes, thus providing no help in favor of its "Romanitas." The main publication calls it Classicizing, but its Classical echoes are certainly quite different from those of the Delphic frieze. The barbarian falling headlong from his horse recalls one of the opponents of Aphrodite on the north side of the Pergamon Gigantomachy, and the concept is also present on the Telephos Frieze.[45] But these motifs were part of the traditional repertoire of equestrian battle scenes, and therefore only the complexity of the composition and the spatial effects can be brought to bear on the comparison. Moreover, the drill is used extensively on the Telepheia, whereas it is almost entirely absent on the Ephesos frieze; this point was made to support a non-Imperial, second-century date, but it clearly cannot be considered probative, especially if the same "school" of sculptors is advocated for the Pergamene and the Ephesian carvings. Finally, one of the main parallels used to confirm a chronology around 160 was the Gigantomachy at Priene—that is, the coffers of the Athenaion, which to me seem convincingly attributed to the fourth century. As already stated above, I do not believe in a stylistic development from one monument to another during the Hellenistic period, and I am wary of dating subjects on purely historical grounds; I shall provisionally accept the official (second-century) chronology for the Ephesos relief, but I shall keep my mind open to the possibility of a completely different assessment, perhaps during the Roman Imperial period.[46]

The comparison with the Priene coffers leads me to mention again in this chapter some temples which I have previously discussed and which I would not assign to the second century. The **Athenaion at Priene,** despite the convincing arguments made by Carter for the fourth-century date of its coffers, continues to elicit suggestions that at least some of the panels belong to the second. Because the main subject of the reliefs is the Gigantomachy, its position relative to the Pergamon Altar is a matter of considerable interest, since even the authoritative entry in the *LIMC,* although citing Carter's chronology, places it within the mid-Hellenistic sequence, after the Pergamene monument.[47] Another such debated monument is the **Athenaion at Ilion.** In this case discussion would seem unnecessary, because the temple should be dated either to the time of Lysimachos or to that of Augustus, who inscribed his name on the architrave. Yet a recent publication has attributed the metopes to the span 150–100 on the basis of some helmet types and compositional patterns that recall fifth- and fourth-century models; even the Classicizing architecture would be in keeping with the proposed date. Recent investigations of the site have not produced conclusive evidence in favor of either a third- or a first-century chronology, but the homogeneous material and technique throughout the structure bespeak a single project, without reused material, as would be the case if earlier metopes had been incorporated into the Augustan rebuilding.[48] Helmet types are not reliable except as *termini post quos*, since various forms continued in use in the visual arts for iconographic purposes; compositional patterns, as we have seen, can be already Classicizing in the early Hellenistic period (or even earlier), and were certainly so during Imperial times. Finally, workmanship in Asia Minor is usually of such high quality that it is impossible to date on technical grounds, and many attested Roman monuments, especially from Aphrodisias, were at first taken for Hellenistic or thought to be considerably earlier than their true time of manufacture.

ALTARS

One of the more interesting architectural features of the second century is the development of monumental altars with figured decoration. Oversized, impressive sacrificial tables existed since the sixth century, but the addition of a figured frieze or other forms of architectural sculpture seems to be a Hellenistic innovation, going back to the third century. I may repeat here that I still believe it possible that the Athenaion altar at Priene belongs to the third century, and we have already discussed the altar of Apollo at Knidos. It now remains to update information on the previously considered altars at Magnesia, Kos, and Tenos, and to consider briefly those at Lagina and Delos.[49]

The **Altar of the Theater at Delos** need not detain us, since its frieze course is now entirely missing. Yet it is attested by an inscription that describes it as carrying figures, and therefore suggests a composition similar to that at Kos. Also similar is the general Π-shape, typical of the Kyklades. A secondary decoration with rosettes and boukrania appeared on the orthostates below the frieze course, together with holes that may have served for bronze attachments to hang wreaths. It is uncertain whether two kneeling satyrs in relief attributed to the structure do in fact belong. The date is impressively precise—179/8—and makes it even more regrettable that we can no longer compare this sculptured frieze with those within the sphere of sculptural influences from Asia Minor.[50]

Equally "irrelevant" would seem to be a renewed discussion of the **Altar of the Artemision at Magnesia**, which is usually dated late in the third century. Yet, having recently re-examined the sculptures from the outer surface of the precinct wall, I am once again impressed by their style, high relief, and volume, which make them closely comparable to the Pergamene Gigantomachy. The over-lifesize figures have the same massive appearance, the same prominent thighs outlined by clinging drapery with deep cavities between folds, the same markings of texture ("press folds"), to some extent even the same elaborate footwear. Equally comparable is the presence of details in very low relief next to highly projecting parts. A discussion of the various architectural elements of the altar points out that some of them have been wrongly attributed, but they do not carry weight for the stylistic assessment of the sculptures. At present, the belief that the altar was built before, or at least exactly at the same time as, the temple seems based on the inscriptional evidence and the famous embassy to Delphi. Yet perhaps even the altar, like the temple, took some time to complete, the sacrificial table receiving attention before the enclosure wall. If this was the case, a second-century date would still be possible for the high-relief figures. The latest reconstruction adds niches in the interior of the precinct wall, each with its own statue, but that program seems far too complex for a functional altar, as the Magnesian one undoubtedly was, and the subtle influence of the Pergamon Altar may once again be subconsciously operative.[51]

Perhaps the most interesting discovery about the Magnesian monument is the recognition that one of its relief figures reproduces a fourth-century original from the Athenian Akropolis. Given the uncertain nature of the altar personages (gods? personifications of the demos? messengers accompanying the embassy?), a definite identification for the Akropolis sculpture could help, although there is no guarantee that the same meaning would have carried across time and space. To be sure, this is the most distinctive among the altar figures, since it wears a net garment probably corresponding to the Greek *agrenon.* Coincidentally, this same type is known through a Roman copy from the Villa of Hadrian at Tivoli and now in the Vatican, so that at least two replicas of the Akropolis statue survive—neither, however, from a meaningful context. The Classical original has been tentatively called Apollo, although other suggestions are also advanced. Since the embassy from Magnesia went to Delphi, this identification would corroborate the theory that sees the event depicted on the outer wall of the altar; yet I would consider it strange for a divine structure to have a quasi-historical representation of a single occurrence—in contrast, for instance, to the timeless ritual of the Parthenon frieze or the possible festival celebration on the Lagina altar. Significantly, the Priene altar carried an image of a seated Muse that also corresponds to an acknowledged type repeated in different chronological versions. It is therefore possible that specific "types" were quoted on these religious structures, without the need for a direct chain of copying from the Athenian monument to Asia Minor and eventually to Tivoli.[52]

If the Magnesia reliefs resemble somewhat those at Pergamon, those of the **Altar of Dionysos at Kos** can be compared to the Artemision frieze at Magnesia, or, perhaps more closely because of subject matter, to the friezes of the temples at Teos and at Knidos—so much so that at first some confusion existed as to the proper connection of the various slabs. This type of carving, with squat, overcrowded figures, is defined as "provincial" by Stampolidis. Since it occurs directly on the barriers around the sacrificial table, on a *Π*-shaped altar, it could be considered the equivalent of the "glorified molding" that has already been postulated as the intended effect of the Magnesian temple frieze, and in intentional contrast to the Magnesian and Priene altars, with their "courtyard" arrangement that could demand a more stately effect for its outer decoration. Yet the altar of Apollo at Knidos, with the same architectural layout as the Koan, has an entirely different frieze. No generalization is possible.[53]

The Koan altar has been dated between 160 and 140, when the island was under Pergamene control. This connection is partly supported by one of the subjects depicted on the altar frieze: a battle of Dionysos and the members of his thiasos (without centaurs, however) against opponents carrying what have been defined as Galatian shields. The "famous" conflict of the Pergamenes against the Gauls would therefore have been translated into a divine contest. I am uneasy about this interpretation. Either the subject carries an element of parody—which would be inappropriate on a sacred structure, especially if built at a time of Pergamene dominance—or historical events have been literally turned into a mythological struggle. The almost contemporary chronology of the Keltomachies prevents them from being compared to the Amazonomachy, for instance, which might have served as an allusion to the Graeco-Persian conflict, or to the Kentauromachy, with the same significance of civilization overcoming barbarism. Divine intervention in a human, historical war was certainly acknowledged—for instance, in the Classical painting of the Battle of Marathon, where gods and heroes are described at the encounter in which Theseus and Herakles supposedly took part (Paus. 1.15.4); yet there the Athenians themselves were shown in action against the Persians, whereas at Kos only the mythological beings are opposing the Gauls. Another suggestion, that the supposed Gauls are instead Indians, would make the relevance of the frieze to the altar much greater, as part of the story of Dionysos struggling to receive acceptance for his cult. Since the topic became known in the Hellenistic period, probably as an allusion to the campaigns of Alexander the Great and Ptolemy Philadelphos, the connection is plausible.[54] That the shields are "Galatian" seems to me a surmountable objection; they may have come to symbolize the armament of any non-Greek enemy, and we have already noted the confusion that may arise in the identification of military equipment.

The Gaulish identification may have indirectly influenced the high chronology of the Koan frieze. Its similarity to Magnesia and the other friezes cited above makes me suspect that a lower date, around 130–120, might be closer to the mark, although the political connection to Pergamon would then be removed. Given the geographic proximity of the sites and their relative distance from the Mysian capital,[55] it makes more sense to imagine the same workmen moving from one commission to the other, even if the subject of the altar frieze may have been inspired by other considerations. This is in fact the second peculiarity of the Koan frieze: at least three topics have been identified as part of the same decoration: Dionysos taking refuge at the altar of Rhea in Phrygia, to escape Hera's wrath; a peaceful Dionysiac thiasos with music-playing maenads; and the already-mentioned battle scene. The last two themes are understandable, since they could be stretched at will, to occupy whatever length of wall was necessary, but the first is surprising—a *unicum*, even if geographically relevant, that might have involved some narrative sequence.

Great similarity between altar and temple, in terms of the sculptural decoration, exists at **Lagina**. Only one corner block survives from the original structure, but its smaller dimensions prevent association with the entablature frieze, despite the correspondence of style and crowning molding. To my knowledge, no reconstruction of the shape has been attempted, and no clear identification of the subject exists. The figures are perhaps somewhat more elongated and slender than on the temple, with slightly greater space in between, but they reach to the top of the field, in single file. We find the same convention of horses disappearing behind their leader, the same personages seated on rocks, the same mixture of what may be divine images next to (probably) humans or personifications. The date of the altar must therefore be very close to the time of execution of the temple frieze.[56]

My last mention is simply an update on the **Altar at Tenos,** since it has been suggested that the four sea monsters and hippocamps found in the vicinity of the Temple of Poseidon and Amphitrite are the akroteria for the altar, on analogy with the Pergamon Altar. Yet the official publication considered the akroterial function but dismissed it in favor of an independent group within the temple. The date of the monsters is given as the beginning of the second century, but the altar seems to have received bronze embellishment at the turn into the first, as a private dedication (by Gaius Pandusinus). Obviously the marine monsters could not have remained in position, had they truly been placed at the altar corners originally, when the bronze sculptures were set up.[57]

HEROA AND TOMBS

The time of kingly graves with elaborate embellishment seems to be over, and private citizens are more likely to set up impressive funerary sculptures for themselves and their families. Yet not many of these can be connected with a proper architectural structure. I have already mentioned the heroon at Messene, on which no more information is available. Another such building, a **Tomb with Karyatids near Rhodes,** is now known through actual photographs rather than newspaper sketches, and has been dated to the second century, although occupancy seems to have been continuous until Roman Imperial times. The photographs of the fragmentary karyatids show them to be fully Hellenistic/Classicizing figures, without hint of Archaism in the preserved portions.[58]

Also a tomb or a cenotaph is the so-called **Skylla Monument at Bargylia** (Karia; Ills. 17–18). It consisted of a rectangular podium with doorway, probably leading to at least two chambers on either side of an entrance corridor, as surmised from the fact that the name of Melas, son of Hermaiskos, is inscribed on the left jamb of the door. An upper story with Doric entablature and four engaged columns per side was surmounted by a pyramidal roof, in its turn topped by an elaborate finial in the form of a Skylla. The total shape is close to that of the so-called Lion Tomb of Knidos—a late Classical or early Hellenistic memorial crowned by a lion that may echo a series of such stepped constructions native to the area—but may also recall victory monuments, such as those at Chaironeia and Amphipolis. The names Melas and Hermaiskos are known from Rhodes, Kos, and Delos (although not in this combination), but also from Attika. A date within the first half of the second century is based on letter forms,

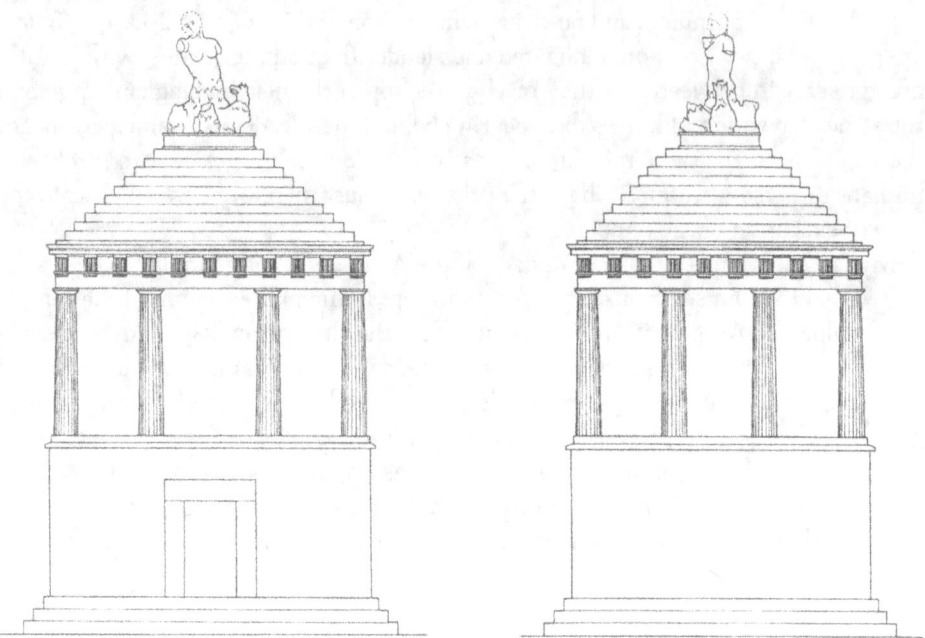

Ill. 17. Reconstruction of the Skylla Monument at Bargylia, front. [After Waywell 1996b, 81, fig. 10]
Ill. 18. Reconstruction of the Skylla Monument at Bargylia, side. [After Waywell 1996b, 81, fig. 11]

architecture, and primarily on the iconography and style of the finial: a fragmentary but impressive, colossal Skylla with two long fishtails set side by side at her back and three canine foreparts emerging from a human torso fringed with seaweed. The sculpture was carved in several pieces, with the sea-dogs (*ketea*) in a darker marble than the white female body. Fragments of human limbs with drapery indicate that this was a "narrative" piece, showing the monster in action as it attacked hapless sailors. It has therefore been postulated that Melas died in a naval disaster, but its nature remains unspecified. A shipwreck (along the rocky coast of Karia) is as plausible as a fatal encounter with pirates, but a historical connection has also been sought in the events of the Second Macedonian War, when Philip V's navy was besieged within the harbor of Bargylia by Pergamene and Rhodian ships (in 201; Polyb. 16.24). Rhodes may have provided inspiration for the Skylla, but other sources are possible.[59]

From that island may be a long block with relief scenes, once belonging to the **Tomb of Hieronymos of Tlos, son of Simylinos**. The piece is now lost, and was originally bought in Alexandria, but it was said to have been found on Rhodes and it has been accepted as such in the scholarly literature.[60] It is usually described as comprising a school scene, and the deceased has been labeled a teacher, but a recent interpretation would see the instruction tableau as a reading of sacred texts for introduction to the Mysteries (nature unspecified), thus making Hieronymos an initiate. The *tabula* inscribed with the name, patronymic, and ethnic of the owner appears centered on the extant block, yet the relief obviously continued on either side, as indicated by figures cut through by the lateral edges. This apparently modest monument is significant for several reasons.

1. It was part of a more complex structure, because of the original presence of additional blocks; it has been suggested that the surviving piece came from the door of a funerary temenos or a tomb, but it could also be a section of a continuous Ionic frieze on a low entablature.[61] We cannot be sure that it belonged to a heroon in the accepted sense of the term, but the deceased seems more exalted than those on standard grave markers.

2. The lower edge of the relief, recessed between framing moldings, carries the signature of the sculptor: *Damatrios epoiese* (the Doric form of the name). This is in keeping with the tendency of the time, as already noted at Pergamon and Knidos.[62]

3. Separators and landscape elements mark changes of setting: a pier or built wall (the "Door of Hades") isolates the "teaching" scene from the next, probably set in the Underworld, and rocky seats near a tree suggest a third environment, perhaps the Elysian fields. One more scene may be depicted at the right edge, divided from the others by a standing female with butterfly wings who gestures toward the right.[63] This procedure recalls the Telephos Frieze. The recurring image of the deceased on either side of the pier would also qualify the Hieronymos relief as continuous "narrative."

4. The "teaching" scene conveys a semicircular arrangement of seated and standing figures that can again be paralleled on the Telephos Frieze (the banquet scene at Argos, panels 39–40). This spatial effect is quite different from the paratactic display of the remaining images on the block and may have been inspired by contemporary mosaics and paintings.

5. If the scenes have been properly reinterpreted, the composition may stress the value of being initiated into the Mysteries. The enthroned male with mantle covering his head is probably Plouton, and the female in front of him Persephone. Farther left is Hermes, identified by his winged shoes. One more standing male, to the right of the throne, should be the deceased being received into the Underworld. The seated Hades is obviously larger than the three standing figures, but these are of equal height, their heads touching the upper border. Therefore, if Hieronymos has been correctly identified, he would be on a par with the deities, although his position "behind" Hades' throne makes him slightly subordinate. He is, nonetheless, exactly placed on the central axis of the block, thus gaining by physical location and height the focus he may lose by hierarchical positioning.[64]

Other points could be made about the relief, specifically its iconography. The male seated on a rock "in Elysium" holds his bent right knee with his clasped hands: this is, in general lines, the pose of the so-called Ares Ludovisi, which goes back to fifth-century prototypes, such as the Ares on the Parthenon frieze, but may acquire funerary connotations with time, since it occurs on the "parapet" of the Sarcophagus of the Mourning Women from Sidon.[65] In the first scene, the "teacher" with open scroll and his companions sit on a semicircular bench with curved legs typically used for philosophers' seats, leaning forward in an equally typical pose.[66] The Psyche with butterfly wings is a popular image of the second century (cf. Pl. 59), although its prototype may have originated in the previous century; and the peculiar image at the right edge, although apparently on her knees or emerging from (or even sinking into) the ground, has a niche-mantle forming a sail behind her head, in the so-called *velificans* type that suggests rapid movement or flying.[67] The accent on Underworld scenes is typical of the times, as contrasted with the more symbolic representations on gravestones.

Plates 39–44 The *velificans* rendering recurs on the **Frieze of Dancing Women from Sagalassos** (Pls. 39–44), which recent literature places within the Augustan period, but which deserves to be mentioned here, since both its initial publications and its style connect it with the second century. As now reconstructed, the Heroon to which the frieze probably belonged consists of a square naiskos with distyle in antis façade, standing on a solid, undecorated podium. Corinthian pilasters appeared at all four corners of the shrine, and a frieze carved with a vegetal chain atop the walls formed the base for a series of slabs depicting a linked line of women dancing and playing musical instruments. Fragments of a colossal statue found nearby have been identified as an image of Alexander the Great, and the Heroon is therefore attributed to the famous ruler, regardless of its actual date; yet the extant head is so idealized that identification seems to me problematic. It is also certain that some parts of the frieze were replaced (or at least repaired) during the second century A.C., as indicated by the carved pupils of the figures and the presence of some mounds for measuring points (*puntelli*), suggesting mechanical copying.[68]

What to me seems surprising is the fact that **another frieze** with Dancing Women and musicians has been found at the same site; yet these slabs cannot be part of the first monument because of their lesser dimensions and poorer execution.[69] In their initial mention, they were dated approximately twenty-five years before those of the Heroon, which was then still placed around 150–130. The redating of the larger frieze may now demand a reconsideration of the smaller, but the presence of two very similar compositions at the same site would require clarification.

As a form of architectural decoration, a chain of mantled dancers and musicians seems an excellent choice. The garments stretching from one woman to the next create an effective horizontal link between them, while the scansion of the figures emphasizes vertical rhythm and clarity; in its total effect, such a frieze functions almost like an alternation of boukrania and garlands, the vegetal festoons being replaced by cloth. At present, only one slab of the larger frieze contains two women: a kithara-player and a *velificans;* all other blocks have a single image, either a dancer in twirling motion or a more quietly standing figure in chiton and himation.

Architectural Sculpture—A Roundup

Drapery is voluminous, helping to give the bodies a pyramidal contour. Deep grooves outline limbs, especially legs and massive thighs. Hems flutter even on static forms, creating patterns—catches at the ankles, "Lykian wavelets," nicks and bends, even a form of ivy-leaf that recalls the famous "Kallimachean Maenads." All sorts of Baroque mannerisms appear throughout, strongly evoking details of the Pergamon Gigantomachy. The *velificans* next to the kithara-player (cf. Pl. 39) resembles one of the akroterial Nikai from Pergamon: her apoptygma is belted high below the breasts and flares out at the wide-spreading hips, echoing in a minor key the pattern of the skirt below—yet, surprisingly, the upper part of the costume, over her breasts, is treated as thin and crinkly, with a slipped strap, while the lower part is heavy and opaque.

This dual texturing is also present on other figures. In general, drapery over the body is rendered as transparent, revealing the underlying folds and occasionally— incongruously—even the navel (cf. Pls. 41–42). Many tension lines are created by muffled arms. In some cases, they are quite effective in conveying the pose; but on a lady with a fringed mantle they appear almost divorced from the rest of the garment, looping between arm and torso like cobwebs (cf. Pls. 43–44). There are other mantles that are long and fringed, as in Isiac contexts; a few, however, are no more than scarves. There is also great variety in hairstyles: loose strands over chest and shoulders, long spiral curls framing the neck, chignons gathered at the nape, perhaps even a melon coiffure; the Roman Imperial head is entirely covered by a tight-fitting veil. Faces are damaged, but what is preserved displays massive contours and heavy jawlines.

The Sagalassos frieze has been considered the predecessor of the Neo-Attic Dancers, and an element in a series of monuments that begins in the late fifth or fourth century (including some bases from the Athenian Akropolis), and continues to Imperial times. Three such friezes (at Samothrake, Antiphellos, and Phanagoria) are clearly Archaistic in style; the others are Classical and Classicizing. Their contexts are not always known, but a few of them have sure funerary function, and it has been suggested that the dancers represent nymphs who protect the dead.[70] Given the chronological span of the type and the difficulty of stylistic dating, solid information is needed to place the Sagalassos frieze within its correct time.

A controversial chronology affects also two slabs of an **Amazonomachy frieze from Soloi** (Cyprus) that probably once decorated a funerary structure. Originally dated to the second century, they were then given to the fourth, on stylistic grounds; a reassessment of the evidence has now returned them to the Hellenistic period. Stylistically, they have little to contribute: the figures are elongated and widely spaced; the Amazons, on horseback, fight with large double axes; the motifs have been called stereotypical.[71]

Firmly dated by inscriptions to 102/1, the **Monument of Mithradates VI** on Delos has been occasionally called a Heroon—yet it was erected during the monarch's lifetime and carried portraits of his allies and generals, thus serving more than one commemorative function. Its anomalous form (almost like an enclosed exedra rather than a naiskos, although Ionic distyle in antis) and its location within the Sanctuary of Foreign Divinities make it difficult to classify.[72]

OTHER BUILDINGS

During the second century, sculptural embellishment is placed also on secular buildings, or at least on structures whose function seems more civic than religious. The **north and east stoas surrounding the Temenos of Athena at Pergamon** are the most conspicuous example of this new tendency. As porticoes, they should certainly be considered public buildings, but their physical enclosure of a sanctuary makes them partake of a religious purpose. Taken in conjunction with the free-standing monuments celebrating Attalid victories that stood within the terrace, the balustrades of their upper story carrying weapon reliefs transform the entire temenos into a Nikephorion.[73]

The idea of decorating balustrades to convey specific messages about a religious precinct may have originated with the Nike Parapet on the Akropolis in Athens. Although the relief slabs there stood free of an actual structure and served the practical purpose of preventing dangerous falls off the Nike bastion, they also provided an allegorical statement of victory in honor of Athens and Athena. Pergamon may have derived its inspiration from the Athenian monument, although no human figures but only military paraphernalia appear on the carved slabs. On the other hand, weapon friezes become increasingly popular in the Hellenistic period, continuing well into the Roman Imperial era. Bouleuteria in particular seem to have favored this type of decoration.[74] The **propylon to the Athena Terrace at Pergamon** has similar balustrades in its upper story. As already mentioned, the narrative panels that used to be attributed to it (cf. Pls. 4–6) are now assigned to Palace V on the citadel; if this were truly the case, more weapon slabs like those from the stoas could perhaps be given to the propylon, continuing the theme of the entire precinct. At any rate, the frieze on the upper entablature of the gateway was also a meaningful complement to the sanctuary, consisting of oak and laurel garlands supported by eagles alternating with bull's heads; above the swags, owls alternated with phialai. The two birds connected with Zeus and his daughter Athena respectively added to the message of power and victory expressed by the types of leaves selected for the festoons and prepared the visitor to enter a terrace dedicated to "Athena Nikephoros."[75]

The **Bouleuterion at Miletos** may have also had a weapon frieze on the entablature of the propylon leading to the courtyard fronting the Council House proper (Ill. 19), but the point is still debated. The gateway, however, provides a firm date for the entire complex through its inscription mentioning a dedication to Antiochos IV Epiphanes, thus between 175 and 163. The bouleuterion itself had shields carved in relief on the screen walls between the engaged columns, alternating with windows.

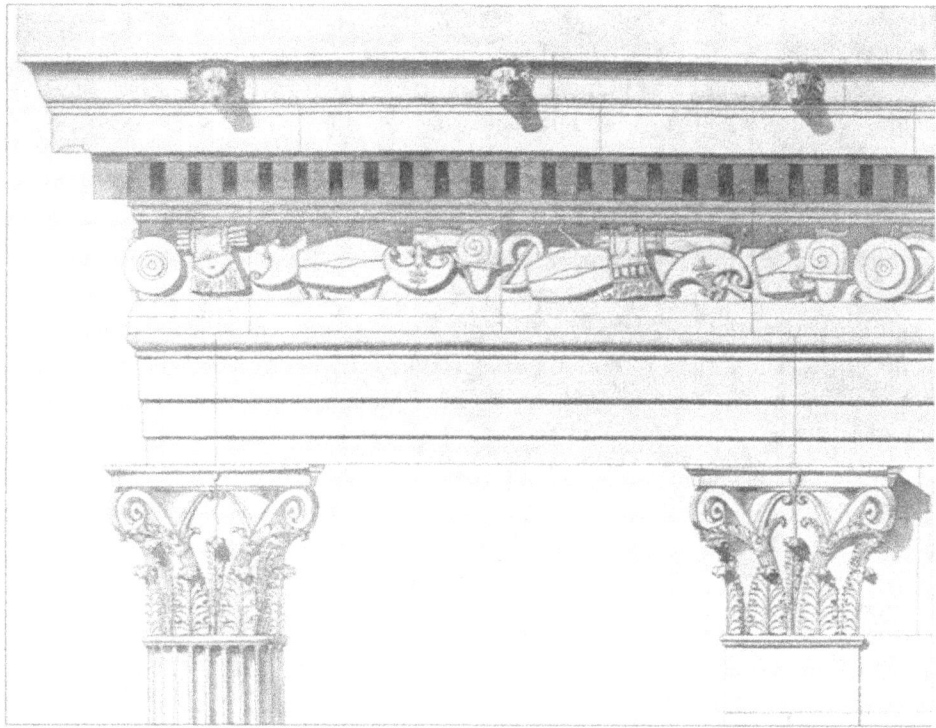

Ill. 19. Miletos, Propylon to the Bouleuterion reconstructed with weapon frieze (drawing by F. Krischen). [Bryn Mawr College Photographic Collection]

Also meaningful, perhaps, was the mixture of Ionic and Doric elements throughout the structure, as if to suggest that both races could find impartial hearing within its walls.[76]

Much more decorative was the **Bouleuterion at Sagalassos,** at present only partially published, which involved a second-story gallery with figured piers. The images in relief may have represented divinities with prisoners crouching at their feet; a Doric frieze had olive wreaths carved in low relief on every other metope, and weapons may have been sculptured on other locations of the building, which is currently dated to the end of the second century but may extend into the beginning of the next.[77]

NON-GREEK ARCHITECTURAL SCULPTURE

At the end of this survey, it seems relevant to mention that some sculptural forms, rare on Greek territory, find instead an unexpected flourishing on Italian territory. Perhaps the most relevant are the many terracotta friezes and pedimental compositions appearing in Etruria or territories under Etruscan influence. Most of these are considered to be under Pergamene influence, not only because of their "pathetic" and

Baroque style, but also because, in some cases, they depict Gauls and may have been inspired by the so-called Smaller Attalid Dedication.[78] The apparent incongruence of a monument *in Athens* being imitated at the moment of strongest Pergamene influence *from Asia Minor* (perhaps, as some would have it, transmitted by Etruscan mercenaries fighting on Asiatic soil) is not openly confronted. Also difficult, to my mind, is the clustering of all such monuments within the second century, with a chronology promoted largely by their alleged Pergamene affinities. It seems possible that we have here typical local forms, only generally influenced by Greek styles that were most probably coming in from the Baroque workshops at Taras, and exploiting Etruscan expressionistic and dramatic tendencies, as well as a more impressionistic medium. It is nonetheless important to note the use of figured friezes and pediments at a time when almost none were produced on the Greek Mainland, and few are attested even for Asia Minor.

One last example is provided by the so-called **Temple of Peace at Paestum**, whose typical Roman plan, with podium and alae, combined Corinthian columns with a Doric entablature below dentils. The building was once thought to have had several phases, but is now assigned to a single one, toward the end of the second century or the beginning of the next, and attributed to the Dioscuri, Castor and Pollux. The sculptured metopes are heavily weathered, but show single figures (with one exceptional panel containing two): warriors or women with fluttering drapery suggesting rapid movement. No topic is clearly indicated, but the very presence of sculptured metopes is of interest in our general context.[79]

As a final comment, we should perhaps speculate about why so much of our evidence for Greek architectural sculpture comes from Asia Minor; yet the answer may be fairly apparent. The Greek Mainland was no longer in a position of dominance, and, in the "old" cities and sanctuaries, the essential buildings were in place long before the second century. New construction occurred only in places without a strong tradition of architectural embellishment, where the focus was, by then, on cult images rather than on the buildings that housed them (we shall discuss the evidence from Lykosoura in Chapter 7). The Greek islands, especially the Kyklades, were equally free from compelling precedents. The only areas that could and did promote architectural sculpture were the sites of Anatolia that were either truly Greek, with a strong Archaic legacy in that field, or the non-Greek cities (e.g., in Karia and Mysia) that were looking—directly or indirectly—to the "golden age" of Athens as a source of inspiration. In Egypt, where the local Pharaonic tradition was never abandoned, the Ptolemies promoted a great deal of architecture, but its embellishment took the form of an enrichment of the surface (a sort of "façade encrustation") that did not require sculpture for its effectiveness. As new surveys and excavations are beginning to show, the use of vegetal motifs in capitals, the segmental (curved) pediment alternating with the triangular form, the broken gable admitting of circular elements within the gap—as we see them in the rock-cut monuments of Petra, or even in some Roman wall paintings—are all in imitation of Alexandrian formulas. Although the buildings of that city are almost entirely lost to us, these echoes have prompted a definition of "Baroque architecture" as a counterpart to the Baroque style in sculpture that flourished elsewhere.[80] The picture we have sketched in the last three chapters, although it makes no claim to be complete, should therefore be not too wide of the mark.

NOTES

1. For quick reference to the problems involved with these structures, see Webb 1996: 104 (Didyma), 144–45 (Hieron at Samothrake); 67 (Pergamon, Temple of Hermes and Herakles); 147 (Hieron at Samothrake, akroterion replaced in Roman times); 72–73 (Temple of Dionysos at Teos; frieze replaced in Roman times). I understand from Prof. Kevin Clinton that there may now be some doubt about identifying the Samothrakian building as the Hieron, but *Samothrace* 1998, 79–86, no. 15, retains the customary explanation (cf. pp. 133–35 and fig. 60 for the Hellenistic Nike akroterion, dated 150–125). The Athenaion at Priene seems to have been under construction from the 2nd half of the 4th c. to the Augustan period: W. Koenigs, as cited by M. J. Mellink, "Archaeology in Anatolia," *AJA* 97 (1993) 126–27; but see also infra. That it was typical of Hellenistic (Asia Minor?) buildings not to be finished at once was brought out in the discussion following Kreeb 1990.

2. F. A. Cooper and D. Fortenberry, "The Heroon at Messene," Abstract, *AJA* 97 (1993) 337. The building is tetrastyle amphiprostyle. But see infra, n. 4, for a Tarentine "heroon." For two possible Numidian heroa (at Simitthus-Chemtou and Kbor-Klib, Tunisia), probably datable to the 2nd c. and decorated with weapon reliefs on their podium walls, under Macedonian influence, see Polito 1998, 85–89, figs. 21–25.

3. For the 2nd c., such shields in relief, with or without central image, appear on the Ionic propylon to the agora at Magnesia, the Temple of Isis, and the Monument of Mithradates VI on Delos (the latter two, perhaps, private dedications of small size), and the Temple of the Upper Gymnasion at Pergamon: Webb 1996, 24, 93–94 (Magnesia, 1st half 2nd c.), 138–39 (Delos, Temple of Isis, ca. 130), 141–42 (Monument of Mithradates VI, 102/1). The sculptures from the Hieron at Samothrake and the Temple at Teos are either questionable, or earlier than the 2nd c.: Webb 1996, 24–25, 146–47; cf. Ridgway 1990, 158–61, but contrast *Samothrace* 1998, 79, 82–83.

4. For stucco metopes that once carried reliefs (a bull's head survives on one, a boukranion on another), see the House of Kleopatra and Dioskourides on Delos (mid-2nd c.): Webb 1996, 138. I may here mention a peculiar **limestone metope from Messene** (*BCH* 115 [1991] 864 fig. 27, tentatively assigned to the Temple of Zeus Soter mentioned by Paus. 4.31.6) because Junker 1993, 160–61, believes it is unique in its treatment of the relief figures that overlap the triglyph and therefore considers it Hellenistic rather than late Classical. The subject (Perseus and Andromeda?) would be a *unicum*.

According to recent research, some of the **Tarentine reliefs** previously assigned to the 3rd c., especially those of the Heroon in Via Umbria, should come down to the period 200–150: Lippolis 1996, 499 and cat. 411.1–5 on pp. 505–507. Note that the new reconstruction drawing, on p. 500, places the decorated metopes on the podium rather than on the entablature above the columns (cf. Ill. 16). The redating is based on a new analysis of the funerary contexts. For previous positions, see Ridgway 1990, 181–84 and Ill. 27. It is important to remember the relatively small scale of all Tarentine architectural sculpture.

On the carved coffers of the Hieron at Samothrake, see now Mantis 1987–90 and 1998; the official 2nd-c. date is questioned by Webb 1996, 23, in light of the chronological pattern of sculptured coffers in general, but seems accepted in *LIMC* 8, s.v. Kentauroi et Kentaurides, no. 223 pl. 440 (between 150 and 125). See also supra, ns. 1 and 3.

5. For such akroteria, see *LIMC* 8, s.v. Nike, 883 and nos. 401–404 (from Ionic tetrastyle prostyle temple on Upper Gymnasion at Pergamon? dated ca. 160; cf. Grote 1992); nos. 405–406 (in Thessaloniki, 2nd half 2nd c.); no. 580, pl. 598 (from Rhodes, ca. 150); nos. 581–82 (from Tyndaris, end 2nd c.; cf. Zanker 1965, and, more important, Gulaki 1981, 247–52, figs. 231–36: "Type Albani-Syracuse," eclectic and early Hellenistic; Danner 1997, 43–44, cat. A 90, pl. 23.4–5: ca. 100); no. 583 (from Pergamon, end 2nd c.); nos. 586–87 (from Hieron at Samothrake, dated 3rd quarter 2nd c. and Roman replacement respectively; cf. supra, n. 1, and infra, ch. 5 n. 35). For a possible Nike akroterion to the Temple of Isis on Delos (ca. 130), see Webb 1996, 138–39. One more Nike, *velificans,* from Halikarnassos, has been variously dated from the Hellenistic to the Late Roman period; it was found under the mosaic floor of a Late Roman villa, with other sculptures of possibly Hellenistic date, and is considered a left-hand akroterion from an unknown building, ca. 100, by comparison with the Tyndaris Nikai: Poulsen 1997, 77–78, figs. 97–100 and ns. 22, 24, 29–30.

Floral akroteria, occasionally with an "akanthos goddess" in their midst, occur on several temples, specifically at Magnesia: cf. Webb 1996, 32. A more unusual form, virtually a high relief against a background plaque, depicts an "akanthos god" as Master of Animals, holding a lion-griffin with each arm; its stylistic assessment (3rd c.?) is based on comparison with minor arts and could allow for a lower chronology, but the piece has unknown architectural connection and specific provenience (although it is from the Chersonesos and is presently in the Hermitage Museum): Möbius 1926, 121–23 and pl. 19; see also Valeva 1995, 341 and fig. 6, within a general study of "akanthos deities." See also infra, n. 22, for the Teos akroterion.

Danner 1997 shows the extreme rarity of extant Hellenistic akroteria from Magna Graecia.

6. Themelis 1994b, 155–64, pl. 53b–d (raking sima of Group C, 2nd c., perhaps from a Temple of Aphrodite near the sanctuary of Poseidon, according to Paus. 4.31.6) and 162, pl. 54a–b (Corinthian capital from the Asklepieion).

7. Reggio cornice figure: Danner 1994, pls. 89–90; cf. Danner 1993 for the Archaic examples.

8. This is Themelis' explanation (1994b, p. 164) for his floral sima from Messene. For the Artemision deer heads, see Webb 1996, 90 and fig. 52, and cf. 92, figs. 60–61, for an akanthos figure as akroterion; see also Rumscheid 1994, vol. 1, 279–81, and cf. supra, n. 5; infra, n. 22.

9. Information on this 1995 discovery was given to me by a student who had participated in the excavation at Fregellae. The male counterpart to the Karyatid seems to be a typically Italic form that diffused to the Greek mainland through Roman influence: note the under-lifesize (0.99 m from head to top of thighs) **Telamon from Thessaloniki,** which, however, cannot be connected to a specific building: Despinis et al., 1997, 58–60, no. 39 (inv. no. 10301), figs. 103–106. A stylistic dating ("later than the Pergamon Gigantomachy, earlier than the Poseidon of Melos") would link it to the establishment of the Roman eparchy of Macedonia in 148, perhaps for a monument commemorating the victory. For Silenoi/Telamones from the theater at Delos, see infra, n. 50.

Architectural Sculpture—A Roundup

10. The epigrams are given by Hebert 1989, 87–89, Q 192–211. For discussion, see, e.g., Webb 1996, 17 and ns. 4–7 (with mention of other possible explanations); add Moreno 1994, 569–70 and fig. 741 (who thinks of the stylopinakia as reliefs framed by small columns, as on later sarcophagi); and Stupperich 1990, who supports a date in the late 160s, and a literal interpretation of the epigrams. If the stylopinakia were simply votive reliefs affixed to columns, as some maintain, they cannot be considered true architectural sculpture. It is not stated whether the temple was dedicated by the city or by the Attalids, but the latter case is preferred. Divinization, although possible during life, is more likely after death.

11. Magnesia Artemision: Ridgway 1990, 155–56; Webb 1996, 89–92. Among the recent discussions, note Bingöl 1990b, who points to two series of capitals in the peristyle, with a third in the cella, indicative of different phases. Linfert 1995, 133, agrees to a long building period and places the temple after the altar, which he connects with the embassy to Delphi and the establishment of the festival in 206 (but see infra). Rumscheid 1994, vol. 1, 25–28, has an extensive discussion of all the chronological evidence and dates the temple surely after 221 (Artemis' epiphany), on Hermogenes' project, but considers a building period "155/0–130" (p. 27); cf. also his pp. 198–214 for a general discussion (esp. p. 207 for the frieze), and vol. 2, cat. 137, pp. 37–39. Osada 1993, 92 and 148, cat. MF20, dates the frieze to 130–120. Moreno 1994, 250–52, although accepting a long period of construction, sees the Amazonomachy as a definite allusion to the victory by the Pergamenes and the Romans over Antiochos III at another Magnesia (on the Hermos) in 190/89, and therefore prefers to date the frieze to the beginning of the 2nd c. A new fragment of the frieze has been identified at the Louvre: Hamiaux 1998, no. 396 (dated 1st quarter 2nd c.).

A brief report in the newsletter from Turkey (M.-H. Gates), in *AJA* 101 (1997) 286, suggests that a window may have been opened on the roof of the temple rather than on the pediment, but the evidence from the Smintheion (supra, Ch. 3 n. 45) makes this statement doubtful.

12. For this suggestion, see Webb 1996, 35, 92, and esp. 97 n. 41, with figs. 54–56 (this last showing the nude Herakles). A previous suggestion (Yaylali 1976) placed two images of Herakles on the S side, which would seem redundant, but the attribution to different locations on the temple seems based primarily on stylistic considerations.

13. Dead Amazons: Yaylali 1976, pls. 7.3 and 32.1, as contrasted with the wounded Greek, pl. 7.2. For a clearer picture, see Moreno 1994, fig. 324 on p. 247. Two more Amazons, slumped on their horses, may be mortally wounded, if not already dead: Yaylali, pls. 25.2, 29.1.

The most complete series of photographs is in Yaylali 1976, but see also *LIMC* 1, s.v. Amazones, no. 104 pls. 455–57, and Moreno 1994, figs. 321–29. The foldout plates in Yaylali, Beil. 1–4, are important to show the gaps in what might otherwise seem an almost fully preserved frieze. For the various meanings of the Amazonomachy through time, see Ridgway 1999, 156–62. It is still remarkable that so few Greeks seem depicted in actual danger, and P. Webb queries whether the original meaning could have been lost, after Alexander's campaigns eastward, and the Attalid dedications in Athens.

14. I owe the idea for this parallel to K. A. Raaflaub, who lectured on "Homer, the Trojan War, and History" at Bryn Mawr College on Sept. 19, 1997. He argued that the Homeric poems reflected the outlook and concerns of a time close to the poet's own, although embodying elements from earlier periods retained in collective memory. On the Skythian axe, see supra, Ch. 3 n. 9. It was suggested to me (by an Aarhus University graduate student) that the varied renderings in the weaponry and attire of the Amazons may suggest an undisciplined, motley

army, as appropriate for barbarians; yet almost as much variety is found among the Greeks. Pattern books are therefore the more likely explanation for the choices.

15. Lykian wavelet: Yaylali 1976, pls. 1.3, 7.2, 31.1. Railroad tracks: e.g., pls. 7.1, 18.2. Many of the patterns analyzed supra in connection with the Pergamene Gigantomachy (transparent drapery, omega folds, rolled mantles) recur on the Artemision frieze, but in a debased version that betrays their automatic repetition. The variety in weapons and costumes for both the Greeks and the Amazons is well summarized by Webb 1996. Yaylali 1976, 142, attributes the frieze to at least three different workshops, with some subgroups and individual hands.

16. Moreno 1994, 151–52.

17. For disproportionate features, see, e.g., the collapsing Amazon on the NW corner block, Yaylali 1976, pl. 1.1. Examples of all the criticized renderings can be found throughout his plates, but some of my comments are based on direct observation of the frieze slabs in Paris, Berlin, and Istanbul. A thorough stylistic analysis is made by Yaylali 1976, 141–73, although his primary goal there seems to be to establish the chronological relationship of the Artemision Amazonomachy to other Hellenistic friezes and sculptures, especially the Pergamon Gigantomachy; he includes more relevant comments in his identification of individual workshops and hands.

18. Yaylali 1976, 99, points out that the drill is used primarily by what he calls the North Workshop; yet his attribution of slabs to locations on the temple is based on his stylistic observations. For press folds, see, e.g., his pl. 5.3; for sternal ribs, e.g., his pl. 8.1.

19. I have been unable to see or to find reference to polychromy or metal attachments on the frieze, and it is likely that the latter were completely omitted, which would add to the molding-like effect. The practice of carving weapons in stone even when they appear in the foreground (see, e.g., the bow on Yaylali 1976, pl. 7.2) produces highly undulating effects; the depth of the background varies considerably.

20. The other instances of an Amazonomachy being used on a temple to Apollo are: Temple of Apollo Daphnephoros at Eretria (pediment; Theseus' Amazonomachy; both the late Archaic and the Classical structure); Temple of Apollo at Aigina (pediment; probably Herakles and Telamon, late Archaic); Temple of Apollo Epikourios at Bassai (internal frieze, Herakles and Theseus, late 5th/early 4th c.). Other Amazonomachies cannot be attributed to a building with certainty or, if safely connected, the deity to whom the building was dedicated cannot be identified. Perhaps the religious link escapes us.

21. The date 130–100 is suggested by Osada 1993, 148–49, cat. MF21, and cf. discussion on pp. 93–94, fig. 59, and bibl. (with other proposed dates) on pp. 136–37, n. 341. Add Rumscheid 1994, vol. 1, 141–45, vol. 2, cat. 8 on p. 3, pl. 3.1 (dating the temple ornament stylistically to the 2nd quarter of the 1st c.!); Webb 1996, 106–107; Stampolidis 1987, pl. 79γ; *LIMC* 1, s.v. Amazones, no. 442. For my earlier comments, see Ridgway 1990, 157–58.

22. I have emphasized "figured" and "temples" because the frieze as an entablature element was already known and it had contained figures earlier, but not in a temple context. Uz 1990, on the basis of a thorough examination of the Tean architecture, would date the core structure to the 2nd c.; an earthquake would have prompted a thorough rebuilding by Augustus, with a second renovation (after another earthquake) in the 2nd c. A.C. He notes three different styles in the frieze blocks, which coincide with changes in types of clamps, dowels, and lifting devices, thus suggesting three different phases of work. Head proportions change from 1:5 to 1:3.

Also the lion-head waterspouts differ (pp. 58–59). A Hadrianic date is proposed for the present frieze, since that Emperor inscribed his name on the architrave of the façade. A clear summary of the situation appears in Webb 1996, 72–74, esp. 74 for skepticism on the pedimental figures as Greek originals, and n. 4 for other suggested dates for the temple. For a dating of the Dionysion at Teos to the late 3rd c., and the identification of it as the earliest temple with figured frieze and dentils in Asia Minor together with the Artemision, see Rumscheid 1995, 39; for a fuller chronological discussion and description, see Rumscheid 1994, vol. 1, 48–51, esp. 49 and n. 425 for the frieze, where a *terminus ante quem* of 204/3 is supported for the beginning of the temple, but a long period of construction is advocated; vol. 2, cat. 354 on pp. 85–86, distinguishes elements by alleged date, including (no. 354.7 on p. 86 and pl. 186.12) what Rumscheid considers a Hellenistic corner akroterion: Dionysos(?) between panthers amid vegetation. For the frieze, see also *LIMC* 8, s.v. Kentauroi et Kentaurides, no. 313, p. 706, pls. 452–53 (2nd c. B.C.); the entry is cross-referenced to Mainades no. 49, p. 787, in the same volume, but the frieze is not listed s.v. Dionysos, despite the obvious presence of the god. For my previous comments, see Ridgway 1990, 156.

23. On the chronological span of the theme, see *LIMC* 8, s.v. Kentauroi et Kentaurides, 706 (S. Drougou); a mosaic at Pella of the late 4th c. shows such a symposion, which may be the earliest visual image extant. I could not detect, at the time of my visit to the Izmir Museum, any traces of hair rendering at the joint of human to equine torsos on the centaurs (as, for instance, on the centaurs of the Belevi coffers) that could also suggest a Hellenistic date.

24. These fragments at the site have been noted by Webb 1996, 73, with list in n. 9.

25. On the scyphi, see Van de Grift 1984, who points to the popularity of the topos in early Imperial literature; the contrast there is between moderation and excess. Cf. *LIMC* 8, s.v. Kentauroi et Kentaurides, 719, no. 484 pl. 480, dated Late Neronian–Vespasianic

26. Knidos frieze slab: most recently, Bruns-Özgan 1995, 263–64, fig. 9, who emphasizes that the relief cannot belong to the altar at Kos, as originally believed; cf. also Webb 1996, 122, with additional refs., and Ridgway 1990, 156.

27. The main publication of the frieze until recently was Schober 1933. A new arrangement for the N and S friezes has now been proposed by Junghölter 1989 (see his foldout plates, Beil. 1–2, for comparison with previous suggestions, and 3–7 for drawings of all the slabs), but see also the review of his book by S. Schmidt, *Gnomon* 63 (1991) 348–51. A thorough stylistic discussion with useful insights is Osada 1993, 64–90. Simon 1993 advocates Hesiodic influences on the frieze—a suggestion already made by Webb in her 1989 dissertation, 266, 271–73, and now repeated in Webb 1996, 108–20, pls. 81–93 (including the altar). Moreno 1994, 674–76, lists most chronological suggestions, including the variant dates mentioned under several entries in the *LIMC* corresponding to the deities supposedly represented on the friezes; they range from 166, on inspiration from the alliance between Karia and Rome (Stewart 1990, 226), to the middle of the 1st c. Smith 1991, 184–85, doubts the historical reference of the "alliance" scene ("surely mythological") and affirms that the dates derived from it "cannot be sustained." He is in favor of a later 2nd-c. chronology. Moreno's figs. 843–46 attempt to reproduce the effect of continuous friezes, usually lost in the more common depictions of single slabs. The discovery of new fragments is reported in "Archaeology in Turkey," *AJA* 100 (1996) 317.

28. These Giants are: figure 4 on slab 226 (attacked by Herakles) and figure 1 on slab 198A (attacked by Hephaistos). They had usually been interpreted as being on their knees, but Osada

1993, 87, argues convincingly that their lower legs are sunk into the ground; he also points out the vertical rendering of the Giant/god composition, and the static lower body combined with an upper torso in motion.

29. For a convenient illustration, see *LIMC* 6, s.v. Hekate, p. 997, no. 100 pl. 661 (dated beg. 1st c.); surprisingly, Hekate wears a helmet; cf. no. 98 for mention of the goddess on the E frieze. As contrasted with the Pheidian Parthenos, the Lagina Hekate has a high belt and narrow shoulders, in keeping with her later date. That the Giant to the right is Artemis' opponent is indicated by her dog, partly carved against the rock on which the Giant kneels. He is usually described as hurling a boulder toward Hekate, but his face is too damaged to show whether it appeared in profile toward that goddess, who certainly does not acknowledge the alleged threat. For other examples of the "velificans" rendering, see infra, ns. 67–68.

30. For illustrations, see again *LIMC* 6, s.v. Kronos, no. 24 pl. 66 (dated 100–80), or Webb 1996, pls. 83–84. This scene has been interpreted as the Birth of Hekate, rather than of Zeus (e.g., Moreno 1994, 676), but the presence of the Kouretes demands the latter, as noted by Webb 1996, 109.

31. Osada 1993, 82–83, well discusses this phenomenon, which Schober 1933 called "Fassadenbildung." Cf. also his p. 88 for a description of the figures as "statuenhaften." I could observe this rendering during a visit to the Istanbul Museum in 1969, although the frieze was not on display in 1995 and 1996.

32. Strong undercutting and two-tiered arrangement are particularly obvious in slab 212: Webb 1996, pl. 85. For Lepcis Magna, see, e.g., Andreae 1977, figs. 557–60. Some of the seated figures have been compared with Rhodian motifs by Osada 1993, 70–71, and (p. 82) with renderings on Late Hellenistic gravestones; but the nymph seen from behind on slab 212 seems to me more closely similar to a Nereid: cf. *LIMC* 6, s.v. Nereides, no. 40 pl. 458 (gilded silver box from Canosa, last quarter 3rd c.; Nereid holds leaf-shaped fan), and commentary on p. 821, where the type, frequent in the Roman period, is said to appear in the 3rd c. For the "dancers" on slab 211, see Webb 1996, pl. 84, and cf. Osada 1993, 69 and n. 252; that the type appears in the 4th c. and diffuses in the East may be shown by the so-called Tribune of Eshmoun from Sidon: cf. Ridgway 1997b, pls. 55a–b; see also *LIMC* 8, s.v. Nymphai, 894, no. 30 pl. 588.

33. This lack of centralization is indeed advocated by Junghölter 1989 (esp. 153–57) for all four sides, since it can no longer be verified on the E (because of missing slabs; he does not accept that Hekate on slab 228 formed the center of the composition), and even the W frieze could be read as a continuum; but see the criticism by Schmidt 1991 (supra n. 27).

34. See Webb 1989, 255–56, and 1996, 111–12, quoting *Theog.* vv. 430–434. Moreno 1994, 676, seems to imply the same identification by his word order when he describes "a warrior and an Amazonian figure" as "Kar and Dea Roma shaking hands." Kar is the eponymous hero of the Karians. For a different iconography of Thea Roma on Delos, see infra, Ch. 5 and n. 11.

35. Rumscheid 1994, vol. 1, 132–39, esp. 139, and vol. 2, cat. 122, pp. 33–34 ("wohl bald nach 81 B.C." on early Hellenistic core). Stewart's suggestion of the alliance of 166 after Rome had freed Karia from Rhodian control (supra, n. 27) may also lead to a similar identification of personages, without demanding a late date for the composition of the frieze. The *senatus consultum*, as often the case, may simply have recognized something that had long been known as a local practice.

36. Osada 1993, 74–79, makes comparisons with gravestones according to the groupings

established by Schmidt 1991; see esp. 78–79 for the "Pferdeprotome" syndrome, and cf. slabs 225 and 219 (bull) on the N side, slab 205 on the S side. On East Greek gravestones, see infra, Ch. 6.

37. For comparisons with the statuary types, see, e.g., Webb 1996, 112, with reference to Schober 1933, 73; she prefers the Townley Aphrodite, reversed, as a prototype for the Lagina image, yet even this is not a proper parallel for the covered arm, which recurs instead on the so-called Venus Marina type, although in conjunction with a distinctive "apron" overfold of the mantle over the legs. For illustrations of these types, see *LIMC* 2, s.v. Aphrodite: no. 526 pl. 51 (Arles A.), no. 546 pl. 54 (Townley A.), nos. 554–55 pl. 55 (Venus Marina type), no. 643 pl. 63 (Melos A.). The standard identifications are accepted by Junghölter 1989 but challenged by Schmidt in his 1991 review (supra, n. 27). On the Poseidon and Aphrodite from Melos, see also infra, Ch. 5.

38. On the Melpomene Type, see *LIMC* 7, s.v. Mousa, Mousai, 995–97, and cf. no. 207 pl. 78, a terracotta statuette from Neapolis now in Thessaloniki, dated mid-2nd c. The comparison is not exact, but all the distinctive features are there: the slipping neckline, the raised leg, the arm propped on the thigh. The leaf-shaped fans that have been mentioned as elements of the funerary repertoire are, of course, also prevalent among terracotta figurines, which often exhibit the elongated proportions typical of the Lagina frieze.

39. The main publication is Oberleitner 1981, with catalogue of all the fragments (32 entries) and a recomposition of the best-preserved section (catalogued as no. 1, but comprising 12 figures on many partly joining pieces) in fig. 38; a single large fragment with a naked horseman and parts of a second horse, cat. 2, is fig. 51; views of the frieze back in figs. 49–50. The height of the slabs is 0.99 m; the recomposed section has a minimum length of 3.27 m. The fragments were found at the turn of the century in the area in front of the theater and near the gate to the main street, but it is excluded that they could have been used on one of its piers or as part of an arch; for the possibility that they formed a base for a bronze(?) group, see p.103, and cf. supra, Ch. 3, esp. n. 34, for the Aemilius Paullus Monument and other ancient examples. Oberleitner 1981 interprets the topic as Galatians against Ephesians (or East Greek troops), and considers it "unthinkable" before the Telephos Frieze and the Aemilius Paullus Monument (p. 103); he gives previous chronological assessments on p. 81. However, Moreno 1994 (252–53 with bibl. in n. 493 on p. 789; his fig. 330 gives only part of the recomposed section) believes that the frieze shows the encounter at the foot of Mount Olympos in Phrygia, in 189, between the Gauls formerly allied with Antiochos III and the Roman troops of the Consul Gn. Manlius Vulso, allied with the Pergamenes. Smith 1991, 186, gives a one-line comment, but in the caption to his fig. 208 (the photograph somewhat more comprehensive than Moreno's, although still partial), he dates the "Gallic battle frieze" to the "3rd or early 2nd c." Osada 1993, 150, catalogues the frieze under MF28 (dating mid-2nd c.) but does not discuss it otherwise. Hannestad 1993, 38 n. 63, considers it Hadrianic on stylistic grounds. Dr. J. Marszal, who has seen the sculptures in Vienna, tells me that he believes a Roman Imperial date is preferable.

40. One such coiffure belongs to figure 4, cat. 1: cf. Oberleitner 1981, fig. 44; the other is a fragment (cat. 9, fig. 56c) comprising a section of forehead and a different knot: strands on either side of a central part are brought forward and tied together.

41. Gauls from Delos and Gizah: Ridgway 1990, pls. 154–55, and cf. pp. 296–99; see also pp. 284–302 for discussion of the so-called Attalid dedications. For the Delos Gaul, see also infra,

Ch. 9 and n. 55. A more detailed article by J. Marszal is forthcoming. As to the different types of shields, I am reminded not only of the difficulties with the Aemilius Paullus Monument but also of the varying armament of the (mythological) combatants on the Artemision Frieze at Magnesia. Note that beards with mustaches are given to Gauls on Roman Imperial sarcophagi: see, e.g., Ridgway 1990, pl. 153 (sarcophagus in Rome, National Museum).

42. The standard at the right edge is a plain shaft planted upright in the ground, and not enough remains to see whether it was embellished further. The standard in the center of the section has three crescent-shaped objects hanging in front (*lunulae*) and terminates in a spear point. Oberleitner 1981, 99, fig. 73, shows many similar standards, but none is identical to that of the Ephesian relief. Moreno 1994, 253, suggests (improbably) that it might be a stylized tree to be completed in paint, an evergreen alluding to the mountainous area where Vulso's encounter with the Gauls took place, but he also admits that the feature could be a standard marking the Keltic encampment.

43. The trophy is described in detail by Oberleitner 1981, under cat. 1, but is not brought up again in discussing the interpretation and the dating of the frieze.

44. The first quotation is from Moreno 1994, 252–53; the second is from Oberleitner 1981, 103–104.

45. Pergamon Giant: Simon 1975, pl. 10. Telephos Frieze (the two Skythian brothers): *Pergamon* 1, 1996, 66–67, cat. 8 (panel 25).

46. Oberleitner 1981 considers the possibility that the relief belongs to a Roman sarcophagus, but believes that those with Gallic battles fall within the 3rd c. A.C. and are therefore quite different. Yet carving techniques in Asia Minor differ from those of Imperial Rome, and the secondary use of the slabs may have removed some important clue. It is perhaps significant, in this respect, that the barbarian horseman of cat. 2 seems smaller than the others, as might be appropriate for the decoration of a short side of a casket. I regret that I have never seen the original relief in Vienna.

47. *LIMC* 4 (1988), s.v. Gigantes, no. 26, with drawing of some coffers on p. 208 (dated ca. 158). For more recent opinions, see, e.g., Linfert 1995, 138–39, attributing probably to Ariarathes IV in 188 or shortly after; see also *LIMC* 8 (1997), s.v. Kybele, 758, no. 82 pl. 514, where the relevant coffer is assigned "zum hellenistischen Umbau" (E. Simon). For Carter's comments, see supra, Ch. 2 n. 45, and cf. my fuller discussion with extensive bibl. in Ridgway 1997b, 135–40 and ns. 45–48. I still believe that the most reasonable account is to be found in Rumscheid 1994, vol. 1, 43–44, with the acknowledgment that the W peristasis may be later than the E but that its coffers may have been prepared in advance, together with the first ones.

48. The 2nd-c. suggestion is made by Schmidt-Dounas 1991. It is rejected by Rose 1994, n. 30 on p. 99; pp. 76–82 propose extensive activity in the temenos during the 2nd c., after the Peace of Apameia in 188, but see infra (Rose 1997) for a possible earlier dating. See also Rose 1992, 45–46, for a revision of his position on the temple as stated in Webb 1996, 47–51, esp. n. 5. Rose 1997, 93–101, discusses Strabo's passage (13.1.26) connecting with Lysimachos both the Temple of Athena and the city walls, and his contradicting statement about the latter. Investigation in 1996 ascertained that, indeed, Strabo must have confused the walls of Alexandria Troas with those of Ilion, since the fortifications of Troy seem to date from the 3rd quarter of the 3rd c. (p. 98), too late for Lysimachos. On the other hand, the Temple of Athena can still be ascribed to that ruler, but Rose does not specify here whether the extant architecture goes back to that phase. Rose 1997, 101, mentions the discovery of a relief fragment showing

Architectural Sculpture—A Roundup

the torso of an Amazon that could be from one of the temple metopes. His report on the 1997 campaign (Rose 1998, 76–87) details other building activity at Troy (in the area of Temples A and B) during the 3rd c. He tells me (*per ep.*, Feb. 4, 1998) that the extant blocks are likely to be from the early 3rd-c. temple, though this fact cannot be proven absolutely. The portico around the temple was built in the mid-3rd c. and demolished by an earthquake in the late 5th c. A.C.— on present evidence, therefore, it seems that it was not destroyed in Fimbria's attack (85 B.C.), and perhaps neither was the temple. I am most deeply indebted to Prof. Rose for sending me copies of his communications in advance of publication.

My previous comments, with additional bibl.: Ridgway 1990, 153–54. A good chronological discussion and assessment in Rumscheid 1994, vol. 1, 18–19, 145–50, esp. on the fleshy flowers of the coffers (pls. 51.9, 52.1–10), said to be certainly *not* early Hellenistic; cf. vol. 2, 23–24, cat. 74. According to this author, the metopes are Augustan Classicizing; Lysimachos' temple, burnt in 85 B.C., is thought to have been thoroughly rebuilt by Augustus as an act of piety toward the venerable site.

49. For a general discussion of luxury altars, see Linfert 1995. Individual monuments are treated by Webb 1996: 94–96 (Magnesia), 99 (Priene), 115–16 (Lagina), 133 (Tenos), 153–54 (Kos). For the Knidian altar, see supra, Ch. 3, n. 53. For my previous comments, see Ridgway 1990: 154–55 (Tenos), 156–57 (Kos), 164–67 (Priene), 167–68 (Magnesia).

Linfert 1995, 138–39, would date the altar at Priene to the 2nd c., shortly after the Peace of Apameia in 188 (as refurbishing of a previous altar), and criticizes Carter's interpretation of the figures on it as Muses, because too many of them (20) would be required by the intercolumniations available; he prefers to think of them as personifications. I still find Carter's identification plausible on the basis of the two figures extant, especially since we cannot tell what other personages might have accompanied the Muses. Rumscheid 1994, vol. 1, 45, vol. 2, 71–72, cat. 294, states that the ornament provides no certain chronological clue; an Imperial inscription on fragments of the architrave does not necessarily indicate a new phase.

50. Delos Altar to Dionysos: Étienne and Braun 1995; the inscription, *ID* 442.B.231–32, mentions an *eidophoros*. For the kneeling satyrs, see figs. 32–33, although cf. p. 83, where their attribution to the altar is doubted; for a reconstruction of the entire structure, see fig. 35 on p. 86. See also Marcadé et al., 1996, 138–39, no. 59 (A 4178, A 4179) for two of the satyrs, clearly wearing a kilt and, originally, a metal wreath "of oak leaves"; and cf. no. 60, pp. 140–41, for a Silenos/Telamon in relief, from the theater.

51. The latest reconstruction is by Hoepfner 1989, 601–19, esp. figs. 15a–b on p. 613 (cf. Webb 1996, figs. 67–68). It is criticized by Webb 1996, 94, and especially by Linfert 1995, 134 and n. 17 (e.g., for misreading clues to the location of steps on some blocks and as having unusually angular niches in the inside, almost like arrow-slits). For attribution of various elements, including later repairs, see Rumscheid 1994, vol. 1, 25–28, 214–17; vol. 2, cat. 138 on p. 39; his cat. 139 lists pieces that do not belong.

52. Akropolis original: Flashar and Mantis 1993, pls. 24–27; for the Vatican statue, see also *LIMC* 2, s.v. Apollon/Apollo, 383, no. 60, where the agrenon is equated to the knotted fillets that decorate the Delphic omphalos. Linfert 1995, 132–34, repeats his earlier suggestion about the embassy, and identifies the figure with agrenon as Apollo Pythios. Webb 1996, 95 and fig. 70, believes the sex of the Magnesian figure is not clear; it could be female, and thus be Britomartis/Diktynna, a nymph assimilated to Artemis.

53. The main publication of the Koan altar is Stampolidis 1987; cf. Webb 1996, fig. 141 for

Stampolidis' reconstruction, comparable to that of the Knidian altar (Webb, fig. 95). See also Rumscheid 1994, vol. 2, 29, cat. 99.

54. For the "Gaulish" shields, see Stampolidis 1987, pls. 7α and 31.12β. For Dionysos and the Indians, see *LIMC* 3, s.v. Dionysos, 418 (A. Veneri, on literary sources), but no Greek representation is cited. See, however, s.v. Dionysos/Bacchus, 558, nos. 241–47, where Roman depictions are listed, often on sarcophagi, and pp. 564–65 for commentary connecting the topic with Imperial conquests in the East, from the Late Trajanic period to that of Lucius Verus and the Antonine emperors (C. Gasparri). A Hellenistic Etruscan frieze from Civitalba may show the Gauls sacking the Delphic sanctuary, when Apollo (with his sister Artemis and his mother Leto) intervened; but Dionysos, although also connected with the Delphic temple, is not shown (although an episode with the god appears on the Civitalba pediment), nor is his participation in that event mentioned by ancient sources. On the Etruscan frieze, see, e.g., Moreno 1994, 495–99, figs. 621, 623, 625; see also Steingräber, forthcoming, and Marszal, forthcoming.

55. Kabus-Preißhofen 1989, 178, defines Koan local style (in free-standing sculpture) as being quite removed from Pergamene influence, and mentions (n. 742) a 1984 work by K. Kalin (available only in typescript) advocating a date for the Koan altar frieze "around 120 at the earliest, but probably closer to 100 or shortly after Lagina."

56. The only recent discussion of the Lagina altar, to my knowledge, is Webb 1996, 115–16 with bibl., figs. 92–93; the height of the altar block is 0.53 m, as compared with the 0.93 of the temple slabs (both figures inclusive of the upper molding). Osada 1993, 151–52, catalogues it as MF32, but (p. 107) mentions only that it should be grouped with Pergamon, Knidos, and Kos in its continuous treatment, as contrasted with the rhythmic, statue-like effect of the decoration on the altars (precincts) at Magnesia and Priene.

57. See Ridgway 1990, 154–55, and n. 3 on p. 200; the official publication is Queyrel 1986, esp. 316–17, nos. 84–85, and 121 for the Gaius Pandusinus dedication (by Agasias of Ephesos) and cf. drawing, pls. 27–29, reconstructing the bronzes at the corners of the antae flanking the altar's central staircase, on the basis of the crowning blocks; for the sea monsters, see his pls. 132–39 and discussion on pp. 279–86, nos. 11–28. See also infra, Ch. 8 and n. 10. The akroterial suggestion for the altar, considered but not endorsed by Queyrel, is advocated by Stampolidis 1991, 295 and cf. his n. 44.

58. For the initial sketch, see Ridgway 1990, 178–79, ill. 26. See now *ArchDelt* 35.2.B (1980, publ. 1988), Chronika, 540–42, pls. 340–41; cf. also Konstantinopoulos 1986, 232, fig. 260; a good photograph in *EAA* Suppl. 2.1 (1971–1994), s.v. Cariatide, fig. 1004 on p. 885.

For a possible redating of Tarentine tombs, see supra, n. 4 (Lippolis 1996).

59. Bargylia Monument: Waywell 1990, pl. 58.3 and drawing on p. 387 (British Museum, BM 1542; initial publication). Waywell 1996a, 111–12, fig. 4 (where the Skylla is discussed in the context of all known representations); Waywell 1996b, with preliminary drawings on p. 81, figs. 10–11 (full publication, including catalogue of hitherto unpublished fragments of sculpture and architecture; comparison with other comparable structures). The British scholar calls the Bargylia monster the earliest extant depiction in marble and on a large scale (p. 75; smaller Skyllas as akroteria are in fact known from earlier Tarentine graves). The figure is reconstructed in the act of lifting a human victim with the right hand, since the torso rotates toward that side and the surviving dog's head looks up and back. A steering oar, as typical for Skylla, may have been held in the left hand. Waywell mentions that the Karian coast was

under Rhodian control at the relevant time, but considers various possible meanings and influences, warning against building circular arguments on the alleged Rhodian connection of the Sperlonga Skylla (p. 96). The Bargylian monster might have been chosen because popular on Rhodes (as shown on "Megarian" bowls, probably from that island—but see de Grummond, forthcoming), or Melas may have been a native of Sicily or South Italy, and have selected a theme distinctive of his origin. Yet, since his name is written on the left door jamb, he probably occupied only the left chamber—nothing is known about the occupant(s) of the other(s). Waywell (1996b, 96) concludes that if the concept of victory is involved in the shape of the building, Skylla may have been selected as an allusion to the triumph of life over death. Moreno 1994, 148–50, color fig. 320, stresses the events of 201. To me, Skylla seems a typical symbol of the perils of the sea, without implication of human agents—neither pirates nor enemy fleet. For the Lion Tomb, see, e.g., Ridgway 1997b, 144, with bibl., and cf. 114–15 and n. 9 for additional mentions (in the context of the Halikarnassos Maussolleion); Waywell 1996b, 95–98, accepts also possible influences from Attic graves and from victory monuments like the Lion of Chaironeia and that of Amphipolis. The total height of the Bargylia Monument is calculated at 12 m. For the inscribed block, see his cat. 54, pp. 114–16, figs. 85–87.

60. Bieber 1961, 127, fig. 490; *DOG* 1979, 500–501, no. 2085 pl. 300; Osada 1993, 48–49, cat. DF12 (comparison with the Telephos Frieze and mosaics illustrating philosophical schools); *LIMC* 4, s.v. Hades, no. 161 pl. 224 (cropped); Palagia 1997a, 69–70, fig. 92 (with the new interpretation of the Mystery reading). The relief has been variously dated from the 3rd c. to the Late Hellenistic period, but comparison with the Telephos Frieze makes me prefer a date in the mid-2nd c., supposedly corroborated by the letter forms of the inscription (*DOG* 1979; see infra, n. 61).

61. The most detailed description of the physical condition of the block is *DOG* 1979, 500–501, no. 2085 pl. 300. The side edges retain small bosses to anchor the additional blocks; the upper surface shows clamp cuttings to the right and left of the block; height, 0.31 m, length, 1.055 m. The piece is said to have come from Trianta, near Ialysos.

62. This Demetrios could be identified with the sculptor (son of Demetrios, perhaps from Antioch) who collaborated with Theon of Antioch on a bronze statue in Lindos: cf. Goodlett 1991, 676–77 (see also supra, Ch. 3 n. 55); if so, a date in the 1st half of the 2nd c. could be assured for the Hieronymos relief. On the other hand, several sculptors with the same name are known, from Rhodes and other areas: cf. *EAA* s.v. Demetrios; nos. 4–5, 7, 9, 10 fall within the relevant timespan.

63. The standard interpretation accepts only two locations, separated by the pier that signifies the door of Hades. There is even some disagreement on where the "teaching" scene takes place: Curtius 1951 takes it to show not a philosophical school but the Seven Sages in Elysium, as contrasted with the other figures within Hades; *DOG* 1979, 500–501, implies that the first scene is located in this world, and that everything to the right of the pier occurs in the Underworld. Yet I believe that the landscape elements in the last third of the relief suggest at least one more environment.

64. The figure's position *behind* Plouton's throne is stressed by Curtius 1951, who therefore identifies it as Aiakos, another of the Underworld judges, or as the first in the row of the condemned (in contrast with the philosophers in Elysium; cf. supra, n. 63). The youth holding his knee would then be Peirithoos or, alternatively, Aktaion, in which case the seated female would

be Maira, according to the "Nekyia" by Polygnotos. This interpretation has not received wide acceptance.

65. Ares Ludovisi: Ridgway 1990, 84–85, pl. 48. Coarelli 1997, 433–37 and n. 198, would place the Ares, as Achilles, on the so-called Ara of Domitius Ahenobarbus (originally a cult-statue base for the Temple of Neptune), together with a Poseidon of the Lateran type and a Thetis "like that from the Stazione Termini area" in Rome, as works of Skopas *minor;* cf. his figs. 98–102 and 104–107, with reconstruction as fig. 110 on p. 441. The Thetis (*LIMC* 8, s.v. Tritones, no. 75 pl. 54; dated 2nd c. A.C.) and the Ares/Achilles are now exhibited side by side at Palazzo Altemps, Rome, and hailed as contemporary in the local newspapers. Yet I would question a Late Republican date for both works, and Prof. O. Palagia kindly tells me (*per ep.,* Sept. 1998) that they are made of different marble. On the male figure, see also *LIMC* 2, s.v. Ares, no. 24 pl. 360; cf. pl. 371, no. 116, for the Ares on the Parthenon E frieze. For the Sarcophagus of the Mourning Women, see, e.g., Boardman 1995, fig. 227 (parapet above pediment). The pose could go back to the "Nekyia."

66. See, e.g., Schefold 1997, figs. 117, 128, 192. *DOG* 1979 mentions that Hieronymos may be the peripatetic who died toward the end of the 3rd c. This philosophical association may be irrelevant, if the teaching scene is in fact a reading of the Mysteries, but its iconography could be nonetheless inspired by standard renderings of philosophical schools: see Osada 1993 (supra, n. 60).

67. On Psyche on the Hieronymos relief, see *LIMC* 7, s.v. Psyche, no. 79 (with cross-ref. to Nemesis, no. 189): 2nd quarter of the 2nd c. The *velificans* type is often used for depictions of breezes or astral beings, such as Selene: cf. *LIMC* 3, s.v. Aurai, nos. 1 and 4, pl. 51, and *LIMC* 7, s.v. Selene, with cross-refs. to Astra. For examples of the "niche mantle" on the Lagina Hekateion, see supra, n. 29; also infra, Sagalassos reliefs, n. 68.

Curtius 1951 identifies the female with butterfly wings as Psyche-Tyche, symbolizing the fate of men (against those who had considered her Nemesis); for him, the *velificans* woman (definitely *not* sinking but rising) would be Nyx. I wonder if she could represent the salvation of an initiate, "rising" into Elysium—yet her gender may be surprising, on a monument for a man. Given the incomplete nature of our evidence, because of the missing figures, only a general assessment of this scene can be given.

68. The main publication of the frieze is Fleischer 1979; see also Fleischer 1984, with acute stylistic analysis in repeated support of a 2nd-c. date, which had been doubted. Rumscheid 1994, vol. 2, 79, cat. 328, prefers an early Imperial to a Late Hellenistic date, but he takes into account pieces mentioned by Fleischer as part of his survey, not as part of the Heroon itself (kind communication by Prof. Fleischer, Jan. 19, 1998). A summary of knowledge up to 1995 appears in Webb 1996, 127–29, who includes information about a lion resting its paw on a bull's head, perhaps topping the monument. For the latest opinion, with redating to the Augustan period, see "Archaeology in Turkey," *AJA* 101 (1997) 277; the naiskos is said to be 7.50 m per side and 3 m high. Cf. the same newsletter, *AJA* 100 (1996) 312, for the discovery of three additional slabs (containing four more dancers: fig. 30 on p. 314) and the evidence of Antonine repairs (fig. 31 on p. 315). The head of Alexander is illustrated by Waelkens 1995, p. 32—it does not look like Alexander to me; yet it is certainly no Roman portrait.

69. These slabs, only 0.50 m high, as contrasted with the 1.17 m of the first frieze, were found reused in a late Roman wall blocking the entrance to a Late Hellenistic fountain house: *Saga-*

lassos I, 1993, 42–43, figs. 20–22. They depict seven dancing girls holding hands and a woman flute-player.

70. For the Akropolis bases, see Studniczka 1907, 27, pl. 1d (Akr. 3363 + 3366; nine women), and 28, fig. 7 (Akr. 1327, six dancers). On Samothrake, Antiphellos, and Phanagoria, see Ridgway 1990, 26–28, ill. 10; also Ridgway 1993b, pl. 77, figs. 152a–b (Phanagoria). The Samothrake frieze is now seen to have surrounded the entire building, which is no longer called the "Temenos" (since it was found to be roofed) but "Hall of Choral Dancers": see *JHS-AR* 41 (1995) 52–53 for the new reconstruction, and *JHS-AR* 43 (1997) 91, for the new name; cf. *Samothrace* 1998, 73–78, no. 17, fig. 33 for the dancers. This largest and most impressive structure within the Samothrakian Sanctuary may have been a Telesterion (as suggested to me by Prof. Kevin Clinton). For other friezes, including the Sagalassos monument, see Osada 1993, 96–100, with several examples; particularly interesting are the two slabs from Narona now in Split: Osada, n. 371 on p. 139, with full bibl. (2nd half 2nd c.); Picard 1963, 1192–94, figs. 468–69. See also the frieze from Dionysopolis (Baltschick) in the Sofia Museum: Venedikov and Gerassimov 1973, 104, 357, pl. 330 (2nd c.). The theory identifying the Dancers as nymphs protecting the dead was advanced by J. Zahle in his doctoral dissertation (in Danish), kindly mentioned to me by Dr. Pia Guldager Bilde.

71. Definition and funerary attribution: Fleischer 1998, 48. For a return to the 2nd-c. dating and an illustration of both slabs, see Hermary 1987, 233 n. 31 and pl. 59.5. Only one slab, with 4th-c. dating, is illustrated in *LIMC* 1, s.v. Amazones, no. 434 pl. 493. From Soloi comes also the late 4th-c. Amazon Sarcophagus in Vienna (Fleischer 1998, Hermary 1987), thus suggesting a local interest in the topic, perhaps because the Cypriot city was thought to have been founded by Theseus' sons Akamas and Demophon together with Phaleron, a descendant of Erechtheus, and later to have been named after Solon. Hermary 1987 does not exclude, however, an allusion to the hostilities against the Persians.

72. The structure was dedicated under Helianax, priest of the Great Gods, as stated by an inscription on façade—his tenancy of the priesthood provides the absolute chronology. For a detailed account, see Webb 1996 (cf. supra, n. 3), fig. 131.

73. This point has been made by Webb 1998, 243–44. See also Webb 1996, 57–60, with a detailed description of the weapons; on relief panels in general, see her pp. 19–20. Extensive discussion and bibl. also in Polito 1998, 91–95, figs. 27–31, who stresses that the variety of armament depicted on the balustrade cannot represent the commemoration of a specific battle. The naval insignia would specifically refute a sole connection with the Gallic wars, as often postulated. Polito (p. 95) notes that, although of excellent quality, this Pergamene weapon frieze did not serve as influential prototype for all subsequent examples of the genre, as many believe—another instance of Pergamenocentrism. It was itself based on earlier models.

74. Polito 1998, esp. 80–81; a brief summary of the weapon motif appears in Webb 1996, 33.

75. On the new attribution of the panels once given to the propylon, see supra, Ch. 2 and n. 31; in general, see Webb 1996, 60–61 (with earlier reconstruction). The propylon and the stoas seem to have been dedications of Eumenes II, therefore datable to the 1st half of the 2nd c. For other, refuted, proposals, see Polito 1998, 93 and ns. 119–20.

76. For a description of the building, see Webb 1996, 102. Although this is not the earliest instance of a mixture of two different orders, I suspect that combinations such as this were intentional and meaningful, not simply a symptom of architectural decadence (as often sug-

gested) or lack of imagination. Cf. also Schaaf 1992, 37–61, esp. 38 on the weapon frieze; Polito 1998, 213–14, definitely dates the latter to the 2nd c. A.C.

77. See *Sagalassos* III, 1995, 25 and fig. 12; the arrangement of the piers as a gallery of an upper story is compared to Macedonian palaces. Cf. also Waelkens 1995, 32 and fig. on p. 29; Webb 1996, 130–31. Rumscheid 1994, vol. 2, 79, cat. 326 and pl. 173.2, dates toward the end of the 2nd c. and mentions additional bibl. Polito 1998, 100 n. 82, seems doubtful about chronology.

78. For a thorough survey of such alleged Pergamene influences in Etruria, not only on architectural sculpture but on all forms of Etruscan art, see Steingräber, forthcoming, and Marszal, forthcoming, with extensive refs. See also the response by de Grummond.

79. The main publication of the temple, with its peculiar mixture of orders, is Krauss and Herbig 1939, with the best illustrations of the carved metopes (pls. 36–41, drawings of some of them on pl. 42) and of the female heads on all four sides of the Corinthian capital (in place of the fleuron; pls. 43–48). The latter show quite a range in their features, with Severizing traits especially in the hairstyle. The metopes are usually carved in one piece with the triglyph, continuing a tradition that goes back to the 6th c. (Foce del Sele "Treasury"); no. 5, surprisingly, may depict a man standing next to a vase-topped pillar and holding a frontal horse. At least one carved panel belongs to one of the long sides. For the recent redating of the temple to a single phase and the new attribution, see Theodorescu 1989, 117–24; a brief summary with tentative attribution to Bona Mens appears in Pedley 1990, 118–19, and figs. 76–78.

Another Italic temple with mixed orders and decorated metopes, at Canosa, is mentioned by Polito 1998, 111–13, and fig. 43 (metope with relief cuirass), but its chronology is uncertain.

80. For definition and analysis of Baroque architecture in Alexandria, see McKenzie 1996, which includes comparisons with Petra. For an earlier review, see Lyttelton 1974, 11–13 (definition), 40–60 (Alexandria), 61–83 (Petra); truly Baroque architecture seems to be Roman Imperial. For comments on the possible influence of Pharaonic tradition on Ptolemaic forms, see Onians 1996, although far more speculative in its approach; note the critical remarks in M. S. Venit's review of Hamma 1996, *AJA* 102 (1998) 453–55, esp. 454

CHAPTER 5

Original Statuary in the Round

We started our survey of second-century sculpture with architectural monuments, because, as mentioned, more than one factor contributes to their chronology. In reviewing statuary in the round, we shall now begin with the few pieces that can be securely dated on external evidence, and shall then discuss those that fall within our timespan on stylistic grounds. In current literature, some of the latter may seem to have a firm chronological basis, especially through connection with specific historical events or patrons, but close examination shows otherwise. Two types of sculpture that could be included in this chapter will be left, however, for later treatment: portraits, since their identification is often based on alleged similarity with coins, and therefore is frequently controversial; and cult images or divine statues attributable to specific sculptors, which will be discussed as part of those masters' oeuvre. Votive and funerary reliefs, albeit original works and occasionally firmly dated, will also be reviewed in another chapter, since they may have derived inspiration from monuments in the round. Statues known only through later copies will receive separate treatment, even if their prototypes have been—more or less convincingly—attributed to the second century.

DATED SCULPTURES

It is regrettable that so few pieces can be included under this rubric, some of them sadly fragmentary or of modest quality. At present count, I can list only seven items, one of them a group. I review them in chronological order, despite the fact that no true stylistic "development" can be noted.

The **statuette of Megiste, Athens NM 710** (Pl. 45) is one such offering. Its relatively inexpensive nature can be inferred not only from its size, but also from the fact that its base was carved from an unfinished Ionic capital—the unusual bottom curve at front and sides, determined by the abacus, and the peculiar projection in the back, corresponding to the echinus between the volutes, are quite understandable once the pedestal is viewed upside down. An inscription states that Megiste, daughter of Architimos from Sphettos, under the archonship of Epikrates, [dedicated the statue] to

Plate 45

the Mother of the Gods. Since the sculpture was found in the Peiraieus, it probably came from the Metroon there. An archon Epikrates is listed for the year 146/5, but the letter forms had initially prompted for the sculpture a date in the Roman period. A revision of our epigraphic knowledge, combined with a stylistic examination, confirms, however, the second-century chronology.[1]

It is assumed that the statuette represents Megiste, rather than Kybele or Aphrodite, because of the lack of suitable attributes. Kybele would probably have been flanked by a lion, and Aphrodite might have had a more revealing costume.[2] Yet the figure's right arm, attached separately and now lost, was once raised so high that the armpit is visible; it is difficult to imagine what the gesture might have been, but it seems significant. Her head is broken off, but there is no trace of hair over her nape and back, so that a rolled-up coiffure can be assumed, unusual for a young girl (which the sculpture is thought to depict because of the flat bosom). Finally, the left arm, which is lowered to hold up the mantle, sports both an armlet and a spiral bracelet probably in the form of a snake.

Megiste's attire is elegant. She wears sandals with a high, layered sole deeply indented between the first two toes. Her himation is looped over the left shoulder, covers the back of the body, and crosses the front over the thighs in a triangular pattern with its apex at the figure's left hand. This triangle is delimited by two twisted rolls of folds; the garment would then have cascaded in a swag along Megiste's left side, but that piece was carved separately and is now lost. Below the mantle, she wears a thin chiton tied high and forming mannered, small kolpoi looping over the belt near the arms; the vertical fall of this garment can be noted beneath the himation, in the typical drapery-through-drapery convention. The hem of the skirt touches the base in a series of stylized waves on her left and forms a niche over that foot, which corresponds to the weight leg. The right leg, trailing, is held so far to the side as to appear almost dislocated, when a body is visualized under the massed cloth. The pose results in a pronounced curve of the left hip that, in conjunction with the tapering width at the shoulders, seems typical for the advanced second century.

A somewhat comparable attire and pose, combined with larger size and much better quality, characterize the **Kleopatra from Delos,** a statue that, together with that of Kleopatra's husband **Dioskourides,** provides one of the best-dated monuments of the second century (Pls. 46–47). The two sculptures were set side by side on a single base in the peristyle of the so-called House of Kleopatra, in the Theater Quarter on the island. The tall, rectangular pedestal carries a long inscription mentioning the woman as the promoter of the monument, in honor of her husband, who had given the two Delphic tripods of silver that stood on either side of the doorway to the Temple of Apollo, under the archonship of Timarchos—therefore in 138/7. The Athenian yearly magistrate is mentioned not only because the island was under Athens' control at the time, but also because both Dioskourides and his wife, as stated in the inscription, were from the Attic deme of Myrrhinous, and must have come to Delos from the

Plates 46–47

Mainland, as had many others. Kleopatra, like her husband, was probably a person of means, since the two sculptures are among the best surviving from Delos, lifesize and comparable to honorary statues set up at public expense on other Aegean and East Greek sites, like Kos and Magnesia. Yet this is a private monument, erected within a private house but on axis with the entrance so that it could be glimpsed from outside and admired fully by any visitor.[3]

The value of the firm date is somewhat weakened by the fact that both the male and the female figure follow standard types; now that both heads are missing, nothing distinctive remains of the couple, and indeed they look as if they might have stepped out from one of the naiskos-like gravestones common on the coast of Asia Minor.[4] What is remarkable is that the two contemporary statues seem to reflect different chronologies: Dioskourides goes back to a late fourth-century prototype—the so-called Lateran Sophokles, perhaps set up under Lykourgos;[5] the Kleopatra wears Hellenistic attire—the diaphanous mantle, probably made from Koan silk, that drapes like a veil and fully reveals the vertical folds of the chiton beneath; the sandals, with high, profiled sole.[6] In addition, her wide hips and narrow shoulders are in keeping with second-century proportions and trends; the pyramidal outline of her figure emphasizes the richness of the chiton and gives the statue an effect of stability and permanence.

Kleopatra holds her right arm across her chest, supporting the left elbow as her left hand reaches toward her face; this is the so-called *pudicitia* pose, meant to express the modesty and restraint of a proper housewife. Yet her silky veil, overample chiton, and elegant shoes indicate also a wealthy woman. Her name, probably inspired by the Egyptian royal family,[7] adds to the impression of high status. Dioskourides, in turn, is shown as a man of letters, since the right arm bent and constrained by the mantle is typical of orators and poets. His free leg is also on that side, yet his pose retains something of the Polykleitan chiasmos, because the tight mantle loop causes the right shoulder to rise, and the lowered left arm corresponds to the left hip pushed up by the weight leg. Surprisingly enough, a simple inversion of the stance, with right arm bent but opposite leg flexed and forward,[8] produces a self-assertive impression absent from the Dioskourides. It is clear that the male and female figures were created as a paratactic group, since both free legs occur on the inside, and the outer contours, emphasized by the weight legs, are compact and balancing, like two parentheses. Note, moreover, the simplicity of Dioskourides' mantle, clearly suggestive of heavy material generating few directional folds, and contrast the criss-crossing patterns of Kleopatra's costume. Yet, although untextured and without chiaroscural effects, Dioskourides' himation shows (regular) press folds, a status symbol, and he wears a tunic below it, as common in East Greek and Roman circles.

The Athenian connection has provided other firm dates for sculptures from Delos. The most impressive is the over-lifesize **Isis from the so-called Serapieion C** on the slopes of Mount Kynthos. It lacks the head with a portion of the upper torso, the arms, and the separately carved feet, but a fragment from a gold diadem has been attributed to it. It is dated by inscriptional evidence to 128/7, when it was dedicated by the Athenian demos. Were it not for its location within the cella of a temple to Isis, we might not have been able to identify what is now simply a colossal female draped in chiton and himation. Its purely Greek iconography and style carry lingering echoes of the Baroque, especially in the many arrow folds over the left side, along the advanced leg. The rich mantle is highly textured but without the drill channels contouring the limbs or the deep pockets of shadow, and its twisted roll across the torso looks almost abraded and flattened. The chiton is expressed by a series of parallel folds grouped in bundles above the plinth, but lying thinly over the abdomen.[9]

The Athenian demos is also involved in another sculpture from Delos—a fragmentary **statuette of Nemesis–Isis**. The inscription on its base states that it was set up by the priest Sosion, son of Eumenes; a second inscription, on an architectural member, mentions that the same man consecrated the naos and the agalma of Isis–Nemesis, to the intentions of the Athenian demos and King Nikomedes [III] of Bithynia, when Dionysios son of Nikon of Pallene was overseer (*epimeletes*) on the island. This information yields a date of 110/109. Regrettably, in sculptural terms we learn little from this broken image, preserved only from the mid-thighs to the base. Once again, the costume of chiton and himation seems entirely Greek; no effects of transparency are present. The one extant sandal (on the trailing right foot) has a high, profiled sole, but the straps were probably indicated only in paint. The drill was used liberally in the chiton and the swag of the mantle hanging at the figure's left side.[10]

It is important to note that so far these Delian dedications have not included master's signatures; they were either entirely private, like the Kleopatra and Dioskourides, or religious, although not quite in the realm of official cult images, within small shrines that belonged to foreign divinities and were acts of personal piety. The next example from the island is also the cult image in a private chapel, but the latter is part of a larger complex, the Establishment of the Poseidoniastes of Berytos (Ill. 20), an agglomeration of residential and public rooms serving a group of merchants from Beirut as a sort of ethnic hostel within the multinational sanctuary. The headless and armless statue is identified as **Thea Roma** by a lengthy inscription that hails the deity as benefactress of the association of traders, shippers, and forwarding agents. A date in the year 110/109 is provided by the mention of the "second thiasos-presidency of Mnaseas son of Dionysios"; the base is signed by Menandros, son of Melas, of Athens. Once again, no attributes are preserved, and the heavily weathered sculpture is not particularly revealing in terms of style. Yet its very Greek costume (chiton and himation), which makes it so similar to one of the Muse types or even the Kleopatra, shows that the sculptor did not attempt to characterize the goddess as a foreigner or a military power. Once again, out of context and without inscription, we would not have been able to establish the identity of the figure. That ethnic characterizations were, however, possible on the island is shown by other works, including some from the very same Establishment of the Poseidoniastes.[11]

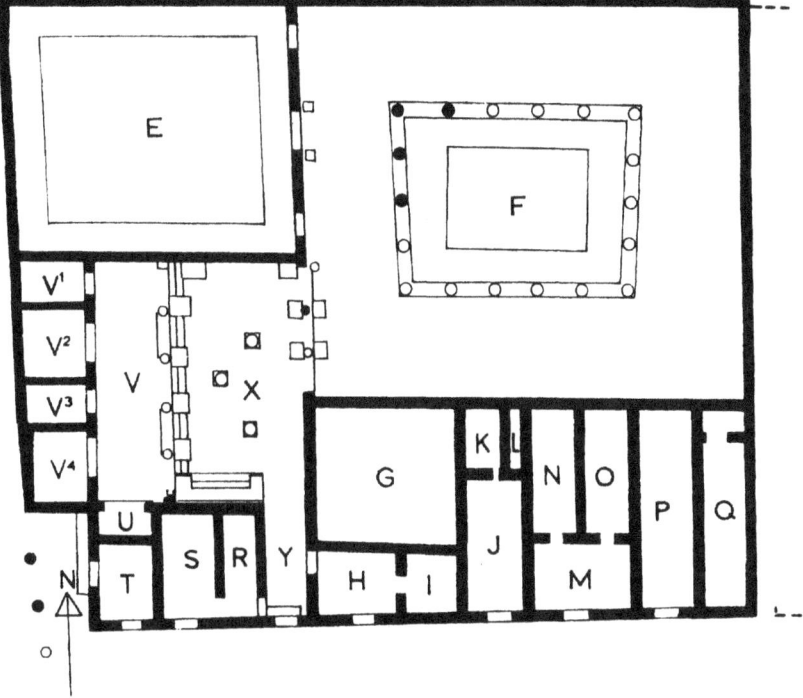

Ill. 20. Delos, plan of the Establishment of the Poseidoniastes of Berytos. Thea Roma stood in chapel V¹; the Slipper-Slapper Group was found in room N. [After *Guide de Delos* (Paris 1966) 115 fig. 20]

The last monument with a firm enough date, just before 100, comes from the same complex, but the residential section rather than the public quarters: it is the famous **Slipper-Slapper Group** of Aphrodite, Eros, and Pan, Athens NM 3335. The work, somewhat under-lifesize, was found in a wing of the building erected around 110 (cf. Ill. 20); its inscription mentions Dionysios, son of Zenon, son of Theodoros, of Berytos, who dedicated the work "on behalf of himself and his children to his ancestral deities," thus allowing for a date at the end of the century on prosopographical and epigraphic grounds, although a slightly earlier date was proposed by some scholars.[12] This time there is no connection with Athens, nor is the sculptor mentioned, but how is the group to be interpreted?

Some commentators have seen it as a genre scene—Aphrodite being attacked by a lascivious Pan and fending him off with the only weapon at her disposal, one of her slippers, and the one more conveniently reachable by her free hand. At the same time, possible underlying meanings have been sought in the slipper itself. Is it an erotic tool meant to enhance the sexual act, as depicted in some scenes of love-making? Is it the symbol of a prostitute, with its suggestive message (*akolouthe*, "follow") written with studs to leave an imprint in the dust? Is it a typical household object with which to perform a routine spanking (Eros is shown on vases being punished by his mother with one of her sandals)? Is it a way of removing a shoe, to obtain the extra power bestowed on the *monosandaloi* in combat situations? Is it a play on words and names: *blaute* (sandal)–blatta–Balaat (the name of the Syrian goddess)?

These suggestions range from the erotic, through the mundane, to the religious, especially since scholars have found it difficult to accept a dedication to the ancestral gods, on behalf of one's children, in the form of a playful, almost burlesque composition. The Syrian nationality of the donor has also validated allusions to Astarte-Balaat, rather than to the Greek Aphrodite. Since the goddess in the group is attempting to cover her genitals with her left hand, a comparison has been established with the Knidia by Praxiteles. This would be the first known sculptural adaptation of the type, perhaps prompted by a donor who had seen the original in the coastal city and realized its own reflection of Asiatic cults. The small Eros has also played a role in the archaeological interpretations; some have seen him as uniting the two fighters, others as helping his mother to repel Pan's advances, still others, and more probably, as neutral, simply needing to touch both figures because of the static demands of the fragile marble. Without presuming to resolve the riddle, I can only offer here some comments of my own.

Aphrodite's gesture of covering her pubes has been given special significance by its similarity to the Knidia's pose, yet the arms are reversed and the hand, in the Delian composition, is more firmly anchored to the body, indeed to cover rather than to point out, as in the Praxitelean image. The inversion, to be sure, is determined by the presence of Pan and by the need to have the right hand brandish the "weapon," but the total effect is different. This is a young but very feminine Aphrodite, plump and curvaceous, with a remarkably dimpled (almost realistically ugly) hand and a coiffed hairstyle that is not only unusual but also quite different from that of the alleged prototype. I wonder how many would have been reminded of the Knidia in looking at the Delian composition—which, moreover, was not meant for public viewing, but for private edification, being located in one of the residential rooms of the club. The muscular Pan is substantially smaller than the goddess, although this discrepancy in size is obvious only from a three-quarter angle; yet the paratactic group seems "one-sided," meant for frontal display, with substantial struts altering the back view. In Greek terms, Pan and Aphrodite appear together much earlier, and Pan and Eros are occasionally depicted as playmates or wrestlers, equal (and small!) in size, under Aphrodite's supervision. Although the Eros is here simply symbolic of an amorous atmosphere, rather than a participant in the action, the combination of the three supernatural beings *per se* is not an Oriental but a Greek concept, or at least a foreign text translated into Greek terms.

To be sure, no text exists to verify the occasion, but the group, usually considered unique, now appears less isolated: a Hellenistic terracotta from Capua shows Aphrodite being embraced by a small Pan; a bronze statuette from the east slope of the Athenian Akropolis preserves at present only the goddess brandishing her sandal, but traces remain of her two companions; a marble fragment of a hand holding a sandal, from Samos, may even suggest that a stone replica of the Delian group existed; finally, a bronze Aphrodite holding up a sandal, of Roman Imperial date, seems to come from Syria, thus implying that the specific iconography held a persistent meaning for the area.[13]

I would hesitate to read the Delian group as confirmation that the Olympians, by the Late Hellenistic period, had descended from their lofty pedestal to a more human, anecdotal level. Yet I also believe that Greek style and iconography reflect here some non-Greek layers of meaning—perhaps an emphasis on the procreative forces of nature, the fertility of men versus the fertility of the earth—that we cannot fully fathom at present. In these terms, the Delian composition serves only to show how realistically the female body could be shown around 100, and how "flat" arrangements were created, perhaps to be set up deliberately for a single viewpoint.

Not as firmly dated, but reasonably bracketed between 159 and 138, is the so-called **Zeus/Hero from Pergamon,** which should therefore be included in this section, although as a separate case. Its chronology is based on the dedication by King Attalos, son of King Attalos—hence Attalos II—of the Temple of Hera, as inscribed over the architrave.[14] The colossal male image, headless and missing its right arm, was found within the cella, in front of a T-shaped base toward the rear of the cella said to be obviously contemporaneous with the building. The pedestal contained cavities for three statues. The central one, seated, must have depicted the temple owner; the Zeus/Hero stood at her (proper) right and one more standing figure flanked her on the opposite side.

Because the preserved neck carries no traces of beard and long hair, the majestic male statue in Istanbul has been thought to depict a heroized Attalos II, the dedicant, who therefore would have stood as *sunnaos* next to the Hera. Yet the Zeus Ammon also from Pergamon, although not a temple image, has equally short hair, and his beard clears the neck to some extent; if the head of the Zeus/Hero was turned toward the central statue, as suggested by the tensed neck muscles, a beard might have jutted out without making contact with the throat.[15] The commanding pose, in reversed contrapposto—the raised right arm (once probably holding a long staff or other attribute) on the side of the weight leg, the left hand on the hip on the side of the trailing foot—is as appropriate for a ruler as for a god, but the wrapping of the mantle that leaves the powerful torso almost entirely bare would seem to favor Zeus. This is a statuary type recurring as early as the late fifth century, in the so-called Dresden Zeus attributed to Agorakritos, but already adumbrated around 460 in the central figure of the east pediment of the Temple of Zeus at Olympia. If the other statue flanking the Pergamene Hera portrayed in fact Zeus—an inevitable conclusion, should the Istanbul figure represent Attalos II—what would have differentiated the human monarch from the immortal consort? A beardless face and a barely visible royal fillet would have been inadequate to spell the difference, and the excessive similarity of "Attalos" to a Zeus type might have been considered hubristic. I could see the Pergamene king shown at slightly smaller scale, perhaps with a tunic below the himation; or I could even visualize an Athena as a pendant to Zeus, thus emphasizing those divinities that recur prominently in the Pergamon Gigantomachy.

Regardless of identification, the Istanbul statue is an impressive original worthy of analysis. It was obviously conceived for a tripartite group—weight leg toward the outside, right shoulder forward, left foot so far back that it touches only with the tip of the sandal—yet its torsion is moderate and a frontal view is equally satisfactory. The figure has been called Classicizing because of its traditional pattern, but the deeply carved cavity between the legs, the dramatic "sail" at the bend of the left knee, the undercutting of the mantle apron, the slashes of the roll around the hips, are clear indications that the idiom of the Gigantomachy was used for this figure in the round: fifth-century devices have been dramatized and exaggerated to produce emotional responses. To be sure, the Zeus/Hero does not show the powerfully fractioned musculature of the Altar sculptures, but his context is epiphanic, not narrative, and a certain conservatism may have been used for a temple image. The imitation of an Athenian monument (the Zeus by Agorakritos?) would also be in keeping with Attalid art. The piecing technique of the Pergamene statue is, however, purely Hellenistic: a major horizontal join separates the upper torso from the draped legs, running just below the mantle roll and partly hidden by small segments of folds added separately. It is significant that this procedure could be used for a temple image, not just for alleged Altar sculptures that could be seen solely from a distance.

PSEUDO-DATED SCULPTURES

With this ambiguous title, I wish to suggest that works traditionally listed in textbooks as firmly dated are instead only tentatively connected to historical events or other circumstances allegedly providing sure chronological underpinnings; in some cases, the association of free-standing sculpture with a building or with a wreck has been taken as a firm date or a reasonably certain *ante quem*, although scholarly debate can continue for individual pieces. I begin my review with perhaps the most famous of all.

Plate 48

The **Nike of Samothrake** (Pl. 48) is one of the glories of the Louvre—one of the "must-see" works in that museum, together with the "Venus de Milo" and the Monna Lisa.[16] We shall discuss the Aphrodite in a later section because of its less definite dating, but the Nike belongs here because it is traditionally associated with the victories obtained in 190/89 by the Rhodian fleet over the Seleukid navy of Antiochos III off Side and Myonnesos.[17] Yet this chronology is based on tenuous grounds, as follows:

1. The style of the Nike is very close to that of the Gigantomachy figures on the

Pergamon Altar. In particular, the rendering of the feathers in the Victory's wings can be paralleled by those of Alkyoneus and of Athena's Nike.

2. The base in the shape of a ship's prow is in Rhodian (Lartian) marble; its importation from that island should mean a dedication by that island.

3. A fragmentary inscription found in the vicinity retains part of the name of a Rhodian, [. . . .]s Rhodios [. . . .], which has been completed as Pythokritos, a known sculptor.

4. Pythokritos signed a rock-cut relief on the akropolis of Lindos, one of the Rhodian cities. The relief is in the shape of a boat's stern, and includes a platform on which a bronze figure stood, probably that of Hagesander, son of Mikion, as suggested by the dedicatory inscription. The combination of a statue and a ship base (probably a trihemiolia) has suggested comparison to the Samothrakian monument.[18] Other ship monuments from Rhodes may indicate a predilection for this type of dedication.

5. In the first half of the second century (especially early during that span, as suggested by argument 1), only the Rhodian fleet was powerful enough to celebrate a naval victory at an island sanctuary.

Each of these points can be rebutted, in order, as follows:

1. The style of the Nike is indeed very close to that of the Pergamene Gigantomachy, but we have seen that the date of the latter is no longer as firm as previously thought. Should a lower chronology be confirmed for the Altar, the Samothrakian monument would be subject to the same shift, thus eliminating connection with the Rhodian naval victories at Side and Myonnesos. Moreover, even authors who accept the similarity with Pergamon (e.g., Carpenter 1960) would stylistically place the Nike *after* the Gigantomachy, further lowering its date. It should also be stressed that there is no evidence of Pergamene style on Rhodes itself, at least as reflected by sculptures found on the island, and that the presence of Rhodians among the carvers of the Altar is no longer taken for granted. Finally, some scholars would date the Nike as early as 250, on the same grounds of style. Point 1, while our most concrete item of evidence, can therefore be viewed with reserve.[19]

2. If provenience of stone were to be considered an index of ownership, the Nike itself should be attributed to Paros! To be sure, Rhodian marble was not frequently exported in antiquity, but its darker, blue-grayish color may have been chosen for contrast with the white medium of the anthropomorphic statue it supported. A Samothrakian sculptor, Hieronymos, worked on Rhodes around 220, and may thus have become acquainted with the type of local stone that he then chose for a monument on his own island.[20] Other scenarios are, of course, possible.

3. Not only is the name entirely restored from a final sigma; it is also uncertain, even unlikely, that the inscription belongs with the Nike, and, as preserved, it gives no indication of being a sculptor's signature rather than, for instance, the name of a dedicant. If other signatures by Pythokritos can be taken into account, he seems to have included his patronymic (son of Timochares) together with his ethnic—and this full

formula is used in the rock-cut monument at Lindos, although he might have been better known on his own island than at Samothrake. In addition, Pythokritos' production is attested only on Rhodes, the nearby Karian coast, and Olympia. Samothrake may have been too far from the sphere of Rhodian activity. We shall return to this issue in discussing point 5; here we may add that Rhodian sculptors are seldom active away from their native territory—except during the (late?) first century, when several seem to have emigrated to Italy—and some are known only through mention in the literary sources.[21]

4. Ship bases are relatively rare; they seem to be primarily a Hellenistic manifestation, the earliest example occurring toward the end of the fourth century. But their distribution is quite wide and forms no pattern: Epidauros, Samothrake, Kyrene, and two from Lindos. The Kyrene ship held a female figure, but certainly not a Nike, at best an Athena, although identification is far from certain, and its associations are with Libya and the Ptolemies. A fragmentary Nike from Tenos, now lost, has occasionally been attributed to a sculptured prow at the site, but there is no assurance that the two went together. The Lindos relief is the parallel most relevant for a Rhodian connection of the Samothrakian monument, yet it is quite different: it consists, first of all, of the stern, not the prow, of a ship; it supported a bronze statue of a human being, probably the man being honored by the demos, Hagesander, in a contrapposto pose suggested by the footprints; finally, it may have included, to the right of the "seats," a sort of naiskos with the relief of a goddess wearing peplos, kalathos, and a foot-length veil—the concept seems entirely at variance with that of the Nike, although allegedly contemporary with it. An earlier ship prow in the round from the Lindian akropolis, backed up against the stoa and facing toward the sea, was also the base for a statue, as suggested by a cutting on the deck, but its nature is unknown, and the fragmentary dedicatory inscription honors a trihemiolia crew of 288 men (= two ships?) as well as two trierarchs: Agathostratos, son of Polyaratos, and Gorgon, son of Archelas. The scale is considerably smaller than that of the Samothrakian monument, and no specific event is cited for the dedication, although the votive can be dated to 265–260 on prosopographical and epigraphic grounds.

To be sure, *monuments* shaped like ships are more numerous, one other being attested for Rhodes, but they supported no sculptured figures and are therefore not comparable. Neither is the narrative Sperlonga group of Odysseus' boat being attacked by Skylla, whose connection with Rhodian masters can only be documented for the end of the first century or later.[22]

One other reference is perhaps relevant. From a private and luxurious house in Segesta, Sicily, come three prow-shaped consoles in limestone, terminating abruptly with a rough surface meant to be inserted into a wall. The prows have holes for metal attachments, and each carries a small square base on the upper deck, perhaps serving a practical function (support for a lamp?) or a commemorative purpose (statuette of divinity, personification, or even house owner?). The house, because of these finds, has been identified as that of "Heraclius, navarchus Segestanus" (Cic. *ad Verr.* 2.5 and passim), who was victorious in a naval battle and died between 73 and 71. The consoles have features in common with the Samothrakian base and have been taken as indication that the local craftsmen had contacts with the East and its monuments. It seems more logical, however, that the Navarch would have embellished his house with replicas of his own fleet—thus invalidating the proposition that the Nike's boat is typically Rhodian.[23]

5. This final point is so strictly dependent on the first one that changes in the first inevitably affect it as well. One additional consideration should be mentioned. As far as is known at present, the Rhodians did not commemorate major events and victories in the same fashion as the Hellenistic monarchs. It has been pointed out that the island "privatized" art and celebrated its maritime power as a global enterprise ascribed to the entire community, thus eliminating propagandistic elements from its sculptures.[24] Individual citizens, magistrates, and admirals were honored by "portrait" statues, but monumental compositions with commemorative character are unknown even from the local sanctuaries. It is surprising that one should have been erected on Samothrake, a site not directly involved in the naval events against Antiochos, and not greatly tied to Rhodes by specific link.[25]

One more corollary could be added to point 5, although less probative than the other arguments. The encounter off Side was "a relatively small-scale affair and not a single ship was sunk." By contrast, that at Myonnesos saw "Rhodes' finest hour." This triumph was achieved primarily through the use of fire baskets: a Rhodian invention that consisted of containers suspended from a pole projecting from the prow that could spill burning material onto enemy ships.[26] Had the Samothrakian monument commemorated such a battle, wouldn't the Nike's base have been equipped with this innovative device? The coins of Demetrios Poliorketes issued for his victory in 306 invariably show the Nike on a boat with a broken prow, suggesting a defeated enemy ship; perhaps this was also the case in Samothrake, but the fragile end of the bow is not preserved, and it is impossible to tell, on present evidence, what the original appearance of the base would have been. Certainly, the Victory was not blowing a trumpet, as on the coins, or holding any other attribute: both of the figure's hands have now been recovered, and both are empty. If Stewart's interpretation is to be credited, the personification (on the symbolic "Ship of State," the victor's ship) would have made a gesture of greeting on entering port; according to Lehmann, the ship (a Samothrakian vessel) was "sailing forth" from the Aegean harbor. It is obvious that many readings of this spectacular monument are possible.[27]

The preceding discussion has served to point out the uncertain basis of all our assumptions. We should now turn to the sculptures themselves, both the ship and the Nike.

I am not competent to answer the question of the type of boat represented by the Nike's base. An expert's opinion I solicited holds that not enough of the vessel is preserved to define it with certainty. The two levels of oars and their box suggest that it is a cataphract, whereas the trihemiolia is an aphract vessel. Were it correct that a tri-hemiolia is depicted, we would be no closer to its ethnic identity, since the type was widely used by all Hellenistic, and even Roman, navies. Anathyrosis on the forward faces of the rounded elements above and toward the rear of the outriggers (oarboxes, parexeiresiai) as currently preserved, together with semicircular beddings in front of them, suggests that some pieces were separately attached, but I do not know whether they served a purely ornamental purpose that might have contributed to identification. Traces of paint on the proper right side of the prow, if they could be read, may supply additional information.[28]

The ship base rests on a series of six slabs carved to resemble rippling waves, with attachment holes perhaps to fasten sea animals or other landscape elements. A deep groove runs diagonally on the upper surface, and probably served for the setting of the ship prow, which at present is, however, axially located. The effect of the "waves" would certainly have been enhanced had water run across them, and indeed one of the major attractions of the entire monument has been the surmise that it once stood in a fountain, on the upper of two basins, the lower one filled with boulders to suggest a perilous shore. Yet it seems now assured that the retaining wall surrounding the basins is of Roman date, that the terracotta pipes within the structure do not lead to it but under it, perhaps to the theater, and may also be Roman; finally, the interior limestone surfaces of both basins were stuccoed, rather than waterproofed or sealed with cement, which is atypical for fountains, since stucco is corroded by water.[29] Although a watery surround would have enhanced the realistic effect of the surging prow, it should be noted that all other ship monuments in the round, even the one at Lindos, were in purely urban settings without illusionistic landscaping; the Samo-thrakian vessel, had it stood in cascading water, would have represented a considerable exception, anticipating by over a century some of the effects obtained by the Romans

Plate 49   (Pl. 49).[30]

Yet some specific planning had gone into the setting of the Nike. The monument was especially visible and accessible not only from the long stoa to the west, but also, as recently argued, from the theater almost directly below it. Indeed, from the orchestra, the Nike and her vessel would have appeared as if towering over the cavea, visually in contact with the last rows of seats. The Aphrodite-like appearance of the Nike —her transparent drapery, her slipping neckline barely covering her right breast— would have emphasized the erotic allure of the figure as traditional since the fifth-century representations, hinting at a connection between Venus and the theater that would have great currency in Roman times. The Samothrakian theater is currently dated around 200, which would almost require for the Nike a later date, if the juxta-position of the two was intentional.[31]

The Victory has usually been described in terms of her tumultuous costume, twirled by the wind against her shapely body. At the site, near the place where the monument was set up, today's visitor can feel the wind blowing uphill from the sea, so that the Nike's rendering would have appeared thoroughly justified. In addition, anyone who has stood on the bow of a moving ship knows the force of the wind generated by the motion even through a calm sea. I am therefore not sure that viewers of the sculpture would have thought of a storm-tossed vessel overcoming difficult circumstances. The boulders on the lower basin may not have been there originally (the area was greatly disturbed by time and various phases of excavations), or, if intentionally placed, would not have been directly in contact with the ship base.

The Nike, originally made from several separate pieces, was recovered in many fragments; her entire right wing and, more significantly, the left shoulder where it meets the other (mostly preserved) wing have been restored in plaster. The arrangement of the mantle on that side is therefore unclear, and partly unclear also is the fluttering panel of cloth that "flares behind the Nike like a rudder to her airborne flight."[32] In antiquity, color contrast would have helped to separate the mantle from the chiton, making the draping intelligible. At present, it takes a second glance to realize that the heavy mantle descending from the left shoulder is worn with an overfold, one tip of which is free to fly out behind the figure, while the main part of the cloth wraps around her right hip and cascades between her legs. From the front, the edge of this overfold is only visible over the right leg, at mid-shin; the true hem of the mantle would have appeared at ankle level, at the place where a smooth surface was created to attach the separately carved foot—yet the material covering the lower leg has been rendered as if thin and transparent, misleadingly suggesting that it is part of the chiton rather than the himation. Only repeated circling around the statue can now confirm the layering of the two garments.

Besides the overfold, the himation also forms a twisted roll that encircles the advanced thigh and falls in between the legs with a highly dramatic effect of light and shadow. The Nike's left leg is entirely free of this covering, in profile creating a long oblique line from trailing left foot to advanced right shoulder, but the visual ascent is broken by the minor accent of the chiton twirling forward, as if blown by its own gusts of wind. On the front, the edge of the chiton meets the mantle roll to create a wide V-pattern over the pubic area; yet this is not a true edge, since the thickness and crinkling of some folds where they turn upward conveys the hint of a double layer. The Nike's chiton should therefore be visualized as belted twice: once, visibly, just below the breasts and then, invisibly, above the hips—the apparent hem of the apoptygma is in fact the lower contour of a deep kolpos. All this doubling of garments—both chiton and himation—could be understandable if the Nike were a young girl not fully grown, dressed in overlarge clothes; yet her body is that of a mature woman, and her proportions in relation to the ship confirm her heroic size. The extra richness of her attire is therefore simply a way of adding movement and contrast to her figure, in a true "Baroque" spirit.[33]

There is no point here in emphasizing the torsion of the Victory's body, the transparency of her garment that reveals the straining ribcage and the swelling abdomen with the indentation of the navel. The surface of the costume is highly belabored, and many arrow folds lead the eye in ever-breaking directions; the layered neckline delimits a smooth expanse of solid flesh over the breasts, and the ruffled feathers provide one more textural contrast. I was able to examine some fragments at close quarters and was amazed at the animation of the feathers' surface with "fingerprint" depressions, almost as if they had been modeled in clay. The sharpness of the carving looks to me different from the more voluminous Pergamene renderings, but the stylistic idiom is the same. The seemingly elongated proportions may have been dictated by the high base and the intended viewpoint.

Who could have dedicated this naval monument? Samothrake was primarily patronized by the Antigonids and the Ptolemies, who left conspicuous traces of their benefactions to the sanctuary. The Ptolemies had an important navy and, during the third century, were in control of the Aegean islands, but the date of the Nike (whether just before or just after the Pergamon Gigantomachy) seems incompatible with a Ptolemaic dedication. The Attalids have been suggested as possible sponsors, yet to my knowledge there are no other traces of their presence on the island. The Macedonians eventually used the sanctuary as a place of asylum, but Perseus, in flight and in fear for his life, would hardly have had time for such an expensive (and triumphant) offering. Philip V may be a better candidate, since he assumed control of the Ptolemaic territories in Thrake around 202–199, and a base for a monumental bronze statue of him has been found in the center of the temenos. The Samothrakians themselves had a fleet, as is natural for an island, and put nautical devices on their coins. At this point, it seems impossible to pinpoint the actual donor of the monument, although the Rhodians seem to me the least probable of the suggested powers: note that the two Lindian ship bases were set up to honor the valor and good will of individuals, not specific events.[34]

Can style provide a better lead to attribution? The Nike of Samothrake seems to stand in dramatic isolation because possible comparisons are either lost or too fragmentary to be better known. It seems logical to look first on the island itself, where presumably sculptural activity was taking place at the so-called **Hieron,** either in the late third or the mid-second century, and since at least one scholar has considered the Nike a commemoration of the Samothrakian navy. Yet parallels are not readily available. The Hellenistic **Nike akroterion,** despite the similar subject, is excessively elongated, gracile in bodily forms, stiff in her drapery, with long straight folds in her himation anchoring her down and virtually no textural differentiation; to be sure, her mantle is worn with an overfold and a waist roll, but it runs across the body in front and barely marks the body beneath. A much better parallel, at least in terms of a general Baroque effect, is the lower half of a **female figure** usually—albeit controversially—attributed to the north (front) pediment of the same building, yet in individual details its difference from the Victory is striking. The figure's short mantle opens up to reveal the advanced left leg covered by a crinkly chiton, but the latter, both above and below the himation, is entirely covered by fine incisions that produce an almost fleecy effect. The himation itself is heavy, with engraved press folds and coarse drill channels slashed through its roll, and with a major valley approximately following the contour of the right thigh.[35]

One particular **Nike, from Tenos,** has been called the "sister" of the Samothrakian Victory. We have already mentioned this piece, now regrettably lost. The one published photograph shows a torso preserved approximately from the breasts (damaged) to mid-thighs, just at the point where the apoptygma of the peplos seems to end. The left leg was forward, partly delineated by adhering drapery; swirling, trumpet-like folds with contrasting motion outlined the stomach area, with navel and swelling abdomen revealed by transparency, although less obvious than in the Samothrakian Nike. The high position of the girdle is also comparable. A true study of this sculpture is lacking, and even its status as a Victory is uncertain; that it stood on a ship prow, simply because one is known to have existed on the island, is pure assumption. Dedicant and occasion are equally unknown.[36]

The island of **Kos** has produced several **Nikai,** one of which is said to resemble the Samothrakian Victory in the unusual rendering of a rounded belt without fluttering ends and visible knot. The lifesize torso is preserved only in the areas just above and just below the girdle, but enough remains to show that a shoulder cord runs from the left armpit to the nape; the costume is probably a chiton with a long apoptygma. The body is described as unusually thick and preserving cuttings for the attachment of wings, presumably in bronze. It is currently dated to the second half of the third century and considered a forerunner of "Euboulides' Nike," but it seems possibly later to me. A **Swinging or Dancing Figure** also from Kos used to be considered a Victory, largely on analogy to the Samothrakian statue, but further study has ascertained the definite lack of wings in the back. The statue, recomposed from two large fragments, lacks head, shoulders, both arms and feet, part of the mantle roll over the left hip, and minor parts of drapery; it is an impressive sculpture nonetheless, with the same effects of transparency over the abdominal area as the Samothrakian Nike. Yet what at first glance look like folds of the thin chiton are instead the fluttering ends of the belt tied high under the breasts with a Herculean knot. The mantle is short, its lower edge barely visible on the thigh just above the break and in between the legs. The right leg is advanced, and acts almost like a prow cleaving the waves formed by the chiton folds on either side of the shin. If the general appearance of the figure vaguely recalls the Nike, once again, individual details are not close enough for immediate comparison. This difference between Koan sculptures and the Samothrakian monument does not, however, provide support against a Rhodian attribution of the latter. As several authors have now noted, despite geographic proximity and traditional assumptions, Kos was not dependent on Rhodes for its artistic inspiration.[37]

One more **torso, in the Boston Museum of Fine Arts** (Pl. 50), has frequently been Plate 50 compared to both the Koan pieces and the Samothrakian Nike; it has even been attributed to Rhodes, but on stylistic grounds, since it was actually found in Rome or its environs. Although the missing back may have been removed in later times, the statue was made in at least five pieces (head and neck, both arms, and lower body at the curve of the mantle roll over the pubic area, of which traces remain). What is now left is therefore the upper torso of a woman wearing a transparent chiton belted high below the breasts by a long cord with looped ends. The navel is so clearly indicated as to look almost uncovered, and fine ridges articulate the major folds of the garment, conveying its diaphanous texture. A slight torsion is suggested by the direction of the hips, which contrasts with that of the breasts. Although an impressive piece of carving, this sculpture cannot help in pinpointing the date and donor of the Samothrakian Nike.[38]

Our final comparison is the **so-called Nike of Euboulides**, already mentioned above in discussing a Koan torso. Both identification and attribution have now been questioned, thus eliminating a more or less firm chronological bracket.[39] Euboulides, son of Eucheir, belongs to a family of Athenian sculptors with recurrent, alternating names, active in the third and second centuries; specifically, the Euboulides in question (III) is usually considered an exponent of the Classicizing movement because an Athena head of colossal size has been attributed to him on the basis of findspot, inscription, and connection with a passage in Pausanias (1.2.5) citing a group of statues that he saw in the area of the Kerameikos. Yet the text can be variously read to state that Euboulides was the maker either of the entire group (Athena Paionia, Zeus, Mnemosyne, the Muses, Apollo, and Akratos) or (as I would agree) only of the Apollo, for which the Periegete specifies that it was dedicated by its artist. Together with the Athena head, a female torso and a second head were found (in 1837), as well as an inscription — *[Euboulides Eu]cheiros Kropides epoiesen* — that was attributed to the remains of a podium allegedly for the entire group. The second female figure was therefore also given to Euboulides and, because of cuttings on her back, was identified as a Nike, although this personification was not included in Pausanias' list. Despite some initial controversy, this became the accepted scholarly position.

The alarm was first sounded by Gulaki (1981), who reviewed the earlier publications and made a strong case for separating the Nike from the Athena. Stylistically, the two are quite different, she argued: the first, a Victory with bronze wings separately added, belongs around 220 and can be fully visualized thanks to echoes in other Nike figures; the second, probably by Euboulides, imitates the Athena Velletri type and may be correctly placed in the late second century. The difference in style between the two heads seems to me so strong that I would agree that they are also chronologically distant, although I find the Athena almost too Classical for the time of Euboulides and perhaps considerably later.[40] The important point here, however, is that by separating the two works we have lost the firm dating for the Nike, which was provided by the connection with a "known" sculptor.

Original Statuary in the Round

Stylistically, however, the comparison with the Samothrakian Nike could still be useful, regardless of the proper identification of the Athenian figure. She appears in motion to her left, although her head is strongly turned to her right; there may still be some doubt about the connection of head and torso, but for our purposes this issue is irrelevant. The colossal goddess wears a chiton belted high below the breast with a flat ribbon; its Herculean knot is flanked by drill holes presumably for the attachment of the two ends. What is preserved of the shoulders confirms a V-neckline without slippage and two full breasts underpinned by regular folds. Under the belt, the garment is characterized by pendant concentric semicircles—a peculiar mannerism conveying the impression of a thick cloth and absent in the Samothrakian Nike. Yet over the abdominal area the rendering becomes "transparent," with the navel clearly indicated and narrowly framed by two trumpet folds. No traces of a mantle are apparent, and the hips are not prominent in the almost cylindrical torso. If these observations carry any chronological value, the Athenian sculpture should be earlier than the Samothrakian Nike, although a date after 200 seems to me possible.[41]

Yet I am wary of making such a suggestion. The stylistic link could lead from the Koan Nike through the Athenian piece to the Samothrakian Victory, in approximate spans of a quarter-century each; nonetheless, I find the leap from the second to the third sculpture almost impossible. Except for an indication of a body in motion, the two have little in common—the Louvre figure shows torsion and balance, and transparent effects are too widespread to suggest influences, although the trumpet folds may be more distinctive. They certainly recur, in many variant forms, on the Pergamon Altar.[42]

To conclude this lengthy review: I would tend—no doubt arbitrarily—to date the Nike of Samothrake around the time of the Pergamon Gigantomachy, perhaps around 160, which could effectively separate it from a Rhodian victory at Myonnesos. I would not exclude Pergamene influences. I would here stress that the piece should no longer be seen in isolation or compared only with other naval monuments, but should be accepted in the context of a series of stylistically related sculptures, although these come from the entire Aegean area—including, to some extent but more remotely, Athens—and none of them can be firmly dated. If indeed a victory commemoration, I would believe the Nike to have been sponsored by a ruling dynasty rather than by an oligarchic democracy, but could accept it as a generic dedication symbolic of power without connection to specific military events.[43]

If, however, the Nike of Samothrake is indeed a monument celebrating a decisive naval encounter, it would fall within the tradition of commemorations that convey success through mythological allusions or symbols. Nike, it has been pointed out, is only a messenger, not an agent, of victory, yet her supernatural status as a personification shifts the glory from the mortals to the immortals. Every other military event seems to have been memorialized by the dedications of captured weapons and rostra, by sculptures of lions (as guardians of the dead and embodiment of bravery, as at Chaironeia), of Nikai (that by Paionios, after the Battle of Sphakteria being perhaps the most famous), or of patron deities (the Colossus of Rhodes, Helios, after the failed siege by Demetrios Poliorketes in 304), or through reliefs narrating mythological battles—Amazonomachies, Kentauromachies, Gigantomachies. Even the relief from Kyzikos (firmly dated to 277/6 because of its inscription) attributes the defeat of the Galatian enemy to Herakles.[44]

A true shift in this tradition may begin with Alexander, who can appear in a fighting context in direct visual relation to his opponents. Yet such depictions occur either in paintings (e.g., the inspiration behind the Alexander Mosaic) or as part of sarcophagi and funerary monuments (Abdalonymos' casket, perhaps the Lefkadia Great Tomb). It has been therefore assumed that a real innovation took place only with the Pergamene dedications commemorating victory not through portrayal of the victorious party, but through that of the defeated enemies *alone.* The emphasis here has been on the absence of the winners and on the shift in focus to the losers, without divine intervention or allusion. But is this notion correct?[45]

This would not be the place to discuss the **Larger and Smaller Attalid Dedications,** which, at best, are known only through Roman copies. I continue to be convinced that even the works that have come down to us are Roman creations and adaptations, *not* true replicas of the monuments in Pergamon and Athens, and strongly decry the scholarly tendency to connect with the events in Asia Minor all depictions of "barbarians," regardless of their findspots and chronology. In addition, I still maintain that both the Smaller and the Larger Dedications were made by Attalos I, thus falling before and even at the very turn into the century under consideration. Here, after discussing the Nike of Samothrake, I simply wish to emphasize that even the monument in Athens—which, on Pausanias' authority (1.25.2), included "the destruction of the Gauls in Mysia"—elevated the event to the mythical sphere by depicting it together with Gigantomachy, Amazonomachy, and Marathonomachy, all encounters of long-standing epic status. Whether we can recapture the appearance of the Akropolis dedication is of secondary importance compared with the undisputed fact that the Pergamenes chose traditional Athenian themes to rank themselves as the next in line after such glorious achievements, thus paying a direct compliment to the Mainland Greeks while indirectly glorifying themselves.[46]

One more pseudo-date is that assigned to a peculiar composition which should count as a relief, in that it was anchored to a background, yet its component figures were worked in the round, thus deserving to be included in this chapter: the **Prometheus Group from Pergamon.** This unusual work consists of three pieces. A male figure reclining on rocky ground is traditionally identified as a personification of Mount Kaukasos, where the mythological event took place; Prometheus is represented by a now headless naked male fastened by means of a dowel to what must have been a rendering of a rock, while an attachment hole on his raised right leg probably served to secure the eagle torturing him; finally, a Herakles in the pose of a shooting archer must have shown the hero freeing the Titan from his punishment. The fragments of this group were found in the debris of the North Stoa within the Athena Sanctuary at Pergamon, and were soon attributed to one of the niches (alternately Doric and Ionic) that were assumed to decorate the wall of the portico at the level of the first story. Attention focused almost immediately on the alleged portrait-like features of the Herakles, and the myth was taken as an allegory of Mithradates VI's efforts to liberate the Greeks in Asia Minor from the Roman threat—a theory supported also on grounds of style, which was considered compatible with a first-century date. Although this chronology was generally accepted, other scholars claimed that the Herakles represented one of the Attalid kings, yet no agreement could be reached on the specific ruler portrayed. In recent years, the group has received renewed attention, partly because it was included in two exhibitions, one of which comprised also slabs from the Telephos Frieze. Yet a thorough study of the monument published in 1998 reaches new conclusions: not only that the composition, as reconstructed, takes up more space than the width of a single niche, but also that the subject should be seen in the context of the entire Athena Nikephoros temenos, as part of a concerted message of Attalid victory propaganda. The specific myth would be a corollary to the Telephos Frieze in emphasizing Attalid descent from Herakles. The date of the sculptures should be more or less contemporary with the erection of the stoa under Eumenes II and perhaps also his brother Attalos II, around 160–150.[47]

This chronology would make the Prometheus Group virtually contemporary with the sculptures of the Great Altar, yet the style of its figures has been described as substantially different. In particular, Prometheus' body, while muscular, appears almost Classical in its rendering, and the mantle enveloping Kaukasos is thick and opaque, hiding the underlying forms. Although these comments are valid, I would rather stress the elements that connect the two works: the many press folds and the tense arrow folds together with the looping grooves of the Kaukasos' himation, the sternal ridges on Prometheus and the drilled grooves delineating his right biceps and left calf, the highly textured lionskin on Herakles that recalls Asterie's dog. Even Herakles' wide eyes can be found on some of the Giants from the Altar, and the spatial arrangement of the figures recurs on the Telephos Frieze.[48] I am convinced that subject matter, level of viewing, and intended location played a large role in determining stylistic conventions and would have no difficulty in dating the Prometheus Group together with the North Stoa.

A similar situation—a "retrospective style" perhaps chosen because of meaning and location—occurs in conjunction with three statues found within the Pergamon Library and probably created at the time of its erection, under Eumenes II. This connection would ensure a placement within the first half of the second century or toward the middle of it, yet, once again, dating is relative, especially since the style is not distinctive or, to put it differently, is not immediately comparable to that of the Great Altar. As usual, we tend to use that monument as the touchstone for every other sculpture from the Mysian city.

One of these statues—a Hera/Aphrodite apparently inspired by Alkamenes' Prokne and Itys from the Athenian Akropolis—is so coherent in its imitation of fifth-century traits that it need not detain us here, although the work is clearly an adaptation rather than a true creation in Classical style. But the **adaptation of the Athena Parthenos** and an **Athena with a crossed aigis** deserve attention, albeit brief, since others have treated them at great length.[49]

The **Parthenos** is the more frankly Hellenistic of the two. Although her drapery pattern follows the general appearance of the Athenian prototype, her cloth has been rendered as thinner, her folds are more belabored, her proportions slenderer, and her stance shows a slight movement (her right shoulder dips) that makes her less hieratic than the original. Also her face seems different, if one can judge from the Roman copies of the Pheidian masterpiece; yet, regardless of its faithfulness, it is important to note the clear drill holes at the corners of the mouth, a technical trait usually attributed to Roman copyists, and the perfunctory finish of the statue's back, obviously not meant to be seen. The slenderness of the figure is at present enhanced by the absence of the attributes that helped to expand the original composition sideways, but a hole in the base, traditionally interpreted as supporting her spear, has now been seen as the fastening point for either the shield or the snake. Even the helmet type, currently restored with a single crest, may originally have held the three of the prototype, added separately in metal. The plaster restoration has misleadingly changed it into a more Hellenistic form—or at least one that recurs on the Altar Gigantomachy and the weapon frieze of the Athena temenos. On the assumption that her attributes were intentionally omitted, it has usually been stressed that the goddess is here portrayed not as the defender of the city but as the source of wisdom, as appropriate for a library; but Niemeier (1985, 118–19) has also noted that by "modernizing" the prototype, the Pergamenes signaled that they not only followed tradition but also carried it forward. We may add that the story of Pandora, repeated from the original for the Pergamene base, may here have had a meaning different from that in Athens, obscure as the latter may still be. In the context of the Library, the myth may have alluded to the contents of the volumes in the building, the gifts of the goddess, or the very creation of sculpture (Pandora, the first *statue*) and therefore of the visual arts.[50]

For all its "modernization," the Parthenos did not share the dramatic style of the Great Altar—yet it could not have been taken for a fifth-century work. By contrast, the **Athena with the crossed aigis** is so eclectic that the statue was initially considered a copy of Myron's Athena for Samos. More recent analyses have emphasized its discrepant traits, especially its pyramidal contour with wide base and narrow shoulders, typical of the Hellenistic period, and the unusual form of the aigis, with its lively snakes that must be a second-century invention. Another invention should be the belt, formed by two snakes tied together—mostly hidden by the kolpos but with heads shown in front, tails on the back of the figure, whose surface is finished as carefully as the front. I would add the slumped pose with shoulders back, which recurs in many Classicizing works. Yet there is no denying the "Severe" rendering of the face and the Classical shape of the sandals, together with a handling of drapery that strongly echoes works datable around 430.[51]

The same building complex (the Library) therefore housed three works chronologically related to the Great Altar but stylistically entirely different not only from it, but also from each other, in their various degrees of imitation of Classical prototypes and forms. That Attalid Pergamon was capable of such a range highlights the danger of dating purely in terms of style. This Classicizing current within the Mysian city has been attributed to its rulers' interest in copying Classical masterpieces; yet Classicizing trends, if defined as deliberate imitation or quotation of earlier forms, occur in other areas of the Greek world, almost simultaneously. The point can be illustrated by our final example of a "pseudo-date."

The piece in question is a colossal statue of **Nike from Hierapytna** (modern Hierapetra) in Crete, now in Venice (Pl. 51). Some misinformation on this sculpture has appeared in previous publications, but recent archival finds and discussion have finally clarified its true position. The story is made more complex by the fact that the image was reworked during the Roman period and turned into an Athena. A large head added at that time (Pl. 52) may have belonged to an akrolithic image of the goddess perhaps contemporary with the Nike, whose original head was probably carved in one piece with the body. Wings in bronze, once set within cuttings in the back, provide identification for a figure whose static pose differs considerably from the lively renderings of Nikai common since the Archaic period, but the type of the Victory at rest begins in the last quarter of the fourth century and was obviously the inspiration behind the Cretan composition, on an island not known for its sculptural production. Also "Classical" is the costume: a chiton visible on the extant right arm below a full peplos with long apoptygma belted below a short, horizontal kolpos. Thin straps tied at the high waist and across the chest meet at a central gorgoneion in metal that may have been added when the folds over the breasts were smoothed to allow the superimposition of a bronze aigis. A lost inscription, poorly transcribed by Onorio Belli in the early sixteenth century, provides the name of the otherwise unknown sculptor, Damokrates from the nearby site of Itanos. The Nike has been dated shortly after 145, when Hierapytna destroyed the neighboring city of Praisos, since a major event must have prompted such a sizable sculpture, but no external evidence exists to support the dating, and the style of the figure is too "Classical" to provide a clearer chronology. I was surprised, on personal inspection, to note how harsh is the rendering of the vertical folds of the skirt, and how shallow and flat that of the chiton pleats over the upper arm. Both recall Roman works; is the provincial location of Hierapetra sufficient to explain these stylistic features? Or was the entire drapery sharpened and

Plate 51

Plate 52

recarved when the iconographic changes were made? Yet the pattern of the costume, if not its ultimate execution, is sufficient to earn the statue its Classicizing label. The Athena head, on the other hand, although cold and smooth, is more in keeping with late second-century forms.[52]

We shall return to the issue of the Classicizing movement in discussing cult images and their masters, but a brief comment should be added here. Under the rubric of "pseudo-dates" we could include several objects recovered from the Mahdia ship, which is currently thought to have foundered during the first half of the first century, perhaps around 70 B.C. The sculptural finds exhibit great range—from figures in Baroque style to others with Classicizing forms, from genre pieces in single version to works known from other replicas and allegedly attributable to specific masters, and even to "signed" objects that may, however, carry the label of a foundry rather than of a sculptor. Because it is difficult to distinguish between items made ad hoc for immediate export and those removed from earlier contexts as a form of trade in antiquities, the *terminus ante quem* set by the approximate time of the shipwreck is of only relative value; yet it should be emphasized that its cargo has already provided a surprisingly early date for some types (e.g., the so-called Stephanos Athlete) that used to be considered products of a much later period. We shall discuss a few examples in the chapter on copies.[53]

SCULPTURES DATED ON STYLISTIC GROUNDS

The majority of original works extant have been assigned to the second century solely on stylistic grounds, which, as we have seen, can be occasionally misleading. Even the tenuous lead of what I have called a pseudo-date is missing, and it is therefore impossible to discuss any item with confidence. In addition, a vast number of pieces belong to the category of honorary statues or of anonymous, unidentifiable subjects, so that only statistical summaries seem meaningful. On the other hand, a few sculptures stylistically dated to our period are among the most famous Hellenistic originals and deserve mention. I shall attempt to strike a balance in discussing individual topics.

My task is made easier by some studies that have covered the entire Hellenistic production of a certain site or have investigated specific sculptural types through the pertinent time range. One such study, by Renate Kabus-Preißhofen, discusses the monuments found on the **island of Kos** and isolates a local sculptural manner that, in her opinion, is distinctive enough to prevail through different chronological and stylistic phases, in turn being quite different from the styles current on Rhodes, Samos, and centers on the coast of Asia Minor. The body types are massive, with limbs barely articulated. Drapery has widely spaced surfaces within bundles of folds leading the eye and emphasizing body contours. A love of details results in distinctive treatment, some of it mannered. Yet the lack of original context (many important monuments from various periods, including the Roman, were found in a cache of sculpture within the substructure of the Roman Odeion) and of external evidence (such as statue bases with helpful inscriptions) means that the sequential arrangement established by the author is inevitably subjective, even if apparently logical, because of the very nature of any formal classification.

In a rough count, from a total of 116 catalogued items ranging from the late fourth century to Roman Imperial times, 35 have been assigned to the second century or to the years immediately around 100, thus implying sustained, if not considerable, sculptural activity during that span of time. Some of the pieces are over-lifesize, including some that were undoubtedly meant as portraits and were therefore honorary; a **colossal female head** may, however, depict a divinity and is the only one to exhibit Pergamene traits: very large eyes, parted lips, triangular forehead framed by ropelike strands of hair crowned by a diadem.[54]

A study by K. Höghammar complements Kabus-Preißhofen's in approaching the Hellenistic sculpture of Kos from an epigraphic and literary angle. Yet even this attempt has provided uncertain dates for the 91 works that are known from inscribed statue bases ranging from the early Hellenistic to the early Imperial period. A high percentage of such statues have significant honorary character, although the line between honorary and dedicatory is often nonexistent. Most statues seem to have been commissioned by Koans for Koans, but no Koan artist signed his pedestals, and therefore no local school can be identified on the basis of signatures. If statistics of this nature can be considered valid (given the absence of absolute chronology), the second century may have seen a decrease in sculptural production, but distribution (town versus Asklepieion versus other locations) appears relatively stable throughout, and no clear preference for marble over bronze is noticeable except for the normal practice of using the latter for portraits and the former for images of the gods. This conclusion contrasts somewhat with the actual remains of sculpture from the island, as catalogued by Kabus-Preißhofen, but bronzes are seldom preserved, and the two pictures coincide in a general sense.[55]

A typological study of **equestrian bronzes** is equally based on pedestals and inscriptions rather than on extant statuary, and it would therefore seem irrelevant for this chapter, but its percentages for the second century reveal the startling penetration of the Romans into the Greek sphere and show that the rider type is no longer the prerogative of kings. Although the Attalids, one Seleukid, one Ptolemy, the Numidian king Masinissa, Prousias of Bithynia, and, potentially, Perseus of Macedonia rated the honor of equestrian monuments, others were erected for private individuals (e.g., Diodoros Pasparos, son of Herodes of Pergamon; Isagoras and Menekrates, sons of Pherekrates of Larisa; Kallikrates of Leontion; Damon of Patras) and for various Roman consuls, praetors, and other officials. These Italians, however, were commemorated only at Delphi and Olympia, the earliest being M. Acilius Glabrio, at Delphi, in 191/90. These epigraphic studies make us realize how much we have lost, and how different our total picture of ancient monuments would be had all these honorary sculptures survived.[56]

Hellenistic Sculpture II

Plates 53a–b

A typological study of **seated female statues** focuses on originals, but despite its wider span (from the Classical through the entire Imperial period) and selection (including terracottas), it lists a mere 148 items, of which only six, in stone, belong to the second century, and five of them come from Pergamon, presumably from the Altar and therefore need not be treated here. The sixth, a **seated figure from Kyzikos** (Pls. 53a–b), is over-lifesize and may represent a goddess because of her scale and her elaborate footstool decorated with vegetal motifs in relief; Kore has been suggested, since her veiled image is shown on the city's coins. The marble figure, headless and armless but with a slight torsion of her upper body to proper right, is in frank Hellenistic style, with narrow shoulders, high waist, and elongated legs. She wears a thin chiton characterized by flat ribbon folds that, over her torso, look almost like individual strips of material; it is belted immediately below the very full breasts, made almost too obvious by the taut material that bunches, however, in V-folds between them. A heavy mantle descends from her (missing) head and covers her lap, but the chiton, now rendered in bundled masses with deep carving between them, reappears over the lower legs. Her attire and pose are typical of a Muse, but this identification is incompatible with her throne (a Muse would sit on a rock). The Kyzikos statue has been dated to the mid-second century, but its treatment is quite different from the almost doughy surfaces of most Pergamene seated figures, and its proportions make me think it might be somewhat later.[57]

Draped standing women of the Hellenistic period have been the subject of two major monographs. The earlier, by R. Horn (1931), includes also Roman copies; the second, by A. Linfert (1976), attempts a distribution by centers. Neither is exempt from difficulties, yet both present a type that we have come to consider typical of second-century creations: a heavily draped figure wearing an extremely transparent, looping mantle or shawl that lies like a cobweb over a female body characterized by wide hips and pyramidal contours, spreading at the base over a rich chiton. The transparency effects of the himatia probably imitated the so-called *Coae vestes* mentioned by Roman writers and made of Koan silk, yet **Kos** itself has retained few examples of the type. **Pergamon** has yielded some more (cf. Pls. 23–25), and we have already discussed the Kleopatra on Delos (cf. Pls. 46–47). One exquisite **statuette**

Plate 54

leaning on an Archaistic support comes from **Melos** (Pl. 54), a larger **statue, from Erythrai,** is signed by the sculptor Apollodoros of Phokaia, son of Zenon, and we have some **examples from Samos** and **from Magnesia,** the latter center being perhaps the one more closely associated with the style. An impressive **figure from the**

Plate 55

north area of the Letoon near Xanthos (Pl. 55), albeit recomposed from innumerable fragments, is of interest also because of its piecing technique—the two main blocks forming the body join along an oblique surface that slants forward and to proper right. The woman's chiton is highly textured, her veil/mantle highly transparent, her contour strongly pyramidal with wide hips. Possible influences from Kos and Magnesia have been suggested; the rendering is, however, too ubiquitous to isolate its origin, although the type, developing from third-century prototypes like the Baker Dancer, deserves to be considered in any survey of the second century.[58]

Other female types are closer to the so-called Tragoidia from Pergamon (cf. Pl. 22) in the lack of transparency of their mantles and the massiveness of their skirts, scored by deep valleys. I shall mention only one under-lifesize **statue from Soloeis (Soluntum),** because of its unusual provenience, from a Punic site in Sicily (Pl. 56). It was found within a private house, probably fallen from an upper floor, where it might have been part of a domestic shrine. Although clearly East Greek in style and marble, this Hera/Demeter type with youthful head and hipshot pose was probably used as an Astarte-Tinit and attests to the export and wide distribution of works produced by Asia Minor/island workshops.[59]

Plate 56

A monograph on **draped standing men** comparable to those on the women seems less satisfactory and somewhat unbalanced. Out of 89 items there catalogued, which include some Roman works, as many as 60 are said to belong to the second century or ca. 100. To be sure, these totals might be affected by the peculiar distribution, the chances of the finds, and the availability of published material, since, of the 60 examples of mantled figures assigned to our specific period, no fewer than 18 are from Rhodes or Kos. Yet some pieces are previously unpublished, and an appendix lists additional works without dates. The figures are grouped according to six standard types (including a few variants), and a seventh category gathers the items that do not follow specific prototypes. Many of the second-century pieces are fragmentary, but some of them are major sculptures, like the already-discussed Dioskourides from Delos (cat. I.1), Zeus/Hero and Zeus Ammon from Pergamon (cat. nos. V.2, 3), and the two male figures currently attributed to the superstructure of the Great Altar (cat. V.22, 23). Some items are statuettes, including two of Sarapis; several represent Asklepios, and a large figure is often considered a depiction of Alexander the Great from Magnesia (cat. V.20; dated third quarter of the second century). A statue of Type III (cat. 6), from Samos, dated ca. 100, is signed by Apollonides Ephesios, underscoring the limited reliability of findspots in determining local styles. That this material can be grouped by types is also an indication of the high degree of standardization prevalent during the Hellenistic period for honorary statues and for some divinities as well.[60]

One major mantled statue is the **Poseidon from Melos,** now in the National Museum in Athens (Pl. 57). This impressive sculpture has received monographic treatment and is often cited, but it has usually been seen in isolation. Technical and compositional similarities, and findspots not widely separated from each other, allow a comparison with the even better known **Aphrodite from Melos,** or, as traditionally called, the Venus de Milo (Pl. 58). Because a thorough treatment of both pieces as products of the same workshop is forthcoming, only a few comments will be made in this context.[61]

Plate 57

Plate 58

It is generally believed that the Aphrodite was found "not far from an ancient theater" (Havelock 1995, 93; Hamiaux 1998, 44), but in reality it lay within a Hellenistic/Roman gymnasion and stadion, in front of one of several niches occupied by statuary. The quadrangular niche closest to the Aphrodite, which in fact still contained some of its fragments, was inscribed: *ΒΑΚΧΙΟΣ Σ ΑΤΙΟΥ ΥΠΟΓΥ[ΜΝΑ ΣΙΑΡΧΗΣ]ΑΣ ΤΑΝ ΤΕ ΕΞΕΔΡΑΝ ΚΑΙ ΤΟ [ΑΓΑΛΜΑ] ΕΡΜΑΙ ΗΡΑΚΛΕΙ—* "Bacchios, son of S[extus] Atius, when he was sub-gymnasiarch, (dedicated) this exedra and the [statue] to Hermes and Herakles." The letter forms, as well as the patronymic of the dedicant, indicate a strong Roman influence that should be no earlier than 166, when Delos became a free port, after which date Roman expansion within the Kyklades flourished. If the Aphrodite indeed stood within the exedra, we know who dedicated it and to whom, and it should not surprise to find the goddess of love at home in a place of high physical activity. In addition, the original appearance of the figure may suggest that she is not a true Aphrodite but an Aphrodite-like personification, or Tyche, of the city of Melos. Although the sculpture is presently exhibited without arms, fragments of both the upper and lower left arm were originally found, with the hand holding an apple. The allusion could be to the golden fruit meant "for the fairest" and given to Aphrodite by Paris. It is, however, also a pun on the name of the island and therefore appropriate for a city symbol.

The rough upper surface of left forearm and hand was not meant to be seen, since they rested, palm up, against a support (probably a pier) inserted in a cavity of an inscribed plinth. The inscription stated: *[ΑΛΕΞ* or *ΑΓΗΣ]ΑΝΔΡΟΣ ΜΗΝΙΔΟΥ [ΑΝΤ]ΙΟΧΕΥΣ ΑΠΟ ΜΑΙΑΝΔΡΟΥ ΕΠΟΙΗΣΕΝ—*"[Alex- or Ages]andros, son of Menides, from Antioch-on-the-Maeander made (it)." This sculptor is not otherwise known, but the practice of signing statues, as we have seen, seems to have become more frequent during the second half of the second century, and place of origin meant relatively little in a period of traveling masters. That this inscribed plinth was not rejoined to the statue, despite its positive connection at time of discovery, is due more to the climate of the 1820s, when the Aphrodite was sent to Paris, than to doubts about its significance. As a gift to Louis XVIII, the Aphrodite was given additional value by a theoretical attribution to Praxiteles or to one of the Classical masters, and it was only Adolph Furtwängler who, in 1893, set the record straight, although letting the Hellenistic date influence his opinion of the sculpture. Regrettably, this part of the plinth is now lost.[62]

That the Aphrodite stood in a niche is confirmed by the unfinished treatment of the back, not meant to be seen; even the sides offered a limited view.[63] This perfunctory carving is especially noticeable in her hair, where it breaks free of the approximately shaped chignon at the nape to descend along the neck in three strands that provide unobtrusive support to the head. Added metal earrings and probably a metal fillet over the marble one (as indicated by attachment holes) would have increased the liveliness of the painted features. A metal armlet on the right upper arm may have served to disguise the join of forearm and hand, which, lowered and supported by a hip strut now removed and covered in plaster, came to rest near the fall of folds over the raised left thigh and must have appeared to hold them.

One of the most interesting features of the sculpture is its technique. The bare upper body is made separately (in a better type of Parian marble than the lower) and joins the lower half where the mantle begins. Sections of the roll of drapery were also carved separately to hide the pouring channels that served to seal in the dowels connecting the two halves of the sculpture (Ill. 21). This daring construction is exactly paralleled in the Poseidon, which was found in the area of the Melian harbor, approximately 300 m (as the crow flies) from the Aphrodite's findspot, although 57 years later. As on the Aphrodite, the rear of the Poseidon is roughly finished; a major join bisects the body at the level of the mantle roll, with pieces added separately to cover and seal it. Like her, the male figure turns his head to proper left while thrusting out the right hip. To be sure, because of the position of his arms, the Poseidon appears more frontal than the Aphrodite, yet both sculptures were made for a restricted viewpoint. When a pillar is restored to the proper left of the female, the composition acquires the wider expansion provided by the restored trident to the proper right of the male. If the mantle of the latter seems more deeply carved and chiaroscural than that of the former, this impression is partly due to the angle of published photographs, since a view directly from the front of the plinth (not of the *base* as presently set in the Louvre) reveals the more dramatic rendering of the folds over the goddess' right leg as contrasted with the partly finished surface over the left thigh. Finally, note the wide-spreading outline of the right foot in both the Aphrodite and the Poseidon, with the little toe short and turned inward—this mannerism may yield a chronological clue.[64]

The piecing technique at mid-body is not unique to these two statues from Melos. The Zeus/Hero from Pergamon mentioned above has a similar construction, and so does the so-called Poseidon occasionally attributed to the superstructure of the Pergamon Altar. A further example is provided by a **male torso from Cosa,** in Italy, which may represent Asklepios and was either brought to the colony as booty or, more probably, made on Italic soil by a Greek immigrant. Some examples from Kos and even from Athens could also be adduced. The provenience of all these sculptures is sufficiently diverse to prevent attribution of their special technique to a single workshop; yet its use may still serve as a chronological indicator, since, on stylistic, epigraphic, or other grounds, these comparable works seem to date around the middle of the second century.[65]

Both the Aphrodite and the Poseidon from Melos have been called Classicizing. The face of the Aphrodite so resembles that of the Praxitelean Knidia (as far as one can judge from the Roman copies of the latter) that, in isolation, it could be misdated. It has also been observed that the figure's proportions are Classical rather than Hellenistic, since the distance between the breasts, measured at the nipples, equals that of the breasts from the navel, which forms the apex of an equilateral triangle. By contrast, Hellenistic Aphrodites exhibit a more elongated torso. Finally, the Melian has

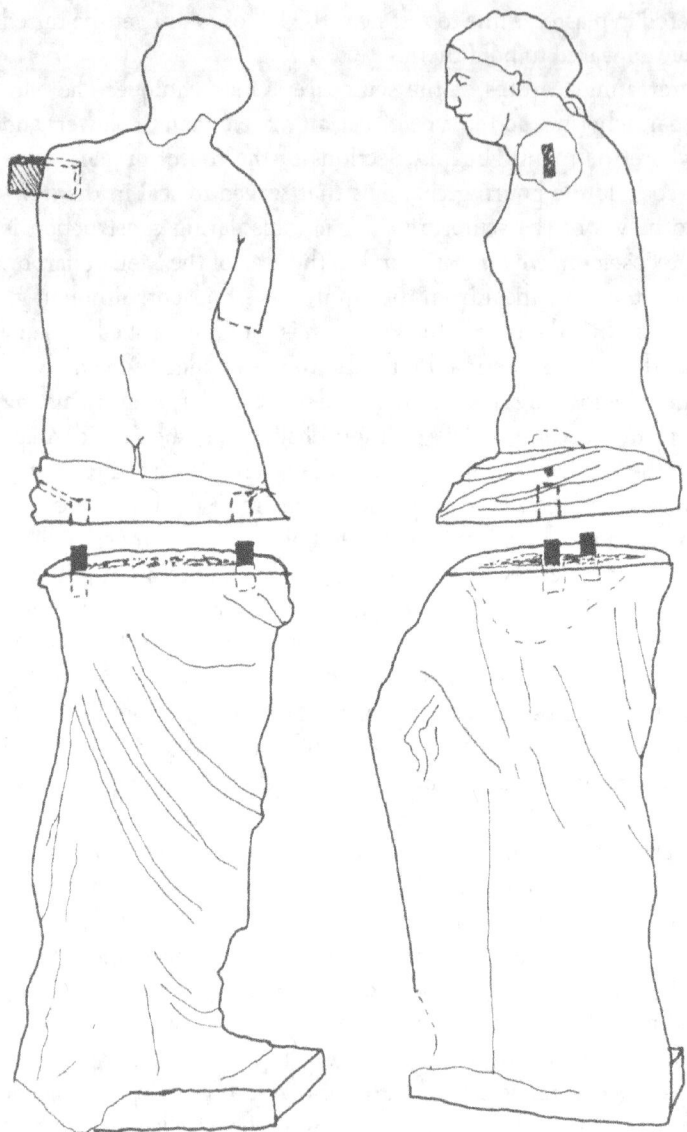

Ill. 21. Aphrodite of Melos, drawing of construction. [After Claridge 1988, 146]

been thought to derive from a fourth-century original of which the so-called Capua Aphrodite would be a more accurate (Roman) copy. Yet at least one author (Havelock) would reverse this relationship, making the Capuan an echo of the Melian, and there is a strong probability that we are dealing here with a type, rather than with a prototype and its derivations.[66] As for the Poseidon, his pose resembles the so-called Hellenistic Ruler type, which may go back to Alexander the Great and was frequently used from late Classical to Late Roman times—we have already noted it in the so-called Zeus/Hero from Pergamon. In both the Poseidon and the Aphrodite, however, specific renderings (the face and beard of the former, the mantle of the latter) leave no doubt as to the Hellenistic date of their execution. Particularly distinctive in the male figure is the trapezoidal shape of the forehead, with its pronounced "Michelangelo bar," the division of the beard into two masses with a central part, and the fleecy appearance of the hair strands, which recalls the head of Teuthras in the Telephos Frieze.

In final summary, originals of the second century have proved to be both varied in their style and largely traditional in their subjects. On the one hand, a dramatic treatment of drapery with almost excessive effects of transparency and chiaroscuro in directional folds produced novel and distinctive creations; on the other hand, uniformity over a wide range of types provided continuity, not simply with the preceding century but even with Classical times. It seems, however, obvious that second-century viewers recognized and accepted very different styles, perhaps only women asking that statues of themselves reflect contemporary fashions in clothing and new proportions in composition. It is important to note that Athens is completely absent from this picture of female honorary statues—not because they did not exist, but because none may have survived or been recognized.[67] To see the possible work of Athenian masters in this field, we have to look to Delos.

In images of female deities and personifications, a belted apoptygma (once the hallmark of fifth-century Athenas) becomes popular and, with it, the use of trumpet folds to delineate the abdominal area. Although this feature appears, in incipient fashion, on one of the pedestals of the Ephesian Artemision, its full development seems to be typical of the second century. Like drapery-through-drapery, therefore, formal devices and mannerisms that began in the third century can be considered distinctive of the following one, if we attempt to isolate characteristics of a "new" style.

Yet the issue that has repeatedly surfaced within this chapter is that of intentional Classicizing, and it is both crucial and difficult. Classicizing intent has been attributed to the makers of divine images, in a desire to stress their connection with the golden age of cult statues such as the Pheidian Athena and Zeus; yet none of the pieces we have examined was a true temple image, with the sole exception of the Zeus/Hero. Moreover, we cannot be sure that the Hellenistic masters had the same idea of period-styles that we have developed. Quotations may have been deliberate in some cases, totally unconscious in others, or the reference may have been to types and models different from those we happen to know. Chronologically, the Classicizing movement used to be given a specific date of inception, but this too has now been revised upward in light of recent new finds. The main problem remains one of proportion: how many Classical traits are needed to define a sculpture as Classicizing, and—if such traits are in the majority—how can we assign to the piece a clear Hellenistic date? As noted above, the three statues found within the Pergamon Library ran the gamut from almost close replica through modernization to eclectic composition, and only the findspot and its history justify attribution to the second century.[68] We should recognize the difficulty and be cautious in our dating.

Many more pieces could be reviewed in this chapter, but my selection has been dictated by degrees of assurance for a second-century date. Other pieces with more uncertain provenience and chronology will be treated in the next chapters.

NOTES

1. Megiste, Athens NM 710: revised chronology and stylistic analysis in Geominy 1985, with mention of previous dates. Total ht. (including base): 1.20m. The statuette undoubtedly belongs with the base because the cutting on the top surface of the pedestal is shifted toward its front and serves to anchor only part of the figure; the folds of her skirt at the back rest directly on the rear projection, which was left in place to accommodate them. The mantle arrangement is compared by Geominy to the Stele of Polybios (see infra, Ch. 6 n. 56); for an illustration, see, e.g., Moreno 1994, fig. 641 on p. 519. See also infra, n. 2.

2. A comparable attire is, however, found on a statuette from Thessaloniki, considered the Goddess of Love because of her more revealing neckline: *LIMC* 2, s.v. Aphrodite, no. 318 pl. 32 (dated 1st c.; the stance is reversed, with the left leg forward); no. 280, from Pella, is another such statuette, now in Oxford (stance also reversed), and is more safely identified because of the presence of Eros. It is considered either a Roman copy or a Hellenistic original, ca. 300; Machaira 1993, 83–84, cat. 56, and p. 193, pls. 58–59, believes it to be Hellenistic, but fully Classical in conception, going back to 4th-c. types. To me the figure seems 2nd c., even comparable (without the strong Baroque emphasis) to the Tragoidia from Pergamon (supra, Ch. 2 n. 76). See also, for the costume, the gravestone of a priestess from Smyrna, Smith 1991, 201 fig. 220.

3. Kleopatra and Dioskourides, in Delos Museum with plaster casts in situ, in the Theater Quarter: e.g., Marcadé 1969, 134, 325–28, pls. 65 (rare back view; cf. also Zanker 1995, fig. 29), 66, 68; Pollitt 1986, 268 fig. 289; Smith 1991, 97, fig. 113; Lewerentz 1993, 19–22 and (for Dioskourides, as part of her male typology, her Type I) 240, cat. I.1, fig. 1; Moreno 1994, 673–74, fig. 817. For the statues and the artistic contents of the entire house, see Kreeb 1988, 17–21, 282–84, cat. 48 (the two sculptures are S48.1–2). The inscription (*ID* 1987; transcribed, e.g., by Kreeb and Lewerentz) leaves it unclear whether the archonship date refers to the gift of the tripods or the erection of the statues; Marcadé, 134, prefers the former interpretation, but in either case the chronological difference should be minimal. Note that the backs of both pieces are perfunctorily finished; they stood originally in a nichelike cavity within the thickness of the peristyle wall, facing the entrance: cf. Kreeb 1988, fig. 2.3 (drawing); Zanker 1995, fig. 14 (after Kreeb). Kleopatra's veil covered also the head; it ends in fringes over the left hip—an

Original Statuary in the Round

Egyptian fashion? She is identified in the inscription as the daughter of Adrastos, he as the son of Theodoros. The two pieces are lifesize (Dioskourides, without feet and head, has a preserved height of 1.36 m).

4. As noted by Zanker 1993, 215, fig. 3—and cf. his figs. 5, 6 (male), 19, 20 (female), 27 (together, at the edges of a three-figure composition), with minor variations in stance and length of costumes. He concludes that the stelai "truly reflect the commonly accepted self-image of the free citizen." Of course, the statement is equally applicable to statuary in the round, given the emblematic value of the stelai. See also Zanker 1995, fig. 13 (Kleopatra and Dioskourides), and cf. figs. 6 (Eretria Youth) and 8 (Aischines); p. 254 comments that to contemporary viewers, the uniformity of the mantled figures spoke of continuity and tradition. Marcadé 1969, 325–26, surprisingly, treats Dioskourides as if he were wearing a *toga exigua*—if found in Italy, he would have been defined as a *togatus cum tunica.* The type is amply treated by Lewerentz (supra, n. 3).

5. See comments and bibl. in Ridgway 1990, 226 and n. 18, on the persistence of this type down to Imperial times (in a discussion of the statue of Aischines). Even Dioskourides' footwear (krepides), although mostly missing, can be compared to a late 4th-c. monument, the Daochos Dedication in Delphi, on the basis of the straps wrapped around his lower legs: Morrow 1985, 110. She mentions, however (p. 121), that similar bindings recur on the Telephos Frieze.

6. See Morrow 1985, 91 and n. 5 on p. 209, listing the Delian Kleopatra. The left foot, inserted separately, is now missing, but the right is still visible. Given the stylistic difference between the two statues, would we have dated them together had they been found apart?

7. Kleopatra II, daughter of Kleopatra I and Ptolemy V, may have been the main inspiration, since she was queen of Egypt with her brother/husband Ptolemy VI, ca. 175/4; two of their children were named Kleopatra (Thea, who married three Seleukid kings in succession; and Kleopatra III, queen of Egypt in 142–101). Ptolemy VIII married both mother and daughter at the same time.

8. Cf., e.g., Zanker 1993, figs. 26, 27. On press folds as status symbol, see Ridgway 1990, 219.

9. Isis from Mount Kynthos: Marcadé 1969, 429, pl. 57; Horn 1931, 77, pl. 29 (rare side view); *LIMC* 5, s.v. Isis, no. 20. The statue is described as leaning on a scepter, but purely because of its hip-slung pose. The inscription giving the chronology is *ID* 2004. The himation, especially from the side, gives the impression of being made of taffeta.

10. Nemesis–Isis: Marcadé 1969, 135, pl. 56 (Delos A 1006). The inscription on the base is *ID* 1062, the other is *ID* 2038; *LIMC* 6, s.v. Nemesis, no. 187 pl. 442.

11. Thea Roma: Marcadé 1969, 128–29, pl. 65; Stewart 1990, 58 (with transcription of the inscription), fig. 832; *LIMC* 8, s.v. Roma, 1053, no. 59 pl. 701; see also p. 1067 for comments on the costume. Only two other monuments are listed within the same category of Roma "in non-Amazonian costume," and both are gems (nos. 57–58, one dated Republican, the other Imperial, 1st or 2nd c. A.C.; one of them is an Athena type). The type in Greek dress is obviously rare. On the other hand, Rauh 1993, 113, makes the point that "the worship of Roma was by and large a Greek rather than a Roman phenomenon." The Greek sculptor would therefore have either ignored or deliberately rejected the Amazonian type current on Italian soil. This is surprising, in view of the many Italians living on Delos, and especially considering the Amazonian Roma(?) on the almost contemporary Hekateion frieze at Lagina (supra, Ch. 4 and n. 34).

Hellenistic Sculpture II

On Delos, the Roma chapel within the complex of the Poseidoniastes is V¹; the statue, still in situ, wears the himation high, with edge crossing between the breasts.

12. Aphrodite and Pan Group: Marcadé 1969, 393–95, 136 (with dating in the 3rd quarter of the 2nd c.), pl. 50, and, with same date, Marcadé et al., 1996, 142–43, no. 61; Niemeier 1985, 30–32 (ca. 130–120, on style of Aphrodite's head); Kell 1988, 50–56, fig. 11 (a formal analysis of group compositions that views the diagonal juxtaposition of the Pan to the frontal Aphrodite as a new direction, and differs from mine); *LIMC* 2, s.v. Aphrodite, no. 514 (= no. 1353) with ample bibl., pl. 50; Stewart 1990, 227, fig. 834 and cf. fig. 831 for a stereometric reconstruction of the Establishment of the Poseidoniastes. The group came from room N, probably a service area underlying the habitation quarters, where it must have fallen from above. Moreno 1994, 680–82, fig. 827, with bibl., thinks of an Oriental sculptor. For an extensive discussion of the group, see Havelock 1995, 55–58, with relevant bibl. in ns. 3 and 6; Dionysios is known to have lived in the Establishment from 110 to 100. The architectural chronology is disputed by Marquardt 1995, 227–34, esp. 228–29, but the same dating of the group is reached (p. 231 and n. 205); her lengthy analysis of the work and its possible replicas concludes that it is an erotic pasticcio. Specific comments in Bruneau 1995, 59–62. For the entire artistic contents of the Establishment, see Kreeb 1988, 21–29 (esp. 25–27), 105–19, cat. 1 (the specific group is discussed on p. 109, cat. S 1.11).

13. *LIMC* 2, s.v. Aphrodite: no. 1352 (= no. 517; terracotta group from Capua, in Naples); no. 515 (bronze statuette from Athens); no. 516 pl. 50 (Roman Imperial bronze, probably from Syria); see also the 11 entries on Aphrodite and Pan, and comments on pp. 128–29 (A. Delivorrias). For the marble fragment from the city of Samos, probably 2nd c. A.C., see *AM* 92 (1977) 189–90, pl. 89. Dionysios' mention of not only his father but also his grandfather in his dedicatory inscription may bespeak eastern practices; the inclusion of his children establishes a family line. This very form of dedication should ensure a serious purpose for the group.

14. For the dedicatory inscription, see supra, Ch. 2 and n. 14; yet the date for the cult-image base may not be as certain as that of the temple: Dörpfeld 1912, 260–61, points out that the T-shaped pedestal is structurally connected with an inscribed base ("d" on plan, pl. 17) for a statue of Adobogiona, wife of the Gallic Tetrarch Brogitaros, which implies a date of the 1st c. (cf. Schmidt 1995, 384, cat. IV.1.147, dated 65–40). He suggests that the cult images too may have been added to the temple at that time, but this notion is not repeated by later literature. He assumes that the third divine figure was Dionysos.

The male statue is Istanbul Arch. Mus. 2767; pres. ht. (without head): 2.10 m; Smith 1991, fig. 63, gives 2.31 m but must include the plinth. *LIMC* 8, s.v. Zeus, no. 249 pl. 229, calls it "Zeus (or hero)" and possibly Z. Ammon. For a three-quarter view, see Pollitt 1986, 108 fig. 112 (dated ca. 200–150). For a recent discussion, see, e.g., Lewerentz 1993, 110–13, 209, cat. V.2, with bibl. A recent description of technical features (main statue made in four pieces, with five smaller elements of drapery added separately along horizontal join at mid-body) is given by Collins-Clinton 1993, 264–65, fig. 14. For a good illustration of the sandaled feet, see Morrow 1985, 129, pl. 107; on p. 119, she considers its footwear "one of the earliest examples of a *lingula* on Greek sandals"; both unprecedentedly elaborate and impractical, the specific form may be imaginary—perhaps confirming a divine identification.

15. Statue considered portrait of Attalos II: Himmelmann 1989, 142; followed by Lewerentz 1993 whereas Pollitt 1986 and Smith 1991 (supra, n. 14) consider it Zeus. Morrow 1985, 119,

may have provided additional support to the latter. Zeus Ammon from Pergamon: supra, Ch. 2 n. 76.

16. "Monna" is an abbreviated form of the Italian "Madonna" (= my lady), and therefore should be spelled with two *n*'s, not one as is common in English.

17. Despite its fame and almost obligatory mentions in all books on Hellenistic (even Greek) art, the Nike has only now been officially catalogued (Hamiaux 1998, 27–32, no. 2, dated ca. 190–180, by a Rhodian or East Greek workshop, on a Rhodian ship and paving). That brief entry should still be supplemented, however, by a detailed treatment that incorporates into the reconstruction all the fragments—mostly from the wings, but also from the drapery and a toe—now catalogued and illustrated for the first time: Hamiaux 1998, 33–38, nos. 4–15, 17–23. For fragments of the ship (some from the ram), see Hamiaux 1998, 38–40, nos. 24–50. These valuable pieces are currently kept in boxes within the storerooms of the Louvre, which I saw in October 1995, thanks to the great courtesy of Alain Pasquier. The study of the monument as a whole, in its Samothrakian setting, is being prepared by I. S. Mark; in the interim, see Mark 1998, and "The Monument of the Victory of Samothrace: Dating Questions," Abstract, *AJA* 100 (1996) 398, where he mentions that some of the pottery (conical bowls) associated with the site may come from a later phase or even from the initial clearing in the 19th c. A second pottery lot is generally Hellenistic, but cannot be dated precisely. Schmidt 1995, cat. X.5 on pp. 507–509, accepts the traditional date for the monument because of the alleged chronology of the pottery found with it. Lehmann 1973 also discusses the wider context, but believes that the Samothrakian sculpture celebrates the local navy, although he retains a date ca. 200. For a Rhodian historical account, see Rice 1991. For stylistic discussion, see: Carpenter 1960, 201–208 (who dates later than the Pergamon Altar, "180–160," and attributes it to Pergamon, commemorating the Attalid fleet's action in 168 in preventing Perseus' further escape from Samothrake, where he surrendered); Stewart 1993b, 130–31,137–53 (date left open; emphasis on the metaphor of the "ship of state"). Smith 1991, 77–79, thinks Demetrios Poliorketes' victory over Ptolemy (I) in 306, at Cypriot Salamis, is the most plausible historical connection for the Nike, although adding that "style might seem to suit the 250's better." Moreno 1994, 366–69, col. figs. 468–71, follows tradition, and attribution to Pythokritos of Rhodes. Goodlett 1991, 676, discusses Pythokritos, active on Rhodes between ca. 203 and 160; 18 statues by him are attested at various Rhodian sites and at Olympia. Isager 1995, 127–28, doubts a Rhodian connection on present evidence; Pollitt, forthcoming, reviews the same information but still favors Rhodes. Knell 1995, the only recent monographic treatment of the subject, is mostly concerned with the location of the monument with respect to the theater, and accepts a ca. 190 date. Cf. also *LIMC* 6, s.v. Nike, no. 382 pl. 589 (dated 190–180).

18. The ship base of the Nike has been discussed by Casson 1973, 102–103, 118–19 (a supergalley, probably a tetreres, a "four"); by Morrison 1996, 219–20, no. 20 ("If the statue is a Rhodian dedication, the warship chosen to bear on its prow the Victory monument is likely to be one of the Rhodian favorites, a τριημιολία"; cf. line drawing 74 on p. 320); by Schmidt 1995, 132–51 (section X), esp. 135 and 142, cat. X.5 on pp. 507–509 (a trihemiolia), in the context of all Hellenistic ship bases (only five); and by Hamiaux 1998, 27 (a trihemiolia). See also infra, n. 28.

19. On various dates for the Nike, see supra, n. 17 (esp. Smith 1991, Carpenter 1960; also Lehmann 1973 and Stewart 1993b). On the lack of Pergamene style on Rhodes, see Merker

1973, 14; more reticent, Gualandi 1976, 15–17. For the issue of a Rhodian connection to the Pergamene Altar, see supra, Ch. 2, ns. 32 and 37. For a history of Rhodes in the period under consideration, see Berthold 1984, and Gabrielsen 1997.

20. Lehmann 1973, 192–93 n. 14, who adds that Hieronymos "has as much claim to the Nike as any other sculptor." For a base said to be in Lartian marble, for a small statue from Soloeis (Sicily), see infra, n. 59. The material was therefore exported to places without suitable local stone.

21. Inscribed fragment: Hamiaux 1998, 41 no. 51, formally excluding it from the Victory. Letters of inscription too small for Nike: Lehmann 1973, 192–93, n. 14; another fragment with larger letters "may belong, but does not help." On Pythokritos' signature, see, e.g., Schmidt 1995, 506–507, cat. X.4: the dedication by the demos of Lindos to Hagesander, son of Mikion, for *arete* and *eunoia* toward the Lindians, by Pythokritos son of Timochares, from Rhodes. Timochares may have been from Eleutherna on Crete, but his son seems to have received Rhodian citizenship. For the distribution of his works, beside Goodlett 1991 (cf. supra, n. 17), see Gualandi 1976, 16 and n. 3; also Moreno 1994, 365. Pliny, *NH* 34.91, lists Pythokritos as one of 26 bronze sculptors (in alphabetical order) who made *athletas autem et armatos et venatores sacrificantesque;* although some names receive added commentary, Pythokritos is not one of those. On the limited travels of Rhodian sculptors, see, e.g., Gualandi 1976, 15–16, who notes that no masters from that island are attested among the many "foreigners" working on Delos.

22. Ship bases: Schmidt 1995, 132–51, section X; she dates the Epidauros base (cat. X.1, pp. 502–503, figs. 159–161) to the late 4th–early 3rd c., but mentions other suggested dates on p. 133 n. 11. Moreno 1994, 367, considers it further commemoration of the events of 190/89. It was reused by L. Mummius ca. 148, and it held a bronze, lifesize statue. See also Rice 1991 and 1993, 242–47 (ship dedications).

Kyrene monument: e.g., Ridgway 1990, 215–17, with range of suggested dates, pl. 99; *LIMC* 6, s.v. Nike [*sic*, although stating "no wing attachment"], no. 381 pl. 588; Moreno 1994, 339–41, figs. 423, 425; Schmidt 1995, cat. X.2, pp. 503–505 (dated 160–end 2nd c.). Nike from Tenos: *LIMC* 6, s.v. Nike, no. 392 ("no wing attachment"); Queyrel 1986, 271 n. 9 ("not from sanctuary"), pl. 164.6, and 276 n. 7 for the fragmentary prow, also now lost but from the sanctuary, tentatively assigned to a cult group; contrast Moreno 1994, 367, who confidently associates Nike and ship base. (This statue will be discussed infra.)

The Lindos relief is described by Schmidt 1995 (supra, n. 18) together with the naiskos of the goddess, but the two could be separate monuments, as perhaps suggested by the semicircular exedra cut into the rock *before* the ship; see also Moreno 1994, 365–66 and col. fig. 463 on p. 369; Morrison 1996, 221–22, no. 21; Gabrielsen 1997, 88–89 with notes, pl. 5. For the other Rhodian ship monuments, see Moreno 1994, 339, 364–65, fig. 453 on p. 359 (ship prow on pedestal, on akropolis of Lindos, facing sea, dated ca. 260; cf. Gualandi 1976, 18 n. 3; Schmidt 1995, 134–35 and cat. X.3, pp. 505–506, surely dated 265–260; Morrison 1996, 203–205, no. 11; Gabrielsen 1997, pl. 4); 366, and fig. 464 on p. 319 (fragment of ram in Rhodes Museum; and cf. n. 655). Other examples are mentioned by Lehmann 1973; some ship monument may have served as base for a statue of a deceased person—a prow from Rheneia, found after Lehmann's publication, comes from a cemeterial area: Couilloud–Le Dinahet 1978, 873 and fig. 30 (Couilloud 1974a, 235, stated that the monument was known only through a reference by an early traveler, as transcribed on p. 344). The Sperlonga groups will be discussed in a later chapter.

Original Statuary in the Round

23. Pugliese Carratelli 1996, 636, cat. 2; the entry (by R. Camerata Scovazzo) illustrates two of the three finds made in 1993 (ht. 0.36 m, l. 0.80 and 92 m; w. 0.39 and 0.40 m), and dates them 150–100. The features listed as similar to the Samothrakian base are: "a) the particular shape of the oars case which, seen from the front, gives the impression of a pair of wings; b) the curve of the lower face of the oars case typical of the Rhodian type and the downward slant of the upper face; c) the particular junction of one of the upper strakes with the base of the oars case."

24. Gualandi 1976, 17–18; cf. Merker 1973, 6: "Rhodian wealth, with its commercial basis, must have been distributed among many individuals, and not concentrated at a central source which could have directed local financial resources toward the execution of large-scale artistic projects. . . . Nor do we know of the emergence to political power of any individual capable of commissioning major sculptural works." Gabrielsen 1997 speaks of a "naval aristocracy" that was based on wealth and skill. Note also the comments by Isager 1995 and by Pollitt, forthcoming.

25. The Kabeiroi, to be sure, were considered the protectors of sailors and may have been worshiped by the Rhodians, especially in the guise of the Dioskouroi in the context of the several foreign *koina* on the islands: see Pugliese Carratelli 1939/40, 195–96 and n. 1, for the special group (i.e., religious, non-commercial, probably elitist) among the associations that was formed by thiasoi of mystai. Within this latter group predominated the initiates of the Soteres of Samothrake and Lemnos, named Soteriastai, Samothrakiastai, and Dioskouriastai; they seem, however, to have been largely composed of foreigners. Cf. lists of pertinent inscriptions, esp. pp. 184–85 (eight mentions of Samothrakiastai), with summary of the situation on p. 200. For possible worship of the *soteres* (the Great Gods of Samothrake), see Rice 1995, 403 n. 44 with refs.; Cole 1984, esp. maps I–III.

26. The two quotations are taken from Berthold 1984, 158 and 161 respectively; for the invention of fire baskets (by the Rhodian Pausistratos), see pp. 154–55 and n. 18. Livy 37.23.4 mentions that at Side the Rhodians had 32 quadriremes and four triremes. On these battles and the war with Antiochos, see also Morrison 1996, 93–109.

27. Stewart 1993b, 141–42. Lehmann 1973, 188; see his p. 184 and n. 7, where both hands of the Nike are discussed. The left, found in a dump in 1967, is said to be somewhat smaller in scale, but still colossal and in the same style as the Nike; the right hand (Hamiaux 1998, 32–33, no. 3; cf. fig. 51 on p. 140 in Stewart 1993b; Moreno 1994, fig. 470) may have been intentionally enlarged for optical purposes. The arms of the Victory have never been found, although an early photograph shows the upper left arm restored; it has now been removed.

28. I am grateful to Dr. Aleydis van de Moortel for discussing the Samothrakian ship with me. The curved elements on the outriggers, although without whatever was separately attached, are clearly visible in the reconstruction drawing (by F. Glaser) published by Horn 1994, 462 fig. 13; cf. Stewart 1993b, fig. 138. Good photographs also in *LIMC* 6, pl. 589; Schmidt 1995, figs. 172 (depression in front) and 173. Morrison 1996, 219–20, perhaps describes them: "at the bottom of the blank side there is on both sides of the ship a wavelike course of what may be louvres, but they seem too small to provide the ventilation required." The bronze revetments with the heads of Dionysos and Ariadne discussed by Horn show how oarboxes could be ornamented, although in different locations.

Schmidt 1995, 142 and 507–508, describes the Samothrakian boat as having two or three rows of rowers, and as being made in three layers: the lowest, in three blocks, is composed of tropis, zoster, and embolon; the middle, in 10–12 blocks, comprises zoster, hypozoma, parexeiresia (outriggers) with two diagonally set tremata (oar openings) per side, proembolion, and akrostolion; the top layer was the katastroma; cf. her figs. 171–73. The blocks were joined by dowels and Π-shaped clamps. In its present state, the ship lacks embolon, proembolion and akrostolion (ram and sternpost) and has been heavily restored. Hamiaux 1998, 27, mentions that the parexeiresiai terminate in front with epotides (in the shape of small lateral spurs), but does not describe the curved elements toward the rear edge, as described above. For this ancient terminology, see Casson 1973, 389–402. Morrison 1996, 220, notes that "the difference in levels between the oarports en échelon on the oarbox face is too small for the ship to be a four." Gabrielsen 1997, 88–89, and ns. 23, 25–26 on pp. 187–88, discusses the Nike base in the context of defining a trihemiolia (pp. 86–94) and considers it a cataphract, therefore not a trihemiolia, but advances no other definition.

The Nike stands on a block with trapezoidal surface that is entirely modern, although something comparable is attested by the remains of dowel cuttings; the Nike's drapery (the feet, separately attached, are now missing) rests on a separate plinth and a further step is provided to support the mantle swag where it falls on the figure's left side: see Stewart 1990, fig. 721, for this detail. I owe the information about the traces of paint to Alain Pasquier.

29. The placement of the Nike is described as I saw it in the Louvre in late 1995; the diagonal groove was visible (for a good photo, see Schmidt 1995, fig. 173), as well as the anathyrosis at the edges of the paving slabs, which implies the original presence of additional stones. Letters engraved on the paving blocks may have served for directions in placing the ship (Hamiaux 1998, 28), but they seem unconnected with the groove; could they bespeak a transfer of the monument from a different initial location? That the findspot of the Nike was not a fountain is mentioned in both publications by Stewart (1990, 215; 1993b, 141 and n. 5) and was stated to me orally by I. Mark, who, in his AIA report (supra, n. 17) specified the Late Republican or early Imperial date of the "boulder retaining wall." This chronology is confirmed by the somewhat laconic entry in *Samothrace* 1998, 102–103, no. 12 (Nike dated early 2nd c.). For comments on the stucco and the pipes, I am indebted to Prof. Ch. Pfaff, who excavated at Samothrake. For early photographs of the niche, see Bouzek et al. 1985, pls. 24–33, and cf. pp. 34–36, where the American position that the theater is later than the Nike is accepted.

30. That Rhodes has been erroneously credited with some of these illusionistic effects is convincingly argued by Rice 1995.

31. This argument is forcefully made by Knell 1995; for a reconstruction of the Nike as visible from the theater, see his fig. 62 on pp. 76–77, and cf. the sight lines in fig. 60 on p. 73. He stresses that the orchestra has no permanent stage building but is bordered by the so-called Altar Court (*Samothrace* 1998, 89–91 no. 14)—yet interpretation of the latter building is controversial: Cole 1984, 18–19 and ns. 154–55. Knell discusses also the similarity between the Aphrodite of Capua type and the Nike of Brescia, as well as the slipped straps of victories on the Nike Balustrade, and notes that the theater of Pompey in Rome (vowed at the triumph of 61, dedicated in 55) was dominated by the Temple of Venus Victrix. For a more extensive discussion of the connection between Aphrodite and theaters, see Pollini 1996, esp. 769–73, 785. The siting of the Nike could also be compared with the arrangement at Praeneste (ca. 100), where the top terrace with curved cavea and colonnade was crowned by a tholos and probably

a colossal statue in black stone (cf. Pl. 49) strongly resembling the Nike: see Romanelli 1967, 91, col. pl. 53; *LIMC* 8, s.v. Fortuna, no. 179 (F. Isis; 2nd half 2nd c.); Gulaki 1981, 153 and n. 999 with additional refs., fig. 239 (beg. 1st c.). For comments on Praeneste, I am indebted to P. Guldager Bilde. Yet these comparisons would almost suggest Roman input, if not a Roman date, for the Samothrakian arrangement. Could the monument have been moved from a previous location in Roman times? Theater dated ca. 200: *Samothrace* 1998, 35.

32. Carpenter 1960, 201. See other quotations in Stewart 1993b, 143–45, and his own explanation of the storm metaphor. Hamiaux 1998, 27, describes the Nike as being made in one piece from below the breasts (at the belt) to the ankles; upper torso (probably including the head), wings, arms, the back of the left leg with the foot, the right foot, and the rear panel of drapery were made separately and attached. I wonder if Hamiaux 1998, fragment nos. 10–11, the more substantial remnants of drapery, may belong to the arrangement of the mantle over the missing left shoulder and to part of its overfold.

33. Hamiaux 1998, 27, describes the costume as consisting of a chiton belted only under the breasts, and a himation falling between the legs and floating in the back, without citing an overfold.

34. Philip V as sponsor of the Nike was suggested by Sophia R. Chaknis, a graduate student at the Florida State University, in a seminar report (Feb. 17, 1997). For the statue of Philip V, see *ArchDelt* 24 (1969) 365–66 and pl. 372c; *JHS-AR* 15 (1968–69) 30, fig. 37; *Samothrace* 1998, 106 and 163, fig. 80 (inscribed base with dedication by the Macedonians to the Great Gods, ca. 200). For Macedonian relationships with the sanctuary, see Cole 1984, 20–25, who stresses that even the Ptolemies were involved with Samothrake because of their Macedonian origin. For Macedonian victory monuments, see, however, supra, Ch. 3 n. 44. For "Philip V's naval ambitions," see Morrison 1996, 68–91 and cf. 109–12 for Perseus' vicissitudes (also Cole 1984, 87–89). For an Attalid dedication, see Carpenter (supra, n. 17). A Ptolemaic dedication would presumably have carried identifying marks on the ship itself, as suggested by the Kyrene monument, and perhaps also by the Athlit ram; for comments on naval parasema used by various powers, see Murray 1991. Theoretically, even the Romans might have been interested in erecting a victory monument on the island, given the connections of the sanctuary with Troy and the ancient belief that the Roman Penates were actually the Samothrakian Gods. For the newly identified Samothrakian cult area at Troy, see Rose 1998, esp. 89–90 and ns. 88–92, with additional refs.

The Lindos relief honors Hagesander for "arete" and "eunoia" toward the Lindians; the ship-prow inscription mentions crew and commanders but does not specify events. Morrison's assumption (1996, 205) that it was once surmounted by a statue of Victory is unverifiable.

35. Samothrake Hieron: most recently, Webb 1996, 144–47; *Samothrace* 1998, 79–86 no. 15, and 133–35, fig. 60 (Hellenistic Nike). That the building may have been misnamed was suggested to me recently by K. Clinton, and several identifications of Samothrakian buildings are currently undergoing revisions (see, e.g., Cole 1984, n. 62 and pp. 11–16). The main publication of the Hieron, Lehmann et al. 1969, has the best photographs: Nike akroterion, 364–68, figs. 317–44 (cf. also Smith 1991, fig. 210); pedimental figure (Vienna, inv. 345; VII.I in pedimental reconstruction), 254–55, figs. 213–14; cf. also old photographs: fig. 253 on p. 295 and fig. 254 on p. 304, which best show the zigzags at the edge of the mantle, with individual folds hollowed out like the pipes of an organ. The crinkly chiton over the left thigh thrusting through

the heavy himation recalls, *mutatis mutandis*, the Medici Athena. The depth of this figure has occasionally cast doubt on its pedimental function; its style seems different from the other, more securely pedimental, pieces, prompting a 3rd-c. date: cf. Ridgway 1990, 158–60, with refs. All these sculptures are said to be in Thasian marble, different from the better-quality Parian of the Nike (on which see supra, Ch. 4, ns. 1 and 5).

36. Nike from Tenos: cf. supra, n. 22. The "sister" definition is by Queyrel 1986, 271 n. 9; cf. also 286 n. 35. Despinis 1995, 329–30 (pl. 68) denies a strong resemblance and points out the different costume. The torso was last seen in Chora ca. 1910.

I call "trumpet fold" the single or double ridge marking a tubular pleat that originates at the waistline (belt) and curves in proximity to the abdomen, usually in the direction of the movement, to end at the edge of an overfold or (more rarely) kolpos; such a fold resembles an upside-down cornucopia or a curved trumpet. Usually two such folds, often in mirror image, delimit the stomach area rendered visible through transparent drapery; in contrast to the 5th-c. pleats that run straight down as the borders of an opaque central panel within an apoptygma, the hallmark of the trumpet folds is their curve in combination with a clinging garment. In the Nike of Samothrake, the most obvious of such trumpet folds is the one over the left hip, closest to the smooth abdominal area and overlapping the mantle roll with an open "mouth." Their vague similarity to 5th-c. drapery patterns notwithstanding, trumpet folds do not occur before the Hellenistic period—perhaps the earliest example in incipient form being on a pedestal of the Ephesian Artemision. They are therefore not listed in Ch. 2 n. 70 among the Pergamene mannerisms derived from the Classical phases, despite the occurrence of transparency over the abdominal area delineated by outlying folds, and their appearance, e.g., on the Doris of the NW risalit (cf. Pl. 12). Trumpet folds are quite prominent on the dancers of the Sagalassos frieze: supra, Ch. 4 and n. 68 (cf. Pl. 39).

37. Nike torso from Kos (in Museum storerooms): Kabus-Preißhofen 1989, 120–21 (with mention of Euboulides' Nike) and 267–68 no. 68 (dated 2nd half 3rd c.), pl. 38.2; *LIMC* 6 s.v. Nike, no. 389 (dated ca. 250). Another almost lifesize torso from Kos (Kabus-Preißhofen 1989, 260 no. 64, pl. 68.1) is also compared to the Samothrakian Nike and to the "Dancer." One more Koan Nike, recomposed from two fragments, is compared by Despinis 1995, 329 pl. 69.

Koan Dancer, Kos Mus. no. 27 (earlier 93; Rhodes Mus. inv. 4662): Kabus-Preißhofen 1989, 158–59 and 264–66, no. 67, pl. 67 (dated ca. 170–160). Pres. ht. 1.30 m (without plinth); the feet, although missing, were on tiptoes; the right hand was clutching the mantle over the thigh, revealing the chiton below. The body's movement is comparable to that of the Nike of Samothrake, and the neckline slips toward the right shoulder, but the proportions are manneristically elongated, with narrow chest and wide hips. The piece is said to be from the ancient city of Kos, but has no precise provenience. The two fragments have now been more correctly joined. For a lengthy stylistic analysis, see Di Vita 1963–64. Kos and Rhodes not artistically connected: Merker 1973, 11–12; Kabus-Preißhofen 1989, 178.

38. Boston Museum of Fine Arts, inv. 97.286: Caskey 1925, 109–110, no. 51 (dated perhaps 2nd c.); Comstock and Vermeule 1976, 58–59, no. 91 (dated perhaps 200–100); attributed to Rhodes by Frel 1971, 124 n. 19. It was initially compared to the Koan "Dancer" by Di Vita 1963–64, echoed by Kabus-Preißhofen 1989, 159.

39. "Nike by Euboulides," Athens NM 233 (pres. ht. from head to groin area, 1.23 m): best discussion and illustrations in Despinis 1995, 321–38, pls. 62–65; cf. Travlos 1971, fig. 542;

Original Statuary in the Round

Stewart 1990, fig. 805. See also the important treatment in Gulaki 1981, 254–61, figs. 241 and 247–48 for the unrestored joining of head and torso; her fig. 242 shows the Athena from the same findspot (Athens NM 234)—cf. *LIMC* 2, s.v. Athena, no. 270 pl. 736 ("so-called by Euboulides," ca. 130); Travlos 1971, fig. 541; Pollitt 1986, 165 and fig. 169 (dated 150–100); Stewart 1990, fig. 804 (ca. 100); Moreno 1994, 553–54, fig. 668; Despinis 1995, pl. 66. *LIMC* 6, s.v. Nike, no. 390, still lists Athens NM 233 as a Victory, although stating that the attachment of wings is not established; but attribution to Euboulides is eliminated and the piece is dated 230–200. Despinis 1990 and 1995, 326, confirms the difference between the two heads, considering the Athena larger, stylistically different, and later, although he is uncertain (also 1995, 325–26) whether the head on the "Nike," which also seems large for the body, is correctly joined. For him, torso NM 233 (with right side of the back worked separately, and only partly finished in the rear) is a Muse, part of Euboulides' group, which stood against a wall: the cuttings in the back would have served to anchor the statue to it. Despinis 1995, 331–32, suggests that the head now on it, because of its greater size, could therefore belong to Mnemosyne, the mother of the Muses, as part of the same group, which he dates ca. 130 or shortly thereafter (p. 335). On p. 337 n. 79, Despinis 1995 provides a stemma of Euboulides' family spanning five generations; the signed block is illustrated on pl. 67. Smith 1991, 240, believes both sculptures were wrongly attributed to Euboulides because of a misreading of Pausanias and calls Athens NM 233 "another goddess ('Nike')." Moreno 1994, loc.cit., follows Despinis 1990 in identifying a Muse in the "Nike," but accepts the head as pertinent and the Athena as part of Euboulides' group.

40. Karanastassis 1987, 416–20, no. B III.1, pl. 47.1–2, lists the Athena head NM 234 as an Augustan adaptation of the Velletri type. See also supra, n. 39.

41. If in fact head and torso go together, at least as part of the same group, "Euboulides' Nike" has a soft, modeled face that finds parallels in some of the female heads on the Pergamon Altar; her hair rendering, although mostly missing because carved on separate pieces, is also comparable in its drill work and volume. See infra, n. 42 for trumpet folds at Pergamon.

42. See, e.g., the Doris on the NW risalit of the Gigantomachy, and, in the Telephos Frieze, King Teuthras rushing to meet Auge (panel 10). For a definition of trumpet folds, see supra, n. 36.

43. I have made a similar assumption for the Aemilius Paullus Monument as originally planned by Perseus: see supra, Ch. 3.

Although concerning a different period, I found striking Strauss' observation (1996, esp. 313, 321) on the invisibility of the obviously powerful and important Athenian navy in texts and artistic monuments of the Classical period. Ship monuments seem to begin only in the Hellenistic period, which might explain an Athenian absence at a time when their navy was no longer politically dominant. We may, however, lack the rostra and cables of conquered ships, if these were in fact displayed in the Athenian Stoa at Delphi; other naval commemorations may have been equally "perishable," and the chance of the finds, both texts and objects, may play a large role in our perception. Could victories at sea have been celebrated only by dedications of actual ships or ship parts, rather than by sculptural compositions? Cf. the *neorion* at Samothrake, newly added to our list of buildings containing ships: *Samothrace* 1998, 109–11, figs. 49–51, dated ca. 250; Ridgway 1990, 172–75 and n. 24.

44. Nike as messenger: Stewart 1993b, 141. Kyzikos relief, Istanbul Arch. Mus. 564: e.g.,

Smith 1991, fig. 211 (with wrong inv. no.); *LIMC* 5, s.v. Herakles, no. 2813 pl. 110. The inscription celebrates the city's successful appeal to Herakles when threatened by the Gauls under Loutarios; the date is provided by the dedicants: the *strategoi* and the *phylarchoi* when Phoinix was *hipparchos*. The hero may be shown killing the Gaulish leader.

I do not take into account here monuments to specific individuals—like Alexander's *hetairoi* who fell at the Battle of the Granikos—because they partake of the nature of honorary statues rather than of victory celebrations. For a good discussion of victory monuments against the Gauls, see Hannestad 1993; a doctoral dissertation on Hellenistic war memorials, by Thomas Brogan, has just been completed; it touches also on earlier commemorations, primarily for Marathon, which seem to have been imitated in later times. See also Rice 1993, esp. on the Rhodian Colossus.

45. For a discussion of this conception, see refs. in Hannestad 1993, with some direct quotations on p. 30; the main proponent is Hölscher 1985, esp. 120–28. Hannestad calls it (p. 32) "perhaps the finest myth created in connection with the Celtic invasions into the Greek world: the myth of victory monuments showing only the agony of defeat, not the triumph of victory, created 2,000 years after the events by European scholars influenced by the concept of the noble savage." She attributes the lack of copies of the winners in such monuments to Roman selectivity and specific interest in the barbarians. Contrast, however, the Tyrannicides erected in Athens in the late Archaic and again in the Severe periods—a sculpture showing only the "winners" without the victim, in an apparent reversal of the Hellenistic approach. Yet even this composition can be explained in terms of an honorary group rather than a victory monument—and I still think that generic bravery in battle, rather than specific encounters, is being shown in such works as the Alexander Sarcophagus and the Alexander Mosaic. Bringmann 1995, 95, who believes that the Altar and the Athenian dedications are contemporary, considers both to be in the spirit of the previous century, but see Marszal 1998. See also infra, n. 46.

46. Previous views on the subject: Ridgway 1990, 284–304. Contrary to what I stated on p. 285, Habicht 1990 has shown that the Attalos and Ariarathes who dedicated the statue of Karneades in the Agora were not the future kings but private Athenian citizens; relationship between the Attalids and Athens did not begin before 200, when Attalos I entered the city and received lavish honors for having saved it from Philip V. Given the sculptural climate of Athens in the second century, one wonders who would have made the Smaller Dedication for Attalos I: Athenian masters or sculptors brought in from Asia Minor? On these historical and artistic issues, see also the forthcoming volume of the Fourth Langford Conference (Gruen, Marszal, Steingräber, de Grummond). See infra, Ch. 8 and esp. pp. 284–85 for a discussion of copies and works that have been grouped around the Smaller Dedication; see also Ch. 9, ns. 53–55, for two more "Gauls," in New York and from Delos.

Prof. Stewart tells me (Sept. 1998) that M. Korres has now identified some bases from the Athenian Akropolis that belonged to the Smaller Dedication; he will publish them as an appendix to Stewart's monograph in preparation on the subject.

47. This theory, by T. Brogan, was first advanced in an unpublished M.A. thesis for Bryn Mawr College in 1990; it is now published in Brogan 1998, and contains a useful summary of previous views and debate. E. Schraudolph, who wrote entry no. 21 for the Telephos Exhibition (*Pergamon* 1, 1996, 86), seems to approximate Brogan's position: "the parallels [for Herakles'

facial features] are too general to allow a particular king to be named. Rather, they probably mean that the god Herakles as the ancestor of the Attalids was envisioned as having facial features similar to these." Brogan's suggestion is, however, more compelling, since it encompasses the program of the other niches and the entire temenos. For a rare illustration of Prometheus' back, see *Pergamon* 1, 1996, fig. 10, clearly showing unfinished areas along the spine, and the dowel hole in the right gluteus; see also figs. on pp. 87–88 for details of the other pieces. Cf. also *LIMC* 7, s.v. Prometheus, no. 73 pl. 427 (dated "159–137 or 88–84 B.C."). For the earlier exhibition, "Herrscher und Athlet," see Himmelmann 1989, 140–42 fig. 57, and cat. 7, pp. 210–16 (Herakles = Attalos II). Brogan's figs. 4.5–6 (1998, pp. 46–47) suggest a possible placement of the group within two niches. Other sculptures from the stoa niches are very fragmentary but the subjects may have included a Leda and the Swan, and a Herakles and Hesione (a female leaning against a column and fragments of a sea monster). Moreno 1994, 598–601 (Herakles = Attalos II), although accepting nearby panels, sees the Prometheus tableau as a fountain ornament (although still within the stoa?), with water emerging from a cavity in the rock under the reclining Kaukasos, whom he identifies, however, as a personification of the river Phasis looking on with right arm raised in surprise—an unlikely suggestion, since the cavity is not pierced through.

48. The style of the Prometheus Group has been seen as different from that of the Telephos Frieze, perhaps because of traditional chronology (*Pergamon* 1, 1996, 86); yet better parallels can be found in the Gigantomachy. Using the illustrations in Simon 1975, cf. Kaukasos' mantle and pl. 23 (the fragmentary "Themis," behind Ouranos, on S frieze); Prometheus' body and pl. 15 (the kneeling Giant in frontal view, Zeus' opponent, on E frieze); Herakles' lionskin and pl. 22 (Asterie's dog, S frieze); Herakles' wide eyes and pls. 10 (Dione's opponent, N frieze) and 18 (Apollo's opponent, "Ephialtes," E frieze).

49. Hera/Aphrodite: Gernand 1975, 23–24, pl. 7; *LIMC* 2, s.v. Aphrodite (uncertain identifications), no. 141 (dated mid-2nd c.) = *LIMC* 4, s.v. Hera, no. 105 (dated 2nd quarter 2nd c.); Niemeier 1985, 111–14, figs. 22, 24 ("Umbildung" after a prototype of ca. 430, from the same findspot and workshop as the Athena Parthenos and the Athena with crossed aigis—but cf. infra, n. 50 [Weber]).

Athena Parthenos: Gernand 1975, 17–24, pl. 12; *LIMC* 2, s.v. Athena, no. 230 pl. 730 (2nd c.; free adaptation); Niemeier 1985, 114–20, figs. 1, 2, 20. Ht. with base: 3.51 m (the original was 11.50 m; therefore Pergamon statue said to be "copy" at one-third scale); cf. Pollitt 1986, 167 and fig. 171. Weber 1993, 103–107, defends the iconographic accuracy of the copy, postulates a larger and wider base (with one additional block on either side of the preserved one) from traces in the Library building, and accepts intentional changes only in the coiffure, which lacks the shoulder locks on the front. She also believes that fragments from another Athena statue now in the Pergamon Museum in Berlin (p. 107, figs. 15–17) come from another replica of the Parthenos that may have stood on the round base of the Athena sanctuary, later to be replaced by an Imperial image. Given the chryselephantine medium of the Pheidian original, mechanical copying is to be excluded.

Athena with crossed aigis: Gernand 1975, 25–34, pl. 6; *LIMC* 2, s.v. Athena, no. 267 pl. 735 (2nd c.); Niemeier 1985, 129–36, figs. 3, 21, 23 ("new conception and creation of Hellenistic Classicizing").

Gernand's article discusses several statues, from Pergamon and elsewhere, that partake of similar Classicizing trends, but are not treated here because their chronology is vaguer. Niemeier 1985 attributes to Pergamon a major role in developing a Classicizing style, sparked by the Attalids' interest in copying earlier works, but see my review, *AJA* 91 (1987) 624–26; see also Steinbruckner 1986, against Niemeier's "lingering" evolutionary approach. Mielsch 1995, esp. 778, makes a strong argument against the alleged Classicizing tendencies at Pergamon, seeing them rather as a conscious reference to Athens, mother city of Ionian cities. In his view, even the building at present identified as the famous Library is instead a sort of Treasury of Athena—which would undermine many of the current notions about the replica of the Parthenos, although it would not seriously affect its date. The Pergamene Library, Mielsch suggests, was probably in the area of the Gymnasion.

Meyer 1997 believes that the Athena with crossed aigis copies the Lemnia by Pheidias; he suggests that even the "Hera/Aphrodite" replicates a Pheidian work, thus completing a trilogy of Athenas by the 5th-c. master. But his evidence (fig. 62: a relief from Libofshe, now in Fier, Albania) seems too tenuous for the Lemnia's identification.

50. For recent speculation on the meaning of the Pheidian base, see Connelly 1996, 72–76; Hurwit 1995. Niemeier 1985, 115, notes that it is impossible to tell how closely the Pergamene base copied the Pheidian original; Weber 1993, 107, suggests that statue and base, in Pentelic marble, were made in Athens and were thus accurate replicas, but cf. infra Ch.7 n. 7.

51. On this Athena, see supra, n. 49; add Ridgway 1970, 130 and bibl. on p. 146, figs. 159–60, for discussion of the piece in Severe terms. Note in particular the oval area of the apoptygma below the belt over the left hip, which recalls the treatment of some Olympia figures. The sandals' soles are high, but their contour is in keeping with 5th-c. forms. The head may not belong, since much plaster joins it to the body and its connection has been doubted; its poor degree of finish in the rear contrasts with the rest of the figure, and no satisfactory headdress has been suggested. Even stucco additions seem unlikely. Niemeier 1985, 134, calls the Athena's pose restless; I see primarily its backward lean, which I consider typical of Classicizing works. See, e.g., a small **Dionysos** figure **from a house in Priene** that burnt down in the late 2nd c. The entry in *LIMC* 3, s.v. Dionysos, no. 101 (with bibl.), dates the piece to the end of the 4th or the beginning of the 3rd c., but I would place it at least 100 years later because of the left shoulder leaning back but without torsion, and the Aphrodite-like head type with chignon and fillet and an almost Archaistic hairstyle above the overly smooth forehead that recalls valances or the ripples of a chiton.

52. Hierapytna Nike (Venice, Arch. Museum 264A): the main publication, with identification of the statue and its provenience, is Beschi 1985; cf. his pl. 3 fig. 4 for the wing attachments. Beschi's conclusions are accepted by Moreno 1994, 535, 545, and fig. 665 on p. 540; the Athena head once placed on the torso but now exhibited separately (Venice, Arch. Museum 264B) is his fig. 669 on p. 543—its helmet was probably in metal, and a modern restoration in plaster has been removed. The two pieces (perhaps originally part of a group) were sent to Venice by Giovanni Mocenigo, but were once, erroneously, attributed to the Grimani collection. That information is repeated by Gulaki 1981, 187–88, who connects the Nike with the Temple of Apollo Pythios at Gortyn—a different Cretan city. According to Beschi 1985, the akrolithic(?) Athena may have belonged to a temple dedicated in common to Apollo, the Twelve Gods, and Athena Polias, as mentioned in a 2nd-c. inscription. The Nike, without head and plinth, is 2.14 m high; with both features added, it might have reached a height of 2.70–2.80 m. It is unclear whether

the elongated proportions of the body are a sign of its times or an optical correction demanded by its size. The right arm is original, but the left is modern.

In July 1998 the Venice Museum was closed and its statues were under protective wraps, but I was able to see both the Nike and the Athena head, through the courtesy of the director, Dr. G.-L. Ravagnan. The Athena head is strongly asymmetrical, bespeaking an original turn to proper right. The slightly parted lips do not reveal the teeth, although these may have been indicated in paint, as the eyebrows probably were, to judge by the smoothed surfaces over the eyes. The prominent Venus ring in the neck contrasts with the emptiness of the tapering face.

53. On the Mahdia wreck, see Hellenkemper Salies 1994, passim, and 1996; also Ridgway 1995b for a summary of the contents of the exhibition volumes. Cf. also infra, Ch. 7.

54. See Kabus-Preißhofen 1989; pp. 176–77 provide a summary of local style and a discussion of possible outside influences, with Magnesia predominating during the 2nd c. Pp. 15–16 review the almost total lack of known contexts, some items being *spolia;* the cache under the Odeion contained an unusually high proportion of portraits, with only two pieces of "ideal" sculpture out of a total of 30 (p. 20). This distribution suggests that some honorary statues of important personages were intentionally salvaged, perhaps after the earthquake of 142 A.C. An important statement occurs on p. 17: the notion that the local marble quarries were opened only at the beginning of the 2nd c. is no longer valid, thus removing one further clue from our chronological assessment.

My rough total of 2nd-c. sculptures breaks down as follows: 14 male statues and torsos (including 3 images of Asklepios, the main god of the island), 14 female statues and torsos, 2 individual male heads (cat. 81, helmeted, a doubtful Alexander), 5 individual female heads; a Rhodian male statue dated to the 3rd quarter of the 2nd c. is catalogued as no. 117, pl. 51.1–3. The Koan sculptures attributed to the 2nd c. include some Archaizing and some Classicizing figures: e.g., cat. 71, and the colossal head mentioned in my text, no. 92, 167–69, pl. 76.1–2, which has been compared to the Pergamon Parthenos: cf. Niemeier 1985, 26–27. Another female head, if not 2nd c., is possibly Antonine (cat. 93). Note that within the catalogue, nos. 1–18 list the sculptures in the round from the Altar of Asklepios.

That honorary statues could be over-lifesize on Kos seems different from Rhodian practices, at least as attested by bases on Lindos, where imprints for bronze portrait statues give a foot length consistent with smaller dimensions and contrasting with those for divinities: see Pollitt, forthcoming, ns. 12–13.

55. Höghammar 1993; see esp. pp. 107–109 for statistics on the various "units" throughout the span under consideration. See also, however, the more critical review by M. D. Fullerton, *AJA* 98 (1994) 787–88, according to whom only 11 examples of sculptures can be attributed to the span 190–70, as against 30 during 330–190. Höghammar 1997 analyzes the (meager) evidence with specific reference to honorary statues of women (mostly private or funerary, with the demos setting up only the statue of a queen [Arsinoe III, shortly before 200] during the span 250–150). What is apparent, however, is the enormous increase in commissions during Roman times—a situation confirmed by other surveys. For comments on types and nature of votive and honorary offerings during the 2nd c., with specific reference to the gymnasion on Delos, and on the desire of citizens to be commemorated in gymnasia, see von Hesberg 1995, esp. 18–23, with additional bibl.

56. On equestrian monuments, see the catalogues and comments by Siedentopf 1968, esp.

pp. 20–27 for the 2nd c. For the monument of M. Acilius Glabrio, see cat. II, 75; there were fewer such monuments for Romans at Olympia than at Delphi. The statue of King Masinissa was dedicated on Delos by Charmylos, son of Nikarchos, of Rhodes.

57. The general study is Koch 1994: it excludes half-naked figures, figures sitting on animals, kourotrophoi, renderings of Isis Lactans, and outright Roman creations, even if eclectic, reviewing only Imperial monuments inspired by Classical or Hellenistic models. Although terracottas are included, only a few statuettes are catalogued. For the Pergamene seated statues, see supra, Ch. 2 n. 77. The Kyzikos statue (Istanbul Arch. Mus. 1356) is her no. 93, p. 103; it was found not far from the south city wall, but it is said not to be funerary because of its large size. For a full publication, see Hoffmann 1965. Cf. also infra, Ch. 9 and ns. 47, 50, for comparison with a statue in Minneapolis.

58. Horn 1931, although outdated, is still an important source of illustrations. On Linfert 1976, see also the critique by Zagdoun 1991, 141 no. 5. The development of the draped female figure is concisely but effectively sketched by Smith 1991, 84–85. A more detailed study, Filges 1997, is limited to figures with mantle roll crossing the chest, and stops its review of originals before our timespan.

For examples of the type from Kos, see Kabus-Preißhofen 1989, cat. 56 (dated end 2nd c., ht. 1.97 m without plinth), pp. 245–48, pls. 63–64 (= Smith 1991, fig. 112), and, to a lesser extent, cat. 53 (ca. 180/170), 239–42, pl. 55 (from the Odeion, type of the "Samian Muse"). For Pergamon no. 68, see Horn 1931, pl. 38.1, and cf. Pergamon no. 54, pl. 21.2 (= Bieber 1961, fig. 514). Melos statuette, Athens NM 238: Horn 1931, 85–86, pl. 44.1; Czapski 1998. Statue from Erythrai, in London, British Museum: Pollitt 1986, 270 and fig. 291 (= Bieber 1961, fig. 521 and p. 131). For an over-lifesize statue from the Samian Heraion (= Horn 1972, 17–20, 82–83, no. 5, pls. 14, 17, 18, dated 160–140) and another from Magnesia, see Bieber, figs. 512 and 520 (for the latter, pp. 131–32 with bibl. in n. 53). For Magnesia, see also Linfert 1976, 34–35, figs. 41–45 on pls. 8–9. Statue (A) from the Letoon: Davesne and Marcadé 1992, 101–106, pls. 37–41 (over-lifesize, dated ca. 165–160 and 150). For the Baker Dancer, see, e.g., Pollitt 1986, fig. 192; Ridgway 1990, 219–22, pl. 102.

59. Female statue from Soloeis (Casa di Leda): Berges 1997, pls. 18.1–2, 19. Ht.: 1.29 m (without base, which was made of Lartian marble with stuccoed front, thus probably supplied locally). The figure leans on a pier to her left, holding a missing attribute, probably a long scepter, with that hand; her right, palm outward, rests on her protruding hip. The head is delicate, with blurred features. The layered-soled sandals show a deep indentation; the raised left foot is neither described nor explained. The type is compared to several East Greek gravestones of wide-ranging provenance, and dated (p. 93) mid-2nd c. For the Pergamon Tragoidia, see supra, Ch. 2 n. 76.

60. Lewerentz 1993; the study is primarily concerned with the iconology of the various types, such as philosophers and poets, orators and politicians. For a synthesis of 2nd-c. styles by 50-year spans, see pp. 205–207, with a change said to appear ca. 100. The two largest typological groupings are Type I (headed by Dioskourides, with the Eretria Youth as cat. I.4; it includes a figure in Cypriot limestone: cat. I.5) and Type V (including the Zeus/Hero and the Zeus Ammon, as well as eight representations of Asklepios from the 2nd c.), each containing 23 items. The smallest group is IV, with a total of six examples. The "Varia" catalogues 10 items (figs. 38–48), many from Melos, and *all* dated to the 2nd c., which seems surprising. Despite frequent cross-references to Kabus-Preißhofen 1989, Lewerentz's attributions of male figures

to the 2nd c. do not entirely coincide with those of the earlier work, even in the determination of provenience (whether from Rhodes or from Kos). For the so-called Alexander from Magnesia, see also Ridgway 1990, 122 (doubtful), and Stewart 1993a, 334–36, fig. 133 (accepted, ca. 160), with bibl. on p. 427. Zanker 1995, 254–55, believes the uniformity of mantled figures speaks of continuity and tradition to contemporary viewers. For the numbers of honorary statues of the same individual erected in a city context, see Raeck 1995. See also infra, Ch. 6, for depictions of men and women in a funerary context.

61. Poseidon of Melos, Athens NM 235 (ht. 2.17 m): main monograph, Schäfer 1968. Lewerentz 1993, 281–82, cat. VI.3, ca. 130/120; Pollitt 1986, 269 and fig. 290 (ca. 150); Smith 1991, 64 ("a dry, second-century original that employs a highly conservative Classical body style to signify elevation and authority"), fig. 304 (2nd c.). *LIMC* 7, s.v. Poseidon, no. 32 pl. 354. Moreno 1994, 352–55, figs. 428, 450, 638, 946, considers the statue Alexandrian in iconography and technique (ca. 180), but with strong parallels in Pergamon and the work of Damophon of Messene. Technical features are illustrated by Schäfer 1968.

Aphrodite of Melos, Paris, Louvre 399/400 (ht. 2.04 m): main monograph, Pasquier 1985. Officially catalogued by Hamiaux 1998, 41–44 no. 52, with additional fragments found with the statue—nos. 53 (hand with apple) and 54 (bare upper arm). No. 55, part of a right forearm with hand, is considered Roman; no. 56, forepart of a sandaled left foot, is said to be too small for the Aphrodite. Hamiaux dates the statue ca. 130–100, as Hellenistic imitation of the late 4th-c. bronze original of the Capua Aphrodite. Niemeier 1985, 31–32 and fig. 10, provides a helpful comparison of the Aphrodite's face with that of Nyx on the Pergamon Gigantomachy (his fig. 14); cf. also his pp. 142–43. See also Pollitt 1986, 167 ("traits of free neoclassicism . . . mixture of diverse baroque and neoclassical traits would seem to place it ca. 150–125 B.C." as supported by letter forms of signature), fig. 172. Smith 1991, 81 ("seeks to give the goddess a more 'classic' dignity: she has a matronly body and heavy, fifth-century features with a blank, solemn expression . . . an original of the second century, but its clear relation to the Capua type reveals the misleading nature, in this context, of the term 'original'"), figs. 305.1–2 (2nd c.). *LIMC* 2, s.v. Aphrodite, no. 643 pl. 63. See Claridge 1990, esp. 145–46 fig. 13, for technical features. Havelock 1995, 93–98, discusses earlier reactions to the statue and suggests that the Capua Aphrodite may derive from the Melian rather than vice versa, as usually believed. See also infra, n. 66.

For a treatment of both statues together, with important historical and stylistic observations, see Maggidis 1998; Dr. Maggidis first presented his theories at a graduate seminar at Bryn Mawr College in April 1991.

62. Thus Hamiaux 1998 states that the connection of statue and inscribed plinth cannot now be proven. The plinth need not have been in two (joined) pieces, which would be unusual, but simply in two levels. The extant surface seems broken all around.

63. Note also how her garment trails in back *below* the level of the plinth's surface. This detail confirms that the plinth was not meant to be sunk into a separate base but constituted the only stand for the statue, which must therefore have been otherwise "protected" from possible breakage. Even the detail of the trailing mantle was intended to provide added support for the ankle area.

64. For photographs of the Aphrodite taken directly from front and back, see Hamiaux 1998, 43. For short fifth toes, see infra, e.g., Ch. 9 n. 34 (Horse and Jockey).

The Poseidon comes from the area of the harbor, where a sanctuary to the sea god might have existed. An inscribed base found nearby mentions a dedication to Poseidon by Theodoridas, son of Laistratos (*IG* 12.3.1096). Remarkably, the same man is attested to have dedicated to Hermes at least one of the three hermaic pillars (also now in the Louvre) found near the Aphrodite, two beardless and one bearded, in one piece with the inscribed base (Hamiaux 1998, 46–50, nos. 57–59; identified, respectively, as bearded Hermes, beardless Herakles, and beardless Herakles with some portrait-like features). Four additional statues were uncovered near the Poseidon: two females (Aphrodite and Amphitrite?; cf. Linfert 1976, figs. 279–80, said to be definitely later), a standing male, and a rider. We cannot deduce from his large size (2.17 m) that the Melos Poseidon was a cult image, since the Melos Aphrodite, a private dedication, is 2.04 m tall.

65. Torso from Cosa: Collins-Clinton 1993; see p. 267 and n. 40 for comparison to the Aphrodite of Melos, pp. 263–64, figs. 9–13, for the Melos Poseidon, pp. 264–65 and fig. 14 for the Zeus/Hero from Pergamon. Other examples (including some from Kos) are discussed within the article. Despinis 1995, 333 and n. 53, compares the technique of "Euboulides' Muse" to that of the Aphrodite.

66. See the useful juxtaposition of frontal views in Niemeier 1985, figs. 9 (the Kaufmann replica of the Knidia in the Louvre) and 10 (the Melian Aphrodite); for the Capua Aphrodite, see his fig. 34 and cf. *LIMC* 2, s.v. Aphrodite, no. 627 pl. 61, with comments on both the Capua type and the statue in the Louvre on pp. 71–72 and 73–74 respectively (discussing previous attributions and relationships). For a monographic treatment of the Capua Aphrodite, see Knell 1993, advocating for it a late 4th–early 3rd c. date—lower than previous commentaries. See also supra, n. 61 (Havelock 1995). For the proportions of the Melian Aphrodite, see Clark 1956, 89.

67. Linfert 1976, for instance, omits Athens entirely from his review of artistic centers producing Hellenistic female statuary. For a review of honorary monuments in Athens, see Stewart 1979, 117–19. He states (p. 119): "Portraits of priestesses and acolytes of Athena, Demeter and others, and of various other private individuals, mostly dedicated by relatives . . . become extremely common in the second and first centuries." His information, however, is derived primarily from statue bases and other evidence. Cf. p. 25: "It may . . . be no coincidence that the years that saw the high-water mark of the baroque in Asia also apparently witnessed the absolute nadir of sculptural style in Athens itself." This judgment should, however, be seen in the context of the Classicizing trend that Stewart believes was predominant in Athens at the time. For honorary statues of women, although primarily with regard to depictions on grave stelai, see Zanker 1995, 261–63; he stresses that costume and pose can be used as clues to differentiate mortals from goddesses.

68. The contents of the Pergamene Library were taken by Antony in 41 and given to Kleopatra VII. No sculptural embellishment is likely after 133, when Attalos III died.

On the issues of intertextuality and Classicizing, see esp. Fullerton 1997, whose comments are relevant also for Hellenistic art, and Fullerton 1998a

CHAPTER 6

Original Reliefs

Funerary and Votive

Previous chapters have already mentioned some possible votive and funerary monuments (the battle relief in Aberdeen [cf. Pl. 34], the so-called Schoolteacher Relief from Rhodes) and drawn parallels between honorary statues (e.g., the Kleopatra and Dioskourides on Delos [cf. Pl. 46]) and contemporary gravestones. We should now attempt to look at these two categories per se, as examples of original sculpture of the second century. I shall begin with tomb markers because they are more abundant and well defined, although, during the second century, the line between a votive and a funerary function becomes faint indeed. This point will receive special attention below.

FUNERARY RELIEFS

It is simpler to begin with areas of little or no production of carved gravestones. **Athens,** for instance, is apparently all but devoid of the figured stelai that were its Classical hallmark, despite the fact that Demetrios of Phaleron's expulsion, in 307, should have allowed discontinuation of his anti-luxury decree. **Boiotia** seems to perpetuate only one of the three types of markers current in the fourth century: the pedimented entablatures in stuccoed poros carved with floral motifs, probably topping high pillars. **Thessaly,** which had a definite figured series of relief gravestones in Classical times, shows a dwindling production that continues only in painting, although some of the purely painted stelai from Pegasai/Demetrias are quite elaborate and remarkable; they belong, however, to the sphere of monumental painting, not to that of sculpture. The series of anthemion stelai, quite widespread within the region, has no figural representation except for a schematically rendered hermaic pillar usually appearing in the lower portion of the slender shaft.[1] **Macedonia** has produced an equally scant crop of funerary reliefs, and recent attention tends to concentrate on the elaborate tombs, also with paintings.[2] The only area on the Greek Mainland with a quantifiable number of carved grave stelai, albeit not figural, is **Achaia**, and its abundant output in the second century, as contrasted with earlier and later times, is attributed to the economic expansion and political prominence engendered by the existence of the Achaian League (dissolved by the Romans in 146). Yet the primary sculptural decoration of these limestone monuments is architectural, in an empty-naiskos format occasionally topped by floral motifs and, in a few instances, underpinned by objects indicated in very low relief against a plain background. Paint was extensively used and would have added immeasurably to the total effect.[3]

Naiskos stelai replete with human figures in relief appear, however, in **Asia Minor**, where they occur in large numbers and provide an essential commentary on local society. Smaller than the latest Classical gravestones from Attika, but very elaborate in their use of symbolic attributes and subsidiary motifs, they have been the focus of attention in recent times, not so much for their stylistic value (especially since chronology is almost always relative) as for their social implications—the expression of a prosperous, self-important citizen class as contrasted with rulers and heroes who could command more complex burial. Not especially known for their gravestones in Classical times, the East Greek cities[4] are clearly thought to demonstrate the impact of their new political and economic conditions in their Hellenistic funerary art—yet a further implication is perhaps present. A smaller group of gravestones comes from the **Greek islands**, especially **Delos** with its cemeteries at **Rheneia**. We shall try to summarize here the relevant aspects of these stelai and to consider the possible reasons for this specific distribution.

East Greek Stelai

In 1977 and in 1979, in two installments, a vast corpus of East Greek gravestones appeared, which had, however, been in the making since 1904. Two German scholars, Ernst Pfuhl and Hans Möbius, were responsible in turn for this daunting undertaking, each of them prevented by death from putting the final touches on his efforts. The two sections (each consisting of one volume of text and one of plates) have become the *locus classicus* for the study of the subject, with material ranging from the Archaic to the advanced Roman Imperial period, and covering not only the cities of the Asiatic coast up to the Black Sea, but also the islands closest to it: Lesbos, Chios, Samos, Kos, and Rhodes. Ample photographic documentation makes accessible in a single source monuments treated in a variety of publications not always available in our libraries and physically scattered throughout museums in Europe and other continents. Yet some problems remain.

Although this major catalogue includes global comments on various aspects of the grave reliefs and their meanings, in the post-Classical section the scenes are listed typologically rather than in approximate chronological order or by provenience. An index of findspots at the end of volume 2 allows some geographic groupings, but no meaningful patterns are made obvious by the chosen arrangement. The task of extracting specific information from the corpus has therefore been attempted by other scholars, in terms of both formal analysis (with a view to a chronological ordering) and semantic message.[5]

Chronology is, however, problematic, since very few clues to external evidence exist; even letter forms and prosopography are of little help, and typology is undermined by the clear recourse to traditional types that originate in the Classical period. It has in fact been argued that the sudden increase in the number of gravestones during the second century, in a variety of locations, is a byproduct of the Classicizing trends visible also in contemporary sculpture in the round. Conversely, the heightened sculptors' activity engendered by large monuments such as the Pergamon Altar and the altar of the Artemision at Magnesia has been seen as the source for much of the labor force active in the funerary field, and thus as the impetus behind its production. It can perhaps be added that reliance on the absolute control of rulers was diminishing, given the uncertain strength of the various Hellenistic monarchies, and this relative decentralization of power led to increased dependence on the benefactions of individuals within the cities themselves, as demonstrated by the corresponding distribution of honorary statues. Funerary monuments could thus be viewed as an additional form of honor, especially since the Smyrnaian stelai, at least, are often set up by the demos, as attested by inscriptions within characteristic wreaths.[6]

If traditional typology and Classicizing trends make it difficult to separate clearly some third- or first-century works from those of the second, it is nonetheless true that changes in conceptions seem to take place by 200, as expressed by epitaphs. According to a recent study, both reliefs and inscriptions shift from a generic representation of equal citizenship to an increasingly specific emphasis on the individual. For instance, the term *arete*, which in the fourth century signified general excellence, by the second century was limited to warriors, thus signaling military valor. The female counterparts, however, may have lost individual rendering in favor of a stereotypical formula that, on the stelai, translated into various iconographic signs symbolic of those virtues and possessions considered appropriate for outstanding women. It seems increasingly clear that such symbolic values were already, if more subtly, expressed by Classical (Attic) stelai, but it is equally true that the proliferation of attributes in second-century gravestones makes such semiotic readings compelling, even if the funerary inscriptions cannot usually be taken as the verbal counterparts of the visual images.[7]

Epitaphs, however, as was true for the Classical period, express more grief than the images themselves. During the second century, only subsidiary figures, usually servants and children, occasionally appear mournful, whereas the dead look unconcerned and detached, often in epiphanic poses that confront the viewers like contemporary renderings of divinities on votive reliefs. This form of gravestone, most frequently of the **naiskos type** with elaborate architectural frame, may depict one, usually two, but even three or more facing figures accompanied by truly diminutive servants. It seldom includes action poses—at most, the gesture of one hand stretched toward another person, or even toward an isolated tree or element of landscape.[8] Whatever meaning is intended to reach the viewer is carried by the many "attributes" or symbols scattered around the main personages, typical of such stelai. Yet even such formal presentations can convey a degree of depth and recession into space, mostly articulated by the lower relief of the objects in the background, or the perspective arrangement of piers and furnishings (Pls. 59–60). In one instance, a low wall separates a leafy tree from a frontal maiden, who nonetheless reaches out as if to pluck a fruit from it, while cradling a doll in her left arm—an indication of adolescence irrespective of apparent scale.[9]

Plates 59–60

Two other dominant types of funerary reliefs appear more "narrative" in their scenes, with figures often in profile or in various poses: the **Funerary Banquet,** prevalent on Samos, Byzantion, and Kyzikos, sporadically attested almost everywhere, and continuing in favor throughout the Roman period; and the **Rider** (or **Horse Leader**) **Type,** sometimes showing two horsemen, and often accompanied by tree and snake, and popular in Pergamon with a distinctive draping of the horseman's chlamys that stretches onto his mount. A fourth possible grouping of gravestones would comprise other formats (for instance, the stelai in more than one register) and scenes too varied and individualized to be gathered under a single heading and thus unable to be characterized as a type.[10]

The Funerary Banquet and the Rider Types carry clear overtones of heroization, occasionally confirmed by inscriptions ("to the hero")—it is important to stress that both iconographic formulas had begun much earlier with a votive function. But even the naiskos stele with frontal figures could imply a special veneration of the dead. Zanker has called attention to a gravestone from Miletos in which three personages— a man, his daughter, and his father—appear to be behind an altar in the foreground, which is encircled by a huge snake; not only does this last detail suggest chthonic cult, but also the fact that all three figures stand on a base, like statues in the round. It has been pointed out that no such statues are known as tomb markers, at least in Smyrna, and that therefore the allusion is to honorary portraits, although as generic types derived from more than one source.[11] Yet the frontal figures between columns are so striking that I wonder whether inspiration may have come from elaborate graves or heroa like the Halikarnassos Maussolleion with its rows of ancestral figures, or even the Pergamon Altar if it too included statuary between and behind its outer columns. The idea of cult, of whatever nature—perhaps simply heroization and veneration rather than actual ritual—would automatically derive from such monumental sources and would find easy acceptance in a territory that was particularly open to the suggestion of royal cult and heroization of the ruler.

I find it significant, in fact, that figured gravestones continue to be mostly absent in Greece proper, especially in Athens, where the tradition for that form of tomb marker was strongest and, toward the end of the fourth century, had included monuments in the size and shape of a small temple. Thessaly and Macedonia are monarchical territories, especially the latter, where the tradition of elaborately painted tombs through the fourth and later centuries—more numerous by now than the known members of the ruling dynasty—probably exerted a comparable influence on painted stelai for individual citizens. That Athens lacked skilled carvers, or did not have the impetus of sustained new constructions, is untenable, in view of the known existence of honorary and divine images, probably even a series of philosopher portraits, and the extensive program of stoas and other civic structures erected within the city during the second century. Nor did all sculptors emigrate to Delos in 166, to rekindle interest in funerary sculpture there. Finally, tendance of the tombs bears no relationship to political activity; that Athens was a backwater in terms of world events should not have affected its funerary traditions and its economic possibilities, especially since prosperity decidedly increased after Delos was given to the city as a free port. Stelai of reduced size and poorer artistic quality (like some of those from Rheneia) could still have been produced, had the need been felt for them.[12] It seems to me that a different explanation is required, especially in view of the fact that both Document Reliefs and, to some extent, votive reliefs peter out in Attika at the same time.

I would tentatively suggest that the remarkable flourishing of figured gravestones in Asia Minor—an area not previously know for its tomb markers—is due to the very "cultic" nature of such reliefs, which straddle the line between funerary and votive. The inspiration for the format may have come from the grandiose tombs of the rulers, and the specific figural types may have resembled honorary statues in the round, but the *need* for such images could have derived from the uncertain political climate of the times, which made reliance on the protection of the dead particularly significant, while the shift in beliefs toward their heroization was a byproduct of eastern religions and philosophies connected with the ruler cult. Finally, we may even surmise some influence from the spreading waves of Italians and Romans into East Greek territory, since ancestral veneration was firmly entrenched in their traditions and must have been carried abroad. The Greek Mainland, by contrast, and especially Athens proved impervious to these conceptions and may have intentionally rejected any form of tomb marking that would imply their acceptance. Heroization of the dead has often been discussed in the context of Hellenistic gravestones; the difference in my proposal is a matter of degree—here stressing the votive over the funerary component—in order to explain proliferation and distribution patterns.[13]

To be sure, some of the depictions on the stelai, even the **naiskos type** of Smyrna, at first glance seem thoroughly mundane and stereotypical. The women are usually in the so-called Pudicitia stance and attire, richly dressed and adorned as befits a proper matron, and with serene, idealized faces; most of the men are tightly wrapped in their mantle (over the "modest" East Greek tunic), and their faces tend to be more realistic, some of them even creased and aging though never truly as elderly as on some Classical gravestones. Both types have been "read" as signifying the typical self-definition of city dwellers who wanted to project an image of virtue combined with sexual allure and luxury in the case of the women, of learning and self-restraint in that of the men. On the other hand, some renderings may not always have carried the symbolic connotations of the alleged prototype (the Aischines, the Sophokles, the Demosthenes statues), and may rather have been chosen and varied according to compositional principles—the stance with a weight leg toward the edge of the field, for instance, or in mirror image to that of a nearby figure; the raised forearm in the Pudicitia type that may, or may not, correspond to the side of the free leg. Thus iconographic selections would be made within workshops and may not correspond to specific requests from the sponsor.[14] Another noticeable similarity—that of the female figures to the approximately contemporary terracottas from Myrina and Tanagra—breaks down in the poses, clearly active in the figurines and less obviously "temporary" on the stelai, despite some hints of outdoor setting, such as a parasol, a sun hat, or a monument in the background. Zanker has pointed out that whereas Classical gravestones depicted women indoors, or at least in neutral contexts, Hellenistic stelai often take them outside the home, perhaps again as a reflection of the honorary statues that stood in agorai or other public places. Yet even these external signs may carry purely symbolic rather than locational meanings—strolling women and men do not normally stand near trees or columns encircled by snakes (cf. Pl. 59), and herms (especially of a mantled Herakles—a hero victorious over death) do not always suggest the environment of the palaistra. One suggestion sees them as marking the boundary of Hades.[15]

A considerable number of gravestones depicting women, whether singly or together with men, belonged to priestesses of various cults—of Isis, of Kybele, especially of Demeter—as shown by inscriptions and attributes, notably the large torches typical of the last-named goddess. Costume is also significant: followers of Isis wear a fringed mantle fastened in a characteristic fashion, while Demeter's acolytes may have one or two chitons (one often with a very low kolpos) and a himation forming a distinctive triangular pattern over the front, below a twisted roll. This arrangement frees their hands for holding the required attributes and may also be suggestive of physical activity. Probably these women are wearing the garments of the respective deities, and the diminutive size of the attendants (whether servants or children) enhances their divine appearance through an entirely unrealistic use of the scale of importance. It seems remarkable that no men should be characterized as priests by the traditional long costume, despite the fact that such functions were easily bought by prosperous citizens. Men holding scrolls have been "read" as projecting an interest in literature and culture, but different suggestions see the scroll as a sacred text, thus implying possible initiation into mysteries, or even as an important possession taken to the grave—a gift to Persephone. Conversely, the inclusion of a horn of plenty among the "attributes" has been taken as indication of *euergasia* and therefore of priestly office, but one stele depicting a couple in *dexiosis* shows two joined cornucopiae (*dikerata*), which may therefore symbolize also marital union and concord, as in the Ptolemaic prototypes of this device (Pl. 61).[16] It should be admitted that several objects on the gravestones allow for more than one meaning, some of which may escape us or be understood according to our own viewpoint.

Plate 61

If slaves and attendants are shown as impossibly small in the naiskos stelai, they seem better proportioned in the other two common types of representations, the Funerary Banquet and the Rider stelai, yet the votive tone is unmistakable in both—which might explain why they are almost entirely missing from Smyrna, where other formulas served the same propitiatory purpose.[17] The so-called **Totenmahl** appears as early as the sixth century and is almost immediately imbued with heroic/chthonic meaning, being used in the heroon for Archilochos on Paros. In the Hellenistic reliefs, changes from the Classical renderings are especially noticeable in the furnishings of the scenes: the kline and other pieces of furniture may have elaborately carved legs, and a new element is introduced, the *kylikeion*, a sort of cupboard for vessels that enhances the impression of a domestic interior (cf. Pl. 63). The general appearance is one of greater luxury, with various objects in the background, including the distinctive horse or horse protome, but an ambivalence comparable to that of the Smyrnaian stelai is obvious in those scenes that add a tree with entwined snake, thus suggesting the outdoors. Another distinctive trait is that the female companion of the reclining male often sits on the kline itself, rather than on a separate throne or stool at the foot of the bed; as a consequence, the woman often faces forward, breaking her visual connection with the reclining man but increasing that with the viewer. Some Rhodian Hellenistic stelai are unique in depicting reclining women, the sole known instances before Roman times (Pl. 62). And some Hellenistic stelai show as many as four men reclining at banquet.[18]

Plate 62

The examples of the type from Samos seem to form a distinctive group. Like other reliefs from the island, they often occupy wide slabs with ample overhead space that give the figures a sense of open-air environment; yet the familiar tree almost never appears (or appears only on late items). Occasionally, however, hangings create a backdrop to the main scene, and architectural elements (in one surprising case an entire façade of a building) are included. A distinctive feature of the Samian Banquets is the frequent presence of armor: shields, helmets, cuirasses. Yet Samos was not particularly warlike, and certainly not more military than Smyrna, where such renderings of weapons are missing. It has been suggested that the Samian attributes derive from the earlier iconography of hero banquets with votive rather than funerary character; yet I believe that a dedicatory purpose continues there throughout the history of the type. It is, in fact, significant that the one epitaph clearly marking the relief as funerary is inscribed on a composition different from the traditional rendering: a youth, Philon, a winner in the pankration, stands naked in the foreground holding a javelin, his own small attendant nearby; a reclining man, a seated woman, another small servant, and a table laden with food form almost a separate scene and must represent the bereft parents. The epitaph is all the more remarkable in that only three are known from the entire island during the Hellenistic period, and the other two occur on undecorated stelai.[19]

Many Banquet Reliefs show several personages around the banqueter, thus conveying a sense of family, but also—I would stress—in some cases, one of worship, so that some scholars would classify as votive a few of the monuments at present listed within the funerary corpus. A distinctive example, probably from Rhodes, shows as many as 10 worshipers (eight men, two women) in stacked rows on either side of the kline on which a heavily bearded man reclines, in front of an architectural background (portico?) that reveals additional figures and one horse protome. On another relief, a banqueter with a Zeus-like head receives the offering of a pig brought in by a miniature slave, while a dignified man (*capite velato?*) stands at the foot of the bed holding a phiale; a tree with snake stretches its branches over the scene, and a rather large servant frames it on either side. A similar pig is being led toward a round altar on a third relief of a reclining man whose wife sits frontally at the foot of the bed in the very distinctive pose and draping of the Tyche of Antioch; on the left side of the panel, a couple with child make a gesture of worship. All three examples are more clearly votive than funerary, especially the last, with its obvious allusion to a personification, but one more item may demonstrate how the two purposes conjoin. A fragmentary stele in two registers (Pl. 63; and cf. Ill. 22, discussed in n. 20, infra) depicts, in the upper, a reclining man with seated wife and another female standing at the head of the kline; a child (rather than a servant, because of his costume) stands in front of the bed, and an elaborate kylikeion appears at the left edge of the scene, but the typical table laden with food is omitted. It appears, however, entwined by a snake, in the lower register, where a mantled man stretches his hand toward Hermes with petasos and kerykeion, in front of a tree and next to a column surmounted by a sundial, on which a servant leans in a mourning pose. The dexiosis motif used with a deity suggests that the deceased has attained superior status, thus confirming the heroizing undercurrent of the funerary banquet, while the sundial alludes to the passing of human time.[20]

The **Rider Reliefs** are even more ambiguous as gravestones than the Banquet scenes, although the two may appear together, as part of two superimposed registers. Several slabs with horsemen have been found in urban and even sacred contexts, and, at Pergamon, specifically in the sanctuary of Demeter; these are therefore unlikely to have been funerary, yet they have the same typology as those coming from cemeteries. In the second century, the type is predominant at Pergamon, perhaps under influence from the royal house, but its diffusion is enormous—from the Iberic peninsula to Asia, from Central Europe to North Africa—and so is its chronological span: reliefs to a heroic horseman begin as early as the late sixth century and are especially popular in the Roman Imperial period. We can here focus only on a few second-century ex-

Plate 63

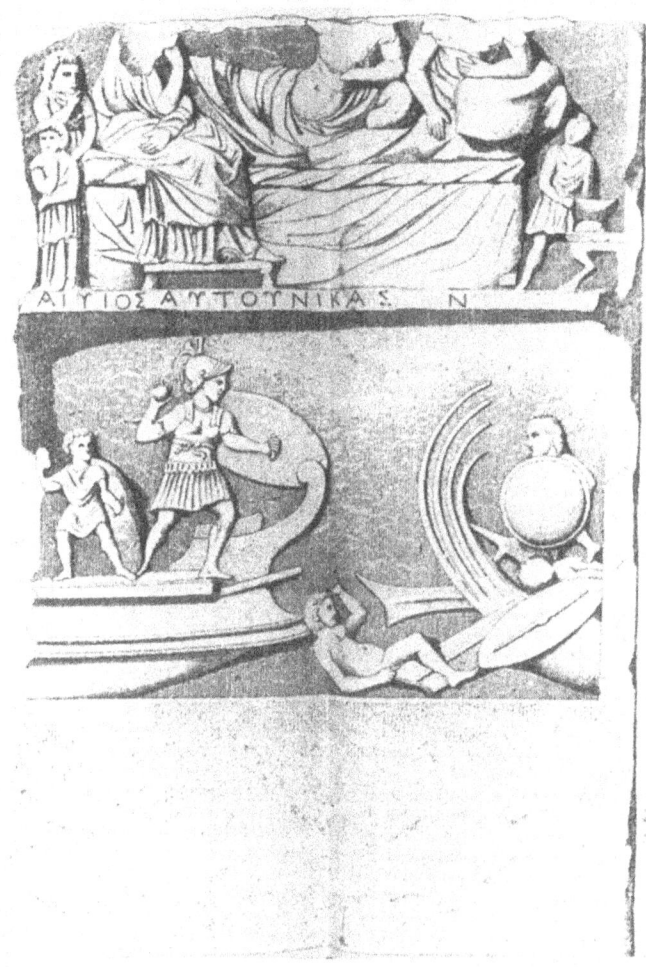

Ill. 22. Now lost stele once in Kios (Gemlik), with Funerary Banquet over
naval encounter (cf. n. 20). [After *DOG* 1979, 310 no. 1227, fig. 79]

amples, choosing primarily among those that are included in the corpus of East Greek
gravestones, although, once again, we stress the uncertainty of their classification or,
rather, the duality of their message.[21]

Although several variations exist, the basic iconography shows the rider either
standing near his horse or mounted. In the latter cases, the animal frequently appears
in motion, almost at a gallop, and its rider's chlamys flies behind him with a hieroglyph for speed, yet the general effect is static, often spoiled by the presence, immedi-

ately in front of the horse, of an altar or a tree with entwined snake. More animated are the scenes in which the horseman is on foot and the animal is restrained, either by himself or by an attendant: it turns its head toward the viewer, and its body disappears behind the standing man, usually with some effects of depth penetration. The Rider may be dressed in a tunic with long chlamys (ephaptis) fastened at the shoulder and rolled around his hips in a triangular pattern in front as he grasps it with his left hand; this is the so-called Polybios motif, since it recurs on the stele of Polybios, to be discussed below, among the votive reliefs. Yet a warlike tone is imparted by the horseman's weapons being held and even worn by attendants, in three cases diminutive.[22] A few reliefs show, however, the hero/rider nude or wearing his chlamys away from his naked body, so that the heroic impression is enhanced. Two such reliefs bear specific description.

The first is a plain **stele from Smyrna**—its architectural frame, if such there was, is now lost. The Rider stands frontally holding what is now just a horse protome, the rest of the animal's body being conceived as vanishing behind the man; he wears his long chlamys as a backdrop, exposing his youthful body with steep groin line. In front of the horse stand two rather sizable attendants, one holding a shield as he moves to left, as if away from the scene. To the proper left of the Rider stands a pillar surmounted by a vase, under the apparently bare branches of a tree encircled by a (largely damaged) snake. In front of both is a round altar decorated with boukranion and garlands. The second **relief** comes **from Pergamon** (Pl. 64): a Hero in the same attire as the previous Rider stretches a phiale in the direction of a veiled woman resting her right hand on a low pier. The libation is meant for a round altar between the two, behind which rises a tree with encircling snake, and in front of which a dog sits, looking up toward his master. Behind the naked youth, a horse is being held by a second young man almost as tall as the Hero; he wears chitoniskos, cuirass, helmet, and shield, and holds the bridle of a horse, again shown only as half a body. It is impossible to tell whether the plaque commemorates one or two personages, since the second man is not simply holding weapons that could be eventually handed over to the almost-naked Hero but is actually wearing full body armor; indeed, other Rider stelai show two men equal in size and attire. Both reliefs here described are notable also for the presence of an altar, which clearly indicates some form of cult. Their date is uncertain, but I would place at least the Pergamene stele late in the second century because of the "vanishing" rendering of the horse and the peculiar mannerism of the man's big toe, carved at some distance from the others. Both semi-nude men—the "hero" in each relief— are in strong Classical poses.[23]

As we have seen, the Totenmahl and the Rider Reliefs, even the occasional naiskos stele, can include altars. On **Rhodes**, free-standing round altars are so numerous and distinctive that they deserve separate treatment, whereas stelai form only one small part of the funerary repertoire. These gravestones, often set up on square bases, resist a strict typology, since many different iconographic formulas are used.

Plate 64

Original Reliefs—Funerary and Votive

We have already mentioned the unusual feature of women reclining at funerary banquets; another is the depiction of warriors, although several are stylistically datable earlier than the second century. One of the most distinctive representations, however, and chronologically set within our timespan, is that of two persons embracing—not only man/woman but also two women (Pl. 65). Both personages are heavily mantled, and only the lack of a tunic under the himation, leaving upper torso and ankles bare, identifies the male partner when the relief is damaged. In the East Greek sphere, these reliefs come only from Rhodes or the nearby islands of Syme and Tilos, but a similar one is said to be in the Tegea Museum.[24]

Plate 65

Other centers near the coast of Asia Minor (thus included in the corpus of East Greek reliefs) show few distinctive traits: some of their gravestones imitate Smyrnaian types, some derive inspiration from Kykladic stelai.[25] We shall therefore turn to the Kyklades to continue our review.

Kykladic Stelai

The most relevant site for our purposes is Delos, although the sacred island allowed neither birth nor death (and thus no burial) on its soil, and women in labor or the dying were hastily transferred to nearby sites, primarily Rheneia. This funerary prohibition probably held until Christianity took over, but the heyday of Delian grave monuments falls between 166, when Athens assumed control of the island, and 88 or 69, when the Mithradatic war and the related sack by the pirates greatly diminished its population and prosperity.[26] A great number of Attic sculptors lived on Delos during that span of time, and most of the gravestones show clear Attic influence, although the iconographic prototypes belong to the fourth century. Other influences and even some imports came from Asia Minor, especially since the island was filled with merchants and slaves of different ethnics. A large Italian population is also attested, and many of the funerary inscriptions mention persons with Roman names and connections, as freedmen or otherwise. In turn, Rheneian stelai diffused to the other Kyklades and to East Greek sites.

Many of the Rheneian stelai and those of the Kyklades as a whole are modest and traditional in both format and iconography, but some distinctive features and preferences may be mentioned. A few monuments are grandiose and deserve specific attention. Chronology is relative, and no stylistic development is readily observed; thus some examples here mentioned may belong to the first rather than the second century.

A format almost exclusively found in the Kyklades during the Hellenistic period is the naiskos stele framed by an arch on piers or columns below an entablature and/or pediment, or hollowed out of the surface as part of the sunken panel with figures. The traditional gabled gravestone is common and may have been used primarily for young people. A distinctive but rarer feature is the large anthemion crown taking up almost the entire width of a stele—an elaborate descendant of the Archaic palmette finial. Another Kykladic form is the stone sarcophagus that must have served as a family chapel; reliefs following the standard typology of free-standing stelai were engraved onto the sides of the chest as more individuals were buried, so that chronology is additive and difficult to assess. Although most caskets are Imperial, some could still belong to the second century.[27]

This suggestion may be confirmed by a spectacular combination of funerary types from Rheneia, as currently reconstructed. The tomb of Tertia Horaria (Ill. 23) consisted of a podium, possibly filled with earth, fronted by three Corinthian columns between antae. These supported a Doric architrave and frieze with plain metopes surmounted by a dentil course and cornice. Above this podium was a large sarcophagus, plain except for a wool basket (kalathos) in relief on its center. The basket was flanked by the valedictory inscription mentioning Tertia Horaria, daughter or liberta of Publius and married to a Publius. The inscription calls her Roman, but the naiskos stele that stood upright above the sarcophagus depicts Tertia as a typical Greek woman, seated with veiled head and transparent drapery and flanked by a small servant with jewel box. A beardless man in tunic and himation that reveal the underlying body stands in front of her, and the two may have joined hands in the dexiosis motif, although their arms are now broken off. The most remarkable part of this stele is the vegetation: from behind the two Corinthian columns emerge two vines that meet in the center of the background with sprays of tendrils, leaves, and grape bunches interspersed with flowers. The resulting effect is that of two persons in the open air, under a grape harbor, seen as if through a window. Above the entablature of the naiskos, a huge oval anthemion (akanthos) occupies almost the entire span of the roof, greatly adding to the richness of the floral decor. Although these vegetal elements, at second glance, prove entirely artificial in both arrangement and appearance, the total composition is overwhelming in its message of luxuriant foliage and, implicitly, of rebirth and afterlife. Paint would have made the monument even more unified and compelling. On prosopographic and stylistic grounds, Tertia's tomb is dated to the last third of the second century.[28]

Iconographically, Tertia's relief falls within the scenes of dexiosis, the most numerous category within the funerary repertoire at Rheneia and in the Kyklades in general. Other motifs are also traditional: women, men, children, seated or standing, alone or with servants. Within female iconography, notable is the rendering of the woman virtually reclining on her *klismos*—legs stretched out, one arm on the backrest—rather than the traditional upright sitting position; other women sit in the pose of the Tyche of Antioch (Pl. 66).[29] The Funerary Banquet is relatively rare, and even rarer is the Rider accompanied by tree and snake—I would imagine, because of the nature of the island. Appropriately, more common is a scene suggesting death by shipwreck—in which case the stele must have marked a cenotaph. It depicts a man seated on rocky ground, usually looking toward the right, often in a mournful or pensive pose with head resting on raised hand; variations include the addition of a servant, a wife, or even part of a ship, although what is shown is not enough to identify its type. This

Plate 66

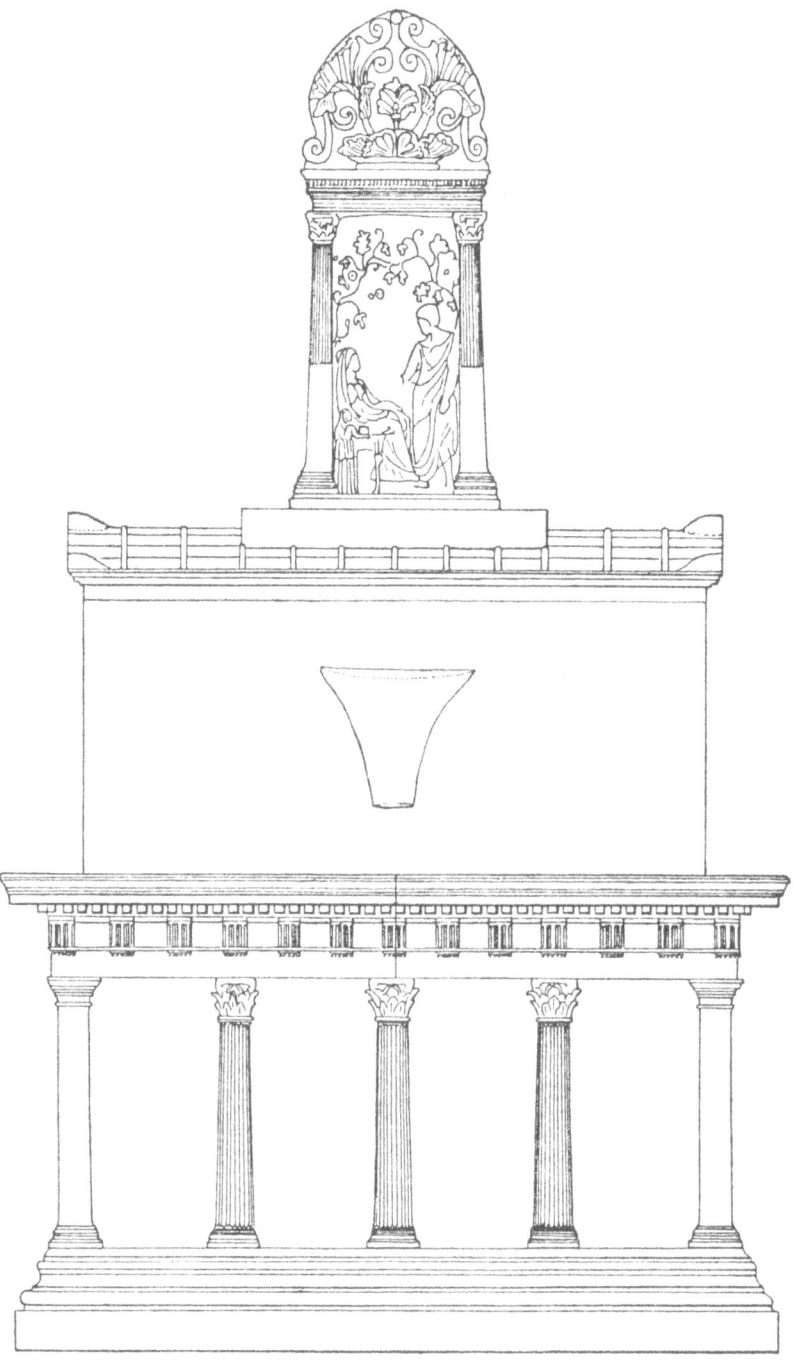

Ill. 23. Reconstruction of monument of Tertia Horaria on Rheneia (Delos). [After Couilloud 1974a, 227 fig. 79]

kind of representation is also known from the East Greek area, as one would expect from coastal or island sites, and it may have originated there, diffusing to Delos. At Rheneia, the drowned men have no attributes of a marine, and death presumably occurred outside a military encounter, although nine reliefs show warriors on ships. It is doubtful, however, that Delos had its own navy. Unique to the sacred island is the actual depiction of a shipwreck, of which three examples exist.[30]

Stelai were not the only form of Rheneian grave markers. Of particular interest are the free-standing sculptures, several of them unfinished, in the shape of humans, lions, and even an unusual, almost entirely anthropomorphic sphinx. The prow of a ship may have served as a statuary base.[31] But another characteristic form is that of the round altar, some examples of which are precisely datable because of inscriptions, which are, however, not limited to the Delian sphere.

Round Altars

This distinctive type, obviously used for votive as well as funerary purposes, is primarily known through examples from Delos, Rhodes, and Kos, so that even altars from elsewhere have been connected with these centers, but many are of unknown provenience and have been found entirely out of context, making classification difficult. Recent excavations in a Rhodian nekropolis have, however, provided important information on the use of such arulae in connection with tomb complexes and funerary plots, and have suggested a revised consideration of the cult of the dead. Typologically, the simplest type of cylindrical altar is decorated with animals' heads or skulls—most frequently bulls (boukephalia or boukrania), but occasionally also deer and rams (cf. Pl. 62). Their horns support garlands, which can also be of two types: either composed of simple leaves or including fruit in varying amounts. Production seems to start late in the third century or the beginning of the second, to continue into the early Imperial period, although on Delos, as for the stelai, the end may come after 69 B.C. Some pieces were appropriated and inscribed in later (Roman) times.[32]

Although falling within the timespan under survey, this type of monument may seem irrelevant to our purposes, yet several features demand consideration: (1) these altars resemble many depicted on East Greek gravestones, as discussed above, and may therefore throw light on the cult of the dead; (2) some examples include human figures (either by themselves or together with the standard garlands and animals' heads) that stress their connection with the funerary repertoire of the stelai; finally, (3) some of them may indeed have a sacred/votive function, thus bridging the gap between the two classes of reliefs. We shall review these points in the same order.

1. Round altars have been noted on some Smyrnaian stelai and Funerary Banquet and Rider reliefs. They are usually plain, without the elaborate moldings and dentil course that crown the Koan and Rhodian types, and certainly without the swags and boukrania of most arulae in the round, although some additional decoration in paint may have now vanished. Yet not only are some Rhodian finds equally plain, but

a few, like those on the reliefs, are encircled by large snakes carved as if coming to partake of the offerings. A good example was found on Knidos, but others are known from Rhodes and Kos, and a remarkable monument from a Rhodian cemetery is in the shape of a handleless bell krater embellished with six lotus- and six akanthos-leaves and surrounded by a snake stretching its bearded head toward a plaque on which two wreaths, like those of the Smyrnaian stelai, are engraved.[33]

Some of the Rhodian altars show clear indications that libations and even burnt offerings were placed on them—although blood sacrifices are not typical of grave cult, they are indeed typical of hero cults since earliest times. The latest studies have therefore suggested that cults of the heroized deceased existed by mid-Hellenistic times, when a marked change toward elaboration in monuments and layout of cemeterial plots can be noted. Inscriptional evidence attests to the help that the living could expect from the dead. In addition, mortuary cult could be grafted onto religious ritual: the second-century will of a certain Epikteta from Thera specifies that a yearly function should be held, with offerings to the Muses on the first day, to Epikteta and her husband on the second day, and to their children on the third. The offerings listed are cakes, barley, bread, cheese, and burnt fish. Connection with the Muses (to perpetuate memory?) is also suggested by several gravestones where figures use the iconography of an established Muse type and by the inclusion of theatrical masks.[34]

That the cult of the dead may have mingled with the ruler's cult is implied by the addition of prominent dikerata (double horns of plenty) between the garlands of many altars from Kos. They are such a typical feature of arulae from that island that they can be considered its hallmark; only one example from Rhodes is known, and seems under Koan influence. Given the strong Egyptian influence on Kos (Ptolemy II was born there), and the appearance of the symbol on Ptolemaic coins, association with their meanings of conjugal concord and "philadelphia" is inevitable, especially since the ribbons tying some of the sculptured garlands end with fringes, like royal diadems. Eventually, the dikerata may have been used also to signify prosperity, but their dominant position on the altars recalls the cornucopiae on the Smyrnaian stelai, for which comparable cultic allusions have been sought.[35]

2. Round altars with human figures have not yet been studied as a group, but several examples have been mentioned in related publications. The simplest carry an inset below the garlands or the animals' heads, depicting different scenes. Two altars from Rhodes show a Totenmahl, yet in both cases the table laden with food is omitted, and in one of them (if not on both) the reclining figure is female. Of the two, the more striking is that inscribed to Archestrata, daughter of Stratokles, wife of Hagesandros, since the rectangular panel is framed by a heavy laurel garland.[36] Another recessed area, on a monument from Kos, shows a frontal man of the Aischines type; over his head, the fourth boukephalion has been turned into a smaller boukranion, to accommodate the inset. From Rheneia, a similar composition uses the frontal man as the total replacement for one of the boukephalia. On an altar from Eresos (Lesbos), a

somewhat amorphous, continuous festoon has no visible means of support, but a man in short costume stands under one "peak," while a horse's head, an oval shield, and a round one respectively appear above the three downward swags.[37]

On more elaborate items, the animals' heads are replaced by Nikai, carrying wreaths and palm branches, and occasionally interacting with other figures; even dancing maenads can support the festoons. The most peculiar case, however, is that of an **altar in the British Museum,** of unknown provenience, where only somewhat more than half the cylinder is occupied by boukephalia connected by hanging garlands; the remaining surface has figures standing on a ledge: a seated woman holding hands with a standing man, with another man next to a pier surmounted by a cone and entwined by a snake, and two small servants. But the most striking image is Hermes holding a kerykeion, behind the seated woman and next to a small support holding a sundial, perhaps as indication that the fateful hour of separation has arrived—as on a gravestone in two registers mentioned above (cf. Pl. 63). A hole piercing the entire altar may have served for libations.[38]

A final example of the combination of garlands/boukrania and figures occurs on a cylindrical **altar in Istanbul** that should be entirely votive: a Tyche figure with horn of plenty in one hand, seated on a rock in front of a flaming altar, is receiving the offerings of eight small Erotes carrying various objects. One of them holds two cornucopiae, one pushes forward a pig—iconography resembling that of funerary monuments; another putto supports a plate of fruits, while the others have different "attributes," including, perhaps, a trumpet. Near the altar, two upright torches mark the sacredness of the spot, contributing to a sense of landscape for the entire scene, as if the overhead festoons were the hangings from the eaves of a stoa.[39]

A somewhat different **altar, from Aigina,** is known only through a drawing. Six Corinthian columns surround the cylinder, creating rectangular areas, two of which are filled by figures in relief: a servant leads a horse toward the next panel, where a mantled man offers a cup to a snake on a tree. The square base of the altar carried an inscription to Pausanias, son of Meidon.[40]

3. Only two monuments, both from Halikarnassos, need mention in this context: a round altar entirely covered with 10 figures in high relief, only recently examined in detail and described as the introduction of a family to the lords of the Underworld; and the so-called Muse Base, catalogued by Berges as a funerary altar although found in a Roman villa west of the Maussolleion. They clearly straddle the line between votive and funerary functions, both in their subject matter and in their appearance. They have both been dated to the second century, although on stylistic rather than typological grounds. I shall refer to the first as the Halikarnassos altar, to the second as the Muse Base, to avoid confusion.[41]

The top of the **Halikarnassos altar** is missing, eliminating the heads of most of the figures, and its surface is weathered, so that its iconographic meaning is unclear. Palagia (1997a) has discussed it in the context of mystery initiations. The clue is given by

Original Reliefs—Funerary and Votive

two men flanking a pillar that supports a herm shaft (top broken off). Each man wears a mantle rolled around the waist over a tunic, and holds a scroll that has been considered a sacred text. The man to the (viewer's) left of the pier has his right arm around the shoulders of a high-waisted woman in chiton and transparent himation who holds a long staff, possibly a torch pointing downward. This iconography has been related to that of several East Greek gravestones, yet in none of them is the torch of a priestess of Demeter held reversed.[42] Another clue to the reading has been seen in a male figure in chitoniskos and fluttering chlamys, in rapid motion to left. Near him a goat stands on its hind legs, and he has therefore been identified as Hermes. Although goats are appropriate to that god, no other attribute is preserved to identify the man; moreover, a second animal, in a similar lively pose, appears near a female figure who stands next to the male and is said to be holding a bunch of grapes while pulling her mantle off her left shoulder. The second animal could, to be sure, be connected instead with the following person (proceeding from left to right), who is seated on a rock and possibly female according to nymph iconography, but in that case it is difficult to explain the smaller servant standing behind the seated person's legs.

Three more personages are next in sequence: a female in peplos (with kolpos and overfold) and back mantle, a male (?) in chiton and himation seated on a throne, and another female standing behind the seat, said to be in bridal attire, who, being near the woman with the "torch," completes the circle. The scene would break down as two couples (the two men near the herm, the two women to the left) framed by Hermes on one side, by Plouton and Persephone on the other, with the "nymph" seated on a rock and the woman/girl with grapes suggesting the nature of the mysteries: Dionysiac.

I have described this monument in some detail because it is little-known and its recent interpretation has a bearing on the function of relief altars. Yet I have some difficulty with the proposed identifications. I find the presence of a servant figure next to a nymph (or maenad) not only unusual but also unjustified. Should the maid be connected with the girl holding grapes, the relationship of the latter to the other personages would remain unclear. The inclusion of a second animal raises questions about the identifying value of the first, and Hermes rushing to collect a soul is surprising.[43] I agree that the peplophoros is a striking antiquarian touch in an otherwise very Hellenistic rendering of female fashions, and should therefore signify a divinity; I would also accept that the men flanking the herm pillar are human rather than divine because of the tunics they wear below the himatia. Yet, despite some admitted connection with the repertoire of the East Greek gravestones, I remain uncertain about the funerary explanation of the relief, as opposed to a mythological one bespeaking a cultic/votive function.

The same difficulty exists about the second monument, the **Muse Base,** although I would be more inclined to accept its sepulchral overtones. Its depiction has been traditionally reviewed in the context of Muses' iconography, but we have seen that these deities could be connected with the cult of the dead, and that certain types were used on gravestones as possible allusions, although not as actual renderings of supernatural beings. The Muse Base is poorly preserved, some figures appearing almost intentionally defaced, but two points should be emphasized.

The composition is divided into apparent groups by the inclusion of two leafless trees. Despite being combined with figures seated on rocks, they convey little sense of landscape, yet add to the overhead space as a way of creating an impression of people steeped in atmosphere. They also recall the devices of narrative friezes, including the placing of figures back to back, as is particularly obvious in the case of the so-called Leaning Muse (Polyhymnia), who turns her back on a seated female with arm raised to her head.[44] This latter is the one image that cannot be reconciled with the standard typology of Muses, whether the "Philiskan" or those known from other sources. I wonder whether it could represent the deceased—a woman with qualities that made her comparable to the Muses, of whom she would be the ninth. Only her gesture would signify mourning.[45]

The second point concerns the eclectic character of both gravestones and figured altars. I continue to believe that the "Philiskan" Muses are a mirage of modern scholarship, although they fully exist as types well known in the Hellenistic period. I accept the early (third-century) date of the Priene Altar to the Athenaion and thus of certain iconographic renderings, specifically that of the Dancing Muse and the "Tyche of Antioch" type (cf. Pl. 66), the so-called Ourania, both included in the Halikarnassos Base. The early existence of this latter type, even before the founding of Antioch in 306, has been dramatically confirmed by a terracotta statuette in a very similar pose found in the Athenian Kerameikos on a destruction level dated around 310. I also find the so-called Venice Muse (cf. Pls. 60, 64) significant, as mentioned in ns. 23 and 34. I believe it possible that types (of Muses?) previously known as monuments in the round were used during the second century as signifiers not only of the Muses themselves, but also of humans possessing their qualities. Specifically, on the Muse Base, I would point out the figure holding a large kithara, whose Archaistic costume recalls the statuette with tragic mask on a Rider Relief from Smyrna. The Muse with the double pipes wears her mantle like one of the Muses on the Mantineia Base.[46] It would seem as if Hellenistic sculptural workshops possessed a standard repertoire, partly derived from Classical Athenian monuments like the Aischines and the Sophokles as well as some female types (Muses?), and partly based on contemporary work within East Greek/Kykladic circles, which they could use as appropriate over a wide geographic area, with selection dictated by specific preferences or ideologies. This communality of patterns is what makes our exegesis so difficult, but its acknowledgment may serve as indication that round altars and gravestones do indeed provide a *terminus ante quem* for the types repeated on them.

VOTIVE RELIEFS

The preceding discussion of some types of gravestones and altars makes obvious the impossibility, without accompanying inscriptions, of a clear-cut division between cultic and funerary functions. Yet a few reliefs are more traditionally considered votive offerings, and some of them have been assigned to the second century. I shall here review only those most significant for the connections they show with the previous funerary monuments and among themselves, as indication of a commonly shared iconographic patrimony and ideology.[47] We may begin with another representation of Muses.

The so-called **Apotheosis of Homer Relief** should by right belong to a review of the second century because it is traditionally placed around 130–120; yet I believe that it dates from the following century. Since I have already treated it in depth in my earlier volume on Hellenistic sculpture (1990), I shall here limit my comments to a review of subsequent bibliography. Perhaps the most important support for my late chronology comes from the various entries of the *LIMC* on the personifications included in the relief. Almost without exception, they appear either exclusively there or there for the first time, all subsequent examples occurring at least one hundred years later. This apparent chronological gap in the comparisons for Archelaos' conception makes me continue to favor the lower date that I based on the findspot (Bovillae, near Rome, in Italy)—which would make it an eclectic commission for a Roman clientele. A higher date (ca. 159) has, however, been advocated by Moreno, who believes the relief was made in honor of Krates of Mallos, head of the Pergamene Library; he would be represented on the slab by the poet's statue on a high base near a tripod. Moreno thus sees Attalos II and his mother Apollonis in the portrait-like depictions of Chronos and Oikoumene crowning Homer. This hypothesis completes the range of proposed attributions of the relief to the important monarchies of the late second century: the traditional one to the Ptolemies of Egypt (the two personifications would portray Ptolemy IV and his wife, Arsinoe III), a more tentative one to the Seleukids (Antiochos VIII Grypos and his mother, Kleopatra Thea), and finally the one to the Attalids. This very range of suggestions should suffice to prove our inability to make a positive identification of two diminutive heads that, in my opinion, correspond to common types rather than to specific individuals.[48]

A recent study, although not specifically concerned with royal identities and dating, has attempted to show that the Muses on the Homer relief appear in the order in which Hesiod had named them in the *Theogony*. This literary approach would, of course, be in keeping with the scholarly climate of Alexandria, but it may have been prominent also elsewhere, as shown by the Lagina friezes and perhaps even the Halikarnassos Base. It would not, however, be amiss in the late first century, as I have suggested by comparing the Apotheosis of Homer to the *Tabulae Iliacae*—especially since Roman paintings of the Neronian-Vespasianic period seem to follow the Hesiodic order of the Muses well before the inception of the better-known sarcophagi.[49]

The literary tenor of the relief has been aptly stressed by the only study, to my knowledge, that has focused on the true nature of the Bovillae relief: not a votive offering, but an educational pinax for a school, a gymnasion, or a library. Its didactic nature would explain why it was found in Italy, probably as the complement for a private library in a Roman villa like that of the Papyri in Herculaneum with its store of Greek and Latin texts. This theory, however, would still place the origin of the work in Pergamon, under Attalos III (he and his mother, Stratonike, would be adumbrated in Chronos and Oikoumene), and in the Stoic climate generated by Krates of Mallos and his followers. Homer would be honored not only in the lowest register of the relief, but also, in heroized form, on the same level as Apollo, by his placement among divine beings in the form of a poet's statue whose head is damaged and therefore cannot be used for corroboration. The significant ties between the Attalids and Rome, not only political and military, but also of a philosophical nature, would have facilitated the transport of Archelaos' panel to Bovillae, once Pergamon had been bequeathed to Rome in 133.[50]

This last theory seems to me quite on target as far as the assessment of the relief itself, yet I would still prefer to see it as a Roman commission, on some of the same grounds. One more point could be made for a late dating. The use of hangings from a colonnade, although effective in separating the mountain scene from the Homeric Apotheosis itself, strongly recalls similar preferences for background fillings in Roman ("Neo-Attic") reliefs, even if of Greek derivation like the famous "Visit of Dionysos to a poet." To be sure, curtains appear as backdrops in some Funerary Banquets, but these are usually datable within the late second or the first century, and the screens are not as encompassing as in the Archelaos relief.[51]

A typical, surely votive example is provided by a **relief in Munich** that has often been compared to the Apotheosis of Homer because of its use of landscape elements—specifically the cloth hanging from a tree that forms a backdrop to an enthroned god and a standing goddess leaning on a pier, both holding tall scepters. The tree itself is unusually realistic, with wide, knobby trunk encircled by votive fillets, a major branch cut off, showing the cracks in the stump typical of split wood, and massive foliage overhanging the scene. Next to the tree, but rendered so as to appear to be receding in the distance, is a tall pillar supporting two statuettes in apparently Archaistic costume. In the center, a rectangular altar receives the offering of a family (father, mother, two children); toward the left edge of the scene, two women wrapped in mantles—one of them wearing a pointed sun hat—and two children stand in front of the tree and therefore in the foreground, yet their size, considerably smaller than that of the other human figures, makes them look as if on a much farther plane. Perspective effects are also obtained through the "porthole viewing" created by the frame, which consists of two antae surmounted by an entablature and a section of tiled roof, like the eaves of a stoa. Note, for instance, how the left anta overlaps the hatted woman's skirt and the edge of the tree stump at the top, while the right anta hides the termination of the curtain (which should be hanging from a second point of support) and the rear of the horned lion-griffin that serves as throne leg.[52]

This apparent separation of frame from picture makes me support a late second-century date for the Munich Relief. Votive panels of the Classical period had also overlapped their borders, but in the opposite direction, stretching their confines so that parts of, or even whole, images appeared on the frame itself. The illusionistic effect of the Munich composition can be found only in a few Archaic renderings, or on Hellenistic monuments. It recalls not only the Telephos Frieze but also, much more closely, the Esquiline paintings with scenes from the *Odyssey*. Similar effects appear on some of the Totenmahl and the Rider Reliefs we have investigated above. Further help for a "late" date can be found in the diminutive worshipers in front of the tree, who resemble the so-called Tanagras—terracotta figurines of elegant ladies in pointed hats that originated in Athens, where they flourished particularly during the third century but continued to be imitated during the second century, not only in Boiotia (hence their name, from the most prolific findspot) but also in Asia Minor. We have noted some of these typical figures on some East Greek gravestones.[53]

Stressing the discrepancy in size between the two groups of worshipers on the Munich Relief, Hausmann (1966) suggested that its composition is an eclectic mixture of two different prototypes: one including only the two deities and the family sacrificing at the altar, and another comprising the second cluster of human figures and their background. He therefore advocated a late second-century date for the panel, in keeping with traditional conceptions of decline and lack of imagination (or even of "Neo-Attic" eclectic tendencies) toward the end of the Hellenistic period. In defense of an earlier chronology, Richter (1968) proposed that the man near the altar depicted Euthydemos I of Baktria (ruled 230–200), thus explaining his size by a scale of importance that made a king intermediate between divinities and mere mortals. As was the case with the Apotheosis of Homer, I find it impossible to believe that a specific portrait was intended for a figure of such diminutive size; I would rather ascribe its relative realism to the same characterizing trends at work for the men on the East Greek stelai, as noted above. Had a different prototype been used for the second group of worshipers, the sculptor of the Munich Relief could easily have adjusted the scale to suit his specific composition, given the care expended on all details of the panel. Once again, as on the Smyrnaian gravestones, totally unrealistic sizes might not have seemed out of place next to larger ones, especially if recession in space was attempted.

In order better to assess its stylistic and chronological idiom, it would be helpful to know where the Munich Relief was made, yet no reliable information is available on this score. The panel was acquired from a dealer in 1882, without provenience. It is often stated that it comes from Corinth, but on no specific evidence. An Attic origin could be advocated on the basis of its tiled frame, but a Rhodian, a Kykladic, and an East Greek workshop have also been suggested, on the basis of unconvincing parallels. Even the two deities that appear on the relief are controversial: they have been called Isis and Sarapis/Osiris, Dionysos and Ariadne, Asklepios and Hygieia,[54] but there is no dedicatory inscription and no attribute is specifically revealing. The tall scepters could suggest Zeus and Hera; the trend of the times would almost require healing or Underworld divinities (Hades and Persephone?).

If the two images atop the pillar could be identified, they might provide a clue, but they are quite small and hard to see. The female may have a phiale in her lowered left hand, while holding on to her companion with her right; the male may be wearing a conical hat (a petasos?) and carries a tall staff (with entwined snake? or is it the tip of his chlamys?). We have already noted a figurine on a pillar in the background of a gravestone, and another appears on a bronze plaque from Delos with Artemis and satyrs at an altar, stylistically dated to 220–210, but a much safer date can be given to a **Document Relief** in Athens that has in fact been compared to the Munich Relief.[55]

One of the very few extant (and legible) from the second century, this inscribed panel was set up in 138/7, under the archonship of Timarchos, by the Orgeones of Aphrodite to honor Serapion of Herakleia (Pl. 67). Although fragmentary, its relief depicts a large female figure, probably Aphrodite, who holds a scepter over her shoulder and stands on one side of an altar. On the other side of it are two smaller mortals: Serapion, with highly distinctive features, and a woman, either his wife or a priestess. In the center distance, a pillar supports a statuette that must be Athena because it wears an aigis and carries a spear, while holding a phiale or a crown in the extended right hand. A bird or other animal appears farther behind. The sense of space, the use of different planes, the individualization of the male figure, the divine image symbolizing sacred space, are all traits that recur not only on the (surely contemporary) Munich Relief, but also on the Apotheosis of Homer, and even, in different combinations, on East Greek gravestones. Once again, we must admit that place of manufacture is not always a reliable indicator of iconography and style, given the widespread diffusion of sculptural trends in the second century.

Plate 67

A drapery pattern that recurs on several reliefs from Asia Minor comes from ancient Kleitor in Arkadia: on the so-called **Stele of Polybios,** which has in fact lent its name to the motif. At first glance, the stele seems firmly identified and dated, yet both points appear less secure on second consideration. A warrior almost 2 m tall stands frontally on a slab terminating with a plain molding. He raises his right hand, palm outward, to express reverence or to salute, and his head, beardless and with short curly hair, is turned in the direction of his gesture; his left arm presses against his shoulder a long spear with "shoe" (*sauroter*) at the bottom. The man wears a chitoniskos (or exomis?) that leaves his right breast free and is belted at the waist, forming a shallow kolpos. A long mantle clasped over his right shoulder envelops his left arm and falls behind him, with the weight at one corner visible against the background next to his left ankle. The other corner forms a swag of folds against the spear, where it is bunched by the left hand after it crosses over the front of the body in a triangular pattern. A large round shield and a crested helmet rest on the ground next to the warrior's right leg and foot; a sword is strapped across his chest on his left side. This relief is now broken into four fragments, so that photographs usually reproduce a cast of it formerly in Berlin but destroyed during World War II. Nothing of the once partly visible inscription can be found on the remains in Greece.[56]

Original Reliefs—Funerary and Votive

Yet identification is based on those fragmentary letters, through analogy with a much later monument. As originally noted on the Arkadian relief, the words ἀντὶ καλῶν ἔργων εἴσ[ατο may have been followed by a name, Πουλυ[βίῳ], of which faint traces were said to have been seen by early German scholars. An inscription of the *third century* A.C. in Olympia used those same words under a statue set up by the polis in honor of a Polybios, son of Lykortas. Since Lykortas was known as the name of the Hellenistic Polybios' father, the recurrence of both names suggested that the man honored at Olympia was a descendant of the Greek historian, which would have prompted an intentional repetition of the honorary formula used on the Kleitor stele four centuries earlier.[57] Yet obviously the "noble deeds" or benefactions for which the Imperial man was honored could not have been of the same nature as those of the Hellenistic predecessor, and the difference in location (a remote place in Arkadia as contrasted with the much more accessible sanctuary at Olympia) may have made the quotation unrecognizable in antiquity—as contrasted with the nineteenth century, when every scrap of Greek inscription was collected and analyzed.

To be sure, the Hellenistic Polybios was repeatedly honored during his lifetime. Born in Megalopolis around 203, he participated in the Achaian League as hipparch, and in 167/6 was taken as a hostage to Rome, where he developed a distinctly pro-Roman attitude. When he returned to Greece after 16 years, around 150 or somewhat later, in connection with the destruction of Corinth, he exercised his influence with the Romans in obtaining from the Senate somewhat better conditions for the vanquished Greeks, thus earning gratitude for his "benefactions." He died at 82 (ca. 120), after a fall from a horse. Pausanias mentions several works in his honor throughout Arkadia: a relief in the double temple of Asklepios and the Letoids at Mantineia (8. 9.1), another in the temenos of Lykaian Zeus within the agora of Megalopolis (8.30.8),[58] a third at Lykosoura, within a stoa near the Temple of Despoina (8.37.2),[59] a fourth at Tegea, near an altar of Ge (8.48.8);[60] at Pallantion, not far from a sanctuary of Demeter and Kore, stood Polybios' portrait statue (8.44.5). Nothing at Olympia or Corinth is mentioned, however, and nothing at Kleitor. Yet it has been assumed that this relief, like all the honorary images mentioned by Pausanias, was erected there for him, after 146, thus when Polybios was in his late fifties or older; the youthful appearance of the warrior on the Kleitor stele has been attributed to an idealizing tendency of the sculptor (Damophon of Messene?), or to the popularity the historian enjoyed within the Achaian League even before being taken hostage to Rome. Following this line of thought, and because of the cavalry spear carried by the man on the Kleitor relief, Moreno has dated the stele around 169, when Polybios was hipparch and considerably younger.

Significantly, the typical pattern formed by the warrior's mantle recurs with some frequency on votive and funerary reliefs of the Hero Equitans type where the main personage is portrayed on foot near his mount. Yet here no horse is present. Perhaps the composition extended onto adjacent slabs, but this hypothesis cannot be verified, given the present state of the extant fragments. The warrior's gesture of adoration might also imply additional figures, even if the relief was set up within a sanctuary; a sign of salute or *adlocutio* seems less probable. As a votive offering, the slab is unusually sizable; it would be more understandable as a gravestone, although this type of funerary marker is very rare in Hellenistic Arkadia. Identification as an honorary monument remains the most plausible hypothesis, but is it really for Polybios? It seems to me that the inscribed formula is too generic, and an Imperial parallel too remote, to warrant attribution to the Hellenistic historian; the traces of Polybios' name could have been "recognized" through logical deduction and wishful thinking, given the Arkadian location of the findspot and the type of relief. The lack of beard in the "portrait" could be explained had the monument been erected after Polybios' Roman stay, when he may be supposed to have adopted Roman customs. As a Greek hipparch in his mid-thirties, Polybios would probably have worn a beard.[61] I would accept a second-century date for the relief, but would leave the issue of identification open; iconographically, given the wide distribution of the type on works of diverse nature, we can probably postulate a more famous or visible prototype, perhaps in the round, that gave rise to repeated imitations throughout the Greek world.

I have left for last the **"Four-Gods Relief" from Delos** because its style, Archaistic throughout, is entirely different from that of the monuments previously examined; yet the plaque is a perfect example of the diffusionistic trends we have been stressing. It depicts Hermes leading Athena, Apollo, and Artemis—we do not know where.[62] The costumes are frankly old-fashioned, with many harsh zigzag edges and pleated effects; hairstyles are equally stylized and artificial, with tied loops over the nape for the men and long tresses over the chest for every figure. The tiptoe stance of the gods is distinctive and contrasts with the more normal stride of the goddesses. Attributes identify each personage: the kerykeion for Hermes, aigis, spear, and crested helmet in the lowered left hand for Athena, a spear and probably a bow (the area is damaged at this point) for Apollo, and flaming torch, quiver, and bow for Artemis, who holds up her skirt in a mannered fashion. Archaistic work of this nature has usually been discounted as purely decorative, meant primarily as a form of embellishment for Roman villas, since many variations of this theme have been found on other slabs and stone vases of Late Republican and Imperial times. Yet the Delian relief is remarkable in that the figures file to left under a border of garlands hanging from boukrania, such as we saw on many funerary and votive altars. A religious component is therefore present on the panel. In addition, some Classical reliefs depicting sacred space include pinakes carrying similar Archaistic figures.[63]

The Four-Gods scenes, from Delos and elsewhere, have traditionally been discussed as either Neo-Attic creations or copies and adaptations of a fourth-century prototype in Athens, the latter theory being the more compelling, since it invoked a possibly famous precedent, from a "good period," in a major artistic center. Recently, it has been forcefully argued that these Archaistic figures constitute "types" that can be used

Original Reliefs—Funerary and Votive

at will and even modified, by judicious alteration of the attributes, whenever necessary. It has been pointed out, for instance, how similar the Athena and Artemis are, in both pose and costume, and how that same female type is known from examples in the round—the so-called Munich-Chigi Athena, which could in turn be used with or without aigis and therefore represent different divinities. Given this interchange between two- and three-dimensional renderings, the issue is no longer one of a specific, famous original, but one of an appropriate formula that entered the repertoire of various workshops through time and could be employed in different contexts.[64]

At the same time, it should be stressed that copying, adaptation, and change of format should not be taken as purely utilitarian devices, depriving the initial image of all meaningful content. As the Hera type(?) from Asia Minor could be turned into an Astarte/Tanit in Punic Soloeis,[65] the Aischines/Sophokles types could be used to convey specific status on East Greek gravestones, and Muses formulas could be combined and recombined in endless permutations for funerary or votive purposes, so Archaistic images could be employed to project an aura of ancient cult and veneration, as confirmed by the sacrificial allusions of boukrania and garlands on the Delian relief. Beyond the confining limits of a specific stylistic evolution, the second century sculptural production can be seen as the result of a massive mingling of trends and sources at the hands of a very varied group of traveling sculptors.

NOTES

1. Helpful general comments on Hellenistic gravestones, also vis-à-vis Classical practices: Schmaltz 1983, 223–49 (esp. 235–36 for chronology); on Hellenistic burials in general: Kurtz and Boardman 1971, 162–69. Athenian gravestones: a few Hellenistic examples of poor quality and retrospective imagery are discussed by Scholl 1996, 77–81; see especially, for the 2nd c., his pls. 26.3–4 and 27, and his cat. 118, 216, and 517. The first (p. 257) is of some interest because the recessed field shows a headless man in the scheme of the Poseidon of Melos, although—in a rather dramatic and overstated pose—he holds a book scroll rather than a trident. I have been unable to consult S. Lymperopoulos, Hamburg dissertation 1985, available only in typescript, dealing with Hellenistic Attic gravestones, but see Zagdoun 1995, 188, no. 326. At any rate, total numbers are minimal; most examples commemorate non-Athenians. See also Schmidt 1991, 43–44 and bibl. in ns. 239–42. Kurtz and Boardman 1971, 166–67, point out that some kioniskoi are decorated with reliefs, but they are minor works compared with earlier gravestones; only in the 2nd c., they state (p. 169), do "relief monuments of some size and magnificence reappear in number," but they give no specific examples, and I am unaware of any.

Boiotian gravestones: Ridgway 1990, 170 (Type 1), with discussion and bibl. on p. 189 n. 49. Three characteristic fragments recently catalogued: Hamiaux 1998, 120–22, nos. 126–28.

Thessalian gravestones; painted (from Pegasai): the basic catalogue remains Arvanitopoulos 1928, but they are currently being restudied in collaboration by a French–German team (cf. Wolters 1979, 81); for recent illustrations, see von Graeve and Preusser 1981, especially 120–45, figs. 1–19 and col. figs. 1–9. One immediate result of the renewed research has been a lowering of the chronology to the beginning of the 1st c. for the end of the series (all examples were found reused in fortification towers whose date is crucial as a *terminus ante quem* for the stelai); cf. Wolters 1979, 87, and Marzolff 1986, especially 78–80. Anthemion series: Wolters 1979, with geographic distribution noted on p. 85; the Demetrias stelai are under strong Attic influence. For the engraved herm, considered typically Thessalian, see p. 86 and pls. 7–9. For all these refs., and for the following ones on Macedonian gravestones, I am deeply indebted to Prof. S. Miller-Collett, who has placed at my disposal her files and sections of her unpublished manuscript.

2. Macedonian gravestones: those found within the Vergina tumulus (and therefore dated by the excavators before 274/3) are published by Saatsoglou-Paliadeli 1984 (they include painted as well as sculptured examples); for chronology, see p. 17. See also Hamiaux 1998, 123–31, nos. 130–37; Voutiras 1989a (production of stelai beginning in late 2nd c.). Brief general comments and bibl. in Schmidt 1991, 32–34 (production peaking in the 2nd c.). For monumental (built) tombs with paintings, see the catalogue in Miller (Collett) 1993; others have since been found but are unpublished.

3. Achaian gravestones: Papapostolou 1993, especially 18, for chronology. From a total of 76 items catalogued (extending from the late 4th c. to the Roman period), ca. 62 belong to the Hellenistic period, and most of them to the 2nd c., though a more precise date is impossible. The most numerous type is the pedimented stele with a sunken panel (cf. fig. 7 on p. 44); others show a simpler naiskos (figs. 8–9 on p. 47); the most elaborate are the composite types, consisting of an upper naiskos and a usually plain lower zone surmounted by a sofa-capital crowning. Two variants of the composite type exist: *A* (fig. 10 on p. 49) exhibits a pedimented naiskos with a single-fascia architrave and a frieze zone like an extended sofa capital decorated with vegetal scrolls in relief; in *B* (fig. 11 on p. 51), the naiskos has a two-fasciaed architrave, its frieze (also of the sofa-capital type with a cyma recta section) is plain, and its top is flat, to be completed by a separately carved finial, probably gable-shaped. Of the stelai with objects carved in low relief on the lower portion, cat. 45, 46, 49, 52 have an amygdaloid motif emerging from an akanthos calyx, probably a bud symbolizing youth; cat. 43 has a four-spoked wheel (perhaps symbolizing life's fortune); the most complex, cat. 47, has a circular object with central "rosette" and suspension loop (a mirror or phiale?), a spindle-shaped unguentarium, and a quadrangular shape with incised central lozenge (a gaming die?). Figural representations in relief are entirely absent. All stelai are inscribed, some of them in prominent positions, and an epigraphic commentary (by A. Rizakis, pp. 110–20) is provided. Paint is said (p. 16) to be the most important characteristic of the stelai.

The Achaian series is considered second only to the Aegean and East Greek gravestones in its variety of types and richness of motifs, especially in contrast to the very limited repertoire elsewhere in the Peloponnesos and NW and Central Greece; cf. p. 17 n. 6 for bibl. and n. 5 for an exceptional carved stele from Skillountia: *ArchDelt* 33 (1978) B¹, 78, pl. 22γ. Some figured stelai from Lakonia have been dated to the 2nd c./Late Hellenistic period (Papaefthimiou 1992, cat. 14, 21, 24, 25, 28, 29) but they are either fragmentary or in poor condition; the most interesting stele in the Sparta Museum (inv. 6661; Papaefthimiou, pp. 160–61, figs. 36a–b: naiskos of Polykratis and Nikandria) is considered an import from Asia Minor, but the floral decoration over its antae makes me think of Kykladic examples, to be discussed infra. The pediment of this stele has a central medallion with gorgoneion, the main panel shows a seated and a standing woman, and a podium is decorated with four Nikai flanking a basket that contains hydriai and amphorae. The gravestone is dated to the 2nd half of the 2nd c. with a Byzantine reuse. The author's contribution on stelai in the Sparta Museum, in O. Palagia and W. Coulson, eds., *Sculpture from Arcadia and Laconia* (1993) 237–44, includes only one Hellenistic item (late 3rd c.).

4. The definition "East Greek" is here used in the geographic sense indicated below, including the neighboring islands.

5. The main publication of the East Greek gravestones is *DOG* 1977 and 1979; reviews of the corpus can usefully be read for a general overview: e.g., B. Freyer-Schauenburg, *Gymnasium* 85 (1978) 261–63, and 87 (1980) 458–60; B. S. Ridgway, *AJA* 82 (1978) 414–15, and 84 (1980) 543–44. Schmidt 1991 provides typological analysis by provenience/place of manufacture, formal development, and investigation of meaning; his coverage extends to Delos and makes brief mention (p. 5 and n. 17, figs. 1–3) of Alexandrian stelai. The sociological aspect of the East Greek material is especially brought forth by Zanker 1993 (with specific reference to Smyrna) and 1995; see also Ridgway 1993a. A brief overview of East Greek and Aegean stelai is given by Smith 1991, 188–90. Each publication includes detailed bibl.

Painted stelai from Egypt (especially Alexandria), Sidon, and South Russia are beyond the scope of our sculptural survey and are therefore not included.

6. Classicizing explanation: Schmidt 1991, 41; he nevertheless attempts to divide the reliefs, according to stylistic development, into stages based on the decreasing volume of the bodies and the increasing symbolism and elongation of proportions. The input from the great altars is advocated by Linfert 1976, 138. Smyrnaian stelai as public monuments: Zanker 1993, 214–15, who points out that, unfortunately, we do not know how these gravestones were displayed; p. 218 stresses that the imagery on these reliefs reflects not the status of a middle class, whose existence he doubts, but rather a value system shared by all citizens. For the changing relationships between rulers and citizens, see von Hesberg 1995, Bringmann 1995, and, more generally, Gruen 1984.

Not only are honorary wreaths typical of Smyrnaian stelai, but also rosettes, perhaps derived from plain Attic gravestones: Schmidt 1991, 9–10, fig. 18; *DOG* 1977, p. 52, e.g., nos. 395 pl. 64, 405 pl. 66, 435 pl. 72. In citing examples from *DOG* 1977 and 1979, I shall attempt to refer only to reliefs that are reasonably likely to date from the 2nd c.

7. Reliefs and epitaphs: Breuer 1995—significantly ending its survey at the 2nd c. Cf. its review, *AJA* 101 (1997) 179–80 (J. W. Day). I would surmise, however, that *arete* meant military valor only in the context of epitaphs, retaining its civic connotation in inscriptions for honorary statues: cf. infra, Ch. 7 n. 53. See also Herrmann 1995, with ample bibl. He makes the important point that, although the city honors its citizens, their professions are not clearly indicated in the inscriptions. Zanker 1995, 263, stresses that the stelai are not purely the visual rendering of the epitaphs: witness the lack of political dimension in the depiction of women, despite their frequent role as benefactresses of the city. Smith 1991, 189, cites the epitaph for Menophila (on a stele from Sardis, his fig. 222 = *DOG* 1977, no. 418 pl. 69, end 2nd c.): "This gracious stone shows a fine woman. Who is she? The letters of the Muses inform us: Menophila. Why then is this white lily and the 'one' (alpha) carved on the stele? Why the book, wool basket, and wreath above? The book is for her intelligence. The wreath tells of her public office (as priestess), the 'one' tells she is an only child. The basket is the sign of her well-ordered virtue. The flower is for the bloom that a daimon stole away. Lightly do I the dust lie upon you. Many

are they to whom you have left tears—dead without husband or parents." This correspondence between image and epitaph is, however, unusual outside of Smyrna (Breuer 1995, 126), and there it bespeaks specific commissions; surprising also is the use of a book in connection with a woman.

For comparable symbolic values in the attributes of 4th-c. gravestones, see Ridgway 1997b, 164 and more discussion with refs. in n. 30 on p. 185.

8. This statement applies primarily to the reliefs where the human figures are shown standing: e.g., *DOG* 1977, nos. 364 pl. 60 (hand toward companion; from Halikarnassos, in British Museum; dated to 2nd half 3rd c. but possibly later, although not as late as 1st c.) and 376 pl. 61 (hand toward tree; from Smyrna, in British Museum, for Isias, a young priestess or devotee of Isis, dated beg. 2nd c.). When one of the personages is seated, the handshake motif (dexiosis) may occur, but in this case the strict frontality of the images is broken and an element of "narrative" is introduced, although the gesture is purely symbolic, and can take place between two women: see, e.g., *DOG* 1977, nos. 1050 pl. 157 (from Priene, in Berlin, dated 1st half 2nd c.) and 1057 pl. 158 (stele of Theophila from Istanbul, 2nd c.). For comments on the changed meaning of the dexiosis motif in the Hellenistic period, see Breuer 1995, 15–39, especially 37–38, contrasting its limited diffusion in Asia Minor with its greater popularity on Delos, probably under Attic influence after 166. She points out (p. 35) that in Late Hellenistic times the gesture can occur with groups and even within the Banquet Relief type (e.g., *DOG* 1979, nos. 1756–58 pls. 255–56, the first two dated ca. 200), but that approximately four-fifths of the handshake scenes involve a man and a woman. See also infra, n. 20 (dexiosis with Hermes).

Besides the minuscule servants, naiskos stelai can include "Maltese" dogs, which interact with, or at least acknowledge, their master/mistress even when the attendants do not, often staring ahead as if unaware of the presence of the dead—one more indication of their attributive nature. For the pets, see, e.g., *DOG* 1977, with males: nos. 114, 116 pl. 27 (from Smyrna and Samos respectively), 131 pl. 30 (from Smyrna); with females: nos. 395 pl. 64 (Tarsos), 397 pl. 65 (Smyrna).

9. Stele of Isomede, daughter of Diphilos, from Ephesos, now in Vienna: *DOG* 1977, no. 371 pl. 61, dated 1st half 2nd c. For a sense of depth and perspective, see, e.g., *DOG* 1977, nos. 382 pl. 62 (from Smyrna [?], woman with nurse holding child in front of diagonally rendered pier; 1st half 2nd c.; cf. Pl. 60), 429 pl. 70 (from Notion, one woman, two attendants, a tree, and a column with mourning Psyche, mid-2nd c.; cf. Pl. 59) and 646 pl. 98 (unknown findspot, probably Smyrna, two men, one woman, with pier and herm; mid-2nd c.). See also infra, n. 11.

Zanker 1993, 220–22, emphasizes that children's iconography treats them as miniature adults, projecting the qualities and achievements they would have had, had they lived. Breuer 1995, 122–31, in an excursus on the regional distribution of epitaphs, notes that most of them are for premature deaths, explaining the lack of poetic inscriptions on the majority of the Smyrnaian stelai on the grounds that the deceased had lived a full term of life, and their predictable death thus caused no excessive mourning (p. 127).

10. I omit here discussion of stelai without human figures, although a few of them belong to the 2nd c. They form the last categories in *DOG* 1979. Among the most interesting, note no. 2225 pl. 317, a quadrangular block inscribed as the Heroon of Dion, son of Artemidoros, of unknown provenience. The face with the inscription shows two snakes, and the other three faces depict a cuirass, a helmet, and a round shield respectively. Also notable are nos. 2269–70

Original Reliefs—Funerary and Votive

pl. 320, by the same workshop, from the environs of Istanbul(?), each depicting various pieces of armor and a bridle with four-pronged metal bit; no. 2269 includes also the prow of a warship. Funerary altars will be discussed separately.

11. Miletos stele now in Izmir: *DOG* 1979, no. 1475 pl. 214 (dated ca. 100); Zanker 1995, fig. 1. The Funerary Banquet and the Rider Types are discussed infra. Lack of funerary statues: Schmidt 1991, 11–12; this statement does not apply to Rheneia/Delos, for instance, where free-standing sculptures have been found in cemeteries (see infra). Perhaps some of the East Greek statues now in our museums without clear findspot and context come from such areas. Note also *DOG* 1979, no. 2318 pl. 327, a Corinthian naiskos from Rhodes where once a statuette in the round of a woman probably stood; the piece, with objects in relief on the short sides, is dated still within the 3rd c.

12. I have not calculated the average size of the Rheneian stelai, but most of them fall within the 0.50–0.70 m range; only a handful are over 1 m high. Zanker 1993, 228, gives estimated dimensions for the Smyrnaian gravestones: they range from 0.40 to 1.70 m, but the majority cluster within the range 0.80–1.20 m; those for children are ca. 0.50 m high; a great number of stelai are fragmentary, and therefore the above figures are only approximate.

13. For remarks on the heroization of the dead on East Greek stelai, see *DOG* 1977, 47–48, with some reference also to Roman practices. Smith 1991, 190, comments: "In epitaphs of the later Hellenistic and Roman periods, 'hero' came to mean little more than the 'late beloved.'" See, however, Schmidt 1991, 141–46, who would accept the "secularization" of the term only in Imperial times, and cites specific epitaphs where reference is made to temene, naoi, and groves for the cult of the dead (144–45, epitaph for three Cretan children, and Smyrnaian stele for Dionysios = *DOG* 1977, 181–82, no. 640 pl. 98). Schmidt also points out that Boiotian gravestones had heroizing connotations even in the Classical period: cf. Ridgway 1997b, 171. This tradition could explain their continuation into the Hellenistic period. See also infra, under Round Altars.

The topic of the ruler cult is too vast to be broached here. For increasing honors to citizens that extended to specifications for their burials, including, exceptionally, interment within the city limits, see, e.g., Herrmann 1995, with added bibl. I have advanced the suggestion of cultic meaning for East Greek stelai in Ridgway 1993a, 234–35, 237–38, and of Roman influence on pp. 236–37. A. Stewart, commenting on both Zanker 1993 and Ridgway 1993a (in Bulloch et al. 1993, 201), mentions that such stelai "link up with a class of monuments that are amply attested by inscriptions but have almost vanished today: the free-standing *naiskoi* with statues of the dead in the guise of Hermes, Demeter, and other gods and heroes before which cult was offered to the dead." For the pervasive presence of Romans see, e.g., a stele from Ergili or Kyzikos (Istanbul Arch. Mus. 5365), with one seated and one standing woman, one man and a small servant in traditional costumes, inscribed three times with the name Μαρκία (Marcia), and dated to the 2nd half of the 2nd c.: *DOG* 1977, no. 1037 pl. 155. This gravestone is also remarkable for the sense of atmosphere created around the figures by their ample spacing and overhead room.

14. Extensive comments on the meanings of both male and female figures, with primary reference to the Smyrnaian stelai, in Zanker 1995, 255–61 and 261–63 respectively; see also Zanker 1993, and my response (Ridgway 1993a), 235–36, on compositional stances. This point is made much more forcefully by Schmidt 1991, 13: "Speziell für die Grabreliefs aus Smyrna

läßt sich auch eine Eigenentwicklung aus kompositorischen Gründen durch die Werkstätten vorstellen." The mantled men appear frequently either in the so-called Aischines or in the so-called Sophokles pose, but the left hand, instead of being held behind the body as in the alleged prototypes, often grasps a fold of the himation in front, usually over the bent leg, suggesting movement. This impression is heightened by the lively mantle swag and edge with sanguisuga fold: e.g., *DOG* 1977, men alone: nos. 156–57 pl. 34 (from Smyrna and Mylasa respectively), 158–61 pl. 35 (all probably or surely from Smyrna); man with woman: nos. 524 pl. 80 (unknown provenience), 546 pl. 85 (from Arabli).

15. On women represented outdoors: Zanker 1995, 261; for depictions of parasols or sun hats, see, e.g., *DOG* 1977, nos. 506 pl. 80 (from Istanbul) and 545 pl. 85 (from Smyrna; both dated 2nd c.). For monuments in the background, see, e.g., *DOG* 1977, 429 pl. 70 (from Notion: female, two attendants, a tree, and a column with snake and Psyche in background, mid-2nd c.). Yet note *DOG* 1977, no. 882 pl. 130 (from Kyzikos, dated still 3rd c., though it seems to me later): in a deep naiskos, a frontally seated woman is attended by a small servant. She should be indoors because of her seat, yet two pillars in the background are topped by sirens and suggest a cemetery setting, which is enhanced by two vessels (lekythos, alabastron) depicted in low relief on the short sides of the naiskos; its Doric frieze is also carried around the corners from the front. Another seated woman with companion, attendant, tree encircled by snake, and pillar with siren, from Smyrna: *DOG* 1977, no. 991 pl. 149; see also p. 46 for general comments on snakes and on herms. On snakes as heroizing symbols: Salapata 1997, 249–55. For hip-herms of Herakles, see, e.g., *DOG* 1977, nos. 161 pl. 35 and 256 pl. 48. A herm on no. 126 pl. 29 is ithyphallic; nos. 114–15 pl. 27 have both a herm and a snake, thus clearly showing the "additive" nature of such signifiers. Herms as marking boundary of Hades: Palagia 1997a, 69 and n. 16.

16. *DOG* 1977, nos. 376 pl. 61 (cf. supra, n. 8; priestess of Isis), 898 pl. 134 (priestess of Kybele), 405–407 pl. 66, 409–10 pl. 67, 872 pl. 129 (here Pl. 61) (priestesses of Demeter; cf. pp. 136–38). See also the stele of Menophila (supra, n. 7). Note no. 855 pl. 125, where the woman standing by a seated man wears an unusual kerchief that recalls some Egyptian renderings.

Priestly garb for men is defined (Mantis 1990, 82–85) as a long chiton with short sleeves, but is usually supplemented by attributes such as knives and kantharoi, and, at least in the Classical period, the men wear a beard. These conventions may no longer apply to the Hellenistic period—Mantis 1990, 97–103, discusses only images of priestesses for that timespan, including eight stelai from Smyrna.

Scrolls as indication of education and philosophical interest: Zanker 1993, 218 (cf. also supra, n. 7, epitaph for Menophila); as sacred texts: Palagia 1997a, 69; as grave goods: Voutiras 1989a, 357; as sign of musical or literary victory: Karo 1943, 35 and pl. 36, left (kioniskos of Demarchos, son of Philon, from Phaleron, in the Athenian Kerameikos, with a relief including a scroll surmounted by a palm branch and inscribed, "He was victorious in the Prytaneion," probably before 250; I owe this ref. to G. R. Edwards). A stele in Leiden, probably from Smyrna, shows a bald man holding a scroll, with two attendants and, in the background, a cornucopia atop a high pillar: *DOG* 1977, no. 170 pl. 37 = Zanker 1993, figs. 6–7; the deceased wears the usual tunic and mantle, but his baldness and a rolled head fillet with central ornament may suggest a priestly function. Zanker 1993, 218 and n. 25, on cornucopiae and priesthood; he mentions the possibility of buying the office; but see also Ridgway 1993a, 237. The stele with joined dikerata is *DOG* 1977, no. 872 (supra); if Zanker is correct, both husband and wife (with Demeter's torch) would therefore have held sacred office. For other examples of the single horn, see *DOG* 1977, nos. 156 pl. 34 (= Hamiaux 1998, 142–43, no. 152), 158 pl. 35, 405 pl. 66.

17. A comparable thought is expressed by Breuer 1995, 127, although with a slightly different emphasis: "Man mag daher annehmen, daß die smyrnäischen Reliefs zumindest insofern nichts anders meinten als andernorts Totenmahlreliefs, als diese hier wie jene dort das repräsentative 'Normalbild' waren." The main difference would be that the Banquet Reliefs show groups, whereas the Smyrnaian gravestones can depict even single figures.

Stelai of the Smyrnaian type are found also outside that city—for instance, at Ephesos, where they may be imports, but also at Erythrai and other sites. For distribution and preference patterns, see Schmidt 1991, specifically pp. 22–24 for those of Pergamon and Samos.

Servant figures are shown improbably diminutive on some banquet scenes from Kyzikos, where their size might have been dictated by the overall small dimensions of the relief fields. For a rapid review by provenience, see Hamiaux 1998, 152–59, nos. 165–74, all of which seem, however, later than the 2nd c. For a 2nd-c. example, see her no. 139, pp. 131–32—a Banquet Relief from Thasos where the reclining man is clearly identified as an initiate of Isis by his Egyptianizing headdress; other cult symbols appear in low relief on the background.

18. Kylikeion: see comments in *DOG* 1979, and cf. p. 365, e.g., nos. 1526–27 pl. 220, 1780 pl. 256, 1872 pl. 268 (all from Samos). Tree with snake in Funerary Banquet scenes: e.g., *DOG* 1979, nos. 1567 pl. 227 (from Pergamon), and 1568 pl. 228 (from Smyrna). Women sitting frontally on kline's foot: e.g., *DOG* 1979, nos. 1544 pl. 223 (from Erythrai), 1554–55 pl. 225 (from Halikarnassos and Kyzikos respectively). The last-mentioned stele, in the Louvre, for Attalos, son of Asklepiodors, is unusually well carved, with many details added separately, including the (now missing) heads of the reclining man and the seated woman, which may therefore have had portrait-like features; Hamiaux 1998, 149–50, no. 162, suggests, however, that the heads were replaced during a period of reuse. The box held by the small servant girl is shaped like a tholos with columns and, originally, a metal finial; it has led to the suggestion that Attalos was an architect and the cista an architectural model. Hamiaux interprets the metal pin as repair for a break, and the tholos as a representation of the Arsinoeion at Samothrake, signifying that the woman had been initiated into the Mysteries of the Great Gods. This Kyzikos stele is also unusual for its many metal attachments (for weapons?) in its upper level. See also infra, n. 19.

Reclining women: nos. 2025–27 pls. 292–93. Four men at banquet: e.g., nos. 2015–16 pl. 291 (from Kyzikos).

For general comments on Banquet Reliefs (Totenmahl), see *DOG* 1979, 353–68 (with special reference to the *realia* of the scenes); Zanker 1995, 253–54, who cites an unpublished Munich dissertation by J. Fabricius (1992), [now *Die Hellenistischen Totenmahlreliefs. Grabrepräsentation und Wertvorstellungen in ostgriechischen Städten* (Munich 1999) (cf. Ridgway, *BMCR*, 99.11.26.] quoted also by Breuer 1995. The Hellenistic Banquet type predominates on Samos, at Kyzikos, and Byzantion and may include "guests," in a widening of the self-definition of the individual. For an analysis of the funerary Totenmahl by areas, see Schmidt 1991, 103–104 (Samos), 104–109 (Byzantion), 110–16 (Kyzikos); also Breuer 1995, 122–24 (Samos), 124–26 (Kyzikos), 126–27 (Smyrna) with specific ref. to epitaphs. See also Ridgway 1997b, 200–201, with additional refs.; for the Parian Archilocheion, see Ridgway 1993b, 243–44, 397–98 with bibl. and comments on the ambivalent nature of Kykladic reliefs in Archaic times.

19. The Samian Banquet Reliefs are conveniently collected by Horn 1972, but I give here the refs. to *DOG* 1979 for ease in comparison: nos. 1583 pl. 230 (tree in background; 1st c. or later), 1511 pl. 218 (curtain hanging in front of column), 1557 pl. 225 (building façade with "broken pediment" showing various objects including an anchor), 1524 pl. 220, 1575 pl. 228, 1581 pl. 230 (weapons), 1821 pl. 262 (stele of Philon the pankratiast; see p. 438 for the epitaph). For refinements on findspots and inventory numbers of the Samian material, see the reviews of both installments of *DOG* by Freyer-Schauenburg (supra, n. 5). Statistics on Samian epitaphs are provided by Breuer 1995, 122–24; she states that on Samos the Banquet Reliefs of the Classical period are votive in nature and acquire funerary connotations only after the 4th c. But note *DOG* 1979, no. 1834 pl. 263, which includes a round altar and a sacrificial animal (ram or bull) and a group of figures with offering basket—an entire cultic scene almost separate from the Totenmahl proper. That Samos was not more military than Smyrna is remarked by Schmidt 1991, 141–42, but *DOG* 1977, 113, mentions that the island was used by the Ptolemies as a naval base. Besides the frequent rendering of weapons, snake and horse protome are consistent features.

20. *DOG* 1979, nos. 1520 pl. 219 (relief from Rhodes[?] with 10 worshipers; note the unusual effect of depth), 1521 pl. 219 (relief from Klazomenai with offering of pig; both large servants and the man with the phiale, remarkably, seem to have long hair; the traditional seated woman is omitted, but a horse protome appears in a "window" at upper right), 1840 pl. 264 (relief with "Tyche of Antioch" and pig; bought in Smyrna), 1831 pl. 303 (unknown provenience; stele in two registers, with Hermes in dexiosis motif; here Pl. 63). Except for this last example, all previously listed reliefs are said to be possibly votive. Perhaps the Banquet type is most clearly funerary when it appears on a multi-register stele, where the other panels narrate something about the deceased: cf., e.g., *DOG* 1979, nos. 1227 fig. 79 on p. 310 (banquet over naval encounter; here Ill. 22), 111 pl. 204 (over hunting scene), 1429 pl. 208 (cuirassed Rider-near-horse scene).

On the other hand, a banquet scene appears on each register of a **two-tiered votive relief from Ephesos,** dated to the mid-2nd c.: Atalay 1985. Its unusually elongated shape resembles the front of the so-called Tribune of Eshmoun (Ridgway 1997b, 211–14, pl. 50a); the return sides of the block were also carved but left unfinished, probably reused in Roman times for funerary purposes. The two registers comprise some 40 personages in various groupings, some inscribed, and some elements of landscape (a rocky frame for the Nymphs). Three human dedicants, labeled Meges, Badromios, and Pozelos, appear with sacrificial animals on the lower register. The upper banquet has three reclining figures (two of them women), the lower one two, perhaps the Dioskouroi. Among the deities are Zeus Ammon (with ram's horns), Kybele, and (labeled) the Horai, the Charites, Phosphoros, Panakea [*sic*], and Hygieia.

21. General comments on the Rider Type: *DOG* 1979, 310–14. See also Schmidt 1991, 17–18 (pointing out a distinctive treatment of the chlamys for Pergamene horsemen; cf. supra, p. 192). Most extensively and recently (1992) *LIMC* 6, s.v. Heros Equitans, 1019–81; remarks on the hero in the Greek world, pp. 1064–73, are by H. Koukouli-Chrysanthaki, V. Machaira, and P. J. Pantos; see esp. pp. 1065–66 for refs. to cult. The entry has a very extensive bibl. A specific case of a historical personage with a hero-cult designation and iconography as Horse-Leader is that of Hephaistion, the companion of Alexander the Great: *LIMC* 6, no. 40 pl. 676 (= Voutiras 1990), relief from Pella inscribed to the Hero Hephaistion, dated last third 4th c.:

within a rocky frame, the hero, in chitoniskos, stands by his horse while a "heroine" pours him a libation. The cult of Hephaistion seems to have been widespread in Alexander's army—the practice of heroization may have penetrated the East in this fashion.

For the Rider scene in conjunction with Banquet Reliefs, see supra, no. 20.

22. Rider on horse, in motion: *DOG* 1979, nos. 1316 pl. 194 (unknown provenience; altar under horse's front leg), 1338 pl. 195 (probably from Ephesos; altar with entwined snake, tree; the rider holds a spear). Rider on foot, in Polybios motif: *DOG* 1977, no. 647 pl. 98 (unknown provenience; horse wears animal-skin saddle, rider accompanied by normal-sized groom, man, and woman, and diminutive servants/children; tree with snake in background), *DOG* 1979, nos. 1430–32 pl. 208 (two from Smyrna include tree with snake; 1431, from Kyme, has horse with animal-skin saddle; diminutive servants carry shield, wear rider's helmet, despite incompatibility of scale). For a similar, fragmentary relief not in *DOG*, now in Basel, see Schmidt 1991, fig. 43 (inscription: Hero Makedon, added in Roman times?) = *LIMC* 6, s.v. Hero Equitans, no. 33 pl. 674, dated 2nd half 2nd c. A dog appears between the horse's legs and a pier (supporting a herm?) behind it, against which two small servants lean; two strigils and two jumping weights are also shown. The horse wears an animal-skin saddle. In front of the animal, at the left-hand break, a raised shield suggests a second person as large as the hero, and a considerably smaller figure (the dedicant?) makes a gesture of adoration.

Note the similarity in rendering between some of these stelai and the Lagina friezes, esp. the north side (cf. Pl 36).

23. *DOG* 1979, nos. 1440 pl. 210 (from Smyrna) and 1477 pl. 214 (from Pergamon = *LIMC* 6, s.v. Hero Equitans, no. 41 pl. 676, dated 2nd half 2nd c.). For the debated dates of this second relief, see *DOG* 1977, p. 43. A third (naiskos) relief which includes the mannered rendering of the big toe, *DOG* 1979, no. 1439 pl. 210 (= Smith 1991, fig. 223), from Smyrna, adds some interesting details to the basic scene: the "hero" wears his chlamys resting on his shoulder and wrapped around his left arm, leaving his Classicizing body free. A servant helping to restrain the horse wears an elaborate helmet (of his master's?), thus connoting military valor, but a dead hare hangs from the leafy tree on the right, and a dog stands in front of it with a second attendant. Both male activities, warfare and the hunt, are thus symbolized by the composition. The panel gives a great sense of space and open-air setting. The horse, wearing an animal-skin saddle, is more completely rendered than on the other two reliefs, although still somewhat diagonally posed in relation to his master.

Rider stelai with two equal personages and two horses: *DOG* 1979, e.g., no. 1461 pl. 212 (from Miletos).

24. On Rhodian funerary monuments, see Fraser 1977; specific comments in Schmidt 1991, 5–8. For women at banquet, see supra, n. 18. On the rare representations of warriors, see *DOG* 1977, 66 and 113; of the seven Rhodian stelai listed, only three (nos. 284–86 pls. 52–53) are dated "Late Hellenistic" and may belong to the late 2nd c.; the others are 3rd c. or earlier. The three that may belong to our span show frontal figures: two (nos. 284–85) are cuirassed, one (no. 286 pl. 53) is mostly naked, with mantle fastened on left shoulder. Most depictions of warriors, from various sites, are Roman in date; some are rock-cut reliefs rather than stelai.

Rhodian embracing couples: *DOG* 1977, nos. 721–25 pl. 108 (no. 723 is from Syme, no. 724 from Tilos [here Pl. 65]; the man/woman stelai are nos. 721–23). The lack of tunic on the male figures marks the difference between these and the Asia Minor renderings. Schmidt 1991, 5–8, comments on Rhodian Hellenistic stelai, and specifically on the embracing figures, mentioning the example in Tegea (p. 8 n. 45). It is suggested that the formula may develop from the Classical stele of Krito and Timarista (*DOG* 1977, p. 196; cf. no. 46 pl. 12), although in the Hellenistic examples both women seem veiled.

25. See, e.g., Schmidt 1991, 20–21 (Ephesos), 21–22 (Chios and Lesbos).

26. The main publication on Delos/Rheneia is Couilloud 1974a (cf. pp. 3, 243–45 for chronology; figs. 13–21 for stele shapes, and discussion on pp. 262–76), corrected and supplemented by Couilloud 1975 and Couilloud–Le Dinahet 1978. See this last, p. 856 fig. 1, for a map of the area with the cemeteries on Rheneia (a small strip of land opposite Delos); figs. 6–11 (pp. 860–62) for drawings of the six prevalent types of stele format, p. 862 for chronology. Production on the other Kykladic islands continued until the 2nd c. A.C., when it deteriorated rapidly for unknown reasons: Couilloud 1974b (chronology: p. 493) and 1975. Schmaltz 1983, 228 n. 533, compares and contrasts Rheneian and Smyrnaian stelai.

27. Arch format: Couilloud 1974a, 249, lists 85 examples of one form of construction, to which five more of different construction can be added; see also p. 268 for discussion. Add Couilloud–Le Dinahet 1978, 862 fig. 11 (drawing, type 6) and stele R 71, p. 866, fig. 21, for an actual example. Arched gravestones are also found on Lesbos, under Delian influence, but they seem to be no earlier than the 1st c.—see, e.g., *DOG* 1977, nos. 199 pl. 41, 404 pl. 67, 857 pl. 126, 1022 pl. 153. They are rare and equally late in East Greece: *DOG* 1977, nos. 191 pl. 40, 198 pl. 41, 400 pl. 65, and comments on p. 54 (cf. Pl. 66). The shape becomes popular in Roman times. Pedimented stelai for youths: Schmaltz 1983, 238, who points out that old age is, by contrast, never shown, even when death occurred very late, as mentioned in the epitaph. Sarcophagi: see Couilloud 1974b, figs. 5–9, all supposedly Imperial (p. 403, and chronology on pp. 404–405 with n. 25), and *DOG* 1977, 53 and nos. 182 pl. 39 (from Rhodosto in Thrake), 218–19 pl. 43 (from Byzantion), also dated early Imperial. For the presence of Hellenistic sarcophagi on Rheneia, see Couilloud 1974a, 225–26 (one lost example [no. 502], some lids), who advocates a short span of manufacture. In Paros, a tradition of sarcophagi standing above ground, decorated with reliefs, is particularly attested for the 2nd c. but goes back to the Archaic period: Schilardi 1986, esp. 19, 23, with bibl.

28. Tomb of Tertia Horaria: Couilloud 1974a, 226–27 fig. 9 for a reconstruction of the entire monument, estimated at a total height of 4.43 m, 2.64 m wide on facade, and 1.60 m on the sides. A somewhat comparable monument existed on 2nd-c. Paros: Rubensohn 1935, 66–67, figs. 11–12 = Kurtz and Boardman 1971, 287 fig. 69 (drawing; sarcophagus surmounted by busts). The Rheneia stele inserted on the sarcophagus lid, with which it was found, is cat. 58, pp. 83–84, fig. 3, and pls. 10, 13, 93 (note that 13.1 is printed reversed). Not only the vines and the finial, but also the akanthos leaves of the Corinthian capitals, would have been painted, possibly in green, to judge from the 3rd-c. Mausoleum of Belevi. Another stele similar to Tertia's is Couilloud 1974a, cat. 57, pp. 81–83, fig. 2, and pl. 12 (pl. 80.2 for inscription), belonging to Ammia, daughter of Zenis(?), and Antiochos, son of Glaukos, from Gaza. The naiskos is framed by Corinthian columns, but has a regular Doric entablature with regulae, guttae, and a triglyph frieze with four relief metopes—the two outer panels with a boukranion, the two inner panels with a rosette. A dentil course lies between the frieze and the akroterial anthemion. The scene within the naiskos, set on a rounded plinth, shows a bearded man shaking hands with a seated woman flanked by a servant, but the man faces forward toward the viewer, and the attendant is impossibly small. The stele is dated to the end of the 2nd or the beginning of the

1st c. That other monumental heroa existed is confirmed by the find of various architectural elements (Doric frieze, column drums, antae) near a stepped platform on Rheneia, erected by a man for his wife in the 2nd c.: Couilloud–Le Dinahet 1978, 858 and fig. 3.

29. My comments are mostly derived from Couilloud 1974a, with additions as indicated. Dexiosis: over one-fourth of the total 371 stelai (figured only, including some early Imperial examples), by my approximate count; Couilloud–Le Dinahet 1978 adds six more. Women "slouching" on their seat: cat. 147–49, pl. 35; this pose recalls the so-called Aphrodite-Olympias, which I have tentatively considered a creation of Julio-Claudian times (Ridgway 1981, 234–37); examples in the two-dimensional arts of the Classical period would not preclude a late translation into statuary in the round (see infra, Chs. 8–9), and the Rheneian stelai confirm the Classicizing revival of the pose in the 2nd–1st cs. For the type, see *LIMC* 2, s.v. Aphrodite, 90–91, nos. 819–41 (including variants and minor arts; dated 5th c.), esp. no. 821 pl. 81, for a sculptural replica. Women seated in Tyche pose: Couilloud 1974a, nos. 132 pl. 32, 169 pl. 40; nos. 159 pl. 37 and 170 pl. 40 are variations on that theme.

30. Funerary Banquet: 14 stelai in total, of which only six are datable to our span (Couilloud 1974a, 299–304, esp. 300–304, distinguishing between Hellenistic renderings considered votive and those considered funerary; pls. 60–63); add Couilloud–Le Dinahet 1978 and, from the Kyklades in general, Couilloud 1974b.

Rider stelai: only two, nos. 311–12 pl. 60, and comments on p. 304; see also infra, under Round Altars.

Men seated on rocks: Couilloud 1974a, 294–98 (four types) and nos. 327–47 pls. 63–68; add Couilloud–Le Dinahet 1978, 868, no. 38 (n. 9 for discussion of cenotaph status). From the Kyklades in general: Couilloud 1974b, cat. 92–95 (no. 94 includes part of a ship), although probably none earlier than the 1st c. For similar renderings from East Greece, see *DOG* 1977, nos. 823 (from Chios, but probably brought there as ballast from Rheneia; showing ship prow), 824–29 pls. 120–21 (from various sites, ranging from 3rd to 1st c.).

Warriors on ship: Couilloud 1974a, 292–94 (suggesting that the Delians, who had no navy, may have nonetheless collaborated with Athens in defending the island from the pirates), nos. 351–59bis pls. 69–70. In the East Greek area: *DOG* 1979, nos. 1275–78 pl. 189 and fig. 79 on p. 310 (for no. 1277, where a naval battle appears in the lower register, below a Totenmahl, ca. 200). No. 1278, from near Bursa and dated to the 3rd c., has a long list of names in two columns, presumably the men who died in the battle. A more unusual relief (*DOG* 1977, no. 283 pl. 52, in the Izmir Museum) shows a cuirassed man with mantle (Polybios pattern), toward whom a kneeling female stretches her arms in supplication(?); a warship prow on rocky ground appears at the right edge of the relief; the inscription is fragmentary.

Shipwrecks: Couilloud 1974a, 298, nos. 348–50 pls. 68–69; the last item shows an overturned ship with no men, the previous two show men falling or reaching toward ships. Note that Type *d* of the "men on rocks" (nos. 341–43 pl. 67) also shows sailors swimming in the waves near a boat.

31. Funerary statues: Couilloud 1974a, 231–35, nos. 1–4 pl. 89 (women; no. 4, a statuette, is kneeling), 5(young man, clearly unfinished)–6 pl. 90 (sphinx near krater, unfinished: Athens NM 1661; cf. *LIMC* 8, s.v. sphinx, 1155 no. 75), 7–9 pls. 90–91 (lions). For the ship prow, see supra, Ch. 5 n. 22. The sphinx is a most remarkable composition, almost entirely anthropomorphic.

32. The latest discussion of (non-figured) round altars from Kos and Rhodes is Berges 1996, 9

and n. 2, and main discussion on pp. 66–71, revising in part the chronology suggested in Berges 1986. How popular this form of monument was is shown by numbers: Berges 1986 (which includes two figured altars) catalogues a total of 113 items (from mid-2nd c. B.C. to beg. 2nd c. A.C.), of which 97 fall within our timespan; Berges 1996 gives a total of 280 altars (perhaps with some overlap with his previous work) but includes no chronology within the entries. The best clues for precise dating are provided by some votive altars from Delos carrying an archon's or a priest's name (Berges 1996, 66 and n. 211), but a few other examples are also helpful. Berges 1996 includes a section (VII) by V. Patsiada, "Grabtische und Grabaltäre in der Nekropole von Rhodos," 84–109; pls. 63.2, 66, 68.3 show altars in their original findspots within the cemetery. Altars with deer and ram heads: e.g., Berges 1996, cat. 28 (pl. 12.4) and 38 (pl. 14.4). A (votive) example with schematic deer heads and smooth garland is inscribed with a dedication to Ptolemy VI Philometor (r. 180–145), his queen, Kleopatra, and their children, by the inhabitants of Thera: Hamiaux 1998, 204–205, no. 220.

Rectangular altars decorated with garlands suspended from boukephalia are also known, but they are beyond the scope of this survey: see, however, Berges 1986, fig. 22, and Berges 1997, pl. 21.6, for an example from Kos that finds a close local imitation in a tufa altar from Punic/Sicilian Soloeis (Soluntum; Berges 1997, pl. 21.5), thus demonstrating the spread and popularity of these insular products.

The highly varied typology of Hellenistic boukrania seems dependent on individual masters and cannot be arranged in a meaningful chronological sequence: see Dinstl 1993, esp. 166, and cf. his figs. 2a–b (on pp. 164–65) for schematic drawings of Hellenistic examples. To be sure, these sacrificial symbols par excellence appear on a variety of structures, not just on altars: cf., e.g., supra, Ch. 3, for the Pillar of Prousias and the carved drums from the Smintheion. For a review of the motif as such, see Webb 1996, 29–30, where the range of occurrences is listed: on "temple, altar, cultic and commemorative building, stoa, propylon, theater, house—with the exception of the heroon." In each case, however, a religious connotation is implied.

33. Knidos altar: Berges 1986, cat. 76, pl. 52.4 = DOG 1979, no. 2228 pl. 317; the inscription was added in Roman Imperial times. Bell krater with snake, from Rhodian nekropolis: DOG 1979, no. 2226 pl. 317 (dated "High Hellenistic"). Altars with snakes: Berges 1986, 84–85, cat. 76–85, figs. 118–25; Berges 1996, 37–38, 64–65, 151 and cat. 275–76, pls. 52.3, 53.1 (from Rhodes), p. 152, cat. 277, pl. 53.2 (from Kos).

For general comments on funerary altars with relief decoration, see DOG 1977, 57–60, where the simple form is credited to early Ionia and a Hellenistic production center in Lesbos is also advocated. Berges 1996, 11, sees the altars from Halikarnassos, Iasos, and Knidos as being influenced by Kos, and those of the Rhodian Peraia (the Rhodian-controlled sites on the Asiatic mainland) and the coast between Kaunos and Phaselis as being of Rhodian inspiration. They are rare outside the Doric hexapolis. The distinction between the Rhodian and the Koan type consists in the upper profile, especially the location of the dentil course: cf. Berges 1996, 46–48, Beil. 1–3 (Koan), 56–59, Beil. 4–6 (Rhodian). Although the types are similar, the two productions have independent development (Berges 1996, 69), and Delos may start later than either, in mid-2nd c. (p. 46). Cf. also Couilloud 1974a, 219–22.

34. Evidence for libations and burnt offerings consists of depressions and barriers on the top surfaces of some altars; it has been suggested that a terracotta or clay element was added to those that were exposed to fire; cf. Berges 1996, 21–22 and 18–20 for discussion of the cult of the dead. Further discussion on pp. 107–109 (V. Patsiada), stressing the drastic change from

Original Reliefs—Funerary and Votive

the plain graves of the 4th and 3rd cs. to the elaborate layouts of the "High Hellenistic" phase. The point is argued against Fraser 1977, 76–81, who had excluded any connection between the round altars and the cult of the dead. See also Berges 1986, 21 (Epikteta's will), 22 and n. 104 (help from the dead to the living), and, in general, 12–26 (function of altars), 26–28 (votive). Muse types on stelai: see, e.g., *DOG* 1977, no. 382 pl. 62 (here Pl. 60), and, in reverse pose, *DOG* 1979, no. 1477 pl. 214 (Pergamon Rider Relief: supra, n. 23—the type is the so-called Venice Muse, or Muse with the Scroll: see *LIMC* 7, s.v. Mousa, Mousai, no. 254d [as part of so-called Philiskos Muses], with mention of other replicas that do not include funerary examples; also Ridgway 1990, 257–58, 266 n. 32, pl. 136). See also "Tyche of Antioch type" (considered Kalliope by Ridgway 1990, 233–37; Ourania type among the Philiskan Muses): supra, ns. 20 (= *DOG* 1979, no. 1840 pl. 264), 29, and infra, n. 36; Ridgway 1994, 34–37, no. 10 (gravestone of Tryphe, from Seleukia on the Orontes, ca 150–100; here Pl. 66). A Rider Relief from Smyrna, *DOG* 1979, no. 1450 pl. 211, includes a pedestal with an Archaistic statuette holding a tragic mask. Cf. the comments in Ridgway 1993a, 237. See also infra, on the Halikarnassos reliefs.

35. Cult of the dead influenced by ruler's cult: Berges 1996, 38–41, esp. 40 n. 120 for fringed tainiai; see also pp. 53, 70 with n. 234. He catalogues 12 Koan altars with dikerata; his cat. 149, pl. 40.4 is the only Rhodian example.

36. On figured altars, briefly, see *DOG* 1977, 57–58; Berges 1996, 63, mentioning an unpublished study by K. Kälin, *Variationen zum Thema 'Nike.' Betrachtet an Rundaltären aus Rhodos und Kos*, Bern 1984 (forthcoming in *HASB?*). See other refs. infra.

Altar of Archestrate, with deer heads: *DOG* 1979, no. 1547 pl. 224 = Berges 1996, cat. 156 pl. 42.3–4 (here Pl. 62; the seated woman is in the pose of the Tyche of Antioch). The second example of Totenmahl is *DOG* 1979, no. 2039 pl. 295 (boukephalia, reclining female).

37. Koan altar with man in inset: Berges 1996, cat. 20, pl. 11.1–2. Rheneian altar: Couilloud 1974a, cat. 498 pl. 87; the barefoot man stands on a separate baseline. Eresos altar: *DOG* 1979, no. 1470 pl. 213; the surface is badly weathered, and it is unclear whether the frontal man stands near an altar; the garland has only three, instead of the customary four, swags. A comparable item, from Mytilene (Lesbos), but datable to the 1st c., has a similar smooth garland, once fully painted, under whose upward curves are rendered, in high relief, the bust of a mantled man, and the heads of a ram and a doe respectively; the upper surface is decorated in relief with two snakes and their offerings: apples, pears, figs, and small cakes: *DOG* 1979, no. 2109 pl. 304.

38. Four Nikai with widespread wings, in himation and chiton with slipped strap, holding garlands with right hand, and, with the left, palm branches, or tainia, or wreath; above swags, birds in different arrangements: Berges 1986, 72, cat. 44, figs. 88a–f (dated by Kählin to the first quarter of the 1st c. but considered possibly earlier). Other Nikai, crowning a cuirassed man, and dancing maenads, are mentioned by Berges 1996, 63.

Altar in British Museum: *DOG* 1979, no. 1105 pl. 166; Palagia 1997a, 68 and n. 10, 70, figs. 87–88. Stele with Hermes (in dexiosis with deceased) and sundial: supra, n. 20 (*DOG* 1979, no. 1831b pl. 303).

39. Altar, Istanbul Arch. Mus. inv. 122: *LIMC* 3, s.v. Eros, no. 448; *LIMC* 8, s.v. Tyche, no. 9 pl. 85. Phialai or rosettes are interspersed with the garlands and boukrania.

40. Aigina altar: Couilloud 1974a, cat. 499 pl. 88, considered one of four Delian reliefs with snake and tree (p. 279).

41. Altar with 10 figures, London, BM 1107: Palagia 1997a is the first study in depth; cf. Fraser 1977, 118 n. 157. Muse "Base," London, BM 1006: the main publication is Pinkwart 1967

(in the context of the Muses of Philiskos); Berges 1986, 23–24, 73, cat. 45 (chronology cannot be confirmed typologically because upper profile is missing; Roman villa was near a cemetery); Ridgway 1990, 258–62, ill. 32; Cohon 1991/92, 78–82 (naming the Muses); *LIMC* 8, s.v. Mousa, Mousai, no. 250 pl. 721 (considered a base).

42. It could be argued that the position symbolizes a flame about to be extinguished, signaling the end of a life, but such funerary signifiers are usually connected with supernatural beings like deities or Erotes. Moreover, the woman's mantle does not describe the triangular pattern that characterizes priestesses of Demeter on Smyrnaian stelai. On the various possible meanings of scrolls on funerary monuments, see supra, n. 16.

43. Palagia 1997a, 69, has noted the incongruity and attributes it to a borrowing from a different context: Hermes leading Plouton's chariot to the Underworld. She also notes the man's peculiar attire, unusual for Hermes in funerary representations. Yet she prefers a funerary to a votive interpretation for the altar, making frequent comparison to the Hieronymos relief (supra, Ch. 4 n. 60); she leaves open the issue of heroization of the dead (p. 71).

44. In the drawing published by Pinkwart 1967 and reproduced in Ridgway 1990, 258, ill. 32, the Leaning Muse marks the beginning, and the seated figure marks the end, of the rolled-out cylinder. Yet a composition in the round has no clear beginning and end; it is therefore obvious that the poses of the two have been considered a caesura. Cf. the drawings in Cohon 1991/92, figs. 4–5, which begin with the Venice Muse and end with the Tyche/Ourania; Cohon, who follows the Hesiodic canon in naming the Muses, identifies the former as Kalliope, the latter as Klio.

45. Berges 1986, 21, comments that the use of Muses on Imperial sarcophagi, where they accompany portraits of the deceased, goes back to Hellenistic prototypes.

46. That the Muses "of Philiskos" may be a modern mirage is argued also by Pollitt, forthcoming; cf. Ridgway 1989, esp. 266–67, and Ridgway 1990, 252–68. Even the discussion in the *LIMC*, 7, s.v. Mousa, Mousai, no. 254, pp. 1001–1002, and the comment on the production of the 2nd c., pp. 1008–1010 (L. Faedo), seem to accept a standard grouping without necessarily subscribing to the attribution to the Rhodian master mentioned by Pliny. Moreno 1994, 409–13, follows the theory of two groups, on Rhodes and for Rome. La Rocca 1996, 619–20, admits that M. Aemilius Lepidus may have commissioned the Muses directly from the Rhodian Philiskos (2nd quarter of 2nd c.), but assumes that the latter's workshop mass-produced many replicas of them, "since various groups of Muses have also been found both in Asia Minor and Alexandria."

Tyche type: supra, ns. 20, 29, 34, 36; for the Athenian terracotta, see Rotroff 1990, 29 fig. 17, and, for the excavation report, Knigge 1980, 264 fig. 14. Venice Muse and statuette with mask: supra, n. 34. Mantineia Base: e.g., Ridgway 1990, pl. 132b, first figure from the left (also holding double pipes).

47. For an unusual relief, probably votive, with a combat scene, now in Aberdeen, see supra, Ch. 3 and n. 56.

48. My previous discussion: Ridgway 1990, 257–66; cf. n. 28 on p. 272, with ref. to the Seleukid attribution; it was first proposed in 1926 (cf. Schefold 1997, 530). The *LIMC* entries, s.v., on the various personifications break down as follows. Sole entry: Historia (vol. 5, pl. 331), Mythos (vol. 6), Physis, Poiesis (vol. 7); first entry, all others uncertain or Roman: Arete (vol. 2, pl. 425), Chronos (vol. 3, pl. 222), Ilias (vol. 5), Mneme (vol. 6), Odysseia (vol. 6), Oikoumene

Original Reliefs—Funerary and Votive

(vol. 7), Pistis (vol. 7, no. 2 pl. 340—but no. 1 is a Roman coin), Sophia (vol. 7). Meaningful exceptions (because of their wider application) are Komodia (vol. 6, no. 7; previous numbers refer to paintings and a single statue in the round, from Thasos), Mnemosyne (vol. 6 no. 2; no. 1 is a lekythos), and Tragodia (sic; vol. 8, no. 5; nos. 1–2 refer to literature or painting, nos. 3–4 are the statues from Thasos and Pergamon). No entry is given for the Batrachomyomachia symbolized on the relief by a mouse and a frog. Publications after 1990: Smith 1991, 187, fig. 216 (late 3rd or 2nd c.). *LIMC* 7, s.v. Mousa, Mousai, no. 266 pl. 73 (on Hellenistic Muse types). Moreno 1994, 561–63, figs. 689 (p. 560) and 737 (p. 593); cf. also p. 416 . Schefold 1997, 336–38, fig. 213, and 530 with extensive bibl. See also infra, ns. 49–50.

49. This position is advocated by Cohon 1991/92, 68–70; he discusses the Archelaos Relief on pp. 70–78, although accepting that it "dates from the third to second century B.C." Identification of the individual Muses is far from certain; nonetheless, the probability that Cohon's argument is correct is high—see his statistical calculations, p. 77 and n. 45.

50. This theory is advanced by Voutiras 1989b; see esp. 167–68, for a discussion of the Italian findspot. He stresses that the relief corresponds to Homeric conceptions of the world according to the interpretation given by Krates and his followers. Krates had spent some time in Rome (having broken his foot while there on a mission) and was said (Suet. *de gramm.* 2) to have introduced *grammatike* to the Italian capital. Archelaos' relief (still dated to the 2nd half of the 2nd c.) would have been taken to Bovillae at the turn into the next century.

51. "Visit of Dionysos to a poet," also known as the Ikarios Relief: e.g., Stewart 1990, 225–26; see also Ridgway 1994, 100–106, no. 32 (A.-M. Knoblauch), esp. 103–104 and ns. 16–19 with added bibl.

52. Relief, Munich Glyptothek 206; its height is variously given as 0.61 m (Smith 1991, fig. 214; Stewart 1990, fig. 824) or 0.79 m (Pollitt 1986, fig. 210). See also Moreno 1994, 344–45 fig. 436 and bibl. in n. 627. It is also variously dated, to the (late) 3rd (Richter 1966, Smith 1991, Moreno 1994) or to the mid–late 2nd c. (Bieber 1961, 126–27 fig. 489 [ca. 160]; Pollitt 1986, 197; Stewart 1990; Hausmann 1960, 89–96, figs. 55–56, with detail of the man next to the central altar). By "porthole viewing" I mean that the composition is seen as if through a porthole that cuts off its edges.

53. Esquiline paintings: Biering 1995 (cf. supra, Ch. 3 n. 4). Tanagras: Uhlenbrock 1990, 48–53 (Attic and Boiotian development), 74–75 (Asia Minor Tanagras). Bieber 1961, 127, believes that *all* the small figures are the children of the couple at the altar, but this theory seems negated by the adult attire of the hatted woman. For examples of the hat on stelai, see supra, n. 15.

Additional support for a late 2nd-c. date can be found in the drapery pattern of the female deity: her heavy peplos with belted apoptygma forms trumpet folds that frame the low-slung, ogival area of the abdomen revealed in incongruent transparency: cf. (with added motion) the so-called Nike by Euboulides (supra, Ch. 5 n. 39).

54. All these identifications are mentioned in Stewart 1990, caption to fig. 824. I could not find the Munich Relief in the *LIMC* despite searching under all the possible headings.

55. Archaistic statuette, holding mask, on Rider Relief from Smyrna: supra, n. 34. Bronze plaque from Delos: e.g., Ridgway 1990, 319–20, pl. 158. Attic Document Relief: Lawton 1995, 72–73 (with comparison to Munich Relief), cat. 61 on pp. 110–11, pl. 32.

56. Polybios Relief: the most detailed publication is by Bol and Eckstein 1975, with good

photographs of the actual fragments in Kato Klitoria, Greece (Beil. 1–7, cf. pls. 40–41; dated not before 146 but not long after, p. 90); they are fully convinced of the correctness of the identification. They mention anathyrosis on the top surface of the slab, which therefore must have carried a crowning element. Most recently, Schefold 1997, 320, fig. 200, with extensive bibl. on p. 528 (considered Neo-Attic Classicizing, late 2nd c.). For an explanation of the attribution on inscriptional evidence, see Richter 1965, vol. 2, 247–48, figs. 1673–74 (skeptical about identification, but rebutted by Bol and Eckstein); nothing new is added by Richter-Smith 1984, 186–87 fig. 148. Moreno 1994, 515–19, figs. 640–41 (dated 169) connects with Damophon. See also supra, Ch. 5 n. 1, for a comparison of the drapery motif on a female statuette.

57. This theory, and the reading of the original inscription, are attributed to A. Milchhöfer, *AZ* 39 (1881) 153ff. (*non vidi*). Another early reading had ἀντί ἄλλων. For a discussion of this inscription, see Bol and Eckstein 1975, 84 and n. 7, 89–90. There were actually two statues at Olympia inscribed with the same name, apparently for two different men: see Richter 1965, vol. 2, 247.

58. According to Pausanias, the inscription on the Megalopolis relief was elaborate: the verses mentioned that "he wandered all over the earth and the sea, he was an ally of Rome, and he ended the Roman anger with Greece" (trans. P. Levi, vol. 2, 449).

59. Interestingly, as listed by Pausanias, the other reliefs within the same colonnade seem to be mythological: the Fates with Zeus Moiragetes, Herakles' and Apollo's Struggle for the Tripod, Nymphs and Pans. The inscription under Polybios' relief stated that "Greece would never have collapsed if they had taken all Polybios' advice, and after it did fail the only help that came to it was through Polybios" (trans. P. Levi, vol. 2, 463).

60. Again, the other relief next to Polybios' mentioned by Pausanias seems to be mythological: Elatos, one of the sons of Arkas. Pausanias' text on Kleitor (8.21.1–4) seems to have a lacuna, but not enough to have eliminated mention of a relief of Polybios, had the Periegete seen one, since he so carefully recorded all others. Bol and Eckstein 1975, 90, mention that Pausanias omitted many other (visible) features of Kleitor, and therefore his lack of notice is not probatory.

61. For the so-called Polybios pattern in Rider Reliefs, see examples cited supra, n. 22; cf. also n. 30, for a cuirassed and mantled warrior near a ship. The pattern has been compared (Moreno) to that of the Prima Porta statue of Augustus. Early observers noted that the pommel of the Kleitor warrior's sword carried an image in relief: either a rider with fluttering chlamys or an Eros riding a panther (Bol and Eckstein 1975, 85); the first possibility would be in keeping with Polybios' rank as hipparch. Originally, the left hand was adorned with a ring, which is now too abraded for verification. The warrior's way of wearing the chitoniskos has been compared to figures on the Parthenon frieze (Schefold 1997), thus confirming the Classicizing character of the sculpture. Other large votive reliefs are known from Arkadia (cf. the so-called Stele of Diotima, Schefold 1997, 108–109, fig. 39, from Mantineia, pres. ht. 1.50 m from feet to base of neck; late 5th c.), but this one remains unusual for the Hellenistic period. We do not know the size of the reliefs with which Polybios was honored at the other Arkadian sites cited by Pausanias. If correctly identified, the Kleitor relief would be the only honorary monument of a famous Greek extant today in the original (Schefold).

62. The Four-Gods Relief: Delos A 9, from the Maison du Lac: cf. Kreeb 1988, 47 (relief came probably from a niche) and 162–66, cat. 9 (the relief is S 9.5 on p. 165); Marcadé et al. 1996,

Original Reliefs—Funerary and Votive

184–85 no. 82. *LIMC* 2, s.v. Artemis, nos. 1167–71 pls. 540–41 (Delos relief: no. 1168 with cross-refs.), and *LIMC* 5, s.v. Hermes, nos. 790–91 pl. 264, mention and show replicas of the types on monuments of different shape and compositions, including one in the Villa Albani of the end of the Republican period. Other examples in panel form, from the Peiraieus, are dated to the early Antonine phase: Tiverios 1989, esp. 389–91, pls. 61.2, 63 (Four Seasons). See Zagdoun 1989, 88–89, 92–94, pls. 20 and 22 for the Delos relief (no. 170 on p. 235, pl. 20.79) and other examples of the individual figures; pl. 18 (cat. 10) shows the Four-Gods Base from the Athenian Akropolis, often considered the 4th-c. original from which some of the Four Gods types were derived. Two other Archaistic reliefs between antae, with garlands and boukrania overhead, show Hermes and the Nymphs and come from the Villa of Herodes Atticus at Loukou, but their date is left open: Spyropoulos 1993, 260, fig. 4.

63. See, e.g., Ridgway 1997b, 196 with refs. in n. 14. The official character of such Archaistic reliefs is also shown by a panel with Hermes and the Nymphs, from Kamiros, inscribed by "epistatai under the demiurgos Dionysios, son of Archidamos": Di Vita 1995, dated between 125 and 102.

64. For this argument, see Fullerton 1997, esp. 435–36 and ns. 33–35; see also Fullerton 1998a, and 2000, passim.

I mention here a **votive relief from Lucanian Herakleia,** now in Policoro, Museo Nazionale della Siritide, because it does not fit into any established category, but it is obviously strongly influenced by Classical (Attic) Nymph Reliefs and by Totenmahl types. Within a cave-like frame, a long-haired and bearded Dionysos reclines on a rocky seat covered by an animal skin. With his left arm, he holds a large cornucopia, and with his right extends a phiale toward a small satyr perched on a rocky prominence. The satyr, seen from behind, is quite muscular, with short tail and a Pan-like horn curving against his forehead hair; he holds a large oinochoe from which he prepares to pour into the phiale. The piece is dated "beginning 2nd c.": Pugliese Carratelli 1996, 721, cat. 273; a better photograph on p. 487. Given the very few stone sculptures from Magna Graecia, this small panel (0.36 × 0.38 m) deserves attention.

65. Statue from Soloeis: supra Ch. 5 n. 59. Cf. also n. 32 in this chapter for a tufa altar at the same site, imitating East Greek formulas

CHAPTER 7

Cult Images and Masters

In previous chapters, we have already had occasion to mention both divine statues found within temples and works that were either directly signed by or could be attributed to specific sculptors—for instance, the Zeus/Hero from Pergamon, the Thea Roma on Delos by Menandros, and the Hierapytna Nike and Athena in Venice, by Damokrates from Itanos. We should here consider some original works that fall within both categories, since, remarkably, the second century seems to witness both a revival in sculptors' signing practices and a special interest in the creation of cult images. Even more important, both Greek sculptors and divine statues find a ready market in Rome, thus providing a clear artistic link between Greece and Italy that goes beyond pure looting of art works or trade in luxury items. Yet, before investigating individual instances, we should clarify the issue of the so-called classical cult statues.

CULT IMAGES

By this modern term, we usually mean the statue of a deity that stood in a temple (whether on Greek or Italian soil) and received offerings or other manifestations of worship. Such an image may have been quite old (of undetermined or "heavenly" origin) and of limited artistic significance, or more recently created (by a known artist) and from costly materials. In either case, we visualize it as having a central position within the temple, usually on axis with the main doorway, even if flanked by other images, perhaps even the earlier venerable statues that preceded the more elaborate versions. A case in point is the chryselephantine Hera in the fourth-century Argive Heraion, made by Polykleitos (the Younger?)—a seated statue (accompanied by an equally chryselephantine Hebe) housed in the same temple as the wooden Hera salvaged from the fire that destroyed the Archaic predecessor at the sanctuary. A more obvious example is the Athena Parthenos by Pheidias, which, however, stood alone within the Parthenon while the earlier wooden image was kept in the nearby Temple of Athena Polias. Some modern authors have suggested that spectacular gold-and-ivory statues like the Parthenos were not truly worshiped and served more as votive objects and repositories of the city's wealth than as recipients of cult; it is clear, none-theless, that they inspired religious awe and received offerings like the earlier simu-lacra.[1]

Yet it has recently been argued that the concept of a cult image is a modern con-struct without ancient validity and that no such classification for statues existed in the minds of the Greeks. Not only was there no specific term to indicate temple images, but ritual offerings could be made to statues away from a temple setting, and even to representations of athletes and other individuals—that is, of mortals, non-divine beings—which were thought to possess special powers.[2] These claims are undoubtedly correct, and it appears that veneration of some sort could attach to two-dimensional (narrative) images as much as to statuary in the round—indeed, the main purpose of Greek architectural sculpture was to provide a didactic and inspirational reminder of divine powers. Yet it is also true that certain temples specifically made provisions for the erection of one or more statues in a prominent position, which would therefore qualify them as "cult images" because of their privileged and prearranged location. A typical example is the Heraion at Olympia, one of the earliest preserved Doric struc-tures (ca. 600), in which the statue base occupied virtually the entire width of the central aisle; another, again, in Classical times, is the Parthenon, with its wide pedestal for the Athena Parthenos framed by a Π-shaped colonnade. Smaller temples, like that of Nemesis at Rhamnous, were almost entirely filled by their colossal images, and the Pheidian Zeus at Olympia was so enormous as to prompt later speculation that, were he to rise, he would take the roof away (Strabo 8.3.30). These points should be kept in mind when we discuss Hellenistic practices.

The importance of these monuments has led, however, to other misleading assump-tions: that all Greek temples were meant to house a cult statue, even when evidence for its presence is missing, and that in fact permanent religious structures began to be erected in order to house such images. Some scholars even postulated the contempo-raneous beginning of monumental sculpture and stone architecture as a cause-and-effect sequence. Further investigation has now shown that Greek practices in the use of cult images varied from area to area, and that the idea of the temple as the house of the divinity is a concept derived from different ancient cultures and religions, not necessarily one native to the Greeks.[3] It seems, however, certain that the fifth cen-tury witnessed the proliferation of elaborate statues, often in precious materials, spe-cifically meant to be placed in a temple, which therefore, from the viewpoint of our restricted definition, can be considered cult images—not because more highly ven-erated and worshiped than others but because of their predetermined purpose. Al-though "temple image" is perhaps a more appropriate terminology than "cult image," I shall hereafter use the two expressions interchangeably.

A great number of chryselephantine statues were made during the fifth and fourth centuries by famous sculptors—or by sculptors who *became* famous because of their creations. Besides the above-mentioned Pheidian Parthenos and Zeus, and the Polykleitan Hera and Hebe, there were, for instance, a Dionysos by Alkamenes, for an Athenian temple, and an Asklepios by Thrasymedes of Paros, for the Epidaurian Asklepieion. More could be listed, but those already cited prove the point.[4] Other materials known to have been used are marble (for instance, the Rhamnousian Nemesis by Agorakritos) and, perhaps exceptionally, bronze—the Athena and Hephaistos attributed to Alkamenes, probably in metal because they stood in the temple of the smith god. By the beginning of the Hellenistic period, however, a new trend seems to have set in: statues made either entirely of gilded wood or in akrolithic technique, that is, with exposed "flesh" made of stone. The result would have been fairly similar to a genuine chryselephantine sculpture but considerably less costly and perhaps of easier manufacture.

To be sure, some late accounts describe divine images made of more exotic materials, typical among them the third-century Sarapis by Bryaxis(?), which is said (Clement of Alexandria, *Protr.* 4.43) to have consisted of a number of different metals and precious stones mixed together and colored blue. I had taken the garbled account to indicate a special alloy for a sculpture basically made of bronze, but I realize now that the description is based on magical texts, primarily Egyptian, used by theurgists for the production of animated statues allegedly endowed with special powers. Although such procedures need not have been followed by more traditional sculptors, authors from the second to the fourth century A.C. may have believed they were, or cited them to discredit, in a Christian vein, the idolatrous practices of the pagans.[5] It is important to realize that much of our information on cult images derived from ancient sources is tinted by the specific biases of the individual writers and should be taken into account with some caution.

An essay by H.-U. Cain (1995) has emphasized the importance that Hellenistic cult images came to assume, not only for the kings but also for the individual towns. Rulers established elaborate festivals and magnificent processions that conveyed allusions to their power and divine connections; democratic Greek cities that could not match the splendor of such monarchical displays nonetheless profited economically from similar events at smaller scale; and all festivities were enjoyed as a form of entertainment. Rituals began to include narrative elements of myths connected with the specific deities, which thus transformed the worshiper from participant to spectator; public banquets complemented the more religious functions; and even architectural layouts were influenced by the processional activities and the desire to showcase cult images as if in a museum setting, when the colossal size and weight of the statues prevented them from being carried around.[6] In such cases barriers separated them from viewers and mosaic floors in front of them often enhanced their appearance. Some distinctive traits of Hellenistic *Kultbilder* were pinpointed by Cain: their costliness, their large size and often akrolithic construction, their creation—and that of their temples—by famous sculptors and architects who served to enhance the reputation of rulers and cities, their mode of display, and finally their political allusions, deriving either from imitation of a famous prototype or from the establishment of new types with meaningful implications.

These are significant points with undoubted validity, but to some extent they can be seen as continuation and enhancement of trends already operative in the Classical period. Costliness, for instance, was certainly a major feature of all chryselephantine temple statues; festivals, competitions, processions, and banquets deriving from sacrifices were as much a part of fifth-century Athens as they were of Ptolemaic Alexandria. What is new there is the lavishness of the "floats" and the objects carried on parade, the inclusion of events (as tableaux vivants) and mythological creatures in the entourage of the gods, and the expensive gifts bestowed upon the viewers of the spectacle. Colossal size and akrolithic construction were also known in earlier times (Pheidias himself made an akrolithic Athena Areia for Plataia), but in the Hellenistic period the two may have been connected, since a statue made partly of wood was less heavy and expensive than one made entirely of stone. A certain lack of good statuary marble (especially for some parts of Greece and certainly for most of Republican Italy, which had to import it from a distance) resulted in more extensive piecing and hollowing out of invisible parts, which, however, were not limited to temple images.[7] Not all Hellenistic cult statues were made by famous masters, as we shall see, and, conversely, some of the Classical ones might have been. Finally, we have already noted the display tendencies of earlier times: the placement of statue bases on axis with the doorway, often emphasized by the arrangement of inner columns; the disproportionate amount of space occupied by the image within certain temples; even the inclusion of windows, upper galleries, and reflecting pools, as we now know to have existed in the Parthenon and the Temple of Zeus at Olympia. The novelty of the Hellenistic period consists in placing the temple itself within its own enhancing setting—surrounded by colonnades, occasionally backing up onto a wall or portico, and set up on the main axis of its precinct. As for the use of metal grilles and mosaic floors in front of the cult images, the first is not unprecedented, and the second seems merely a technical development of the times, perhaps replacing perishable carpets.[8]

What, by its very chronology, should be primarily a Hellenistic feature is the imitation of famous prototypes and earlier styles—so much so that the Classicizing trend is occasionally thought to have originated through the production of cult images, which were not only conservative par excellence but also patterned after *opera nobilia* for religious and political purposes. Yet here too some precedents can be cited. We have repeatedly noted that retrospective stylistic traits occurred in various types of statuary as early as the Classical period proper, and imitation was already at work in the Epidaurian Asklepios, said to echo the Pheidian Zeus. Cain himself cites the statue of Ephesian Artemis set up by Xenophon in his estate at Skillous near Olympia, and accepts a date at the end of the fourth century for the replica of the Parthenos at Priene. In the first instance, the desire to transfer the specific cult together with the replicated image (ἀφίδρυσις) may have been at work, but in the second, the Prieneians' intent seems more clearly political—to suggest a link to Athens as their metropolis. In the case of "new" cult images (that is, the non-replicas), the long-robed depictions of Dionysos and Apollo may have indeed echoed and legitimized the almost effeminate luxury (τρυφή) of the Hellenistic kings, but the types had already been introduced by ca. 350, and so had that of the standing Asklepios as the quintessential burgher.[9]

Cult Images on Greek Territory

The problem with these theories is that often the alleged cult image is visualized through depictions on coins that are not always contemporary with the statue in question. This is the case with the by-now notorious **Asklepios by the Athenian Phyromachos,** which was made for Pergamon and stolen by Prousias of Bithynia when he raided the area in 156/5. A recent series of writings by a single author and a special collection of essays on the master have made him appear as one of the most influential sculptors of the second century, yet many ambiguities still exist. The coins adduced as evidence for the appearance of his Asklepios considerably precede his creation, if the latter has been correctly dated around 168–156, and they show two different types —a standing and a seated image—thus obviously demanding a choice. The numismatic closeup of an Asklepios head has prompted comparison with a marble piece in Syracuse, said to be an Augustan lock-for-lock replica of the Pergamene original. Yet that work seems to me entirely Roman, most probably a Iuppiter, and certainly a generic type of elderly bearded deity in imitation Greek style. Finally, not only the original location (Asklepieion, Nikephorion, or Upper Gymnasion?) but also the medium of Phyromachos' statue is in doubt, some advocating bronze, some marble, and some gold and ivory.[10] That several names can be associated with Phyromachos, as his teacher, associates, and pupils, speaks for the abundance of known sculptors within the Hellenistic period, especially the second century, but their styles and personalities remain nebulous and their creations phantoms; to attempt their reconstruction amounts to shadow-boxing.

What is significant, however, is that so many cult statues should have been made during the Hellenistic period. This point has received insufficient stress because of the general belief that each temple, from early times on, possessed a "cult image." Yet, as noted, this was not always the case. The three centuries after Alexander the Great saw, however, an unprecedented production of divine statues meant for temple locations, some of which have survived in more or less fragmentary state. I shall here mention only a few that present some features of special interest.

Excavations at the site of **Pheneos in Arkadia** have uncovered two small temples next to each other, both containing large pedestals for statues. Those of the northern shrine have not been found, but the shrine to the south has yielded a colossal female head and two pairs of feet, one set wearing elaborate sandals. The base inscribed with second-century letter forms states that, when Therilaos, son of Heroidas, was priest of Asklepios, he had the statues made—by Attalos, son of Lachares, the Athenian.

Cult Images and Masters

They were undoubtedly akrolithic, as indicated by the female head that terminates in a rounded shallow tenon, typical of this technique, and must have represented **Asklepios** and **Hygieia**. At the time of Pausanias' visit, they may have been covered by the hillside against which the shrines stand, since he did not mention the complex.[11]

The Asklepios has been visualized as seated, with a standing Hygieia next to him. That the goddess was wearing a long costume is indicated by her bare feet, of which only the front part was made in marble. The male sandals, with holes for metal attachments, seem an unusual mixture of two forms (trochades and krepides). The female head is startling because it has retained its inserted eyes, still fringed by massive bronze lashes; the strong asymmetry of the features suggests that the goddess turned toward her male companion. Her hair is parted in the center and pulled back in a series of frizzy strands that contrast with the polished, almost empty surface of the face; they are surmounted by a crown of braids, but the back of the head is hollow, perhaps to be covered by a veil in gilded wood—matronly attire somewhat unusual for Hygieia.[12]

This complex at Pheneos epitomizes all the points made about Hellenistic practices related to cult images. Pedestal and statues filled the entire back of the main room of a small temple, and were fronted by a mosaic floor. The statues were colossal (three times lifesize), akrolithic, Classicizing in style, with inserted eyes that either derive from the chryselephantine technique or imitate works of the Severe period. Even their base—in dark stone crowned by a now missing molding probably in white marble— recalls Classical formulas; it was signed by the sculptor, in keeping with Hellenistic customs. He was an Athenian—that is, from a major center of production of temple statues—also credited (Paus. 2.19.3) with making the cult image of Apollo Lykeios for his temple in Argos. At Pheneos another Athenian, Eucheir, son of Euboulides, therefore another second-century master, had made a Hermes for the temple of that god seen by Pausanias (8.14.10). If the statues recovered from the Kerameikos in Athens can indeed be assigned to Euboulides, we can expect the Hermes to have been equally Classicizing in style.[13]

An interesting mixture of styles occurs in a complex that involves one of the Hellenistic sculptors best represented by original, extant works: the statues of **Despoina and her associates** from her sanctuary at **Lykosoura in Arkadia**, made by **Damophon of Messene**. The group consisted of two colossal statues, of Demeter and her daughter Despoina/Kore, seated on a projecting central platform flanked by two narrower segments of the same pedestal, on which stood smaller statues of Artemis with her hunting dog (next to Demeter) and the cuirassed Titan Anytos (next to Despoina). The two main goddesses, holding torch and scepter respectively, sat on an elaborate throne with arm supports in the shape of a Triton and a Tritoness on each side (one female element replaced in repairs of Hadrianic times); their feet rested on a footstool decorated in front with separately attached figures (of Kouretes and Korybantes, according to Pausanias), laterally by lions in relief, on either side of a tympanon. A barrier separated the sculptures from the viewers, and a mosaic floor extended before them, again as typical of Hellenistic displays. This famous group, described in detail (if somewhat erroneously on technical matters) by Pausanias (8.37.1–6), echoed by Imperial coins of Megalopolis, and frequently cited in the modern literature, presents some unusual aspects that deserve individual mention.[14]

1. *Construction.* Although Pausanias believed that the main figures and throne were made from one piece of stone, they were in fact built up from many hollowed parts doweled together. They were not akrolithic, in that even the drapery was of stone—one of the most distinctive features is indeed the swag of the mantle that crossed Despoina's lap and fell alongside her left leg. But the Titan Anytos was constructed differently: his cuirass lappets were made from very thin, narrow pieces attached to a core, thus resembling the chryselephantine technique. Painting enhanced the total effect: a curtain behind the seated goddesses was dark blue, Despoina's mantle was purple-red, and Demeter's chiton may have been black. These colors are partly derived from a third-century sacred law from the sanctuary that lists what visitors to the temple were forbidden to wear, probably so as not to replicate what was worn by the main divinities: no jewelry, no purple, flowered, or black dress, no sandals, no curled hair . . .[15]

It has been assumed that the hollowed-out parts, especially the heads, were to be completed in wood or stucco, but I wonder whether this was truly the case. Areas invisible from the front need not have been finished, and it was impossible, given the barrier and the size, for the viewers to gain a good lateral view of the main deities. Anytos may have worn a (metal?) helmet, and the small holes in his forehead locks were meant for metal pegs probably supporting additional stone pieces.[16] The eyes of Artemis and Anytos were inserted separately, but, surprisingly, those of Demeter were not, although the eyeballs were grooved, perhaps for the inlay of colored rims for the iris. Despoina's head is missing and therefore this feature cannot be verified, but one wonders why the more startling effect of eyes and lashes in different materials should have been omitted for the more important personage(s). Could paint and even an iris in a different medium have been more effective?

2. *Symbolism.* Demeter's black costume may have been not only a sign of mourning but also a local feature: in Arkadia, Demeter had the epithet Black (Melaina), after an encounter with Poseidon. Allusions to that god are present not only in the armrests, but also in the decoration of Despoina's mantle with its wave border and its frieze of Nereids riding marine creatures. The figured composition (imitating woven or embroidered patterns) has been described in allegorical/narrative terms: a depiction of a free, happy world under Zeus' control, symbolized by the eagles and thunderbolts of the topmost register. The large Nikai with incense burners carved on the widest zone are acolytes in the cult, while the representation that has aroused the greatest interest—the cortege of figures in female clothing and animal heads—might show the participants in an actual festival procession at the site or, to my mind, be a further allusion to Demeter and her transformation into a horse.[17]

Cult Images and Masters

It should be stressed that, in Arkadia, familiar cults and divinities often assume different traits and local peculiarities. The amount of symbolism included in the Lykosoura group is, however, fully in keeping with the overload of allusive details in Classical cult images. At Lykosoura, Demeter's arm on Despoina's shoulder signified their mother–daughter relationship; Artemis was thought to be Demeter's daughter as well (Paus. 8.37.6), besides being the third Megale Thea of Arkadia; Anytos, being a Titan, belonged to an earlier generation and, as kourotrophos of Despoina (Paus. 8.37.5), symbolized the antiquity of her cult; the tympana and lions of the footstool, together with the Kouretes and Korybantes, alluded to Kybele, the mother goddess, to whom Pausanias instinctively refers by mentioning the size of the Meter statue in Athens. Other, more obvious symbols are the cista on Despoina's lap, the torch, and the scepter cited by Pausanias. Note, however, that traditional iconography has been reversed, the scepter being held by the daughter rather than by the mother.

Another unusual detail appears on the Artemis: a fragment of her left arm preserves traces of snakes entwined around the elbow, confirming the Periegete's description; her right hand held another torch. Her and Anytos' smaller scale in comparison to the main goddesses may not only signify relative importance but also embody a narrative (processional?) element, as if the two smaller figures were seen at a greater distance, both spatial and temporal.

3. *Style.* Although the group has often been labeled Classicizing, it is more frankly eclectic, as best exemplified by the three preserved heads: the Artemis recalls late fourth-century works in her melon coiffure and smooth face with small mouth; the Demeter is more obviously Hellenistic because of her overlarge eyes, undulating lips, and impressionistic hair strands pulled away from the smooth face, some of them actually engraved against her veil; the Anytos is positively Baroque, with wispy, almost fleecy hair and beard, plastically rendered eyebrows, highly modeled forehead, and trapezoidal contours. Subject matter, therefore, seems to determine the rendering; note that the original Tritoness has an equally Classicizing face although her double tails are a Hellenistic development.[18] Equally Hellenistic is the tendency to render mouths open, with teeth showing. Although slightly parted lips had already appeared in earlier periods, teeth were never so obvious. Drapery, where preserved, seems crisp and "modern," but Demeter's chiton clings to her body with transparency and catenaries that recall some Parthenonian pedimental figures. All traits noted at Lykosoura can now be confirmed in other works plausibly attributable to Damophon and his collaborators, to be mentioned below.

4. *Chronology.* It had usually been assumed that the Lykosoura group dated after 183, when an earthquake probably damaged the Olympia Zeus, because Pausanias (4.31.6) states that Damophon repaired its breaking ivory. Familiarity with Pheidian works would have inspired the Messenian's own "revivalist" style. According to other hypotheses, Damophon's Classicizing was a conscious reaction to the Asiatic Baroque of the Pergamon Altar. The picture has now changed considerably. Not only is it currently recognized that Classicizing elements existed before the second century, but

much more information about Damophon and his family has come to light through the recent excavations at Messene, suggesting a peak of activity well before the inception of the Pergamon Gigantomachy. Interpretation of the new data is not without controversy, but it would place the Lykosoura group before the repair work on the Zeus, between 200 and 190, considerably earlier than usual. This timespan is based on the fact that a second-century inscription engraved on a Doric column mentions Damophon's generous gesture of forgiving the Lykosourans a debt of 3,546 silver tetradrachms due to him for some unspecified transgression related to his work terms. The sum is expressed in the so-called "Alexanders," which no longer circulated in the Peloponnesos after approximately 190, thus providing a *terminus ante quem* for Damophon's contract. Even a somewhat wider chronological bracket would not considerably alter our notion of the sculptor's *floruit*, to be placed between 214 and 182 on other grounds.[19]

The above-mentioned inscription has yielded a wealth of additional details on **Damophon and his family**. It has provided a sure patronymic (Philippos, not the Xenophilos previously inferred from the name of one of his sons), and an idea of his widespread activity, for which seven cities honored him: Oiantheia (in western Lokris), Krane (on the island of Kephallenia) and Leukas (another western island), Melos and Kythnos (in the Kyklades), Gerenia (on the border between Messenia and Lakonia), and Lykosoura (in Arkadia). The sculptor made cult statues for three of those cities: an Aphrodite Limenis for Leukas, another Aphrodite for Kythnos, and the Despoina group at Lykosoura. Pausanias mentions other works, including an Artemis Laphria for Messene (4.31.7) that must have copied the image at Kalydon for the requirements of that local cult. But many more divine images have come to light at Messene in secondary contexts, although connected with the Asklepieion complex.[20]

Many attributions to Damophon, from Messene and other sites, have now been made on the basis of the ancient sources and comparison with the Lykosoura sculptures. These attributed pieces are mostly fragmentary and exhibit a great variety of styles, including Severizing; the best-known among them is a slightly over-lifesize **head of Apollo** with inserted eyes and holes for a metal wreath, which strongly recalls the Arkadian goddesses in its rounded oval face and soft mouth.[21] These sculptures have now been usefully collected and discussed and need not detain us here, except to note that they consistently represent divine and heroic images, in which Damophon seems to have specialized, as contrasted with other Messenian masters who were his approximate contemporaries but are known exclusively from their signatures on statue bases of victorious athletes at Olympia.[22]

Damophon's production is so abundant that he must have had a considerable workshop, even if not manned by his family: he could use a whole range of styles, and even copy earlier works (Artemis Laphria); he could handle ivory, as shown by the repairs to the Zeus, although no chryselephantine image by him is attested; he made mostly statuary in stone and wood (as part of the akrolithic technique), and perhaps also in bronze, although this is an inference rather than a fact.[23] Despite lack of evidence, an **akroterial figure from the Temple of Despoina** (Artemis? Nike?) has been attributed to him on comparison with the Artemis within; yet traditional practices would suggest that the main sculptor concentrated on the cult images, and the precise date of the Doric, hexastyle prostyle building is not known. If a product of his workshop, however, this lively figure recalls some of the statues discussed in Chapter 5 in connection with the Samothrakian Nike.[24]

Damophon was paid enormous sums for his work, yet he is mentioned only by Pausanias, and his statues do not seem to have been copied in later times, or to have been taken by the Romans—a salutary consideration, given the common assumption that the Romans looted, collected, copied, and especially cited only sculptures by famous masters. That some were reworked in Imperial times may also suggest that their artistic value was not highly prized; Themelis in fact makes the important point that Damophon's colossal works were best appreciated from a distance. Although some female heads found in Italy have been attributed to him, there is no evidence that Damophon went to Rome—any apparent resemblance is due to the general stylistic trends of the time.[25]

A **male head** frequently compared to the Lykosoura Anytos comes **from Aigeira** in Achaia. It used to be considered the Zeus by the Athenian Eukleides mentioned by Pausanias (7.26.4) together with a chryselephantine Athena, but a reassessment of the evidence has cast serious doubts on this attribution. The main points of the argument are that the small shrine within which the colossal head and a pertinent left arm were found stood near the theater, not visited/noted by Pausanias. In addition, its tetrastyle prostyle plan makes it closely comparable to the Dionysion in Athens; its mosaic floor has a central panel depicting an eagle and a snake, of uncertain significance, but it is surrounded by Dionysiac symbols: griffins, kantharoi, and thyrsoi. Finally, Pausanias describes the Zeus as being of marble, whereas the treatment of head and arm clearly indicates that they were part of an akrolithic figure. Not only is the head hollowed out, but its cavity extends through the neck, thus suggesting a supporting wooden pole. In the second piece, the large tenon hole through the left biceps implies insertion into a sleeved upper arm probably in wood, and the total figure is therefore likely to have been in mixed media. Finally, and most important, the locks framing the deity's forehead end abruptly in flat surfaces pierced by holes for metal attachments. It has been suggested that parts of the tufts were completed in stucco and that a gold wreath overlay them. I see no reason for plaster additions (except perhaps alongside the cheeks) and can almost visualize the wide leaves of the crown through the shapes of the truncated locks. The total statue was therefore a Dionysos, probably seated, in the akrolithic technique; it can no longer be connected with the Eukleides who made the Zeus, and that sculptor may even be redated to the fourth century, on the basis of a mention in Plato's will and Pausanias' statement (7.25.5) that he made four cult statues for Boura, destroyed by earthquake in 373.[26]

In stylistic terms, the Aigeira Dionysos seems to me more Classicizing than the Anytos, but this impression may be influenced by the less visible hairstyle. The small mouth reveals the teeth through the parted lips, which seem more sharply contoured than on Damophon's heads. The central part in the beard is a Hellenistic feature, but the orderly, horizontal arrangements of the curls on either side of it is quite different from the Baroque roughness of the Anytos or even of the Melian Poseidon, despite their equally present, but much less obvious, central part. The inserted eyes, now missing, would have added to the impressiveness of the colossus.

The male head was found in 1916. A second **akrolithic head from Aigeira, female,** came to light in 1987. Preserved in two non-joining pieces, the face is too fragmentary for complete stylistic assessment, but its triangular forehead framed by crisp waves allows comparison with the head of the **Fortuna Primigenia in Palestrina**. Its hollowed out back and its scale (twice lifesize) confirm identification as a cult image, although no name can be definitely assigned to this youthful deity. The find must remain another example of the popularity of akrolithic and Classicizing temple statues in the Peloponnesos.[27]

One more instance is made less clearly identifiable by the lack of a pertinent head. Fragments of **two hands and two sandaled feet** in marble from within the **Temple of Apollo at Bassai** had been recognized as parts of an akrolithic cult image but had been thought to belong to the Classical period. A study of the footwear has, however, shown that its type cannot be earlier than the mid-Hellenistic period. The cut of the feet clearly suggests their connection with a draped figure, and the ornamentation of the sandals led to identification as a female image, thus probably not the temple "owner." A more recent proposal would return to the original interpretation and attribute the feet to an Apollo Kitharoidos in a long garment; it would also, however, lower its date to Augustan times, in keeping with information about Augustus' removal of ivory statues from Greece as a form of punishment. The akrolith would then be a replacement made shortly after the Bassai Temple had been left without its much earlier cult image.[28] On present evidence, I find it difficult to decide between a Hellenistic and an early Imperial date, although known trends would seem to favor the second century. I can accept that a feminine type of sandal might have been appropriate for Apollo, a god often depicted in a belted peplos or a sleeved chiton; yet Dionysos was also frequently given womanly garb, as discussed above. Could the grape leaf decorating the Bassai sandals allude to the god of wine? He had close connections with Apollo, and the hand fragments with their attributes are not sufficiently readable for determination. Were we certain that the Bassai image was male, however, we would gain further insight on the allusions made possible by the use of specific types of footwear.

A similar issue arises with the remains of the **colossal group of cult images from Klaros,** in Asia Minor. Found in pieces within the large temple, it consisted of a central, seated Apollo flanked by a standing Artemis and Leto. Their enormous size (ca.

7 m) is best exemplified by a recent photograph showing two restorers at work with the fragments. These have now been replicated in lightweight casts to facilitate re-composition, and can be seen in their approximate relationship, although still incomplete. All three figures are headless and armless, but the Leto is almost entirely preserved, and the Artemis lacks only the weight-supporting right leg; of the Apollo, however, only the draped legs remain—his feet, carved in one with the lower legs, although visible solely in their frontal half, exhibit elaborate sandals. At the point over the instep where the thongs separate and the *lingula* ends, the footwear is provided with a heart-shaped ornament decorated by a frontal sphinx (or siren?) in relief. These sandals are identical to those worn by the **Hermaphrodite from Pergamon,** which may therefore come from the same workshop. The mixture of tongue and straps has been seen as a formula combining male and female forms of footwear, which would be highly appropriate for a Hermaphrodite. Should the same point be made for the heavily draped Klarian Apollo?[29]

Despite their enormous size, the three cult images were entirely in marble and assembled from a number of separate pieces, some of them fastened by large metal dowels. The Leto wears a chiton and a himation/shawl so thin that it reveals the vertical folds of the underlying garment; the Artemis sports a peplos with apoptygma belted high under the breasts, over which the strap of her quiver crosses. All three figures show clinging cloth over the advanced thighs, distinctive press folds, and stylistic traits that suggest a dating around 170–160, but they echo fourth-century prototypes. The Artemis has been compared to the bronze Peiraieus Artemis occasionally attributed to Euphranor, and indeed the stacked V-folds of the Klarian apoptygma recall the same rendering on the Apollo Patroos; I would also cite the latter for a parallel to the distinctive pattern of addorsed catenaries on the outer surface of the right knee on the Klarian Apollo.[30] The missing heads might have confirmed a Classicizing approach.

In this connection, a beautiful **female head from the Letoon near Xanthos** (Pl. 68) deserves mention because it was also made from separate parts and shows traces of tooling even on its top surface, yet it is approximately lifesize and in frankly Hellenistic style—indeed very close to some goddesses of the Pergamene Gigantomachy in the ropy treatment of her hair strands and her softly modeled mouth. The piece was clearly intended for insertion into a draped body, and it has been suggested that its rear portion, with a peculiarly stepped surface, was completed in marble, whereas other areas of the hairstyle were perhaps rendered in stucco and even paint. I am always hesitant to believe in plaster additions, especially outside the Alexandrian sphere, and wonder whether this exquisite head, although not akrolithic and colossal, might have belonged to a cult image (or to a location in a high niche?) to be seen from a distance and from below, as perhaps implied by the tooled upper surface of the cranium and the definite downward slant of the left eye. Be that as it may, the strong connection to the style of the Great Altar is worth noting in an area at some distance from Mysia (cf. Pls. 69a–b).[31]

Plate 68

Plates 69a–b

A workshop that produced statuary in both akrolithic and full-marble forms, not only for cultic but also for honorary purposes, both in Greece and in Italy, is that of the **family of Polykles,** from Thorikos, from which many signatures are preserved. Various attempts at defining the stemma of these masters have been made, with somewhat different results, and it is beyond my competence—and the focus of my work—to trace here the difficult steps in the evidence that establish the intricate relationships among its members. I shall therefore concentrate on the actual sculptures that contribute to our understanding of the second century, this time taking us definitely into the world of Rome and its new needs.[32]

In Greece proper we have fragments from a colossal marble statue of **Athena Kranaia** seen by Pausanias (10.34.4) at Elateia in Phokis, made by **Timokles and Timarchides,** sons of Polykles (II); the Periegete mentions also that the figures on its shield copied those of the Parthenos in Athens, thus establishing the two brothers as "Neo-Attic" sculptors. No secure date can be given for this work, but from the general span of the masters' activity, it should fall within the third quarter of the second century. For the same city (Paus. 10.34.3), they also made the cult image of Asklepios, of which nothing remains.[33] A more complete statue, well over lifesize but regrettably headless, was found on **Delos,** within a niche on the western side of the Agora of the Italians (Ill. 24). An inscription on its base identified it as a **portrait of C. Ofellius Ferus,** an Italian probably from Campania, and the work of **Dionysios,** son of Timarchides (I), and **Timarchides** (II), son of Polykles (IV)—therefore Dionysios' nephew. A slightly revised chronology would set this work around 110.[34]

The remarkable points about this statue are several, perhaps the most important being its enormous size despite its being the portrait of a living person, a wealthy (slave-?)merchant (*negotiator*). Equally significant is its nudity, with only a (fringed!) chlamys gathered on the left shoulder and wrapped around the bent arm—for a true Roman, this mode of representation would have been exceptional, conceivable only in the mixed world of Delos or the Hellenized tendencies of South Italy. The type, as often noted, is that of a Classical Hermes (Richelieu Type, characterized by the distinctive draping of the chlamys over the left shoulder, here slightly modified), but the object once held in Ofellius' left hand was probably a sheathed sword or dagger, although inappropriate for the honorand. Since no official titles are listed on his base, Ofellius could not have been depicted as a magistrate or military commander, and his compatriots therefore immortalized him as a benefactor (*euergetes*) with the iconography adopted for Alexander and his successors—he had in fact subsidized the erection of the Agora west portico, as mentioned by an inscription on its architrave.[35] It is important to note that a male torso attributed to Damophon and identified as **Asklepios' son Machaon, from Messene,** makes use of the same prototype and changes the kerykeion into a sheathed dagger, whose rounded tip is still preserved against the figure's left biceps. Thus an Athenian and a Messenian workshop could adopt similar formulas and solutions, although Machaon's military connotations were more readily justifiable than Ofellius'.[36]

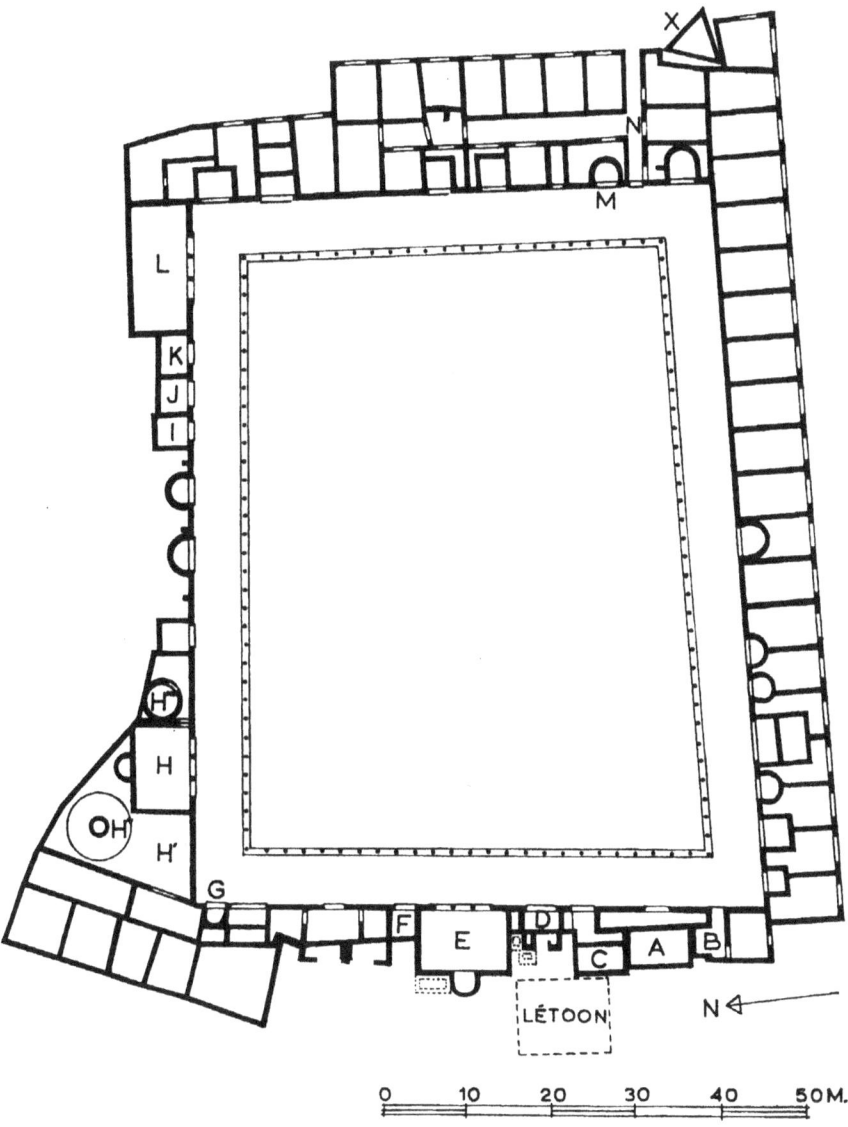

Ill. 24. Delos, Agora of the Italians; the niche of C. Ofellius Ferus is item F on plan. [After *Guide de Delos* (Paris 1996) 108 fig. 181]

Cult Images on Italian Soil

With the family of Polykles, we have crossed over into the realm of works commissioned from Greek masters by Italians—not only the Ofellius Ferus for Delos (still on Greek territory, although it is uncertain whether the statue was carved on the island or in Athens), but also several akroliths for temples in Rome, which must have required the installation of a workshop in Italy. A **Polykles** is mentioned by Cicero (*ad*

Att. 6.1.17) as having made a **Herakles,** which has been recognized in a colossal, hollowed out head (but without inserted eyes) from the west slope of the Capitoline. Perhaps the same Polykles and **Dionysios** (his brother, who worked for Delos) are said by Pliny (*NH* 36.35) to have created a statue of Juno Regina that is tentatively identified in a similarly treated **head in Rome** of unknown findspot. Other divine images attributed by the same source (a Iuppiter Stator by Polykles, an Apollo holding a kithara by his father, **Timarchides**) have not been recovered except perhaps in later, debatable copies.[37] These statues belong entirely to the second century, and only the last scion of the family, **Timarchides II,** known through inscriptions as "the younger" (*ho neoteros*), would reach past 100 B.C.

Several other alleged cult images, mostly heads of colossal size and in the same akrolithic technique, or at least with hollowed-out cranial cavities, but not always with inserted eyes, have been gathered by Martin (1987), but their date is often as hypothetical as their connection with specific cults and temples. Only the already mentioned head of Fortuna Primigenia, from a probably seated statue at Praeneste, can be considered certain. One more **female head from Largo Argentina (Rome)** has a reasonable chance of being identified as the *Fortuna huiusce diei* (Today's Luck), since it was found by Temple B—an association that would date it to 101/100, when the structure was erected by Q. Lutatius Catulus. Its maker is unknown, but the head —with its emphatic central part in the wiglike hair, its large (non-inserted) eyes, its heavy lips revealing the teeth, and its massive, almost smooth face—impresses more for its size than its artistry, although it fits well within the tradition of similar cult images.[38]

Certainly associated with the cult of Diana Nemorensis are three sculptures from **Nemi** that have received recent attention. The first, a **female head in Copenhagen,** recalls the head from the Xanthian Letoon in the piecing technique of its flat back with stepped and tooled surfaces, but its size is colossal and some additions were definitely made in marble, although some curls may have been in stucco, and rough transitions between pieces (especially the curl section to the proper right of the central part) were probably filled and covered in plaster. Pieces of drapery carved from a thin slab of marble may belong to the same figure and would have been attached to a wooden core. This is somewhat the same technique used for the Anytos at Lykosoura, which can be considered akrolithic, although I would reserve the term for statues where only the uncovered flesh parts were rendered in stone. The whole statue is calculated to have been approximately 3 m high, thus suggesting that it was a temple image, and the youthful features, together with drapery appropriate for hunting garb (chitoniskos with mantle wrapped around the waist), would fit Diana. The graceful head stands somewhat tilted on a long neck, and shows asymmetries indicating a turn to proper right. The hairstyle, in its present state almost a form of the *Melonenfrisur,* frames a smooth, triangular forehead; taking piecing into account, it may have been a bow-knot coiffure with locks trailing along the neck. The eyeballs are not inserted, but their surface has been tooled to differentiate the iris from the rest; their slanted surface conveys a downward look, as befits the figure's size. The small mouth reveals the upper teeth. The Classicizing style is inspired by fourth-century forms, and a date in the last quarter of the second century has been proposed.[39]

A second **female head** from Nemi **in Philadelphia** seems heavier, in my opinion closer to fifth-century styles, and although still over-lifesize, it is smaller than the Copenhagen head. Its piecing technique is different, consisting of the entire back of the head and neck along a straight surface, with a flattened top and some recessed tooling suggesting a separately added diadem or veil. The lower part of the neck tenon, however, is roughly finished, as if to join a body in a different material, so that this piece too probably belongs to an akrolith. The relatively small, non-inserted eyes, look straight ahead, and the heavy lips are parted showing the upper teeth. No specific date for it is suggested, except for a general connection with a major remodeling of the sanctuary in the second half of the second century; identification as Diana and the use of the rare and expensive marble again prompt a definition as cult image.[40]

The third piece from Nemi, **the bust of a bearded deity in Nottingham**, approximately lifesize, provides some added features of interest. Head and chest are carved from a single block of marble, but the former is hollowed out, whereas the latter is cut flat, with traces of tooling. It was therefore suggested that the piece was either unfinished or cut down from a complete statue. Traces of green stains may, however, imply that it was set on a draped body made of (gilded?) bronze, a mixture of media not uncommon on Italian soil. The complete figure has been visualized according to the iconography of Asklepios, but identified as Virbius, a local hero who probably had healing functions and is mentioned by an ancient source as having a cult image in the sanctuary. Not only is the bust interesting because of its possible connection with a bronze body; it was also made from separate parts—most of the hair and an extensive portion of the beard had to have been added in stucco. The upward tilt of the head, the large (non-inserted) eyes, the modeled cheeks and lively hair strands, wherever preserved, make it remarkably similar to a torso of **Asklepios from Mounychia**, which may have been entirely in marble, although it retains more of his facial hair and had separately inserted eyes. Since the Asklepios was found within that god's sanctuary in the Peiraieus, it was probably its temple image by an Athenian sculptor, but there is no way of assigning the Italian bust to a specific master. It should be noted, however, that a Baroque style was adopted for the male type, whereas Classical formulas were used for the two Nemi goddesses, although all three pieces are likely to be contemporary.[41]

The second-century date of the Mounychia Asklepios already validates the chronology proposed for the Virbius, but a second comparison, although perhaps not as "lock-for-lock" as the previous one, could also strengthen it. In the trapezoidal shape of his face (especially at the forehead), the separation of the curls from the cheek contour (a distinctive second-century trait), the pathetic expression, the modeling of the surface with a pronounced Michelangelo bar, both the Asklepios and the Virbius resemble the Poseidon from Pergamon, thus attesting to the spread of specific models and styles over a wide geographic range.[42]

Plates 70a–b

One more over-lifesize female head in Philadelphia, the so-called **Hope Goddess** (Pls. 70a–b), deserves mention here because this impressive work is relatively little known. Although of unknown provenience, it may belong among the Italian cult statues because its unusual coiffure finds its only parallel on a bronze from the Villa of the Papyri at Herculaneum. The strands of hair around the forehead conform to the *Melonenfrisur,* but those originating from the area of the temples rise over the crown of braids that surrounds the top of the head. The beautiful marble piece, in Classical style but with parted lips and both upper and lower teeth indicated, as typical of the Hellenistic period, was definitely part of an akrolithic statue: not only was it hollowed out and roughly tooled around all possible contact surfaces, thus precluding stone additions, but its neck was pierced through, as for the insertion of a wooden pole supporting an interior armature. Although stylistic dating is dangerous, technique, size, and medium would support a time of manufacture around 100 or slightly earlier.[43]

The list of cult images made by Greeks for the Romans and Italians could be considerably expanded, especially taking into account the ancient sources and first-century examples. Not all such sculptures were akrolithic; the colossal **seated Herakles found at Alba Fucens** was entirely in marble, and a statue of Iuppiter Capitolinus, by Apollonios (the Athenian?), was in gold and ivory.[44] Here it suffices to stress the phenomenon, and to correlate it with a similar trend on Greek soil, which cannot therefore have been spurred by the need to replace temple statues looted by the Romans, nor have been prompted by increased religiosity or even by the establishment of new cults, since many of the images listed above were made for pre-existing shrines or sacred areas. It seems confirmed once again that style could be determined by subject matter, rather than by pure imitation and allusion or even aesthetic reaction. Thus Classicizing forms were considered appropriate for certain types of divinities (the younger and more aloof, perhaps, like Artemis, Athena, Apollo), whereas the more mature, humane, suffering types (Demeter, Asklepios, a Titan like Anytos) could be rendered in Baroque style.

MASTERS

According to a recent count, over one hundred Athenian sculptors who worked in marble or bronze during the Hellenistic period are known by name. They were active not only in Athens, but also abroad. On Delos, approximately 50 works by 16 Athenian sculptors, before and after 167, are documented by signed bases; 15 similar inscriptions are known from Delphi, 13 from Rhodes. Attic activity is attested from 10 cities in the Peloponnesos, and as far afield as Olbia on the Hypanis (Bug) and Apollonia in Cyrenaica.[45] As already mentioned, moreover, Phyromachos and his colleague/teacher(?) Nikeratos, both Athenians, were active at Pergamon at the turn into the second century, and several members of Polykles' family moved to Rome.

Non-Attic sculptors are also well represented during the Hellenistic period. Rhodes seems at first to have employed itinerant masters from a variety of areas, but to have restricted its patronage to stable local ateliers after 167. It has been calculated that "between ca. 150 and 100 B.C., 15 of the 21 signed statues were produced in only two workshops; 81% of the bronze sculpture known from surviving bases is from identifiable workshops." Although sculptural production in Rhodes shows two major peaks— between ca. 250 and 168, and then between ca. 100 and 50—the making of statues by residents is best attested during the "low" phase of the second century. Among these sculptors, Pythokritos has already been mentioned in connection with his rock-cut ship relief at Lindos; his father was probably from Crete, but the son became a Rhodian citizen and collaborated with other naturalized masters, predominantly from Soloi, who eventually established their own workshops and a long line of active sculptors. Thus "Rhodian" does not always mean a native of the island.[46]

The same problem arises with works apparently signed by Ephesian artists. It has been argued that initially only pieces meant for export included the sculptor's ethnic but that, from the early first century, "Ephesian" was used as a mark of quality, probably because of the reputation of an established line of production in that East Greek city, and thus did not reflect the true birthplace of either the master or the dedicant. Likewise, many sculptures found in Italy may have been signed by an "Athenian" to indicate simply that they came from Greece or that their maker worked in the Greek tradition.[47]

This unsettling possibility should be viewed within the larger issue of sculptors' signatures and the art trade—even the location of signatures on a statue becomes significant. Archaic and Classical bases carrying the traditional formula, "so-and-so made (*epoiesen*)," are well known, but only a few figures (I would say, primarily those from East Greek areas, or places under strong influence from Near Eastern countries where statues could be used as virtual billboards for extensive statements) were directly inscribed, perhaps because writing on a human body destroyed the impression that a living being was portrayed and stressed the inanimate nature of the object. But the Hellenistic period produced sculptures that were often meant for distant markets and were thus more easily transported without a cumbersome and not-strictly-necessary base. Masters therefore began to sign their name on inconspicuous but integral, non-removable areas of their work—not only on items of clothing but especially on plinths, minor attributes, tree-trunk supports, and arm-stumps of herms. We shall consider an example of this last location, which raises further questions about the relationship of master's signature to workshop owner and issues of original versus copy.[48]

Among the many pieces recovered from a shipwreck off the coast of Tunisia (Mahdia) in the early years of the twentieth century, the bronze **herm of a turbaned, Archaistic Dionysos** carries a signature, *ΒΟΗΘΟΣ ΚΑΛΧΗΔΟΝΙΟΣ ΕΠΟΙΕΙ*, on its right (shorter) arm-stump.[49] It was at first supposed that the herm served as the support for the raised right elbow of a winged youth crowning himself with a wreath of wild olive, who was then identified as Agon (or Eros Enagonios), the personification of (an Olympic) contest—the signature would have applied to the entire composition and not to the relatively minor herm. In 1994, however, a thorough examination and conservation of all the material from the Mahdia shipwreck in Bonn, Germany, resulted in some major discoveries. Among them was the realization that the Eros (for such it must be, without agonistic connotations) was not joined to the herm, which was therefore an independent work, by a Boethos of Kalchedon, a city on the Sea of Marmara across from Byzantion, on the Anatolian coast. In addition, another **herm (now in the Getty Museum** in Malibu), remarkably similar to the one from the wreck but of unknown provenience, proved also closely comparable in alloy and measurements, and therefore likely to be an unsigned product of the same workshop. The name Boethos was already known from several ancient literary sources and inscriptions; although it was always suspected that more than one person was involved, various statues of children had been connected with a second-century sculptor by that name. After the recent findings, however, the issue has become more complex and requires a different approach, despite the fact that old theories are hard to kill. I shall here outline what I consider the relevant points of the problem.[50]

1. *How many Boethoi were there, and from what city?* The inscription on the Mahdia herm was cut into the wax model, before casting—it was therefore part of the production of the piece and not a later addition, although we do not know whether it was a true signature or the equivalent of a factory stamp. It does not date the herm precisely except for a *terminus ante quem* of ca. 70 B.C., the approximate time of the wreck. The Archaistic style of the herm also precludes a firmer stylistic dating, now that the "Agon" can no longer be factored into the equation. The important point is that, whether signature or stamp, the inscription states clearly that **Boethos** (father unnamed) is **from Kalchedon.**

An inscription from Ephesos, however, gives the ethnic of **Boethos, son of Apollodoros,** as *KAPXEΔONIOΣ*, that is, from Punic Karchedon, which the Romans called Carthago—Carthage. That this is not a stone-cutter's mistake is shown by a mention in Pausanias (5.17.4); the Periegete, in the Heraion at Olympia, sees a statue of a naked boy in a sitting pose, which Boethos of Karchedon had crafted (*ἐτόρευσεν*) in gilded bronze—although this text is often emended in translation to read "Kalchedon." A Punic connection may be further proved by Cicero's statement (*in Verr.* 4.14.32) that Verres stole from Pamphilos of Lilybaion (a Punic naval base) a heavy and famous hydria by Boethos.[51]

The Kalchedonian family may have moved more strictly within Greek territory. According to an inscribed base, **Boethos, son of Athenaion, Kalchedonian,** made (*ποιήσας*) and dedicated a thank-offering (probably a lifesize statue) to Athena Lindia, likely in gratitude for having been appointed proxenos in that Rhodian city, during the priesthood of Nikagoras, son of Panaitios.[52] This information translates into the year 184. Objects in the Athenaion at Lindos by a silversmith named Boethos are also mentioned (without patronymic or ethnic) by Pliny (*NH* 33.155), but they cannot be connected with the inscribed base mentioned above—and the Ciceronian passage may even be used to argue that it was the Carthaginian Boethos who was the silversmith. Pliny's confused note-taking is well known; yet in his book on bronzes (*NH* 34.84) he repeats that although Boethos was better known for his silverwork, he also made a statue of a boy strangling a goose. This passage has had the greatest impact for all attributions of sculptures to the master.

The proxenos Boethos may be the man who signed a base for a statue of Antiochos IV on Delos, which must fall between 166 (the beginning of Athenian control) and 163, when the Seleukid king died. This same man is thought to be the sculptor whose name recurs on the Mahdia herm, since he still identifies himself there as Kalchedonios; yet on the Delian base no ethnic is cited, and the patronymic (son of Athenaion) is included instead. A firm also in Delos might have produced the many bronze fittings for luxury beds found in the Mahdia wreck, although at an uncertain time, and perhaps sent them to Athens, where the shipment originated. This theory is based on a puzzling reference (Porph. *In Q. Hor. Flacc. Epist.* 1.5.1) to *lecti Boethici*, and interpreted as the equivalent of *lecti deliaci*—a type of luxury klinai with metal furnishings.[53] After the sack of the sacred island, the "Kalchedonian" family (and its firm) might also have moved, since a **Boethos son of Diod[otos]** inscribed his name on the upper part of the Elgin throne—a Neo-Attic work probably made in Athens, since it carries a relief of the Tyrannicides on one of its sides. **Diodotos, son of Boethos** seems to have signed a Hermes in Gaeta, Italy, (as transcribed in the sixteenth century by Pirro Ligorio), thus confirming that the name ran in the family. Yet this branch of the household may have reached Athens (if at all) from Nikomedeia, because a statue of Herakles in Rome is said (again by Pirro Ligorio) to have been signed on its club by **Menodotos and Diodotos, the sons of Boethos of Nikomedeia**. Since the capital of Bithynia (modern Izmit), which was founded by Nikomedes in 264, is not too far from Kalchedon, such a move is not implausible.[54]

A Delian presence through the second century is proved by a **Boethos** who, together with (his brother?) **Theodosios**, signed a base for an honorary statue of Epigenes, son of Dios, from Melite (an Attic deme) dedicated to Apollo. Epigenes' office on the island (as epimeletes) is datable to 126/5, thus making this Boethos a descendant (grandson or nephew) of the one who produced the Antiochos.[55] Finally, two epigrams inscribed on a base found in Rome within the Trajanic Baths mention that a statue of an infant Asklepios, dedicated by the doctor Nikomedes of Smyrna, was made by a Boethos. The date of both the statue (missing) and the epigrams is uncertain.[56]

According to this heterogeneous information, therefore, we would have a family of sculptors divided into several branches: one that from Kalchedon went to Rhodes (Lindos), Delos, and eventually Athens, where it was established as a (Neo-Attic?)

firm by the early first century; a second branch that went to nearby Nikomedeia and perhaps merged in some fashion with the main line; and a third branch that almost simultaneously moved to Carthage (when it was still Karchedon) and may have specialized in silverwork.

In sketching this outline, I have primarily followed Linfert's tentative theories (1994), but other scenarios are possible. As Peter Green reminds us, it is a "usual temptation to succumb to that notorious academic fallacy, the belief that all *surviving* evidence must be in some way interrelated and cohesive."[57] In particular, I want to stress that the name Boethos seems quite at home in Phoenician/Punic territory, thus requiring no emendation to Pausanias' text. Not only are two homonymous philosophers (one of the second century, the other of the Augustan period) from Sidon, but a mid-second-century inscription from Kition, a Phoenician city on Cyprus, honors a Boethos, son of Apollodoros—the same combination of names that occurs on the Ephesos base.[58]

It is also generally assumed that the two Delian bases signed by a Boethos are by two different masters separated by at least one generation, since a sculptor active on Lindos in 184 and on Delos around 166–163 could not have been still working in 126/5 when Epigenes was made epimeletes. Theoretically, however, the Lindian proxenos from Kalchedon, because of his office, could have remained on Rhodes and thus be different from the Delian sculptor Boethos, son of Athenaion, (a cousin?) who has the same patronymic but does not specify his ethnic. In this case, the latter could have made both the Antiochos and the Epigenes. This second statue, as a work of his advanced years, may have required the collaboration of a younger sculptor, Theodosios, probably an apprentice—no ethnic and no patronymic are given in the signature, and there is no assurance that the collaborating sculptors were brothers, as suggested by Linfert's stemma.[59] That no ethnic was included for either the Antiochos or the Epigenes may imply that Boethos' workshop was well established on the island—he may even have originally gone there from Athens, given his dates.

If the Boethos who made the Antiochos for Delos was also the maker of the Mahdia herm, why did he omit his patronymic on the bronze and include instead an ethnic considered superfluous on the island? That the piece was meant for export does not explain the inclusion, especially if the Dionysos had already been set up once. It is clear that Boethos would entertain commissions for similar herms, as shown by the existence of at least one more example from the same workshop—yet "Kalchedonios" in the signature would not have revealed that the objects could be acquired on Delos, nor was it a mark of excellence, since the East Greek city was not particularly famous for its sculptures, as has been postulated for Ephesos. This consideration leads us to the second point of importance.

2. *Was Boethos the actual maker of the herm or simply the creator of the type?* Despite the complexity of the situation described above, the tendency remains to believe in a "famous" sculptor Boethos who was active during the first half of the second cen-

tury, made the Boy Strangling the Goose mentioned by Pliny and other statues of children, and produced the Mahdia herm.[60] This last piece, although recovered from a wreck, is thought not to have been part of an ad hoc shipment, since it had already been installed and forcibly removed from its original base. It was thus an "antique" meant to fetch a good price from a Roman collector of Greek *opera nobilia*. Yet even these "facts" are open to other interpretations.

The previous installation of the Mahdia herm is postulated on the basis of a lead plug at the bottom of the shaft, which still retains a fragment of the original marble base. According to a plausible reconstruction, a stone plinth was carved with a pyramidal boss in the center, pierced through for the insertion of a metal rod leaded in place that would have served to stabilize the herm if overturned. The rod seems to be lost, but traces of the lead solder remain. Over the roughly finished surface of this stone tenon, the massive lead plug that fastened the herm was poured. When the herm was pried up from its base, the pressure deformed the front plate of the bronze shaft and produced a fracture that eventually resulted in the present hole at the lower left corner; the marble boss was chiseled off because it could not be separated from the lead plug, which is clearly visible in unrestored photographs through the above-mentioned break. Many aspects of this scenario still puzzle me.[61]

A herm removed from a sanctuary—during the sack of Delos in 88?—could have been taken to Athens and then shipped for sale to Rome. But how do we explain, then, the very close similarity of the Getty herm, which extends even to the alloy? In addition, two marble heads, probably from herms, one from Vaison (Roman Vaiso) in France, and one from Pompeii, seem to reproduce the type with considerable fidelity.[62] Seeing it within the context of the Mahdia wreck, we get the impression that Boethos' herm was one of those pieces manufactured by workshops exclusively for the Roman trade, often shipped out in multiple copies, which could then continue to be reproduced from the original model or from the exported objects themselves. Given the mass of architectural elements in Pentelic marble carried by the Mahdia ship (no fewer than 60 or 70 monolithic columns, at least five "Chimaera capitals," approximately 20 Attic-Ionic capitals and bases), the chances of an Athenian origin are strong for both the marble sculptures and the bronze objects.[63] Only four small votive reliefs and five short inscriptions of minimal value (also from Athens and the Peiraieus) can definitely be dated to the fourth century, and they may have been, if not actual ballast, given their relatively insignificant weight, at least fillers to stabilize the heterogeneous cargo.[64]

With these few exceptions, no object from the Mahdia wreck can be confidently dated before the mid-second century, and most of them have been stylistically placed around 120–100; yet the wreck itself happened at least 20 to 40 years later. The enormous investment of capital represented by the architectural elements, the huge marble kraters, and the bronze parts for beds (even if all statuary is disregarded) would speak against the stockpiling of inventory so far in advance of the time of shipment.[65]

The only evidence that would link the Archaistic herm to an earlier period is Boethos' name and the peculiar mention of the ethnic "Kalchedonios."

From a sculptural point of view, it has been noted that the Mahdia herm received considerable attention directly in the wax, after the molding but before the actual casting, in a combination of direct and indirect process. By contrast, the Getty herm appears simplified, although retaining all the basic traits. Does this "personal touch" justify Boethos' signature as against a more mechanical reproduction? Or was Boethos the originator of the basic type, which could then be repeated in cheaper (faster) casts or even marble translations? Note that the Getty herm has its own low base cast in one piece directly in bronze, perhaps more economical than a stone pedestal. Given the multiplicity of sculptors named Boethos, the ambiguity of the ethnic in conjunction with a possible Athenian shipment, and the many reproductions of the type, we should entertain the notion that "commercial" works need not reflect the originator of a type but—like the herm of Polykleitos' Doryphoros signed by the Athenian Apollonios, son of Archias—simply identify the maker of a specific object.[66] In this light, there is no need to connect the Mahdia herm with a famous Boethos.

3. *How many works can be validly assigned to the "famous" second-century Boethos?* Interpretation of the sources has played a major role in this respect. Pliny's mention that Boethos made a **Boy Strangling a Goose,** and Pausanias' attribution of a seated child at Olympia had seemed confirmed by the youthful appearance of the Mahdia Eros when it was connected with the herm. Thus Boethos was thought to specialize in representations of children—a Hellenistic interest apparently attested by Herondas' Fourth Mimiamb (third century), describing a child throttling a goose (by an unnamed artist) as a possible dedication at an altar. A group of a boy wrestling with a large gander, known from several marble replicas, was at first identified as Boethos' work, but because of Herondas' date, it had to be placed in the early third century, although prosopographic and stylistic considerations (albeit based on somewhat invalid comparisons, like the Pasquino Group or the Ludovisi Gaul) would have favored a later chronology. It was also pointed out that the goose named by Herondas was a much smaller type (an Egyptian *chenalopex*) than the bird represented by the marble replicas, and one more composition (known in a Roman copy from Ephesos) was then proposed as Boethos' creation. Despite this uncertainty, a large number of other attributions have been made on the basis of these "prototypes." To list only the most recent ones: (*a*) the original of the children/satyrs splashing water, four of which were found on the Mahdia wreck and at least three (one of them well preserved) at Sperlonga; (*b*) the Eros/Agon, even if it does not go with the herm; (*c*) the other bronzes from the wreck, as work of the firm, including the "Neo-Attic" marble kraters as reproductions perhaps of originals in precious metals; (*d*) the type of the Herakliskos strangling the snakes; (*e*) the Eros and Psyche group; (*f*) the child Herakles with lionskin and Apples of the Hesperides.[67]

In my opinion, none of these attributions can be substantiated. To begin with the literary sources, the earliest (Herondas), especially given the type of animal he mentions, could easily reflect Egyptian figurines. It has even been suggested that his poetic description is not based on actual monuments but is a literary genre, and certainly not to be located at Kos—whose proximity to Rhodes might have supported a connection with a Boethos active at Lindos.[68] Pliny insists on Boethos' skill in silver and, when he mentions the Boy with the Goose in his book on bronzes, does not specify its size—that too could have been a small-scale work, in keeping with the practices of a silversmith (remember the Herakles Epitrapezios allegedly by Lysippos!). Even Pausanias does not state whether the gilded child at Olympia was a lifesize figure. Since the infant was seated, a small object can readily be envisioned; by the second century A.C., the Heraion had become a repository for precious antiques, not all of which were large. A Carthaginian Boethos, a silversmith, could easily have produced all these works as figurines, which therefore would not at all be representative of the tendencies of a second-century, Kalchedonian Boethos who made honorary and/or divine statues. Whether any of the silversmith's child-compositions were later enlarged and translated into marble is a question that cannot be answered, but we do know that "Neo-Attic" workshops often drew their inspiration from two-dimensional representations or from objects of the minor arts.

This seems to be the case with the **Eros and Psyche,** a subject exemplified by terracottas said to be datable before the mid-second century. Yet the dating of the figurines is uncertain, and the marble replicas belong exclusively to the Roman Imperial period, when the popularity of both Eros and Psyche had considerably increased together with their metaphysical meaning.[69] Linfert finds confirmation for the attribution in the position of Eros' legs, which recall the Silenos with baby Dionysos attributed to Lysippos, in keeping with what he sees as an intentional imitation, if not parody, of Classical works in Boethos' production. The Child Strangling the Goose (large type) would echo Herakles Wrestling the Nemean Lion; the **Baby Herakles with the Apples of the Hesperides** would be a lighter version of the Herakles Farnese type.[70] This type of quotation of Classical motifs in a humorous vein or projected into a different timeframe seems to me typical of the very late Hellenistic phase, when production was almost entirely dictated by the tastes and needs of the Roman market, and even more so of the Imperial period, when royal children (or even mature emperors) could be depicted in divine guises with allegorical meanings, as a form of official flattery.

How messages can change from Greek to Roman times is shown by the replicas of the **Infant Herakles Strangling the Serpents.** The type in isolation originated as a numismatic symbol, first on coins of Kyzikos datable to the mid-fifth century or slightly later, then on those of Thebes. By the end of the fifth century or around 395, a new type was invented there, but was also used almost simultaneously (393) by the Aegean maritime states that had formed an alliance against Sparta. Byzantion, Ephesos, Samos, Knidos, Lampsakos, Iasos, Kyzikos, and Rhodes—the allied cities— used their own device on the reverse but the same image of Herakles and the serpents as the obverse. It obviously implied not only a connection of some of those states with Herakles (as especially clear for Thebes, his birthplace), but a powerful force against human enemies, with the two kings of Sparta perhaps symbolized by the two snakes. Surprisingly, some early coins show a bearded Herakles rather than an infant, as the myth would require. In Roman times, this imagery was resumed to identify an emperor (e.g., Geta), and the child type was translated into three-dimensional sculpture, frequently used for funerary purposes and given a portrait head. For the Romans, therefore, the dead child was assimilated to Herakles and his ultimate triumph over death, the royal scion was glorified through the promise of his prowess from infancy, while the mature versions completed the Herculean equation. I see no reason to believe that the sculptural renderings originated in the mid-Hellenistic period, when the league coinage would have been best known.[71]

The only composition that can definitely be dated before Imperial times is the **"splashing child"** of the Sperlonga/Mahdia type, and its date is more likely to be the early first century than the early or mid-second, given the unlikeliness of stockpiling, as suggested above. The presence of mirror-images is attested from the wreck (as well as at Sperlonga), thus indicating a specific decorative purpose for the pieces, or at most the possibility that a buyer could choose the replica that best suited his layout—like chairs in a modern classroom equipped for both right- and left-handed students. Small variations in the coiffure (and perhaps the ears) between the Mahdia and the Sperlonga versions already imply modifications of the original model and a form of ancient mass production.[72] The same kind of repetition and pairing is exemplified on the wreck by two statuettes of the same Artemis type and the four marble kraters—two of the Borghese type showing a youthful Dionysos, and two of the Pisa type showing the god of wine as elderly. This is factory output, and if a master lent his name to it, we can no longer recover it.

To be sure, the **Eros (ex-Agon)** must also be dated to the late second/early first century, but it is no longer to be attributed to Boethos, *pace* Linfert and others. Its alloy is different from that of the Dionysos herm, and so is the lead of its dowel. The youthful figure is instead stylistically closer to another bronze Eros from the wreck, and analysis of its core seems to show that it matches those of a "grotesque" (the dancing dwarf F 215) and a pantheress belonging to a bronze candelabrum. In brief, this new examination of the Mahdia cargo has conclusively demonstrated that style alone is insufficient to establish chronology. It has also removed one more reason to connect a "famous" second-century Boethos with figures of children.

I have dealt at some length with this specific issue to demonstrate the complexities of identifying masters, and the dangers of speculation, once sculptural production is no longer geared to a Greek clientele but serves the demands of Roman customers. The different purposes, meanings, and manufacturing conditions that obtain under such circumstances increase the difficulties of our task and the impossibility of distinguishing between "original" and "copies." Other sculptural works signed by masters and with a similarly ambiguous nature—the Borghese Warrior, the Sperlonga groups—will be discussed in the next chapters.[73]

NOTES

1. Hera in Argive Heraion: e.g., Ridgway 1997b, 25–28 and esp. n. 9 (earlier image in pear wood). Athena Parthenos, as votive or object of cult: most recently, Donohue 1997, 37–38 and n. 35; Stewart 1998, 271–73.

2. Donohue 1997, with a historiographical discussion on the origin of this modern concept; note, however, that she defines a cult statue as "an image of a god that is the focus of worship," as distinct from another divine representation that does not receive such attention (pp. 31–32). For statues of athletes that received "worship," see also Jones 1998.

3. Temples meant to house cult statues: see, e.g., Dinsmoor 1950, 40: "It was not until the gods had become personified and embodied in statues of considerable size that they would have required specially built shelters." Others are cited by Donohue 1997, 32 n. 5 (her point 2). Additional statements in the same vein have been collected by J. Griffin Miller in her unpublished Ph.D. dissertation for Bryn Mawr College: "Temple and Statue: A Study of Practices in Ancient Greece" (1995), which reviewed early Greek practices in the context of other contemporary Near Eastern and Egyptian usages. See her "Temple and Image: Did All Greek Temples House Cult Images?" Abstract, *AJA* 101 (1997) 345. Session VD of the 98th Annual Meeting of the Archaeological Institute of America was entirely devoted to a Colloquium on "'Cult' Statues of the Ancient World"; see *AJA* 101 (1997) 382–83 for Abstracts of the papers presented on Mesopotamian, Egyptian, Hittite, Greek, and Roman images.

For a more recent position on cult images, see Stewart 1990, 44–46. I would accept his statement that "since it housed the cult statue, the temple was thought of as the house (oikos) of the god" (p. 46), even if this concept may not have prevailed from the start. I would thus translate differently the two Greek passages cited by Donohue 1997, 39: Origen quoting Celsus quoting Herakleitos, *Contra Celsum* 1.5: ὅμοια, ὡς εἴ τις τοῖς δόμοις λεσχηνεύοιτο, ποιεῖν τοὺς προσιόντας ὡς θεοῖς τοῖς ἀψύχοις; and Herakleitos' statement as reconstructed from Clement, Origen, and Aristokritos: καὶ τοῖς ἀγάλμασι δὲ τουτέοισιν εὔχονται, ὁκοῖον εἴ τις τοῖς δόμοισι λεσχηνεύοιτο, οὔ τι γινώσκων θεοὺς οὐδ' ἥρωας οἵτινες εἶσι—not "those who approach lifeless things as gods act like a person who holds conversations *with houses*" and "And they pray to these statues, as if someone, not knowing who the gods and heroes are, were to chat *with his house*" (my emphasis), but "the houses *of the gods*"; that is, as if they were talking to the temples, which are also lifeless. I thank R. Hamilton for advice on these passages.

4. K. D. S. Lapatin, *Chryselephantine Statuary in the Ancient Mediterranean World*, is forthcoming; in the interim, see Lapatin 1997, with copious refs. To be sure, statues in gold and ivory were made before the Classical period, but they were of relatively small size, as contrasted with the later creations. Akrolithic images are attested from the early 5th c.

5. Bryaxis (probably a Karian sculptor later than the Athenian homonymous master) and his Sarapis: Ridgway 1990, 95–97 with refs. in n. 45; add Ridgway 1997b, 250–51; Stewart 1990, 300–301, T 149, for Clement's text and discussion; Cain 1995, 116 and n. 5 (with additional refs., and apparent belief in the ancient text). For theourgoi and their use of magical texts, see

Kane 1998, esp. 148–50 with many examples; she mentions Clement's description (n. 32), but relates it to the making of a Sarapis bull rather than a statue of the god.

6. Many ancient sources mention (wooden?) statues being carried in procession, but for an actual example of an idol (a draped herm?) being carried by a female initiate, as immortalized in a stone sculpture from Messene, see Themelis 1994a, 116 and figs. 19–20 (statue no. 245, 1st c.), who discusses the ritual of Artemis Ortheia at Messene.

7. Even areas with local supplies of good stone could import marble from elsewhere for specific reasons: the Athena Parthenos for the Pergamene library, for instance, was in Pentelic, as well as its base. Unless, with Weber 1993 (cf. supra, Ch. 5 n. 49), we believe both to have been made in Athens, Attic marble may have been chosen to strengthen the link between prototype and replica. Since the back of the Pergamene Athena is perfunctorily finished, thus implying knowledge of its intended setting, I would be more inclined to believe in local production from imported material. Whether Greek sculptors made cult statues for the Romans in Greece for later shipment, or on Italian soil with imported marble, considerations of weight would have been important. For the extensive piecing of much 2nd-c. statuary, see supra, Ch. 5. That the Romans also used chryselephantine statues is shown by the Iuppiter Capitolinus made by an Apollonios to replace the image by Vulca destroyed in the fire of 83 B.C.: Schwarz 1988, 241; see also infra, n. 44.

8. Cain 1995 provides examples and discussion of all these features (esp. 123–25 for the showcasing of images and parallels with palace practices), but he does not emphasize the elements of continuity that to me seem important. He is also scrupulous in pointing out that votive offerings were displayed in the same manner as (and together with) the temple images. One of his lesser-known examples is the chapel of Dionysos Kathegemon within the Royal Palace at Pergamon, which also included bronze barriers and a mosaic floor (p. 124).

9. Cain 1995, 120, cites several examples of aphidrysis, including the Skillous Artemis (Xenophon, *Anab.* 5.3.12) and the Priene Athena, for which he accepts the date given by Weber 1993, 97. On the latter statue, see also Ridgway 1997b, 135 and 154 n. 45. Cain (p. 119) acknowledges a strong Classicizing trend "at least as early as the 2nd c.," but stresses other possible motivations for the imitation of earlier images. See his pp. 116–19 for the establishment of *new* cult images—Dionysos (Sardanapalos), Apollo (Kitharoidos), Asklepios—although he cites the 4th-c. precedents.

10. Andreae has devoted several writings to Phyromachos, of which only those related to the Asklepios and the most recent are here cited. For the essays collected on the master, see Andreae 1990, esp. 45–100; 1989, 239 and 241 no. 26 (as fixed chronological point, 168–156); and 1992. He advocates a bronze seated statue in the Nikephorion. For criticism of his position see: Queyrel 1992, esp. 372–78 (collection of sources) and 378–89 (discussion of three homonymous sculptors: end 5th c., early 3rd c., ca. 230–168 for the maker of the Asklepios); Müller 1992 (statue had to be in Asklepieion, in marble). Stewart 1993 (cf. supra, Ch. 2 n. 33, review of Andreae 1990) would accept the Syracuse head and a chronology (220/10–180/70: p. 713) lower than the one he postulated in 1979 (p. 16: probably considerably earlier than 190). As more recently stated (*per ep.* Sept. 11, 1998), Stewart would now basically agree with Queyrel's chronology.

Coins used to reconstruct the statue date from 240–230/20: cf. *LIMC* 2, s.v. Asklepios, 866–67, for comments on the difficulty of distinguishing types, and 894, for the possibility that Phyromachos' statue was not returned to Pergamon but was replaced by another image; see also p. 896 for additional hypotheses (B. Holtzmann). Aelius Aristides (42.4) describes a 2nd-c. *Imperial* statue, not that by Phyromachos (Müller 1992, 198 n. 17). See also Moreno 1994, 263–68 (Asklepios was chryselephantine, in Asklepieion; not lost because mentioned in the present tense by Diod. Sic. 31.35 = Stewart 1990, 302–303 T 154), and 790–92 ns. 517–22 (long discussion of ancient sources and Phyromachos' pupils).

Syracuse head: Andreae 1990, pls. 20–23, 25–35 (pls. 24, 37.1–2 for coin comparison); Moreno 1994, 483 fig. 610, 493 ("deity," considered copy of Pergamene work). Roman Jupiter: Wilson 1990, app. 1, and esp. Landwehr 1990, 105, 107 (G3) and 112 (dated between 113 and 138 A.C.); her entire contribution stresses the *Romanitas* of certain father-god types.

11. Excavation report: Protonotariou-Deilaki 1961–1962; cf. Papachatzis, vol. 4 (1980), 230–32, esp. caption to fig. 203 with plans of the two temples, figs. 204 (colossal feet) and 208 (Hygieia head). Smith 1991, fig. 300; Moreno 1994, 555 and figs. 670, 672 (Hygieia).

12. On the sandals, see Morrow 1985, 117 and pl. 104 on p. 128. She does not refer to the metal attachments, but I was able to see the fragments in the local museum, in Fall 1988. Cf. *LIMC* 5, s.v. Hygieia, no. 216 and p. 572 for comments on the unusual matronly form of the Hygieia, more appropriate to Hera; a tainia is mentioned, but not the braid. Her neck is marked by "Venus rings." See Protonotariou-Deilaki 1961–1962, pl. 64γ, for a view of the back of the head.

13. Mosaic floor: Protonotariou-Deilaki 1961–1962, pl. 66; Papachatzis, vol. 4 (1980), fig. 207. The Hygieia head is 0.80 m high. Inserted eyes, "not since the Severe period": Schwarz 1988, 243 (but some examples in stone statuary occur also in the 4th c.). Signatures of sculptors on cult images of the Classical period are known only from doubtful literary sources: Donderer 1996, 93; but see his comments for Hellenistic practices. Attalos' work is not otherwise known, but he has been dated to the mid-2nd c. on letter forms and the assumption that he was a contemporary of Eucheir; Trummer 1993, 152 n. 100, would date his sculptures to the last quarter on stylistic grounds. See supra, Ch. 5 n. 39 for Euboulides and the Kerameikos finds; also infra, this chapter. On Eucheir and his work, see Despinis 1995, 338; he would accept a Hellenistic type of Hermes in marble, standing near a herm, as shown on Roman coins of the city: cf. Papachatzis, vol. 4 (1980), fig. 209 on p. 234. Madigan 1991, 509 n. 30, and 1993, 118 n. 22, lists additional akroliths in the Peloponnesos, all from the 2nd c.: a Dionysos in Argos, by unnamed master, and a Kore and Aphrodite at Megalopolis (Paus. 8.31.2–6), an Eileithyia at Aigion (Paus. 7.23.5), all by Damophon of Messene, on which see infra. See infra also for two heads from Aigeira and the fragments from Bassai.

14. Lykosoura group: main descriptions by Stewart 1990, 93–96 figs. 788–92, with Pausanias' text on p. 304, T 156; Pollitt 1986, 165 (with text of Pausanias), figs. 166–68; Smith 1991, 240–41, figs. 301.1–3; Moreno 1994, 504–14 (cf. 504, fig. 629, for the Severan bronze coin = *LIMC* 1, s.v. Anytos, no. 2 pl. 697, with erroneous number); Papachatzis, vol. 4 (1980), 334–40, figs. 323–26 (temple and plan of sanctuary), 327–38 (statues), 339 (coin). For a description within the compass of Hellenistic cult images, see Cain 1995, 124–25. For a rare photograph of the footstool, see *BCH* 96 (1972) 1002, fig. 42; for the Triton and Tritoness, Themelis 1996, figs. 104–105 (originals) and 130 (Hadrianic repair). See also *LIMC* 1, s.v. Anytos, no. 1 pl. 697 (with erroneous number); 2, s.v. Artemis, no. 1184 pl. 542; 3, s.v. Despoina, no. 1 pl. 278 (mantle, feet, right arm with cista); 4, s.v. Demeter, 880, no. 436 pl. 596; 8, s.v. Triton, no. 24 pl. 49. Artemis' right hand holding torch: Themelis 1996, fig. 125.

15. Construction: Kourouniotes 1906–1907; see 381 and fig. 21 for Anytos' cuirass. Colors

and sacred law: Stewart 1990, 94–95. For a 2nd-c. addition to the sacred law on a recently found fragment, see Loucas and Loucas 1994.

16. Additions in stone, wood, or stucco; Anytos' helmet: Themelis 1996, 178, citing Trummer 1993. Yet my study of the Philadelphia head (Ridgway 1997a) makes me doubt that all such cranial cavities were meant to be completed. Moreno 1994, 510, believes that stucco additions and pieced locks were influenced by Alexandrian techniques, on the basis of an inscription from Messene (birthplace of Damophon and one of his main markets) signed by Demetrios, son of Apollonios of Alexandria (Moreno, p. 506; *SEG* 23, 1968, 85–86, no. 225). Pausanias (4.32.1) indeed states that statues in the Messenian Gymnasion were Egyptian works, but does not specify their date, and Moreno's assumption that Damophon learned his sfumato technique from them is unwarranted. Themelis 1994a, 115 and n. 22, dates Demetrios' inscription to the 1st c. B.C.–1st c. A.C., well after Damophon.

17. Demeter, Poseidon, and story of transformation into horse: Stewart 1990, 94; see 95 for description of mantle decoration by registers. The allegorical/narrative interpretation is Cain's (1995) 125, who stresses the processional layout of the temple, fronting a large area flanked by a long stoa and containing three altars. On Arkadian cults, see Jost 1985, esp. 172–78, 326–37. Many terracottas in human form but with animal heads were found at the sanctuary.

18. Although other creatures were given double fishtails before (e.g., Skylla), Triton was usually shown with a single pisciform lower body; the earliest example of two legs/tails is on a mosaic from Rhodes, of the early 3rd c.: *LIMC* 8, s.v. Triton, no. 12 and commentary on p. 84; the Grimani Triton (no. 22) is probably a Roman copy and may not go back to an original by Skopas; the Pergamene Tritons from the Great Altar have a single tail.

19. This chronological information is derived from Themelis 1996, esp. 168–72. Moreno 1994, 808 n. 814, prefers to place Damophon's activity between 183 and 168, but his suggestion may be based on an erroneous interpretation of a numismatic issue. Moreno believes that the Alexander coinage was replaced by the *first* triobols of the Achaian League only after the destruction of Corinth, on the evidence of a hoard from Poggio Picenze (Abruzzi). Yet the article he cites (Boehringer 1991) states only that the League coinage *continued* to be issued after 146, especially in northwest Arkadia (see esp. p. 166, no. 7, for the coinage of Megalopolis before and after 146). This position is reaffirmed by Warren 1993. Thus the Italian hoard has no consequence for the terminal date of the "Alexanders" in the Peloponnesos, as accepted by Price 1991 (cf. esp. 155, under "The Peloponnese": "During the unsettled period of the early third century BC, during the last quarter of the same century, and during the early second century BC there were occasions on which Alexanders were the preferred form of coinage"), and as summarized by Themelis 1996, 170. I am deeply grateful to Carmen Arnold-Biucchi for help with bibl. and interpretation of the numismatic evidence.

The Hadrianic date briefly proposed because of a misreading of the evidence for the Lykosoura repairs is no longer considered possible: Pollitt 1986, 312 n. 2; Stewart 1990, 304.

Themelis 1996, 180, notes the similarity between the Tritons at Lykosoura and the (later) Pergamene Giants (*not* the akroterial Tritons), but derives both renderings from Classical prototypes.

20. On the inscription from Messene, see Themelis 1996, 168–69, and 184–85 on Damophon's family; n. 160 mentions that his stemma will be published separately; p. 183 states (in contrast to earlier publications) that Damophon's sons and grandsons were not necessarily sculptors, although they set up statues at Lykosoura to honor members of their family. More or

less the same sequence of generations is reconstructed by Moreno 1994, 504–507, with stemma on p. 807 n. 803. The list of works by Damophon compiled by Stewart 1990, 304, on the basis of sources can now be considerably extended, as well as its geographic range. For the recent finds, see Themelis 1996—an important compendium and updating of many previous publications—and Themelis 1994a, specifically for the Artemis complex, with fragments of the colossal cult image (figs. 13–14a–b: Artemis with a torch = Phosphoros).

21. Themelis 1996, 157–58, nos. 2 and 3a, figs. 97–99 (Severizing heads, identified as Podaleirios and Machaon, Asklepios' sons), 160–61, no. 1a, figs. 102–103 (head of Apollo). For the latter, cf. Moreno 1994, figs. 628, 631; Smith 1991, fig. 302. Statues of Muses, which may have accompanied the Apollo at Messene, were recut as male statues during the Imperial period: Themelis 1996, 161; he dates the Asklepieion complex between 214 and 182 (p. 172).

22. Themelis 1996, 184, outlines the following family of sculptors: Agias I, his sons Pyrilampos [sic] and Aristomenes, and the latter's son, Agias II. For Pyrilampes, cf. Paus. 6.3.13, 6.15.1, and 6.16.5; Maddoli 1989 distinguishes between a Pyrilampes from Sikyon, of unknown date, and one from Messene, but he dates the latter to the 1st c.

23. Themelis 1996, 173: statue of Artemis Hegemone for Lykosoura; cf. Paus. 8.37.1.

24. Lykosoura akroterion: Themelis 1996, 164 and n. 50, fig. 121; note the trumpet folds of her transparent apoptygma (belted below the breasts), which frame the low-slung abdomen. The temple was a peculiar construction, with walls consisting of orthostates and baked bricks with mortar, but entablature in marble. If damaged during the earthquake of 183, it was probably repaired before 146 (on inscriptional evidence), and must have been refurbished under Hadrian. It is unclear how many phases are represented by the extant structure.

25. Damophon in Rome: Schwarz 1988, 244–45; other authors are cited by Themelis 1996, 183 n. 158, who does not credit their theories; see also p. 181 for the comment cited.

26. Madigan 1991 makes a strong case for reidentifying the Aigeira head, as I have summarized. Some of his points are not equally strong: the temple near the theater (naiskos D) was too small to have housed a colossal Zeus and a chryselephantine Athena—but we have seen how crowded Hellenistic temples were; Pausanias says the Zeus was in Pentelic marble, whereas the extant fragments are not—but Pausanias was not a geologist and may have been mistaken. Yet, although he is occasionally wrong in assessing whether sculptures were in one piece (cf. Lykosoura), would he have missed an akrolithic statue? That the handling of the fleshy portions of the head suggests the sensuousness of Dionysos rather than the majesty of Zeus is a more subjective argument, although based on a correct analysis of the "boneless" treatment of the face.

Madigan's article appeared too late to be considered by Trummer 1993, who retains the traditional identification but is the best source for photographs of the head (Athens NM 3377, pls. 64–67, and figs. 5–6 for views of the back) and the related arm (NM 3481, pl. 68, figs. 2–3); discussion (pp. 141–48, with extensive bibl. on p. 143 n. 13) dates the "Zeus" between 150 and 125. For additional photographs, see Pollitt 1986, fig. 170 (conveniently illustrated near the Anytos), and Smith 1991, fig. 299 (opposite Anytos = fig. 301.2), which well shows the rasped surface of the truncated forehead locks. An interesting comparison of beards with central parts can be made by looking at pls. 48–79 in Landwehr 1990.

27. Trummer 1993, 148–55, pl. 69a–b and fig. 8; see fig. 10 for the Fortuna Primigenia. Cf. LIMC 8, s.v. Tyche/Fortuna, no. 4 pl. 90 (mid-2nd c.); Martin 1987, 234–35, cat. 14, pl. 31.

28. First study of the sandals: Morrow 1985, 96–97, figs. 9d, 12d, and pls. 77–78, dated dur-

ing or after the 2nd half of the 2nd c., although a Roman date is not excluded. The Augustan date is argued by Madigan 1993, who reads the hand fragments as holding a kithara or lyre and a plektron; his article contains useful comments on the akrolithic technique.

A possibly similar case occurs at Tegea, where the Archaic ivory Athena was taken by Augustus and replaced with a statue of the goddess removed from the town of the Manthoureans (Paus. 8.47.1). This image was flanked by an Asklepios and a Hygieia said to be by Skopas, but it has recently been argued that the master in question was Skopas Minor, a 2nd-c. sculptor; the two figures were depicted on a votive relief that serves as a basis for the revised chronology: Lebendis 1993; cf. Ridgway 1997b, 49 and n. 63. Yet Skopas Minor seems to have worked primarily in Rome: Ridgway 1997b, 252 and esp. n. 47.

29. At present, the main publication of the Klarian statues is Marcadé 1994; see fig. 20 for the men working on the Leto, and fig. 29 for the assembled casts and a hypothetical human to scale. For the Apollo's feet, see figs. 9–11 (note the short little toe bent up and inward), figs. 7–8 for frontal sphinx and Hermaphrodite's sandals = Morrow 1985, figs. 123a–b. Morrow, 139–40, attributes the mixture to the figure's double nature, but Marcadé is skeptical. For the Pergamon statue, see also *LIMC* 5, s.v. Hermaphroditos, no. 18 pl. 191; cf. Ridgway 1990, 328. A paper on the cult images at Klaros, by M. Flashar, was delivered on July 4, 1997, at a Memorial Symposium for A. Linfert; its publication (*Hellenistische Gruppen*) is forthcoming [now 1999, pp. 53–94] (I thank Dr. C. Häuber for this information).

30. Date: Marcadé 1994, 453 and n. 20 ("not later than 170–160 and probably earlier"); Artemis torso, figs. 21–23, and cf. p. 454 for 4th-c. comparisons. Peiraieus bronze (large) Artemis and Apollo Patroos: e.g., Ridgway 1997b, 328 and 335–37 respectively; cf. my pl. 80a and Marcadé 1994, fig. 1 (fold pattern at knee). Marcadé states that a more precise chronology may be given by the final study of temple and inscriptions. The date of the temple is left uncertain by Rumscheid 1994, vol. 1, 20: it was at least begun by the 3rd c. and had an Imperial phase "connected with the cult images."

31. Letoon head (Antalya Museum 2.18.77): Marcadé 1976; pres. ht. (measured from jugular depression and without cranial calotte): 0.285 m. For comparisons with Pergamene heads, see figs. 5 (Aphrodite) and 6 (cast of "Nyx"). Özgen and Özgen 1988, 94 no. 110 (col. ill.) and cat. entry on p. 207 (pres. ht., with neck, given as 0.38 m).

A somewhat comparable piecing of the cranium occurs on a beautiful **female head and upper torso** (shoulders and beginning of left arm) in the **Toledo** Museum of Art (acc. no. 1937.5; preserved ht. 0.332 m; Pls. 69a–b). The piece may have been cleaned too forcefully when first found (it was sold in Rome in 1914), and thus appears somewhat blurred, especially in the area of the lower lids. But the type of bust join recalls the Fanciulla d'Anzio (see infra, Ch. 8), and the style is in keeping with the late 2nd c. or the beginning of the 1st. The proper left side of the face is less carefully finished than the right and was probably not visible; a hole and a groove circling the chignon may have secured a metal band. I am grateful to Dr. Sandra Knudsen for the information that a test of the marble suggests a Parian origin; her article (in collaboration with C. Craine and R. H. Tykot) is forthcoming in Herrmann et al., eds., *The Study of Marble and Other Stones Used in Antiquity* (ASMOSIA Conference 5, held in Boston in 1998), to be published as a *JRA* Supplement.

For earlier opinions ("Praxitelean"), see Richter 1917.

32. The most recent study of Polykles and his family is Despinis 1995, 339–72, with stemma on p. 362; he lists five men by that name, of whom four represent four different generations;

the other recurrent name in the family is Timarchides (I and II); active related sculptors are Timokles and Dionysios. For additional recent discussions, see Moreno 1994, 521–30, 541–43, 545–46 (with a different stemma on p. 809 n. 832); Queyrel 1991, 448–64 (with three possible stemmata on pp. 461–62, and table of works attributed to the family on p. 463); Stewart 1990, 304–305 (with ancient sources T 157–60); Martin 1987, 60 (with attributions of Roman cult images); Pollitt 1986, 162–63, 173–75, 313 n. 12 (stemma closer to Despinis' but less complex and beginning with Polykles II). Other reconstructions are mentioned by Despinis, whose theories will be basically followed here.

33. Athena Kranaia: Despinis 1995, 339–47 and 347–49 (attributed head, NM 4817), 363 and n. 180 (date), 369–72 (list of all fragments from Elateia in Chaironeia Museum, of which only nos. 1–4 are colossal), pls. 70–72.1, 73–75.2, 76, 80, 81.1. For discussion of the Neo-Attic term, see Cain and Dräger 1994 (p. 814 on Polykles' family).

34. The main publication on the Ofellius Ferus is Queyrel 1991 (restored ht. 2.80 m), with extensive bibl. up to 1990 on pp. 389–96; the statue came from niche 18 within the Agora of the Italians (cf. plan on p. 399 fig. 14; F on plan of Ill. 24); the date suggested there is 130–120, with repairs in antiquity (p. 404). Lower date: Despinis 1995, 361; see 363–64 for discussion of a special technique corresponding to that of the Athena Kranaia and maybe a workshop practice: shallow rectangular cuttings for the attachment of separate pieces leaded in place; cf. Barthe and Besnainou 1988, 416–17 figs. 5–7. For illustrations, see, e.g., Pollitt 1986, 75 fig. 78; Stewart 1990, fig. 839; Smith 1991, fig. 316; Moreno 1994, 550–52, figs. 673, 676, 949 (after cast in Rome; he considers the sculptors cousins); Marcadé et al. 1996, 190–91, no. 85.

On the possible purpose of the Agora of the Italians (a palaistra with various functions), see Rauh 1993, 289–338 (dedications found there are listed on pp. 295–322); but see also the rebuttal by Bruneau 1995, 45–54 (multifunctional uses of a gathering area with open square surrounded by porticoes, and a display place for the Italians on Delos).

35. Fringed mantle with traces of polychromy: Queyrel 1991, fig. 22; object in left hand, 405–406, fig. 19, and cf. reconstruction drawing, fig. 22, with spear in right hand; prototypes and iconographic meanings are extensively discussed and illustrated, with ruler type proposed. Moreno 1994, 550, erroneously states that Ofellius had paid for the *northern* portico of the Agora of the Italians. For the Hermes Richelieu, see also Ridgway 1997b, 337 and pl. 82, with additional refs.

36. Machaon from Messene: Themelis 1996, 158, no. 3b, figs. 100–101; the torso is said to go back to a "statue of Diomedes related to the Doryphoros of Polykleitos," yet comparison with the Ofellius Ferus is provided in n. 24, and the Machaon's similarity to the 4th-c. Hermes Richelieu Type seems to me closer because of the precise draping of the chlamys over the left shoulder. If the head in Severe style (Themelis 1996, 3a, fig. 99) goes with torso 3b, it would confirm Damophon's eclectic approach.

37. That Ofellius Ferus might have been made in Athens is suggested by Queyrel 1991, who also postulates the later workshop in Italy. Youthful, beardless Herakles from the Capitoline, in Conservatori Museum: Despinis 1995, 363–65, pl. 77 (either by Polykles III, son of Polykles II, or by Polykles IV, son of Timarchides I, according to his stemma; the lionskin over the head was probably added in marble, not in stucco as generally surmised); see also Moreno 1994, figs. 648–49; *LIMC* 4, s.v. Herakles, no. 1307 pl. 529. Female head (with originally inserted eyes), once Albani Collection, now in the Capitoline Museum: Despinis 1995, 365–66, pl. 78 (earlier than the Herakles, but not necessarily Juno Regina, closer to Pergamene sculp-

ture); Moreno 1994, fig. 646; *LIMC* 5, s.v. Juno, 823 (discussion of other possibilities) and no. 40 = *LIMC* 2, s.v. Aphrodite, no. 1068 pl. 107; Martin 1987, 209–10, cat. 3, pls. 6–7 (dated ca. 146). Apollo with kithara: Despinis 1995, 366–68 with refs. (against the usually attributed type of Apollo from Kyrene, since an akrolithic statue would have been draped). See also *LIMC* 2, s.v. Apollon, no. 586, and cf. s.v. Apollon/Apollo, 367 no. 7. For the Kyrene Apollo, see, e.g., Moreno 1994, figs. 642, 645; *LIMC* 2, s.v. Apollon, no. 222 pl. 202, and cf. s.v. Apollon/Apollo, 383–84 no. 61, with discussion. Martin 1987, 50 and 207 cat. 1, lists the Apollo by Timarchides as the first example in Rome (ca. 179) of the use of marble as a statuary medium; pl. 1 illustrates an attributed fragmentary hand, pls. 2a–b show the Kyrene Apollo.

A more recent survey of Greek masters in Republican Rome is provided by La Rocca 1996; cf. p. 618 for his discussion of Polykles and Timarchides.

38. Fortuna Primigenia: see supra, n. 27. Head from Largo Argentina in Braccio Nuovo, Conservatori Museum: Moreno 1994, 555 and fig. 671; Guldager Bilde 1995, 198. Martin 1987, 103–11 and figs. 26a–b, discusses findspot and other relevant marble fragments (arm, sandaled feet); the body would have been in bronze; see also 213–15, cat. 5, pls. 13–14.

39. Head from Nemi, Copenhagen, Ny Carlsberg cat. 87 (inv. no. 1517): Guldager Bilde 1995, 195–99, figs. 3–6, and drapery fragment (in Nottingham), 199–200, figs. 7–10; cf. p. 199 for date, 200–201 for reconstruction of hairstyle, 213 for technique, 194 for findspot. Other mentions: Martin 1987, 182–91, 236–37, cat. 15, pls. 32–33 (last quarter 2nd c.); Moltesen 1997, col. fig. 59 on p. 88 and cat. 2 on p. 129 (see also infra, n. 40); *LIMC* 2, s.v. Artemis, no. 869, and s.v. Artemis/Diana, no. 108 pl. 605 (both entries date it early Imperial, after 4th-c. original).

40. Head in Philadelphia, Museum of the University of Pennsylvania, MS 3483: Guldager Bilde 1995, 202–205, figs. 12–15; cf. p. 195 for findspot and date. See also Moltesen 1997, 90 figs. 60–61, and infra, n. 41.

41. Nottingham torso, Castle Museum N832: Guldager Bilde 1995, 206–13, figs. 19–24, and fig. 25 for comparison with Mounychia Asklepios; see also p. 194 for findspot, p. 213 for technique, and pp. 213–15 for important comments on piecing and the use of marble in the Late Hellenistic period. Other mentions: Moltesen 1997, 91 fig. 62, and 129–30, cat. 3; all three cult images from Nemi, and other possible examples from the sanctuary, are discussed (P. Guldager Bilde) on pp. 197–200 (English trans.).

Mounychia Asklepios: Stewart 1979, 48–50 (with discussion of technique), pls. 10–11, 15a, c, e; *LIMC* 2, s.v., no. 346 pl. 663. On Virbius, see also *LIMC* 2, s.v. Artemis/Diana, 794, and *LIMC* 5, s.v. Hippolytos I, 445–46.

42. Poseidon from Pergamon: supra, Ch. 2 n. 78. The "lock-for-lock" correspondence between the Virbius and the Asklepios was verified by Dr. Guldager Bilde (*per ep.*).

43. Hope Goddess, in the Museum of the University of Pennsylvania, Philadelphia, 30-7-1: Ridgway 1997a; Waywell 1986, 93, no. 49, pl. 57.2–3. For the bronze head from Herculaneum (Naples Nat. Mus. 5592), see Ridgway 1997a, figs. 5–6; Mattusch 1996, 102–21.

44. Alba Fucens Herakles, in Chieti Museum: usually discussed in the context of the Herakles Epitrapezios by Lysippos: see Ridgway 1997b, 297–98 and n. 30 with bibl., 294–304 for the issue of the Epitrapezios. I am convinced that the statue in Chieti ranks with the other cult images made for the Romans in Classicizing style—here quite Baroque. See also Moreno 1994, 492 and figs. 611, 613 (considered an export to Italy, without mention of Lysippos); *LIMC* 4, s.v. Herakles, no. 986 pl. 512; Martin 1987, 225–27, cat. 10, pls. 23–24 (dated first decades of 1st c.). On the chryselephantine Iuppiter Capitolinus, see supra, n. 7; Martin 1987, 133 with n. 665,

134. There is some debate on whether that image belonged to the Sullan or the Domitianic period: cf. *EAA* s.v. Apollonios 9°. The source citing it (Chalcidius, commentary to Plato, *Tim.*) dates from the 4th c. A.C. Martin 1987 catalogues a total of 17 possible remains of cult statues, and adds 3 in appendix.

45. My figures are derived from Habicht 1997, 112; cf. his n. 41 for mention of possible additions to Stewart 1979, 157–74, where names of sculptors are listed. These numbers may include masters active during the late 4th, 3rd, and 1st centuries, but preserved evidence seems to favor 2nd-c. masters; cf. also infra, Ch. 9 and n. 58. See also Cain and Dräger 1994, esp. 812–13. For sculptors active in Athens (Euboulides and Eucheir) cf. supra, Ch. 5. For Athenian activity in the Peloponnesos, see supra in this chapter (e.g., Attalos at Pheneos). For Delian signatures, see also Marcadé 1969, 56–61.

46. Information based on Goodlett 1991: see p. 674 and fig. 1 for dating of sculptural peaks and graph charting them, p. 675 for quotation, p. 676 on Pythokritos and workshops by masters from Soloi, pp. 679–81 for discussion of the various possible meanings for the ethnic "Rhodios." Cf. supra, Ch. 5, for the Lindian rock-cut relief and other attributions.

47. Donderer 1996, esp. 101; he points out the apparent gap in signing practices (from the early 5th c. to the 2nd half of the 2nd c.: pp. 93–94), and argues that signatures may have first been used on sculptures in retrospective styles, but were soon applied to contemporary works: cf. his figs. 11–12 for a mantled man signed by Apollonides Ephesios on an area visible only from the side. See also infra, Ch. 8.

48. For Archaic signatures and their location, see Ridgway 1993b, 70, 101–102 n. 24, 430–31. Many examples of all periods (including refs. in ancient sources) have been collected by Donderer 1996; see also supra, n. 47. Late Hellenistic and Roman Imperial signatures, especially on alleged "copies," are mentioned by Richter 1951, 45 (with ns. 1–3)–49.

49. There is no established term for the projections that occur on either side of a herm shaft in place of the arms; they are variously called arm-bosses, side brackets, or side tenons. I prefer arm-stumps.

50. On the wreck in general, and the 1994 exhibition in Bonn, see the comprehensive two volumes by Hellenkemper Salies et al, 1994; for mention of subsequent publications, Ridgway 1995b; add Barr-Sharrar 1996, and a useful review by a marble expert, *AJA* 101 (1997) 182–84 (J. C. Fant). Hellenkemper Salies 1996 adds new findings and viewpoints, and provides a bibl. of reviews and additional publications on pp. 218–19. On the bronze herms (in Tunis, from Mahdia, and in Malibu, Getty Museum): Mattusch 1994a; 1994b, 796–98; 1996, 169–90 (all with numerous and detailed illustrations); also Willer 1994a and 1994b, for technical details of restoration and installation. On the so-called Agon (Eros): Söldner 1994, and new photographs in Hellenkemper Salies 1996, 211–15, figs. 9–14; also Söldner 1998, and, on the restoration, Willer 1998. On Boethos: Andreae 1994 (connection with marble figures at Sperlonga). Linfert 1994, with hypothetical reconstruction of movements (p. 835) and possible stemma of *five* Boethoi (p. 836), systematically discusses literary sources, inscriptions, and attributions; I derive most of my information from this source. All inscriptions are conveniently transcribed and illustrated in Marcadé 1957, s.vv. Boethos (with various ethnics and patronymics), Diodotos, and Menodotos. Although pre-Bonn, Aneziri and Damaskos 1989–90 provide useful information grouped by patronymic and ethnic (with extensive bibl.) and reach different conclusions (three Boethoi). For pre-Bonn opinions on "Agon" and Boethos, see also, e.g., Ridgway 1990, 232–33 with bibl. in n. 23; Stewart 1990, 305–306. Donderer 1996, 94, considers the Mah-

dia herm the earliest example of a signed Hellenistic work, perhaps in keeping with its retrospective style, but his chronology may be influenced by the presumed connection with a mid-2nd.-c. Boethos.

51. The Ephesos inscription (Aneziri and Damaskos 1989–90, 184; Linfert 1994, 833, no. 8; Marcadé 1957, 34, s.v. Boethos, son of Apollodoros, Carthaginian) is problematic, in that it occurs on a reused base—one of eight set up in honor of Tiberius. Yet the use of "Karchedonios" instead of "Karthagennesios" shows that the inscription was faithfully transcribed from the original formula, which must have predated Carthage's destruction in 146 and the Caesarian refounding under Roman name. It is unclear what type of monument the base held, but it was sizable and could not have been a vase. Linfert's stemma (supra, n. 50) acknowledges a Carthaginian Boethos ("around 180") but does not connect him directly with the other members of the reconstructed family line. Marcadé is in favor of considering Pausanias' mention a scribal error in transcription.

52. Lindos inscription: Marcadé 1957, 28, s.v. Boethos, son of Athenaion, Kalchedonian; Linfert 1994, 832, no. 5.

53. Delos inscription, honoring Antiochos for his excellence (*arete*) and his benevolence toward the Athenians: Marcadé 1957, 28; Linfert 1994, 833, no. 6. *Lecti Boethici* (or *Boethiaci*: Marcadé 1957, 29) is, however, an emendation for the textual *a boetos oboeotos*, which is nonsensical. Although plausible, it seems to me that the correction is not assured. Rolley 1996a, 285, points out that the phrase *lecti deliaci* defines a type of object, not a place of manufacture.

54. Elgin Throne (now in the J. Paul Getty Museum in Malibu): Marcadé 1957, 35 (discounting the inscription as a signature because on the edge of the back, near the location where the left shoulder would have rested); Linfert 1994, 833–34, no. 10 (throne dated variously, from 3rd to 1st c.). Gaeta inscription: Marcadé 1957, 40, s.v. Diodotos, son of Boethos, of Nikomedeia (he suggests that the "Hermes" was actually a herm, since the inscription consists of four single words in a column, as appropriate for a herm shaft; no ethnic is here included); Linfert 1994, 834, no. 11 (contrary to Marcadé, he is uncertain about Ligorio's accuracy). Statue of Herakles: Marcadé 1957, 72, s.v. Menodotos and Diodotos, sons of Boethos, of Nikomedeia (the statue was seen by Ligorio in the house of the sculptor Leonardo, near S. Marco Palace); Linfert 1994, 834, no. 12.

55. Delian statue of Epigenes: Marcadé 1957, 32, s.v. Boethos and Theodosios (another statue of Epigenes was made by Hephaistion, son of Myron, q.v.; it is not certain that this Boethos was even related to the son of Athenaion); Linfert 1994, 833, no. 7.

56. Marcadé 1957, 30–31 (dating the base 3rd c. A.C.); Linfert 1994, 833, no. 9 ("perhaps" 3rd. c. A.C.); *LIMC* 2, s.v. Asklepios, p. 892 (= *AnthGr* 3, 92, 9–10).

57. Green, forthcoming; note his additional statement about "that old fallacy . . . the firm belief that whatever items survive from a period, however fragmentary or intermittent, must, of necessity, be integrally connected." I am aware that I am falling into the same temptation, despite my intention to resist it.

58. The Kition inscription was found too late to be considered by Marcadé 1957, but it is not mentioned by Linfert 1994, and is cited by Aneziri and Damaskos 1989–90, 191, only in n. 48. The initial reading (Nicolaou 1969, 84–85, no. 13, from the Larnaka District) has been modified by Bagnall 1973 (121–23, no. 1), who assumes that the stone-cutter twice wrote υ for ν. The text would therefore state that Apollodoros son of N[. . .], one of the *philoi* of the king, honored his own son Boethos, one of the *hegemones* (= an officer at arms), with an image. The king in

question is either Ptolemy VI Philometor or Ptolemy VIII Euergetes II, since the inscription is datable around the middle of the second century. Obviously nothing connects these persons with sculptural activity, and we do not know who made Boethos' statue.

For the two philosophers from Sidon, see *OCD*³ s.v. Boethos 3 (a Stoic philosopher, 2nd c.) and 4 (an Aristotelian of Augustan times). Hellenkemper Salies 1996, 210, repeats Ch. Börker's statement (made at the Bonn Colloquium in Jan. 1995), that from the Greek islands alone 30 Boethoi are known; Linfert's stemma was considered too reductive—at least four families must be represented by the known signatures. See also Rolley 1996a, 284, for further criticism.

59. Contrast the inscription transcribed by Ligorio on Herakles' club, where Menodotos and Diodotos are clearly identified as brothers: "hoi Boethou, Nikomedeis."

60. See, e.g., Mattusch 1994a, 437; 1996, 175–76; Andreae 1994, 372; Linfert 1994, 835 and n. 12.

61. For this explanation of the evidence, see Mattusch 1994a, 432 and fig. 1; Willer 1994a, 953, and esp. 1994b, 968, figs. 15–16 on p. 967, and col. pl. 34.1, after p. 951. The point is reiterated by Willer 1996 within a wider context on the installation methods of bronze statues through the centuries. At the 1995 Colloquium, it was agreed that the "Agon," the herm, and the marble tondi were shipped as antiques; the possibility that the "Agon" was loaded on board with its base was considered absurd and received no further discussion: Hellenkemper Salies 1996, 202–204 and esp. n. 20.

I am still not sure (despite Willer's more recent arguments) that all lead plugs within bronze statues indicate that the piece had been previously set up: see Ridgway 1995b, 344. The marble tenon still embedded within the lead filling of the shaft would seem to confirm the case for the Mahdia herm. This work (if not the "Agon") could theoretically have been shipped together with a marble base, although it seems unlikely that the central boss would have broken off without intentional chiseling, as a consequence of the shifting cargo in the wreck—*if* its size in proportion to the shaft itself is correctly reproduced in the drawing, Willer 1994b, fig. 16. Contrast the CT image (fig. 15), which shows it smaller and less centered. Since the lead plug still fills the bottom of the herm shaft, I do not see how the central rod could have been lost; had it been of iron, corrosion and concretion should have retained its approximate shape. Excavations of other wrecks have in fact yielded much smaller iron nails that could be reproduced by pouring plaster into the cavity left by the disintegrating iron within its concretion. A hole for a rod remains within the bronze itself, and it is suggested that a metal bar served to support the inner core during the casting (cf. Willer 1994b, 959, figs. 2, 10–12). Could this be the same rod that perforated the marble tenon and was then removed with the core? Could the lead plug be the stabilizer for a top-heavy herm with a hollow shaft, rather than a means of securing it onto a stone base?

62. See Mattusch 1996, figs. 5.21 (Vaison head) and 5.22 (Pompeii head); other works, in marble and terracotta or on gems, are less closely comparable (figs. 5.16–20).

63. Some columns are also in either Doliana or Dokimeion marble; for the dispute over the interpretation of this evidence, see Hellenkemper Salies 1996, esp. 208; also 214–16. Carol Mattusch reminds me that heterogeneous marbles and bronzes were found in the so-called Peiraieus cache, presumably from different proveniences (on this issue, see now Palagia 1997b, esp. 189). Perhaps the Mahdia cargo was equally made up of objects from different sources simply gathered in Athens for shipment together with the architectural elements.

64. Even this opinion can be disputed: cf. Kuntz 1994, esp. 896.

65. The more recent theories would even place the date of the wreck somewhat later: cf. Hellenkemper Salies 1996, 205–206; also 254–70 (M. Palaczyk), and 271–75 (S. Rotroff). It seemed generally accepted (p. 214) that the cargo bespeaks serial production, and was unlikely to have been commissioned and bought ca. 20 years before actual manufacture.

66. I am indebted to Carol Mattusch for sharing with me the important information that samples taken by her during 1998 showed the Doryphoros herm from Herculaneum to have an alloy comparable to those of the Amazon bust and the head of the pseudo-Seneca from the same villa, indicating manufacture by the same workshop.

67. The two epigrams mentioning an infant Asklepios (supra, n. 56) may also have influenced attributions of children. See Andreae 1994 (with suggestion that the "Sperlonga type" was at first exported in marble, then in plaster casts from which new replicas were made: p. 372); Linfert 1994, esp. 837–43 (all attributions illustrated); Mattusch 1996, esp. 177 and n. 83 for Boy Strangling a Goose. Her figs. 5.14a–c show three replicas, all from the Villa of the Quintilii, where they were used as fountains, now in the Vatican, the Louvre, and the Munich Glyptothek respectively; fig. 5.14d shows a seated child with duck in the Villa Borghese, different from the one in Vienna (= Linfert 1994, fig. 3) usually proposed as an alternative attribution to Boethos (note that the labels for Mattusch figs. 5.14c and d have been reversed). Since Pliny mentions that the child is choking the bird by embracing it (*amplexando*), the Ephesos type cannot qualify; perhaps we should visualize a child holding an animal against his chest, like one of the Brauron "bears." Cf., e.g., a young girl with bird, Fethiye Mus. 862: Smith 1991, fig. 115 (dated 3rd c. but perhaps somewhat later). The type of boy with the large goose seems to have been conceived in marble—a highly artificial pyramidal structure resting on two legs per side (from front, clockwise): (1) both legs of the boy; (2) right leg of boy and of goose; (3) both legs of goose (and tail); (4) left leg of goose and of boy. For my earlier comments, see Ridgway 1990, 232–33, pl. 114.

68. See Ridgway 1990, 163 and refs. in n. 15. The altar described by Herondas is almost certainly not that of the Asklepieion at Kos. That the ancient terminology does not differentiate between a full-scale statue and a statuette is argued by Bartman 1992, 14–15.

69. Eros and Psyche: Linfert 1994, 840, fig. 5, list of replicas in n. 24, mention of terracottas and their date in n. 26. Yet later or more uncertain dates are suggested for the terracottas illustrated in *LIMC* 3, s.v. Eros (no. 413b pl. 630—1st c. B.C./A.C.) and 7, s.v. Psyche (no. 121 pl. 455—2nd/1st c.; no. 122 pl. 455—3rd/2nd c.). For the marble groups, see *LIMC* 7, s.v. Psyche, no. 141a–c pl. 458 (considered Roman copies of an original dated between beg. 3rd c. and end 2nd c.). Kell 1988, 109–13, believes the concept originated in Alexandria because of the terracottas and the literary refs., but considers the marble group "nachhellenistisch" (1st c. B.C.), diffusing to Rome when Egypt fell under its control.

70. *LIMC* 4, s.v. Herakles, no. 1226 pl. 527, points out that the oversize quiver along the child's left side may imply that he is really Eros, albeit wingless, carrying Herakles' weapons; see p. 786 for the comment (O. Palagia) that the idea is probably Late Hellenistic but that most of the examples date from the 2nd c. A.C., some with portrait heads (e.g., no. 1231 pl. 528), possibly carrying funerary connotations. To me the anachronistic imagery of a *child* Herakles wearing the lionskin and holding the Apples seems entirely Roman. The type is usually in statuette format, but by the mid-3rd c. A.C. it could even be rendered at colossal size and in green basalt (no. 1236 pl. 528), thus increasing the incongruence of the concept but enhancing its symbolism: see esp. La Follette 1994, 67 no. 2, and discussion, 73–78, figs. 28–29.

Cult Images and Masters

71. I have derived my information and some of my comments from Berthold 1984, 25–26, and esp. Woodford 1983; see also her discussion in *LIMC* 4, s.v. Herakles, 831–32, nos. 1598–1647 pls. 552–55; no. 1619 pl. 553 (Thebes, stater, ca. 440) seems to me to show Herakles as an adult; certainly mature is the Herakles on a coin of Geta from Herakleia Pontica, no. 1623 pl. 553 (209–212 A.C.). For a three-dimensional rendering of the kneeling type, see no. 1624 pl. 553—a statuette in Florence ("Roman, but deriving from a Hellenistic prototype"). Cf. Linfert 1994, 839 and fig. 4; he rejects the idea that the Florence figure is a parody of the Laokoon, yet would accept the comparison to lower its date to the mid-2nd c., "nach dem Laokoon-Urbild." See his n. 22 for the suggestion that, should the comparison lower the date even further, a statue of the seated type in the Capitoline would support an earlier chronology for a different version of the type: *LIMC* 4, no. 1634 pl. 554 (dated late 2nd c. A.C., perhaps Caracalla; cf. Arata 1993). It is remarkable that the sculptural replicas listed in the *LIMC*, whether kneeling (nos. 1624–28), seated (nos. 1634–38) or standing (no. 1643 pl. 555), with only two exceptions, are described as statuettes. They show such diversity in pose and rendering that an iconographic concept, rather than a specific prototype, seems to me to have been used.

For my earlier comments, see Ridgway 1990, 339–40, with additional refs.

72. The ears of the best-preserved child from Sperlonga are pointed, suggesting a satyr; the heads of the Mahdia examples are too corroded for this detail to be noticeable, but in both cases no tail is visible. Was the intended location of the pieces known in advance, so that this detail could be omitted? Dr. A. Salza Prina Ricotti tells me (oral communication, November 1995) that, in her opinion, the Sperlonga "satyrs" could not have sat on three sides of the square basin (the water triclinium), as presently reconstructed (e.g., Andreae 1994, 371 fig. 11), because the dining couches would have occupied those positions; she would place them on the terrace in front, with piers. Andreae himself (1994, 370 and n. 12) speaks against the duplication of images in a true Hellenistic environment, and considers it typical only of Roman villas. One more adaptation of the type (late 1st c. A.C.), with satyr's ears but transformed into an Eros by the addition of bronze wings and quiver (probably in the Renaissance), and in a slightly different pose (holding an object in the left hand): von Bothmer 1990, 236, no. 171 (M. L. Anderson).

73. On the problems created by the duplication allowed by bronze-casting techniques, see Mattusch 1996, passim, and the review of her theories by Hurwit 1997, esp. 589–90

CHAPTER 8

The Problem of Copies

In the previous chapter we considered sculptures carrying a master's name without being able to determine with confidence whether such objects were originals meant for export and signed by their maker or items produced in series bearing the equivalent of a factory stamp. The suggestion of mass production is perhaps more applicable to bronzes, which could be repeated almost unchanged from a basic model; it seems less credible in the case of marble statuary, which could indeed duplicate specific prototypes (as the Mahdia and Antikythera wrecks have demonstrated), but was also subject to modifications and approximations sufficient to allow us to consider each piece an individual creation.

The issue of copies and replicas, with all the various shades of meaning implicit in such additional terms as variant, imitation, interpretation, adaptation, derivation, and similar words, has finally begun to receive some positive attention. An early, negative position that implicitly considered any copy inferior, and pronounced "original" all works of good quality and in generic Greek style, seems now almost entirely superseded. In the last decade, several publications have emphasized the originality of sculpture created for purposes and locations different from those of the presumed model, and have actually attempted to look *at* each monument per se, rather than looking *through* it in order to glimpse its alleged prototype. Specifically, it has been acknowledged that even statuary first created during the Roman Imperial period could be duplicated and repeated in various combinations, without laying claim to the prestige of a Greek pedigree. Yet many are still reluctant to abandon the idea that *Kopienkritik* is a valid method of reaching back into the Greek past in order to recover lost *opera nobilia*, especially if mentioned by literary sources. I have repeatedly expressed my own opinions, in earlier publications and throughout the previous chapters of this book. I shall now summarize briefly what I consider the most likely scenario for the last two centuries B.C. and the subsequent Roman Imperial period.[1]

There is no question that true copies existed: the marble replicas of the bronze Tyrannicides, and the many versions of the Erechtheion Karyatids, from very faithful to approximative, are enough to prove the point. Cases where the Greek prototype is no longer extant are more difficult to prove, but some could be accepted—for instance, the many reproductions of the Doryphoros, albeit with varying fidelity in measurements and changes of expression. "Quotations" of previous styles were always possible, from the late Archaic period onward, usually with specific meanings that may have changed from object to object and place to place. Whether such quotations were meant to be perceived by the viewer, or were simply expedient for the sculptor who relied on pattern books, casts, and traditional repertoire, cannot be easily determined; certainly, reproductions like the Pheidian Athena Parthenos, as we have already discussed, carried deliberate meaning proportionate to the relevance of the model for the sponsor. Each case has to be judged on its own merit.

By the second century B.C., Roman expansion within the Mediterranean area was considerable and constantly increasing. So was the demand for Greek artifacts, sparked at first by objects taken as booty and paraded in triumph through Rome, but certainly fueled also by Italian presence on Greek lands. We have tended to look at this picture with a prejudiced eye, believing that all inspiration moved from East to West. We are beginning to acknowledge that the so-called West played its own significant role: Etruscans and other Italics moved with more frequency than usually realized, and Taras, with its pre-second-century Baroque, had made a major impression on the Etruscan artistic repertoire.[2] Most important, the conception of public and domestic space in Italy was different from the Greek, and "melting pots" like Delos and Rhodes were bound to reflect the influx of Roman foreigners. From the mid-second century onward, most Greek workshops were active, at least in part, to satisfy the demands of an Italian clientele.

For an Italy not yet aware of its own marble quarries, marble objects were particularly appealing. Candelabra, huge kraters with relief figures, elaborate column capitals, and columns themselves formed a large part of such exports, as we have learned from the Mahdia wreck. But statuary in the round with didactic, narrative, or epic character was also appreciated, indeed demanded for the creation of *ambience* in villa gardens and the atria of houses open to the typically Roman phenomenon of the *clientes*.[3] The establishment of private libraries was also important in promoting an appetite for images of appropriate poets and philosophers of the past—even when no such previous portraits existed. The demand sparked the imagination of the carvers.

The value of quotations to the Romans might have been minimized by the fact that few could have had direct knowledge of the models. It was more important to have something that looked Greek in style, whether Classical or Hellenistic (or even Archaistic and Severizing), with an *ethos* that might have trickled down through the centuries to acquire its own particular value in a Roman context.[4] Types, prevalent since earliest times (what, after all, better defines a kouros or a kore, even if each had individual meaning?), became highly diffused—another aspect of the phenomenon that had already produced stock (formulaic) bodies for honorary statues and gravestones. When epic or mythological content was involved, such types were drawn from a variety of sources, such as reliefs, paintings, and minor arts. Figurines, whether in terracotta or precious metals, and even attachments for vessels, could be and were magnified to lifesize proportions. The lively and more narrative, more realistic inventory of molded bowls and architectural friezes was mined for inspiration. I am convinced that two-dimensional representations provided a rich repertoire of forms and conceptions for sculptors who translated them into the third dimension. And if, in the process, some lack of depth, some reduced sense of volume, gave the complex figures the appearance of appliqués or works à jour, the effect came eventually to be regarded as a plus, one more form of that *trompe l'oeil* that was concurrently explored by the so-called Second Style of mural painting. Artistic eclecticism—a term that has carried a modern stigma—was highly practiced, not as a consequence of an exhausted creativity and a decadent taste, but as a form of aesthetic freedom, an emancipation from rules that pleased through its novelty and contrast.[5]

To be sure, it is impossible for us to tell whether a motif or concept originated first in the minor arts and was then appropriated by large-scale sculpture, or whether the exact opposite is true. The very same artifact can reasonably be viewed by dissenting scholars as either a source of inspiration or a reflection of a pre-existing composition, with a circular argument that cannot be resolved on available evidence. Yet when a *type* exists in two-dimensional form long before its extant rendering in the round, even the chances of survival cannot fully explain the chronological gap. Specific instances may be debated, but the basic principles of motif-borrowing and typological replication should be explored before the theory of an alleged (and famous) prototype being faithfully copied is formulated.

AMBIGUOUS SECOND-CENTURY MONUMENTS

The Slipper-Slapper Group, uniting a modernized Knidia with a Hellenistic Pan, has already been discussed among the dated monuments (Chapter 5). Since the prototype of the Aphrodite is known, we can theoretically state that the sculpture partly copies an earlier work; yet both rendering and conception are varied enough to rank the Delian piece with original creations.

An over-lifesize statue that has surprisingly dropped out of recent surveys of Hellenistic sculpture is the **so-called Juno Cesi** (Pl. 71), named after the collection that once housed it, now in the Capitoline Museum in Rome. It has alternatively been called a Pergamene original or a Roman copy after Pergamene prototypes, especially the so-called Tragoidia from the Pergamon Altar (cf. Pl. 22). Its voluminous drapery, the textured mantle rolled below the high-belted waist with long overfold forming a triangular apron, the deep carving of the folds that outline the forward leg, the many-layered, deeply indented sole of her sandals, bespeak the stylistic idiom of the mid-second century. The two variant positions could be reconciled if the statue is seen as an original in Baroque style made by an itinerant Greek artist for a Roman temple.

Plate 71

The Problem of Copies

The lack of a master's signature (although perhaps included on the now lost original pedestal) could be explained by the religious function of the sculpture, although statues of Iuno Regina in wood continued to be dedicated in the capital as late as the first century, and the lack of arms, and therefore of attributes, prevents a positive identification of the Cesi marble.[6]

A more difficult case is presented by the so-called **Borghese Warrior** in the Louvre, which some believe to be a Greek original carrying the name of its maker—Agasias, son of Dositheos, Ephesian—whereas others think that the sculptor signed as copyist, having derived his model from one of the Attalid dedications in bronze.[7] The situation is complicated by the fact that the statue was found at Porto d'Anzio, within the same villa owned by the emperor Nero that produced the famous **Fanciulla d'Anzio**—another monument often debated in terms of original versus copy.[8] In addition, the male figure is said to be in Pentelic marble, its sculptor signs as an Ephesian, and another work by him (a fragmentary base with identical formula and, apparently, letter forms) was found at Halos in Thessaly. That the signature in this case was placed on the pedestal rather than on the sculpture itself has prompted the suggestion that only pieces meant for export were inscribed directly.[9]

In this particular instance, despite its findspot, I tend to believe that the Warrior belongs still within the second century, but was made in fact for the Roman market; the pedestal in Thessaly confirms that this sculptor was active in Greek territory as well. It is unclear whether he was related to the Agasias, also of Ephesos, son of Menophilos, who for Tenos made two bronze groups (Nike, Eros, and Anteros) dedicated by Gaius Pandusinus within the sanctuary of Poseidon and Amphitrite around 100. This same Agasias, son of Menophilos, is also amply attested on Delos (ten signatures are sure and three more are attributable to him on good grounds); in addition, a Menophilos, son of Agasias, may be his father, since his inscriptions on Delos have been dated to the second half of the second century. It would therefore seem as if a family of sculptors from Ephesos (comprising both men named Agasias, although with different fathers) was active on the sacred island, in the Kyklades, and on the Greek Mainland, as well as producing statuary for export. It is perhaps significant that both Menophilos, son of Agasias, and Agasias, son of Menophilos, continue to use the ethnic definition "Ephesios," despite what must have been a protracted stay on Delos. Whether Agasias, son of Dositheos, was instead based at Ephesos remains unclear.[10]

Those who consider the Borghese Warrior a copy seek its bronze prototype in the victory groups dedicated by the Attalids in Pergamon, Delos, and possibly other Greek sites. Yet many have already recognized the affinity between the Warrior's pose and a lunging figure on the Amazonomachy frieze of the Halikarnassos Maussolleion. Indeed, the pose is almost standard in violent combat scenes; it recurs, for instance, on the battle side of the Alexander Sarcophagus from Sidon—the mostly naked man on the right half of the composition, holding the bridle of an Oriental rider's horse with his raised left hand.[11] But our comparisons are influenced by the strong diagonal view of the Louvre statue that seems preferred by most illustrations. That this was not the intended viewpoint may be shown by the plinth, recomposed from five fragments, whose front corresponds to the frontal aspect of the left leg and of the head, despite its strong upward tilt to proper left. From this angle, also, the inscription on the tree trunk is most visible, as well as the strong torsion of the body, otherwise not as pronounced. Hamiaux further points out that the oblique outline is at present enhanced by the lack of the shield the Warrior once held on his left arm, and by the restoration of the right arm, which is stretched out toward the back, whereas it could originally have been strongly bent at the elbow.[12]

Although this last comment is entirely appropriate, I suspect that the restoration is correct. *Mutatis mutandis*, the Warrior's pose strongly recalls a pattern highly favored in the Severe period—for instance, the Herakles fighting the Amazon on one of the metopes of Temple E at Selinous, and its probable prototype, the Aristogeiton of the Tyrannicides by Kritios and Nesiotes. To be sure, these images are flattened, as it were, for a two-dimensional view—the Herakles because of its true relief nature, the Aristogeiton because of the pairing with Harmodios. Yet the spread-out limbs are the same, and so is the limited compositional depth, surprising in the Warrior because of his pronounced torsion. He therefore fits well within the creations of the late second–early first century that, in my opinion, produced the Niobids in comparable poses. Somewhat similarly posed, although probably later in date, is the so-called Wineskin Bearer from the Blinding of Polyphemos at Sperlonga—another figure that may go back to a "type" rather than a prototype.[13]

These last-named statues differ from the Warrior in that one of their legs is raised onto a rocky elevation; what gives the Borghese statue its élan is the position with both feet on the ground, one leg frontal, one in profile, torso twisted on its axis toward proper right, left arm stretched forward in defense, head sharply turned toward an opponent presumably on horseback. The almost flayed rendering of the musculature is proverbial; the back is particularly impressive, suggesting that perhaps more than one view of the figure was indeed possible. The neck with its many creases contrasts with a small head that almost resembles fourth-century renderings. It has been called Lysippan, although we have nothing original by the Sikyonian master to go by, and the pronounced undulation of the contour from forehead to nose tip seems to me more typically Hellenistic.[14]

The scale of the statue—small lifesize—surprises at first glance, because photographs suggest heroic proportions. Were these reduced dimensions chosen as part of a group composition, with an enemy towering above on his/her mount? Nothing suggests nationality or context for the Warrior, so that even an equestrian Amazon could be postulated as his opponent, in keeping with the Maussolleion inspiration. It is more likely, however, that he was one of what have been termed single-figure groups (*Einfigurengruppen*)—works in which only one member is shown but a second is implied by action and context, requiring a viewer's imagination to complete the subject.[15]

The Problem of Copies

From this point of view, the above-mentioned comparison of the Borghese Warrior with one of the Tyrannicides may be illuminating. In that case, the two conspirators were rendered at the moment of their fatal attack, but the victim, not included, had to be mentally supplied by the knowledgeable Athenian spectator. In later sculpture, it is assumed, only the victims were shown on the Akropolis: the Gauls, the Persians, the Amazons, and the Giants of the Attalid Dedication. The Borghese Warrior goes one step farther in this imaginative direction in that it is impossible to tell, on present evidence, whether he is a victim or a victor. His next presumed motion could well plunge a sword or spear into the chest of a horse or even manage to dismount his enemy; on the other hand, he could succumb to a dominant force. This ambivalence seems again typical of the elusive, tantalizing conceits of the Late Hellenistic phases.[16] In conclusion, I can only reiterate my opinion that the Borghese Warrior is a type, not a copy, created in a Hellenistic mode and with spatial and compositional principles typical of the late second century, to serve a Roman market that was perhaps not yet defined in its nature, as contrasted with a specific commission. Ignorance of its intended setting may explain the various viewing angles allowed to the statue, where even the back of the plinth corresponds to an interesting aspect of the sculpture.

The issue of the intended viewpoint involves another monument attributed to the second century, either as a true original or an Imperial copy: the so-called **Farnese Bull (Toro)**, depicting the **Punishment of Dirke**. There is almost complete agreement in dating to the Severan period the extant marble group now in Naples, carved for the specific location within the Baths of Caracalla in Rome where it was found; yet one scholar has put forth a spirited argument for identifying the (now highly restored) sculpture with a Hellenistic work cited by Pliny (*NH* 36.34); another has strongly maintained that it is a Claudian copy, on stylistic and ideological grounds.[17]

According to the Roman writer, Apollonios and Tauriskos made Zethos, Amphion, Dirke, the bull, and even the rope, from the same block (*ex eodem lapide*). In Pliny's day, the group, taken from Rhodes (*a Rhodo advecta*), stood in the *Monumenta Asinii Pollionis*, a complex that has been connected with the *Atrium Libertatis*, to the north of the Forum of Caesar, erected by Asinius Pollio, a friend of Mark Antony, with the proceeds of his victory over an Illyrian tribe, the Parthini, in 39. The place contained several other works of art—many, if not all of them, dating from the Late Hellenistic period—until it was demolished at the turn into the second century A.C. to make room for the Forum of Trajan. The fate of its contents is not known, but technical details and general composition have been used to argue that the Farnese Bull is an adaptation of the Rhodian creation, made ad hoc to serve as a fountain within Caracalla's Baths. Alternatively, if a Claudian date is accepted, the early Imperial copy would have originally stood in a public place, perhaps the group of parks on the Esquiline supplied by the *Aqua Claudia*, or even the *Horti Tauriani*, named after the cognomen of T. Statilius Taurus, for which a bull composition would have been particularly appropriate.

I shall state immediately that I agree with those who date the sculpture in Naples to the late second–early third century A.C. Yet several problems remain: is it a true copy of a second-century B.C. original, or was it considerably modified to suit its intended location? Was there a single, Rhodian prototype, or was there also a Pergamene version? When did Apollonios and Tauriskos work, and were they "copyists" or original masters? I shall treat these issues in reverse order.

We have no information on the two sculptors except for the above-cited Plinian passage. In the same context, the Roman writer mentions another work (*hermerotes*) by a Tauriskos from Tralleis, whom he differentiates from an engraver (*caelator*) about whom nothing else is known. It is therefore generally assumed that Apollonios and Tauriskos were both from Tralleis, although active on Rhodes. Pliny adds that the two sculptors caused a controversy about their parents (although *parentum hi certamen de se fecere* may also be translated as "they gave rise to a competition of parents"), in that Menekrates appeared to be their father, while in effect it was Artemidoros. This passage has now been interpreted to mean that the style of Apollonios and Tauriskos resembled that of Menekrates, who could therefore have been assumed to be their father/teacher, whereas in reality another man was. Other scholars prefer to read the statement as spelling the difference between an adoptive (Menekrates) and a biological (Artemidoros) father. In either case, because of the presumed connection among Menekrates, Rhodes, and the Pergamon Altar, Pliny's text has been used to support a date around 150 for Apollonios and Tauriskos' activity, and consequently for their Punishment of Dirke. As we have seen, however, the notion of a Rhodian Menekrates at Pergamon is based on highly questionable evidence, and nothing excludes a later date (mid-first century B.C.) for the two masters.[18]

This is the position taken lately by Moreno, who believes the two copied an original Rhodian bronze made by Phyles, son of Polygnotos, of Halikarnassos, around 223. He thus sees Apollonios and Tauriskos in the same light as Hagesandros, Polydoros, and Athanodoros, the Rhodian sculptors who signed one of the Sperlonga groups—skillful copyists and adaptors of earlier Hellenistic compositions in another medium. The Sperlonga groups will be treated later in this chapter. For the moment, I shall only acknowledge the possibility that Apollonios and Tauriskos, even if active on Rhodes, belong chronologically together with the ("Neo-Attic") masters who made the other works assembled by Asinius Pollio in his *Monumenta*. I also note that Pliny does not mention the size of their composition; that it was colossal is only inferred from the Severan version, scaled to the Imperial baths, and from Pliny's admiration for the single block of marble from which it was carved. But his admiration may simply be due to the difficulty of rendering a rope in this fragile medium—it may also have been misplaced, as seems to have been the case for the Laokoon.[19]

Moreno's theory, based on his belief that two Hellenistic versions of the Punishment of Dirke existed, brings us to our second question. According to the Italian scholar, the earlier rendering, Rhodian, would have been donated to the island by the Halikarnassian master, who, in consequence, received from the city the title of benefactor (*euergetes*), as attested by his signatures after 223. The later version of the myth originated in Pergamon and was inspired by a painting. It occurred, in relief form, on one of the *stylopinakia* on the Temple of Queen Apollonis at Kyzikos, as mentioned by a Late Roman literary source; it was then adapted for Etruscan urns of the second century, and was known in the Kyklades during the first, since it was used as decoration for a cuirassed statue of Mark Antony on Naxos around 40.[20]

Since nothing is known about Phyles and his style, I find it difficult to accept Moreno's admittedly "hypothetical" attribution. A presumed similarity between the Farnese Bull and a pyramidal arrangement on the Amazonomachy Frieze at Halikarnassos implies no more than traditional compositional schemes. Indeed, the Farnese Amphion resembles also the naked Greek restraining a horse in the center of the Alexander Sarcophagus, already cited above in connection with the Borghese Warrior, and it seems plausible that the pattern of a horse-tamer should have been used for a hero restraining a bull. These comparisons have no true chronological or geographic value beyond their relatively early *terminus post quem*.[21]

The theory of two different versions is, moreover, based on minor differences in the various replicas of the subject known to us. As far as I can see, almost all could be reconciled through the need to adapt a three-dimensional version to a two-dimensional surface; in some cases, however, artists may have devised their own compositions for the retelling of a well-known myth, without necessarily having recourse to a specific visual prototype. The apparent support for a late third- or even a mid-second-century sculpture provided by Etruscan urns seems to me misleading: Moreno wants them dependent on his Pergamene version because they are somewhat different from the Farnese Bull, but three South Italian vases—the earliest examples of the topic within the extant iconographic repertoire—offer possible (pictorial) precedents for this unusual theme on the very soil of Italy, which eliminates the necessity to postulate Pergamene migrations of motifs and style.[22]

The impressive cuirassed torso recovered on Naxos is, as far as I can see, the earliest genuine echo of a specific sculptural group, which I concur in considering the work by Apollonios and Tauriskos on Rhodes, eventually taken to Rome. The apparently symmetrical arrangement of the two brothers on either side of the bull is demanded by the surface to be decorated—as Lambrinoudakis has noted, each man appears to stand with his rear leg on a loop of the *cingulum* tied around the waist, thus lending the scene tectonic stability. Yet dependence on a rendering in the round is shown by the omission of Zethos' left arm and one of the bull's front legs. Of particular importance is that Dirke on the cuirass is not reclining semi-nude, as in the Toro Farnese, but is fully dressed in transparent chiton (revealing the navel) and himation rolled around the waist; she is, moreover, kneeling in profile to right while grasping in supplication Amphion's right leg. According to Lambrinoudakis, this rendering is truer to the original composition, since it recurs in other examples, and it is the seated Dirke of the Naples group that deviates from the prototype. Although kneeling figures are known earlier (on the already cited Maussolleion Amazonomachy, for instance), they are prominent in the Pergamon Gigantomachy, and the Greek scholar would therefore accept a second-century date for the Rhodian group.[23]

The reclining Dirke of the Toro Farnese leads us to examine our first question: how close is the Severan composition to its Rhodian prototype? Kunze readily admits that the figure of Antiope standing behind her children must be an addition of the Imperial sculptor, and so must the *boukolos*—the young shepherd seated on the ground in front of the bull, a genre figure—together with his dog and the other animals carved in various levels of relief around the rocky pedestal. His analysis (*pace* Heger and Andreae) convincingly places all these elements within the tradition of the Severan period. Without them, the work returns to the core personages listed in Pliny's passage (and attested by the Naxian cuirass), yet Kunze argues for an original square arrangement of the group with a main viewpoint from the front of the rocky base. I am not so sure. The schematic drawing of the figures' placement (his fig. 16), without Antiope, reveals a major lacuna in the rear right corner, which to me suggests an intentional squaring of the composition to suit a central location accessible from all sides.[24]

It is instructive to note how fragmentary the Severan group was when found, and how extensively pieced together it is at present. Although the earlier restorers have been shown to have used unusual perspicacity in reading all available clues for the reconstruction of the figures in relation to one another, it should be emphasized that all heads (except that of the bull and of the "Imperial" boukolos) are modern, and that the Dirke is ancient only in a small part of her lap (with the beginning of her naked torso) and a stretch of drapery adhering to the rock between her widespread legs. Her reconstructed pose is surely correct, but even its alleged similarity to that of nymph statuettes of the Hellenistic period—which has been used to connect the prototype to Rhodes—is undermined when the group is viewed from a corner position that reveals Dirke's right leg to be almost in profile.[25]

The Farnese Bull seems therefore to be only a relative echo of the group by Apollonios and Tauriskos. To use it stylistically and compositionally to support a date for the prototype in the mid-second century appears methodologically unsound; in addition, comparison with the Ludovisi Gaul, the Pasquino, and the Laokoon increases rather than dispels the uncertainty.[26] At present, the original Punishment of Dirke in the round is best visualized through the Naxian cuirass. The torso has plausibly been attributed to a statue of Mark Antony, who controlled the island in the 40s. His image seems to have suffered a sort of *damnatio memoriae* and its base to have been reinscribed after 27 B.C., thus confirming its original identification. The connection between Antony (who styled himself the new Dionysos) and the god of wine is strengthened by a statuette once supported by the cuirassed figure's right hand—a Nike-like type plausibly interpreted as a maenad. Both the bull and the context of the Dirke myth stress the Dionysiac overtones so apparent also through various attributes on the Farnese group. Is this allusion sufficient to provide a chronological clue for the creation by Apollonios and Tauriskos?

It has been suggested that the presence of the topic among the stylopinakia at Kyzikos served to emphasize the filial piety of Eumenes II and his brother. But would a group in the round, outside the larger context of the other myths, have conveyed the same message? Even if the two brothers Zethos and Amphion were meant to symbolize the Attalid siblings, in isolation within the Dirke story they could only have appeared as avengers of a wrong and thus hardly appropriate for a donation from Pergamon to Rhodes.[27] Once again, we should note the scholarly tendency to attribute every important monument to Pergamon, maximizing the importance of a state that was, after all, only one of the players on the complex Hellenistic stage. I am, as usual, wary of seeking political implications in each rendering of an ancient legend, despite the obvious use of epic and myth by the Pergamenes to legitimize their dynasty. Should this ideological connection be challenged, one more possible chronological clue would be lost. At present, I can only assert that a Punishment of Dirke in the round existed by the 40s B.C., but this *terminus ante quem* is insufficient to place the prototype within the second century. Nor can we establish its style as typically Rhodian, Pergamene, or Karian.[28]

One final note on the Naxian cuirass: another interesting instance of a decorated thorax occurs on four statues from Tenos showing an armed Greek attacking a centaur. The scene is repeated four times with minor variations, especially in the position and rendering of the monster's head. The type of armor is Hellenistic, and the scenes recall not only the Belevi coffers but also (without cuirass) the duel on the helmet of the elderly warrior within the Pasquino Group. The fragmentary torsos (with cavities for separately inserted heads) are currently dated to the Julio-Claudian period rather than to the Late Hellenistic–Late Republican phase with a possible Claudian reuse, but the tradition of decorating cuirasses with mythological scenes has been considered earlier than the famous Prima Porta statue, and the Kentauromachy theme has been labeled typical of Tenos, where other examples occur. The Naxian torso (if correctly identified as Antony) seems to me to locate the practice within the Kyklades, and to confirm a date in the second half of the first century B.C.—a date that I continue to advocate for the original of the **Pasquino Group**. Since I have already discussed the latter in my previous Hellenistic book, I shall only update the topic by referring to recent research that provides additional pertinent bibliography and support for a late chronology of the sculpture.[29]

The use of rocks and elements of landscape within a statuary composition—as in the Farnese Bull—has been considered typically Rhodian, on the assumption that the islanders used their natural features as realistic setting for their art. An influential article by H. Lauter (1972) pointed out not only the many grottoes on Rhodes, but also statue bases shaped like rock formations, which he considered unique to the island. He suggested that veritable ancient pleasure parks existed, adorned with sculpture, and his opinion has been enthusiastically followed by other scholars, leading to the Rhodian attribution of monumental complexes like the alleged prototypes of the Sperlonga groups. Recent reassessments, however, have somewhat altered this picture.

Perhaps the "line of least resistance" is offered by the **rock-shaped statue bases**. Only nine examples are known, six of them unpublished, and they are limited to Lindos and Kameiros; used to support single statues, perhaps divine, those from the latter site were found within a sacred temenos. They usually present an irregular surface everywhere except for the bottom, meant to rest on an understructure, and the area smoothed out to carry the dedicatory inscription, whose formula indicates no special reason for the selection of that type of pedestal. The earliest base has been dated to the second half of the third century, and therefore the rock pedestals are taken as typical expression of the Hellenistic imitation of natural forms that includes the ship bases already discussed (Chapter 5).[30]

To be sure, several statues with a Rhodian provenience, verified or alleged, incorporate a rock formation in their composition—for instance, a reclining satyr adorning a fountain, a nymph presumably dipping her toes in a pool, the bronze Eros asleep on a boulder now in New York—but many others exist with similar devices and different origins: an Aphrodite from Kos with a small Eros perched on a stone pile learning to shoot the bow, an Aphrodite from Kyzikos with foot raised on a rock, and, among the Roman copies, the so-called Polyhymnia type of Muse probably at home in Asia Minor, and the female partner of the "Invitation to the Dance."[31] Many more such works could be cited; yet, admittedly, a statue base separate from the sculpture it held is different from these examples. Perhaps the convention arose because the intended dedication was to be in bronze, but the practice seems to have been limited and short-lived. Given the paucity of examples, the inattention to (and even the difficulty of identifying) such rock bases, and the wide distribution of sculptures with rocky ground required by composition, it seems unlikely that the Rhodian pedestals signify a unique Rhodian penchant for the exploitation of natural forms.

Even less tenable is the assumption that **ancient parks** existed on Rhodes. This point has now been extensively discussed by Rice (1995) in her analysis of grottoes on the akropolis of Rhodes. Although the latter may have been dedicated to the Nymphs, and certainly housed small votive sculptures and offerings in rock-cut niches, they were not dissimilar to cave shrines on the slopes of the Athenian Akropolis and other Greek locations, and therefore cannot be considered specifically Rhodian. As to the parks, she suggests that they are "a misconception based upon a romantic modern view of 'urban playgrounds'." Rodini, the most frequently cited example, was certainly an ancient cemetery and as such far from a pleasure park exemplifying a special love of nature. A rock-cut courtyard adorned with reliefs (now badly effaced) within the nekropolis of Karakonero is said to be unique on Rhodes and influenced by Alketas' Tomb at Termessos and other East Greek funerary layouts, thus belying a local tradition; a thorough study places it, however, within the context of the local *koina* and sees in the reliefs elements of Alexandrian art.[32]

The Problem of Copies

Similar warnings against visualizing major sculptural compositions in natural settings on Rhodes had previously been sounded by Rice herself and, even earlier, by Merker, with specific reference to the **Sperlonga groups,** yet in recent years two powerful voices have been raised in support of locating on Rhodes the bronze prototypes of the marbles in Italy: Andreae's and Moreno's. The first scholar would attribute to the Greek island only the Skylla/ship complex, which he dates around 188 and 168, filling the apparent gap between the Nike of Samothrake and the Pergamon Altar. The second scholar, however, sees Rhodian creativity behind all the Sperlonga compositions: prototypes for the Blinding of Polyphemos (accompanied perhaps by an Offering of the Cup), the Theft of the Palladion, and the Pasquino would date between 228 and 166, during Moreno's First Rhodian Phase; those for the Skylla/ship and the Laokoon would belong to the Second Phase, since they betray the influence of the Pergamon Altar, and date around 140. Literary and historical connections are offered for each suggestion.[33]

I find it irrelevant to discuss here the various theories surrounding the epic groups found in 1957 within a cave at Sperlonga, on the Italian coast near Terracina, south of Rome. They have been usually described as representing a cycle of deeds focusing on Odysseus, although other explanations have periodically been put forth. Since I believe that they do not fall within my intended chronological compass, I shall not analyze them in detail. I shall only list the reasons why the inclusion of the topic within this chapter could be justified, and state my personal opinion of the moment.[34]

1. The Sperlonga ship carries on its rudder box the signatures of three Rhodian masters—therefore, it falls into the same approximate category as the Borghese Warrior. Indeed, at some point after the initial discovery, some of the marbles from the cave were briefly considered High Hellenistic originals.

2. The style of the various groups reflects the Baroque traits of the Pergamon Altar: pathetic expressions, exaggerated musculature, straining poses, dramatic situations. It is therefore conceivable that they should be attributed to the same period that produced the Attalid Gigantomachy, albeit as later replicas.

3. Given that the extant signatures belong to three Rhodians, and that Rhodian participation in the Pergamon Altar has long been thought likely, or even preponderant, the temptation to connect possible prototypes to Rhodes is understandable. If, moreover, the grotto location at Sperlonga is seen as a more grandiose example of Rhodian naturalism and love of nature, the equation makes additional sense. I leave aside the postulated connections to literary works and historical events, since none of them is provable on objective grounds.[35]

These points can be countered as follows:

1. Signatures alone cannot prove or disprove the "originality" of a work of art. True creations could be signed by their masters—yet, at least in the case of the Doryphoros herm by Apollonios, son of Archias, the Athenian, we know that what we would consider bona fide copies could also rate a signature. Sculptors may have wanted to ad-

vertise their ability to provide casts or replicas of famous works, or they may have been proud of their own skills regardless of the greater or lesser degree of originality in their production. Indeed, plagiarism and personal styles are modern constructs that most likely did not apply in antiquity. In the case of the Sperlonga groups, I believe we are dealing with monuments only relatively dependent on specific models. Each composition was probably drawing on established iconographic patterns, but combined and adapted to the specific setting of the Italian grotto, thus ranking as veritable creations. As terra-sigillata vessels carried the stamps of the workshop that produced them without necessarily being by the hand of its owner, so statuary could carry the signature of the sculptural atelier that made it even if many more hands were involved in its execution. At the time of the Sperlonga marbles (probably around 30–20 B.C. by latest reckoning),[36] we are at the threshold of the great Augustan movement to embellish the capital, when master carvers would have been in great demand and Greek activity on Italian soil, already established during the previous century, was taken for granted.

2. By the end of the second century, every style was available to sculptors, who could choose what was most appropriate for their subject. Stylistic analysis alone is not an adequate measure of correct date; moreover, several points of comparison between some Sperlonga renderings and Late Republican/early Augustan portraits and monuments have also been suggested.[37]

3. Rhodian dominance on the Pergamon Altar has already been challenged, and so has the Rhodian alleged love of nature and impressionistic settings. That the makers of the Sperlonga groups, or at least of the Skylla/ship, were Rhodian "copyists" would still say nothing about the location of their alleged models, which they could have derived from anywhere in the ancient world—in fact, Moreno's list of Rhodian prototypes is considerably reduced by Andreae, who attributes most of the original groups to Pergamon. The suitability of the Sperlonga topics to Italian soil, where most of the adventures depicted were thought to have taken place, makes them obvious choices for an Italian commission, especially considering that some of them had numerous antecedents in Etruscan and Tarentine works.[38]

One important point about the Sperlonga groups is in fact the acknowledgment that similar iconographic patterns can be found in the minor arts of Hellenistic times. Those who consider them echoes of famous monuments in the round take such gems, seals, and relief ware as *termini ante quos* for the creation of the sculptures; yet the opposite argument is made by those who see in them the antecedents of the large-scale renderings, especially when the artifacts date considerably earlier (third or even fourth century) than the postulated second-century statuary originals. It is impossible to obtain certainty with this somewhat circular methodology (a sort of chicken or egg game), but I tend to side with those who emphasize the priority of the two-dimensional *iconography* that could have provided inspiration for more monumental, three-dimensional works.[39]

The Problem of Copies

A second consideration of possible importance is the fact that all sculptural works attested in Pergamon by the extant statue bases deal with commemoration of contemporary victories or with divine/mythological subjects—none of them, to my knowledge, uses themes taken from the Trojan epic. The earliest date at which such subjects can be documented in sculpture in the round is that of the Antikythera wreck, approximately the mid-first century, since its cargo contained at least two figures of Odysseus, recognizable by his distinctive pilos. Attalid propaganda used the arts to glorify the dynasty as the defender of Hellenism and to provide for it a legitimacy that was perhaps felt to be on shaky ground, as contrasted with that of the Diadochoi and their successors. Pergamene sculptural and architectural dedications, both at Pergamon and abroad, were *public* and royal, significantly rooted in the tradition of previous Greek victory monuments. Their inherent messages were meant to be read and understood by a great variety of viewers, regardless of their language. But the Sperlonga groups speak a different idiom: they focus on the adventures of heroes who fought at Troy and cannot be reconciled with the Attalids and their history; their almost *private* character seems addressed to a selected audience. To attribute their "originals" to Pergamon or even to Rhodes would require a leap of faith based only on a chain of modern attributions.[40]

In my current opinion, therefore, all the Sperlonga compositions can be considered original creations of the late first century, only generically patterned after Baroque forms. They are usually discussed in terms of an Imperial program, given the magnitude of the enterprise, and the Sperlonga villa has been linked to Tiberius and the first decades of the first century A.C. An earlier date, as now proposed, would eliminate that link, or at least would place the embellishment of the grotto among the luxury arrays of Late Republican private villas, as attested by the intended market for the definitely pre-Imperial Mahdia cargo.[41] One more work has, however, been recently mentioned to support the Sperlonga sculptures as Tiberian, or at least Imperial commissions: the so-called **Centaur from the Esquiline**.

This impressive head could have been treated in our previous section, because it falls in that ambiguous position of being considered alternatively a Hellenistic (Pergamene) original or a Roman copy. It was found in an area of Rome corresponding to the *Horti Lamiani*, or even the nearby *Horti Maecenatiani*, which in Tiberian times were Imperial property. Not only is it improbable that a Pergamene original would have been set up in that location, but the similarity between the Sperlonga sculptures and the centaur's head strongly suggests that they were all products of the same workshop and should be similarly dated toward the end of the first century B.C. I concur with this assessment, although the possibility of Tiberian ownership seems tenuous.[42]

Another statue found in the *Horti Lamiani*—the **Old Shepherd Carrying a Lamb** —gives me a chance to review my position on the subjects that I have called "**Old Destitutes**," especially since many of them have been attributed to prototypes of the second century. I continue to believe that the original of the Seneca Type may go back to the third century, but a spirited rebuttal of my mythological identification (Glaukos?) deserves to be acknowledged. The statue would depict a man who, despite his advanced age and weak body, pursues his goal of bringing offerings to the gods—an object to be viewed with pleasure and not with pity. Yet the image would not be a portrait of the donor, and thus would not follow the earlier tradition of linking the deity and the dedicant. It would rather provide the more affluent classes an opportunity for contemplation of a different social level, embodying perhaps an "ideal of innocence." I do not believe that earlier dedications necessarily portrayed the donor (honorary statues of individuals, even if set up in sanctuaries, are a different case because of their specific purpose and were usually erected by others), and I do not see any obvious connection between rulers and genre subjects, as implied by the theory. If an early date for the Seneca/Fisherman Type can be supported, I would still maintain that a cultic reason stands behind the choice of subject, making it justifiable on religious/mythological—not on social—grounds and explaining its widespread replicas.[43]

The chronological issue returns to the fore with statues of **Old Women,** whose prototypes have usually been attributed to the late third or, more often, to the second century. Here support for my theory that they may all belong to the Late Republican/early Imperial phase has come from a discussion of a head in a private collection at Oslo, dated to the Augustan period. In contrast to the statues of fishermen and shepherds, usually preserved in single replicas, this type of a toothless hag with head framed by voluminous folds is known through several variants linked by their wrinkled faces, half-open mouths, and variously covered hair. The Oslo woman's hairstyle furnishes an important clue, in that it can be matched in portraits of Livia, Augustus' wife; other examples within the group have been compared to male portraits, from which they may have derived inspiration. The new interpretation is based on the premise that statues of old women, when fully preserved, show details of costume and jewelry that bespeak a comfortable social position; they "are not 'have nots' or 'have beens' [but] are clearly among the 'haves' of this world." They depict devotees of Dionysos who exemplify the dangers of excessive indulgence and the consequent disorderly behavior, subverting the implicit role-model their age should make them. They could appear ludicrous but also sinister—a message that would not be lost on viewers of the early Imperial period who had seen Julia, Augustus' daughter, banned for her drunken and dissolute conduct. More important, from my point of view, the theory stresses the quasi-mythological character of these sculptures, an approximate counterpart to the intoxicated Herakles *mingens*.[44]

This interpretation also imparts a moralizing, didactic purpose to sculpture—which seems typical of Roman art. We have already mentioned it in connection with the Teos frieze, and we may repeat it here with regard to the **Young and Old Centaurs with Eros,** two works best known from the second-century A.C. statues in *bigio morato* (dark stone), once in Hadrian's Villa at Tivoli, signed by Aristeas and Papias of Aphrodisias, although several other replicas of the group are known. So far we have been dealing mostly with pieces extant in only one exemplar or at least in fairly close versions of a type. We can now review a few monuments that have come down to us in many close copies, thus proving that the "originals" were famous, or at any rate well liked. Yet this popularity should not be taken as indication of a second-century date — to the contrary. It may be the symptom of a society different from the Greek, one that saw sculpture as more public than private, more anecdotal than strictly religious in content, more appropriate for a wider variety of settings, and certainly more capable of being reproduced.

The pair of centaurs has been thought to copy a second-century bronze prototype, especially because of the "Pergamene" pathetic traits of the old centaur's face as he is tormented by the small Love on his back. But we have already seen that these stylistic traits are no longer sufficient to postulate true Hellenistic originals behind the Roman "copies." That centaurs in the round existed at the time of the Great Altar is demonstrated by its possibly akroterial figures and the examples from the Pergamene Asklepieion, but the conception of contraposing the young to the old, and the joyful potential for love in youth to the tortured frustration of advanced age, seems to me entirely Roman.[45]

An equally moralizing intent could be behind the original and some of the many replicas of the **Hanging Marsyas,** a work known through 59 reproductions in the round and at least two types, the so-called White and Red Marsyas. There is general agreement that these two types are not simply somewhat modified versions of the same original but go back to two different models, the red more often copied than the white, although some features of one type have occasionally been introduced into the other. The terminology is confusing as well, in that the Red Marsyas, so called because several of its replicas are in pavonazzetto marble, was also reproduced in white stone, and conversely the white marble of the White type may once have been painted, thus minimizing the difference between the two versions. Finally, it is unclear whether one type is earlier than the other, and if so, which. The Marsyas has generated a great amount of literature, but has fairly recently received comprehensive treatment, and I can therefore limit my comments to a brief summary and some personal thoughts.[46]

The satyr is shown hanging from a tree, his arms bound above his head, his musculature agonizingly stretched. In general terms, the Red type conveys the impression that he has already been flayed, in punishment for his hubris in challenging Apollo to a musical contest; there is more torsion to the body, the facial features are strongly asymmetrical, and the expression of suffering is more pronounced. The White type seems less pathetic and more symmetrically organized along a central axis, and its musculature appears less emphatic. Yet, as noted above, the types were occasionally conflated, and many replicas are either headless (thus eliminating an important clue to classification) or have been extensively restored after discovery, thus presenting possibly misleading elements. It is unclear which type was accompanied by additional statues: a Skythian sharpening a knife, in preparation for the flaying, and an Apollo enjoying the result of his musical performance.

Some scholars, connecting the Marsyas to political events, see it as a victory monument commemorating the so-called Elephant Battle of Antiochos I in 268; others read in it an allusion to the atrocious punishment of Achaios, who had tried to usurp the throne of Antiochos III and was executed in 213. They thus would date the composition to the end of the third century; still others, emphasizing its similarities to Pergamene art, place it in the second. For some, the White type is the earlier, and the Red is a more realistic reworking of the White, in Pergamene terms. Weis' sequence dates the Red around 120–80, and the White to the mid-first century A.C. Complete certainty is impossible, given the difficulty of assessing style, especially through copies, as often mentioned above.

More significant, perhaps, is the fact that hanging from a tree seems to be a typically Italic form of punishment. Although the flaying of Marsyas by a Skythian executioner, in the visual arts, goes back at least to Classical times, the details of the torture are not explicit, and the only *terminus ante quem* for the sculptural composition is a poem (*AnthPal* 7, 696) currently dated before 90 B.C. Weis, who initially made the Italic connection, has suggested a possible link to Sulla. I am uncertain about reading political implications in works of art, but I am struck by the fact that several monuments attributable (albeit debatably) to the first century B.C.—the Laokoon, the Farnese Bull, the Niobids, the Hanging Marsyas—emphasize divine punishment. Could the conquering Romans have felt the need to justify themselves as instruments of divine intervention? Conversely, although executions by Hellenistic rulers could be as barbaric as any mythological torture, the arts of the period were never fully explicit in depicting such horrors. In particular, I doubt that a flayed (or about-to-be-flayed) Marsyas would have been appropriate within the kingdoms of Asia Minor, whether Seleukid or Attalid, since the satyr was venerated by the Phrygians, considered a defender against the Gauls, and mourned there with reference to local topography. Roman iconography, by contrast, is noted for its brutal realism. In summary, I could accept a late second-/early first-century date for the Hanging Marsyas, but as part of that Greek production catering to Roman demand, and in that Baroque style that seems to have been preferred for tragic and epic subjects, no matter how removed in time from the Pergamon Altar.[47]

At this point, it should be noted how frequently certain works have been compared to one another, without any of them being able to provide a firm chronological anchor for all the comparisons. Specifically, in terms of facial features, the Giants of the Pergamon Altar are traditionally considered similar to the Laokoon, the dead Giant in Naples (usually thought to copy a figure from the Smaller Attalid Dedication), the Odysseus and the Steersman from Sperlonga, the older warrior in the Pasquino

The Problem of Copies

Group, the Centaur from the Esquiline, the Old Centaur of the pair mentioned above, and the Hanging Marsyas. Only the first item in this list is firmly attributed to the second century and can be considered "original." All the remaining monuments are either known solely through copies or, if no other replica is extant, may be dated to the first century B.C./A.C. If musculature is considered together with the pathetic and highly contorted faces, the Borghese Warrior can be added to the list. The key note resonating through all these works is the use of Baroque formulas to create emotional effects. This practice may be understandable for monuments with a mythological or epic content, but I want to end this review with an example that has usually been classified as portraiture.

A statue of the Cynic philosopher Antisthenes (lived ca. 445–365) was made (in Athens?) by Phyromachos, as attested by a reinscribed signature on a base for a bronze statue found at Ostia. The statue is lost, but the portrait is known through several herms, one labeled with the philosopher's name, from Tivoli, and another, unepigraphic, from Pergamon, which has strengthened the supposition that the Athenian sculptor who worked for the Attalids may have made a duplicate for the East Greek city. The complete figure has been reconstructed from a terracotta statuette found at Pompeii together with one of Pittakos, which, despite its scale, seems to have the same physiognomic traits as the herms. The figurine has been used by Andreae to connect Phyromachos with the Attalid sculptures, especially the Dead Giant of the Smaller Dedication, which he attributes to Attalos II, thus strengthening his chronological argument for the master's mid-second-century activity.[48]

In reality, the head of Antisthenes as we know it through the Roman versions has all the Baroque qualities of the various sculptures of elderly types we have listed above, although slightly less distorted than the centaurs and the Marsyas, but certainly close to the older warrior of the Pasquino Group and even the Laokoon. That Phyromachos made a statue of Antisthenes seems certain, but his "portrait" was at best over a century later than the lifetime of the philosopher and was therefore imaginary. Moreover, we cannot tell what his statue looked like, and the debate on the correct chronology of the master (or even his identity, given the many homonymous sculptors) prevents a stylistic assessment. As for the herms, I believe in their similarity to the terracotta statuette, but the latter has been argued to have been made, free-hand, to depict one of the Seven Wise Men, like Pittakos, and therefore cannot be used to identify the Cynic philosopher. The coroplast would have been using his imagination, patterning his product on a generic philosopher type, to supply the demand of his Roman clientele.

Could we reverse the situation and imagine that an image appropriate for one of the Seven Wise Men was later labeled Antisthenes by a copyist who had been requested to produce an image for which he had no prototype available? The very adaptable nature of the Baroque style would make the hypothesis credible, although unprovable. On the other hand we know that sculptors working for the Romans freely invented "portraits" of individuals who lived long before their time and were probably never immortalized by the Greeks themselves. I have long held this theory for the so-called Aspasia, Perikles' companion, and other similar cases can be cited.[49]

WORKS REFLECTING PLAUSIBLE SECOND-CENTURY PROTOTYPES

After this sweeping statement against recognizing second-century models in so many traditional attributions, can anything be salvaged for the sculpture of that period? My previous chapters have purposely concentrated on undoubted Hellenistic originals to dispel the notion that nothing can be known about Hellenistic sculpture of the middle century.[50] On the other hand, I have to admit that I am always uneasy about accepting as Hellenistic echoes works extant only in Roman "copies." In addition, I find it increasingly difficult to separate the production of the second from that of the first century, since so much material was then being made primarily to satisfy the Roman market.

Among the works generally attributed to the third–second century, although more recently downdated toward ca. 100, are several groups of satyrs frolicking with nymphs or hermaphrodites, and of Nereids and sea centaurs or other marine creatures. They belong to a world of Mischwesen and personifications that seems to have become highly popular toward the end of the second century. Proof lies in the subjects of the dedications on Tenos by Gaius Pandusinus (Nike, Eros, and Anteros), the Slipper-Slapper Group, or the Nymph being disrobed from behind by a Satyr, which, as appliqués, adorned a wall of the House of the Poseidoniastes on Delos. These all seem to cluster around the turn into the first century.[51]

A literary mention (Pliny, *NH* 36.35) tells us of a marble group depicting **Pan and Olympos,** struggling or wrestling (*luctantes*), which stood in the *Porticus Octaviae*, perhaps set up there in the 20s. It was made by Heliodoros, a sculptor thought to have worked around 100, and has been visualized in a composition of which the best replica is now in the Naples Museum. How faithfully this marble copies the original is difficult to tell: the head of the youth looks impossibly Classicizing, the "advances" of the goat-god (if "wrestling" is given erotic connotations) seem rather directed at teaching the youth how to play the shepherd pipes, and it has been suggested that Pliny confused Olympos with Daphnis, since Marsyas is usually considered Olympos' teacher. Other interpretations have also been proposed.[52]

The problem with the literary mentions is not as important, for my purposes, as the fact that the head of the Naples Pan (for that figure is Pan, without any question, regardless of his companion's identity) is remarkably similar to a **"relief" from the Mahdia wreck**. It too was an appliqué meant to be fastened to another surface, and its large size implies that it was for a wall rather than a votive plaque or a metope. It was found together with a similar piece, but rather than depicting a youth, this second head is that of a woman with a *Melonenfrisur*, probably a nymph. The composition would therefore be somewhat comparable to that of the other appliqués mentioned above, from Delos, which are in turn partly comparable to scenes on "Neo-Attic" reliefs and kraters.[53]

The date of the Mahdia wreck, despite some uncertainty, falls surely within the first half of the first century B.C., and some of the works within the cargo may have been as early as the previous century. The Pan head from Mahdia shows unquestionably that the type of the group in Naples was already in existence by the time of the wreck, in that it could even be combined with other personages into novel compositions. Pliny states that the "symplegma" by Heliodoros was the second best-known in the world; on the other hand, its fame might have derived from its being in Rome. The Pan of the Mahdia wreck suggests rather that its "prototype," or at least its "type," was available in the Greek world (Athens? Delos?) from which the ship sailed off on its last voyage. Its evidence serves primarily to confirm a late second-century date for this type of "genre," and to give further confirmation of the eclectic ways in which sculptors' ateliers performed.

I feel less confident about the chronology of other such "genre" works. The group of **Hermaphroditos Struggling with a Satyr** has been recently treated and its prototype dated after 100, partly because of its "flat" composition with one primary point of view. This same consideration applies to the Delian appliqués, the Slipper-Slapper Group, and the original of the Pan/Daphnis, thus lending some credence to this late dating, although, on these same grounds, one or two decades before the turn into the next century would also be plausible. To be sure, the Satyr/Hermaphroditos group has at least another valid viewpoint (the rear of what can be considered the primary side), but the truly suggestive angle is the one that reveals both the feminine breast and the masculine penis of the hermaphrodite, despite the fact that his/her body faces in the opposite direction. In fact, quite an impossible torsion of the human body and head has been demanded by the composition, which therefore shows the motivation of its maker — to shock and interest the viewer with his topic and to increase admiration for his carving skill.[54]

An intriguing aspect of the group is the fact that the struggle of the two Mischwesen results in an impasse. Although Hermaphroditos pushes away the satyr with his/her right hand on the satyr's face, he/she also twists his/her right leg so that it hooks the satyr's right leg, thus preventing the creature's escape. This arrangement may reflect the need to prevent breakage of the fragile marble, but it may also bespeak the ambivalence of the protagonists' mood and the uncertainty of their actions' outcome. A somewhat comparable pose occurs in the **Nymph Carried Away by a Sea Centaur** (Amymone kidnapped by Triton for Poseidon?), exemplified by a single group in the Vatican that once served as a fountain. Nereids riding sea monsters are known from Classical times, usually in the context of carrying the weapons of Achilles, but this is a violent scene, the kidnapper has the front legs of a horse, and two Erotes ride in the rear. The victim seems in distress, yet her left leg (restored) is hooked onto her aggressor's right. Is this again a technical expedient or a compositional device? The Vatican group has been compared to the Nymphs carried by Centaurs (*centauri nymphas gerentes*) said to have been made by the Tarentine Arkesilaos in the first century (Pliny, *NH* 36.33), but other dates have also been suggested, placing it almost contemporary with the Punishment of Dirke in the mid-second century. I have already expressed my doubts about this high chronology for the work by Apollonios and Tauriskos, and would be inclined to place even the Nymph/Sea Centaur in the early Augustan period.[55]

A **Satyr-Attacking-Nymph** composition is known in two versions: one that shows the female in the position of the Crouching Aphrodite with the attacker behind her—both at ground level—and another with the satyr sitting on a rock, the nymph almost upright and twisting against his left thigh and arm. In both cases, she pushes the aggressor away with her right arm by grabbing his hair—in the first group at the level of the temple, in the second at the top. Generally dated to the second century, the first type has also been labeled *nachhellenistisch* and attributed to the first third of the first century because of its single viewpoint; the second type has been thought to mark "the end of Hellenistic creations" at the end of the second century. Because both groups involve motifs and types known also singly or in different combinations, I hesitate to see them as anything other than eclectic, popular subjects much appreciated by the Romans and therefore incapable of precise dating, especially when only "copies" are extant. I can perhaps note that Pan and Daphnis, Marsyas and Olympos are still subjects grounded in specific mythology and thus suitable for public display, whereas a generic satyr grappling with a generic nymph widens the reference and becomes better suited to a private environment. If this distinction has any validity, these "anonymous" groups in the round may not be earlier than the first century.[56]

In summary, these "genre" compositions aim at creating a magic natural world inhabited by Dionysiac/Aphrodisiac creatures meant—I emphasize—for a Roman clientele. The cargo of the Mahdia wreck with its bronze Erotes, its relief kraters, and its marble tondi underscores the market's demand for such subjects. The line between Hellenistic and Roman becomes harder to draw, since in fact no solution of continuity exists between the two—only the purposes to which sculpture was put may vary. Even when invented and manufactured in Greece proper, to me these erotic groups seem most appropriate in the luxurious gardens of Roman villas like that of Poppaea at Oplontis (where in fact some of the types discussed above have been found), and their "variations on a theme" appear the product of workshops that could draw from a vast repertoire of established icons in the minor and even the major arts, thus making our stylistic analysis moot.

NOTES

1. For my earlier statements, see esp. Ridgway 1984. For more recent pronouncements, see, e.g., Landwehr 1990, Gazda 1995a and esp. 1995b with abundant refs., Bergmann 1995 (with

specific focus on painting), Fullerton 1997 and esp. his review of O. Palagia and J. J. Pollitt, eds., *Personal Styles in Greek Sculpture* (Yale Classical Studies 30, Cambridge, 1996): *Bryn Mawr Classical Review* 9.3 (1998) 265–71. The papers produced by an NEH Seminar on "The Roman Art of Emulation" in Summer 1994 are forthcoming. Hurwit 1997 takes a more moderate position. For the traditional approach, see, e.g., Moreno 1994. My own thinking has now been partly influenced by discussions with Mark Fullerton. The picture I am sketching is, of course, highly simplified.

2. On this point, see the important contributions by de Grummond and Steingräber, both forthcoming, with extensive bibl.

3. Various articles on this topic can be found, e.g., in Gazda, ed., 1991; Hellenkemper Salies et al. 1994; and two symposia held at Philadelphia, under the sponsorship of the University of Pennsylvania: "Roman Architecture: On the Villa" (April 21–22, 1990), and a symposium on Roman gardens (Nov. 18–19, 1995): see W. F. Jashemski, ed., *The Gardens of the Roman Empire I*, forthcoming.

4. On the issue of repetition and acquired ethos, see esp. Gazda 1995b.

5. Some of these concepts are also expressed by Himmelmann 1995; see esp. p. 53 for his definition of eclecticism, although focused primarily on the Augustan period. The literature on the two-dimensionality of three-dimensional works has a long history that cannot be summarized in these pages. See, most recently, Häuber, in *Hellenistiche Gruppen* [now 1999, 158–80]. I am grateful to Dr. Häuber for sending me her text in advance of publication. For stone figures to be applied to walls, see Marquardt 1994, esp. 332, for two examples from the Mahdia wreck and discussion of parallels from Delos (a satyr disrobing a nymph from behind), on which see also infra in this chapter.

6. Juno Cesi: the best illustration remains BrBr 359—note the press folds and the arrowhead patterns on the almost leathery mantle; for the sandals, see Morrow 1985, 173, 216 n. 7, and fig. 15 on p. 169 ("copy"). For the vicissitudes of the statue after discovery, see Haskell and Penny 1981, 242–43, no. 51. Bieber 1961, 119, considers it a copy of a Pergamene work like the Tragoidia; the entry in *LIMC* 4, s.v. Hera, no. 136, sees it as an original of the Pergamene Baroque from the 1st half of the 2nd c., and leaves its identification open, since arms and attributes are modern restorations. La Rocca 1996, 619 (and fig. on p. 618) calls it Pergamene, but does not exclude the possibility that the statue could have been made by "one or more artists who arrived in Rome with a victor." I had advanced a similar suggestion: Ridgway 1990, 357 and n. 12. For the Late Republican response to Attalid culture and art, see Kuttner 1995, although this piece is not mentioned. For wooden images of Iuno dedicated in Rome, see *LIMC* 5, s.v. Iuno, nos. 37–39, and comments on p. 855.

7. Borghese Warrior, Louvre Ma 527: Hamiaux 1998, 50–54, no. 60, with select bibl. and opinions ("ca. 100 B.C.? Asia Minor? Greece?"); the statue has recently been cleaned and consolidated, although some modern restorations were not removed: cf. p. 8 (A. Pasquier). See also: Donderer 1996, 100–101, figs. 13–14 (with discussion of the inscription on the tree trunk); Moreno 1994, 683–85, figs. 830, 834–36 (dated too late? early 1st c.; hints at honorary monument); Smith 1991, 53, fig. 54 ("copy after an original of 3rd c."); Stewart 1990, 224, figs. 110–11 (text places letter forms ca. 100; caption states: "Roman copy, original ca. 100–75."). Stewart 1979, 91 n. 25, mentions that Agasias signs the Borghese Warrior "as an *exporter*, not necessarily a copyist."

8. Fanciulla d'Anzio: Ridgway 1990, 228–30 and bibl. in n. 21 on p. 242, pls. 111a–c. For a rare view of the back, see Weis 1998b, 265 and fig. 26.18 on p. 268—which should confirm that the statue was made for the specific niche in which it was found. Cf. Moreno 1994, fig. 402; his text, 308–18 and figs. 395, 399–400, considers it copy of a bronze of the late 3rd c., set up (in his stoa at Delphi?) by Attalos I to honor a Pythia, Phaennis, who had prophesied his victories a generation before the arrival of the Gauls in Asia: Paus. 10.15.2—yet Paus. 10.12.5 implies that Phaennis was a prophetess at Dodona, not at Delphi. Smith 1991, fig. 110, labels it "copy of an original of 3rd c. B.C." Stewart 1990, 214, figs. 721–22, dates it ca. 200–150 (therefore as a Greek original), in "the richly declarative Asian manner." I continue to believe that the work was made in the Roman Imperial period, after the style of the mid-2nd c.

9. Donderer 1996, 100; for the Halos base, see Marcadé 1957, s.v. Agasias, son of Dositheos, 2–3, pl. 25.1, dated ca. 100.

10. Agasias, son of Menophilos: Marcadé 1957, s.v., 4–8 (Delos), 9 (Tenos), 10–11 (four signed bases on Delos further inscribed by Aristandros, son of Skopas, as restorer, presumably after Mithradates' sack in 88—but cf. Ridgway 1997b, 276 n. 46). See also s.v. Menophilos, son of Agasias, 73–74 (three Delian signatures). From whatever evidence is available, this Agasias seems to have worked both in marble and in bronze. Marcadé leaves uncertain any connection between Agasias, son of Menophilos, and Agasias, son of Dositheos, although he includes the latter in his book on Delian signatures, despite the fact that this master is not epigraphically attested on the island. If indeed the Borghese Warrior is in Pentelic marble, a Delian or an Attic origin, rather than an Ephesian one, would seem more likely. For the Tenos groups, see supra, Ch. 4 n. 57. Additional comment in Donderer 1996, 100–101.

11. Maussolleion frieze: e.g., Stewart 1990, 224, cf. figs. 532–33 (London, BM 1020); Moreno 1994, 684 and fig. 116 on p. 96. For the Alexander Sarcophagus see, e.g, Moreno, fig. 106 on p. 89; Smith 1991, fig. 226.2. I have chosen this specific example because motifs from this sarcophagus appear from Pella in Macedonia to the Phoenician territory of its owner, Abdalonymos, thus implying the wide use of pattern books. On the Attalid dedications and their inflated attributions, see infra, Ch. 9 and ns. 53–56; also Marszal, 1998 and forthcoming.

12. Preferred diagonal views: e.g., Smith 1991, fig. 54; Stewart 1990, fig. 811; even Moreno 1994, fig. 835, although taken mostly from the back. For the proper viewpoint, see Hamiaux 1998, fig. on p. 52.

13. For the Severe parallels, see Ridgway 1970, figs. 32 (metope from Temple E), 115 (Aristogeiton, Conservatory replica); and cf. fig. 28 (Borghese Warrior), there compared (p. 22) to the lunging Lapith on the Olympia west pediment. For the Niobids, see Ridgway 1990, 82–84 (there compared to the Borghese Warrior and the Wineskin Bearer), and cf. figs. 45–46. For the best illustrations of the Sperlonga statue, see *AntP* 14, pls. 10–13, esp. 10.

14. For a closeup of the Warrior's profile, see Stewart 1990, fig. 810; note that the right ear (visible in the photo) is entirely restored. The so-called Sandalbinder, also attributed to Lysippos but by me dated much later (with the Borghese Warrior), shows a similar twist of the neck, but seems to have a smoother facial profile, to judge from the extant copies: Ridgway 1990, figs. 40–43a–b.

15. See Ridgway 1990, 322 and n. 16 on p. 343 for ref. to the inventor of the term.

16. On the issue of whether victims were shown with victors, see supra, Ch. 5 and n. 45. Note that Moreno 1994, 684, considers the Warrior an "evocation of the military action in which

the protagonist distinguished himself." He suggests that a subject from the Maussolleion Ama-zonomachy was adapted to celebrate a Roman's military valor. The Warrior would therefore not be a victim, even if the monument were funerary/commemorative.

17. The monument (Naples, Arch. Mus. 6002) is called the Farnese Bull (It. Toro) because after its discovery in 1546, it was owned by the Farnese family in Rome. It was taken to Naples in 1789, and to its museum in 1826. It has been extensively studied in all its aspects: *Toro Farnese* 1991; see esp. pls. 10–23 for drawings of the original fragments, and the color-coded restorations of the 16th, 18th, and 19th centuries with their systems of assemblage. For a con-cise listing of the main restorations, see, e.g., Moreno 1994, 375. Cf. also *LIMC* 3, s.v. Dirke, no. 7 pl. 503; the entry's author (F. Heger) strongly advocates the identity of no. 7 (which he dates ca. 160–150) and no. 1 (the work cited by the Plinian passage); cf. esp. pp. 641–43. The most extensive discussion of the Farnese Bull is Kunze 1991, who supports an intended view-point from the front of the plinth (his pl. 2), rather than from the front left corner (cf. pl. 1), as proposed by other scholars (including Moreno 1994: see his fig. 476). See now also Kunze's 1998 monograph with catalogue of all known representations of the subject, and my extensive review of it in *JRA* 12 (1999) 512–20. For the original use of the Farnese Bull as a fountain, see *Toro Farnese* 1991, 62–65, figs. 55–57 (G. Prisco), disputed by Kunze 1998, 7, and 21–23, who attributes the related cuttings to Michelangelo's intended installation. That the sculptures gathered by Asinius Pollio were "Neo-Attic" in date is argued by Becatti 1960; cf. Isager 1991, 163–67.

The Claudian date for the Farnese Bull is championed by Andreae 1993, with many stylis-tic comparisons and interpretations; see esp. 129–31 for parallel manifestations and possible location of the group before its transfer to the Baths of Caracalla. The marble original by Apol-lonios and Tauriskos, given by Pergamon to Rhodes, would have been made between 165 and 159: cf. Andreae 1989, 242 no. 29 and 243 n. 5. Andreae 1996 is a more popular, more heavily historical discussion of his 1993 theories. *Contra*, Kunze 1998, 36–38.

La Rocca 1996, 624 (and fig. on p. 625), suggests that the Toro Farnese (the actual group in Naples) may have been executed around the mid-1st c. B.C.

18. Börker 1986 advocates stylistic rather than filial connections; he reads Pliny's comment as an allusion to a possible self-laudatory epigram on the work of the two sculptors, which he theoretically reconstructs (p. 44); see his p. 42 and ns. 4–10 for the ubiquitous earlier men-tions in scholarship of Menekrates as the adoptive father of Apollonios and Tauriskos. Kunze 1991, 24–25 and 33, accepts the idea of stylistic imitation promoted by Börker, and thinks that Apollonios and Tauriskos worked in the tradition of a famous master (Menekrates) of the pre-ceding generation. See, however, his n. 70 (p. 41), where he cites a signature in Magnesia (Kern 1900, 138–39, no. 213b) by a sculptor Apollonios of Tralleis, son of Tauriskos, datable to the 1st c. B.C./A.C. on epigraphic grounds. Kunze considers him a descendant of the Dirke master, several generations later, but the juxtaposition of the two relevant names seems striking. See also Kunze 1991, n. 72, and 1998, 78–80, esp. n. 345, against identifying Menekrates with the architect mentioned by Ausonius (*Mos.* 306–307), which may be an erroneous transcription for Metagenes. For discussion of Menekrates in connection with the Pergamon Altar, cf. supra, Ch. 2 n. 32; Börker 1986, 48 and n. 37, admits that no Rhodian is attested by the Pergamon Altar inscriptions, yet he assumes (49) that Apollonios and Tauriskos' works could be compared to Menekrates' in terms of colossal size and virtuoso handling of marble.

Andreae 1993, 109–10, rejects as speculative any connection with either Menekrates the architect or even Menekrates the sculptor, whom he believes to have been a subordinate figure in the carving of the Pergamon Gigantomachy, at a time when the Punishment of Dirke was also being created; but his main concern seems to be to defend his theory that the mastermind behind the Pergamon Altar was Phyromachos. Since Pliny mentions *another* Tauriskos as being from Tralleis, Andreae assumes that the two makers of the Punishment of Dirke were *not* from that city. To the contrary, Özgan 1995, 144, and esp. 147–51, discusses Apollonios and Tauriskos within the context of sculpture from Tralleis, but he adds nothing new to the traditional argument; he continues to consider Menekrates the adoptive father of the two masters, and suggests that Eumenes II would have called in the best active sculptors for the Altar, including the Trallianoi, as perhaps attested by a fragmentary signature (. . . ιανοι; pp. 146 and 151). He dates the Magnesia inscription (supra) to the 1st c. B.C. (p. 144 and n. 894).

19. Moreno's theory (1994, 372–79 and esp. 650–52) will be discussed immediately infra. He seems to imply that the Punishment of Dirke in marble was commissioned by Asinius Pollio, although the Plinian expression (*a Rhodo advecta*) may suggest forcible removal. The island was sacked by Cassius in 42; Kunze 1991, 17, thinks that the sculpture may have passed into Asinius Pollio's hand when his friend Mark Antony and Octavian divided the spoils of Caesar's killers, Brutus and Cassius, after their defeat at Philippi. For the meaning of *ex eodem lapide*, see Kunze 1991, 17; 1998, 42. See also *Toro Farnese* 1991, 61–62 (G. Prisco), with ref. to the Laokoon; it is there argued that the group in Naples was originally carved from a single, huge block of marble, perhaps in imitation of the prototype, but this statement can only reflect on the skill of the Imperial masters rather than on that of the Hellenistic ones.

20. Moreno 1994, 372–79 (Rhodian version), 493–94 (Pergamene version); he dates the Kyzikos temple ca. 166 (cf. supra, Ch. 4 and n. 10). Most of the monuments cited as antecedents of, or derivations from, both versions are illustrated by Moreno, but see esp. *Toro Farnese* 1991 and *LIMC* 3, s.v. Dirke (cf. also *LIMC* 1, s.v. Antiope). Phyles of Halikarnassos is attested on Rhodes by at least 15 signatures for bronze statues made between 250 and 215; after 223 he signs as *euergetes:* cf. Marcadé 1957, 89–97 (also two signatures from Delos, one from Astypalaia). Goodlett 1991, 676, states that Phyles never signed a base jointly with other sculptors, but her understanding is based on the absence of a linking καὶ, which, according to her criterion, connotes collaboration; Marcadé 1957, in fact, lists statues by Phyles next to others by Hieronymos of Samothrake (p. 98), Mnesitimos and Tleson (p. 99), and Ploutarchos son of Heliodoros (p. 100), all on Lindos. Moreno's attribution of the Punishment of Dirke to Phyles uses as corroborative evidence a base apparently of vast proportions found on Rhodes in 1977, but the monument is described (Kontorini 1980, 381 n. 6) as a group of members from one family for which Phyles produced (and signed under) five statues—quite different from a mythological composition. For Phyles' practice of signing individually under each of his contributions, see also Marcadé 1957, 92v–93 (base from Lindos) and 93 (base from Kameiros); the sculptor seems to have specialized in honorary portraits. For such forms of paratactic groups, see Merker 1973, 11 and 15 with refs.

Cuirassed statue of Mark Antony: Lambrinoudakis 1989. The armor was also decorated with other reliefs: Herakles struggling with the Nemean Lion, below the central knot of the *cingulum;* Dionysos leaning on a thyrsos, next to a panther, below a vine, on the central lappet; and an eagle grasping a serpent, below the right armpit. See also Kunze 1998, 86–88 with ns. 368–69, and, on the Kyzikos stylopinakion, pp. 74–77.

The Problem of Copies

21. Moreno 1994, 372; the quotation is from p. 374; see his fig. 474 for the Maussolleion slab (BM 1009) with a kneeling Amazon—her hair grasped by a Greek—reaching toward an approaching companion. Many other slabs from the Halikarnassos Amazonomachy use similar three-figured pyramidal patterns. Cf. supra, n. 11, for the man on the Alexander Sarcophagus.

22. F. Heger, *LIMC* 3, s.v. Dirke, 640–41, postulates at least three painted versions: one exemplified by the South Italian vases, ca. 410–400; a second, possibly a cycle, attributed to Aristeides of Thebes, in the 1st quarter of the 4th c.; and a third at the beginning of the Hellenistic period. The transition from pictorial to plastic would have originated with the Kyzikos stylopinakion. The Rhodian group in the round would have been a Pergamene royal commission. All three South Italian vases have recently been connected with Euripides' tragedy *Antiope* (Taplin 1998), but their different iconographic approach, perhaps independent from actual stagings of the drama, is recognized. I thank G. R. Edwards for this ref. See also Kunze 1998, 43, nos. 1–3, pl. 9a–b, and p. 47.

The same uncertainty about different prototypes applies to the much later (4th-c. A.C.) contorniates depicting the Punishment of Dirke: see Forsyth 1981, esp. 91 ("The designer of the reverses on the contorniates was obviously able to draw on several versions of this scene and may well have created his own composition"). Kunze 1991, 18, stresses that the Plinian group in Rome served as the basis for all reproductions of the theme in the early Imperial period (since most of them appear to cluster around that time), but he also cites evidence that other groups in the round (although perhaps patterned after the one in Rome) existed in Asia Minor during the 2nd and 3rd cs. A.C. See also Kunze 1998, 105–108.

The most frequently cited Etruscan urn (*LIMC* 3, s.v. Dirke, no. 8 pl. 504; Kunze 1991, 24 fig. 14) shows a *velificans* Dirke that seems to me quite different from other renderings and peculiarly "local," as well as incongruent, since the two brothers are depicted still harnessing the bull. Andreae 1993, 110–11, lists the Etruscan urns as the first replicas after the Rhodian (marble) prototype, but he seems to dismiss any representation earlier than ca. 150–130 as irrelevant to his subject. For a more extensive discussion, see now Kunze 1998, 70–73, pls. 16–17a.

23. Lambrinoudakis 1989, 344, and 346 respectively. His thoughts on composition and chronology are summarized on pp. 346–47; he advocates a single prototype in the round—the sculpture by Apollonios and Tauriskos—from which all other renderings derive; he admits, however, that a connection of the group's creators with the Pergamon Altar remains "in the realm of pure speculation." Andreae 1993, 124–25, accepts all of Lambrinoudakis' conclusions except those on the Dirke.

24. Kunze 1991, 21–22; 1998, 34 with n. 159, and 64–68. Cf. also *Toro Farnese* 1991, 43–46 (P. Zanker). Andreae 1993, 118–20, would accept the dog and even the boukolos (which he considers a personification, the god of the place) as part of the original composition, stating that it is better to assume one too many figures than one too few. He, however, agrees (121–22, 128–29) that the Antiope is an Imperial addition, meaningful within the Claudian copy because typologically patterned after the Venus Genetrix—the group would have emphasized Claudius' relationship with his mother, Antonia, and his brother, Germanicus. Andreae also stresses the squaring of a composition that originally may have had quite a different form.

25. Nymph figures: Gualandi 1976, 56–63, nos. 15–17, figs. 31–35; see esp. p. 60 for discussion of the Dirke connection. The type has been found elsewhere, as well as in Rhodes, so that an island origin is not assured. A catalogue of 11 items is provided by von Prittwitz und Gaffron

1988 (his Type 3, pp. 30–60), who connects the general image with Aphrodite but dissociates the Dirke from the group (p. 52). *LIMC* 2, s.v. Aphrodite, no. 879 pl. 87, also lists the type as depicting the goddess. Kunze 1991, 25, minimizes the value of the statuettes as chronological indicators; see also Kunze 1998, 80–82. Lambrinoudakis 1989, 349 n. 58, suggests that the Farnese Dirke might have been patterned after the Aphrodite type, rather than vice versa. Indeed, an Aphrodite type, if well known in the Hellenistic period, would seem a peculiar choice for a devotee of Dionysos, as Dirke is characterized by the wearing of a goatskin (original traces remaining: *Toro Farnese* 1991, 57 fig. 42). Özgan 1995, 150, accepts that the Rhodian nymph statuettes (dated ca. 150 or shortly after) provide a *terminus ante quem* for the Dirke group, which he places in the 2nd quarter of the 2nd c.

26. Cf. Kunze 1991. I shall briefly discuss his comparisons infra.

27. Andreae 1993, 125–29, provides additional meanings for a possible Attalid donation: Eumenes II had established in Thebes a sanctuary of Dionysos Lyseios, who would be recalled by the Bull in the group commemorating a Theban legend; Dirke (according to an earlier suggestion by A. Linfert) may have had the hairstyle of a Gaulish woman, thus alluding to the punishment of the Gauls by Dionysos, main god of the Pergamenes. See also Andreae 1996, 78–80, where the abundant hair of the "so-called dead Amazon" in Naples (considered a dead Galatian by Andreae) is compared to that of the Dirke on the Farnese cameo (his fig. 7). I find it even harder to believe that a female figure would have been used to symbolize the Gallic enemy; alternatively, the personification of Galatia, the region, would be unusual before Imperial times: cf. *LIMC* 4, s.v. Galatia.

Moreno 1994, 372–74, believes that the original bronze by Phyles (cf. supra, n. 20) was given to Rhodes in commemoration of the earthquake that so severely damaged the island in 227/6 (the bull being a symbol of the earth tremor). In addition, Moreno argues that the punishment of Dirke signifies divine meting out of suffering beyond the human sense of justice—again, an allusion to the consequences of the natural disaster. His position is criticized by Himmelmann 1995, 73, as an example of the new approach meant to lend flesh and blood to Hellenistic art history ("Man sieht hier sehr schön, wie die hellenistische Kunstgeschichte durch die neue Methode an Farbe und Plastizität gewinnt").

Kunze 1998, 83–90, stresses the "Victorious Rider" allusions of the composition, accepts the analogy Zethos/Amphion = Dioskouroi = Eumenes/Attalos, and, albeit tentatively, suggests that the original monument could have been set up in the Sanctuary of Dionysos by the Rhodians, to honor the Pergamene rulers as their defenders and patrons.

28. A similar opinion (an eclectic work of the 1st c. B.C.) is held by Himmelmann 1995, 33 and n. 59, with promise of a thorough discussion forthcoming.

29. Tenos cuirassed torsos: Queyrel 1986, 289–92, nos. 30–33, pls. 142–48; nos. 30 and 33 are more carefully carved than nos. 31–32; for discussion, and mention of the Pasquino, see pp. 298–302—however, on the cuirasses, the Greek uses his foot, not his knee, on the back of the centaur, and stabs him in the neck with his sword. The centaur raises his right arm as if to grab the weapon, but his fist is in front of the blade.

On the Pasquino: Ridgway 1990, 275–81, pls. 237–38; Himmelmann 1995, 13–19, 60–62, pls. 18–23 (different viewpoint suggested for the group: pl. 20); Weis 1998b and forthcoming. A contribution by D. Grassinger on the Pasquino and the Achilles/Penthesileia groups is in *Hellenistische Gruppen* [now 1999, 323–30]. See also infra, under Sperlonga.

The Problem of Copies

Although decorated helmets existed in Classical times, their ornament traditionally consisted of single items (owls, griffins, etc.); the use of mythological scenes may begin only toward the end of the Hellenistic period, together with the decorated cuirasses, thus helping to support a 1st-c. date for the Pasquino. I also would retain a similar chronology for the related group of **Achilles and Penthesileia** (Ridgway 1990, 281–83); for recent new evidence, esp. from Carthage, in possible support of an earlier date, and for arguments against it (after the Pasquino), see Himmelmann 1995, 58–60, pl. 27.

30. These rock bases were first mentioned and illustrated by Lauter 1972; they are now discussed by Schmidt 1995, 193–96, and catalogued (only three examples, pp. 538–40, figs. 197–99). The earliest base is signed by Mnasitimos, son of Teleson, member of a large family of sculptors (cf. Goodlett 1991, 675 fig. 3, 676); the offering (in bronze) was set up by the Demiourgos Hagesistratos, son of Hermokles, ca. 215. Smith 1991, 140, mentions that similar bases for bronzes have also been found on Delos, but he gives no reference, and I have not been able to trace them.

31. Satyr from fountain: Merker 1973, 29, no. 55, figs. 37–39 ("probably still Hellenistic"); cf. also *LIMC* 8, s.v. Silenoi, 1130, no. 219 for the subject as fountain sculptures, of which ca. 80 are known. Nymph dipping toes in pool: Merker 1973, 27, no. 13, figs. 13–15; see also the Aphrodite/nymph types on rock, mentioned supra, n. 25. Eros in New York: Ridgway 1990, 326–28, pl. 164; Mattusch 1996, 160–68, esp. 161–65, fig. 5.9 (no date possible). Aphrodite and Eros, from Kos (possible replica of the Melian A.): *LIMC* 2, s.v. Aphrodite, no. 632 pl. 62 (dated late Hellenistic–1st c. B.C.; cf. the same rocky rendering on two ring bezels, nos. 634–35, dated to the 3rd c.); Kyzikos Aphrodite: *LIMC* 2, s.v., no. 647 pl. 63 ("Hellenistic"), and cf. Merker 1973, 26–27, no. 12, figs. 9–12 (many other examples of the type exist). Polyhymnia type: Ridgway 1990, 257, 262, pls. 134–35; cf. also supra, Ch. 6, under "Votive Reliefs." Invitation to the Dance (if such a group ever existed): Ridgway 1990, 321–24; Kell 1988, 14–20, fig. 1 (dated shortly before mid-2nd c.); Smith 1991, 130, figs. 157.1–4 ("3rd–2nd c."); *LIMC* 8, s.v. Nymphai, 895, nos. 39 (coin) and 40 pls. 591–92 (dated end of the 3rd/2nd c., after original by Doidalsas). See also infra, n. 53. [Now W. Geominy, *Hellenistische Gruppen* 1999, 141–55.]

32. Rice 1995: the quotation is from p. 403; see esp. 402–404 on the function of the Rhodian grottoes, and n. 46 for a rebuttal of Lauter's 1972 theories; cf. also p. 399 and n. 24 for Greek cave shrines. On the Karakonero courtyard, see Moreno 1994, 361 fig. 454 (called a tomb). The most extensive study is by Guldager Bilde 1999, who interprets the scenes as the Return of Hephaistos, centering on Dionysos; I am grateful to her for sending me proof of her article before publication (her paper was delivered in 1994). The rock-cut reliefs include elements attached separately and areas completed in stucco. For a brief mention with reference to Alketas' Tomb, see E. E. Rice, "A Sculptured Funerary Precinct from Hellenistic Rhodes," Abstract, *AJA* 101 (1997) 374. For Alketas' Tomb, see, e.g., Ridgway 1990, 36–37, with refs. For rock-cut niches and reliefs on the Athenian Akropolis, see, e.g., Ridgway 1997b, 197–99 and n. 22 on p. 224.

33. Earlier warnings: Rice 1986, and cf. 1995, 400 n. 34; Merker 1973, 24 n. 90; now also Himmelmann 1995, 36. The bibl. on Sperlonga has become enormous, but for a specific expression of chronological viewpoints and attributions of prototypes, see, e.g., Andreae 1989, 241, and in *Ulisse* 1996, 298–315, 362–64. Moreno 1994, 359–64 and figs. 454–58, defends the idea of Rhodian love of nature and illustrates grottoes on the akropolis of Rhodes; for the

attribution of monuments to the First Phase, see 379–85 (Pasquino), 385–87 (Theft of Palladion), 391–95 (Offering of the Cup to Polyphemos), 395–405 (Blinding of Polyphemos). For attribution of the Skylla/ship to the Second Phase, see Moreno 1994, 613–24.

The **Laokoon** should be discussed together with the Sperlonga groups, since it was obviously carved by the same sculptors who signed the Skylla/ship composition. I shall not enter into its problems, however, because they are similar to those of the Sperlonga marbles and have been treated in the same literature; see, most recently, Kunze 1996b, esp. 139–52. I would accept the Laokoon as an original creation (after earlier motifs) of the late 1st c. B.C. or somewhat later. See also Pollitt, forthcoming, and comments on "epic" compositions, infra, n. 40.

34. For a brief account of the Sperlonga sculptures, see, e.g., Smith 1991, 110–11, figs. 144–47. A great deal of information on various published viewpoints on the subject can be found in Himmelmann 1995 and Weis 1998a and 1998b. See also de Grummond, forthcoming, where a strong defense for a possible Italic background to some of the myths and compositions is provided.

35. For instance, Andreae has repeatedly suggested that the Skylla group was originally set up on Rhodes as a memorial to those who had lost their lives fighting against the pirates. The Rhodians were indeed active within the Aegean against Cretan and other piratical forces, but earlier—during the 3rd c. The 2nd c., by contrast, saw a retrenching of their efforts and a loss of their effectiveness: cf. Berthold 1984, passim and esp. 223–25 (Diod. 31.38). Other Rhodian commemorative monuments seem to have had a non-mythological appearance: cf. supra, Ch. 5, ns. 22 and 34. The *Alexandra* by Lykophron is too vague in its allusions to be connected with actual sculptures, *pace* Andreae. That the Sperlonga ship is a trihemiolia can be debated, and its type may, at any rate, have no corroborating value: see the controversy about the Samothrakian ship, Ch. 5. See also infra, n. 40, on "epic" groups and their chronology.

36. Latest chronological assessment, based on the type of masonry employed within the Sperlonga cave: Kunze 1996b, but see also the points made by Weis, forthcoming. A paper by V. M. Strocka, on the dating of the Sperlonga groups, is in *Hellenistische Gruppen* [now 1999, 307–22]. On possible iconographic prototypes for the Sperlonga sculptures (mostly in the minor arts), see Himmelmann 1995. Comparison with relief ware may extend even to the practice of using originally unrelated motifs to create new meaningful combinations. For an example of contacts between media, see supra, Ch. 3 n. 32 (Samos frieze). Doryphoros herm signed by Apollonios: e.g., Stewart 1990, 230, figs. 380–81.

37. See, e.g., Kunze 1996b, 204–21, figs. 23–26, 35–43.

38. Cf. *Ulisse* 1996, passim. This last point is properly developed by two forthcoming papers of the Langford Conference: Weis and de Grummond. See also Steingräber, forthcoming, for a summary of alleged Pergamene influences on Etruscan artifacts. Should Pergamon be considered the true inspiration behind (some of) the Sperlonga groups, it would be difficult to tell whether such input came directly or was mediated by Etruria. The irrelevant ethnic of the "copyists" is stressed also by Pollitt, forthcoming.

39. Minor arts as echoes: e.g., *Ulisse* 1996, passim (B. Andreae). Minor arts as inspiration: e.g., Himmelmann 1995. See Weis 1998a, and Ridgway, *BJb* 197 (1997, publ. 1999) (both reviewing Himmelmann 1995).

40. For the point on the propaganda purposes and tone of the Attalids, see Gruen, forthcoming. The distinction I am making is between mythological heroes, such as Herakles or even the

The Problem of Copies

Dioskouroi, whose parents were actual gods, and epic heroes known through the *Iliad* and the *Odyssey*, who are at present sculpturally attested only for the Italian market. Interest in the Homeric poems may be said to begin with Archelaos of Priene and the "Apotheosis of Homer" relief, but even this work, in my opinion, can be connected with a Roman commission (see supra, Ch. 6). Perhaps a revival of interest in the Trojan roots of the Romans during the Late Republican period is responsible for the phenomenon.

It could be argued that Agamemnon and Achilles appear on the Telephos Frieze, but they are not seen in the context of the Trojan War, and the whole narration centers on Telephos, Herakles' son and ancestor of the Attalids, in keeping with other propaganda messages. The Pasquino, the Achilles/Penthesileia, the Laokoon, are only "Pergamene" by inference and stylistic attribution, not by hard evidence. In addition, my emphasis is on *free-standing* statuary, since Trojan themes may have appeared in architectural sculpture as early as 5th-c. Athens (Ilissos, Nike Temple, and Hephaisteion friezes), are well known for the 4th, and during the Hellenistic period seem attested for the Athenaion at Ilion and the Smintheion at Chryse.

41. For a Tiberian possession (the *Praetorium Speluncae*), see esp. Andreae's writings, as cited in *Ulisse* 1996, passim; this author would read the entire sculptural program in the light of Tiberius' ancestry and ideological connections. The identification of the villa is accepted, albeit with some reservation, by Himmelmann 1995, 54–55. It is rejected (together with a Tiberian program), also in view of the Antikythera cargo, by Kunze 1996b, 160–65; see esp. ns. 67, 72, 82. Hafner 1996 holds an intermediate position: an Imperial villa, but not Tiberius'.

42. Centaur head: Rome, Conservatori Museum no. 1137, over-lifesize. The Imperial findspot is stressed by Himmelmann 1995, 63–65, who adds (p. 73) that a 1995 unpublished manuscript by E. La Rocca reached similar conclusions vis-à-vis the Sperlonga sculptures and the Laokoon. Himmelmann in turn supports the connection (previously noted by Hecht 1956, 138–39, figs. 1–8, when the Polyphemos was still in a private collection) between the frontal view of the centaur's head and that of the Polyphemos head in Boston (cf. his pls 28–29), although the similarity disappears in profile (pls. 30–31). The Boston Polyphemos is said (Himmelmann 1995, p. 65) to be a Trajanic work, perhaps copying hair patterns of a "Homeric" composition of Late Republican date. For the similarity between the centaur and the Odysseus of the Polyphemos Group at Sperlonga, see his pls. 32–33. Moreno 1994, 405–407, figs. 515, 517, 586, identifies the Esquiline centaur with the "Cheiron teaching Achilles" cited by Pliny, *NH* 36.29, as being in the *Saepta*, and by the Italian scholar considered a marble copy (by the Sperlonga workshop) of a Rhodian bronze original contemporary with the Pergamon Altar. This identification had previously been advanced and refuted. For a discussion of scholarly opinions on the Esquiline head, see the thorough summary in Häuber 1986: that the head belonged to a centaur is suggested by its pointed, equine ears, but a human leg was also found with it and the piece could therefore depict a giant. For another illustration of the work, cf. Smith 1991, fig. 164 ("copy after an original of c. 200 B.C.").

43. For my previous position, see Ridgway 1990, 332–38, esp. 333 and n. 34 for the Old Shepherd from the *Horti*, and 334–36, pl. 173, on the Seneca/Fisherman; the article by C. Häuber announced there in my n. 35 is now being developed into a monograph, but see a mention, by the same author, in Jashemski, ed. (forthcoming, supra n. 3), where she pinpoints the Roman findspot of the statue in the Louvre and tentatively connects it with one of the sanctuaries there or with Seius Strabo's private art collection. The Fisherman has also been discussed, within

its wider context, by Moreno 1994, 345–50, figs. 437–39, 444; attributed to Alexandrian realism, the type is visualized as standing in a pool. For the rebuttal of my mythological theory,
see Völker-Janssen 1993, 229–59, esp. 233 n. 23, in an essay titled "Überlegungen zu einer
höfischen Funktion hellenistischer Genredarstellungen." The author seems to believe in great
nature parks of the Hellenistic period (at Alexandria, Antioch-Daphne, Rhodes) where such
statues may have been displayed with a social function (cf. p. 249), because too many replicas
of the Seneca Type exist to suggest location of the original in a private garden; n. 47 makes
the important point that no fisherman is ever shown fishing while standing—indeed, other ancient examples are in a sitting position. Somewhat the same point (genre statues dedicated by
the wealthy elite) is made by Smith 1991, 138–39; the Seneca/Fisherman (fig. 179) is labeled
"copy of an original of c. 200 B.C.," and its 17 replicas are considered extraordinary.

44. Sande 1995; the quotation is from p. 44, the comparison to the urinating Herakles on pp.
45 and 47. For a tentative chronology, see p. 43: "Myron's old woman" is dated ca. 100 or a little
later, as the earliest example of the "Old Hag" type; others belong in the last quarter of the
1st c. (including the "Old Market Woman" in the Metropolitan Museum), while the rest could
copy originals from that period or "works from the 1st–2nd centuries A.D. based more loosely
on earlier models." For illustrations of the above-mentioned types, see Smith 1991, figs. 174–
76 (considered copies of 3rd–2nd-c. originals). For the intoxicated Herakles, see *LIMC* 4, s.v.
Herakles, nos. 875–910 pls. 504–506. Amedick 1995, on the other hand, believes that the type
of the old woman originated in the Hellenistic period as a counterpart to bucolic literature, but
was adapted in Roman times to many contexts, including mythological (divine nurses), sacrificial, and ritual (festivals). Additional refs. to Myron's Hag in Meyer 1996a, 96, n. 33 (dated
3rd c.); for a short monograph, see Zanker 1989.

45. Centaurs at the Great Altar: supra, Ch. 2 n. 81; cf. also Ridgway 1990, 324–26. Centaurs
on the Teos frieze and the Berthouville scyphi: supra, Ch. 4 ns. 22 and 25. Young and Old Centaurs: Smith 1991, 132, figs. 161–63; *LIMC* 8, s.v. Kentauroi et Kentaurides, p. 719, no. 483 pl.
479 (comments on p. 721), listed among Centaurs in Roman art, but related to no. 303 p. 697
(comments on p. 706), prototype for the group, dated 1st half of 2nd c., by comparison with a
bronze statuette in Boston, MFA, with traces of attachment for Eros on shoulder: no. 304 pl.
451 (from a stand or an item of furniture, dated 2nd c.). For Pergamene originals in bronze, see
Bieber 1961, 140–41, figs. 581, 583–84; she stresses the similarity between the young centaur's
face and that of the "Fauno colla Macchia" in Munich (her fig. 582). To my mind, this comparison proves the general adaptation of types from one "monster" to another, thus virtually
belying precise copying from a specific original. Bronze originals are postulated on the dark
marble of the (heavily restored) replicas from Tivoli, but Roman choice of colored stone seems
to have been unsystematic: cf. Weis 1992, 21 n. 36. Kell 1988, 29–30, figs. 4, 7, has a different
theory: only the Old Centaur goes back to the 2nd half of the 2nd c. or, more precisely, the
beginning of the last third; the Young Centaur would have been created in Roman times; but
his grounds are purely compositional and stylistic.

46. Hanging Marsyas: most extensively, Weis 1992, with list of all replicas and rich bibl.; also
LIMC 6, s.v. Marsyas, no. 61a(red)–b(white), pl. 192, and comments on pp. 376–78 (A. Weis).
A third type (no. 62), made to look earlier than Hellenistic (Severe) is considered a 2nd-c. A.C.
recasting. Smith 1991, 106–107, mentions a much more limited number of copies, and reverses
the proportion of red to white replicas, but he also summarizes possible political implications;
his figs. 135a–b show two replicas of the Marsyas, and fig. 136 gives the single known copy in

the round of the Skythian slave (the so-called Arrotino, Italian for knife-sharpener), although a now lost second replica is known to have existed: cf. Weis 1992, 3 n. 9, and 47–56 for its connection with a Marsyas type and a Roman date. The Apollo type is much less clearly defined. See also Moreno 1994, 240–44 (White Marsyas and Arrotino), figs. 307–10, 312, 314; 671–72 (Red Marsyas), figs. 810–14, 816.

Meyer 1996a discusses a table leg with Marsyas and Skythian, said to be from the Philadelphia area near Mount Tmolos, but considered "modern?" by Weis 1992, 211–12, no. 57. Meyer revisits his previous positions, summarizes latest opinions, and sees the White Marsyas, in group with the Arrotino, as a possible victory monument celebrating Antiochos I Soter's victory over the Galatians (with Marsyas representing the barbarians), and dating before the mid-3rd c.; the Red Marsyas would date ca. 100 years later; for additional "replicas" see his pp. 118–19. He distinguishes the two types by the binding of the wrists — together for the Red Type, separately for the White, resulting in arms spread farther apart, but this detail is most often missing in the replicas. My acceptance of a 3rd-c. date (1990, 335) refers to the Seneca Fisherman, *not* to the Marsyas, as cited by Meyer 1996a, 97 and n. 48. A paper on the "flayed" Marsyas, by C. Maderna-Lauter, is in *Hellenistische Gruppen* [now 1999, 115–40].

47. Punishment of Achaios: the theory, by Fleischer 1972–75, is followed, e.g., by Smith 1991 and Moreno 1994 (see supra, n. 46) for the White Marsyas, which they regard as earlier. Pollitt 1986, 118–19, is one of the scholars who would date to the 2nd c. and connect to Pergamon; Meyer 1996a, 110, considers this possibility, but prefers Antiochos I and the mid-3rd c. For a full review of previous opinions, see Weis 1992. That the Red Type was earlier than the White was first suggested by Borbein 1973. For the Marsyas myth in Classical art, see, e.g., the Mantineia Base: *LIMC* 6, s.v. Marsyas I, no. 24 pl. 187; Ridgway 1997b, 206–209 (and cf. Herod. 7.26). The connection with an Italic form of punishment is made by Weis 1982; cf. Weis 1992, 66–73 for a link between the composition and Sulla; 107–11, for the origin of the White Type in the Maiandros Valley. Yet the same author, in *LIMC* 6, s.v. Marsyas I, 377–78, states that the evidence for attributing to the sculpture political or symbolic meaning, as well as specific dates, is "circumstantial." That Marsyas was venerated by the Phrygians is also pointed out by Smith 1991, 106–107, who cites Paus. 10.30.9 for the satyr's defense against the Gauls (which would make an Attalid or even a Seleukid monument implausible); yet he accepts the Achaios theory. The emphasis on subjects of "Divine Punishment" in (late) Hellenistic sculpture has been noted by R. R. R. Smith, review of B. Andreae, *Laokoon und die Gründung Roms*, in *Gnomon* 63 (1993) 351–58.

48. Antisthenes, by Phyromachos: Andreae 1980, dated 1st half 2nd c.; this date is narrowed down (168–156) by Andreae 1989, 241. Himmelmann, in Andreae et al., 1990, 13–23, believes the statue was by a 4th-c. Phyromachos; other scholars have variously dated the Hellenistic sculptor (see supra, Ch. 7 n. 10). The Antisthenes is discussed by Smith 1991, 36, fig. 34 (inscribed herm from Tivoli, dated "later 3rd c."); Moreno 1994, 203–205, figs. 265, pp. 268–71, figs. 335, 343, 562 (the last, the replica from Pergamon; see p. 204 for the theory of bronze duplicates in Athens and in Mysia) with chronology based on Phyromachos' work for Attalos I (see also infra, n. 49); Schefold 1997, 168–71, figs. 78a–c (bibl. on pp. 502–503), and 280–81 fig. 161, for the terracotta statuette from Pompeii, dated ca. 75 A.C. (bibl. on p. 524). Andreae 1990, 80–81, pls. 44–46, would date the terracotta ca. 100 B.C. But cf. Koch 1993 for the value of the figurine.

49. Herm of Aspasia, in the Vatican Museum: Ridgway 1981, 240–41. I understand that a

date in the 1st c. B.C. and a Roman purpose have been proposed by S. Sande, "Die Aspasia-Herme und verwandte Bildnisse," in *Ancient Portraiture: Image and Message* (Acta Hyperborea 4, Copenhagen 1992) 43–58 (*non vidi*). For another possible example of "Roman" imagination in portraiture, see Ridgway 1998 (the Anakreon). The Pergamon replica of the Antisthenes, found with other portraits of philosophers and one of Euripides, was dated by the excavators to the late Hadrianic or early Antonine period; since all other known copies of that portrait cluster within Italy, it is likely that its model stood there and was furnished to Pergamon by Italian workshops: cf. Ridgway 1984, 98 and n. 7.

50. I avoid the term "mid-Hellenistic," which means different things to different authors. I simply mean the span 200–100.

51. Tenos dedications: supra, n. 10, and ch. 4 n. 57. Slipper-Slapper Group: supra, Ch. 5 n. 12. Delian appliqués: supra, n. 5; for the nymph, see also Havelock 1995, 57 (erroneously called a fragmentary statuette) fig. 14; *LIMC* 8, s.v. Nymphai, 895 no. 49a pl. 594 (with one Neo-Attic comparison).

52. The situation is made more confused by another Plinian mention (*NH* 36.29) of a marble group by uncertain master that was a counterpart to Cheiron teaching Achilles in the *Saepta Iulia* (cf. supra, n. 42): Pan and Olympos. It has been suggested that this second group showed instead Marsyas and Olympos, whereas Pan and Daphnis were depicted in the group within the Porticus Octaviae. Others would consider both groups mentioned by Pliny as depictions of Pan and Daphnis. See *LIMC* 3, s.v. Daphnis, no. 7 (mention of Saepta group) and no. 8 pl. 261 (Naples group, dated ca. 120), but cf. *LIMC* 7, s.v. Olympos I, no. 39 (Saepta group = Daphnis, no. 7) and no. 40 (= Daphnis, no. 8). Both entries include bibl. See also Marquardt 1994, 331 and ns. 27–28 (Pan and Daphnis in Naples copy the work by Heliodoros). A full discussion of all the replicas (18 at large scale, of which six are complete) and single reproductions and adaptations of the Pan/Daphnis group is in Marquardt 1995, 182–206, pls. 19–20.1–2 (cf. p. 198 for Pliny's mistakes—in Saepta, it should be Marsyas instead of Pan; in Porticus Octaviae it should be Daphnis instead of Olympos—and p. 202 on unclear meaning of *luctantes*); the Mahdia piece is mentioned only on p. 207 n. 106, within a list of imitative works; the original (by a Rhodian Heliodoros?) is dated ca. 100 or just after the turn of the century, on compositional and stylistic grounds (*Kopienkritik*). Häuber forthcoming (supra, n. 5) would accept a *bronze* Marsyas and Olympos openly struggling. On the works displayed in the Porticus Octaviae, as discussed by Pliny, see Isager 1991, 160–62.

53. Appliqués from the Mahdia wreck: Marquardt 1994, figs. 1–2 (nymph) and 3 (Pan); cf. her figs. 5–6 for the Neo-Attic echoes. On the date of the Mahdia wreck, see supra, Ch. 7 n. 65, esp. Hellenkemper Salies 1996. For a group in the round, juxtaposing Pan to a nymph of the Invitation to the Dance type, see Marquardt 1995, 255–57, pl. 25.3 (Vatican Magazines; dated to Antonine times).

54. On this group and its many replicas (at least 30, mostly from Rome and its environs): Häuber, forthcoming (I warmly thank the author for letting me read her manuscript in advance of publication). She stresses that the main viewpoint is the one showing Hermaphroditos from the back, the satyr in profile; the "rear" of the group would show Hermaphroditos from the front, although the satyr would still be quite visible. Her proposed chronology (early 1st c.) is later than that suggested by Kell 1988, 21–28 (close in time to the Telephos Frieze and the Smaller Attalid Dedications: p. 26), and by Smith 1991, 130, fig. 159 ("3rd–2nd c."). *LIMC* 5, s.v. Hermaphroditos, no. 63d–u pls. 195–96, lists several sculptural replicas; comments on

p. 278 (A. Ajootian) compare to the Heliodoran group dated around 100. Note that the pose of the satyr being toppled back by his raised right foot occurs also on groups of **Pan Extracting a Thorn from a Satyr's Foot**: e.g., Bieber 1961, fig. 635; Marquardt 1995, 212–26, pl. 22, dated mid-1st c. (p. 217). This topic is also known from another variant, with the satyr sitting more upright: *LIMC* 8, s.v. Pan, 934, no. 213 pl. 628 ("copy of Hellenistic" [*sic*]); Marquardt 1995, pl. 23.1–2, dated also mid-1st c. (p. 222), although compositionally different from the first type — one more instance of the eclectic nature of these genre scenes.

Another group of **Hermaphroditos and a Satyr** (*LIMC* 5, no. 64c–j for sculptural examples, pl. 196, and p. 279 for comments), in which the former is the aggressor rather than the victim, is compositionally known since the mid-2nd c. on Calenian relief ware, but the statuary replicas seem to me entirely Roman rather than Hellenistic in spirit, especially in the disharmonic proportions of the two protagonists.

55. Nymph/Sea Centaur, in Vatican Museum, Sala degli Animali: *LIMC* 1, s.v. Amymone, no. 92 (the Sea Centaur is kidnapping the nymph — not a Nereid — for Poseidon, which explains the Erotes, and perhaps the female's effort not to fall into the waves); *LIMC* 6, s.v. Nereides, no. 140 (compared to Arkesilaos' works, dated 1st c.); *LIMC* 8, s.v. Triton, no. 33 pl. 45; Bieber 1961, fig. 640. For restorations (including both legs of the Sea Centaur and both lower legs of Nymph with feet), see *Helbig*[4], no. 100 (H. von Steuben), where the group is considered a possible original of the 1st c. that would have stood in real water (the present wave is a modern restoration). Kunze 1991 compares it with the Punishment of Dirke. On Nereids and Tritons/centaurs, see also Lattimore 1976, 56 and passim. The composition has been adapted for a **Sea Centaur Carrying Silenos**, in the Louvre; Bieber 1961, 150, fig. 641, considers it a parody of the first group, but others reverse the order: cf. *LIMC* 8, s.v. Triton, no. 35 pl. 46 ("Pergamene school, ca. 200"). Both works are also treated by Kell 1988, 69–78, who compares the Louvre group to the composition of the Nymph/Satyr (Capitoline Type, see infra, n. 56) and thus considers it "nachhellenistisch" (= 1st c. B.C.); while seeing the Vatican group as eclectic and Roman, at the earliest from the end of the 1st half of the 1st c.

56. Group with Satyr sitting on ground, kneeling Nymph (Capitoline Type, seven replicas): Kell 1988, 57–64, figs. 12–13 (1st third of the 1st c.); Smith 1991, fig. 158 ("3rd–2nd c."); Bieber 1961, 147, fig. 627. An unfinished replica in Athens, found on the grounds of the Olympieion, is made with mechanical means and should therefore be Imperial; it is said to be after a prototype from the 1st c.: Palagia 1987, 80, fig. 3. Its presence in Athens is important, given that most replicas of the type come from Italy. See also H.-H. von Prittwitz und Gaffron, in *Hellenistische Gruppen* [now 1999, 181–86].

Group with Satyr seated on rock, almost standing Nymph (Terme Type, seven replicas known as well): Kell 1988, 44–49, figs. 9–10 (no echo in the minor arts); Ridgway 1972, 63–64, no. 22, figs. 5–7; Marquardt 1995, 255, dates the original of this type to the 3rd quarter of the 2nd c., in discussing an adaptation of it that uses Pan instead of a satyr, and Hermaphroditos instead of a nymph: pl. 25.4 (once de Clerq collection, then art market Genf; dated Hadrianic).

Kell's dating of Late Hellenistic and "nachhellenistisch" groups is based mostly on compositional and stylistic principles, which leave me doubtful when dealing with non-originals, since many alterations could and were introduced by the Imperial copyists. On the other hand, helpful summaries of previous opinions are provided for the items under discussion, thus clearly indicating the range of dates that have been proposed for each. The current tendency is to lower most dates toward the 1st century, thus recognizing the creativity of that "commercial" phase.

CHAPTER 9

Odds and Ends

In the previous chapter, we briefly touched on an alleged portrait known only through later copies. In this last section, where "odds and ends" are gathered, we shall be dealing with a mixture of originals and copies, and therefore, briefly, with portraits as a category.

PORTRAITS

Readers of my work on sculpture have noted that I usually shy away from portraits. I truly fear the subject, not only because of the relative lack of identifiable Greek originals, but also because I am skeptical of Roman "copies" inscribed with the names of famous poets or philosophers of Greek times. I have already mentioned the widespread (and fully recognized) willingness of Imperial sculptors to provide their clients with whatever image they desired, whether or not a prototype for it existed. The number of replicas of a given portrait, usually taken as proof of a famous, or at least accredited, original, is also, to my mind, not probative, since the inception of a type in the Late Republican period or within an Italian workshop could automatically produce through several generations a series of duplicates fully in keeping with the trend of the times, already accustomed to the copying of official Imperial portraits. Indeed, we need not wait until the reign of Augustus to find, in Etruria, several renditions of what, at first discovery, had been considered a distinctive portrayal of a specific individual. The elderly and corpulent man reclining on the lid of a stone sarcophagus had appeared so realistic as to qualify as an intended likeness—until subsequent finds of similar funerary images inscribed with different names proved conclusively that we were dealing with a type, the "fat Etruscan," symbolic of ruggedness, prosperity (hence his prominent stomach), and noble lineage, to be repeated on demand.[1]

Other startling points need to be considered. In that great gallery of portraits that was the **Villa of the Papyri at Herculaneum**, rulers, orators, philosophers, and even divinities mingled, those within the large peristyle perhaps *without permanent labels*. The alleged identities and pairings of the latter are based on assumptions, none of which, in my opinion, can be proven with confidence, and one wonders to what extent an ancient viewer could have recognized all intended personages—or was the anonymity intentional? The busts of monarchs are thought to represent heads of dynasties (Ptolemy I, Seleukos I, Philetairos, but even Pyrrhos and Demetrios Poliorketes); significantly, however, the most magnetic and perhaps most recognizable of all rulers, Alexander the Great, is not included. A new study of all bronze busts from the Villa, with special emphasis on technique and repairs, is currently in progress and may eventually help us determine if all portraits were set up simultaneously after being manufactured by a single foundry, as claimed. If this were the case, the apparent similarity between the heads currently identified as two different rulers could be explained as workshop variations on a single model, for the client's satisfaction. In practical terms, the logistics of assembling within a single workshop a gallery of rulers' portrait-casts from such disparate sources as Pergamon, Seleukia, and Alexandria seem beyond the capabilities of the times, even under the *Pax Augusta*. If the bronzes are truly overcasts, as suggested, the approximate correspondence of measurements for what should have been originals from different sources once again appears improbable.[2]

Another important feature of the category of portraits is that most extant images, whether of rulers or of philosophers, seem to cluster within the third century. A rapid glance through a popular handbook such as Smith 1991 reveals that his figs. 21–43 are all based on works said to go back to late fourth-/third-century prototypes, or depict personages who died before 200. Virtually the same is true of Smith's portraits of rulers (figs. 3–20), with a definite gap between the "copy of an original of c. 200 B.C."—identified, controversially, as Antiochos III—and another "of c. 100–90 B.C."—Mithradates VI. To be sure, a search through Richter's collection, *The Portraits of the Greeks*, would partly fill this gap, but with equal uncertainty; the more specialized selection by Schefold, based on periods of creation (not the lifespan of the subject), yields only five examples of statuary types considered copies of originals ranging from ca. 180 to ca. 140, most of them doubtfully identified.[3]

A group of **male portraits from Delos** is certainly composed of Greek originals, some of them by Athenian masters, even if identification is uncertain. Yet here too a comparable phenomenon is apparent. According to the chronology advocated by Stewart (1979), the majority of extant heads should fall, at the earliest, between 130/120 and 69, with the largest group further bracketed between 100 and 88, but other dates have also been suggested, mostly bringing the upper *terminus* down; excavational context is not often helpful except as an *ante quem*. Statistics of signed versus unsigned portraits based on inscriptional evidence from the bases yield larger numbers for earlier periods, but the respective sculptures no longer survive. In terms of production in Athens itself, a comparable picture is obtained from the Agora material, all essentially Roman in subject and late within the first century.[4]

The apparent realism of the portraits from Delos, and the strong Italian presence on the island, have given rise to the suggestion that the extant heads depict Romans, or some of those Greeks who were so strongly pro-Roman as to have desired for their images Roman physiognomic traits as an expression of their allegiance. Scholars who believe that the Delian portraits pre-date the Late Republican veristic examples maintain instead that the apparent individualization of the features comes from the East, where gravestones, as we have seen (Chapter 6), show women with idealized faces, but men with marked traits and signs of mature age. Whatever full statues, albeit often headless, are preserved on Delos, moreover, seem to follow entirely the Greek tradition: the naked, muscular, and over-lifesize body of the "pseudo-athlete" (dated ca. 100), the man wrapped in his mantle (never a toga), the cuirassed torso displaying a Hellenistic, not a Classical, type of armor. Only the soft boots occasionally preserved are the Roman *calcei* instead of the Greek krepides.[5]

A recent essay has claimed for Pharaonic Egypt the right to be considered "the birthplace of portraiture" intended as "the discernible likeness of a specific individual," since images needed to be recognizable in order to function properly. By contrast, **Ptolemaic portraits** are said to be "homogenized" and remarkably difficult to identify because of their apparent similarity to one another, whether in sculpture in the round or in relief.[6] Yet a second essay within the same collection of papers argues almost the opposite point: that a few portraits of second-century Ptolemies, both in Greek and in Egyptian form, appear to have been based on an official court type disseminated within a system of image-control comparable to that used in the Roman Empire.[7]

To be sure, the identifying features in such "copies" are primarily limited to the hair rendering above the forehead, which in turn can be compared to that ruler's image on coins. Even granting that the appearance of hair below the forehead band of an Egyptian *menes*-headdress is unparalleled except in Ptolemaic portraits, one wonders whether it is appropriate to use for them the same criteria that apply to the considerably later heads of the Julio-Claudians. Similar, albeit not identical, patterns of forehead locks occur on some of the Delian heads—those that do not sport the typically Roman crewcut—and even on a portrait from the Athenian Agora. Are we therefore dealing with workshop mannerisms rather than with identifying features? Would the very appearance of forehead hair on an Egyptian royal portrait convey the ethnic "Greek" without meaning to specify the individual Ptolemy, otherwise named by the inscription? In one case, it is not the hair but the facial features—fleshy cheeks, wide eyes—that correlate with the depictions on coins; yet here too a series of non-royal heads in Egyptian stones may reveal somewhat the same stylization. The staring, enormous eyes of most Ptolemaic portraits are certainly a convention rather than a physical trait, and one that may be rooted in a local tradition.[8]

As a footnote, we may comment on the sfumato technique, allegedly a "Praxitelean" feature of many Ptolemaic royal portraits with blurred facial traits. Actual influence from the Athenian sculptor has already been disputed, and the wide diffusion of the technique noted, thus eliminating it as an Alexandrian characteristic. Now

Odds and Ends

it has been argued that all the apparently undefined features of Ptolemaic statuary would have been sharply accentuated by paint, and that the entire surface might have been tinted, in order to eliminate the contrast between the parts executed in marble and those added in stucco. The highly polychrome face of "Alexandria" in Roman mosaics has been taken as indication of how a finished royal portrait might have appeared with its original coloring in place.[9]

The relative abundance of surviving portraits of the Ptolemies contrasts with the paucity of **Seleukid images in the round**—only seven, including usurpers, according to Fleischer (1991), and one of his attributions (the so-called Attalos I from Pergamon) is highly controversial. Bronze statues were erected more often, during the ruler's lifetime, but these were frequently melted down; marble sculptures had a better chance of survival, but these carried divinizing overtones and were traditionally idealized and generic. Yet even more significant is the relative lack of statuary in general from the entire Seleukid realm. Analysis and identifications are usually limited to coins, and these as well show a clearly defined type only beginning with Antiochos IV Epiphanes (ruled 175–164), conforming to it thereafter until the end of the dynasty. I am not qualified to comment intelligently on numismatic matters, noting only the youthfulness of the depictions, the relative paucity of divine attributes, perhaps even the slight ambiguity in the rendering of curls over the temples that, in overlapping the royal fillet, may recall the horns of some third-century issues.[10]

If we move away from likenesses, however, is there a statuary formula for a ruler type?

RULER TYPES

A typical example of how a statue can convey a concept even when the identity of the subject is uncertain is provided by the so-called **Hellenistic Ruler in the Terme Museum** (Pls. 72a–b). This over-lifesize bronze has been the subject of heated controversy ever since its discovery in 1885, not only in terms of identification but even in terms of chronology. Dated from the fourth to the first century B.C., it has been called the portrait of a Greek, a Roman, and even a Carthaginian. Among the Greek names, those frequently cited are Alexander Balas (ruled 150–146), Perseus of Macedonia (178–168) or his father Philip V (220–178), Antiochos II or Demetrios I of Syria (261–246 and 162–150 respectively), Ptolemy VI (180–145), and Eumenes II and Attalos II of Pergamon (197–160, 160–139). Among the Romans, Agrippa, Lucullus, Sulla, Titus Quinctius Flamininus, and an unnamed general have been proposed. Identification as Hannibal—either around or before 200, or after the Carthaginian joined Antiochos III in 195—has found no resonance, and the nude rendering makes it improbable.[11]

Several features of this impressive bronze are distinctive. Perhaps the best known is the fine engraving of the facial hair: the beard, which extends onto the throat down to the level of the Adam's apple; the mustache, which merges with the beard; and even the short hair over the nape, at the point where the plastic curls end. In each case,

Plates 72a–b

the growth is rendered as individual, triangular tufts with curving tip, within which one or two shorter lines may be incised. These tufts have absolutely no volume (at a cursory glance, the man looks clean-shaven) and contrast with the tousled curls over the cranium, which form a definite shelf over the bulbous forehead. The more plastically rendered eyebrows seem knotted, yet it is only the prominence of the frontal muscle that makes them appear so, together with the unusually small ocular cavities and their crow's feet, as if the man were squinting. Note that the superciliary muscle does not overlap the upper lid at the outer corner, as is common in athletic figures of the late Classical and Hellenistic periods, including portraits of Alexander the Great — a trait that perhaps denoted athleticism. Yet the Ruler's ears are swollen (the so-called cauliflower rendering), especially the more exposed left, as appropriate for a boxer or wrestler.[12]

The entire head of the Ruler is remarkable in itself. The cheeks look flaccid, belying the apparent youthfulness of the over-muscular body; the nose is hooked, the slightly parted lips are almost too fleshy, and the mouth seems too small in relation to the other features. The whole head, in fact, appears somewhat out of proportion to the body — an effect that would have been enhanced if the bronze was originally set up on a column or high pedestal, as usual for an honorary monument.

But was this the statue's true function? The distinctive facial features have always been considered portrait-like, regardless of the proposed identification. The very dimensions of the head — of natural size as against the heroic scale of the body — could confirm that an ideal, stock torso was given a portrait head taken from an official model, thus creating the discrepancy. The practice is well known for Imperial statues, sometimes with ridiculous results. Yet the aesthetic effect of the Ruler is satisfactory, quite different from the slight shock produced by the so-called Pseudo-Athlete from Delos with his bald head, protruding ears, and bourgeois features that appear incongruous over a Polykleitan ideal body.[13]

The idealized physique, the nakedness, and the pose with left arm raised, holding a spear, and right arm bent behind the back, combine to convey the impression of a victorious ruler — an allusion to "spear-won land." The type has been said to go back to a Classical model, the so-called Alexander with the Spear attributed to Lysippos and known only through later statuettes; it was much appreciated during the Roman Empire, when several emperors had themselves portrayed in that fashion. Yet it is usually overlooked that the spear of those examples is more often held by the right arm, as if in readiness and in position of command. The Terme Ruler, by contrast, is obviously relaxed, not resting on his weapon but actually leaning forward in a stance that looks seriously unbalanced when viewed in direct profile. His left foot is so far back that it touches only with the tips of its toes, undermining the obvious Polykleitan comparison. Moreover, the right hand on the buttock, it has been argued, is the sign not of a victorious but of a challenged hero, one who has to overcome great obstacles: a Meleager or a Herakles, not a triumphant Alexander.[14]

Odds and Ends

To be sure, other ruler types seem patterned after different models, especially Hermes, but also Apollo and even Dionysos. We have already mentioned this point in connection with the Ofellius Ferus on Delos, who used a "benefactor" type reproducing a Hermes figure, with mantle bunched up on a shoulder. Other renderings include a cuirass or a chlamys; some figures are standing but others can be seated. In general, it can be said that only a virile, highly muscular, nude or semi-nude body and a commanding pose combine with a portrait head to suggest a ruler, but no specific formula exists. It is perhaps the contrast with the other accepted types—the citizen fully wrapped in his himation, occasionally with underlying tunic; the philosopher, usually seated because elderly, therefore venerable, and in a teaching pose, with shoes on his feet—that gives the ruler statuary its recognition. The athletic type is similar, but more specific in attributes and pose, besides being rarely preserved from the Hellenistic period, as we shall see below. It lacks, moreover, that touch of "divinity," of the superhuman, that makes the ruler image distinctive, even if its scale is not always colossal.[15]

The Terme Ruler qualifies for his epithet on two counts: he has a heroic figure and a portrait head, even if he does not wear a fillet, which would mark him definitely as a monarch. Therefore the scholars who consider him a Hellenistic Greek have suggested individuals who had not yet assumed the royal title, such as a young Attalos II or Demetrios I during his Roman exile. Equal importance has been given to the short beard: it has been called a mourning beard (and again, appropriate circumstances have been adduced to support various identifications, for both a Greek and a Roman), or that of a pretender to the throne, or even of a general during a campaign, who would neglect to shave.[16] In all these cases, the date given to the statue depends heavily on its identification. Comparisons with coin profiles have been so extensively used and abused that little credence can attach to them.

Stylistic considerations have only relative value, if we accept that a heroic, Classical body could be used at any time for a portrait head, as we have mentioned above. For the Terme bronze, the bulging muscles, especially the knobby digitations over the right, compressed side, and the somewhat inflated appearance of the pectorals and the whole torso, have prompted reference to the Baroque anatomy of the Great Altar. A **colossal marble torso from Elaia,** the harbor of Pergamon, with (missing) head turned to proper right and right arm broken off from a possibly raised position, looks almost like a mirror image of the bronze—but no specific date is available for it, and influence from the Altar Gigantomachy, as we have seen, was widespread over time.[17]

A meaningful comparison has been made with a **bronze head in the J. Paul Getty Museum,** in Malibu, California (Pls. 73a–b). It is truly clean-shaven, its cheeks firmer, its nose straight; the ears are normal, the eyes larger, and the engraved eyebrows have a more regular pattern, but the forehead hair is fairly close, if more orderly. One scholar wants to recognize in it a portrait of the same individual, Attalos II, but the provenience of the piece is unknown, although said to be Asia Minor.[18]

Plates 73a–b

Findspot and context of the Terme Ruler are of limited help. It was found in uncontrolled digging at the foot of the Quirinal, within the basement of a structure not far from the Baths of Constantine, so that it is likely that it belonged to their decoration, together with the equally famous statue of the **Seated Boxer** found nearby a month later, as recorded by Rodolfo Lanciani.[19] It seems fairly certain that the latter was made during the first century B.C., and those who wanted to group the two bronzes together therefore gave a similar date to the Ruler. Yet recent scholarship has tended to dissociate the two and to consider the Ruler a second- or (less plausibly) a third-century creation. It is surprising that a bronze of the second century B.C. should have survived until the time of Constantine, who is actually known for having transported so many Greek originals to his new capital of Constantinopolis. But the same argument could be made for the Boxer, which has not been challenged.

One other item could provide evidence that the Ruler stood in Rome by the end of the Republic. On the Ruler's stomach, the letters L.VI.P.L.XXIIX were cut at some later time; their meaning is unclear, but the first three have been read as "loco sexto," as part of an official inventory of works of art in the city, and dated to the Republican period. This date seems supported by similar inscriptions on two other monuments—a bronze horse from Trastevere in the Museo Nuovo Capitolino, once carrying a rider, and a base for the (missing) statue of the early Republican dictator M. Minucius—but inventories of this nature are also known from other periods of Roman history, including the Late Imperial, and the date of the two monuments is equally uncertain. On the Ruler's right thigh a second, pointillé monogram, MAR, is still unexplained.[20]

The temptation to find parallels for the technique of the Ruler's unusual beard—not for identification purposes but for chronology—is strong. A **bronze head from Kyrene** has a comparable engraving of the beard high on the cheeks, but strands become independent of the face below the jaw, although only a small fringe is rendered. The portrait has been thought to depict a young North African, but primarily because of its findspot. Its context was secondary and provides no chronological indication, although dates proposed range from the early fourth to the early third century. Theoretically, the piece could even be Roman.[21] A **second bronze head in the J. P. Getty**
Plates 74a–b **Museum** (Pls. 74a–b), appears to be a well-established fourth-century type, yet has a finely engraved beard, mustache, and sideburns that recall the peculiar facial hair of the Ruler. To be sure, the rendering of the Getty head is due to the engraving of the strands on the original wax, whereas that of the Ruler is said to be the product of cold work on the surface of the finished bronze; yet most of the wisps have the same triangular shape with curving tips and inner detailing, and the basic approach is comparable. Regrettably, as for all pieces of questionable provenience, this second Getty head cannot be precisely dated, but the suggestions that it comes from Boubon in Pisidia and that it was made in the second century A.C. cannot be entirely discounted. The Malibu piece had been tentatively attributed to an athletic bronze torso in the Burdur Museum that comes from the Boubon Sebasteion, but further study of both fragments has shown that they cannot go together. If not from the Sebasteion,

however, the Getty head could still have originated in Asia Minor. What is of further interest in our context is that the body in Turkey can be connected with an inscribed base within the Sebasteion that proves it to be an image of Valerianus the Younger (Caesar in 257–258). It thus confirms that Classical-looking statues were still being produced in the advanced third century A.C.[22]

I had thought at first that the technique of the Terme Ruler betrayed some affinity to Late Etruscan bronzes with pointillé beards, although the stippled effect of the latter is different from the precise definition of the Ruler's tufts. But two further possibilities now come to mind: this very fine down may translate into bronze the effect produced by paint on marble faces—in which case no chronological clue is provided, since this technique on stone goes back to the Archaic period; or it may parallel the experiments on marble prevalent during the third century A.C. to convey closely cropped hair and beard. In some of these Roman statues, the beard extends down along the throat, very much like that of the Terme Ruler.[23]

How this same experimentation with texture may have looked on contemporary bronzes is perhaps shown by two **heroic royal images from the Yemen**, inscribed not only with their respective names (in South Arabian script), but also with that of their maker, Phokas, a Greek. The statues represent King Damar alay Yuhabirr and his son Tharan, known to have ruled together in the last decade of the third century A.C. Significantly enough, the statue of the younger man is in the very pose of the Terme Ruler.[24]

To be sure, the Classicizing long hair and the somewhat undefined musculature of the younger king from the Yemen are a far cry from the coherent style and modeling of the Terme bronze. Yet place and date would lead us to expect such difference. More remarkable is the fact that the extant bronzes from the Boubon Sebasteion could all easily be taken for Classical/Hellenistic works, were it not for their portrait heads or their connections to inscribed bases: the Marcus Aurelius, now in Cleveland, looks like a typical Hellenistic citizen, in his Sophokles Type pose, Greek mantle with press folds, and underlying tunic; the Lucius Verus now in the Levy Collection has a fully Classical body, and so do the Septimius Severus in the Dorothy Wendell Cherry Collection in New York, the Caracalla, and the already mentioned Valerianus.[25]

I do not want to go so far as to suggest that the Terme Ruler is Roman Imperial, made for the Baths of Constantine or only somewhat earlier. Yet the remarkable group of statues from the Sebasteion has clearly shown how close to Greek originals Roman bronzes could be, although the heads are true contemporary portraits. Even some technical details, such as the separately cast toes, can be paralleled from the fifth century B.C. to the third A.C., and only occasionally does an unusual procedure or, more tentatively, a distinctive alloy suggest a specific date.

ATHLETES

One would imagine athletic statuary to represent another well-defined category, but we are left with remarkably little from the Hellenistic period, and especially the second century. Many statue bases from Olympia and elsewhere, and mentions in Pliny and Pausanias, attest to the existence of such monuments, but most were in bronze and have not survived. That they have not been "recognized" among Roman marbles may confirm that dedications in sanctuaries could not be copied and may not even have had an intrinsic interest for the Romans.[26]

On the basis of what remains, there seems to be virtually the same ambiguity in athletic iconography as there was for ruler types. This was to be expected, since rulers were intentionally given the best possible body and comparable nakedness. Yet athletes could have been distinguished by their activities and lively poses, and this seems not to have been the case. A typical instance is provided by Smith's uncertainty in labeling a **youthful marble torso from Pergamon:** "Ruler or athlete, from the gymnasium. Later 3rd or 2nd cent. B.C." Were it not for its findspot, the small figure, with its separately added calotte and missing but extended arms, would certainly have been considered royal.[27]

Monographs on athletes and athletics usually have recourse to vases, reliefs, small bronzes, and statues often known only from "copies"—yet most of these are lifesize or over, whereas victors' images, by rule, were always at less than natural scale. Given the strictures mentioned above, these Roman works are therefore open to suspicion on more than one count. Even so, we are struck, once again, by the peculiar gap apparent for the second century, although some pieces could perhaps move up or down the chronological scale.[28] I shall therefore briefly review the few items that may raise a claim to belong within this survey, but we should first mention some evidence that may explain this peculiar situation.

The gymnasion as an institution was indeed central to Hellenistic life. We would expect to find there the best examples of athletic statuary, yet lists of dedications suggest that different objects were instead preferred. An inventory of bronzes from Delos drawn up under the archonship of Kallistratos (156/5) shows that, before 166, sculptural dedications in the gymnasion consisted of images of officials, or of statuettes of Erotes, Herakles, Apollo kitharoidos, all small and supported by piers, columns, or high bases. The victors in the lampadedromia dedicated their torches and the statuette of a female holding a vase(?). Such offerings continued even after 166, when Athens assumed control of the island, but the main emphasis shifted to the activities of the magistrates, or to the existence of athletic groups previously unattested (the *Ephebeusantes*, who dedicated to Apollo, Hermes, and Herakles lists of names of their members; and the *Aleiphomenoi*). Among other offerings, the Delians gave 41 marble herms, 83 shields with different forms of decoration, many votive pinakes, even one sundial. Herakles becomes especially important within the gymnasion, and his herms are frequently set up there.[29] From Melos, we have already noted three second-century hermaic pillars, one with a Classicizing, bearded Hermes head, the other two with heads of a youthful Herakles, which were found in the proximity of the famous Aphrodite, itself a dedication in a gymnasion.[30]

Odds and Ends

The Delian gymnasion also had images of Mithradates VI and his brother, as well as other rulers, and an altar for the peoples of Rome and Athens.[31] The desire to be honored in the gymnasion is an interesting phenomenon of the second century, which recognizes the place as the "crucible for the future ruling class of the city," where the citizen benefactors are revered as virtual new founders, therefore as if in a second agora. This state of affairs is probably reflected in the anecdote repeated by Vitruvius (7.6.5–6), in which the citizens of Alabanda are accused of lacking a sense of propriety: "In their gymnasium the statues are all pleading causes, in their forum, throwing the discus, running, or playing ball."[32] We can perhaps assume that the sculptures in the agora were symbolic of athletic activities rather than being victors' portraits. On the other hand, such fine distinctions between locales may be a modern construct: the fifth-century Athenian Agora held a racecourse for Panathenaic competitions, and the track was overlooked by one of the most famous honorary monuments of antiquity, the Tyrannicides.[33]

Perhaps the most convincing athletic monument from the second century is the bronze group of a **Horse and Jockey from Cape Artemision** (Pl. 75). This important sculpture has finally been the subject of a detailed study and thorough technical analysis of its casting features, but these have regrettably provided no new information as to its exact date. It is at least assured that the jockey goes together with the horse, since a piece of his drapery joins the back of the animal—even this point was initially debated, disparate dates having been given, on stylistic grounds, to the two components of the group. The foundered boat from which the bronzes came, regrettably, has defied proper excavation, and a recent listing of wrecks in the Mediterranean gives it a wide temporal bracket: 200–80.[34]

Plate 75

At first glance, the sculpture could be categorized as genre, since the jockey is a boy with a "street urchin" face. Scholars debate whether he has negroid features, but his typically Greek hair contradicts the theory; perhaps age rather than ethnicity is implied in his rendering, or he may be representative of the mixed races that must have been common in Greece and Asia Minor after Alexander's campaigns. The boy is equipped for a race, with spurs on his feet and probably a goad in his right hand, and his pose suggests that he is inciting his mount as if close to the goal—bent forward, torso twisted, arms stretched in opposite directions, legs spread out, his short garment flying out behind him. When removed from the horse, as some photos show him, the jockey seems even more active than when placed on it, as he certainly was in antiquity.

The animal itself is in full motion, almost in a flying gallop. Though parts of it are extensively restored (including the entire tail), the modern reconstruction is correct. It has been noted that the jockey looks too small for the horse, perhaps intentionally to emphasize the courser over its rider. What is less noticeable, given the inherent monumentality of the composition, is that both horse and jockey are smaller than life-size, as required by a victory monument. That such the group was is suggested by the brand on the horse's right hind thigh: a flying Nike holding out a wreath. The symbol, of course, could simply indicate the horse's stable and its owner, but its message of victory could not have escaped the viewers.

The group is remarkable for several reasons. It is the only surviving evidence of horse-racing monuments in the round; we know of several chariot groups dedicated in antiquity after a victory—for instance, the one on which the famous Delphi Charioteer once stood, or those on the tall pillar monuments erected by and for the Attalids in Athens—but this is the only extant sculpture in the round commemorating a horseback-riding event. It is also evidence that riders could be quite young, yet this is not an athlete competing in a youth category, but probably a hired jockey for a wealthy sponsor: the very costliness of the bronze group demands it. It would be tempting to read this sculpture as the vignette of an impromptu race among peers, such as those of young Bedouins in the African desert which I witnessed in my childhood. But the horse is properly harnessed, as Hemingway has noted, the jockey is too well appointed for his task, and the purpose of a monument with such a subject would be difficult to visualize. Finally, while other Classical athletic sculptures, or even other equestrian groups, usually showed the moment after the event, or a relatively quiet pose, this is a daring rendering of violent motion caught in mid-action, as only bronze could allow.[35]

Classical features in the horse had prompted dates as early as the fifth century for it; the jockey is clearly Hellenistic, but no objective evidence exists for his chronology. Connection with historical personages is impossible, although suggestions have been made (Moreno would like to ascribe the group to Pergamon), and the location of the wreck is not particularly illuminating. Stylistically, the sculpture has a touch of the Baroque mixed with Classicizing elements, but, as we have seen, this assessment is insufficient to pinpoint its creation.[36] Aesthetically, the horse looks too thin when viewed frontally, but it was probably set up so as to be seen from both sides—the right because of the brand on the horse's thigh, the left because it offered a glimpse of the jockey's face. Polychromy greatly added to the total effect: the horse's hooves were patinated black, its eyes (and those of the boy) were inserted, its brand was inlaid (perhaps in silver), and its tongue was probably in red copper. Tooling and texturing (the horse's mane, the boy's costume) increased the richness of the monument.

Another group that seems caught in mid-action is that of the **marble Wrestlers in Florence,** yet appearances may be misleading, and here too no precise date is possible. The sculpture is so extensively reconstructed that even the pose may be erroneous, and originally no clear winner would have been suggested, thus eliminating the piece as the copy of a victory monument. A recent suggestion would consider it a decorative work for a palaistra or a gymnasion. A drawing by Cavalleris shows that *both* wrestlers' heads were missing when the group was found, and those we see at present seem to be based on the Niobids also in Florence. Given this fact, even the presumed Lysippan influence diminishes, since it was hypothesized primarily on the head type.

Odds and Ends

The composition is known through only one exemplar, thus preventing further speculation; it is usually assigned to the early Hellenistic period, most often the third century, but I see no obvious grounds for the assumption. As discussed above, we have no clear evidence, from the inventories, that Greek gymnasia and palaistrai were "decorated" with demonstration sculptures, like the statuary outside modern stadia symbolizing the various sports, and the often-quoted anecdote in Vitruvius may not only express concepts of his own time and place, but also reflect a true situation, not one peculiar to Alabanda. The wrestlers' group could easily be a Roman creation.[37]

Roman demand may also lie behind the **two bronze youths from the Villa of the Papyri** at Herculaneum. They too are usually considered wrestlers, to be placed opposite each other as if ready to grapple. Yet they are not mirror images but duplicates, and a recent study has suggested that they were set up as parallel runners, at the beginning of their race. In the garden peristyle of the villa, they probably stood on either side of the long basin, which would have visually functioned as the separation of their lanes on a racetrack, while the steps leading to the upper, inner peristyle would have served not simply as their goal but also as a vantage point for the statues to be viewed by visitors, like a grandstand. The alleged Lysippan cast that is responsible for the traditional third-century date is just as appropriate for a late first-century one, contemporary with the busts and other bronzes from the villa.[38]

My last example is another bronze, and equally controversial: the **Izmir Runner** (Pl. 76). It was found at sea, near Kyme, and with a height of 1.54 m could clearly qualify as a victor's monument. Yet he is not an Olympionikos, since the wreath he wears is of oak. He may also have carried a torch in his left fist, and he turns his head in the same direction and slightly upward, rather than in the direction of his movement. It has been noted that he has the body of a youth and the head of an older man, yet this is not quite correct, since the fine sideburns along his cheeks may indicate the first bloom of youth; in that direction signify also the lack of pubic hair and the undetailed musculature of the abdomen. To be sure, the face is distinctive, with its strong nose, dimpled chin, and partly open mouth, but not sufficiently characterized to suggest a portrait. The bronze has been dated to the first century B.C. or the first A.C. (perhaps Tiberian), but comparisons have been proposed with the Eros (formerly Agon) and with the bronze (oil) lampadephoroi from the Mahdia wreck, which would carry a late second-century chronology. On the other hand, the runner's hair, coming to a peak in the center of the forehead, has been more tentatively said to recall portraits of the soldier emperors and of private citizens from the third century A.C. This disturbing range echoes my comments on the Terme Ruler and increases our uneasiness about the dating of ancient bronzes.[39]

Plate 76

SCULPTURE AS FURNITURE

The comparison between the Izmir Runner and the two bronze lamps from the Mahdia wreck leads us to investigate another category of sculpture: statues that had a practical as well as a decorative function within a household. The two lampadephoroi from the wreck are unusual in that the entire body is the container for the oil; one of them is a Hermaphrodite, the other an Eros, but they are virtually identical except for the modifications and additions required by the two different identities. Their size (0.49 m), however, qualifies them as statuettes, perhaps to be fastened to a wall, and their date is possibly so close to the turn into the next century that they need not concern us excessively for our survey. What is more important is that they are part of a type known also at a larger scale, which finds literary mention as early as the Homeric poems and is well attested from Roman villas. In terms of material evidence, little remains from the Greek sphere, perhaps because statues that have lost their attributes can no longer be recognized as functional. The primary reason for the situation, however, may be the fact that a Hellenistic household differed substantially from a Roman one, and only royal palaces would have had the luxury of such servant-statues.[40]

The contradiction of having a human figure act as a functional object may appear stronger to us than to the ancients, so accustomed to the presence of youthful slaves catering to their every need. Yet some sense of propriety may have encouraged the use of antiquarian traits in such utilitarian images, to imply a different span of time, or perhaps even the very quality of "statue" as an immobile item separate from the contemporary sphere.[41] To judge from the Roman examples, such figures were often given Severizing hairstyles and androgynous head types; perhaps their very nakedness would have been a definite signifier within a household context. One other formula made use of Archaistic or Archaizing style: recently, a bronze youth from the House of Polybius at Pompeii has been illustrated, and two other pieces, in marble— a draped female statue and a headless torso—have been discussed as a pair of servant figures from Palace V at Pergamon. These latter are therefore Hellenistic, fairly well dated to the second century by their findspot.[42]

Plates 77a–b

The more completely preserved figure, in **Berlin** (Pls. 77a–b), is usually called a **Dancer,** because it lifts the "skirt" of the long himation with the left hand and steps forward with the left foot; the outstretched right arm, now missing from mid-biceps, may have held a lamp. The **torso** (Pl. 78), now **in Istanbul,** was found in a mosque at

Plate 78

Bergama, the modern city over the ancient site, and was therefore removed from its original context; it is not identical to the figure in Berlin, in that both arms (carved separately and now lost) were clearly stretched forward, but they may have held a tray, thus still creating a reasonable counterpart to the torch-bearer. Differences in its costume and hairstyle are subtle enough to ensure comparison and connection with the statue found in the Palace while also establishing a distinct persona.

The differences between the two have also been interpreted as appropriate for a group originally composed of three elements and representing the Charites, whose iconography involves precisely such slight variations. Pausanias (9.35.6) mentions that Charites by Boupalos stood at Pergamon in the *thalamos* of Attalos, and it was once argued that the two figures in question were part of such a group and that Boupalos was a Hellenistic sculptor, perhaps homonymous with one from the sixth century. The theory did not receive much credence but has been revived now, in connection with two heads found on the Demeter terrace at Pergamon, which duplicate the unusual hairstyle of the so-called Dancer. It has been suggested that they belong to the two missing Charites from the Palace, or that they represent a duplicate group set up in the Demeter precinct; the torso in Istanbul, although influenced by that work, would be by a different hand and probably from a different context.[43]

ARCHAISTIC/ARCHAIZING SCULPTURE

Whether or not the two statues from Pergamon can be considered "furniture," they can certainly be classified as Archaistic/Archaizing, or rather as typical of the form of archaizing that developed in Asia Minor and, to a lesser extent, on Rhodes. Since the Hellenistic, second-century date of the figure from Palace V cannot be doubted, the existence of such a stylistic trend within our period is confirmed—it had already been postulated on the evidence of reliefs and gravestones (Chapter 6).

The distinction between Archaistic and Archaizing is perhaps conceptual rather than factual, and a spirited attack on all such prescriptive (as well as descriptive) terms has recently been launched. These strictures are undoubtedly correct, but I still see some value in my own definition of the two terms, used in order to convey a mental image, although not to suggest a chronology. I call Archaistic a work that at first glance looks almost coherently Archaic, with only a few mannerisms or anachronistic traits betraying the fact that it was made after 480. By contrast, I call Archaizing a work made in the *style* of its own period—most explicitly, the Hellenistic Baroque— but whose underlying *pattern* is Archaic. A brief analysis of the Berlin "Dancer" may explain my meaning more clearly.[44]

The figure's twisted pose, with right shoulder forward, left arm held back, shoulders aslant, head turned to proper right, is undoubtedly *not* Archaic. Only the stiff legs with straight knees might recall the typical sixth-century korai, yet even this feature could be explained by the specific step of a dance or, if accepted, the utilitarian function of the sculpture. The face, it has been noted, resembles the Artemis of the Pergamon Gigantomachy, and the elongated proportions of the body give the hint of a high waist, despite the lack of a proper belt under the breasts. The chiaroscural drapery, moreover, is openly Baroque, with its cascade of catenaries framed by straight folds, the deep carving that outlines the outer contours of the body, the twisted bundle of the mantle crossing between the breasts, the many arrow folds that slash the right side of the torso, and the crêpelike texturing of the chiton. What is Archaic about this figure is its *pattern:* the emphasis on the vertical axis provided by the bundled folds that end in swallow-tails, the symmetrical arrangement of the subsidiary folds in the apopytgma of the mantle, the framing function of the himation massed on either side of the body, the effect of transparency that reveals both legs despite their many-layered envelope. To be sure, some of these features—catenaries, transparency, texturing—could be paralleled in Classical, fifth-century sculptures, but not the apparent "law of frontality" (in its Archaic meaning) that dominates the composition despite its hint of motion. The mannered pose of lifting a garment to one side is also a typical Archaic gesture. Here it appears motivated by the need to step forward or to dance, yet further analysis reveals that the skirt of the chiton—the only potentially impeding item of the costume—remains unmoved, and its hem retains its horizontal level above the feet.

Whether or not the "Dancer" is called Archaizing or Archaistic, its basic principles seem to have influenced a good number of works that have been helpfully collected by others and shall not, therefore, be repeated here. What is important is to note the extension of this style through the subsequent centuries into the advanced Imperial period. Also significant is the fact that **Rhodes** has produced a slight variant of the form in hieratic, motionless types, the so-called (Archaistic) **Artemis-Hekate** figures, Plate 79 of which several have been found on the island (Pl. 79). They eschew the chiaroscural, Baroque effects of the Pergamene statues, and thus seem closer to Classical/Archaistic works from the Greek Mainland, but from their period they retain the elongated proportions, the high waist, and the narrow shoulders over wide hips. Archaistic female figures in slightly different attires are also known from other islands of the Kyklades and, somewhat more rigidly, from Athens, thus attesting to the wide diffusion of the general trend during the second century. It should be stressed, however, that regional characteristics are much more evident in Archaistic/Archaizing productions than in sculptures in "Hellenistic" styles.[45]

That the Archaistic style extended to Rome is shown by the two **Diskouroi from the Fountain of Juturna,** near the Temple of Castor. The marble statues are highly fragmentary, but show the two young men in heroic nudity, standing next to their horses (each animal's belly is supported by a palm tree, probably added as needed during a Tiberian repair). They were at first thought to be truly Archaic, or perhaps Severe, even part of the booty taken from Greece by Aemilius Paullus after Pydna. A review of the evidence has now provided a date in the mid-second century, as a thank-offering erected by the victorious general in a style that would recall the antiquity of the cult.[46] If this interpretation is correct, it would throw additional light on the Delphic pillar monument as a typically Greek rather than as a Roman expression.

I end my review of second-century sculptures with two puzzling pieces that deserve to be better known, although their identity, place of origin, status (original or "copy"?), and therefore chronology are uncertain. In this respect, they are fully representative of the problems we encounter in dealing with Hellenistic material and can be treated here to summarize issues and suggest leads for future research.

Plates 80a–b   The first is a **female figure in Minneapolis** (Pls. 80a–b). When first extensively discussed in the scholarly literature, it was on the art market, after its discovery in 1885 "near the Tiber"—hence its nickname, the Tiber Muse—and its many years in an Italian private collection. It shows a young woman dressed in a thin chiton and a himation that wraps only around the lower part of her body. Her left foot is propped on a layered support that suggests a stratified geological formation — or, as one scholar has orally proposed, the prow of a ship. The prop is damaged at the front, and so are the toes of the raised foot, but the figure as a whole is remarkably well preserved; missing are, however, the foot of the right leg supporting the weight, the head, the separately inserted right arm from the shoulder, and the left forearm below the elbow. We lack, therefore, whatever attributes she held, which would once have revealed her identity. The woman leans forward, probably turning slightly to her right, so that her neckline slips down revealing the top of the right breast; in addition, the garment forms an open loop over her right side, uncovering part of her body. This is an unusual rendering, for which not many parallels are known.[47]

Since only a few strands of hair remain over her nape, the Tiber Muse probably wore a chignon like the Melos Aphrodite. The alluring "slipped strap" is a common trait in the iconography of the goddess of love, but other deities are also shown in this fashion, including Hera and Hygieia, and even the Drunken Woman usually connected with Myron's name, although hers may be a ferocious satire on old age.[48] What the Minneapolis statue has in common with the hag in Munich, however, is also the way in which her chiton is held by twin straps over the shoulders. The rendering is not identical, but confirms a Hellenistic fashion that goes with the border along the neckline. Other Hellenistic features in the Minneapolis statue are the armlet with an inset stone and the high belt, tied with a Herakles knot, as well as the small cylinders at the sides of her sandal.[49]

The loop of the chiton below the right armpit recurs in a seated statue from Kyzikos (cf. Pl. 53) that has been tentatively identified as Kore but could easily be another goddess. She is also close to the Minneapolis statue in the general rendering of her costume: the chiton with thin, ribbon-like folds and the mantle encircling the lower body. This convincing comparison has prompted the suggestion that the Tiber Muse originally came from Asia Minor and, like the Kyzikos sculpture, should date to the third quarter of the second century. To be sure, the Minneapolis statue shows a more plastic treatment of the chiton folds over the front, which, however, may be justified by the leaning pose; the folds change into linear pleats over the sides and on the long, curving back.[50]

Can this stylistic similarity suffice to attribute the Tiber statue to an East Greek city? Less conclusive is an analysis of the pose and type, which seem highly diffuse. They recur in sculptures of Muses, and are clearly attested for the mid-second century by a terracotta statuette that was found in a tomb in Neapolis, in Northern Greece. Even the slipping neckline of the chiton is comparable. The presence of a terracotta kithara from the same tomb suggests that it was once held by the figurine, confirming its identity as Melpomene. A marble Muse also dated to the second half of the second century, in two fragments (one of them recovered some years after the first) comes from **Macedonian Dion;** she too holds her left foot on a rock and wears the same two garments, but her chiton remains in place, her torso is erect, and her body shows little torsion. Although she holds a lyre against her left side, she has been called Terpsichore, yet the propped foot and the static pose seem unsuited for the Muse of the dance. The same stance may be used to imply different modes: not only that of a body at rest, or the inner tension and introspection of a Hellenistic ruler, but also simply a listening attitude. In this sense, we find it again in the iconography of Muses on fifth-century vases.[51]

Given its Italian findspot, I would postulate that the Tiber Muse may have come from Sicily, where at least one more sculpture, the goddess from Soloeis (cf. Pl. 56), attests to the presence of East Greek products on the island. That Muse statuary was known there is shown by three examples in **Syracuse,** from a Nymphaion on the terrace above the theater, where they were perhaps set up by an actors' guild late in the second century—a rare instance of Hellenistic marble sculpture from Sicily. One of them is a variant of a well-known type usually identified as **Artemis–Hekate** and extensively represented **on Rhodes,** although also widely distributed, with minor changes, from Athens to Kyrene. Obviously, no specific iconography for certain Muses had yet been established in the second century, so that some popular types were adapted to the different functions and demands. This approach to iconography and this stylistic koine make assessment of Hellenistic sculpture proportionately difficult.[52]

In suggesting that the Tiber Muse came from Sicily, we have automatically implied that we consider it a Greek original rather than a "Roman copy." It could, of course, be a work made by a Greek master in Rome for a Late Republican customer, like the many other sculptures cited in Chapter 7. It seems less likely that it could be an Imperial reproduction of a second-century prototype, although, admittedly, only its high quality (a notorious trap!) and perhaps its type of marble militate against the possibility. This same problem arises with our second piece.

Plates 81a–b
The remarkable **Gaul in the Metropolitan Museum,** New York (Pls. 81a–b), is the lower part of a marble figure in striding pose; his bent right knee and the direction of his movement have suggested that he is attacking an enemy set up on a separate plinth to (viewer's) left, but a slight torsion in what remains of the man's torso (note especially the shelflike fold over his genitals) implies that he was partly facing the front, and we have already noted several other statues of fighters without opponents. The upper part of the statue was carved separately and doweled in place; it is now missing, but the legs down to the ankles are covered by tight-fitting trousers with a few tension folds, and holes for the attachment of a metal dagger on the right hip correspond to the Gallic practice of wearing the weapon on that side, as contrasted with Greek custom. The dagger hung from a remarkable belt which probably imitates a leather item with metal elements, and which vaguely recalls that worn by the Eros riding the Old Centaur in the Louvre.[53]

Mostly because of its identification, the statue has been published as a Roman copy of one of the Attalid dedications—another example of the tendency to ascribe to Pergamon anything remotely connected with Gauls. Yet according to a reliable source, the piece comes from the Italian/Etruscan site of Cerveteri, not especially known for its sculptures during Imperial times. Its marble seems Greek, and the use of metal attachments is not typical of Roman copies. Finally, the costume is more in keeping with that of the European Kelts than of the Asiatic Galatians.[54] This excellent work could have been made, probably by a Greek, for a Late Republican general, perhaps even Caesar, victorious in one of the many encounters with Keltic populations at the end of the second and during the course of the first century B.C.

In its general orientation (parallel to the front of the plinth) and animated pose, the Gaul in New York has been compared to the marble **Warrior from Delos** (Pl. 82), now in the National Museum in Athens. This well-known statue comes from the Agora of the Italians, and it used to be connected with the pedestal of a monument in honor of Marius, who had won victories against the Keltic Cimbri and Teutones in 102–101 B.C. This association has now been rejected on several grounds, yet the figure is still thought to depict a Gaul because it rests its right knee on the cheekpiece of a horned helmet, considered typically Keltic. It has therefore recently been suggested that the statue may belong to the end of the third century, as part of a monument celebrating the victory of Attalos I over all the Galatians, which stood in front of the northern end of the South Stoa on Delos.[55]

Plate 82

Several objections can be raised against this attribution. Although the top block of Attalos I's monument is missing, the other two Pergamene dedications on the island consisted of bronze sculptures, and it is unlikely that the third one would have used a different medium. As far as we know, all such victory monuments by the Attalids were in bronze. It is also impossible to disregard the actual findspot of the marble warrior—the Agora of the Italians—where indeed a great number of monuments were erected in marble, according to Italian practices. Even the helmet next to the Warrior is a hybrid form, combining Macedonian and Italo-Keltic elements, and thus could also be Italic. Finally, the warrior is entirely nude and wears a baldric supporting a scabbard on his left side, according to Greek custom. If the head is pertinent, it does not show the wild hair and barbaric features associated with the iconography of the Gauls. Perhaps the sculptor who made it, unlike the master of the New York statue, was not directly acquainted with Galatians, either those in the East or those in the West, and therefore used the generic motif of a fighter—as Polykles and Timarchides, who made C. Ofellius Ferus, used a Greek Hermes/ruler type for the honorary monument of a Roman merchant. Given the date of the Agora of the Italians, the Warrior should be approximately contemporary with the Ofellius, and whatever his true ethnic, he had to be relevant for the Italians who frequented the Delian place. Like the Gaul in New York, he should not be viewed through the distorting lens of Pergamene perspective.[56]

CONCLUSIONS

With these last two statues, both under "the shadow of the Pergamon Altar," yet both probably made for Romans, we have come full circle to where we began. We have seen how the evidence from a major and well-preserved monument has influenced most of our Hellenistic attributions, coloring interpretations and historical reconstructions, even leading us to disregard some excavational data. And we have seen the important role played by the new power within the Mediterranean. It is now time to attempt some general conclusions on second-century styles and sculptures.

To be sure, this book does not purport to be a handbook of all monuments produced during that span of time, and it is certainly not representative in *geographic terms.* In part, these omissions are due to the uncertain nature of the evidence, and especially the chance of the finds. A notable gap is the material from **ancient Alexandria,** where new underwater finds offer some promise to fill in the picture.[57] Sculpture from **Syria** may remain scarce, although Robert Fleischer plans a second volume on the Seleukids. **Sicily and South Italy** are underrepresented on my pages, partly because a lack of marble in those areas prevented more extensive production, but partly also because different habits of adornment of public places may have prevailed and because the heavy-handed Roman control did not lend itself to large-scale commemorations. Without tyrants and rulers, the once splendid Sicily lacked the incentive—and the events—to set up civic monuments. The few marble pieces for private consumption, at modest sizes, may have come from Asia Minor or the islands.

Athens has not fared well in these chapters, yet Athenian masters were very active on Delos and elsewhere, and the high standards of craftsmanship in the area are documented by the finds of high-quality relief ware from the Agora. General prosperity is attested by the colossal cult images made by Athenians and, eventually, by the so-called Neo-Attic production (witness the cargo of the Mahdia shipwreck); yet Athenian sculptors went abroad—a practice not limited to them but significant in the context.[58] **Asia Minor,** by contrast, has been seen as the hotbed of innovations and artistic activity—in part correctly, because of the image the nouveau-riche Attalid dynasty wanted to project, in part because the Greek element along the coast had a longstanding tradition that found expression in buildings and monuments, with a new line of production in gravestones. **Macedonia,** however, is underrepresented, perhaps because its courtly climate preferred manifestations of luxury other than sculptural embellishment. The **Aegean islands,** both those of the Dodekanesos and the Kyklades, especially Melos, seem quite active, although much of what has been found remains at the level of the artifact and "commercial" production. Exact copying seems to begin in this century, perhaps not in, and for, Pergamon, as some advocate, and not even in Athens, as the Neo-Attic products would suggest, but certainly in the general Greek area, as documented by the Diadoumenos of Polykleitos found on Delos, whose faithfulness to a model is supported by additional replicas.[59]

Can the presence of **Rome** be felt in the available artistic evidence? Not necessarily, unless we count it negatively, in the relative lack of Greek victory monuments after the mid-century, and, positively, in the introduction of a few hybrid forms that penetrate footwear and armor. Italy certainly provided a major market, to be exploited by producers of a variety of luxury objects, not just sculpture. On Greek soil, the great number of honorary statues erected in many Greek centers speaks to the political impact of Roman nationals, and some of the religious images and structures were set up by the Romans themselves, but they remain in the Greek spirit and use Greek types, so that unless inscriptions provide proof, they cannot be assigned with certainty. Equally intangible is the alleged Roman contribution to the veneration of the dead that may have resulted in heroizing overtones in East Greek and Kykladic gravestones and funerary altars. The best information comes from Italy itself, where Greek masters emigrated and worked, albeit for new masters and requirements. Findspots can be ignored only at the risk of mistaking the message, although some sculptures might have entered Roman territory as booty or purchases. Much of the statuary that seems "Roman" in concept and purpose (e.g., the satyr/nymph groups, the moralistic "punishments") belongs, I suspect, to the following century.

In *stylistic terms*, several trends are present, and cannot be arranged in a logical temporal sequence; subject matter seems to dictate preferences. Perhaps the most obvious is the **Baroque style** of—indeed—the Pergamon Altar, but as something already existing and widely diffused before its adoption by the multinational masters working for the Attalids. It continues throughout the second century and into later times. The **Classicizing style**, long a viable option, remains current, especially for images of deities; it can appear on gravestones, for instance, where a more idealized female may stand next to a male figure of Baroque or realistic appearance. **Archaistic and Archaizing**, in different proportions, are also attested throughout—closer to Archaic formulas on the Greek Mainland and the islands, closer to contemporary fashions on the Anatolian coast, with a regionalism that contradicts the wider stylistic picture. The so-called **Rococo style**, canonized by Bieber's influential book,[60] escapes me as a definable trend. It may perhaps be equated with realism, yet many of its alleged products seem later, and perhaps Roman in spirit and commission. It could also be characterized as a playful vein, a light-hearted arrangement of figures within the world of nature, but I cannot pinpoint satyrs, Erotes, and children as definitely part of our time bracket.

Perhaps the most tangible **elements of style** to be attributed to this century (but not to it alone) are the extreme effects of transparency: both drapery through drapery and the contouring of forms under several layers of clothing; the use of arrow folds with directional effect resulting in surface tension; the introduction of trumpet folds in fluttering overfolds to define abdominal areas—a mannerism indirectly deriving from fifth-century patterns. In faces, mouths are often open, more so than on Classical works, revealing the teeth; beards may have a clear central part. Proportionately, figures seem more elongated, the females with narrow shoulders, high waistlines, and broad hips, forming a sort of pyramidal outline when covered with their luxurious garments. A shoulder-back stance has also been noted, and, especially for males, a wide "stride" with trailing foot touching only at the toes. Footwear has many-layered soles with deep indentations between the first two toes; the latter may be carved wide apart in a bare foot; a very short fifth toe may be a recurrent mannerism.

In *technical terms*, stone sculpture is remarkable for the extent of its piecing: not simply attributes, heads, limbs, or small details carved separately, but entire trunks joined at mid-torso, and panes of drapery. Backs are occasionally hollowed out, surfaces can remain unfinished or uncarved, and a return to the akrolithic technique includes a penchant for inserted eyes, perhaps with divine implications; but there are fewer metal attachments, probably none in architectural sculpture. Bronzes are increasingly frequent, but not many have survived. Their casting and joining methods, as far as we can judge, remain traditional, so that it is hard to date on technical grounds; the reuse, with ad hoc modifications, of single models makes dating by stylistic features equally hazardous. The repetition of standard types in both stone and bronze seems a feature of workshop (mass) production, yet sculptors' signatures reappear and increase in frequency through the century, not only on free-standing monuments but also on architectural sculpture. Mechanical copying by measuring points is also attested.

Iconographically, I do not yet find the Homeric compositions and allusions that are supposedly behind the Sperlonga sculptures. If they existed, they were probably made for the Romans, on Italian soil. Myth was still extensively used, often for propaganda purposes, but in my opinion the Trojan War as a subject, although popular in architectural sculpture, was apparently not yet exploited in the round, at least in Greek cities proper. It eventually became so as part of an incipient trend toward transforming previously narrative and/or attributive images into three-dimensional statuary—witness the creation of river-god statues. Athletic sculpture may have been rarer; it was mostly in bronze and has not survived. Ruler statues were instead common, but even those have left behind a generic reflection rather than actual evidence; they were, at any rate, probably patterned after images of divinities. The majority of sculpture we have examined is somewhat amorphous and anonymous. A tendency existed to use well-established types for a variety of purposes, almost a return to Archaic practices, when a few generic formulas could be turned into specifics. We have noted it for the Muses and other deities. Some male types—the citizen, perhaps even the seated philosopher—were derived from the fourth-century repertoire of the Attic gravestones.

East Greek and Kykladic funerary monuments seem to reach a peak within the second century; standard types like the Funerary Banquet continue in use with a distinctive distribution, but new forms develop that, in the frontality of the figures and/or the proliferation of attributes, hint at heroization. Yet even figureless structures like the Achaian naiskoi convey the same suggestion of veneration, perhaps indicative of turbulent years and need for divine protection. The separation between funerary and votive reliefs (especially of the Rider type) is vague indeed.

Architecturally, the type of structure most likely to have been embellished with sculpture was the altar, although here too the third century offered precedents. Such decoration could take the form of relief or of statuary in the round set up over the projecting wings of a Π-shaped formation. Temples in Asia Minor continued to be built, but construction was prolonged over time, and size could prevent meaningful compositions or artistic high quality. Tombs diminished in importance, *pari passu* with the diminution in stature of the various rulers. Palaces may have been decorated with reliefs, but the evidence is ambiguous; private houses, however, began to use ornamentation, although often in stucco. Civic buildings prospered, but they were less likely to be embellished in traditional manners. A different form of display enhanced the architecture in lieu of sculpture: axiality, backdrops, terracing, dramatic vistas.

In *summary*, we may have to admit that the shadow of the Pergamon Altar is almost inevitable, as that is the only representative structure that can securely be assigned to the second century, regardless of its actual position within those hundred years. With its enormous size and number of sculptures in relief and in the round, it fills our mental vision and provides the only legitimate picture within a highly confused scenario. Yet it should not prevent us from looking further and farther, with clear mind and eyes, fighting the tendency to fall under its spell, and recognizing the complexity of what can legitimately be classified as Hellenistic sculpture.

NOTES

1. For general comments on Etruscan sarcophagi and portraits, see Brendel 1978, 390–95, and, for the 2nd c., 420–23 (by E. Richardson).

2. The study of the bronzes from the Villa, by C. C. Mattusch and H. Lie, has already produced some results: see supra, Ch. 7 n. 66. Prof. Mattusch kindly tells me (*per ep.*, Sept. 1998) that, in her opinion, the bronzes are not overcasts, and have different sizes and styles; three "dynastic" portraits, however, stylistically and proportionally similar, have the same alloy and will be attributed to a single purchase. The marbles have a single style and size and should come from one workshop (probably not the same one that made the bronzes). Smith 1988, 70–78, provides some totals: of the nearly 80 extant sculptures from the Villa, more than half are portraits of famous Greeks (one of them a full-scale statue of Aischines), three are of Romans. Only seven small bronze busts are inscribed; at natural scale, there are 15 bronze busts, probably from herms, and 13 marble herms. On two marble herms there are faint traces of painted inscriptions identifying Archidamos III of Sparta (r. 361/0–338) and Panyassis (a 5th-c. epic poet)—why were the labels only painted, and not also incised, as was more common? and were the bronze busts labeled on their marble shafts, now lost? (Some, but not all, of the table busts, like the Doryphoros', have inscriptions incised either on the base or on the chest.) One wonders whether "identification" was left to the last minute, according to the owner's wishes. Of the 28 large-scale "portraits," 10 (five in bronze, five in marble) are thought to depict rulers. The bronze busts, according to Smith 1988, are overcasts, the marble ones accurate copies, of Hellenistic originals, made as a group in early Imperial times, when a refurbishing of the Villa added the large peristyle garden. Yet, among them, only the Panyassis and the so-called Pseudo-Seneca are known through additional replicas from elsewhere. Moreover, not even Delos or Athens could have provided prototypes (and casts) for all the rulers represented at the

Herculaneum Villa. Other areas are not known for their commercial reproduction of statuary models. Smith 1991, 22, seems to nuance his previous position, acknowledging "varied scale and style" among the 10 ruler portraits.

For an annotated bibl. on the "program" of the Villa of the Papyri, see Queyrel 1990, 111. See also Ridgway 1990, 126–27 and ns. 38, 41–42 with refs. I do not deal here with these portraits as such, because they allegedly go back to prototypes of the 3rd, not of the 2nd, c. I shall only repeat (cf. Ridgway 1990, 112) that I am puzzled by the fact that the so-called royal diadem on some of these heads ends over the nape instead of continuing with loose ends over the shoulders, as clearly rendered on coins; the only (marble) bust with this rendering is "unidentified" (Smith 1991, fig. 14). Yet the fashion is attested for images of Herakles and was certainly possible, from a technical standpoint, in both marble and bronze statues.

3. Schefold 1997, section on "High Hellenism" (all dates here cited to be understood as "after original of"): nos. 148 (Hippokrates, ca. 180), 149–50 (Pseudo-Seneca from Villa of the Papyri, Aristophanes? ca. 180), 151 (seated poet in Copenhagen, Pindar? ca. 180/170), 152–53 (Homer, ca. 150). The section on Greeks of Roman time includes only one bust: Karneades, ca. 140 (nos. 197–98). I do not count here the stele of Polybios, already discussed supra, Ch. 6, and several terracotta statuettes with realistic heads, which do not truly belong among portraits. Even von den Hoff 1994 covers only the span ca. 310–170.

The so-called Hellenistic Ruler in the Terme, Rome, mostly dated to the 2nd c., will be discussed infra. For additional, if controversial, identifications of rulers' portraits and wide-ranging bibl., see Queyrel 1990.

4. Stewart 1979: 71–72 (chronology of extant portraits), 66 (statistics based on inscriptions; a total of 128 portraits, both signed and unsigned, for the period 166–100 [of which 94 are dated between 124 and 100], corresponds to a total of 91 for the period 99–0). Stewart is primarily interested in identifying works by Athenians, although he stresses that the "expatriates" on the island had no contact with the mother city (p. 67). He also outlines the evolution of portraiture in Athens itself from ca. 50 onward, following what he calls "the prolonged period of sterility following the collapse of the neo-classic manner c. 100" (p. 80). I do not believe in the water-tight sequence of styles, as repeatedly mentioned, nor can I subscribe to a Baroque trend beginning in Athenian portraiture of the late 3rd c., which Stewart had based on his original (high) chronology for the Antisthenes by Phyromachos (Stewart 1979, 16–17; but cf. supra, Ch. 7 n. 10). Almost two decades later, one of Stewart's former students could — surprisingly — consider *Classicism* a Hellenistic phenomenon impelled especially by Pergamon (Kuttner 1995, 158).

For more general accounts of the Delian portraits, see, e.g., Pollitt 1986, 73–75; Smith 1988, 126–27.

5. See, e.g., Pollitt 1986, fig. 73 (Pseudo-Athlete: ht. 2.55 m); Marcadé 1969, pls. 68–70 (men in himation), 75–76 (cuirassed torsos), 78 (calcei). For the term "philorhomaioi," albeit applied to rulers of the 1st c. B.C., see Smith 1988, 130–32. Smith considers it more likely that Italian businessmen brought the realistic trend in portraiture with them from Rome to Delos, rather than that the aristocratic Romans followed the lead of some Delian merchants.

6. Kozloff 1996; the quotations are from pp. 249–50. The tradition of identifiable portraits is said to be as early as the beginning of the third millennium. The difficulty in telling one Ptolemy from another seems not to be due to the quality of the carvings, which is considered uniformly good. She also suggests that the Greek Ptolemies did not like to be depicted

in the darker stones available in Egypt, including limestone, which was traditionally painted red for male skin (n. 19 on p. 259, although it is not quite correct to state that the Greeks left marble skins unpainted—ganosis would have tinted the stone). The lack of local white marble would have made sculptures in the Greek tradition costly, within an economic system that relied heavily on exporting a lot and importing very little; this situation may have led to the use of stucco and plaster for corrections and additions to sculptures when sufficient marble was not available.

7. Smith 1996, 204, 206. The point is established by comparing portraits of Ptolemy VI (r. 180–145) in Greek style and marble to some of his portraits in Egyptian granite and other hard stones: figs. 3–4; also a marble head of Ptolemy VIII Euergetes Physkon (r. 145–116) on loan to Yale University is compared with a diorite head in Brussels: figs. 5–6. Other examples are adduced.

8. Smith 1996 uses the hair pattern to identify Ptolemy VI; cf., however, Stewart 1979, pls. 18a (Delos A 4192) and 25b (Athens NM 320); for crewcuts, see, e.g., his pls. 18c, 19c–d (Delos A 2912, 4191, 4186). Fleshy features and wide eyes of Ptolemy VIII (Physkon): cf. some of the heads in Bothmer 1996; private individuals could, of course, imitate distinctive royal features, but the argument may also be circular; Bothmer lists features previously, but erroneously, thought to reflect Greek influence, and stresses the complex origins of two of them (inserted eyes and corkscrew curls). For other features of Egyptian heads (tilt, mood, increased naturalism, open mouth, even the Macedonian kausia), he would however accept Greek input (p. 226). That "a variety of styles coexisted throughout the Ptolemaic Period" is stated by Stanwick 1992, 135, q.v. for other significant comments. For additional bibl. on Ptolemaic portraits, see Ridgway 1990, 130–31.

9. "Praxitelean" sfumato as an Alexandrian feature: Ridgway 1990, 13 and n. 1 on pp. 60–61, 130–31 with refs. (royal portraits), 363–66, esp. 364. On the origin of the theory and its applicability to a wide area: Stewart 1996b, esp. 235–38 (origin) and 239 (diffusion). High polychromy, by comparison with mosaic *emblemata:* Daszewski 1996. For the mosaics, see *LIMC* 1, s.v. Alexandria, nos. 73–74 pls. 371–72 (among the uncertain representations, dated 2nd half 2nd c.). For a review of the various papers included in Hamma 1996, see Venit (supra, Ch. 4 n. 80).

10. Fleischer 1991, esp. 116 (paucity of sculptural finds and list of accepted portraits), 134 (coin type beginning with Antiochos IV), 135–36 (difference between marble temple-statues and bronze *eikones*); for Antiochos IV and his coin type, see 44; for divine attributes and their allusions (even in connection with non-Seleukid coins), 132–33. On the functions of royal statues and on attributes, see also Queyrel 1990. Bergmann 1998 discusses astral symbolism: section I and pp. 13–84 for the Hellenistic period.

11. Hellenistic Ruler: Rome, Museo Nazionale delle Terme 1049. For an extensive bibl. with specified identifications, see Fleischer 1991, 107 (Demetrios I). Add Moreno 1994, 418–27, figs. 531, 533, 536–37, 941 (T. Quinctius Flamininus, dedicated in Rome by Eumenes II after 196); Knell 1995, 69 and n. 123, (statue of Philip V that stood on Samothrake; cf. supra, Ch. 5 and n. 34); Mattusch 1996, 77 fig. 3.2, 119 and n. 50 (no identification, regrettably little technical discussion); Meyer 1996c, with description and previous opinions (Eumenes I, who did not assume royal title, hence lack of diadem, mid-3rd c.); Hafner 1997 (Demetrios I, made before 162 when the hostage prince fled Rome). For the best photographs, see Himmelmann 1989, pp. 143–47, 205–207, with discussion on pp. 126–49 (Attalos II, before assuming the royal title);

technical comments on pp. 180–84 (M. R. Sanzi Di Mino, A. M. Carruba: probably a Roman general). Cf. also Smith 1991, fig. 3 ("undiademed prince or dynast, 3rd–2nd c.") and comments on pp. 19–20; *LIMC* 3, s.v. Dioskouroi/Castores, 614, no. 21 pl. 490 (doubtful identification, dated mid-1st c.). Identification as Hannibal was suggested by V. Poulsen, *Fran Grottörna till Rom* (Stockholm 1965) 260–61 and supported by J. D. Breckenridge, "Hannibal as Alexander," *AncW* 7 (1983) 121ff., both cited by Meyer 1996c, 133 and ns. 54–56. The idea itself, regardless of sculptural identification, is not as improbable as it may seem at first, since three statues of Hannibal, dedicated by the Thourioi in three different areas of Rome, are mentioned by Pliny, *NH* 34.32.

12. For good details, see the color photographs in Himmelmann 1989, on pp. 145–46 and 207, fig. 4d. Note the regular arc of the eyebrows (on which tufts of hair were "applied," probably in the wax), the space between them and the very shallow vertical grooves (frown lines) that frame it. The bulging eyebrow muscle overlapping the lid at the outer corner is usually called Skopasian, after works attributed to that master. For an analysis of the facial features, see Himmelmann 1989, 130, with comparison to Lysippos' Apoxyomenos, although probably because of physiognomics, not because of style; the technical analysis (p. 181) defines beard and mustache as cold work. A connection with the (late) Lysippan School is tentatively supported by Meyer 1996c, esp. 144–46.

13. Pseudo-Athlete from Delos, Athens NM 1828 (ht. 2.25 m): e.g., Smith 1991, fig. 315; Stewart 1990, fig. 840. The Hellenistic Ruler is slightly smaller: ht. (from top of head), 2.04 m; (to top of raised left arm) 2.37 m. For a distinctly disproportionate Imperial example, see, e.g., *Fire of Hephaistos* 1996, 349 fig. 1: Trebonianus Gallus (r. 251–253), Metropolitan Museum of Art 05.30, ht. 2.41 m.

14. This last theory is proposed by Hafner 1997, who identifies the Ruler as Demetrios I of Syria, before 162 when he fled Rome to assume power—hence the lack of royal fillet and the pose; see his fig. 5 on p. 133 for the forward lean, and fig. 13 on p. 140 for a restoration with cuirass by the free leg, which looks improbable. See also Himmelmann 1989, left-hand fig. on p. 147; the slant could be blamed on the modern restoration, yet the statue seems further unbalanced when viewed directly from the rear (right-hand fig. on same page), with strong lean to proper left, enhanced by the curved spinal groove. For a comparable forward slant, see *Fire of Hephaistos* 1996, 224–31, cat. 23 (a youthful Dionysos from Syria), esp. figs. 23c–d, unless this piece as well has been damaged. The area of its findspot has yielded Roman remains no earlier than the 2nd c. A.C. (cf. p. 230 and n. 18).

For the position of the Ruler's trailing foot, albeit in reverse stance, cf. the Antikythera Youth (e.g., Stewart 1990, fig. 530), which is, however, better balanced. See also infra, n. 25.

The expression "spear-won land" goes back to Alexander: cf. Smith 1991, 19–20 (on meaning of ruler's pose); Queyrel 1991, 431–33 and figs. 49–51 (Baltimore "Alexander Lépine," although Smith 1991, fig. 2, calls the statuette "king, 3rd–2nd c."). For other bronze statuettes of Alexander, see, e.g., Stewart 1990, figs. 564–65 (the Fouquet and the Nelidow Alexander), both labeled "Roman copies" although the Nelidow figurine has been also considered Renaissance. See also his figs. 566 (Herakles' pose, Farnese type) and 549 (Meleager type). The Terme Ruler has also been compared to a Dioskouros: cf. supra, n. 11, and Himmelmann 1989, 136–37, and figs. 52.6, 9 on p. 129 (Pergamene coins), although the hand position differs.

For rulers' imitation of Herakles, see the judicious analysis by Palagia 1986, although she does not include the Terme bronze. In some cases, Hellenistic monarchs patterned themselves after the divinized Alexander-Herakles rather than after the hero himself, although not all examples are considered valid; the Ptolemies are a separate case because they claimed descent from Herakles, and so did Marc Antony. True assimilation to Herakles among the Roman emperors begins with Caligula and Nero, and continues, with gaps, until Maxentius.

15. Ofellius Ferus: supra, Ch. 7 and n. 34; the ruler type is discussed by Queyrel 1991, 433–35 (with mention of the Terme Ruler), and 437–43 for implied meanings. For a similar type, but headless and **smaller than lifesize,** from Pergamon, see Smith 1991, fig. 181 ("Ruler, late 3rd or 2nd c."; but the Berlin Museum label says Roman).

Contrast between citizen and ruler types: Smith 1993 (who makes the point that the city portraits continue from the 4th c., but the royal images are new in the 3rd); Himmelmann 1989, 100–25 (his fig. 45, from Pergamon, is an example of a **seated ruler**—cf. Smith 1991, fig. 191, "seated hero? Later 3rd or early 2nd c."), and the review by Queyrel, *RA* 1991, 380–82. A tradition of cuirassed statuettes in ruler pose existed also in Italy: Richardson 1996, 108–16 (Group III, "small imitations of the lazier Hellenistic ruler portraits").

16. For this last theory, see Queyrel's review of Himmelmann 1989 (supra, n. 15), and his 1990 annotated bibl. with discussion of other suggestions.

17. For a good photograph of the right digitations of the Ruler, see Himmelmann 1989, right-hand fig. on p. 147; note also the inflated neck muscle. Marble torso from Elaia, in London, British Museum: Smith 1991, fig. 190 ("colossal seated god. 2nd c."). I am not sure the figure was seated. I am grateful to Dr. Pia Guldager Bilde for alerting me to the similarity between the Terme Ruler and the marble torso.

18. Head in Malibu, J. Paul Getty Museum, no. 73.AB.8: Himmelmann 1989, 131–32, figs. 53a–b (compared to the Terme Ruler, but with awareness of the stylistic differences; close to portraits of Mithradates VI, thus early 1st c.); Queyrel 1990, 142 no. 315 (same individual, Attalos II, ca. 140); Stewart 1990, 223–24, fig. 803 ("Sulla, ca. 100–75," with "ruthless, even brutal character"); Meyer 1996b, 170–71, 190–91, figs. 40, 77 (early 3rd c., probably Hephaistion, perhaps in group with Alexander).

19. Seated Boxer: Rome, NM 1055. For the best photographs, after cleaning and restoration, Himmelmann 1989, pp. 165–71, 201–203, with comments on pp. 150–74 (dated 2nd quarter of 1st c.), technical discussion on pp. 175–78 and diagram fig. 67 on p. 179; a brief essay by P. Moreno, pp. 178–80 (late 4th c., attributed to Lysippos). See also Smith 1991, fig. 62 ("3rd–2nd c."); Moreno 1994, 60–66, figs. 15, 59, 66, 68, 72, 74–76, 78 (dated before Alexander's death); Rausa 1994, 156–58, figs. 43–46 (eclectic, Late Hellenistic after Classical models, perhaps even Neo-Attic); Meyer 1996a, 96 (compared to Arrotino and Myron's Old Woman, all 3rd c.).

20. See, e.g., Himmelmann 1989, 205–207, where the comments on the Ruler's inscriptions are credited to J. Fabricius. The bronze horse from Trastevere, inv. no. 1064, has occasionally been attributed to Lysippos, as part of the original group of the *Hetairoi* brought to Rome from Dion (Calcani 1989, 31 and ns. 103–109, 110–16, figs. 48, 50–55), but a more likely theory, on the basis of a bronze rider's foot with elaborate sandal, from the same findspot (inv. no. 2164), assigns it to the mid-1st c., pre-Augustan period (Bergemann 1990, 103–105, no. P50, pls. 1a, 3b, 5b, 7c, d, f; for the foot, see pl. 86g–h). The vegetal scrolls on the bronze sandal make me wonder whether it could belong to a deity (a Dioskouros?) rather than a mortal. The horse is inscribed L.I. XXIIX = *loco primo*—28? But note the alleged number, which corresponds to that of the Ruler—a peculiar coincidence.

The base for Minucius carries the inscription L.I.XXVI, but the statue is missing. Later inventories are attested, e.g., by the refurbished "signatures" of Skopas Minor on a base for a statue of Hercules Olivarius (ca. 100? cf. Ridgway 1997b, 275 n. 47), and of Praxiteles and Pheidias on the Dioscuri of Montecavallo (ca. 170–180 A.C.; cf. Geppert 1996, 133–47, esp. 133, dating the added inscriptions after the mid-4th c. A.C., although possibly later, but before 1089, because mentioned by Benzo d'Alba, who died at that time).

21. Head from Kyrene, London, BM 268: Mattusch 1996, 80–83, figs. 3.4 ("no clue as to the date . . . beyond . . . the history of the site," which she takes down only to the Ptolemaic annexation in 322. In *Fire of Hephaistos* 1996, 308, fig. 1, she finds it "tempting" to date before 322.

22. Malibu, J. Paul Getty Museum, head no. 71.AB.458: *Fire of Hephaistos* 1996, 311–15 cat. 44, with extensive bibl. That this head did not belong to the headless bronze body from the Sebasteion in Boubon was already demonstrated by Inan 1977–78, 283–84 no. 13, pls. 91–92 (head, compared to the Terme Ruler), 285 no. 15, pls. 93–94 (body in Burdur Museum), 285–87, pl. 95 (wax cast of head added to torso, connection rejected). Inan 1993, 230–33 no. 12, connects the Burdur torso with the Sebasteion base carrying inscription no. 16, confirming identification as Valerianus the Younger.

Fire of Hephaistos 1996, 314–18, cat. 45 (**head of young man,** loaned by Dr. and Mrs. Raymond Sackler), demonstrates that work comparable to the Terme Ruler could be created within the late 2nd/early 3rd c. A.C. This date is provided by the peculiar technique of the neck join covered by saw-tooth patches, which recurs on datable Imperial portraits and seems limited to that period (cf. Jones 1994). This head combines the shelf of curls over the forehead with a much flatter rendering of incised hair strands at the top of the cranium. Significantly enough, this head was once thought to be a posthumous portrait of Alexander Balas (see cat. bibl.). See also a **bronze head of Hadrian** from the river Thames, in London, where plastic forehead curls combine with an engraved beard and mustache: *Fire of Hephaistos* 1996, 152 fig. 8 (possibly 122 A.C.).

23. Etruscan heads, from Bovianum and from Lake Bolsena: *Fire of Hephaistos* 1996, 126 and ns. 8, 11 on p. 135 (B. S. Ridgway); these heads have been dated to the 4th–3rd cs. For examples of painted facial hair on early Greek statues, see, e.g., the so-called Blond Boy, Akr. 689: Ridgway 1970, 57 and bibl. on p. 74. Roman statues: e.g., three marble figures with Polykleitan bodies and portrait heads, dated mid-3rd c. A.C. (von Heintze 1962, esp. pls. 5, 11–12, 17–18). Beards extending low onto the throat do not seem to be a Greek practice, and not even a Hellenistic one, despite some coin portraits that sport very short hair along the jaw line: cf. the conveniently collected numismatic illustrations in Fleischer 1991, passim.

24. Yemen kings (now in Sana Museum): Weidemann 1983, esp. 16–18 (inscriptions and chronology), 26 (more precise dating), pls. on pp. 14–15 (younger Ruler) and details of face on pp. 17, 20. The father too holds his spear with the left hand, but has the right arm along the side, rather than bent toward the back, as the son's is; his beard appears somewhat more plastic than that of the younger man, perhaps to suggest age differentiation: pl. on p. 26. The bronzes have been restored to a height of 2.37 and 2.38 m respectively (without spears), but these dimensions are made uncertain by the highly fragmentary conditions of the statues when found.

25. On the Boubon material and Valerianus, see supra, n. 22. All figures range somewhat over 2 m in height. Inan 1993 considers 14 statues as belonging to the Sebasteion, in a program of husband/wife pairings, and ranging from the Julio-Claudians to Gallienus, thus over a span of 200 years, until the mid-3rd c. A.C.: pl. 26 fig. 29 (Marcus Aurelius), pls. 27–28 figs. 30–

32 (Lucius Verus), pl. 30 fig. 34 (Septimius Severus), pl. 35 fig. 46 (Caracalla torso; goes with head of figs. 44–45). Cf. also Inan 1977/78: pls. 80 (Lucius Verus), 85 (Septimius Severus), 89 (Marcus Aurelius), 90.2 (Caracalla). See also *Fire of Hephaistos* 1996, 331–39, cat. 50 (Lucius Verus in the Levy Collection), and p. 345 fig. 2 (Marcus Aurelius in Cleveland). All the athletic bodies from the Sebasteion, except for the Valerianus, have a wide stride with trailing foot on tiptoes, like the Terme Ruler. The Lucius Verus in the Levy Collection is said to be "caught in motion": von Bothmer 1990, 240–41 no. 174 (M. L. Anderson). I would rather believe that the pose was chosen to impart liveliness to the figure, but not to suggest actual forward progress.

Meyer 1996b, 185–87, addresses the "Sebasteion Problem" in connection with a highly restored bronze statue in the Levy Collection, perhaps part of a pair (cf. figs. 8–15 and 60–61 with p. 178; bibl. in n. 1). He believes that the two were portraits of Eumenes II and Attalos II (ca. 170, as against the official dating of the Levy bronze "no later than the last quarter of the 1st c.": von Bothmer 1990, 238–40, no. 173, "Statue of a man" [M. L. Anderson]), and suggests that the bronze "Emperor" in Houston, officially considered late 2nd c. A.C. (but not from the Sebasteion), is instead Hellenistic, copying the same prototype as the Levy statue. I find these theories hard to credit.

26. Bases at Olympia and elsewhere: evidence is collected by Rausa 1994 (first section); cf. also Lehmann 1997, 123 and n. 22 for the Late Hellenistic base of Lastenes, with footprints indicating a Polykleitan stance. Here see infra, n. 28, and, e.g., supra, Ch. 7 n. 22, refs. in Themelis 1996 and Maddoli 1989. The cited passages in Pausanias refer to such statues; add, e.g., Paus. 6.4.5 and 6.12.8 for boxers' statues by Polykles and his family. See also the 26 masters (including Eucheir and Timarchides) listed in Pliny, *NH* 34.91, as having made statues of athletes. For the likely prohibition against copying in sanctuaries, see Ridgway 1984, 37 and passim.

27. Smith 1991, 156 and fig. 182; the marble is now in the Izmir Museum. Smith 1991, 51–55, has a brief section on "Athletes," but it is heavily slanted toward the late 4th c., a few possibly 3rd-c. examples (in Roman copies), pieces like the "Agon" from Mahdia (now known to be an Eros), the Borghese Warrior (who is not shown as an athlete), and the Izmir Runner, on which see infra.

28. The issues of scale and prohibition of copying are raised also by Weber 1996, esp. 33–35 and n. 23, with analysis of footprints on bases at Olympia. Since she focuses on the late 4th c., and primarily the Lysippan Apoxyomenos, she has to conclude that the Scraper represented an athletic ideal, rather than a specific victor. For other treatments of the subject, see Rausa 1994 (heavily dependent on Roman copies and attributions), Himmelmann 1989, 150–74 (with emphasis on the Terme Boxer and boxing).

29. I have derived most of my general information from von Hesberg 1995, who in turn summarizes Jacquemin 1981. The latter tries to match actual remains with the mentions of the inventory inscription (ID 1417; A.I, lines 118–154, refer to the gymnasion). The bronzes are all lost, but Jacquemin visualizes them not only through the extant pedestals (fig. 7, for a statuette of Herakles; fig. 14, a base holding a small marble herm shaft) but also through graffiti on some of them (figs. 3–5, Eros shooting arrows, holding torch). One Eros statuette was described as holding Herakles' weapons. Another unusual offering was a Palladion, given by Satyros of Kephisia, probably in 166/5. The gymnasion in question is identified as the so-called *Palestre du Lac:* Tréheux 1988 and Bruneau 1990. In general, for Delos under the Athenians, see Habicht 1997, 246–63.

See also Vorster 1989, esp. 284–85, for the importance of Herakles and his herms in the palaistra and the gymnasion; and Achenbach-Kosse 1989 (infra, n. 37).

30. Herms from Melos: Hamiaux 1998, 46–50, nos. 57–59; cf. supra, Ch. 5 n. 64.

31. The statues of Mithradates VI and brother Chrestos were given by the gymnasiarch Dionysios in 116/5; an image of Mithradates V was set up by Seleukos in 129/8, and one of Nikomedes III of Bithynia by Dioskourides in 119/8. The altar was dedicated by Archias in 114/3. A statue of a gymnasiarch is attested for the year 126/5. See Jacquemin 1981, 164–65.

32. The first quotation is from Gauthier 1995, 10; the second, from M. H. Morgan's translation of Vitruvius. The anecdote is cited by von Hesberg 1995, 22–23, who makes somewhat the same point as Gauthier.

33. See Ajootian 1998, esp. 7 fig. 1.5 for a plan of the Agora with an indication of the base for the Tyrant Slayers.

34. The recent, thorough study is by Hemingway 1997, from which some of my information is derived; see also Hemingway 1998 for previously unnoticed details of the horse's harnessing. A monograph by the same author is forthcoming. For recent illustrations and general discussions, see Pollitt 1986, 147, fig. 159 (the jockey); Stewart 1990, 225, pls. 815–16; Smith 1991, 54, fig. 58 (jockey's face); Moreno 1994, 296–302, with detailed photographs: figs. 368, 370, 371 (Nike brand), 371–73, 374–75 (jockey's feet—note the very small fifth toe), 377, 379. In the list of Mediterranean wrecks transporting ancient works of art (by F. Geldsdorf, in Hellenkemper Salies et al. 1994), the Artemision wreck is no. 41 on p. 765, with number corresponding to location on map, fig. 1 on p. 759.

35. Equestrian compositions in relief often show horses resting on only the hind legs or even just one hoof, but these poses would have been impossible in the round in a medium other than bronze. Battle monuments, such as that commemorating Attalid victories on the Pergamene akropolis, probably included similar rampant horses, but they have not survived, and this difficulty would confirm, in my opinion, the lack of later copies. How the Pergamene ones might have looked, judging from traces on the long base, is suggested by Marszal, forthcoming.

36. The jockey's feet display a remarkably short fifth toe: cf. Moreno 1994, figs. 374–75 on p. 297. But I cannot be sure that this detail is chronologically significant.

37. For most of these comments, including the connection with the Niobids, see Achenbach-Kosse 1989, who lists (p. 78 and n. 46) a sampling of typical offerings by wealthy citizens for the embellishment of gymnasia during Hellenistic times; see her pp. 79–80 for discussion of the heads. Because of their alleged 3rd-c. date, the Wrestlers are not discussed by Kell 1988, but receive a thorough treatment in Künzl 1968, 60–65 (prototype dated 260–240). Rausa 1994, 158–61, deals with wrestlers at large ("a topic preferred by Hellenistic sculptors") and does not devote to the Uffizi group a catalogue entry, although he illustrates them (figs. 47–48); he sees them as within the Lysippan tradition. Smith 1991, 53 and fig. 57, dates to the 3rd c. A study of wrestling groups in the Hellenistic minor arts, by R. Thomas, is in *Hellenistische Gruppen* [now 1999, 199–211].

38. Bronzes in Naples, Nat. Mus. nos. 5626, 5627. For the runners theory, see Warden and Romano 1994, although the two authors may still favor a Greek date and interpretation for the "prototypes." For a "Roman" interpretation, see *Fire of Hephaistos* 1996, 133, fig. 10, and n. 35 (B. S. Ridgway). Rausa 1994 (supra, n. 37), figs. 41–42, considers them wrestlers, dates their "originals" to the last third of the 3rd c., and places them in a clear Lysippan tradition,

but his comparisons (e.g., the seated Hermes from the same villa) would rather prove my case. C. C. Mattusch tells me that their differing alloys may suggest different workshops, or at least non-simultaneous casts.

39. Runner from Kyme, Izmir 9363: the official publication is Uçankus 1989 (I thank Drs. D. Romano and A. Brownlee for making this article and its illustrations available to me); he dates the bronze to the Tiberian period, but on very tenuous stylistic grounds and comparisons, although the hair rendering indeed recalls Julio-Claudian portraits: cf. his figs. 25–27 for details. A good technical analysis is still lacking. See also Smith 1991, 55 fig. 61 ("1st cent. B.C. or A.D."); for the Mahdia comparisons, see Hellenkemper Salies et al. 1994, 350 and n. 30 (S. Lehmann, "Agon"), 523 and n. 26 (H. Hiller, lampadephoroi); for the 3rd c. A.C. date, but without autopsy, see Weber 1996, 35 (with additional bibl.). Rausa 1994, 166 and n. 73, calls it a Roman original inspired by Classical Greek prototypes.

40. Mahdia lampadephoroi: Hiller 1994; see esp. 525–27 for discussion of servant statues; the Homeric passage is *Od.* 7.100–103 (in the palace of Alkinoos). The author makes the important point that all the "silent servants" known so far from the Hellenistic period seem to be Erotes or Hermaphrodites shown in motion, as part of the Dionysiac-erotic sphere so abundantly represented by contemporary terracottas, whereas the figures found in Roman villas are usually adolescents with Polykleitan or Severizing bodies in static poses (cf. her n. 35 for refs.).

I have long suspected that the so-called **Marathon Boy** (Athens NM 11518) may have been such a servant statue, perhaps from Herodes Atticus' villa: cf. pls. 84b–c in Ridgway 1997b, 343–44 and ns. 38–39. Another statue that may have served practical purposes (cf. Ridgway 1990, 227–28) is the so-called **Praying Boy in Berlin,** although a recent technical examination and reproduction of the (probably Rhodian) bronze repeats the traditional identification: Zimmer and Hacklander, eds., 1997, with an account of the bronze's history, 25–34. For an archaeological discussion, see Lehmann 1997, who dates it (p. 125) to the 320s, acknowledging, however, that no real chronological indication is to be derived from its technique (p. 118 n. 7). Although he admits that no individualization is given to the facial features, Lehmann considers the image that of a boy victor in the Halieia, a festival in honor of Helios—figs. 11–12 on p. 128 draw the reconstructed statue with boxing straps on the missing hands, but the undamaged, non-swollen ears of the youth seem to me to speak against his interpretation as a victorious athlete raising his arms to heaven in prayer or thanksgiving. I would visualize the figure as holding up two "torches" (or a torch and another object), as a lychnouchos. Perhaps significantly, Heilmeyer 1996, although citing it only as a stylistically different forerunner (p. 43), groups the Praying Boy with other "functional" bronzes. He moreover points out (chart and p. 34) that its legs have the same length as those of the Youths from Salamis and Antequera; yet the statue in Berlin is ca. 0.10 m smaller than the other two.

For a review of the difference between the use of sculpture in Greek and Roman houses, see Kunze 1996a, esp. 112–15 and ns. 22–42.

41. On the other hand, one can look at this practice as another expression of the phenomenon already noted at the Pergamon Altar, where the Giants of the risalits crawl on the same steps negotiated by the human worshipers. This blurring of the lines between the real and the make-believe world of sculpture is also adumbrated—in somewhat different terms—by statues of deities leaning on Archaistic "idols" (cf., e.g., the statue from Melos, Athens NM 238: supra, Ch. 5 n. 58).

42. Bronze from the house of C. Iulius Polybius: Mattusch 1996, 139 and col. pl. 5. She describes the piece as an Apollo, because of its resemblance to the Piombino bronze now in the Louvre, which indeed depicts the god; but the Pompeii youth was found with remnants of a candelabrum and perhaps even a tray that he probably held in his outstretched arms, and is therefore unquestionably a servant figure. Since he probably dates from the 1st c., he need not concern us here. For the female statues, see Kunze 1996a, figs. 5–6 (servant figures); for a summary of previous scholarship on the same two sculptures (as Charites), see Brahms 1994, 261–65, and 361–63, cat. 91–92, figs. 97–99. For a perceptive analysis of their costume, see Fullerton 1987, 266–68, pl. 18.1–2. On the semantic distinction between "Archaistic" and "Archaizing" as stylistic terms, see Fullerton 1998b, 72–73; also discussion infra.

43. This theory is by Brahms 1994, 264–65 and n. 1152; the two heads from the Demeter terrace are still unpublished; the issue of whether a Hellenistic Boupalos existed is left open. For the initial suggestion and identification, see Heidenreich 1935, revised in 1988 to make Boupalos as late as the Augustan period. Fullerton 1987, 269, seems to accept the Berlin Dancer as a possible Charis or nymph, regardless of authorship. For a likely connection of Archaizing traits with the nymphs, see also the Knidian altar discussed supra, Ch. 3 and n. 53, and cf. Ch. 3 n. 25 (Telephos Frieze).

44. The "attack" is Fullerton 1998b, where valid objections are raised to all ambiguous terminology that relies on matters of degree. He is also completely correct in pointing out the presence of Classical, as well as Archaic, traits in some works that could, therefore, be open to more than one classification; finally, he is equally right in claiming that we cannot possibly discern the intent behind such "hybrids" and whether the sculptor was deliberately Classicizing or Archaizing, or even quoting a specific precedent. The issue becomes even more complex when "Lingering Archaic" and the concept of copies are factored into the equation. For my amplified definitions of the terms, see Ridgway 1993b, 445–46; cf. also 460–61, for the Asiatic form of Archaizing, and p. 12 for a definition of the "law of frontality."

45. Rhodian Artemis-Hekate: Fullerton 1987, 261–65; cf. *LIMC* 2, s.v. Artemis, no. 525 pl. 487 (from Rhodes, under "Uncertain representations"). See also Zagdoun 1995, 157 no. 52, for her 1993 communication on Rhodian Archaistic to the International Congress. Brahms devotes a section to Hellenistic representations: cf., e.g., her cat. nos. 39, 45, 47, for statues from Rhodes, nos. 55–59 for examples from Delos (some unpublished; generally dated to the Hellenistic period), and concluding comments on pp. 275–78. Both Fullerton 1987 and Brahms 1994, 265–69, follow the development of the Pergamene type into Roman times; other examples of that specific pattern in the advanced Imperial period, from the Balkans, are mentioned by Heidenreich 1988, including a 2nd- or 3rd-c. A.C. relief with two Nemeseis holding up their skirts: cf. *LIMC* 6, s.v. Nemesis, no. 146, from Tomis; other Archaistic types are no. 147a–b pl. 440.

For a recently published Artemis from Athens, see Palaiokrassa 1991, 101–102, statue Γ 13, pls. 10–11.The figure, holding a torch, with head and right arm inserted separately, is dated to the 2nd c. Its style is Archaistic, i.e., by my definition, much closer to a true 6th-c. work. According to Brahms 1994, 276–77, nothing new occurs in Attika during the Hellenistic period, and its Archaistic style is said to be a phenomenon of its Classicizing.

46. Most recent mention: La Rocca 1996, 619 (dedication by Aemilius Paullus; an expression of religious conservatism); *LIMC* 3, s.v. Dioskouroi/Castores, no. 56 pl. 493 (dated late 2nd c.,

with mention of Tiberian restoration). Helbig[4], no. 2067 (H. v. Steuben), suggested that the statues (dated 470–460) may have been made in Magna Graecia. The theory that they may be booty brought from Greece proper is tentatively advanced by Clarke 1968, on the basis of a passage in Minucius Felix' *Octavius*, 7.3.

47. "Tiber Muse," Minneapolis Institute of Arts no. 56.12; ht. 1.21 m. The main publication is Neutsch 1956, written when the statue was on the art market, from the collection of Domenico Vitali; cf. his pls. 13–17. He calls its material "Greek island marble." The suggestion that the support is the prow of a ship was made orally by A. Alföldi and cited by Rieche 1973, n. 38 on p. 34 (cf. fig. 25). See also infra, n. 51.

48. On the motif of the slipped strap, see supra, Ch. 3 and n. 13 (esp. Delivorrias 1991). Myron's Old Woman: supra, Ch. 8 n. 44; see, e.g., Smith 1991, fig. 174.

49. On cylindrical loops, see Morrow 1985, 92, pls. 67, 70, considered a common feature after 150.

50. The comparison is made by Fuchs 1966, 49 n. 32. For the Kyzikos seated statue, see supra, Ch. 5 and n. 57. The chiton loop, although on the opposite side, appears also on an image of the so-called Venus Victrix in the Vatican Belvedere: Neutsch 1956, 48 and pl. 20.1. He also makes a general comparison for style and pose with a marble statuette in the Vatican Magazines (pp. 54–55, pl. 18). He considers the latter a Pergamene original of the 2nd c., and would date the Tiber statue to the following century because "more academic." Although I see the resemblance in both pose and costume, the statuette seems to me a simplified version of the same type, hardly reason for establishing a chronological sequence; her mantle is draped lower on the back, and her chiton is so transparent that the beginning of the division between the glutei is revealed as a shadowy accent.

51. Terracotta statuette from Neapolis, in Saloniki, Arch. Mus. 2809: *LIMC* 7, s.v. Mousa, Mousai, 997, no. 207 pl. 718; cf. also no. 205 (Louvre CA 799) pl. 718, from a tomb in Aigina, dated 3rd quarter of the 3rd c. Both figurines hold their left foot on a rocky elevation. For terracotta Muses in tombs, see comments on p. 1007. Neutsch 1956, in exploring possible identifications for the Tiber statue, had thought in terms of a "light" Muse like Thaleia or Terpsichore, because attributes had left no traces on the figure. For the "Terpsichore" from Dion, Demeter sanctuary, see the various excavation reports: *BCH* 1983, 786 fig. 83; *AR* 30 (1983–84) 43 fig. 73; *Prakt.* 1982 (publ. 1984) 66, pl. 49.2 (mentioning lyre similar to tortoise shell).

For the first two meanings of the pose, see Neutsch 1956, 46–47, who cites Oidipous in front of the sphinx, and Argo watching Io. For a listening pose while Muses play musical instruments or poets recite, see, e.g., *LIMC* 6, s.v. Mousa, Mousai, no. 14 pl. 385 (RF hydria in Berlin, ca. 450–425) and no. 81 pl. 396 (RF lekythos in Basel, ca. 420–410). See also Ridgway 1990, 262, for other examples on vases. The pose, together with comparable iconographic details, recurs also on the Lagina frieze: see supra, Ch. 4 n. 38.

Von Prittwitz und Gaffron 1988 discusses the Minneapolis statue as his cat. 4.2.7 (pp. 82–83), within the context of his Type 4 (pp. 61–89), despite the fact that the Tiber figure is neither a statuette nor semi-nude. He would date it to the 1st half of the 1st c. He believes that the iconography of a semi-nude female with foot propped on a rock may have originated with Aphrodite.

52. Statue from Soloeis: see supra, Ch. 5 and n. 59. Muses from Nymphaion in Syracuse: Bonacasa 1996, 426 (connected to a Rhodian workshop); one of the three, headless, is cat. 391

on p. 753 (pres. ht. 0.82 m); best photograph in Langlotz and Hirmer 1968, pl. 161 and comments on p. 312 (mention of other replicas), with addendum on p. 318 attributing to an East Greek workshop, for "export," a great number of these Hellenistic statues diffused in the Greek cities from Smyrna to Barcelona. Cf. also *LIMC* 7, s.v. Mousa, Mousai, 993, no. 173, and comments on p. 1010. The Syracuse Muse wears a very transparent chiton belted just below the breasts, and with her right hand holds her mantle roll across her body to the level of the left hip; the other end of the mantle falls from the crook of her left elbow. Her bent left leg is completely revealed and outlined by deep carving, despite being covered by two different garments. She is considered a variant of the type with mantle swag falling in between the legs, the so-called Rhodian Artemis–Hekate, used also for Aphrodite: cf. Gualandi 1976, 130–37, with mention of distribution, and *LIMC* 2, s.v. Artemis, 686–87, nos. 875–77 pls. 511–12. See also Ridgway 1990, 216–17 and n. 8 on pp. 239–40. For the Nymphaion, see Lavagne 1988, 386, and Neuerburg 1965, 108–109 no. 4.

53. Gaul in New York, Metropolitan Museum 08.258.48: Richter 1954, 205–206 no. 205, pl. 145; considered copy of a late 3rd–early 2nd-c. Attalid dedication at Pergamon, because too large (pres. ht. 0.93 m, ca. lifesize) to have been part of the Athenian Smaller Dedication. Stated to be a "translation" from a bronze because a tree-trunk support (now partly broken) strengthened the advanced leg—but cf. the Borghese Warrior. Both legs are broken off below the knees, but the right foot with part of the ankle to mid-shin shows that the hose reached the level of the sandals. Front and (viewer's) left edges of the plinth are preserved. The more extensive discussion is by Wenning 1978, 30–31, pl. 13.3, who objects to the theory of an opponent. See also infra. The piece is briefly mentioned, as a comparison for an Alexandrian work, by N. Bonacasa, *ArchCl* 12 (1960) 177–78 (considered Alexandrian).

Centaur and Eros in the Louvre: e.g., Smith 1991, fig. 161. See also supra, Ch. 8 and n. 45. To my knowledge, a doctoral dissertation by Doris Stupka, "Der Gürtel in der griechischen Kunst" (Vienna 1972), has never been published, but I understand that belt buckles and hooks are rare in true Greek examples. A new study of this topic is highly desirable.

54. This point is made by Wenning 1978, 31, who cites also the belt and the sandals, and accepts identification as a Gaul, but lists the New York statue among representations of barbarians *not* to be associated with Pergamon. He claims it is a late 2nd-c. original from the Italian/Etruscan sphere, and I would concur. For Etruscan and Italic representations of Gauls, see Marszal, forthcoming, and Steingräber, forthcoming. A comparable sentiment, although in a different context, is expressed by Meyer 1996a, 109: "The *art-historical legend* that among the Hellenistic depictions of Gauls those attributed to the Great Attalid Dedication take precedence over anything Alexandrian . . ." (my emphasis).

55. Delos Gaul, Athens NM 247: see, e.g., Ridgway 1990, 297–99 and refs. in n. 31, pls. 154a–b; ill. 38 on p. 298 shows the location of Attalos I's Galatian monument. The honorary monument to Marius (for *arete* and *euergasia*, the traditional formula for benefactions) does not mention his victories and gives his title in the accusative, thus implying that the sculpture represented Marius himself. The recent theory is by Moreno 1994, 302–305 and n. 579 with additional refs., figs. 376, 386 (dated late 3rd c.). The comparison with the New York Gaul is by Wenning 1978, 30. Marcadé et al. 1996, 204–205, no. 92, date the statue to the late 2nd c., but, given its findspot, see in it a possible allusion to Attalos III's bequest of Pergamon to Rome. See also infra, n. 56.

56. The helmet form is discussed by Dintsis 1986; under "Kappenhelme," p. 156 and n. 74, he mentions the horn decoration of the Delos Warrior as a form developed in Italy. See also his p. 162 and n. 114 for additional comments on the Italo-Keltic type of helmet with motifs influenced from Macedonia. Yet Dintsis compares it also with weapons depicted on the balustrade reliefs from the Athena terrace at Pergamon, and therefore dates the Delos Warrior to the time of Eumenes II (197–159). See his cat. 260 on pp. 295–96, pl. 70.5 (drawing), and Beil. 12 no. 432. Note that a horned helmet is worn by the Athena head on some Hellenistic terracotta antefixes from Troy: Miller (Collett) 1994, pl. 84.

Wenning 1978, 24–26, pl. 13.1, discusses the Delian figure under non-Pergamene representations and may not consider him a Gaul. Stewart 1990, 227 and pl. 838, believes him "inspired" by Pergamene dedications and dates ca. 100. For inflated Pergamene attributions, see also supra, Ch. 8 n. 11 (Borghese Warrior).

C. Ofellius Ferus: supra, Ch. 7 and ns. 34–35.

57. For a popular announcement, see, e.g., "Newsbriefs," *Archaeology* 49.1 (Jan/Feb. 1996) 22–23. Mid-2nd-c. Alexandria is credited with the invention of the **reclining Nile** in the round, but only echoes of it exist in two statuettes (one in marble, one in limestone) and a lead figurine that are said to be Hellenistic (I am not sure): Klementa 1993, 7, and cat. nos. A1–3 on pp. 9–12, pl. 1.1–2. All other extant sculptures of river gods are Imperial. River personifications are known since the early Classical period (if not the pediments of the Temple of Zeus at Olympia, certainly coins and Nymph Reliefs), and they recur in Hellenistic architectural sculpture (e.g., the altar in Knidos and the Telephos Frieze, supra, Ch. 3). But, once again, the emphasis here is on sculptures *in the round*.

Hellenistic Cyrenaica seems to have produced little sculpture, and virtually nothing during the 2nd c.: Beschi 1996, 442.

58. For comments on the quality of Hellenistic pottery from Athens, I am indebted to G. R. Edwards. Habicht 1997, 112–13, offers some statistics on Athenian sculptors (cf. supra, Ch. 7 and n. 45); although his coverage is wider than ours (from Alexander to Antony) and is partly based on Stewart 1979, his figures are worth repeating. Slightly over 100 sculptors in marble and bronze are known by name from 320 to 31 (including some overlooked by Stewart); 15 worked in Attika and abroad—Delphi, Delos, Rhodes, Boiotia, and Rome. From 180 onward, they also worked at Pergamon. We have already discussed the Athenians who worked for Rome (supra, Ch. 7). Note, however, the danger of considering the entire Hellenistic period as a whole, so that distinctions from century to century are not apparent and the picture may look more consistent than it was in reality.

59. Delos Diadoumenos, Athens NM 1826: see, e.g., Stewart 1990, 226–27, figs. 383–85. For copying beginning at Pergamon, see supra, Ch. 5 n. 49: Niemeier 1985 and Weber 1993, but also my review of Niemeier, and Steinbruckner 1986; in support of an even earlier Pergamene date (2nd half of the 3rd c.), see Meyer 1996b, 187–88. On Neo-Attic workshops, see Cain and Dräger 1994. On Hellenistic sculpture from Melos, see Trianti 1998.

60. See a brief history of the term, and some attributions, in Pollitt 1986, 127–41; this sensible scholar manifests reservations comparable to my own; cf. p. 131: "The question of what much of that sculpture which is classed as 'Hellenistic rococo' was for remains mysterious," and, on p. 141: "Whether one can legitimately . . . say that there was a definable rococo phase in Hellenistic art is doubtful."

List of Monuments
Bibliography
Credits for Plates
Selective Index

List of Monuments

Works are listed in the order of mention and by their provenience, when known, rather than by present location (* = copy; † = perhaps copy)

Works Accepted as Second Century

Pergamon, Reliefs from propylon/andron

Pergamon Altar (ca. 160–133): Gigantomachy Frieze; standing and seated figures in the round; akroterial figures; Telephos Frieze

Delphi, Pillar of Prousias (180/79): Boukranion Frieze

Delphi, Aemilius Paullus Monument (174–167): Battle Frieze

Chryse, Temple of Apollo Smintheus (ca. 160–130): frieze, decorated column drums

Knidos, Altar of Apollo Karneios: reliefs (190–140?)

Magnesia, Temple of Artemis (150–120?): Amazonomachy Frieze

Delos, theater altar (179/8): rosettes and boukrania, satyrs (?), figured frieze now lost

Lagina, Temple of Hekate (120–100): frieze

Kos, Altar of Dionysos (160–140 or 130–120): frieze

Delos, Monument of Mithradates VI (102/1): medallions with portraits, akroteria

Pergamon, stoas on Athena Terrace (ca. 195–150): balustrade reliefs

Pergamon, propylon to Athena Terrace (ca. 195–150): frieze with eagles, owls, garlands; perhaps relief panels

Peiraieus, statuette of Megiste (146/5)

Delos, Kleopatra and Dioskourides (138/7)

Delos, Isis from Serapieion C (128/7)

Delos, Nemesis/Isis (110/9)

Delos, Thea Roma (110/9)

Delos, "Slipper-Slapper Group" from House of Poseidoniastes of Berytos (110–100)

Pergamon, Zeus/Hero from Temple of Hera (159–138)

Melos Aphrodite (ca. 130)

Melos Poseidon (ca. 130)

Works Possibly Second Century

Samos, pillar monument: Erotes frieze

Veria (Beroa): Chariot-race frieze

"Iphigeneia" Relief in Izmir (from Pergamon?)

Termessos, frieze with scenes from Iphigeneia's legend

Termessos, Temple of Zeus Solimeios: Gigantomachy frieze

Battle Relief in Aberdeen

Messene, Temple of Zeus Soter (?): metope with Perseus and Andromeda (?)

Taras, reliefs from some funerary monuments

Thessaloniki, Telamones

Fregellae, terracotta Telamones

Kyzikos, Temple of Apollonis: stylopinakia(?)

Alabanda, Temple of Apollo Isotimos: Amazonomachy frieze

†Teos, Temple of Dionysos: frieze and pediment

Knidos, Temple of Dionysos (?): frieze

Ephesos Gallic Battle Relief

Magnesia, altar of the Artemision: frieze

Lagina, altar of the Hekateion: frieze

Rhodes, Karyatid Tomb

Bargylia, Skylla Monument

Frieze from Tomb of Hieronymos of Tlos

†Sagalassos: large Dancers' Frieze

Soloi, Amazonomachy frieze

Paestum, Temple of Peace: metopes

Nike of Samothrake (ca. 160?)

Praeneste, black stone figure (Fortuna/Isis?)

"Euboulides' Nike"

Boston torso (female)

Pergamon, Freeing of Prometheus (160–150?)

Pergamon, adaptation of Athena Parthenos

Pergamon, Athena with crossed aigis

Priene, Dionysos statuette from private house

Hierapytna "Nike"

List of Monuments

Works Accepted as Second Century

Many gravestones: from Smyrna and other areas of Asia Minor; from Rhodes; from Delos/Rheneia and other areas of the Kyklades; Banquet Reliefs from Samos; Rider Reliefs, especially from Pergamon

Round altars with boukrania/boukephalia and garlands: from Delos, Kos, and other areas

Athens, Document Relief in honor of Serapion of Herakleia (138/7)

Pheneos, Asklepios and Hygieia by Attalos, son of Lachares

Lykosoura, four-figure group by Damophon of Messene

Delos, C. Ofellius Ferus by Dionysios and Timarchides (ca. 110)

Mahdia "Pan" appliqué (ca. 100)

Pergamon "Dancer" from Palace V (ca. 150)

Works Possibly Second Century

Hierapytna Athena Head

Kyzikos, seated female figure

Letoon (Xanthos), draped woman

Melos, statuette of Aphrodite leaning on Archaistic idol

Soloeis, female figure

Cosa, male torso

Halikarnassos altar

Halikarnassos, Muse Base

Munich Votive Relief with offering scene

Kleitor, Stele of "Polybios"

Delos, Four-Gods Relief

Herakleia (Lucania), votive relief with Dionysos

Messene, various sculptures by Damophon and others

Aigeira, head of Dionysos

Klaros, cult triad (Apollo, Leto, Artemis)

Letoon (Xanthos), female head

Toledo, female bust from Italy

Various colossal heads in Rome

Praeneste, head of Fortuna Primigenia

Nemi, two heads of Diana, torso of Virbius

Mounychia, Asklepios

Eros (ex-Agon) from Mahdia wreck, and other bronzes

†Juno Cesi

Borghese Warrior

*Fanciulla d'Anzio

*Hanging Marsyas

Delos, some male portraits

Artemision, Horse and Jockey

Mounychia, Archaistic Artemis

Rome, Dioscuri from Fountain of Juturna

Tiber Muse in Minneapolis

Syracuse, three Muses from theater Nymphaion

Cerveteri, Gaul in New York

Delos, Warrior from the Agora of the Italians

Bibliography

Abbreviations of periodicals and standard works follow the guidelines set forth in the *American Journal of Archaeology* 95 (1991) 4–16.

Achenbach-Kosse, M., 1989: "Die Ringergruppe in Florenz," *AntK* 32, 71–81.

Ajootian, A., 1998: "A Day at the Races: The Tyrannicides in the Fifth-century Agora," in Hartswick and Sturgeon 1998, 1–13.

Akten XIII, 1990: *Akten des XIII. Internationalen Kongresses für klassische Archäologie, Berlin 1988* (Mainz).

Amberger-Lahrmann, M., 1996: *Anatomie und Physiognomie in der hellenistischen Plastik: Dargestellt am Pergamonaltar* (Stuttgart).

Amedick, R., 1995: "Unwürdige Greisinnen," *RM* 102, 141–72.

Andreae, B., 1977: *The Art of Rome* (New York).

Andreae, B., 1980: "*ΑΝΤΙΣΘΕΝΗΣ ΦΙΛΟΣΟΦΟΣ ΦΥΡΟΜΑΧΟΣ ΕΠΟΙΕΙ*," in *Eikones: Studium zum griechischen und römischen Bildnis* (Festschrift H. Juker, *AntK* BH 12) 40–48.

Andreae, B., 1989: "Fixpunkte hellenistischer Chronologie," in *Beiträge zur Ikonographie und Hermeneutik: Festschrift für Nikolaus Himmelmann* (*BJb* BH 47, Mainz) 237–44.

Andreae, B., 1992: "Phyromachos, Schöpfer des Pergamonaltares," *AntW* 23, 65.

Andreae, B., 1993: "Auftraggeber und Bedeutung der Dirke-Gruppe," *RM* 100, 107–31.

Andreae, B., 1994: "Statuetten eines sitzenden Knäbleins," in Hellenkemper Salies et al. 1994, 365–74.

Andreae, B., 1996: *Der Farnesische Stier: Schicksale eines Meisterwerkes der pergamenischen Bildhauer Apollonios und Tauriskos von Tralleis* (Freiburg im Breisgau).

Andreae, B., 1997: "Dating and Significance of the Telephos Frieze in Relation to the Other Dedications of the Attalids of Pergamon," in *Pergamon 2*, 1997, 120–26.

Andreae, B., et al., 1990: *Phyromachos-Probleme* (*RM* EH 31, Mainz).

Aneziri, S., and Damaskos, D., 1989–90: "*BOHΘOΣ*," *ΑΡΧΑΙΟΓΝΩΣΙΑ* 6 (publ. 1992) 183–91.

Arafat, K. W., 1996: *Pausanias' Greece: Ancient Artists and Roman Rulers* (Cambridge).

Arata, F. P., 1993: "Lo *Hercules infans dracones duos strangulans* del Museo Capitolino: Contributo all'iconografia imperiale d'età antonina," *BullComm* 95, 73–96.

Arvanitopoulos, A. S., 1928: *ΓΡΑΠΤΑΙ ΣΤΗΛΑΙ ΔΗΜΗΤΡΙΑΔΟΣ–ΠΑΓΑΣΩΝ* (Athens).

Atalay, E., 1985: "Un nouveau monument votif hellénistique à Éphèse," *RA*, 195–204.

Bagnall, R. S., 1973: "Three Notes on Ptolemaic Inscriptions," *ZPE* 11, 121–27.

Bankel, H., 1997: "Knidos. Der hellenistische Rundtempel und sein Altar. Vorbericht," *AA*, 51–71.

Barber, E. J. W., 1992: "The Peplos of Athena," in J. Neils, ed., *Goddess and Polis: The Panathenaic Festival in Ancient Athens* (Princeton) 103–17.

Barr-Sharrar, B., 1996: "The Mahdia Masterpieces," *Archaeology* 49.1 (Jan./Feb.) 54–59.

Barthe, G.-L., and Besnainou, D., 1988: "Restauration de l'effige-portrait de Caius Ofellius Ferus à Délos," *BCH* 112, 413–32.

Bibliography

Bartman, E., 1992: *Ancient Sculptural Copies in Miniature* (Leiden).

Bauchhenss-Thüriedl, Ch., 1971: *Der Mythos von Telephos in der antiken Bildkunst* (Würzburg).

Becatti, G., 1960: "Letture pliniane: le opere d'arte nei *Monumenta Asini Pollionis* e negli *Horti Serviliani*," in *Studi in onore di A. Calderini e R. Paribeni* (Milan) vol. 3, 199–210.

Belson, J. D., 1980: "The Medusa Rondanini: A New Look," *AJA* 84, 373–78.

Bergemann, J., 1990: *Römisches Reiterstatuen: Ehrendenkmäler im öffentlichen Bereich* (Mainz).

Berges, D., 1986: *Hellenistische Rundaltäre Kleinasiens* (Freiburg im Breisgau).

Berges, D., 1996: *Rundaltäre aus Kos und Rhodos* (Berlin).

Berges, D., 1997: "Neue Forschungen zum gräco-punischen Solus," *AntK* 40, 89–101.

Bergmann, B., 1995: "Greek Masterpieces and Roman Recreative Fiction," *HSCP* 97, 79–107 (pls. on pp. 108–20).

Bergmann, M., 1998: *Die Strahlen der Herrscher: Herrscherbild und politische Symbolik im Hellenismus und in der römischen Kaiserzeit* (Mainz).

Berthold, R. M., 1984: *Rhodes in the Hellenistic Age* (Ithaca/London).

Beschi, L., 1985: "La Nike di Hierapytna, opera di Damokrates di Itanos," *RendLinc* 40, 131–43, pls. 1–8.

Beschi, L., 1996: "Sculpture in Greek Cyrenaica," in Pugliese Carratelli, ed., 1996, 437–42.

Bieber, M., 1961: *The Sculpture of the Hellenistic Age* (2nd ed., New York).

Biering, R., 1995: *Die Odysseefresken von Esquilin* (Studien zur antiken Malerei und Farbgebung 2, Munich).

Bingöl, O., 1990a: "Der Oberbau des Smintheion in der Troas," in Hoepfner and Schwandner 1990, 45–50.

Bingöl, O., 1990b: "Zu den neueren Forschungen in Magnesia," in Hoepfner and Schwandner 1990, 63–67.

Blanck, H., 1969: *Wiederverwendung alter Statuen als Ehrendenkmäler bei Griechen und Römern* (Rome).

Blümel, W., 1992: *Die Inschriften von Knidos*, vol. 1 (Bonn).

Boardman, J., 1995: *Greek Sculpture: The Late Classical Period* (London).

Boehringer, C., 1991: "Zur Geschichte der Achaischen Liga im 2. und 1. Jh. v. Chr. im Lichte des Münzfundes von Poggio Picenze (Abruzzen)," in A. D. Rizakis, ed., *Achaia und Elis in der Antike* (Akten des 1. Internationalen Symposiums Athen, May 19–21, 1989; Athens) 163–67.

Bol, P. C., and Eckstein, F., 1975: "Die Polybios-Stele in Kleitor/Arkadien," *AntP* 15, 83–93, pls. 40–41, Beil. 1–7.

Bonacasa, N., 1996: "Sculpture and Coroplastics in Sicily in the Hellenistic-Roman Age," in Pugliese Carratelli, ed., 1996, 421–36.

Borbein, A., 1973: "Die Statue des hängenden Marsyas," *MarbWPr*, 37–52.

Börker, C., 1986: "Menekrates und die Künstler der Farnesischen Stieres (zu Plinius xxxvi 39)," *ZPE* 64, 41–49.

Bothmer, B. V., 1996: "Hellenistic Elements in Egyptian Sculpture of the Ptolemaic Period," in Hamma, ed., 1996, 215–30.

Bouzek, J., et al, 1985: *Samothrace 1923/1927/1978: The Results of the Czechoslovak*

Bibliography

Excavations in 1927 Conducted by A. Salač and J. Nepomucký and the Unpublished Results of the 1923 Franco-Czechoslovak Excavations Conducted by A. Salač and F. Chapouthier (Prague).

Brahms, T., 1994: *Archaismus: Untersuchungen zur Funktion und Bedeutung archaistischer Kunst in der Klassik und im Hellenismus* (Frankfurt).

Brendel, O. J., 1978: *Etruscan Art* (Pelican History of Art, Penguin Books, New York).

Breuer, C., 1995: *Reliefs und Epigramme griechischer Privatgrabmäler: Zeugnisse bürgerlichen Selbverständnisses vom 4. bis 2. Jahrhundert v. Chr.* (Cologne).

Bringmann, K., 1995: "Die Ehre des Königs und der Ruhm der Stadt: Bemerkungen zur königlichen Bau- und Feststiftungen," in Wörrle and Zanker 1995, 93–102.

Bringmann, K., and von Steuben, H., eds., 1995: *Schenkungen hellenistischer Herrscher an griechische Städte und Heiligtümer* (Berlin).

Brogan, T., 1998: "The Prometheus Group in Context," in Hartswick and Sturgeon 1998, 39–52.

Brommer, F., 1963: *Die Skulpturen der Parthenon-Giebel*, 2 vols. (Mainz).

Brommer, F., 1967: *Die Metopen des Parthenon*, 2 vols. (Mainz).

Brommer, F., 1970: "Neue pergamenische Köpfe," *JBerlMus* 12, 191–210.

Brommer, F., 1977: *Der Parthenonfries*, 2 vols. (Mainz).

Bruneau, P., 1990: "Deliaca (VIII)," *BCH* 114, 553–91.

Bruneau, P., 1995: "Deliaca (X)," *BCH* 119, 35–62.

Bruns-Özgan, C., 1995: "Fries eines hellenistischen Altars in Knidos," *JdI* 110, 239–76.

Bulloch, A. W., et al., eds., 1993: *Images and Ideologies: Self-Definition in the Hellenistic World* (Berkeley/Los Angeles/London).

Cain, H.-U., 1995: "Hellenistische Kultbilder: Religiöse Präsenz und museale Präsentation der Götter im Heiligtum und beim Fest," in Wörrle and Zanker 1995, 115–25.

Cain, H.-U., and Dräger, O., 1994: "Die sogennanten neuattischen Werkstätten," in Hellenkemper Salies et al. 1994, 809–29.

Calcani, G., 1989: *Cavalieri di bronzo* (Rome).

Callaghan, P. J., 1981a: "On the Date of the Great Altar of Pergamon," *BICS* 28, 115–21.

Callaghan, P. J., 1981b: "The Medusa Rondanini and Antiochos III," *BSA* 76, 59–70.

Callaghan, P. J., 1982: "On the Origin of the Long Petal Bowl," *BICS* 29, 63–68.

Carpenter, R., 1929: *The Sculpture of the Nike Temple Parapet* (Cambridge, Mass.).

Carpenter, R., 1960: *Greek Sculpture* (Chicago).

Carter, J. C., 1975: *The Sculpture of Taras* (*TAPS* 65.7, Philadelphia).

Carter, J. C., 1983: *The Sculpture of the Sanctuary of Athena Polias at Priene* (London).

Caskey, L. D., 1925: *Catalogue of Greek and Roman Sculpture* (Museum of Fine Arts, Boston).

Casson, S., 1973: *Ships and Seamanship in the Ancient World* (Princeton; reprinted 1995).

Childs, W. A. P., and Demargne, P., 1989: *Le Monument des Néréides: Le décor sculpté* (Fouilles de Xanthos 8, Paris).

Claridge, A., 1990: "Ancient Techniques of Making Joins in Marble Statuary," in *Marble: Art Historical and Scientific Perspectives on Ancient Sculpture* (Malibu) 135–62.

Clark, K., 1956: *The Nude: A Study in Ideal Form* (New York).

Clarke, G. W., 1968: "The Dioscuri of the Lacus Iuturnae," *Latomus* 27, 147–48.

Coarelli, F., 1997: *Il Campo Marzio: Dalle origini alla fine della Republica* (Rome).

Bibliography

Cohon, R., 1991/92: "Hesiod and the Order and Naming of the Muses in Hellenistic Art," *Boreas* 14/15, 67–83.

Cole, S. G., 1984: ***Theoi Megaloi:*** *The Cult of the Great Gods at Samothrace* (Leiden).

Collins-Clinton, J., 1993: "A Hellenistic Torso from Cosa," in R. T and A. R. Scott, eds., ***Eius Virtutis Studiosi:*** *Classical and Postclassical Studies in Memory of Frank Edward Brown (1908-1988)* (Studies in the History of Art 43, Washington, D.C.) 257–78.

Comstock, M. B., and Vermeule, C. C., 1976: *Sculpture in Stone: Museum of Fine Arts* (Boston).

Connelly, J. B., 1996: "Parthenon and *Parthenoi:* A Mythological Interpretation of the Parthenon Frieze," *AJA* 100, 53–80.

Couilloud, M.-T., 1974a: *Les monuments funéraires de Rhénée* (Exploration Archéologique de Délos 30, Paris).

Couilloud, M.-T., 1974b: "Reliefs funéraires des Cyclades de l'époque hellénistique à l'époque impériale," *BCH* 98, 397–498.

Couilloud, M.-T., 1975: "Autels et stèles des Cyclades (Compléments)," *BCH* 99, 313–29.

Couilloud–Le Dinahet, M.-T., 1978: "Tombes d'Ano Generale: Recherches à Rhénée," *BCH* 102, 853–73.

Crawford, M., ed., 1996: *Roman Statutes* (*BICS* Suppl. 64, London).

Curtius, L., 1951: "Redeat Narratio," *MdI* 4, 10–34.

Czapski, C. S., 1998: "NM 238: A Hellenistic Statue and Its Archaistic Support," in Hartswick and Sturgeon 1998, 53–59.

Danner, P., 1993: "Figuren an Simaecken: Eine Form ostgriechischer Architekturdekoration im griechischen Westen," in J. Des Courtils and J.-C. Moretti, eds., *Les grands ateliers d'architecture dans le mond égéen du IVe siecle av. J. C.* (Paris) 253–60.

Danner, P., 1994: "Ein architektonisches Terrakottafragment hellenistischer Zeit aus Reggio Calabria," in N. A. Winter, ed., *Greek Architectural Terracottas of the Classical and Hellenistic Periods (Symposium Dec. 12-15, 1991),* (*Hesperia* Suppl. 27) 305–8.

Danner, P., 1997: *Westgriechische Akrotere* (Mainz).

Daszewski, W. A., 1996: "From Hellenistic Polychromy of Sculptures to Roman Mosaics," in Hamma, ed., 1996, 141–54.

Davesne, A., and Marcadé, J., 1992: "Les sculptures," in A. Bourgarel et al., *Fouilles de Xanthos 9: La Region nord du Letoon* (Paris) 79–146.

de Grummond, N. T., forthcoming: "Gauls and Giants, Skylla and the Palladion: Some Responses," in de Grummond and Ridgway, forthcoming.

de Grummond, N. T., and Ridgway, B. S., eds., forthcoming: *From Pergamon to Sperlonga: Sculpture and Context* (University of California Press).

Delivorrias, A., 1991: "Problèmes de conséquence méthodologique et d'ambiguïté iconographique," *MEFRA* 103, 129–57.

Despinis, G., 1990: "Zu einigen Künstlern der späthellenistischen Zeit," in *Akten XIII* 1990, 151.

Despinis, G., 1995: "Studien zur hellenistischen Plastik I: Zwei Künstlerfamilien aus Athen," *AM* 110, 321–72.

Despinis, G., et al., 1997: *Catalogue of Sculpture in the Archaeological Museum of Thessaloniki* I (Thessaloniki).

Dickins, G., 1920: *Hellenistic Sculpture* (Oxford).

Bibliography

Dinsmoor, W. B., 1950: *The Architecture of Ancient Greece* (London/New York).

Dinstl, A., 1993: "Ein Bukranienfries aus Limyra," in J. Borchhardt and G. Dobesch, eds., *Akten des II. Internationalen Lykien-Symposions, Wien, 6.-12. Mai. 1990* (Vienna) 161–67.

Dintsis, P., 1986: *Hellenistische Helme* (Rome).

Di Vita, A., 1963–64: "Statua di Nike da Cos," *ASAtene* n.s., 41–42, 25–26, 25–37.

Di Vita, A., 1995: "Due rilievi tardoellenistici da Camiro," *RM* 102, 101–13, pls. 25–26.

DOG 1977, 1979: E. Pfuhl and H. Möbius, *Die Ostgriechischen Grabreliefs*, vols. 1 and 2 respectively (Mainz).

Donderer, M., 1996: "Bildhauersignaturen auf griechischer Rundplastik," *ÖJh* 65, 87–104.

Donohue, A. A., 1995: "Winckelmann's History of Art and Polyclitus," in W. G. Moon, ed., *Polykleitos, the Doryphoros, and Tradition* (Madison) 327–53.

Donohue, A. A., 1997: "The Greek Images of the Gods: Considerations on Terminology and Methodology," *Hephaistos* 15, 31–45.

Dörig, J., 1977: *Onatas of Aegina* (Monumenta Graeca et Romana 1, Leiden).

Dörpfeld, W., 1912: "Die Arbeiten zu Pergamon 1910–1911," *AM* 37, 233–76.

Dyabola: Computer database, Archaeological Bibliography and Subject Catalogue of the Deutsches Archäologisches Institut in Rome, 1956–.

Dyggve E., Poulsen, F., and Rhomaios, K., 1934: *Das Heroon von Kalydon* (Copenhagen).

Edwards, G. R., 1975: *Corinthian Hellenistic Pottery: Corinth VII.3* (Princeton).

Étienne, R., and Braun, J.-P., 1986: *Tenos I: Le sanctuaire de Poseidon et d'Amphitrite* (Paris).

Étienne, R., and Braun, J.-P., 1995: "L'autel monumental du Théatre à Délos," *BCH* 119, 63–87.

Étienne, R., and Le Dinahet, M.-T., eds., 1991: *L'espace sacrificiel dans les civilisations méditerranéens de l'antiquité* (Actes du Colloque, Lyon 1988; Paris).

Fehr, B., 1997: "Society, Consanguinity and the Fertility of Women: The Community of Deities on the Great Frieze of the Pergamum Altar as a Paradigm of Cross-Cultural Ideas," in P. Bilde et al., *Conventional Values of the Hellenistic Greeks* (Studies in Hellenistic Civilizations 8, Aarhus) 48–66.

Ferrari, G.: see Pinney.

Filges, A., 1997: *Standbilder jugendlicher Göttinnen: Klassische und frühhellenistische Gewandstatuen mit Brustwulst und ihre kaiserzeitliche Rezeption* (Cologne).

Fire of Hephaistos 1996: C. C. Mattusch et al., *The Fire of Hephaistos: Large Classical Bronzes from North American Collections* (Catalogue of Exhibition, Harvard University Art Museum, April 20–August 11, 1996; Cambridge, Mass.)

Flashar, M., and Mantis, A., 1993: "Ein wiedergewonnenes attisches Original: Zum Typus Vatikan, Museo Pio Clementino Inv. 934," *AntP* 22, 75–83, figs. 2–15 on pp. 84–86.

Fleischer, R., 1972–75: "Marsyas und Achaios," *ÖJh* 50, Beibl., 104–22.

Fleischer, R., 1979: "Forschungen in Sagalassos 1972 und 1974," *IstMitt* 29, 273–307, pls. 71–91, 136.

Fleischer, R., 1984: "Zur Datierung des Frieses von Sagalassos," *AA*, 141–44.

Fleischer, R., 1991: *Studien zur Seleukidischen Kunst I: Herrscherbildnisse* (Mainz).

Fleischer, R., et al., 1998: "Der Wiener Amazonensarkophag," *AntP* 26, 7–54.

Forsyth, N. R., 1981: "The Punishment of Dirce and the Death of Laocoon on Contorniate Reverses," *RN* 23, 6th ser., 80–95.

Bibliography

Fraser, P. M., 1977: *Rhodian Funerary Monuments* (Oxford).

Frel, J., 1971: "The Rhodian Workshop of the Alexander Sarcophagus," *IstMitt* 21, 121–24.

Froning, H., 1988: "Anfänge der kontinuierenden Bilderzählung in der griechischen Kunst," *JdI* 103, 169–99.

Fuchs, W., 1966: "Zur Rekonstruktion einer weiblichen Sitzstatue in Chalkis," *JBerlMus* 8, 32–49.

Fullerton, M. D., 1987: "Archaistic Statuary of the Hellenistic Period," *AM* 102, 259–78.

Fullerton, M. D., 1997: "Imitation and Intertextuality in Roman Art," *JRA* 10, 427–40.

Fullerton, M. D., 1998a: "Atticism, Classicism, and the Origins of Neo-Attic Sculpture," in Palagia and Coulson 1998, 93–99.

Fullerton, M. D., 1998b: "Description vs. Prescription: A Semantics of Sculptural Style," in Hartswick and Sturgeon 1998, 69–77.

Fullerton, M. D., 2000: *Greek Art* (London).

Gabrielsen, V., 1997: *The Naval Aristocracy of Hellenistic Rhodes* (Aarhus).

Gauthier, P., 1985: *Les cités grecques et leurs bienfaiteurs (IVe–Ier siècle avant J.-C.): Contribution à l'histoire des institutions* (*BCH* Suppl. 12, Paris).

Gauthier, P., 1995: "Notes sur le role du gymnase dans les cités hellénistiques," in Wörrle and Zanker 1995, 1–11.

Gazda, E., ed., 1991: *Roman Art in the Private Sphere: New Perspectives on the Architecture and Decor of the Domus, Villa, and Insula* (Ann Arbor).

Gazda, E., 1995a: "Roman Copies: The Unmaking of a Modern Myth," *JRA* 8, 530–34.

Gazda, E., 1995b: "Roman Sculpture and the Ethos of Emulation: Reconsidering Repetition," *HSCP* 97, 121–48 (pls. on pp. 149–56).

GdDm, 1991: *Guide de Delphes: Le Musée* (Ecole Française d'Athènes, Paris).

GdDs, 1991: Bommelaer, J. F., and Laroche, D., *Guide de Delphes: Le site* (Paris).

Geominy, W., 1985: "Die Statuette Athen NM 710," *AM* 100, 367–75, pl. 81.

Geppert, S., 1996: "Die monumentalen Dioskurengruppen in Rom," *AntP* 25, 121–47.

Gernand, M., 1975: "Hellenistische Peplosfiguren nach klassischen Vorbilder," *AM* 90, 1–47, pls. 1–12.

Gogräfe, R., 1996: "Strenger Stil oder Klassizismus? Die Bronzestatue des Apollon aus Isriye," *AntW* 27.5, 353–58.

Goodlett, V. C., 1991: "Rhodian Sculpture Workshops," *AJA* 95, 669–81.

Green, P., 1972: *The Shadow of the Parthenon: Studies in Ancient History and Literature* (Los Angeles/Berkeley).

Green, P., ed., 1993: *Hellenistic History and Culture* (Berkeley/Los Angeles/Oxford).

Green, P., forthcoming: "Pergamon and Sperlonga: A Historian's Reactions," in de Grummond and Ridgway, forthcoming.

Grote, U., 1992: "Bauplastik aus Pergamon," in *ΜΟΥΣΙΚΟΣ ΑΝΗΡ: Festschrift für Max Wegner zum 90. Geburststag* (Bonn) 179–87.

Gruen, E. S., 1984: *The Hellenistic World and the Coming of Rome* (Berkeley).

Gruen, E. S., 1992: *Culture and National Identity in Republican Rome* (Ithaca).

Gruen, E., forthcoming: "Culture as Policy: The Attalids of Pergamon," in de Grummond and Ridgway, forthcoming.

Gschwantler, K., 1993: "Bäume, Säulen, Mauern: Zum Fugenschluss der Reliefs vom

Bibliography

Gölbaşi-Trysa," in J. Borchhardt and G. Dobesch, eds., *Akten des II. Internationalen Lykien-Symposions, Wien 6.–12. Mai 1990* (Vienna) vol. 2, 77–85, pls. 17–20.

Gualandi, G., 1976: "Sculture di Rodi," *AS Atene* 54, n.s. 38, 7–259.

Gulaki, A., 1981: *Klassische und klassizistische Nikedarstellungen: Untersuchungen zur Typologie und zum Bedeutungswandel* (Bonn).

Guldager Bilde, P., 1995: "The Sanctuary of Diana Nemorensis: The Late Republican Acrolithic Cult Statues," *ActaArch* 66, 191–217.

Guldager Bilde, P., 1999: "Dionysos among Tombs: Aspects of Rhodian Tomb Culture in the Hellenistic Period," in V. Gabrielsen et al., eds., *Hellenistic Rhodes: Politics, Culture, and Society* (Studies in Hellenistic Civilization 9, Aarhus) 227–46.

Gunter, A. C., 1995: *Labraunda. Swedish Excavations and Researches 2.5: Marble Sculpture* (Stockholm).

Guthrie, W. K. C., 1935: *Orpheus and Greek Religion* (London).

Habicht, Ch., 1990: "Athens and the Attalids in the Second Century B.C.," *Hesperia* 59, 561–77.

Habicht, Ch., 1997: *Athens from Alexander to Antony* (London).

Hafner, G., 1996: "Das 'Praetorium Spelunca' bei Terracina und die Höle bei Sperlonga," *RdA* 20, 75–78.

Hafner, G., 1997: "Verhinderte Helden," *ÖJh* 66, 129–41.

Hamiaux, M., 1998: *Les Sculptures Grecques II: La période hellénistique (IIIᵉ–Iᵉʳ siècles avant J.-C.)* (Catalogue, Musée du Louvre, Paris).

Hamma, K., ed., 1996: *Alexandria and Alexandrianism* (Papers Delivered at a Symposium by the J. Paul Getty Museum and the Getty Center for the History of Art and the Humanities and Held at the Museum April 22–25, 1993; Malibu).

Hannestad, L., 1993: "Greeks and Celts: The Creation of a Myth," in P. Bilde et al., *Centre and Periphery in the Hellenistic World* (Studies in Hellenistic Civilization 4, Aarhus) 15–38.

Hannestad, N., 1994: *Tradition in Late Antique Sculpture: Conservation, Modernization, Production* (Aarhus).

Hansen, E. V., 1971: *The Attalids of Pergamon* (2nd ed., Ithaca/London).

Harrison, E. B., 1972: "The South Frieze of the Nike Temple and the Marathon Painting in the Painted Stoa," *AJA* 76, 353–78.

Hartswick, K. J., and Sturgeon, M. C., eds., 1998: *ΣΤΕΦΑΝΟΣ: Studies in Honor of B. S. Ridgway* (Philadelphia).

Haskell, F., and Penny, N., 1981: *Taste and the Antique: The Lure of Classical Sculpture 1500–1900* (New Haven/London).

Häuber, C., 1986: "Testa di centauro," in M. Cima and E. La Rocca, eds., *Le tranquille dimore degli dei: La residenza imperiale degli* horti *Lamiani* (Rome) 97–99, fig. 67.

Häuber, C., 1999: "Vier Fragmente der Gruppe Satyr und Hermaphrodit vom Statuentypus 'Dresdner Symplegma' des Museo Nuovo Capitolino in Rom," in *Hellenistische Gruppen* (Mainz) 158–80.

Hausmann, U., 1960: *Griechische Weihreliefs* (Berlin).

Havelock, C. M., 1995: *The Aphrodite of Knidos and Her Successors: A Historical Review of the Female Nude in Greek Art* (Ann Arbor).

Bibliography

Haynes, D. E. L., 1972: "Alte Funde neu endeckt," *AA*, 731–42.

Hebert, B., 1989: *Schriftquellen zur hellenistischen Kunst: Plastik, Malerei und Kunsthandwerk der Griechen vom vierten bis zum zweiten Jahrhundert* (Gratz).

Hecht, R. E., Jr., 1956: "A Colossal Head of Polyphemos," *MAAR* 24, 135–45.

Heidenreich, R., 1935: "Bupalos und Pergamon," *AA*, 668–701.

Heidenreich, R., 1988: "Griechisches aus Turkmenien," *AA*, 81–85.

Heilmeyer, W.-D., 1994: "*ΘΕΟΙΣ ΠΑΣΙ*—Rhodos, Pergamon und Rom," in *La ciutat en el món romà* (Acts of the 14th International Congress of Classical Archaeology, Tarragona, Sept. 5–11, 1993; Tarragona) vol. 2, 201–3.

Heilmeyer, W.-D., 1996: *Der Jüngling von Salamis: Technische Untersuchungen zu römischen Grossbronzen* (Mainz).

Heilmeyer, W.-D., 1997: "New Arrangement and Interpretation of the Telephos Frieze from the Pergamon Altar," in *Pergamon* 2, 1997, 127–28.

Hellenistische Gruppen 1999: *Hellenistische Gruppen: Gedenkschrift für Andreas Linfert* (Mainz).

Hellenkemper Salies, G., et al., 1994: *Das Wrack: Der antike Schiffsfund vom Mahdia* (Kataloge des Rheinischen Landesmuseum 1.1–2, Bonn) 2 vols.

Hellenkemper Salies, G., et al., 1996: "Neue Forschungen zum Schiffsfund von Mahdia," *BJb* 196, 199–337, esp. "*Das Wrack:* Eine Bilanz nach zwei Jahren," 199–219.

Hemingway, S. A., 1997: "The Horse and Jockey Group from Artemision: A Bronze Equestrian Monument of the Hellenistic Period" (Ph.D. Dissertation for Bryn Mawr College).

Hemingway, S. A., 1998: "A Bridle for the Bronze Horse from Artemision," in Hartswick and Sturgeon 1998, 115–18.

Heres, H., 1994: "Telephos Frieze, Pergamon," in *LIMC* 7, s.v. Telephos, pp. 856–62, no. 1, drawing on pp. 858–59, pls. 590–94.

Heres, H., 1997: "The Myth of Telephos in Pergamon," in *Pergamon* 2, 1997, 83–108.

Hermary, A., 1987: "Le sarcophage d'un prince de Soloi," *RDAC*, 231–33.

Herrmann, P., 1995: "*ΓΕΡΑΣ ΘΑΝΟΝΤΩΝ:* Totenruhm und Totenehrung im städtischen Leben der hellenistischen Zeit," in Wörrle and Zanker 1995, 189–97.

Hiller, H., 1994: "Zwei bronzene Figurenlampen," in Hellenkemper Salies et al. 1994, 515–30.

Himmelmann, N., 1989: *Herrscher und Athlet: Die Bronze vom Quirinal* (Milan).

Himmelmann, N., 1994: "Mahdia und Antikythera," in Hellenkemper Salies et al. 1994, 849–55.

Himmelmann, N., 1995: *Sperlonga: Die homerischen Gruppen und ihre Bildquellen* (Nordrhein-Westfälische Akademie der Wissenschaften, Vorträge G 340, Opladen).

Hoepfner, W., 1989: "Zu den grossen Altäre von Magnesia und Pergamon," *AA*, 601–34.

Hoepfner, W., 1990: "Von Alexandria über Pergamon nach Nikopolis: Städtebau und Stadtbilder hellenistischer Zeit," in *Akten XIII*, 1990, 275–85.

Hoepfner, W., 1991: "Bauliche Details am Pergamonaltar," *AA*, 189–202.

Hoepfner, W., 1993: "Siegestempel und Siegesaltäre: Der Pergamonaltar als Siegesmonument," in Hoepfner and Zimmer 1993, 111–25.

Hoepfner, W., 1996a: "Der vollendete Pergamonaltar," *AA*, 115–34.

Bibliography

Hoepfner, W., 1996b: "Zum Maussolleion von Halikarnassos," *AA*, 95–114.

Hoepfner, W., 1996c: "Zum Typus der Basileia und der königlichen Androness," in Hoepfner and Brands 1996, 1–43.

Hoepfner, W., 1997: "The Architecture of Pergamon," in *Pergamon 2*, 1997, 23–57.

Hoepfner, W., and Brands, G., eds., 1996: *Basileia: Die Paläste der hellenistischen Könige* (Internationalen Symposon in Berlin, Dec. 16–20, 1992; Mainz).

Hoepfner, W., and Schwandner, E.-L., eds., 1990: *Hermogenes und die hochhellenistische Architektur* (Kolloquium Berlin, July 28–29, 1988; Mainz).

Hoepfner, W., and Zimmer, G., eds., 1993: *Die griechische Polis: Architektur und Politik* (Tübingen).

Hoffmann, E., 1965: "Eine weibliche Sitzfigur aus Kyzikos," *IstMitt* 15, 65–70, pls. 30–32.

Höghammar, K., 1993: *Sculpture and Society: A Study of the Connection between the Free-standing Sculpture and Society on Kos in the Hellenistic and Augustan Periods* (Acta Universitatis Upsaliensis, Boreas 23, Uppsala).

Höghammar, K., 1997: "Women in Public Space: Cos c. 200 BC to c. AD 15/20," in I. Jenkins and G. B. Waywell, eds., *Sculptors and Sculpture of Caria and the Dodecanese* (London) 127–33.

Hollinshead, M. B., 1992: "Steps to Grandeur: Monumental Stairs and Hellenistic Architectural Complexes," in T. Hackens et al., eds., *The Age of Pyrrhus: Papers Delivered at the International Conference, Brown University, 8–10 April 1988* (Archaeologia Transatlantica, Louvain) 83–96.

Hölscher, T., 1985: "Die Geschlagenen und Ausgelieferten in der Kunst des Hellenismus," *AntK* 28, 120–36.

Horn, H. G., 1994: "Dionysos und Ariadne: Zwei Zierbeschläge aus dem Schiffsfund von Mahdia," in Hellenkemper Salies et al. 1994, 451–66.

Horn, R., 1931: *Stehende weibliche Gewandstatuen in der hellenistischen Plastik* (*RM EH* 2).

Horn, R., 1972: *Samos 12: Hellenistische Bildwerke auf Samos* (Bonn 1972).

Howard, S., 1983: "The Dying Gaul, Aigina Warriors, and Pergamene Academicism," *AJA* 87, 483–87.

Hübner, G., 1993: *Die Applikenkeramik von Pergamon: Eine Bildersprache im Dienst des Herrscherkultes* (Pergamenische Forschungen 7, Berlin).

Hübner, G., 1994: "*Calices Pergami* und die Scherbenfunde aus des Großen Altar," in *Third Conference for Hellenistic Pottery, 24–27 September 1901, Thessaloniki* (Athens) 282–93.

Hurwit, J. M., 1995: "Beautiful Evil: Pandora and the Athena Parthenos," *AJA* 99, 171–86.

Hurwit, J. M., 1997: "The Death of the Sculptor?" *AJA* 101, 587–91.

Inan, J., 1977/78: "Der Bronzetorso im Burdur-Museum aus Bubon und der Bronzekopf im J.-Paul-Getty-Museum," *IstMitt* 27/28, 267–87 (with Epigraphic Appendix by C. P. Jones, pp. 288–96).

Inan, J., 1993: "Neue Forschungen zum Sebasteion von Boubon und seinen Statuen," in *Akten des II. Internationalen Lykien-Symposions* (Vienna), vol. 1, 213–39.

Ippel, A., 1912: "Die Inschriften" (von Pergamon), *AM* 37, 227–303.

Isager, J., 1991: *Pliny on Art and Society: The Elder Pliny's Chapters on the History of Art* (London/New York).

Isager, J., 1995: "The Lack of Evidence for a Rhodian School," *RM* 102, 115–31.

Jacquemin, A., 1981: "Notes sur quelques offrandes du gymnase de Délos," *BCH* 105, 155–69.

Bibliography

Jacquemin, A., and Laroche, D., 1982: "Notes sur trois piliers delphiques," *BCH* 106, 191–218.

Jacquemin, A., Laroche, D., Lefèvre, F., 1995: "Delphes, le roi Persée et le romains," *BCH* 119, 125–36.

Jeppesen, K., 1992: "*Tot operum opus*: Ergebnisse der dänische Forschungen zum Maussolleion von Halikarnass seit 1966," *JdI* 107, 59–102.

Jessen, H. B., 1968: "Ein neuer Fund aus Pergamon," *AA*, 794–95.

Jones, S. C., 1994: "The Toledo Bronze Youth and East Mediterranean Bronze Workshops," *JRA* 7, 243–56.

Jones, S. C., 1998: "Statues That Kill and the Gods Who Love Them," in Hartswick and Sturgeon 1998, 139–43.

Jost, M., 1985: *Sanctuaires et cultes d'Arcadie* (Paris).

Junghölter, U., 1989: *Zur Komposition der Lagina-Friese und zur Deutung der Nordfrieses* (Frankfurt).

Junker, K., 1993: *Der ältere Tempel im Heraion am Sele: Verzierte Metopen im architektonischen Kontext* (Cologne/Weimar/Vienna).

Kabus-Preißhofen, R., 1989: *Die hellenistische Plastik der Insel Kos* (*AM* BH 14).

Kähler, H., 1948: *Der große Fries von Pergamon* (Berlin).

Kähler, H., 1965: *Der Fries vom Reiterdenkmal des Aemilius Paullus in Delphi* (Berlin).

Kane, S., 1998: "Two Limestone Goddesses From the Sanctuary of Demeter and Kore/Persephone at Cyrene, Libya," in Hartswick and Sturgeon 1998, 145–53.

Karanastassis, P., 1987: "Untersuchungen zur kaiserzeitlichen Plastik in Griechenland. II: Kopien, Varianten und Umbildungen nach Athena-Typen des 5. Jhs. v. Chr.," *AM* 102, 323–428.

Karo, G., 1943: *An Attic Cemetery: Excavations in the Kerameikos at Athens* (Philadelphia).

Kästner, V., 1994: "Gigantennamen," *IstMitt* 44, 125–34.

Kästner, V., 1997: "The Architecture of the Great Altar and the Telephos Frieze," in *Pergamon* 2, 1997, 68–82.

Kell, K., 1988: *Formuntersuchungen zur spät- und nachhellenistischen Gruppen* (Saarbrücken).

Kern, O., 1900: *Die Inschriften von Magnesia am Maeander* (Berlin).

Kleiner, G., 1956: "Ein pergamenisches Relief im Museum zu Izmir," *AM* 71, 202–4.

Klementa, S., 1993: *Gelagerte Flußgötter des Späthellenismus und der römischen Kaiserzeit* (Cologne).

Knell, H., 1993: "Die Aphrodite von Capua und ihre Repliken," *AntP* 22, 117–39.

Knell, H., 1995: *Die Nike von Samothrake: Typus, Form, Bedeutung und Wirkungsgeschichte einer rhodischen Sieges-Anathems im Kabirenheiligtum von Samothrake* (Darmstadt).

Knigge, U., 1980: "Kerameikos: Tätigkeitsbericht 1978," *AA*, 256–65.

Koch, L., 1993: "Die Sitzstatuetten des Antisthenes und Pittakos aus Pompeii," *AA*, 263–69.

Koch, L., 1994: *Weibliche Sitzstatuen der Klassik und des Hellenismus und ihre kaiserzeitliche Rezeption* (Münster).

Konstantinopoulos, G., 1986: *ΑΡΧΑΙΑ ΡΟΔΟΣ* (Athens).

Kontorini, V., 1980: "*ΕΝΑΣ ΝΕΟΣ ΡΟΔΙΟΣ ΟΛΥΜΠΙΟΝΙΚΗΣ*," in *ΣΤΗΛΗ* (in memory of N. Kontoleon, Athens) 380–82.

Kourouniotes, K., 1906–1907: "The Mechanical Construction of the Group," in G. Dickins, "Damophon of Messene, II," *BSA* 13 [357–404] 384–89.

Bibliography

Kozloff, A. P., 1996: "Is There an Alexandrian Style—What Is Egyptian about It?" in Hamma 1996, 247–60.

Krauss, F., and Herbig, R., 1939: *Der korinthisch-dorische Tempel am Forum in Paestum* (Berlin).

Kreeb, M., 1988: *Untersuchungen zur figürlichen Ausstattung delischer Privathäuser* (Chicago).

Kreeb, M., 1990: "Hermogenes—Quellen- und Datierungsprobleme," in Hoepfner and Schwandner 1990, 103–15.

Kreikenbom, D., 1992: *Griechische und römische Kolossalporträts bis zum späten ersten Jahrhundert nach Christus* (JdI EH 27, Berlin).

Krumeich, R., 1997: *Bildnisse griechischer Herrscher und Staatsmänner im 5. Jahrhundert v. Chr.* (Munich).

Krumme, M., 1993: "Das Heiligtum der 'Athena beim Palladion' in Athen," *AA*, 213–27.

Kuntz, U. S., 1994: "Griechische Reliefs aus Rom und Umgebung," in Hellenkemper Salies et al. 1994, 889–99.

Kunze, Ch., 1991: "Dall'originale greco alla copia romana," in *Toro Farnese* 1991, 13–42.

Kunze, Ch., 1996a: "Die Skulpturenausstattung hellenistischer Paläste," in Hoepfner and Brands 1996, 109–29.

Kunze, Ch., 1996b: "Zur Datierung des Laokoon und der Skyllagruppe aus Sperlonga," *JdI* 111, 139–223.

Kunze, Ch., 1998: *Der Farnesische Stier und die Dirkegruppe des Apollonios und Tauriskos* (JdI EH 30, Berlin).

Kunze, M., 1986: *"Wir haben eine ganze Kunstepoche gefunden!" Ein Jahrhundert Forschungen zum Pergamonaltar* (Katalog der Sonderausstellung in Pergamonmuseum, Nov. 1986–April 1987; Berlin).

Kunze, M., 1990: "Neue Beobachtungen zum Pergamonaltar," in Andreae et al. 1990, 123–39.

Künzl, E., 1968: *Frühhellenistische Gruppen* (Cologne).

Kurtz, D. C., and Boardman, J., 1971: *Greek Burial Customs* (Ithaca).

Kuttner, A., 1995: "Republican Rome Looks at Pergamon," *HSCP* 97, 157–78.

La Follette, L., 1994: "The Baths of Trajan Decius," in *Rome Papers* (JRA Suppl. 11) 6–88.

Lambrinoudakis, V., 1989: "Neues zur Ikonographie der Dirke," in *Beiträge zur Ikonographie und Hermeneutik: Festschrift für Nikolaus Himmelmann* (BJb BH 47, Mainz) 341–50, pls. 52–54.

Landwehr, C., 1990: "Die Sitzstatue eines bärtigen Gottes in Cherchel: Zur Originalität römischer Vatergottdarstellungen," in Andreae et al. 1990, 101–22.

Langlotz, E., and Hirmer, M., 1968: *L'Arte della Magna Grecia: Arte greca in Italia Meridionale e Sicilia* (rev. ed., Rome).

Lapatin, K. D. S., 1997: "Pheidias ΕΛΕΦΑΝΤΟΥΡΓΟΣ," *AJA* 101, 663–82.

La Rocca, E., 1996: "Greek Artists in Republican Rome: A Short History of Sculpture," in Pugliese Carratelli 1996, 607–26.

Lattimore, S., 1976: *The Marine Thiasos in Greek Sculpture* (Monumenta Archaeologica 3, Los Angeles).

Lauter, H., 1972: "Kunst und Landschaft: Ein Beitrag zum rhodischen Hellenismus," *AntK* 15, 49–59.

Bibliography

Lavagne, H., 1988: *Operosa Antra: Recherches sur la grotte à Rome de Sylla à Hadrien* (Paris).

Lawton, C. L., 1995: *Attic Document Reliefs: Art and Politics in Ancient Athens* (Oxford).

Lebendis, I., 1993: "*ΤΑ ΑΓΑΗΜΑΤΑ ΤΟΥ ΑΣΚΗΠΙΟΥ ΚΑΙ ΤΗΣ ΨΓΕΙΑΣ ΣΤΟ ΝΑΟ ΤΗΣ ΑΘΗΝΗΣ ΑΛΕΑΣ ΣΤΗΝ ΤΕΓΕΑ,*" in O. Palagia and W. Coulson, eds., *Sculpture from Arcadia and Laconia* (Oxbow Monographs 30, Oxford) 119–27.

Lehmann, K., 1973: "The Ship Fountain, from the Victory of Samothrace to the Galera," in *Samothracian Reflections: Aspects of the Revival of the Antique* (Bollingen Series 92, Princeton) 179–259.

Lehmann, Ph. W., et al., 1969: *Samothrace 3: The Hieron* (Bollingen Series 60.3, Princeton).

Lehmann, S., 1997: "Der 'Betende Knabe,'" *ÖJh* 66, 117–28.

Levi, P., 1993: "People in a Landscape: Theokritos," in Green 1993, 111–27.

Lewerentz, A., 1993: *Stehende männliche Gewandstatuen im Hellenismus: Ein Beitrag zur Stilgeschichte und Ikonologie hellenistischer Plastik* (Hamburg).

Liampi, K., 1990: "Der makedonische Schild als propagandistisches Mittel in der hellenistischen Zeit," *Meletemata* 10 (Research Centre for Greek and Roman Antiquity) 157–71.

Linfert, A., 1976: *Kunstzentren hellenistischer Zeit: Studien an weiblichen Gewandfiguren* (Wiesbaden).

Linfert, A., 1994: "Boethoi," in Hellenkemper Salies et al. 1994, 831–47.

Linfert, A., 1995: "Prunkaltäre," in Wörrle and Zanker 1995, 131–46.

Lippolis, E., 1996: "La produzione in pietra," in E. Lippolis, ed., *I Greci in Occidente: Arte e artigianato in Magna Grecia* (Taranto) 493–507.

Loucas, I., and Loucas, E., 1994: "The Sacred Laws of Lykosoura," in R. Hägg, ed., Ancient Greek Cult Practice from the *Epigraphical Evidence* (Proceedings of the Second International Seminar on Ancient Greek Cult organized by the Swedish Institute at Athens, Nov. 22–24, 1991; Stockholm) 97–99.

Love, I. C., 1972: "A Preliminary Report of the Excavations at Knidos, 1971," *AJA* 76, 393–405.

Love, I. C., 1973: "A Preliminary Report of the Excavations at Knidos, 1972," *AJA* 77, 413–24.

Luschey, H., 1961: "Der Kopf der Aphrodite aus dem grossen Fries von Pergamon," *IstMitt* 11, 1–4.

Lyttelton, M., 1974: *Baroque Architecture in Classical Antiquity* (Ithaca).

Machaira, V., 1993: *Les groupes statuaires d'Aphrodite et d'Éros: Étude stylistique des types et de la relation entre les deux divinités pendant l'époque hellénistique* (Athens).

Maddoli, G., 1989: "Pyrilampes, dimenticato scultore di Sicione, e la cronologia di Pyrilampes di Messene (Paus. VI 3, 13)," *DialArch*, ser. 3, vol. 7, 65–69.

Madigan, B., 1991: "A Transposed Head," *Hesperia* 60, 503–10.

Madigan, B., 1993: "A Statue in the Temple of Apollo at Bassai," in O. Palagia and W. Coulson, eds., *Sculpture from Arcadia and Laconia* (Proceedings of an international conference held at the American School of Classical Studies at Athens, April 10–14, 1992; Oxbow Monograph 30, Oxford) 111–18.

Maggidis, Ch., 1998: "The Aphrodite and the Poseidon of Melos: A Comparative Study," *ActaArch* 69, 175–97.

Bibliography

Mantis, A., 1987–1990: "*ΤΟ ΑΝΑΓΛΥΦΟ ΤΟΥ ΜΟΥΣΕΙΟΥ ΘΑΣΟΥ, Λ* 3255, *ΚΑΙ ΤΑ ΑΝΑΓΛΥΦΑ ΦΑΤΝΩΜΑΤΑ ΤΟΥ ΠΡΟΝΑΟΥ ΤΟΥ ΙΕΡΟΥ ΤΗΣ ΣΑΜΟΘΡΑΚΗΣ,*" in *Thrakike Epeteris* (volume in honor of G. Bakalakis' 80th birthday, Komotini) 159–70.

Mantis, A., 1990: *ΠΡΟΒΛΗΜΑΤΑ ΤΗΣ ΕΙΚΟΝΟΓΡΑΦΙΑΣ ΤΩΝ ΙΕΡΕΙΩΝ ΚΑΙ ΤΩΝ ΙΕΡΕΩΝ ΣΤΗΝ ΑΡΧΑΙΑ ΕΛΛΗΝΙΚΗ ΤΕΧΝΗ* (Athens).

Mantis, A., 1998: "*ΤΑ ΑΝΑΓΛΥΦΑ ΦΑΤΝΩΜΑΤΑ ΤΟΥ ΙΕΡΟΥ ΤΗΣ ΣΑΜΟΘΡΑΚΗΣ,*" in Palagia and Coulson 1998, 209–25.

Marcadé, J., 1957: *Recueil de signatures des sculpteurs grecs,* vol. 2 (Paris).

Marcadé, J., 1969: *Au Musée de Délos* (Paris).

Marcadé, J., 1976: "Tête féminine du Létoon de Xanthos," *RA,* 113–20.

Marcadé, J., 1994: "Rapport préliminaire sur le groupe cultuel du Temple d'Apollon à Claros (état de mai 1995)," *REA* 96, 447–63.

Marcadé, J., et al., 1996: *Sculptures Déliennes* (Paris).

Mark, I. S., 1998: "The Victory of Samothrace," in Palagia and Coulson 1998, 157–65.

Markle, M. M., III, 1977: "The Macedonian Sarissa, Spear, and Related Armor," *AJA* 81, 323–39.

Markle, M. M., III, 1978: "Use of the Sarissa by Philip and Alexander of Macedon," *AJA* 82, 483–97.

Marquardt, N., 1994: "Die Reliefköpfe," in Hellenkemper Salies et al. 1994, 329–37.

Marquardt, N., 1995: *Pan in der hellenistischen und kaiserzeitlichen Plastik* (Bonn).

Marszal, J. R., 1998: "Tradition and Innovation in Early Pergamene Sculpture," in Palagia and Coulson 1998, 117–27.

Marszal, J. R., forthcoming: "Ubiquitous Barbarians: Representations of the Gauls at Pergamon and Elsewhere," in de Grummond and Ridgway, forthcoming.

Martin, H. G., 1987: *Römische Tempelkultbilder: Eine archäologische Untersuchung zur späten Republik* (Rome).

Marzolff, P., 1986: "Grabbauten von Demetrias," in *Studien zur klassischen Archäologie* (Festschrift Friedrich Hiller, Saarbrücken) 73–90.

Mattusch, C. C., 1994a: "Bronze Herm of Dionysos," in Hellenkemper Salies et al. 1994, 431–50.

Mattusch, C. C., 1994b: "The Production of Bronze Statuary in the Greek World," in Hellenkemper Salies et al. 1994, 789–800.

Mattusch, C. C., 1996: *Classical Bronzes: The Art and Craft of Greek and Roman Statuary* (Ithaca).

McKenzie, J., 1996: "Alexandria and the Origins of Baroque Architecture," in Hamma 1996, 109–25.

Meischner, J., 1972: "Beobachtungen zu einem bärtigen Reliefkopf in Pergamon," *IstMitt* 22, 113–32.

Merker, G. S., 1973: *The Hellenistic Sculpture of Rhodes* (Studies in Mediterranean Archaeology 40, Göteborg).

Meyer, H., 1996a: "The Hanging Marsyas Reconsidered: A Roman Table Leg, Early Seleukid Art, and the School of Lysippos," *BullCom* 97, 89–124.

Meyer, H., 1996b: "The Levy Bronze: On Portraiture and Copying under the Attalids," *BullCom* 97, 149–96.

Bibliography

Meyer, H., 1996c: "The Terme Ruler: An Understudied Masterpiece and the School of Lysippos," *BullCom* 97, 125–48.

Meyer, H., 1997: "Athena Lemnia (Typus Fier-Berlin-Richmond): Zur Identifizierung des meistgerühmten phidiasischen Werkes und seines Überlieferung," in G. Grath et al., eds., *Komos: Festschrift für Thuri Lorenz zum 65. Geburtstag* (Vienna) 111–17.

Mielsch, A., 1995: "Die Bibliothek und die Kunstsammlung der Könige von Pergamon," *AA*, 765–79.

Miller (Collett), S. G., 1993: *The Tomb of Lyson and Kallikles: A Painted Macedonian Tomb* (Mainz).

Miller (Collett), S. G., 1994: "Architectural Terracottas from Ilion," in N. A. Winter, ed., *Greek Architectural Terracottas of the Classical and Hellenistic Periods (Symposium Dec. 12–15, 1991) (Hesperia* Suppl. 27) 269–73.

Möbius, H., 1926: "Eine dreiseitige Basis in Athen," *AM* 51, 117–24.

Moltesen, M., 1997: *In the Sacred Grove of Diana: Finds from a Sanctuary at Nemi* (English title of bilingual version, *I Diana Helige Lund: Fund fra en Helligdom i Nemi*; Exhibition, Ny Carlsberg Glyptotek, Copenhagen).

Moreno, P., 1994: *Scultura ellenistica*, 2 vols. (Rome).

Morrison, J. S., 1996: *Greek and Roman Oared Warships* (Oxford).

Morrow, K. D., 1985: *Greek Footwear and the Dating of Sculpture* (Madison).

Moser von Filseck, K., 1990: "Noch einmal zum Strigilisreiniger Ephesos-Wien: Klassik oder Klassizismus?" *ÖJh* 60, 1–5.

Moustaka, A., 1993: *Grossplastik aus Ton in Olympia* (*OlForsch* 22, Berlin).

Müller, H., 1992: "Phyromachos im pergamenischen Nikephorion?" *Chiron* 22, 195–226.

Müller-Wiener, W., 1982: "Neue Weihgeschenke aus dem Athena-Heiligtum in Priene," *AA*, 691–702.

Murray, W. M., 1991: "Provenience and Date: Evidence of Symbols" (Ch. 4), in L. Casson and J. R. Steffy, eds., *The Athlit Ram* (Nautical Archaeology Series 3, College Station).

Neuerburg, N., 1965: *L'architettura delle fontane e dei ninfei nell'Italia antica* (Naples).

Neutsch, B., 1956: "Weibliche Gewandstatue im römischen Kunsthandel," *RM* 63, 46–55.

Nicolaou, I., 1969: "Inscriptiones Cypriae Alphabeticae VIII, 1968," *RDAC*, 70–97.

Niemeier, J.-P, 1985: *Kopien und Nachahmungen im Hellenismus* (Bonn).

Oberleitner, W., 1981: "Ein hellenistischer Galaterschlachtfries aus Ephesos," *JKSW* 77, 57–104.

Onians, J., 1996: "From the Double Crown to the Double Pediment," in Hamma 1996, 127–40.

Osada, T., 1993: *Stilentwicklung hellenistischer Relieffriese* (Frankfurt).

Özgan, R., 1995: *Die griechischen und römischen Skulpturen aus Tralleis* (Asia Minor Studien 15, Bonn).

Özgen, E., and Özgen, I., eds., 1988: *Antalya Museum* (Catalogue).

Özgünel, C., 1990: "Das Fundament des Smintheion," in Hoepfner and Schwandner 1990, 35–44.

Palagia, O., 1986: "Imitation of Herakles in Ruler Portraiture: A Survey, from Alexander to Maximinus Daza," *Boreas* 9, 137–51.

Palagia, O., 1987: "Les techniques de la sculpture grecque sur marbre," in *Marbres*

Bibliography

Helléniques: De la carrière au chef-d'œuvre (Catalogue de l'exposition à Bruxelles 1987–88; Gand) 76–89.

Palagia, O., 1997a: "Initiates in the Underworld," in I. Jenkins and G. B. Waywell, eds., *Sculptors and Sculpture of Caria and the Dodecanese* (London) 68–73.

Palagia, O., 1997b: "Reflections on the Pireus Bronzes," in *Greek Offerings: Essays on Greek Art in Honour of John Boardman* (Oxbow Monograph 89, Oxford) 177–95.

Palagia, O., and Coulson, W., eds., 1998: *Regional Schools in Hellenistic Sculpture* (Oxford).

Palaiokrassa, L., 1991: *ΤΟ ΙΕΡΟ ΤΗΣ ΑΡΤΕΜΙΔΟΣ ΜΟΥΝΙΧΙΑΣ* (Publications of the Greek Archaeological Society 115, Athens).

Papachatzis, N. D., 1974–1981: *ΠΑΥΣΑΝΙΟΥ ΕΛΛΑΔΟΣ ΠΕΡΙΕΓΕΣΙΣ* (Athens; vol 1: 1974; vol. 2: 1976; vol. 3: 1979; vol. 4: 1980; vol. 5: 1981).

Papaefthimiou, W., 1992: *Grabreliefs späthellenistischer und römischer Zeit aus Sparta und Lakonien* (Munich).

Papapostolou, J. A., 1993: *Achaean Grave Stelai* (Athens).

Pasquier, A., 1985: *La Vénus de Milo et les Aphrodites du Louvre* (Paris).

Pedley, J. G., 1990: *Paestum: Greeks and Romans in Southern Italy* (London).

Pergamon 1, 1996: R. Dreyfus and E. Schraudolf, eds., *Pergamon: The Telephos Frieze from the Great Altar*, vol. 1 (San Francisco).

Pergamon 2, 1997: R. Dreyfus and E. Schraudolf, eds., *Pergamon: The Telephos Frieze from the Great Altar*, vol. 2 (San Francisco).

Pfanner, M., 1979: "Bemerkungen zur Komposition und Interpretation des Grossen Frieses von Pergamon," *AA*, 45–57.

Picard, C., 1963: *Manuel d'archeologie grecque: La sculpture*, vol. 4.2 (Paris).

Pinkwart, D., 1967: "Die Musenbasis von Halikarnass, London B. M. 1106," *AntP* 6, 89–94, pls. 53–57.

Pinney, G. (Ferrari), 1988: "Pallas and Panathenaea," in *Proceedings of the Third Symposium on Ancient Greek and Related Pottery* (Copenhagen) 465–77.

Polito, E., 1998: **Fulgentibus Armis:** *Introduzione allo studio dei fregi d'armi antichi* (Xenia Antiqua Monografie 4, Rome).

Pollini, J., 1996: "The 'Dart Aphrodite': A New Replica of the 'Arles Aphrodite Type,' the Cult Image of Venus Victrix in Pompey's Theater at Rome, and Venusian Ideology and Politics in the Late Republic and Early Principate," *Latomus* 55, 757–85.

Pollitt, J. J., 1974: *The Ancient View of Greek Art: Criticism, History, and Terminology* (New Haven/London).

Pollitt, J. J., 1986: *Art in the Hellenistic Age* (Cambridge).

Pollitt, J. J., 1993: "Response" to Martin Robertson, in Green 1993, 90–103.

Pollitt, J. J., forthcoming: "The Phantom of a Rhodian School of Sculpture," in de Grummond and Ridgway, forthcoming.

Pouilloux, J., 1960: *Choix d'inscriptions grecques: Textes, traductions et notes* (Paris).

Poulsen, B., 1997: "The Sculpture from the Late Roman Villa in Halicarnassus," in I. Jenkins and G. B. Waywell, eds., *Sculptors and Sculpture of Caria and the Dodecanese* (London) 74–83.

Price, M. J., 1991: *The Coinage in the Name of Alexander the Great and Philip Arrhidaeus* (A British Museum Catalogue, vol. 1; Zurich/London).

Bibliography

Protonotariou-Deilaki, E., 1961–1962: "ΑΝΑΣΚΑΦΗ ΦΕΝΕΟΥ," *ArchDelt* 17.2, Chron., 57–61.

Pugliese Carratelli, G., 1939–1940: "Per la storia delle associazioni in Rodi antica," *ASAtene* n.s. 1/2, 147–200.

Pugliese Carratelli, G., ed., 1996: *The Greek World: Art and Civilization in Magna Graecia and Sicily* (Catalogue of Exhibition "The Western Greeks," held at Palazzo Grassi, Venice, March–Dec. 1996; Rizzoli, New York).

Queyrel, F., 1986: "Appendice IV, Les Sculptures," in R. Étienne and J.-P. Braun, *Ténos* I: *Le sanctuaire de Poséidon et d'Amphitrite (BEFAR* 263) 267–320.

Queyrel, F., 1990: "Portraits princiers hellénistiques: Chronique bibliographique," *RA*, 97–172.

Queyrel, F., 1991: "C. Ofellius Ferus," *BCH* 115, 389–464.

Queyrel, F., 1992: "Phyromachos: Problèmes de style et de datation," *RA*, 367–80.

Radt, W., 1981: "Der 'Alexanderkopf' in Istanbul: Ein Kopf aus dem großen Fries des Pergamon-Altars," *AA*, 583–96.

Radt, W., 1995: "Pergamon: Vorbericht über die Kampagne 1994," *AA*, 575–95.

Radt, W., 1996: "Pergamon: Vorbericht über die Kampagne 1995," *AA*, 443–54.

Radt, W., 1997: "Pergamon: Vorbericht über die Kampagne 1996," *AA*, 415–29.

Raeck, W., 1995: "Der mehrfache Apollodoros: Zur Präsenz des Bürgers im hellenistischen Stadtbild am Beispiel von Priene," in Wörrle and Zanker 1995, 231–38.

Rauh, F., 1993: *The Sacred Bonds of Commerce: Religion, Economy, and Trade Society at Hellenistic Roman Delos* (Amsterdam).

Rausa, F., 1994: *L'immagine del vincitore: L'atleta nella statuaria greca dall'età arcaica all'ellenismo* (Treviso/Rome).

Reeder, E. D., ed., 1988: *Hellenistic Art in the Walters Art Gallery* (Baltimore).

Retaining the Original 1989: *Retaining the Original: Multiple Originals, Copies, and Reproductions* (Studies in the History of Art 20, Washington, D.C.).

Rice, E., 1986: "Prosopographika Rhodiaka, Part ii: The Rhodian sculptors of the Sperlonga and Laocoön Statuary Groups," *BSA* 81, 245–50.

Rice, E., 1991: "The Rhodian Navy in the Hellenistic Age," in W. R. Roberts and J. Sweetman, eds., *New Interpretations in Naval History: Selected Papers from the 9th Naval History Symposium* (Annapolis) 29–50.

Rice, E., 1993: "The Glorious Dead: Commemoration of the Fallen and Portrayal of Victory in the Late Classical and Hellenistic World," in J. Rich and G. Shipley, eds., *War and Society in the Greek World* (London/New York) 224–57.

Rice, E., 1995: "Grottoes on the Acropolis of Hellenistic Rhodes," *BSR* 90, 383–404.

Richardson, E. H., 1996: "The Muscle Cuirass in Etruria and Southern Italy: Votive Bronzes," *AJA* 100, 91–120.

Richter, G. M. A., 1917: "A Greek Head in the Goldman Collection," *Art in America* 5 (April) 130–34.

Richter, G. M. A., 1951: *Three Critical Periods in Greek Sculpture* (Oxford).

Richter, G. M. A., 1954: *Catalogue of Greek Sculptures in the Metropolitan Museum of Art* (Oxford/Cambridge, Mass.).

Richter, G. M. A., 1965: *The Portraits of the Greeks*, 3 vols. (London).

Bibliography

Richter, G. M. A., 1966: "The Votive Relief in Munich Once Again," in *Mélanges offerts à K. Michalowski* (Warsaw) 625–27.

Richter-Smith, 1984: *The Portraits of the Greeks*, revised and abbreviated by R. R. R. Smith (Ithaca).

Ridgway, B. S., 1970: *The Severe Style in Greek Sculpture* (Princeton).

Ridgway, B. S., 1972: *Classical Sculpture* (Catalogue of the Classical Collection, Museum of Art, Rhode Island School of Design, Providence).

Ridgway, B. S., 1979: "The Ludovisi Head," in *Studies in Classical Art and Archaeology* (Festschrift P. von Blanckenhagen, Locust Valley, N.Y.) 153–61.

Ridgway, B. S., 1981: *Fifth Century Styles in Greek Sculpture* (Princeton).

Ridgway, B. S., 1984: *Roman Copies of Greek Sculpture: The Problem of the Originals* (Jerome Lectures, 15th ser., Ann Arbor).

Ridgway, B. S., 1988: "The Study of Hellenistic Art," in Reeder 1988, 27–34.

Ridgway, B. S., 1989: "Musings on the Muses," in *Beiträge zur Ikonographie und Hermeneutik: Festschrift für Nikolaus Himmelmann* (*BJb* BH 47, Mainz) 265–72.

Ridgway, B. S., 1990: *Hellenistic Sculpture I: The Styles of ca. 331–200 B.C.* (Madison).

Ridgway, B. S., 1993a: "Response" to R. R. R. Smith and P. Zanker, in Bulloch et al. 1993, 231–41.

Ridgway, B. S., 1993b: *The Archaic Style in Greek Sculpture* (2nd revised and expanded ed., Chicago).

Ridgway, B. S. et al., 1994: *Greek Sculpture in the Art Museum, Princeton University: Greek Originals, Roman Copies and Variants* (Princeton).

Ridgway, B. S., 1995a: "Lo stile severo: Lo stato della questione," in N. Bonacasa, ed., *Lo stile severo in Grecia e in Occidente: Aspetti e problemi* (Studi e materiali, Istituto di Archeologia, Università di Palermo, no. 9, Rome) 35–42.

Ridgway, B. S., 1995b: "The Wreck off Mahdia, Tunisia, and the Art-Market in Early 1st c. B.C.," *JRA* 8, 340–47.

Ridgway, B. S., 1997a: "A Goddess in Philadelphia," in B. Magnusson et al., eds., ***Ultra Terminum Vagari:*** *Scritti in onore di Carl Nylander* (Rome) 271–77.

Ridgway, B. S., 1997b: *Fourth-Century Styles in Greek Sculpture* (Madison).

Ridgway, B. S., 1998: "An Issue of Methodology: Anakreon, Perikles, Xanthippos," *AJA* 102, 717–38.

Ridgway, B. S., 1999: *Prayers in Stone: Greek Architectural Sculpture ca. 600–100 B.C.E.* (Sather Classical Lectures 63, Berkeley).

Rieche, A., 1973: "Die Kopien der 'Leda des Timotheos,'" *AntP* 17, 21–51.

Robertson, M., 1993: "What Is 'Hellenistic' about Hellenistic Art?" in Green 1993, 67–90.

Rohde, E., 1964: *Pergamon: Burgberg und Altar* (Berlin).

Rohde, E., 1976: "Das verlorene Haupt des Zeus: Stellungnahme zu einem Anpassungsversuch am Pergamon Ostfries," *IstMitt* 26, 101–10.

Rolley, C., 1996a: "Les bronzes grecs et romains. Recherches récentes. XXIII. Statuaire et bronzes figurés grecs," *RA*, 269–91.

Rolley, C., 1996b: "Sculpture in Magna Graecia," in Pugliese Carratelli 1996, 369–98.

Romanelli, P., 1967: *Palestrina* (Cava dei Tirreni, Napoli).

Bibliography

Rose, C. B., 1992: "The 1991 Post–Bronze Age Excavations at Troia," *Studia Troica* 2, 43–60.

Rose, C. B., 1994: "The 1993 Post–Bronze Age Excavations at Troia," *Studia Troica* 4, 75–104.

Rose, C. B., 1997: "The 1996 Post–Bronze Age Excavations at Troia," *Studia Troica* 7, 73–110.

Rose, C. B., 1998: "The 1997 Post–Bronze Age Excavations at Troia," *Studia Troica* 8, 71–113.

Rotroff, S. I., 1990: "Building a Hellenistic Chronology," in Uhlenbrock 1990, 22–30.

Rubensohn, O., 1935: "Parische Künstler," *JdI* 50, 49–69.

Rumscheid, F., 1994: *Untersuchungen zur kleinasiatischen Bauornamentik des Hellenismus,* 2 vols. (Mainz).

Rumscheid, F., 1995: "Die Ornamentik des Apollon-Smintheus-Tempels in der Troas," *IstMitt* 45, 25–55, pls. 1–26, 56.

Saatsoglou-Paliadeli, Ch., 1984: *ΤΑ ΕΠΙΤΑΦΙΑ ΜΝΗΜΕΙΑ ΑΠΟ ΤΗ ΜΕΓΑΛΗ ΤΟΥΜΠΑ ΤΗΣ ΒΕΡΓΙΝΑΣ* (Thessaloniki).

Sagalassos I, 1993: *Sagalassos I: First General Report on the Survey (1986–1989) and Excavations (1990–1991),* ed. M. Waelkens (Leuven, Acta Arc. Lovaniensia, Monographiae 5).

Sagalassos III, 1995: *Sagalassos III: Report on the Fourth Excavation Campaign of 1993,* M. Waelkens and J. Poblome, eds. (Leuven 1995).

Salapata, G., 1997: "Hero Warriors from Corinth and Lakonia," *Hesperia* 66, 245–60.

Samothrace 1998: *Samothrace: A Guide to the Excavations and the Museum,* ed. J. R. McCredie, (8th rev. ed., Thessaloniki).

Samuel, A. E., 1993: "The Ptolemies and the Ideology of Kingship," in Green 1993, 168–92.

Sande, S., 1995: "An Old Hag and Her Sisters," *SymbOslo* 70, 30–52.

Schaaf, H., 1992: *Untersuchungen zu Gebäudestiftungen in hellenistischer Zeit* (Cologne).

Schädler, U., 1991: "Attizismen an ionischen Tempeln Kleinasiens," *IstMitt* 41, 265–324.

Schäfer, J., 1968: "Der Poseidon von Melos," *AntP* 8, 55–67.

Schefold, K., 1997: *Die Bildnisse der antiken Dichter, Redner und Denker* (Basel).

Schilardi, D. U., 1986: "A Fragment of a Marble Relief-Sarcophagus from Paros," in H. Kyrieleis, ed., *Archaische und klassische griechische Plastik* (Mainz) vol. 2, 13–26.

Schmaltz, B., 1983: *Griechische Grabreliefs* (Darmstadt).

Schmidt, I., 1995: *Hellenistische Statuenbasen* (Frankurt am Main).

Schmidt, S., 1991: *Hellenistische Grabreliefs: Typologische und chronologische Beobachtung* (Cologne/Vienna).

Schmidt, Th.-M., 1990: "Der späte Beginn und der vorzeitige Abbruch der Arbeiten am Pergamonaltar," in Andreae et al. 1990, 141–62.

Schmidt-Dounas, B., 1991: "Zur Datierung der Metopen des Athena-Tempels von Ilion: Bemerkungen zur Architektur," *IstMitt* 41, 411–15.

Schober, A., 1933: *Der Fries des Hekateions von Lagina* (IstForsch 2).

Scholl, A., 1996: *Die attischen Bildfeldstelen des 4. Jhs. v. Chr.: Untersuchungen zu den kleinformatigen Grabreliefs im spätklassischen Athen* (*AM* BH 17, Berlin).

Schwarz, G., 1988: "Die Rezeption des klassizistischen Götterbildes bei den Römern," in *ΠΡΑΚΤΙΚΑ ΤΟΥ* XII *ΔΙΕΘΝΟΥΣ ΣΥΝΕΔΡΙΟΥ ΚΛΑΣΙΚΗΣ ΑΡΧΑΙΟΛΟΓΙΑΣ* 4–10 *ΣΕΠΤ.* 1983 (Athens), vol. 3, 241–45.

Bibliography

Siedentopf, H. B., 1968: *Das hellenistische Reiterdenkmal* (Waldsassen/Bayern).

Simon, E., 1975: *Pergamon und Hesiod* (Mainz).

Simon, E., 1993: "Der Laginafries und der Hekatehymnos in Hesiods *Theogonie,*" *AA*, 277–84.

Smith, R. R. R., 1988: *Hellenistic Royal Portraits* (Oxford).

Smith, R. R. R., 1991: *Hellenistic Sculpture: A Handbook* (London).

Smith, R. R. R., 1993: "Kings and Philosophers," in Bulloch et al. 1993, 202–11.

Smith, R. R. R., 1996: "Ptolemaic Portraits: Alexandrian Types, Egyptian Versions," in Hamma 1996, 203–13.

Söldner, M., 1994: "Der sogennante Agon," in Hellenkemper Salies et al. 1994, 399–429.

Söldner, M., 1998: "Der Eros von Mahdia," *AntP* 26, 61–71, pls. 27–34.

Spyropoulos, Th., 1993: "*ΝΕΑ ΓΛΥΠΤΑ ΑΠΟΚΤΗΜΑΤΑ ΤΟΥ ΑΡΧΑΙΟΛΟΓΙΚΟΥ ΜΟΥΣΕΙΟΥ ΤΡΙΠΟΛΕΩΣ,*" in O. Palagia and W. Coulson, eds., *Sculpture from Arcadia and Laconia* (Oxbow Monographs 30, Oxford) 257–67.

Stähler, K., 1968: "Zu den Iphigeneienreliefs in Termessos," *AA*, 280–89.

Stähler, K., 1978: "Überlegungen zur architektonischen Gestalt des Pergamonaltares," in *Studien zur Religion und Kultur Kleinasiens* (Festschrift K. Dörner, Leiden) 838–67.

Stampolidis, N. C., 1984: "Der 'Nymphenaltar' in Knidos und der Bildhauer Theon aus Antiochia," *AA*, 113–27.

Stampolidis, N. C., 1987: *Ο ΒΩΜΟΣ ΤΟΥ ΔΙΟΝΥΣΟΥ ΣΤΗΝ ΚΩ. ΣΥΜΒΟΛΗ ΣΤΗ ΜΕΛΕΤΗ ΤΗΣ ΕΛΛΗΝΙΣΤΙΚΗΣ ΠΛΑΣΤΙΚΗΣ ΚΑΙ ΑΡΧΙΤΕΚΤΟΝΙΚΗΣ* (*ArchDelt* Suppl. 34, Athens).

Stampolidis, N. C., 1991: "Altar, Krateutes, and Acroteria: A Contribution to the Study of *Π*-shaped Altars," in Étienne and Le Dinahet 1991, 291–96.

Stanwick, P. E., 1992: "A Royal Ptolemaic Bust in Alexandria," *JARCE* 29, 131–41.

Steinbruckner, S., 1986: "Zu Jörg-Peter Niemeier, *Kopien und Nachahmungen im Hellenismus,*" *HASB* 11, 19–26.

Steingräber, S., forthcoming: "Pergamene Influences on Etruscan Hellenistic Art," in de Grummond and Ridgway, forthcoming.

Stewart, A., 1979: *Attika: Studies in Athenian Sculpture of the Hellenistic Age* (*JHS* Suppl. 14, London).

Stewart, A., 1990: *Greek Sculpture: An Exploration* (New Haven/London).

Stewart, A., 1993a: *Faces of Power: Alexander's Image and Hellenistic Politics* (Berkeley/Los Angeles/Oxford).

Stewart, A., 1993b: "Narration and Allusion in the Hellenistic Baroque," in P. J. Holliday, ed., *Narrative and Event in Ancient Art* (Cambridge) 130–74.

Stewart, A., 1996a: "A Hero's Quest: Narrative and the Telephos Frieze," in *Pergamon* 1, 1996, 39–52.

Stewart, A., 1996b: "The Alexandrian Style: A Mirage?" in Hamma 1996, 231–46.

Stewart, A., 1998: "Nuggets: Mining the Texts Again," *AJA* 102, 271–82.

Stewart, A., forthcoming: "*Pergamo ara marmorea magna:* On the Date, Reconstruction, and Functions of the Great Altar of Pergamon," in de Grummond and Ridgway, forthcoming.

Strauss, B. S., 1996: "The Athenian Trireme, School of Democracy," in J. Ober and

Bibliography

C. Hedrick, eds., *Demokratia: A Conversation on Democracies, Ancient and Modern* (Princeton) 313–25.

Strobel, K., 1996: *Die Galater. Geschichte und Eigenart der keltischen Staatenbildung auf dem Boden des hellenistischen Kleinasien. 1. Untersuchungen zur Geschichte und historischen Geographie des hellenistischen und römischen Kleinasien* I (Berlin).

Studniczka, F., 1907: *Kalamis* (Leipzig).

Stupperich, R., 1990: "Zu den Stylopinakia am Tempel der Apollonis in Kyzikos," in E. Schwertheim, ed., *Mysische Studien* (Asia Minor Studien 1, Bonn) 101–9.

Sturgeon, M. C., forthcoming: "Pergamon to Hierapolis: From Theatrical 'Altar' to Religious Theater," in de Grummond and Ridgway, forthcoming.

Tancke, K., 1990: "Wagenrennen: Ein Friesthema der aristokratischen Repräsentationskunst spätklassisch-frühhellenistischer Zeit," *JdI* 105, 95–127.

Taplin, O., 1998: "Narrative Variation in Vase-painting and Tragedy: The Example of Dirke," *AntK* 41, 33–39, pls. 8–9.

Themelis, P. G., 1994a: "Artemis Ortheia at Messene: The Epigraphical and Archaeological Evidence," in R. Hägg, ed., *Ancient Greek Cult Practice from the Epigraphical Evidence* (Proceedings of the Second International Seminar on Ancient Greek Cult, organized by the Swedish Institute at Athens, Nov. 22–24, 1991; Stockholm) 101–22.

Themelis, P., 1994b: "Hellenistic Architectural Terracottas from Messene," in N. A. Winter, ed., *Greek Architectural Terracottas of the Classical and Hellenistic Periods (Symposium Dec. 12-15, 1991),* (*Hesperia* Suppl. 27) 141–69.

Themelis, P., 1996: "Damophon," in O. Palagia and J. J. Pollitt, eds., *Personal Styles in Greek Sculpture* (Yale Classical Studies 30, Cambridge) 154–85.

Theodorescu, D., 1989: "Le forum et le temple 'dorique-corinthien' de Paestum: Une experience pré-Vitruviènne," in H. Geertman and J.J. De Jong, eds., **Munus non Ingratum:** *Proceedings of the International Symposium on Vitruvius'* **De Architectura** *and the Hellenistic and Republican Architecture* (Leiden, Jan. 20–23, 1987; Leiden) 114–25.

Thimme, D., 1946: "The Masters of the Pergamon Gigantomachy," *AJA* 50, 345–57.

Thompson, H. A., and Wycherley, R. E., 1972: *The Athenian Agora 14: The Agora of Athens* (Princeton).

Tiverios, M. A., 1989: "Archaistica II," in *Beiträge zur Ikonographie und Hermeneutik: Festschrift für Nikolaus Himmelmann* (BJb BH 47, Mainz) 389–97.

Toro Farnese 1991: *Il Toro Farnese: La "montagna di marmo" tra Roma e Napoli* (Naples).

Travlos, J., 1971: *Pictorial Dictionary of Ancient Athens* (New York).

Tréheux, J., 1988: "Une nouvelle lecture de l'inventaire du gymnase à Delos," *BCH* 112, 583–89.

Trianti, I., 1998: "*ΕΛΛΗΝΙΣΤΙΚΑ ΑΓΑΛΜΑΤΑ ΤΗΣ ΜΗΛΟΥ*," in Palagia and Coulson 1998, 167–75.

Trummer, R., 1993: "Zwei Kolossalköpfe aus Aigeira," *AntP* 22, 141–55.

Uçankus, H. T., 1989: "Die bronzene Siegerstatue eines Läufers aus dem Meer von Kyme," *Nikephoros* 2, 135–55.

Uhlenbrock, J. P., 1990: *The Coroplast's Art: Greek Terracottas of the Hellenistic World* (New York).

Ulisse 1996: *Ulisse: Il mito e la memoria* (Catalogue of an exhibition held in Rome, Palazzo delle Esposizioni, Feb. 22–Sept. 2, 1996; Rome).

Bibliography

Umholtz, G., 1994: "Royal Patronage of Greek Architecture as an Instrument of Foreign Policy in the Hellenistic Period" (Ph.D. Dissertation for the University of California at Berkeley).

Uz, D. M., 1990: "The Temple of Dionysos at Teos," in Hoepfner and Schwandner 1990, 51–61.

Valeva, J., 1995: "The Sveshtari Figures (an Attempt to Specify Several Hypotheses)," in *Studia in Honorem Alexandri Fol* (*Thracia* 11) 337–52.

Van de Grift, J., 1984: "Tears and Revel: The Allegory of the Berthouville Centaur Scyphi," *AJA* 88, 377–88.

Venedikov, I., and Gerassimov, T., 1973: *Thrakische Kunst* (Vienna/Munich).

Vokotopoulou, J., 1982: "Phrygische Helme," *AA*, 497–520.

Völker-Janssen, W., 1993: *Kunst und Gesellschaft an den Höfen Alexanders d. Gr. und seiner Nachfolger* (Quellen und Forschungen zur antike Welt 15, Munich).

von Bothmer, D., ed., 1990: *Glories of the Past: Ancient Art from the Shelby White and Leon Levy Collection* (New York).

von den Hoff, R., 1994: *Philosophenporträts des Früh- und Hochhellenismus* (Munich).

von Graeve, V., and Preusser, F., 1981: "Zur Technik griechischer Malerei auf Marmor," *JdI* 96, 120–56.

von Heintze, H., 1962: "Drei spätantike Porträtstatuen," *AntP* 1, 7–31.

von Hesberg, H., 1988: "Bildsyntax und Erzählweise in der hellenistischen Flächenkunst," *JdI* 103, 309–65.

von Hesberg, H., 1995: "Das griechische Gymnasion im 2. Jh. v. Chr.," in Wörrle and Zanker 1995, 13–23.

von Prittwitz und Gaffron, H.-H., 1988: *Der Wandel der Aphrodite: Archäologische Studien zu weiblichen halbbekleideten Statuetten des späten Hellenismus* (Bonn).

von Vacano, O., 1988: "*Regio instratu ornatus:* Beobachtungen zur Deutung des Reliefs des L. Aemilius Paullus in Delphi," in *Bathron: Beiträge zur Architektur und verwandten Künsten* (Festschrift H. Drerup, Saarbrücken) 375–86.

Vorster, C., 1989: "Bonner Abguß einer verschollenen Heraklesherme," in *Beiträge zur Ikonographie und Hermeneutik: Festschrift für Nikolaus Himmelmann* (*BJb* BH 47, Mainz) 281–87.

Voutiras, E., 1989a: "*Libelli . . . Persephonae maxima dona,*" in *Beiträge zur Ikonographie und Hermeneutik: Festschrift für Nikolaus Himmelmann* (*BJb* BH 47, Mainz) 355–60.

Voutiras, E., 1989b: "*ΠΕΡΙ ΤΗΣ ΚΡΑΤΗΤΕΙΟΥ ΑΙΡΕΣΕΩΣ: ΣΚΕΨΕΙΣ ΓΥΡΟ ΑΠΟ ΤΟ ΑΝΑΓΛΥΦΟ ΤΟΥ ΑΡΧΕΛΑΟΥ ΑΠΟ ΤΗΝ ΠΡΙΗΝΗ,*" *Egnatia* 1, 129–68 (German summary 169–70).

Voutiras, E., 1990: "*ΗΦΑΙΣΤΙΩΝ ΗΡΩΣ,*" *Egnatia* 2, 123–62 (German summary 163–64).

Waelkens, M., 1995: "Rise and Fall of Sagalassos," *Archaeology* 48.3 (May/June) 28–34.

Warden, P. G., and Romano, D. G., 1994: "The Course of Glory: Greek Art in a Roman Context at the Villa of the Papyri at Herculaneum," *Art History* 17, 228–54.

Warren, J. A. W., 1993: "Towards a Resolution of the Achaian League Silver Coinage Controversy: Some Observations on Methodology," in M. Price et al., eds., *Essays in Honour of Robert Carson and Kenneth Jenkins* (London) 87–99.

Waywell, G. B., 1986: *The Lever and Hope Collections: Ancient Sculptures in the Lady Lever*

Bibliography

Art Gallery, Port Sunlight, and a Catalogue of the Ancient Sculptures Formerly in the Hope Collection, London and Deepdene (Berlin).

Waywell, G. B., 1990: "The Scylla Monument from Bargylia: Its Sculptural Remains," in *Akten XIII*, 1990, 386–88.

Waywell, G. B., 1996a: "Scilla nell'arte antica," in *Ulisse* 1996, 108–19.

Waywell, G. B., 1996b: "The Scylla Monument from Bargylia," *AntP* 25, 75–116, pls. 59–66.

Webb, P. A., 1989: "Figural Sculpture in Hellenistic Architecture: Asia Minor and the Aegean Islands" (Ph.D. Dissertation for Bryn Mawr College).

Webb, P. A., 1996: *Hellenistic Architectural Sculpture: Figural Motifs in Western Anatolia and the Aegean Islands* (Madison).

Webb, P. A., 1998: "The Functions of the Sanctuary of Athena and the Pergamon Altar (the Heroon of Telephos) in the Attalid Building Program," in Hartswick and Sturgeon 1998, 241–54.

Weber, H., 1966: "Zum Apollon Smintheus-Tempel in der Troas," *IstMitt* 16, 100–114.

Weber, M., 1993: "Zur Überlieferung der Goldelfenbeinstatue des Phidias im Parthenon," *JdI* 108, 83–122.

Weber, M., 1996: "Zum griechischen Athletenbilde: Zum Typus und zur Gattung des Originals der Apoxyomenosstatue im Vatikan," *RM* 103, 31–49.

Weidemann, K., 1983: *Könige aus dem Yemen: Zwei spätantike Bronzestatuen* (Mainz).

Weis, A., 1982: "The Motif of the *Adligatus* and Tree: A Study in the Sources of Pre-Roman Iconography," *AJA* 86, 28–41.

Weis, A., 1992: *The Hanging Marsyas and Its Copies: Roman Innovations in a Hellenistic Sculptural Tradition* (Rome).

Weis, A., 1998a: "Sperlonga and Hellenistic Sculpture," *JRA* 11, 412–20.

Weis, A., 1998b: "The *Pasquino* Group and Sperlonga: Menelaos and Patroklos or Aeneas and Lausus (*Aen.* 10.791–832)?" in Hartswick and Sturgeon 1998, 255–86.

Weis, A., forthcoming: "Odysseus at Sperlonga: Hellenistic Hero or Roman Heroic Foil?" in de Grummond and Ridgway, forthcoming.

Wenning, R., 1978: *Die Galateranatheme Attalos I: Eine Untersuchung zum Bestand und zur Nachwirkung pergamenischer Skulptur* (Pergamenische Forschungen 4, Berlin).

Willer, F., 1994a: "Die Restaurierung der Herme," in Hellenkemper Salies et al. 1994, 953–58.

Willer, F., 1994b: "Zur Herstellungstechnik der Herme," in Hellenkemper Salies et al. 1994, 959–70.

Willer, F., 1996: "Beobachtungen zur Sockelung von bronzenen Statuen und Statuetten," *BJb* 196, 337–70.

Willer, F., 1998: "Die Bonner Restaurierung des Eros von Mahdia," *AntP* 26, 73–89.

Wilson, R. J. A., 1990: *Sicily under the Roman Empire: The Archaeology of a Roman Province, 36 B.C.-A.D. 535* (Warminster).

Woodford, S., 1983: "The Iconography of the Infant Herakles Strangling Snakes," in *Image et céramique grecque: Actes du Colloque de Ruen, 25-26 Nov. 1982* (Publications de l'Université de Rouen 96, Rouen), 121–29.

Wolters, C., 1979: "Recherches sur les stèles funéraires hellénistiques de Thessalie," in *La Thessalie* (Actes de la Table-Ronde, July 21–24, 1975, Lyon; Collection de la Maison de l'Orient Méditerranéen 6), 81–110.

Bibliography

Wörrle, M. and Zanker, P., eds., 1995: *Stadtbild und Bürgerbild im Hellenismus: Kolloquium, München, 24. bis 26. Juni 1993* (Munich).

Yaylali, A., 1976: *Der Fries des Artemisions von Magnesia am Mäander* (*IstMitt* BH 15).

Yfantidis, K., 1993: "Beobachtungen an zwei pergamenischen Köpfen in Schloss Fasanerie bei Fulda," *AM* 108, 225–38.

Zagdoun, M.-A., 1988: "Bulletin Archéologique. La Sculpture: Reliefs Hellénistiques," *REG* 101, 113–69.

Zagdoun, M.-A., 1989: *La sculpture archaïsante dans l'art hellénistique et dans l'art du Haut-Empire* (Paris).

Zagdoun, M.-A., 1991: "Bulletin Archéologique. La Sculpture: La Ronde-Bosse Hellénistique (1960–1987)," *REG* 104, 140–97.

Zagdoun, M.-A., 1995: "Bulletin Archéologique. La Sculpture Hellénistique," *REG* 108, 150–89.

Zanker, P., 1965: "Zwei Akroterfiguren aus Tyndaris," *RM* 72, 93–99.

Zanker, P., 1989: *Die Trunkene Alte: Das Lachen der Verhöhnten* (Frankfurt).

Zanker, P., 1993: "The Hellenistic Grave Stelai from Smyrna: Identity and Self-image in the Polis," in Bulloch et al. 1993, 212–30.

Zanker, P., 1995: "Brüche im Bürgerbild? Zur bürgerlichen Selbdarstellung in den hellenistischen Städten," in Wörrle and Zanker 1995, 251–63.

Zimmer, G., and Hacklander, N., eds., 1997: *Der Betende Knabe: Original und Experiment* (Frankfurt).

Credits for Plates

1–3, 21–29, 49	B. S. Ridgway
4–6	D. Pullen
7, 12–15, 17, 20, 77a	Staatliche Museen zu Berlin
8	J. Laurentius, Antikensammlungen, Staatliche Museen zu Berlin, Preussischer Kulturbesitz, neg. no. PM 8154,22.1
9a–b	Antikensammlungen, Staatliche Museen zu Berlin, Preussischer Kulturbesitz, neg. no. PM 7342
30	Antikensammlungen, Staatliche Museen zu Berlin, Preussischer Kulturbesitz, neg. no. PM 7756
31	Poster from San Francisco Exhibition
32	Prof. Niels Hannestad
33	Courtesy Prof. C. Özgünel
34	Courtesy Anthropological Museum, Marichal College, Aberdeen
35	Bryn Mawr College Collection
36	Courtesy Dr. P. Webb
37	Kunsthistorisches Museum, Vienna, neg. no. II 27335
38	Kunsthistorisches Museum, Vienna, neg. no. II 27333
39–44	Courtesy Prof. R. Fleischer
45, 57, 67	Athens National Museum
46, 47	R. Carpenter Collection
48, 58	The Louvre, Département des Antiquités grecques, étrusques et romaines
50	Courtesy Museum of Fine Arts, Boston
51–52	Venice Archaeological Museum
53a–b, 64	Istanbul Archaeological Museum
54	C. Czapski
55	D. Greenewalt
56	DAI Rome, neg. 95.362 b
59	After E. Pfuhl and H. Möbius, *Die Ostgriechischen Grabreliefs*, vol. 1 (Mainz 1977) no. 429 (hereafter *DOG* 1977)
60	After *DOG* 1977, no. 382
61	After *DOG* 1977, no. 872
62	After E. Pfuhl and H. Möbius, *Die Ostgriechischen Grabreliefs*, vol. 2 (Mainz 1979) no. 1547 (hereafter *DOG* 1979)
63	After *DOG* 1979, no. 1831

Credits for Plates

Selective Index

This index focuses on Hellenistic monuments and topics as discussed in the text. References to notes (which should be consulted in conjunction with the text) have generally not been included, except in cases where they provide additional information. Architectural sculpture (as well as some sculpture in the round, where applicable) is listed by provenience rather than by museum; statues of deities and heroes are listed by name, group compositions and well-known works are mentioned under their most common appellation.

Selective Index

Selective Index

Selective Index

Hellenistic art/period (*continued*)
54, 84, 86, 117, 128, 165, 241; schools, Rhodian, 11, 12, 151, 277
"Hellenistic Ruler" in the Terme Museum (**Pls. 72a–b**), 305–09, 313. *See also* Statue types, Hellenistic Ruler
Hephaistion: votive relief to, 220–21 n. 21
Herakles: from Alba Fucens, 246; with the Apples of the Hesperides, 252, 253; child, strangling serpents, 252, 253–54; Epitrapezios, 253; in gymnasia, 168, 188 n. 64, 310; *mingens*, 282; pose, 306, 326–27 n. 14; in Rome, from Capitoline, 244. *See also* Pergamon Altar, Telephos Frieze
Herculaneum, Villa of the Papyri, 266 n. 66; bronze runners ("Wrestlers"), 313; Doryphoros herm, 252, 279; female bronze head ("Sappho"), 246; portraits, 302–03
Hermaphrodite: lampadephoros, 314; from Pergamon, 241; struggling with satyr, 286, 287, 301 n. 55
Hermes, 204, 205; by Eucheir, 235; on gravestones (**Pl. 63**), 196; in gymnasia, 168, 310; Richelieu type, 242; as ruler's type, 306–07, 319. *See also* Four-Gods Reliefs
Hermogenes (architect), 32, 84, 109, 110
Hieronymos (sculptor), 151, 292 n. 20
Hieronymos Relief (so-called Schoolteacher's). *See* Rhodes
Homeric bowls. *See* Relief pottery
Honorary statues. *See* Statue types
Horse and Jockey from Cape Artemision. *See* Athens, National Museum
Horse Leader Reliefs. *See* Rider Reliefs
Horses: akroterial at Pergamon, 28, 43, 45–46; bronze, from Trastevere, 308; on funerary/votive reliefs, 195, 196–98; on Lagina Friezes, 113, 121; riderless (motif), 80; turning back, 80, 82, 85
Hygieia, at Pheneos, 235

Ilion: antefixes with Athena head, 335 n. 56; Athenaion, 117–18; Athenaion, new metope fragment, 137 n. 48; cult of Samothrakian Gods, 179 n. 34
"Invitation to the Dance" Group, 278
Iphigeneia. *See* Izmir; Termessos
Isis: costume, 194; from Delos, 145–46
Isis/Nemesis, from Delos, 146
Istanbul, Archaeological Museum: "Alexander" from Pergamon, 35–36
Izmir: Iphigeneia Relief, 85; Runner from Kyme (**Pl. 76**), 313

Juno Cesi (**Pl. 71**), 270–71

Kalydon: Heroon of Leon, 53 n. 26
Karakonero, funerary complex. *See* Rhodes
Kentauromachy, 120, 277; at Teos, 110–11. *See also* Centaur, Centaurs

Klaros: altar, 25; cult images, 240–41
Knidos: altar to Nymphs/Apollo Karneios (**Ills. 14–15**), 56 n. 44, 87, 119; Lion Tomb, 121; Temple of Dionysos, frieze, 110–11
Kos: altar frieze, 101 n. 55, 109, 110, 118, 119–20; colossal head, 165; dancer's statue, 157; local style, 164; Nike statues, 157, 159; round (funerary/votive) altars, 202–03, 224 n. 33; sculpture from, 164–65
Krates of Mallos (philosopher), 33, 207–08
Kyme, bronze runner. *See* Izmir
Kyrene: bronze head from (London, BM 268), 308
Kyzikos: Banquet relief for Attalos, 219 n. 18; relief to Herakles, 160; seated female (**Pls. 53a–b**), 166, 317; *stylopinakia*, 106, 275, 277; Temple of Apollonis, 106–07

Labels on relief sculpture, 33–34, 71–72, 88–89
Lagina, altar, 119, 120–21
Lagina, Hekateion, 111–15; Friezes, 55–56 n. 42, 100 n. 47, 109, 117, 207, 221 n. 22; Friezes, Birth of Zeus (east side), 112; Friezes, Gigantomachy (west side), 111–12, Apollo, 35, Hekate, 112; Friezes, North side (**Pl. 36**), 112–13; Friezes, South side, 114
Landscape elements, 101–02 n. 55, 206, 208; on Derveni Krater, 70; on gravestones (**Ill. 23**), 192, 195, 196, 198, 200; on Hieronymos Relief, 123; on Knidos altar, 88–89; at Lagina, 111; on Nereid Monument, 69; on Punishment of Dirke, 276, 277; rocky seats and bases, 43, 114, 121, 123, 204, 205, 229 n. 64, 278; on Smintheion, 85; on stelai, 194; on Telephos Frieze, 68, 71, 72, 73, 74; at Trysa, 74. *See also* Odyssey Landscapes
Laokoon, 10, 54 n. 37, 267 n. 71, 276, 279, 284, 285, 296 n. 33
Largo Argentina (Rome): female head, 244
Lecce Frieze, 80, 82
Letoon (near Xanthos, Lykia), 54 n. 36; draped female (**Pl. 55**), 166; female head (**Pl. 68**), 241
Limyra: Heroon of Perikle, 73, 94 n. 20; Ptolemaion, 31, 104
Lindos, rock-cut relief. *See* Pythokritos of Rhodes; Ships, bases and monuments
Lion, lioness: at Pergamon, 28, 34, 43, 46; on Telephos Frieze, 72; as waterspouts, 49 n. 10, 52–53 n. 26
Literary sources, 10, 13, 20, 34, 76, 82–83, 106, 248–49, 252, 284; Christian writers, 232; Euripides, 69–70, 86, 293 n. 22; Hesiod, 33, 113, 114–15, 207; Homer, 34, 108, 131 n. 14, 297 n. 41, 314, 322; Kallimachos, 58 n. 53; Lykophron, 296 n. 35
Ludovisi (Suicidal) Gaul. *See* Attalid Dedications
Lykosoura: cult statues, 59 n. 57, 235–38, 244; Temple of Despoina, akroterial figure, 239
Lysippos, Lysippan, 10, 11, 253, 272, 306, 312, 326 n. 12

Selective Index

Selective Index

Selective Index

(East Greece), 190–99, 205, 210, 304, 322; in Athens/Attica, 189, 192–93; in Boiotia, 189, 217 n. 13; *dexiosis* motif, 195, 196, 200, 216 n. 8, 220 n. 20; epitaphs and inscriptions, 191, 195–96, 215 n. 7; heroization and cult, 192–93, 202–03, 321; influence on architectural sculpture, 113, 134 n. 32; from the Kyklades, 199–202, 214 n. 3, 322; in Lakonia, 214–15 n. 3; in Macedonia, 189–90, 193; naiskos type, 191–92, 193–95; painted stelai, 189, 190, 215 n. 5; from Rhodes (**Pl. 65**), 198–99; from Skyllountia, 214 n. 3; in Thessaly, 189, 193. *See also* Banquet scenes; Rheneia; Rider (Horse Leader; Hero Equitans) Reliefs; Smyrna

Reliefs, votive, 206–13, 220 n. 20, 229 n. 64; altars, 224 n. 32. *See also* "Apotheosis of Homer" Relief; Banquet scenes; Four-Gods Reliefs; Munich Relief; Rider (Horse Leader; Hero Equitans) Reliefs

Rheneia: ship base, 176 n. 22; stelai (**Ill. 23**), 193, 199–202

Rhodes, 5–6, 15 n. 9, 32–33, 89, 269; altars, 198, 202–03, 224 n. 33; altar, of Archestrate (**Pl. 62**), 195, 203; Artemis/Hekate, Archaistic (**Pl. 79**), 316; Artemis/Hekate, Hellenistic, 318; banquet scenes, 195, 196; connection with Kos, 157; connection with Menekrates, 32, 54 n. 32, 274; connection with Pergamon, 55 n. 37, 151; connection with Samothrake, 153; funerary relief of Hieronymos, 94 n. 19, 122–24, 189; gravestones (**Pl. 65**), 198–99; Karakonero complex, 278, 295 n. 32; monument by Phyles, 292 n. 20; nymph statuettes, 276; pleasure parks, 277–78; sculptors' activity, 152, 247; Tomb with Karyatids, 121. *See also* Hellenistic art/period, schools, Rhodian

Riace Warriors, 9

Rider (Horse Leader; Hero Equitans) Reliefs (**Pl. 64**), 192, 196–98, 200, 209, 211, 322

"Riderless Horse" motif, 80

Rococo, style, 11, 286–88, 321

Rome, Roman: commissions, 207–08, 217 n. 13, 230, 254–55, 288, 319; cult images, 239, 240, 243–46; expansion and influence, 5–6, 15 n. 9, 34, 47, 115, 168, 185 n. 55, 193, 200, 269, 320–21; meanings, 110, 253–54, 269, 282, 283, 321; Penates cult at Troy, 179 n. 34; statues of Romans/Italians, 165, 242, 303–04, 305, 309, 320–21; technique, 110, 115; tendencies and effects, 11, 69, 74, 76, 103, 154
  monuments: Ara of Domitius Ahenobarbus, 140 n. 65; Ara Pacis, 34; Ephesos relief, 115–17; Lepcis Magna, 112

Sagalassos: Bouleuterion, 127; frieze of Dancing Women (**Pls. 39–44**), 104, 124–25, 180 n. 36; smaller frieze, 124

Samos: banquet scenes, 195; Erotes frieze from pillar monument, 96 n. 32; female statues, 166

Samothrake: Altar Court, 25; Dancers Frieze, 125; Hieron sculpture, 103, 129 n. 3, 130 n. 4, 156–57; Nike of (**Pl. 48**), 8, 130 n. 5, 150–59, 180 n. 36, 239, 279; statue of Philip V, 156; theater, 154

Sarapis, by Bryaxis, 232

Sarcophagi (Greek), 199–200

Sardis: stele of Menophila, 215–16 n. 7

Satyrs: as children, splashing water, 252, 254; at Delos, 118; as fountains, 278, 295 n. 31; and Hermaphroditos, 287, 301 n. 54; at Knidos, 110; and Nymph, 286, 288; on Pergamon Gigantomachy, 39, 74; on Telephos Frieze, 74; at Teos, 110; on votive reliefs, 210, 229 n. 64

Sculpture, technique: akrolithic, 232, 233, 235, 239, 240, 244, 246, 322; bronze casting, 8–9, 251–52, 265 n. 61, 303, 308, 309, 322; chryselephantine, 230, 231, 236, 238, 246; degree of finish, 43, 45, 71–72, 168, 169, 183 n. 47, 322; "disembodied heads," 74, 84, 114; hollowing, 38, 233, 235, 236, 244, 322; inserted eyes, 54 n. 35, 235, 236, 238, 240, 245, 261 n. 37; metal attachments, 45, 63 n. 77, 95 n. 23, 99 n. 44, 109, 118, 162, 168, 235, 322; piecing, 42, 43, 46, 150, 155, 158, 169, 233, 241, 244, 245, 260 n. 31, 310, 321–22; relief technique, 74, 108; struts, 42; use of patterns, 35, 59 n. 58, 61 n. 69, 80, 90, 108, 275, 280, 315. *See also* Color; Drapery; Hellenistic art/period, schools; Terracotta sculpture

Seated Boxer in the Terme Museum, 308

Segesta: ship consoles, 152–53

Seleukids and Syria, 5–6, 116, 207, 284, 305, 320

Seven Wise Men, 285

Severe/Severizing, style, 235, 238, 314

Ships: bases and monuments, 151, 152, 153–54, 202, 278; on gravestones (**Ill. 22**), 200–201, 223 n. 30

Shipwrecks, on gravestones. *See* Ships

Sicily/South Italy, 5–6, 104, 106, 152–53, 167, 229 n. 64, 242, 275, 318, 320. *See also* Taras

Signatures, 151, 165, 168, 230, 309; on Halikarnassos Maussolleion, 56 n. 44; on Knidian plaque, 101 n. 54; on Knidos altar, 88–89; on Pergamon Altar, 32, 34, 55 n. 37; at Sperlonga, 279; on statues, 158, 163, 166, 167, 168, 247, 271; on Tomb of Hieronymos, 123

Silenos, carried by sea centaur, 301 n. 55

Skopas, Skopas *minor* (sculptors), Skopasian, 10, 140 n. 65, 258 n. 18, 260 n. 28, 326 n. 12, 327–28 n. 20

Skylla: at Bargylia, 121–22; on Rhodes, 296; at Sperlonga, 152

Slipper-Slapper Group. *See* Delos

Smintheion (Temple of Apollo) at Chryse (Troad) (**Pl. 33**), 32, 82, 84–85, 224 n. 32

Smyrna: gravestones from (**Pls. 60–61**), 191, 193–95, 209; Rider stele, 198

Soloeis (Soluntum): altar, 224 n. 32; female statue (**Pl. 56**), 167, 213, 318

Selective Index

Plates

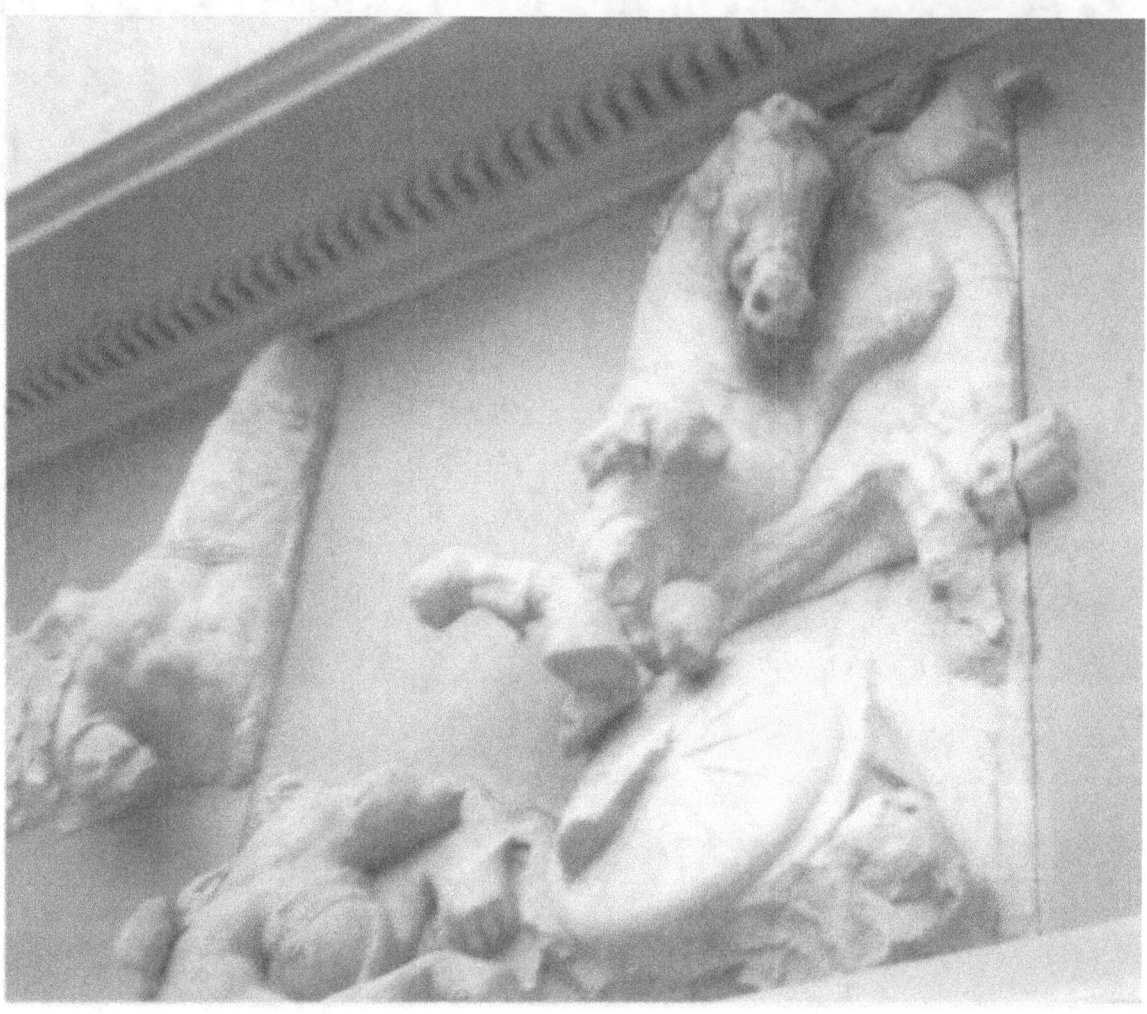

Plate 1. Pergamon Altar (as displayed in Berlin Museum), Gigantomachy, east side: Giant with starburst shield, under Hera's winged horses. Note the height of the relief.

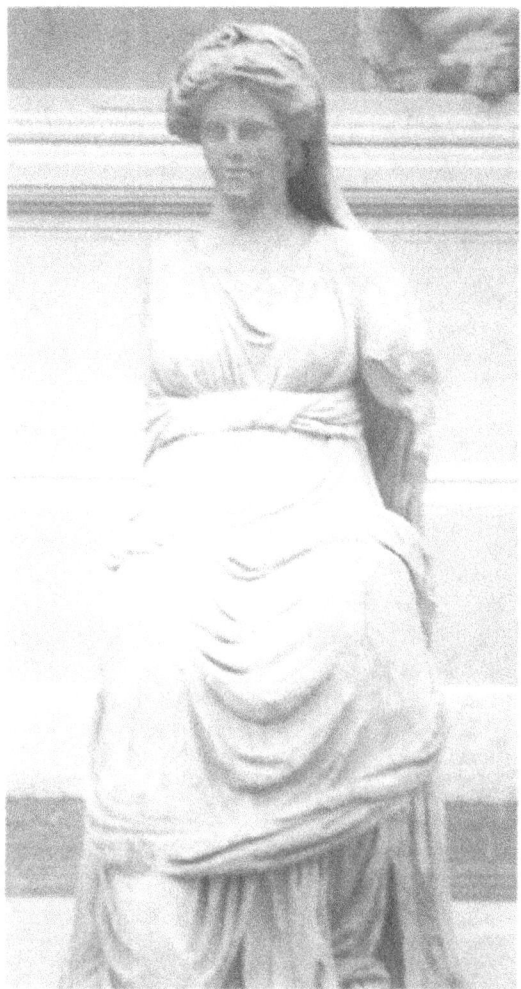

Plate 2. Berlin Museum: seated figure from Pergamon
(from Altar? = *AvP* 7, no. 62).

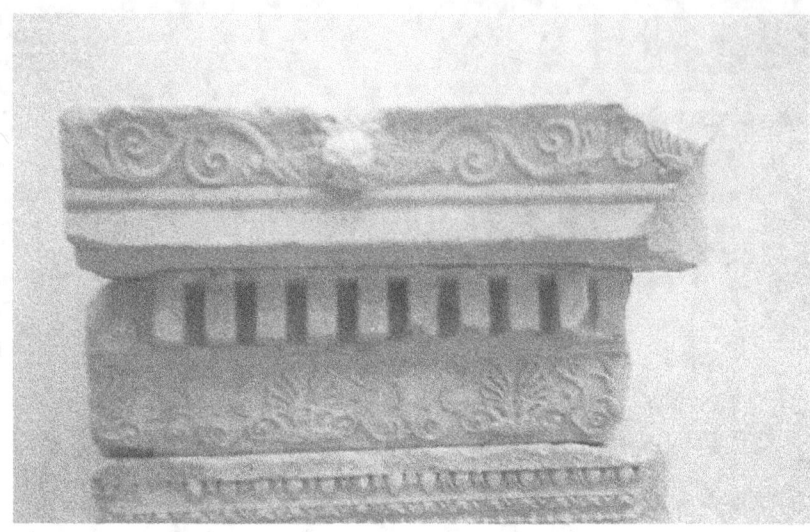

Plate 3. Berlin Museum: cornice blocks from Pergamon attributed to the sacrificial table of the Great Altar.

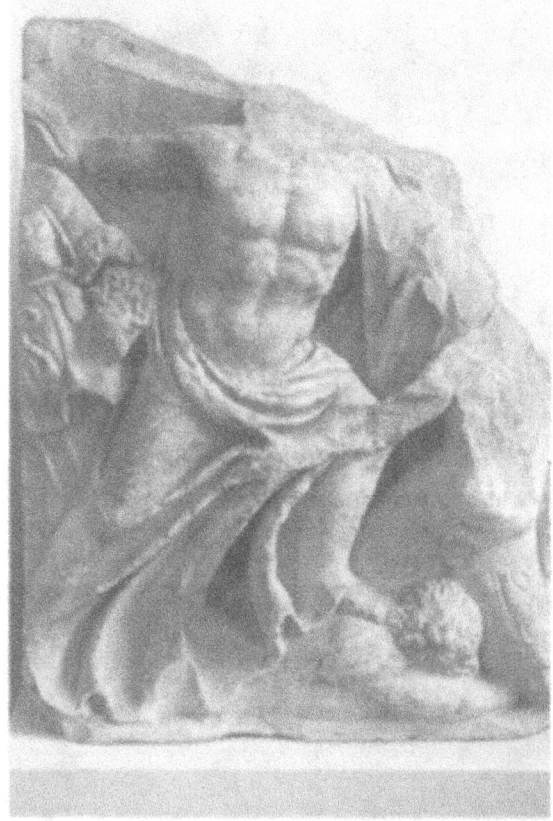

Plate 4. Berlin Museum: slab with Gigantomachy, from Pergamon—Palace V?

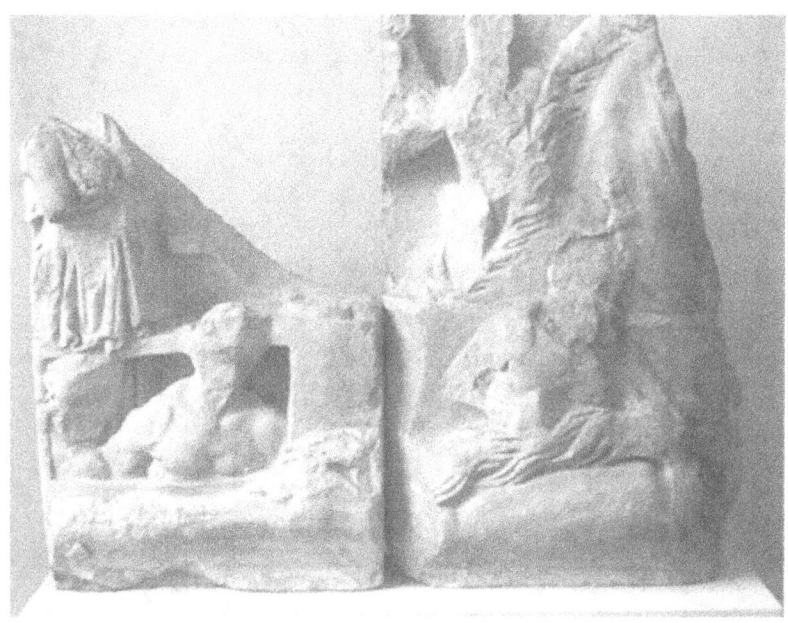

Plate 5. Berlin Museum: slab with Trojan Horse, from Pergamon—Palace V?

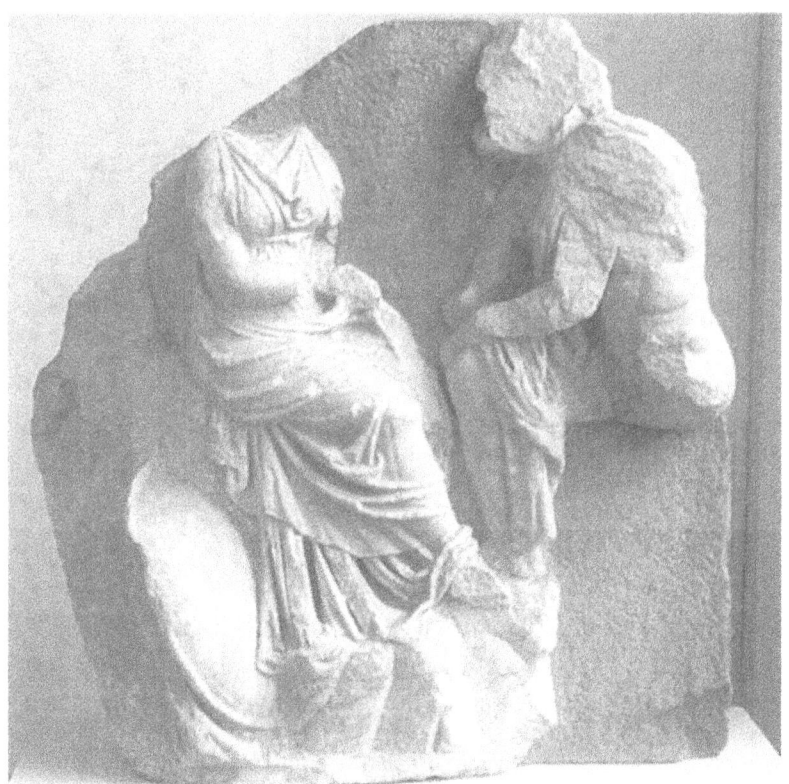

Plate 6. Berlin Museum: slab with Athena and male figure—from Palace V?

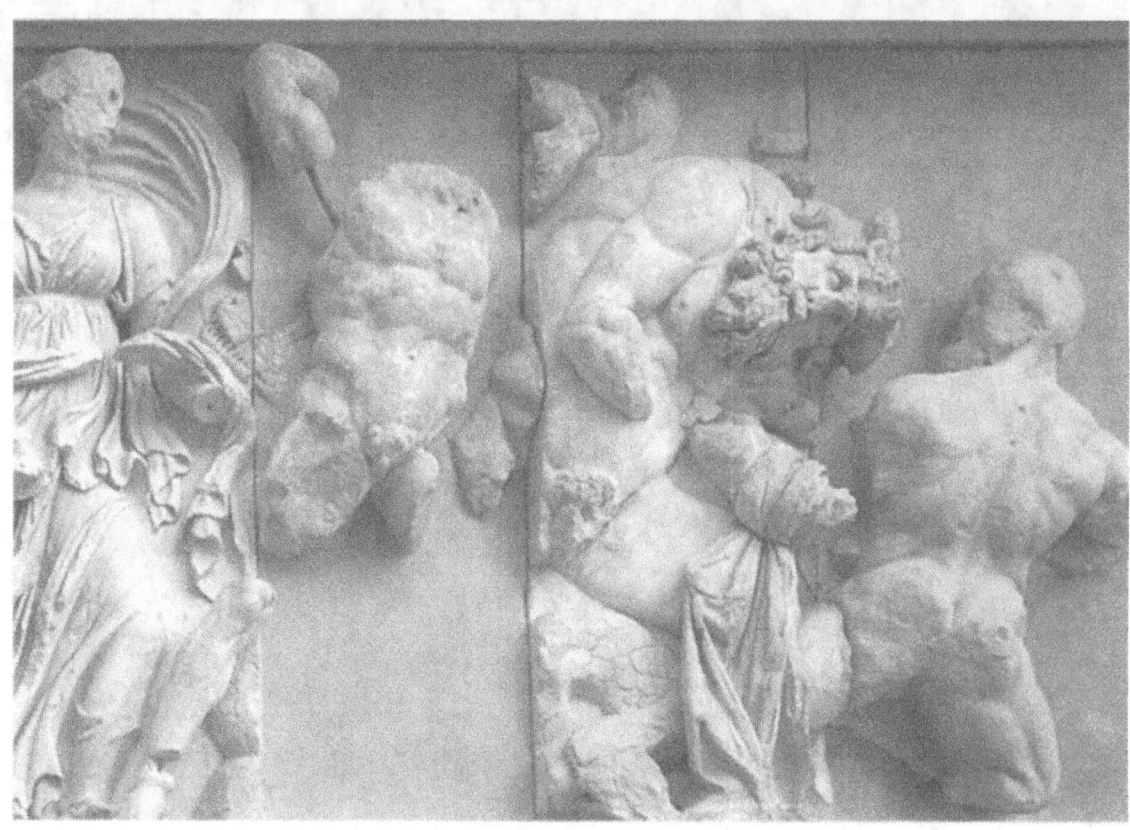

Plate 7. Pergamon Altar (as displayed in Berlin Museum), Gigantomachy, south side: bull-giant; his opponent is the so-called Worksop Torso, found in England.

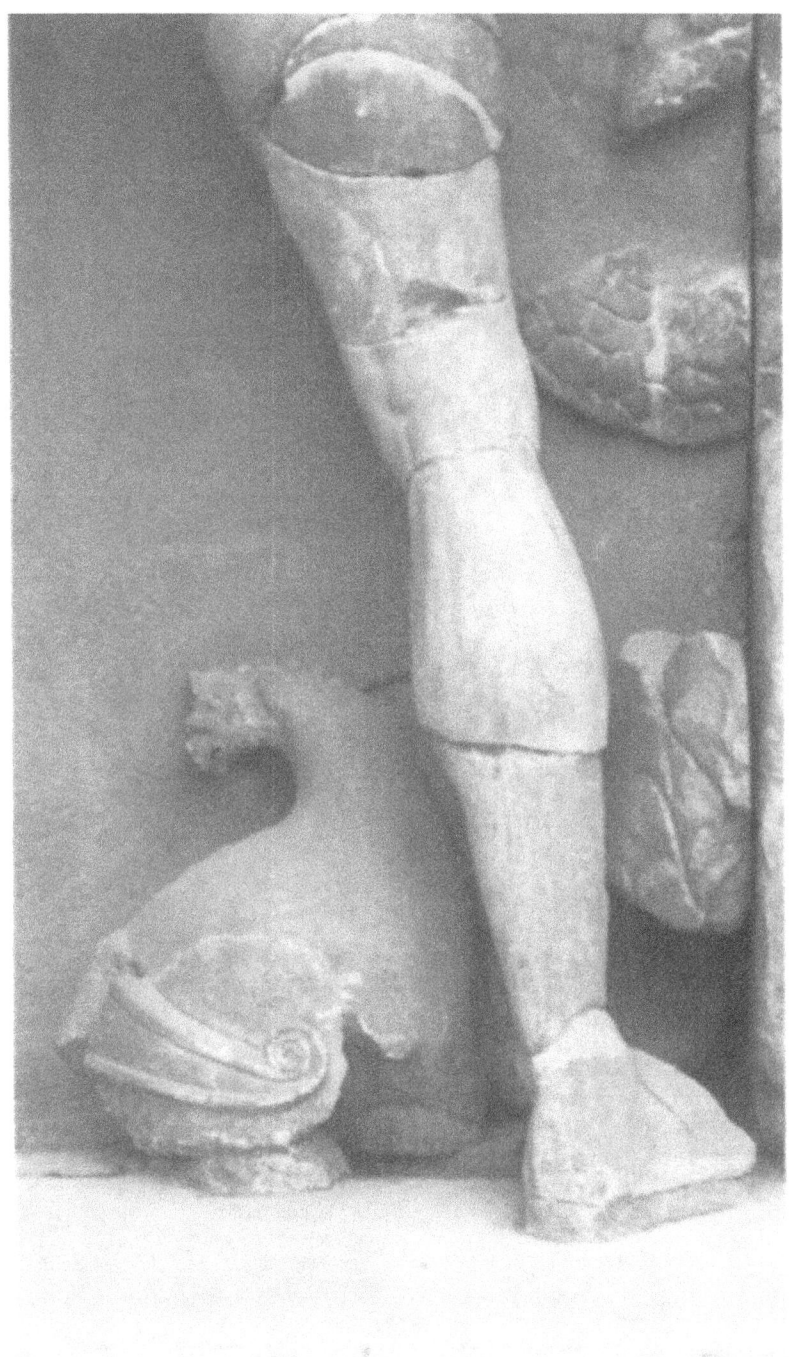

Plate 8. Pergamon Altar (as displayed in Berlin Museum), Gigantomachy, north side: detail of griffin-topped helmet.

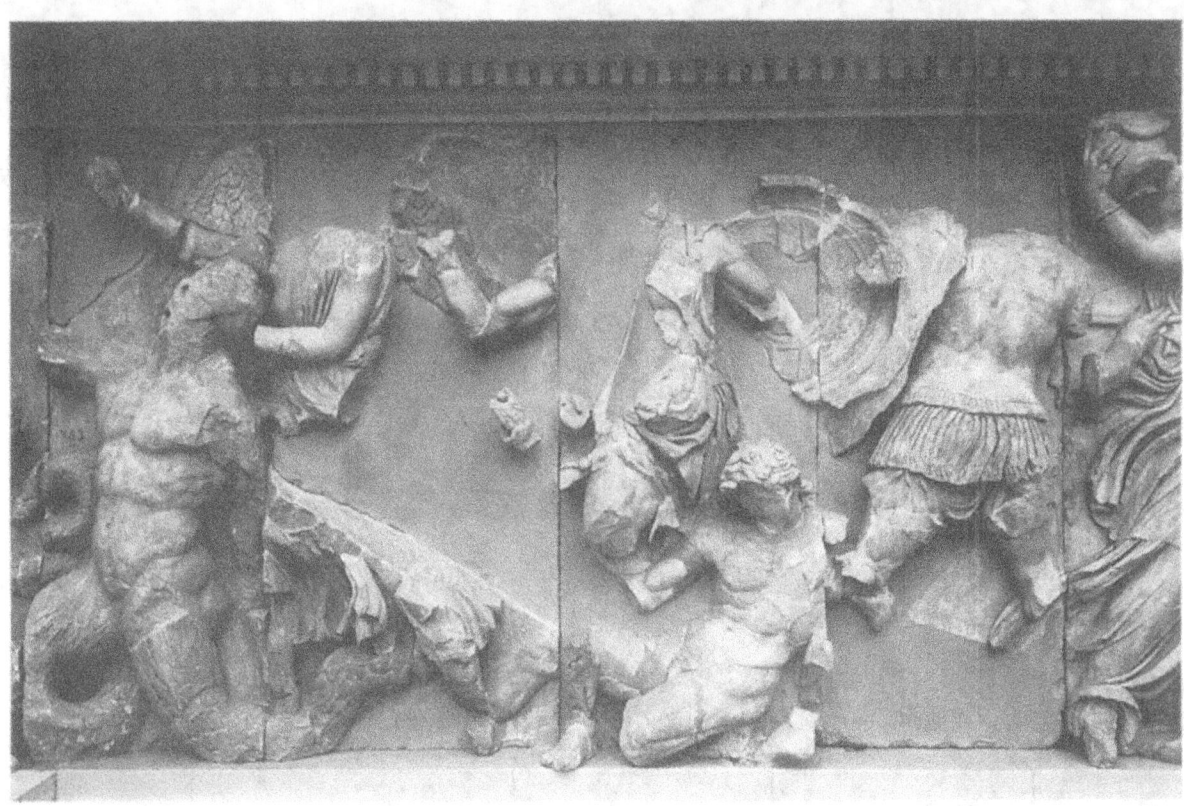

Plate 9a–b. Pergamon Altar (as displayed in Berlin Museum), Gigantomachy, north side—(a) full view; (b) detail of cuirassed Giant. Note winged thunderbolt on his shield rim.

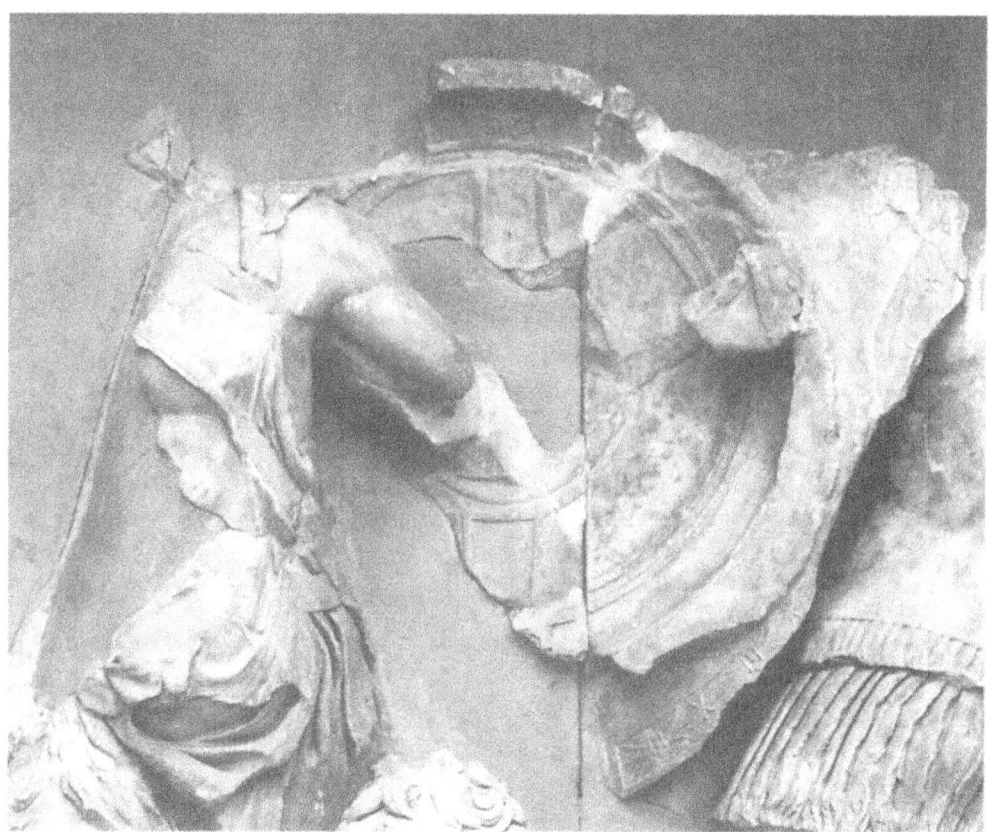

Plate 9b.

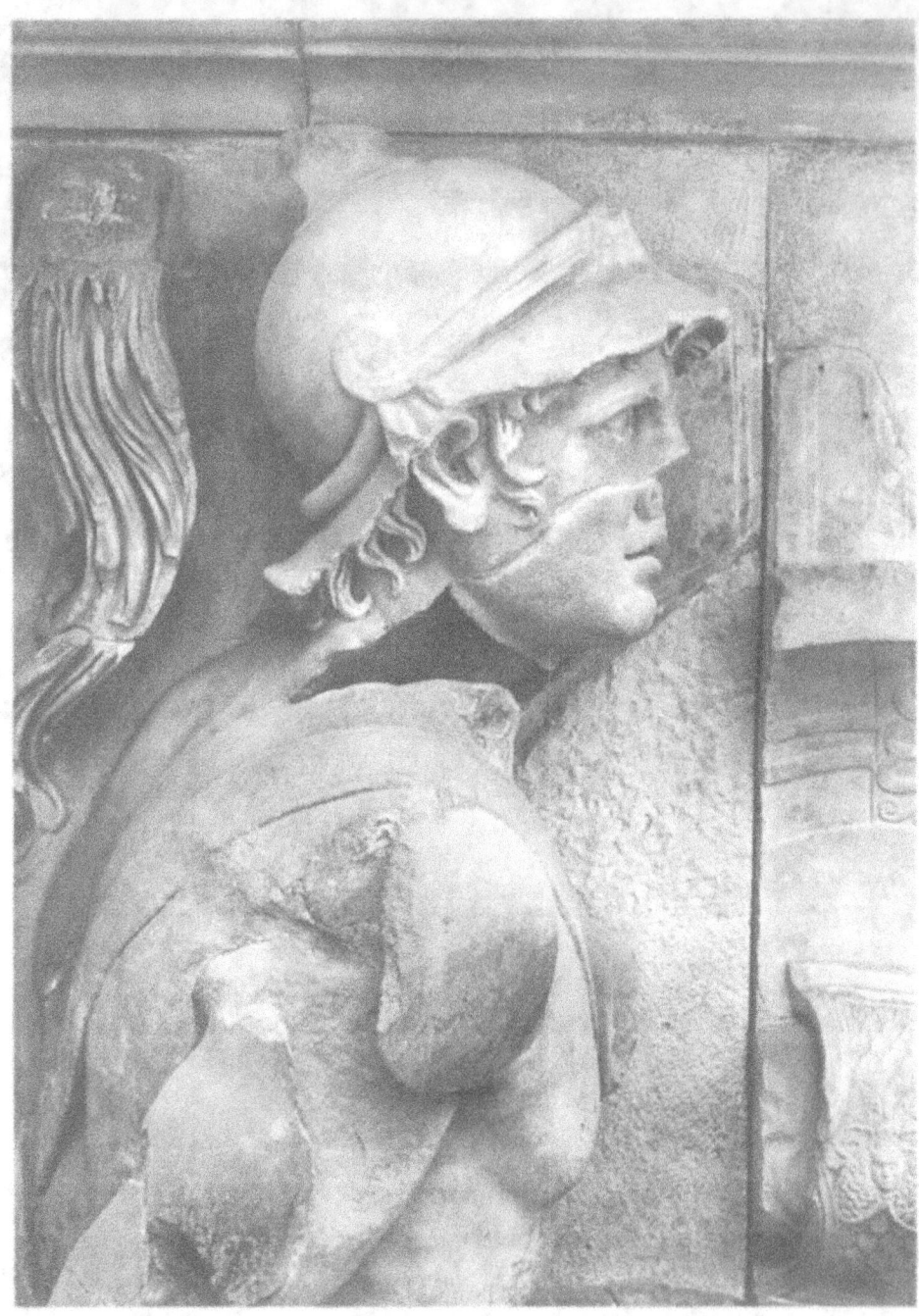

Plate 10. Pergamon Altar (as displayed in Berlin Museum), Gigantomachy, east side: detail of "Otos" (Artemis' opponent). Note the gorgoneion against the aigis on his shield strap.

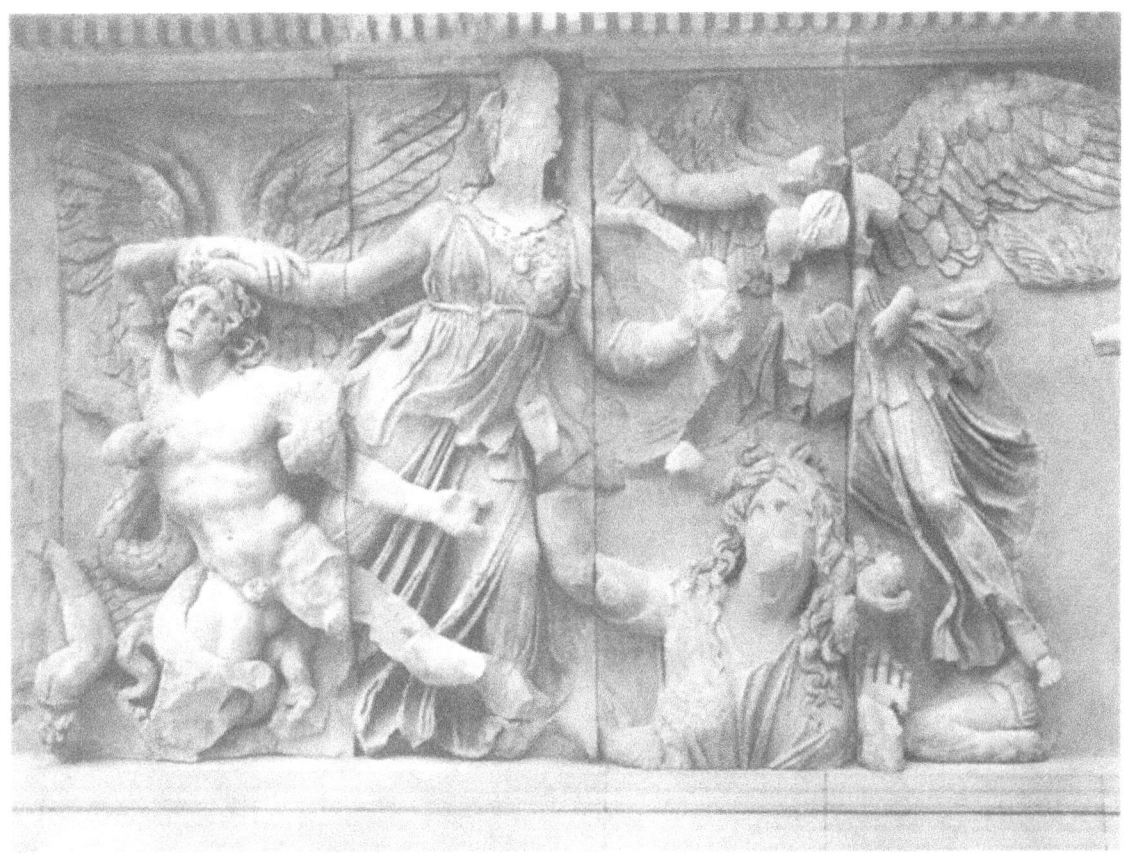

Plate 11. Pergamon Altar (as displayed in Berlin Museum), Gigantomachy, east side: Athena being crowned by Nike while defeating Alkyoneus, in the presence of Ge.

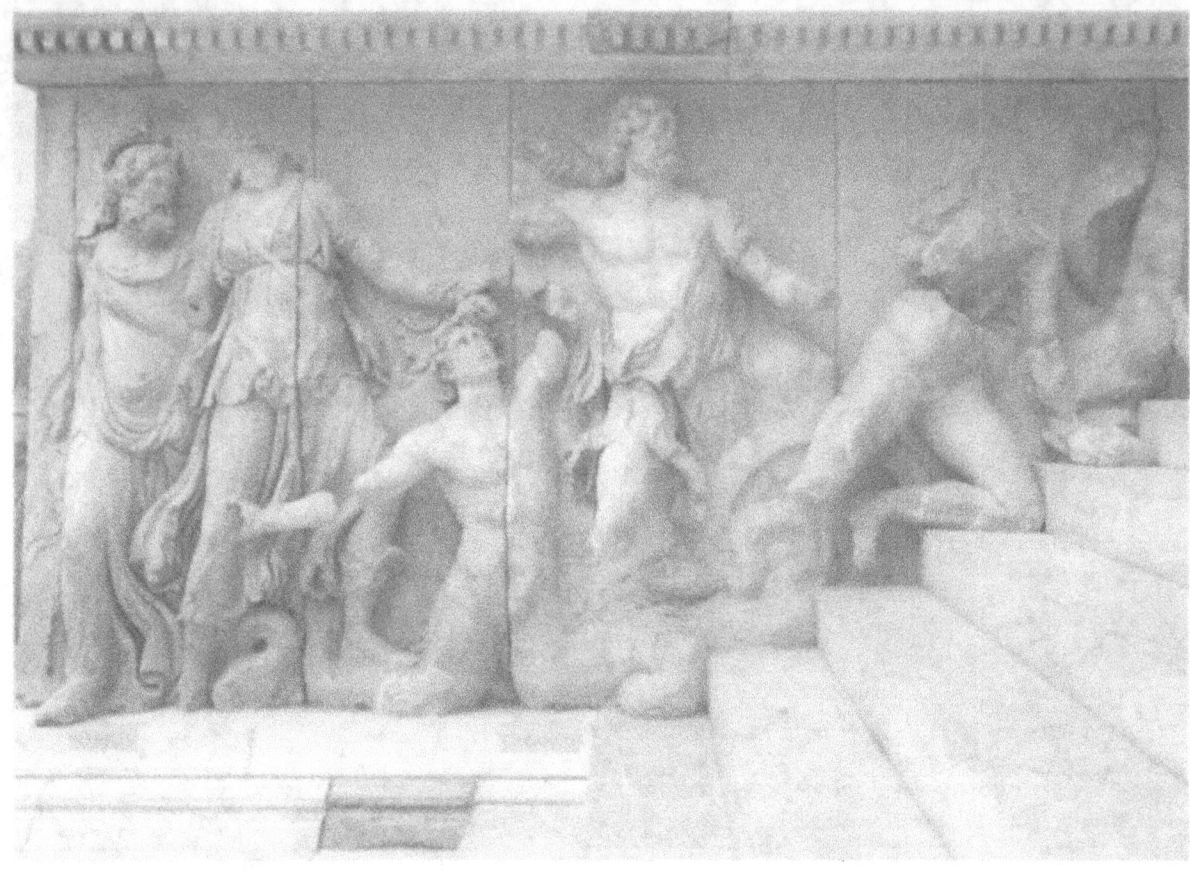

Plate 12. Pergamon Altar (as displayed in Berlin Museum), Gigantomachy, northwest risalit: sea divinities (Nereus, Doris, Okeanos) and Giants.

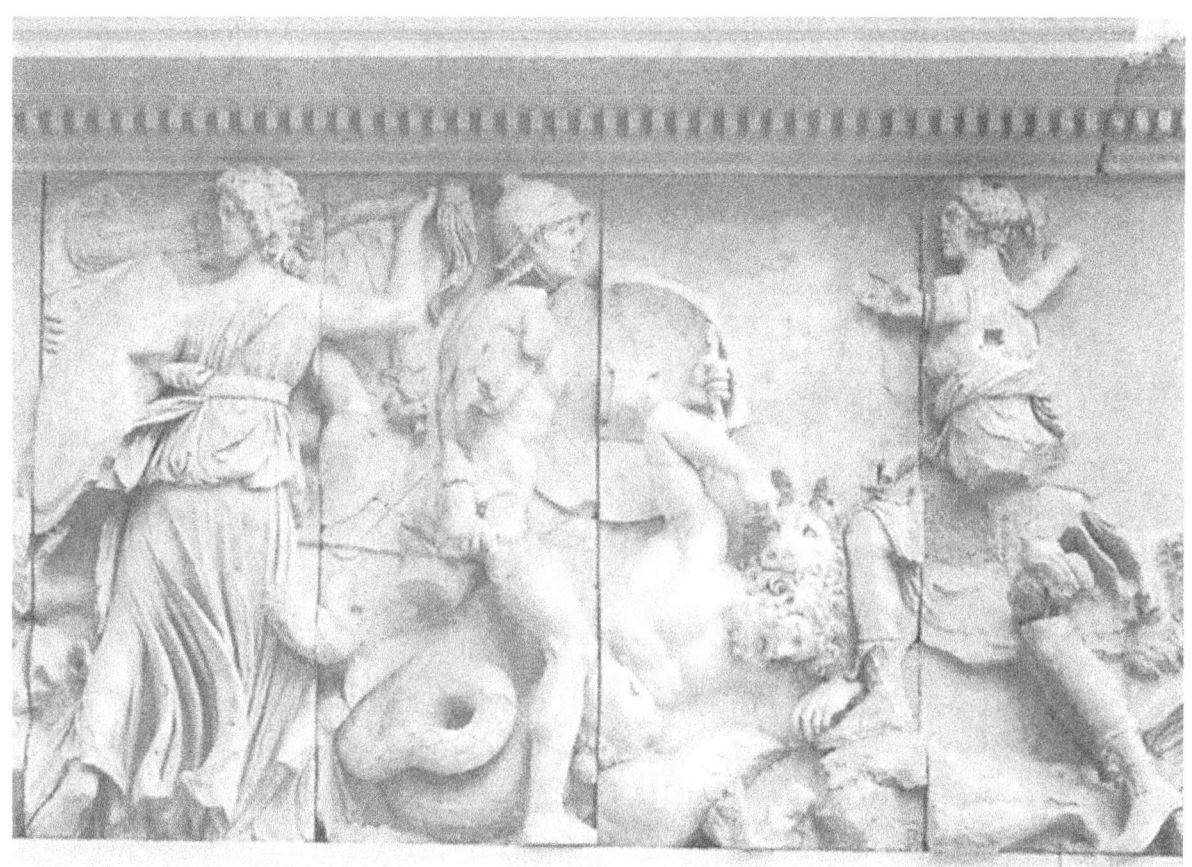

Plate 13. Pergamon Altar (as displayed in Berlin Museum), Gigantomachy, east side: Hekate, "Otos," Artemis. Note the snake biting Hekate's skirt, and the Giant gouging the dog's eye.

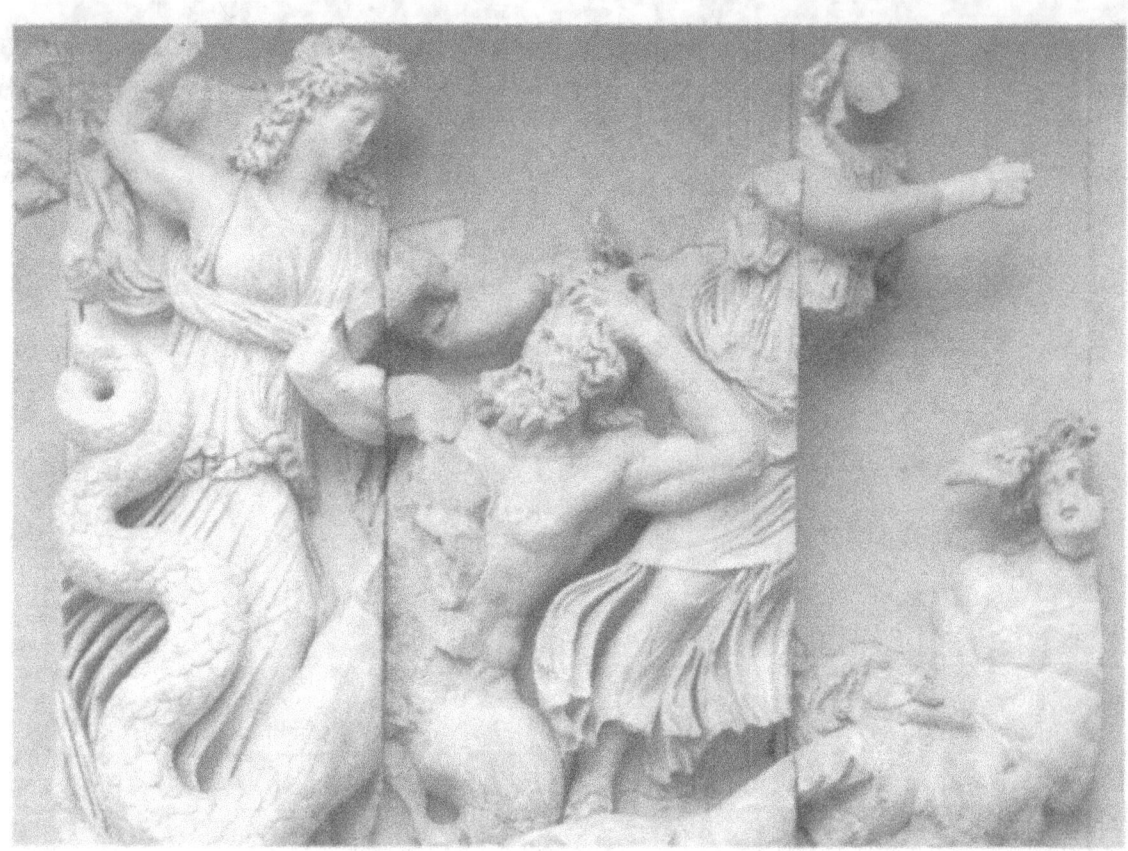

Plate 14. Pergamon Altar (as displayed in Berlin Museum), Gigantomachy, north side: the Moirai.

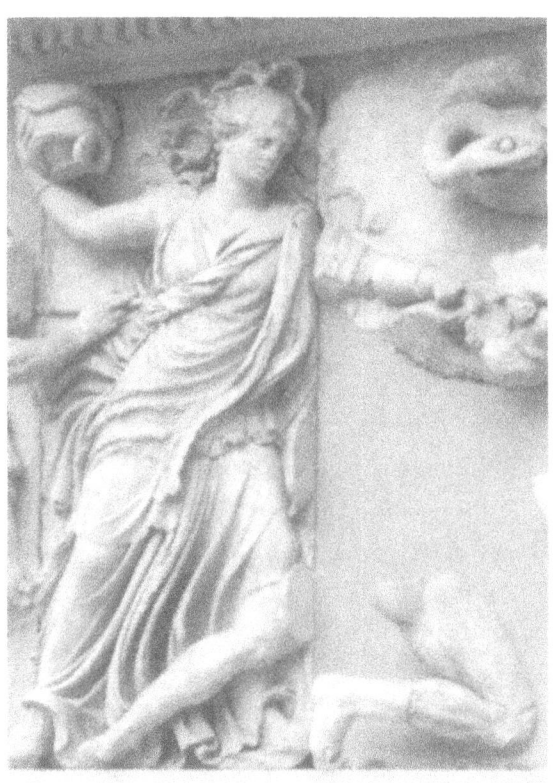

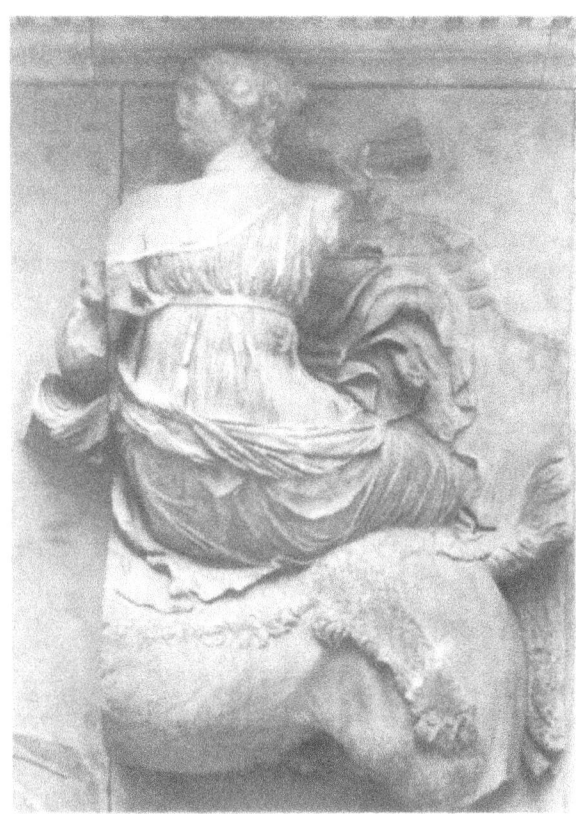

Plate 15. Pergamon Altar (as displayed in Berlin Museum), Gigantomachy, north side: Nyx (or Persephone).

Plate 16. Pergamon Altar (as displayed in Berlin Museum), Gigantomachy, south side: Selene. Note contrasting textures.

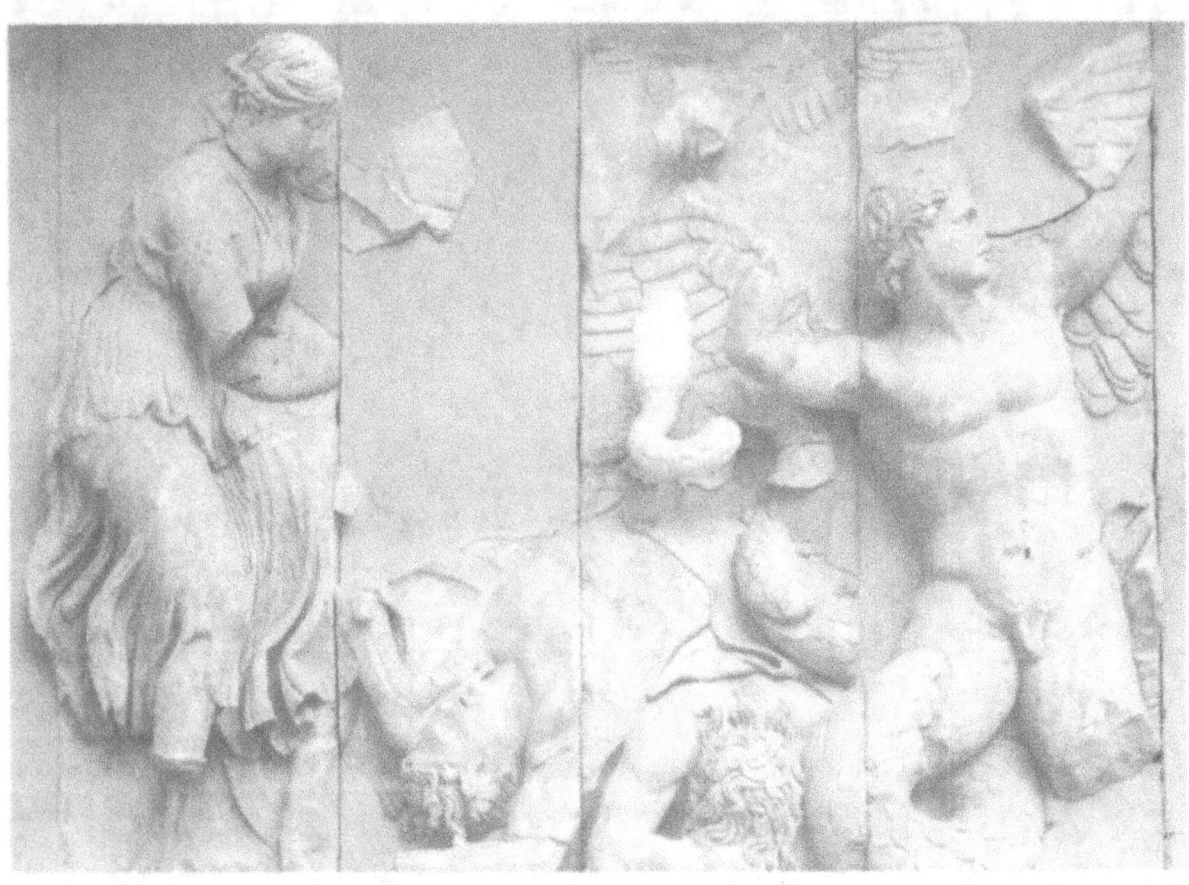

Plate 17. Pergamon Altar (as displayed in Berlin Museum), Gigantomachy, north side: Aphrodite and Eros (note his small body and wings above the kneeling Giant's right wing).

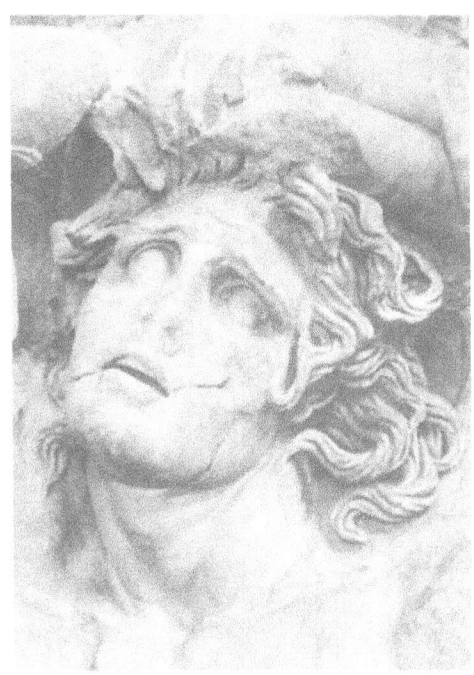

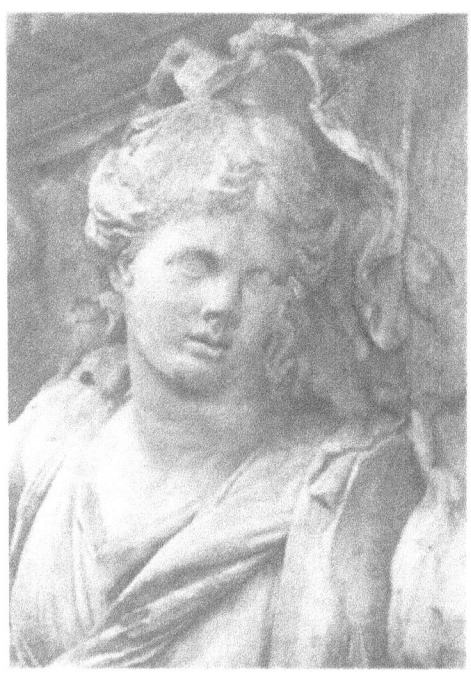

Plate 18. Pergamon Altar (as displayed in Berlin Museum), Gigantomachy, east side: detail of Alkyoneus. Note the drillwork around the eyes and the hair strands.

Plate 19. Pergamon Altar (as displayed in Berlin Museum), Gigantomachy, north side: detail of Nyx/Persephone.

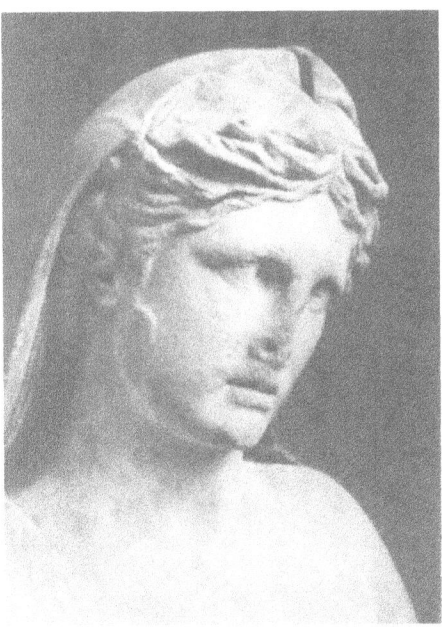

Plate 20. Berlin Museum: head of seated figure from Pergamon (Muse? from Altar? = *AvP* 7, no. 50).

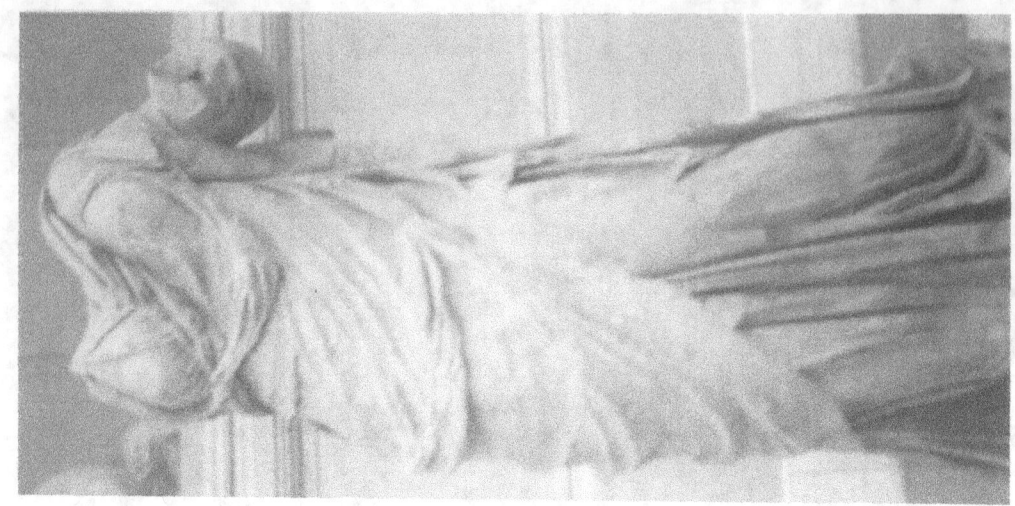

Plate 23. Berlin Museum: standing figure from Pergamon (from Altar? = *AvP* 7, no. 54).

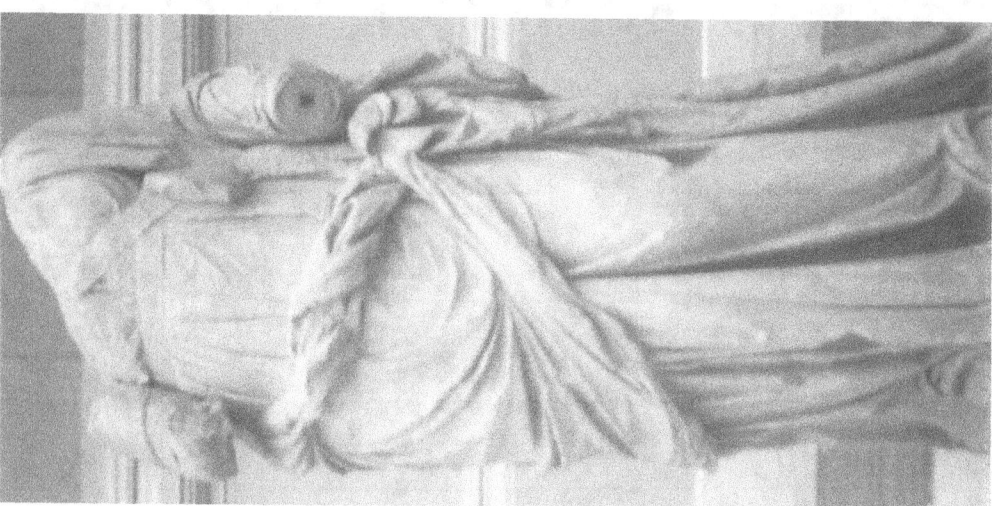

Plate 22. Berlin Museum: so-called Tragoidia from Pergamon (from Altar? = *AvP* 7, no. 47).

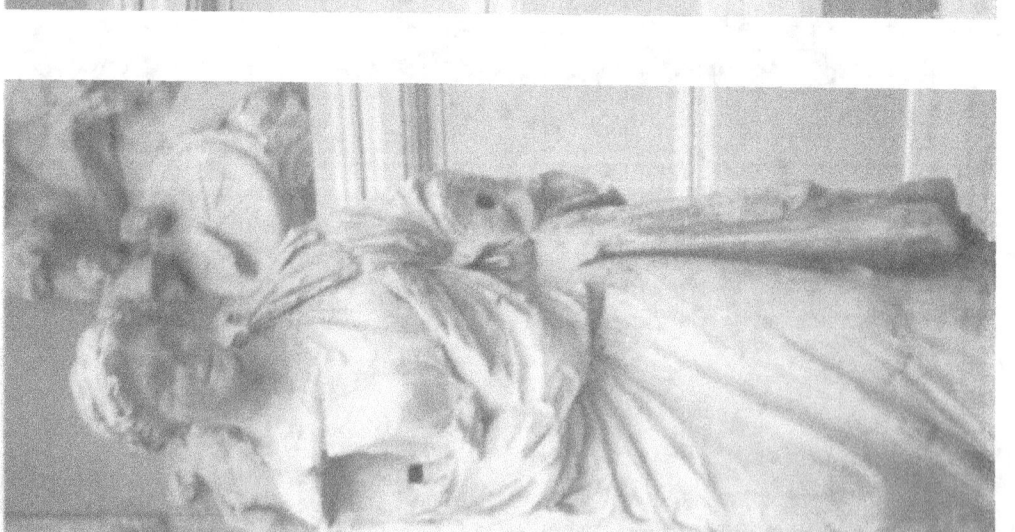

Plate 21. Berlin Museum: standing figure from Pergamon (from Altar? = *AvP* 7, no. 69).

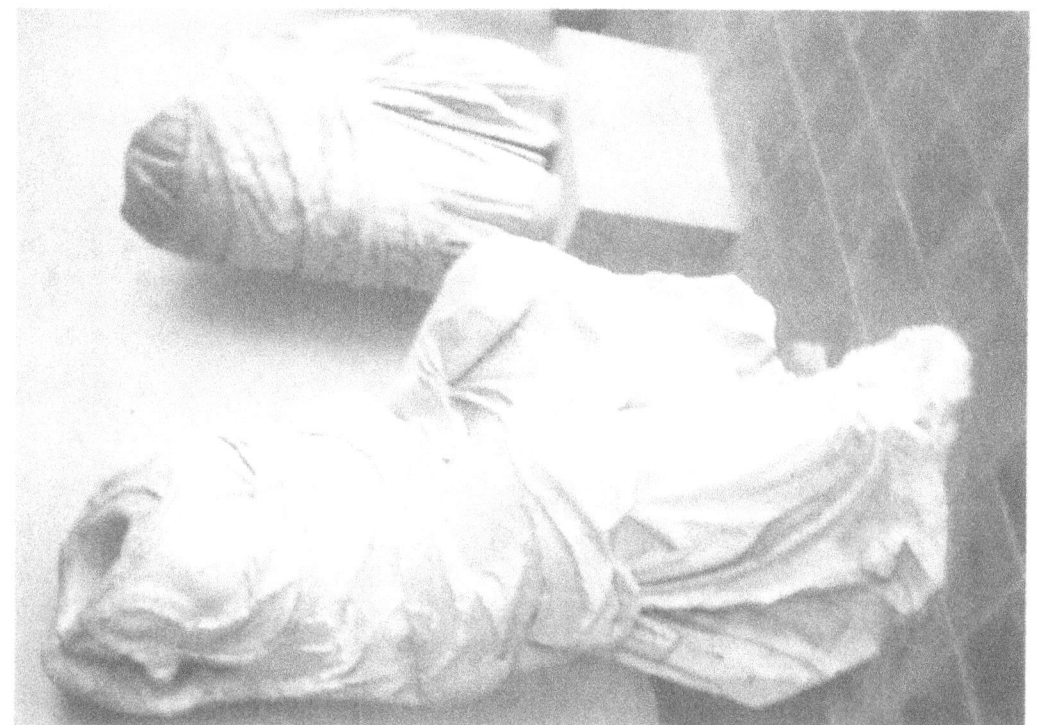

Plate 25. Bergama Museum: seated and standing figures from Pergamon (from Altar? = *AvP* 7, nos. 63 and 58 respectively).

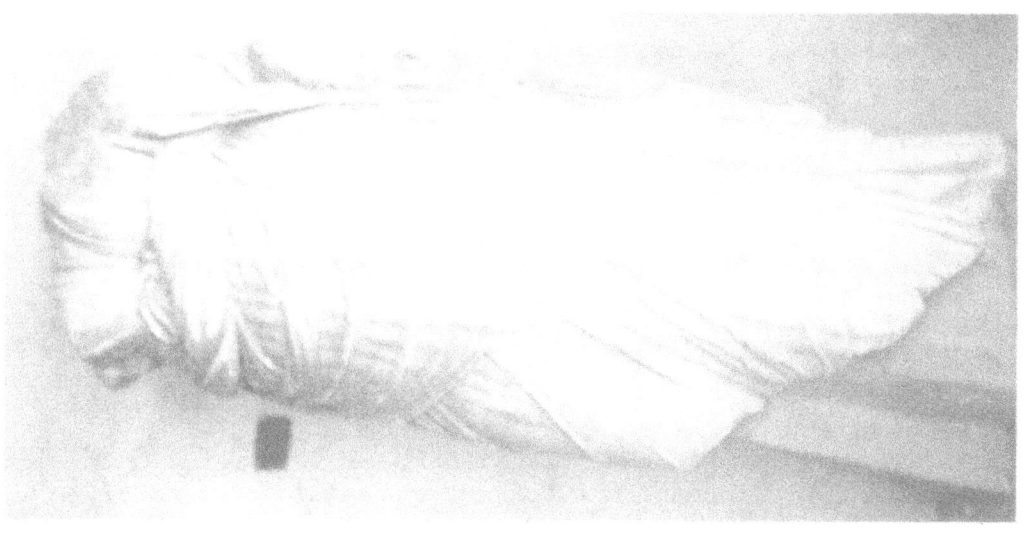

Plate 24. Bergama Museum: standing figure from Pergamon (from Altar? = *AvP* 7, no. 85).

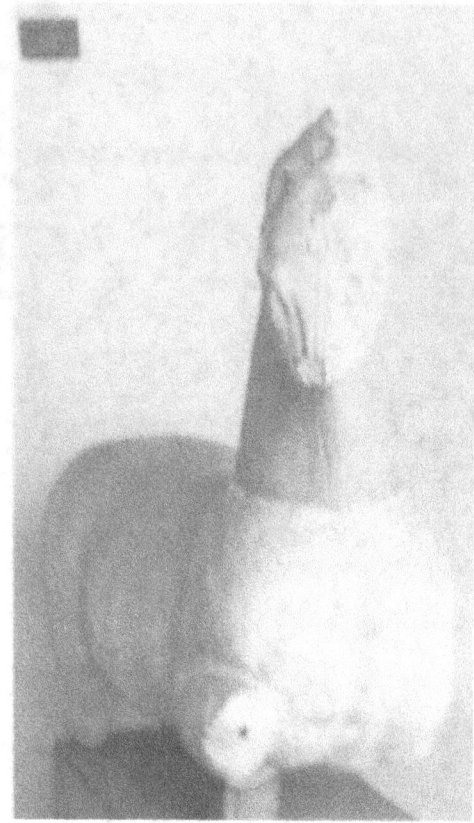

Plate 26. Bergama Museum: horse from roof of Pergamon Altar.

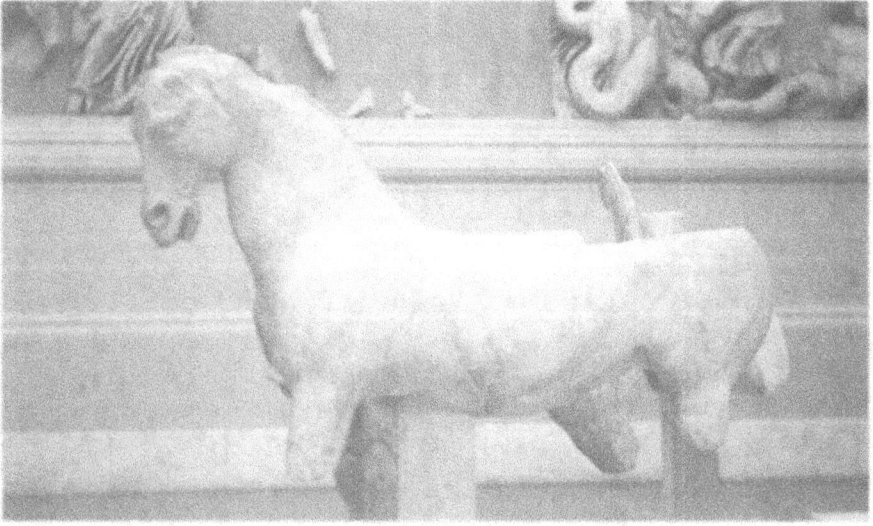

Plate 27. Berlin Museum: horse from roof of Pergamon Altar.

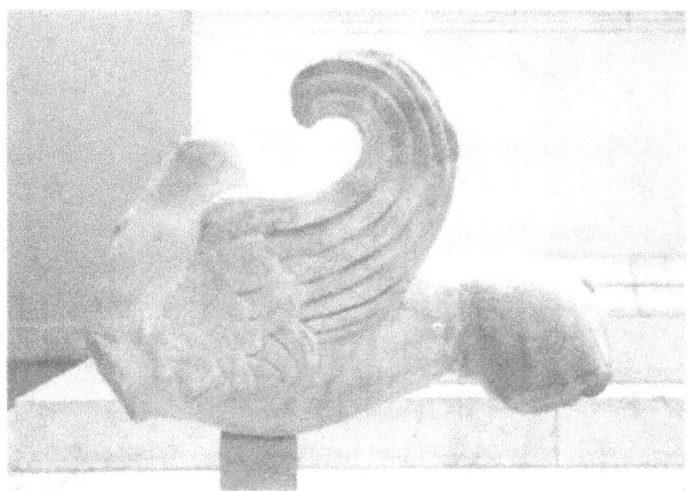

Plate 28. Berlin Museum: griffin from roof of Pergamon Altar.

Plate 29. Pergamon Altar (as displayed in Berlin Museum), Telephos Frieze: east wall, panel 14. Telephos' ship for trip to Mysia. Note the stylized rendering of the waves and the peculiar "eye" of the boat, shaped like a human ear(?).

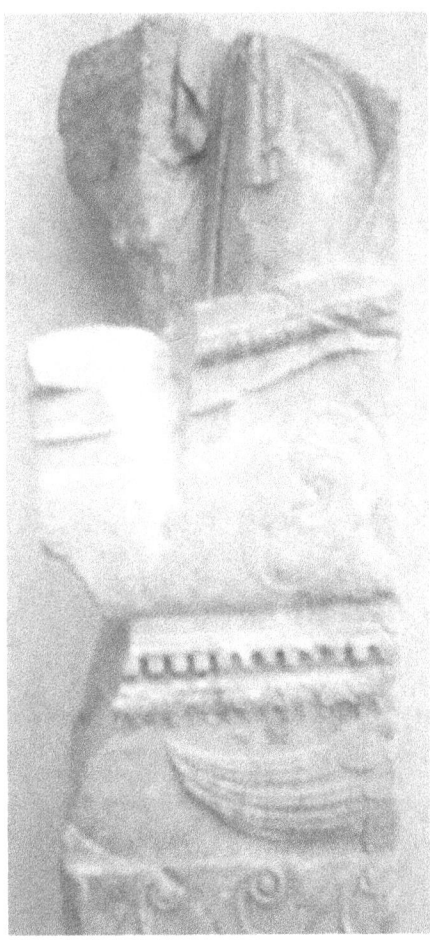

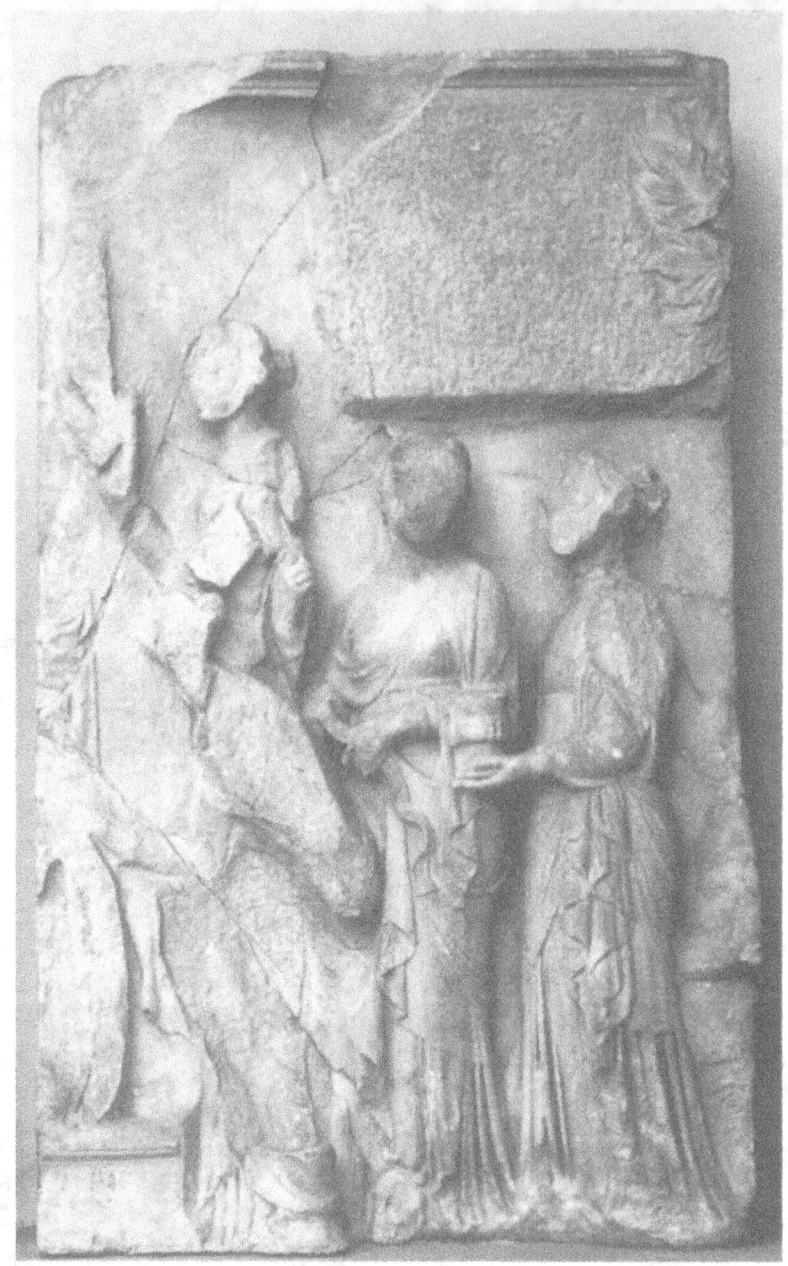

Plate 30. Pergamon Altar (as displayed in Berlin Museum), Telephos Frieze: north wall, panel 11. Auge establishes the cult of Athena at Pergamon. Note the slipping of the chiton neckline and the Archaistic zigzagging of the mantle folds.

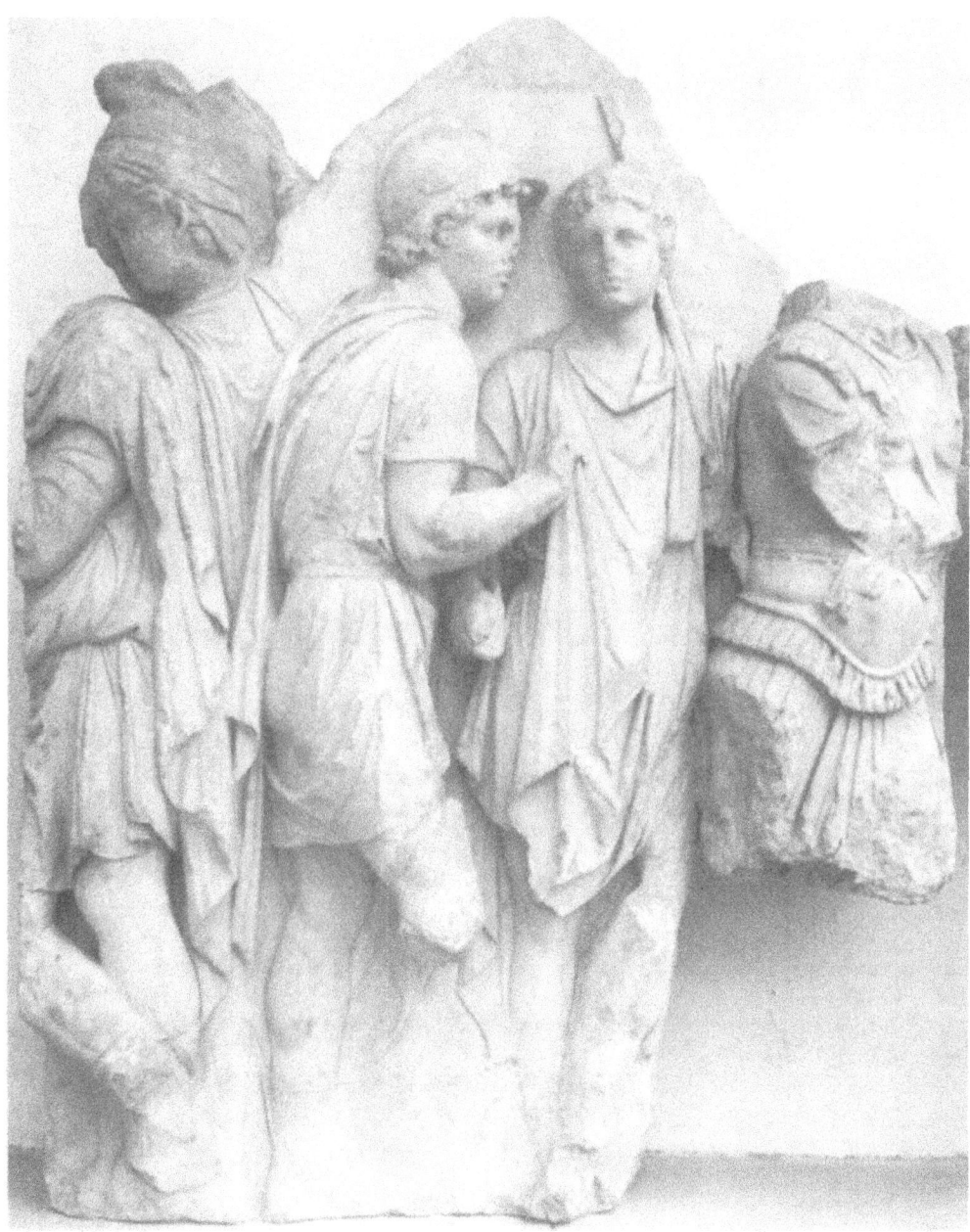

Plate 31. Pergamon Altar (as displayed in Berlin Museum), Telephos Frieze: east wall, panel 16. End of one scene, beginning of Telephos' arming scene. Note the drilled grooves outlining some figures.

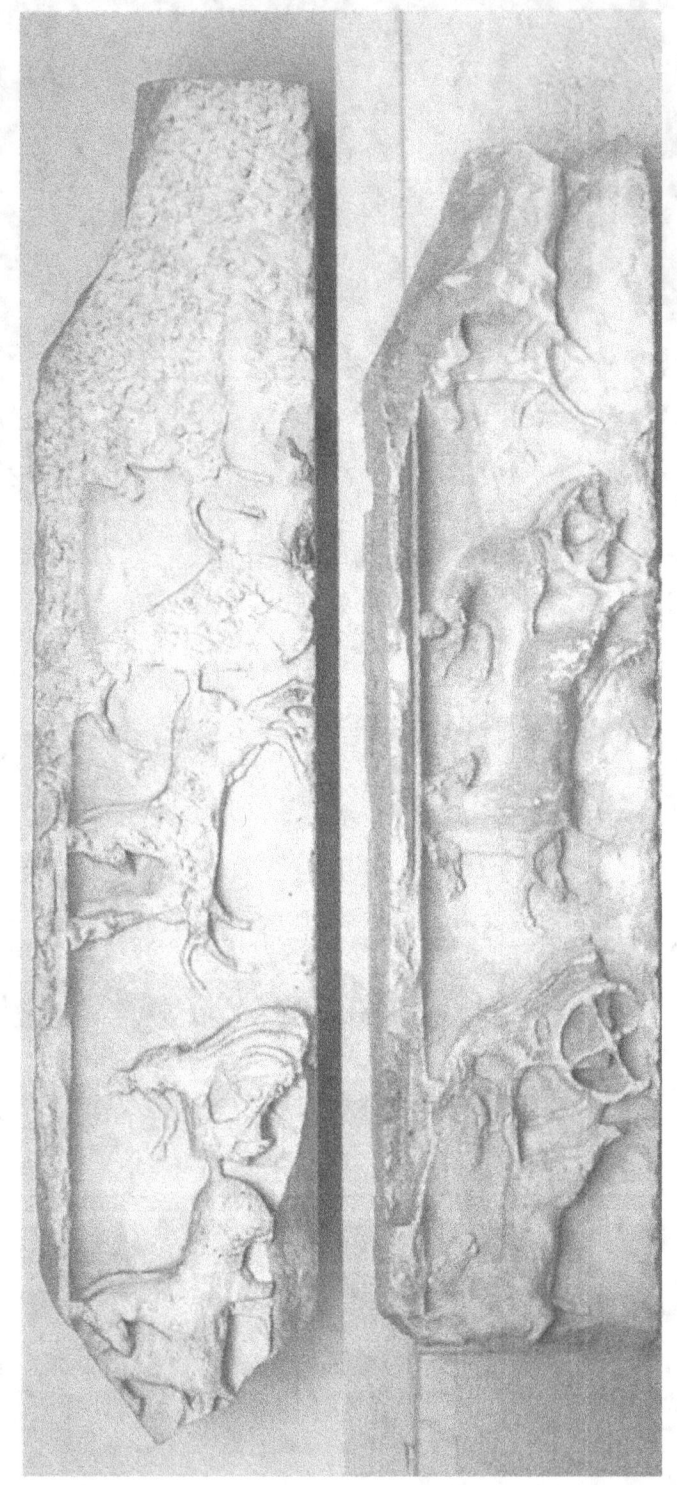

Plate 32. Veria Museum: Chariot frieze, probably from a Macedonian tomb. Note the horse turning back.

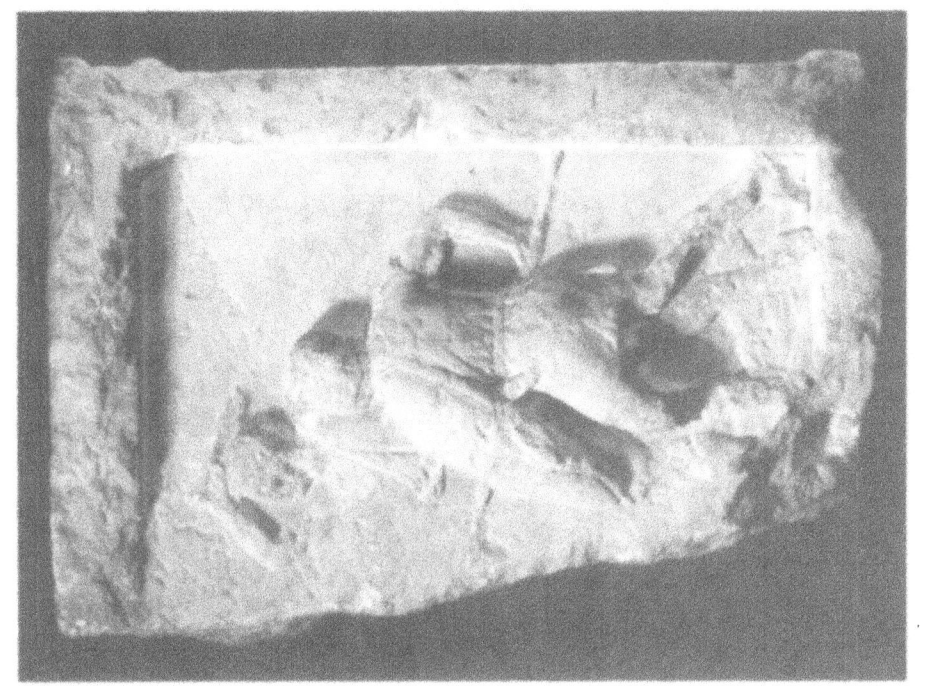

Plate 34. Aberdeen, Scotland, Anthropological Museum, Marichal College. Votive relief of unknown provenience.

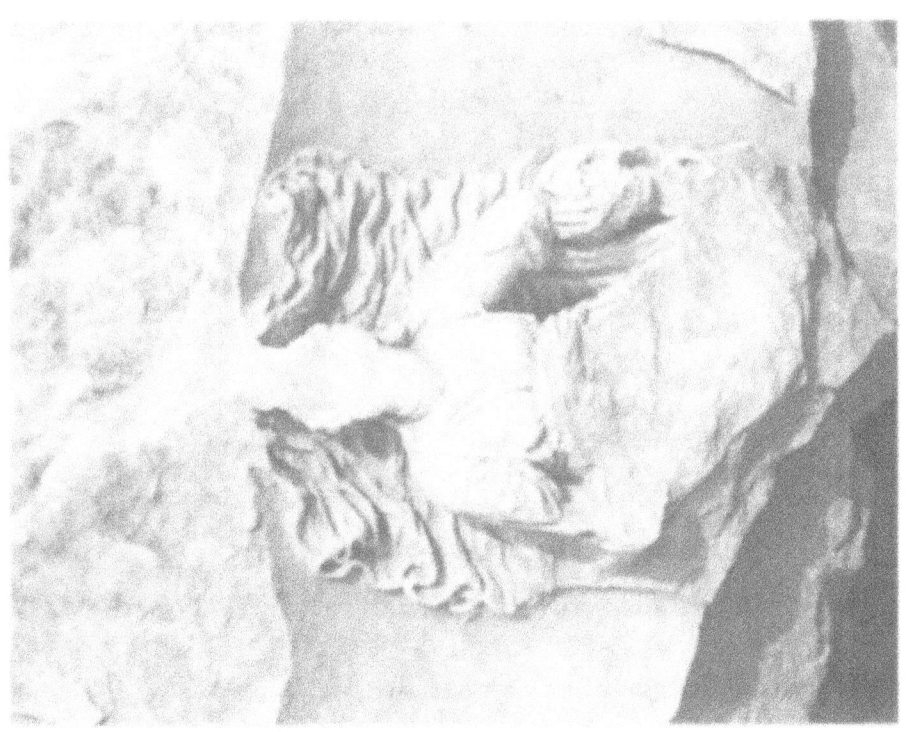

Plate 33. Chryse, Temple of Apollo Smintheus, fragment from frieze: Andromache?

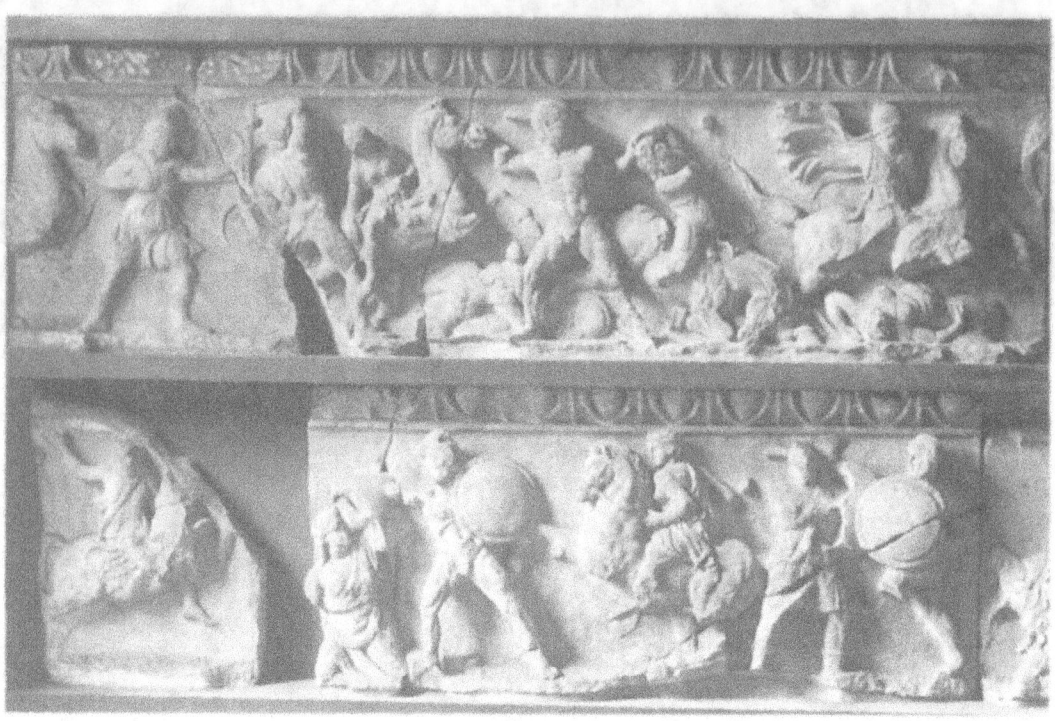

Plate 35. Paris, Louvre: sections of frieze from Temple of Artemis at Magnesia.

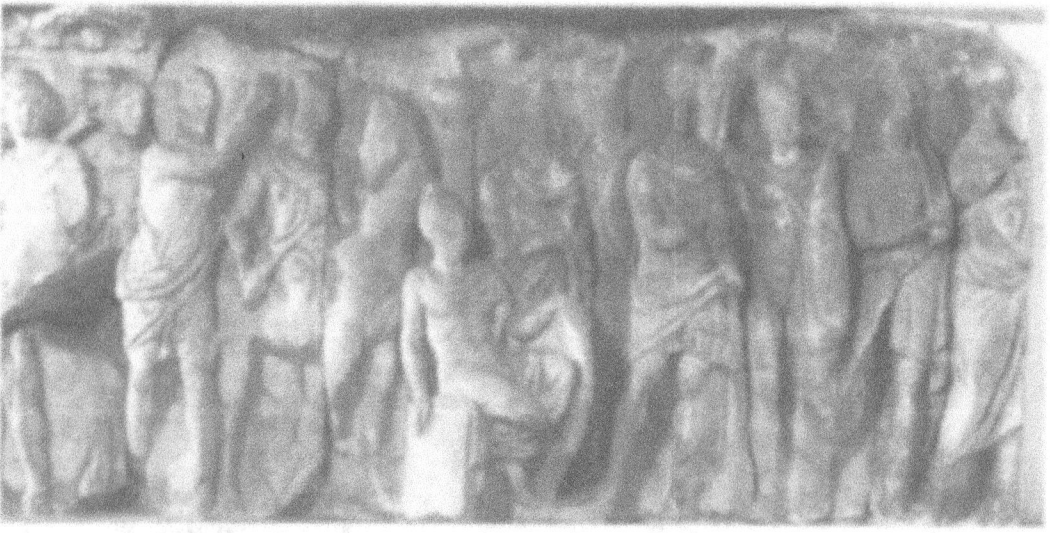

Plate 36. Istanbul Archaeological Museum: section of north frieze from Hekateion at Lagina.

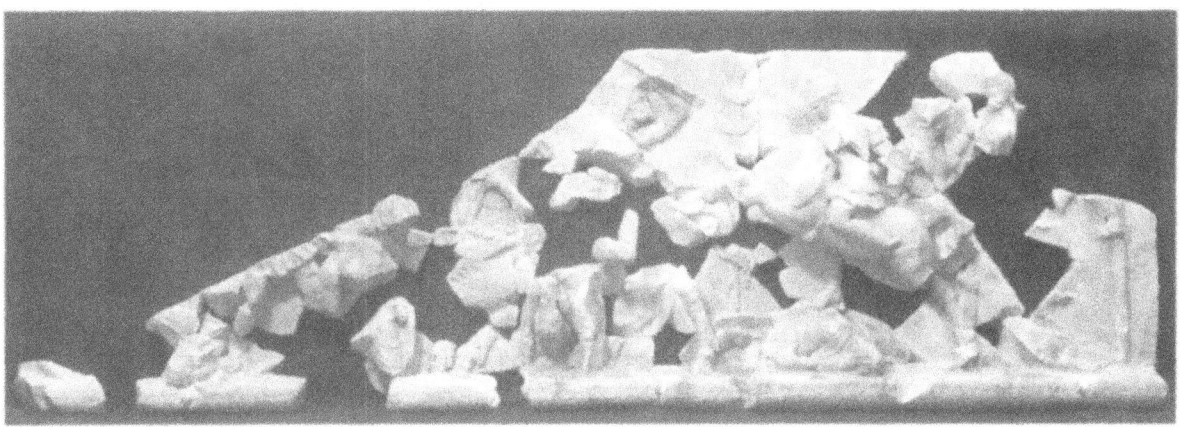

Plate 37. Vienna, Kunsthistorisches Museum: Galatomachy frieze from Ephesos.

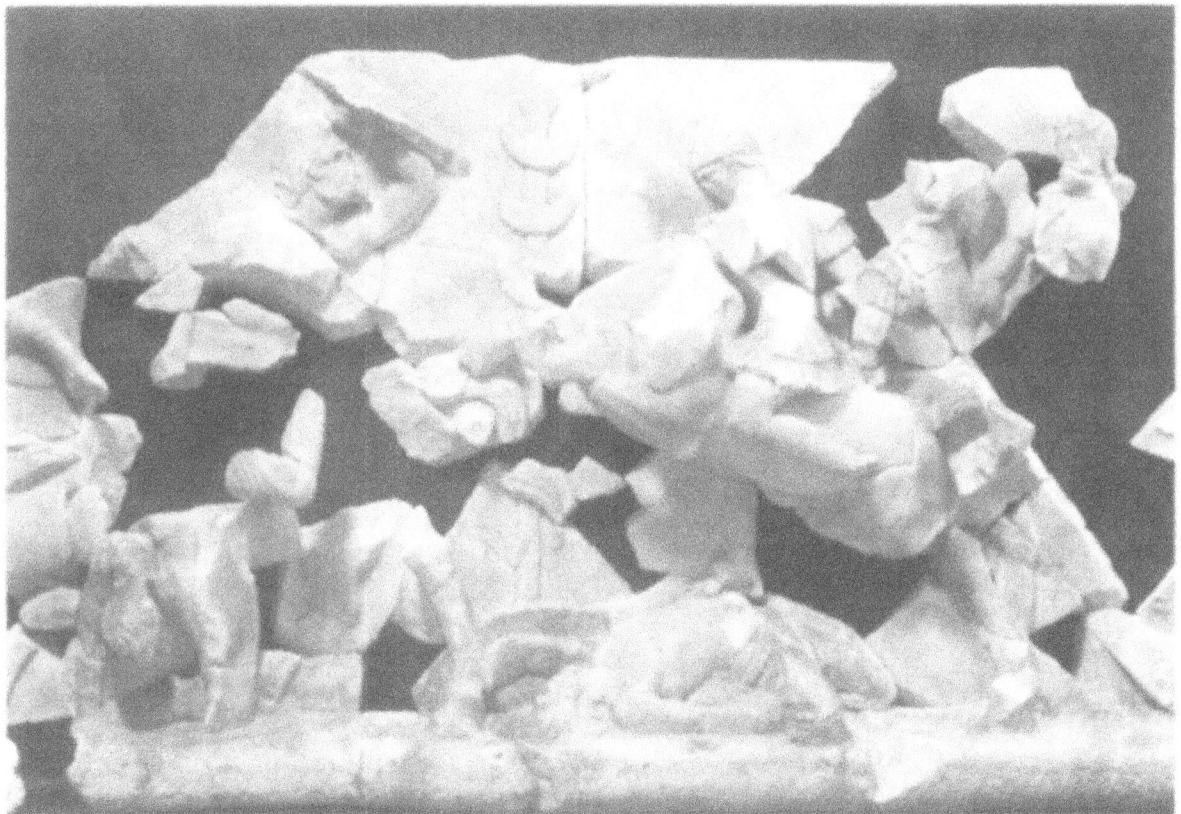

Plate 38. Vienna, Kunsthistorisches Museum: Galatomachy frieze from Ephesos, detail.

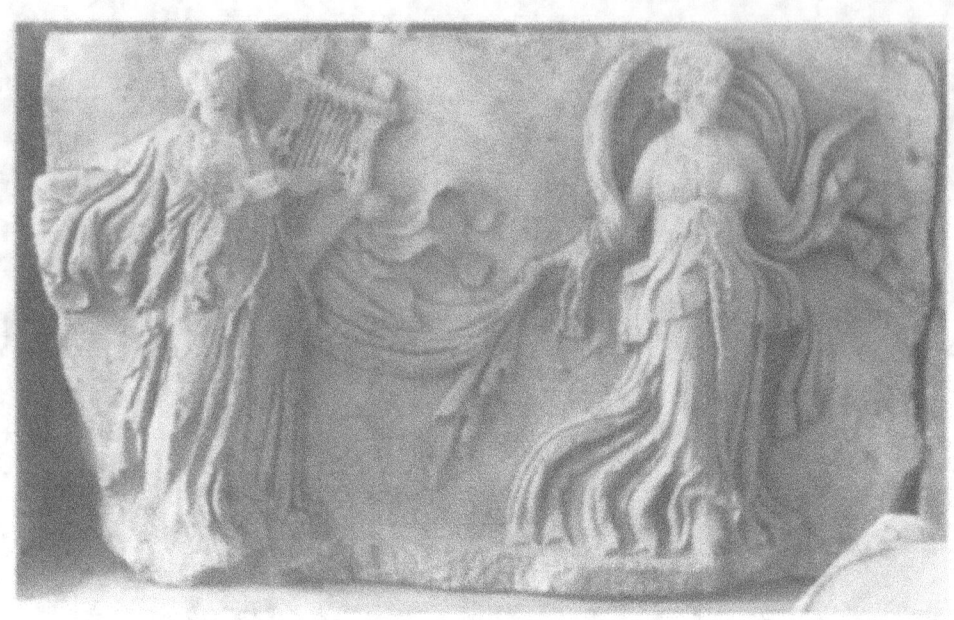

Plate 39. Sagalassos, Frieze of Dancing Women: kithara-player and *velificans*.

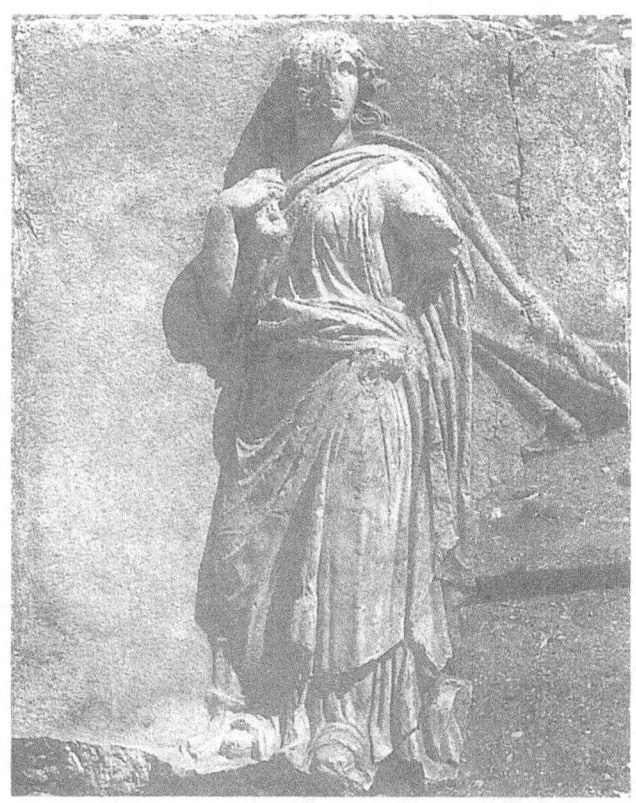

Plate 40. Sagalassos, Frieze of Dancing Women: leader of the chorus(?)

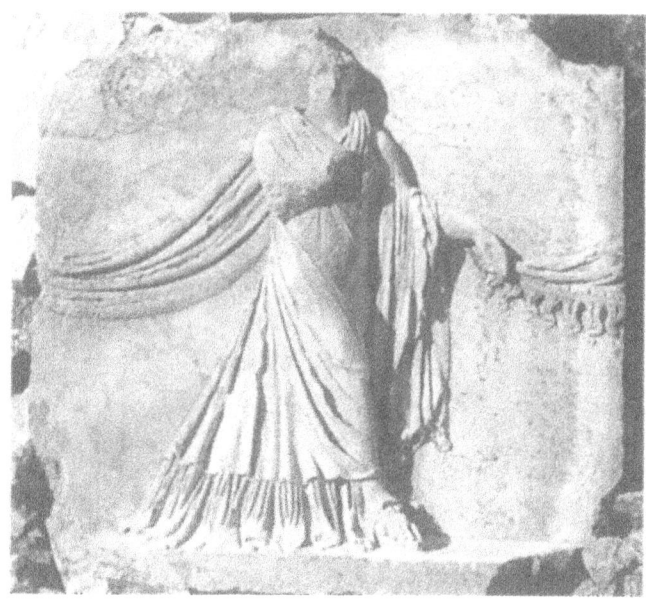

Plate 41. Sagalassos, Frieze of Dancing Women: dancer holding on to fringed scarf.

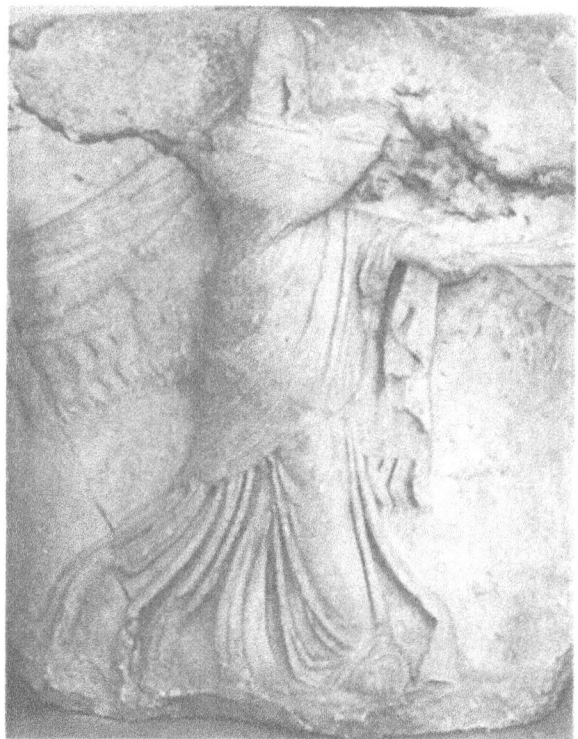

Plate 42. Sagalassos, Frieze of Dancing Women: dancer with fringed mantle.

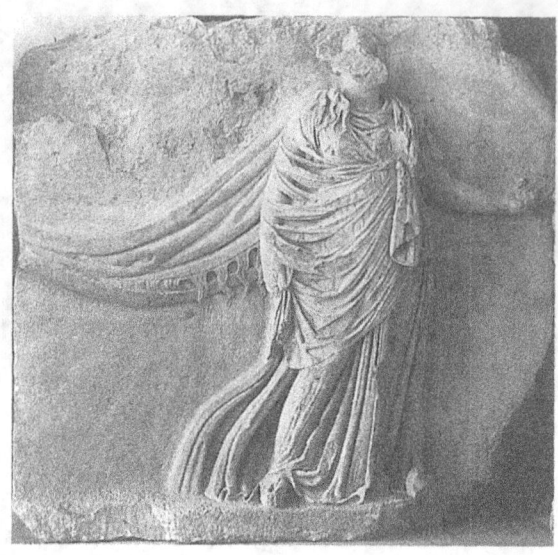

Plate 43. Sagalassos, Frieze of Dancing Women: dancer with "cobweb drapery."

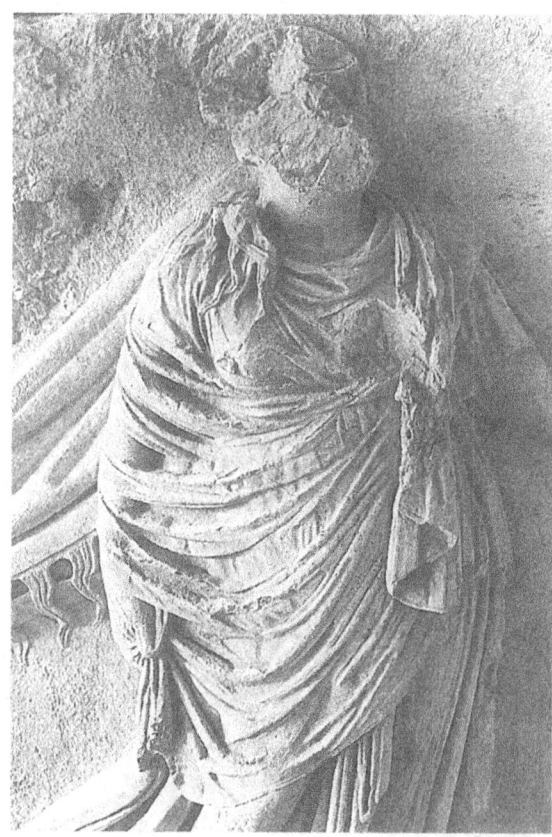

Plate 44. Sagalassos, Frieze of Dancing Women: detail of Pl. 43.

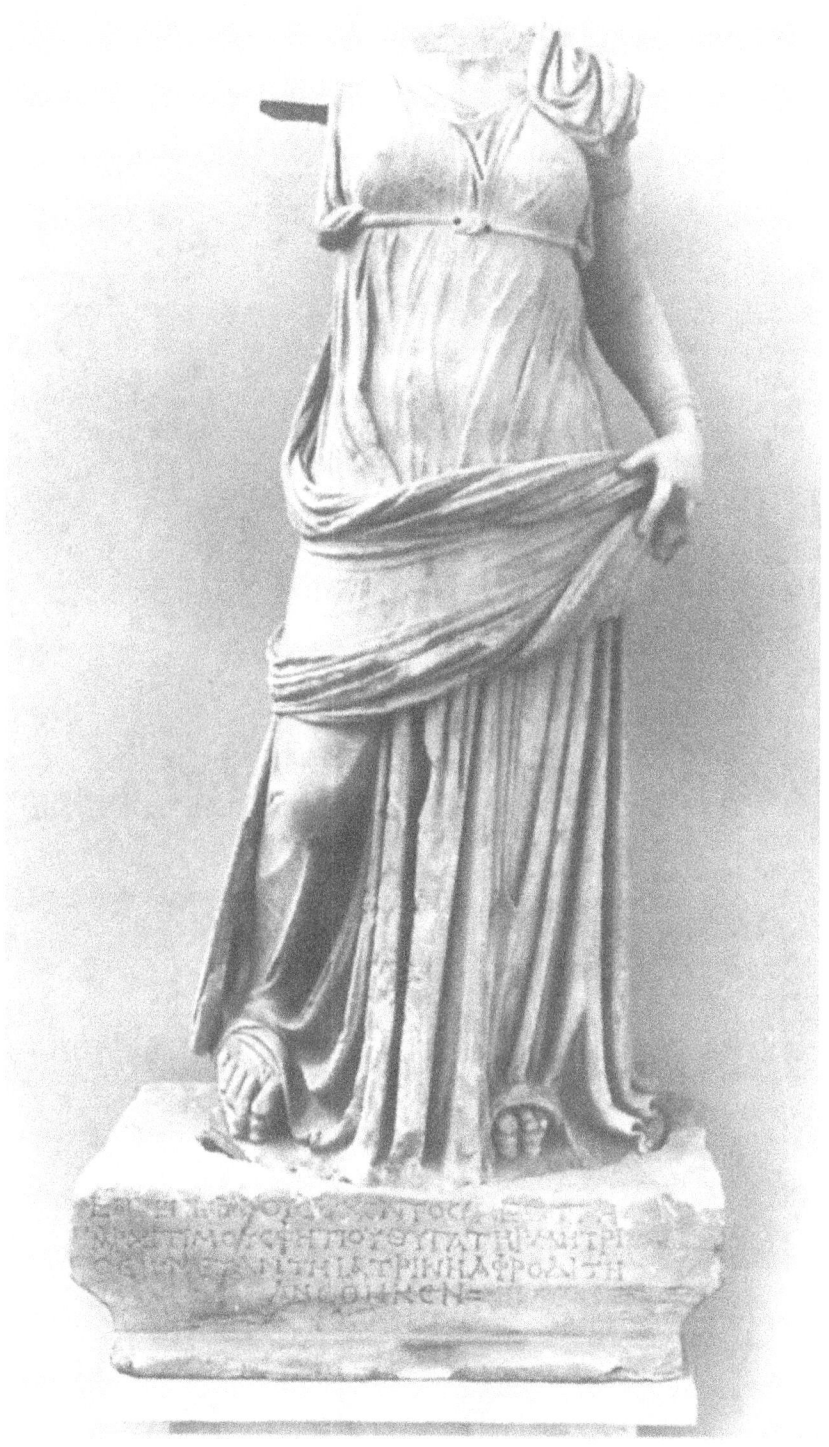

Plate 45. Athens, National Museum no. 710: statuette of Megiste.

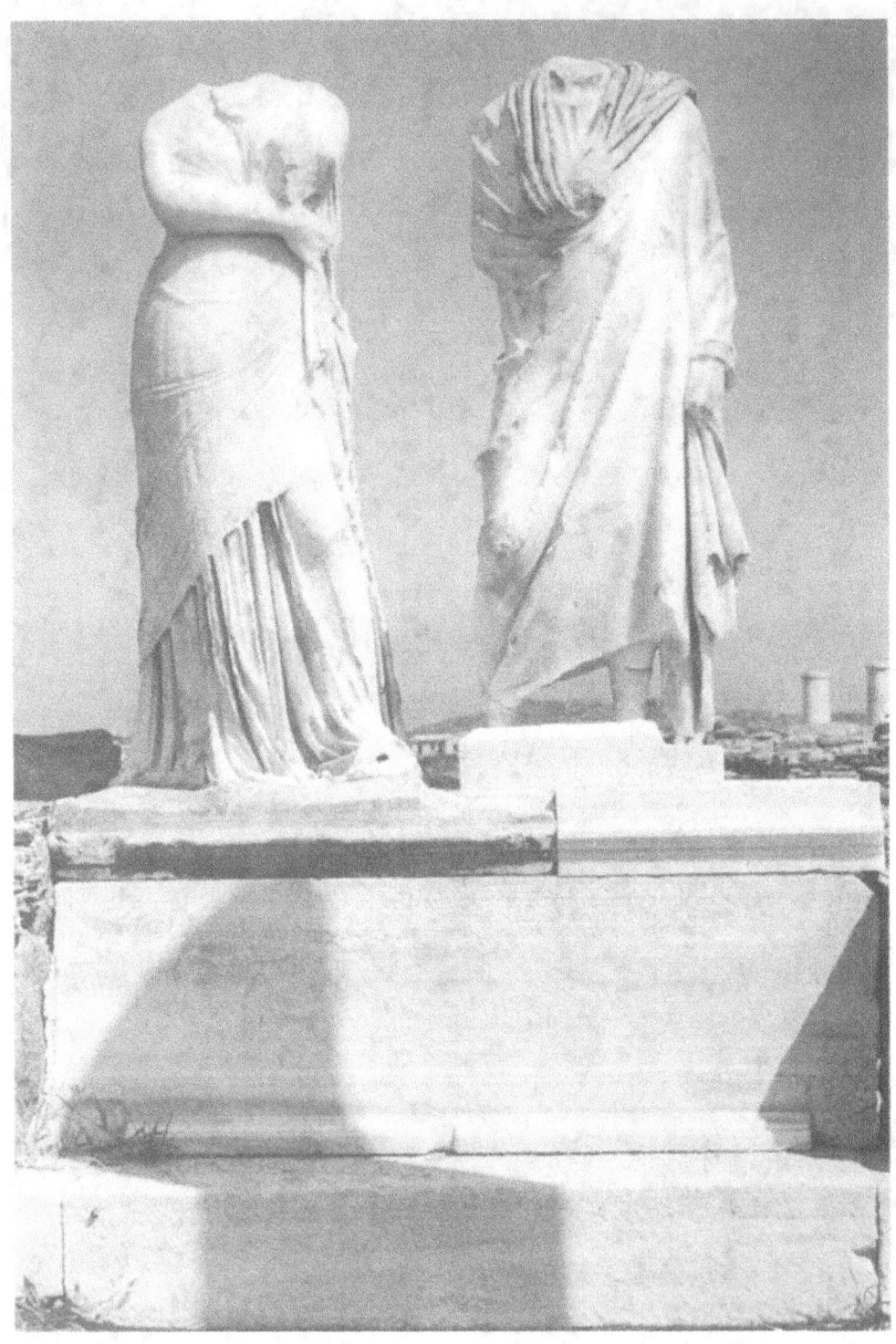

Plate 46. Delos, House of Kleopatra: statues of Kleopatra and Dioskourides.

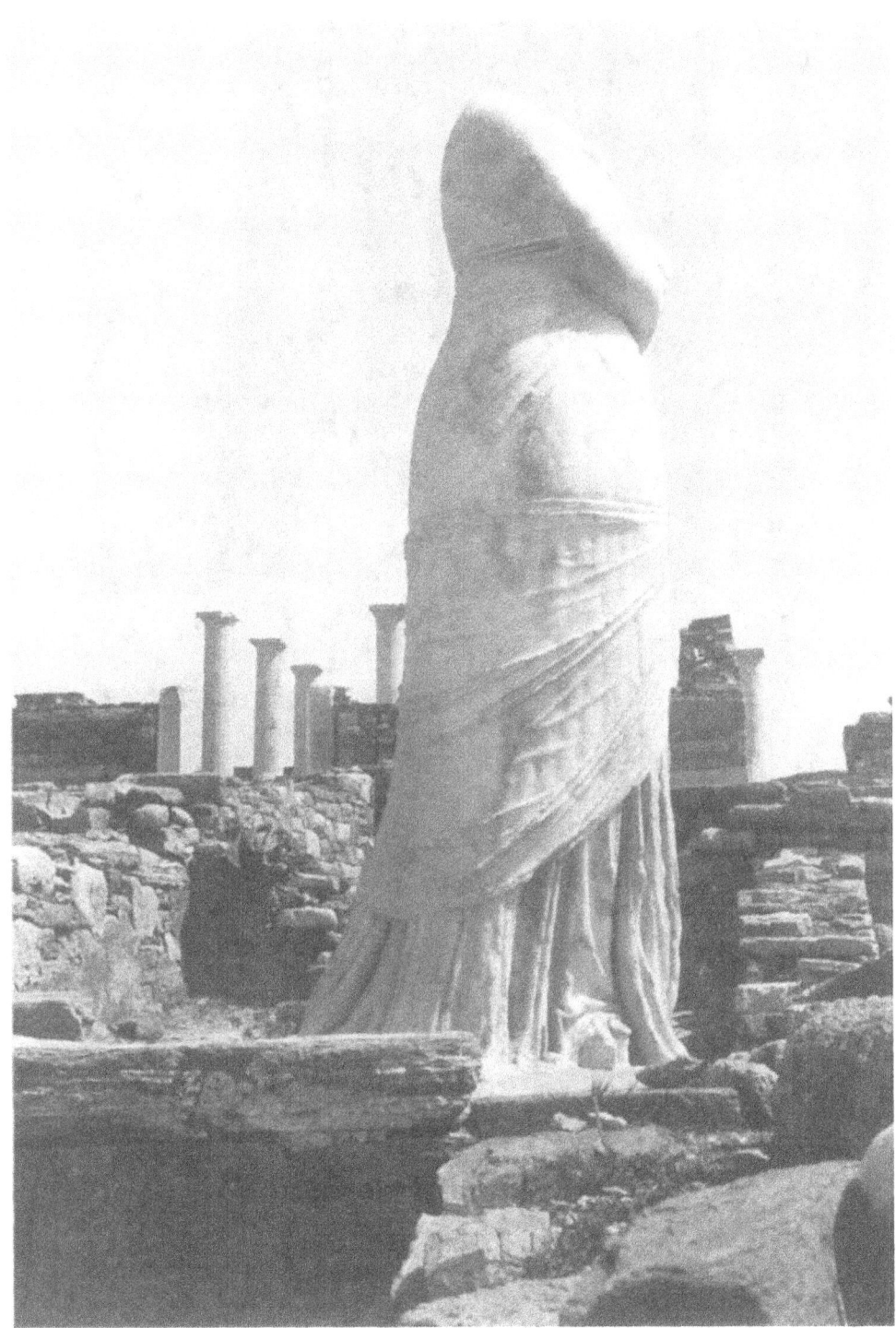

Plate 47. Delos, side view of Kleopatra of Pl. 46.

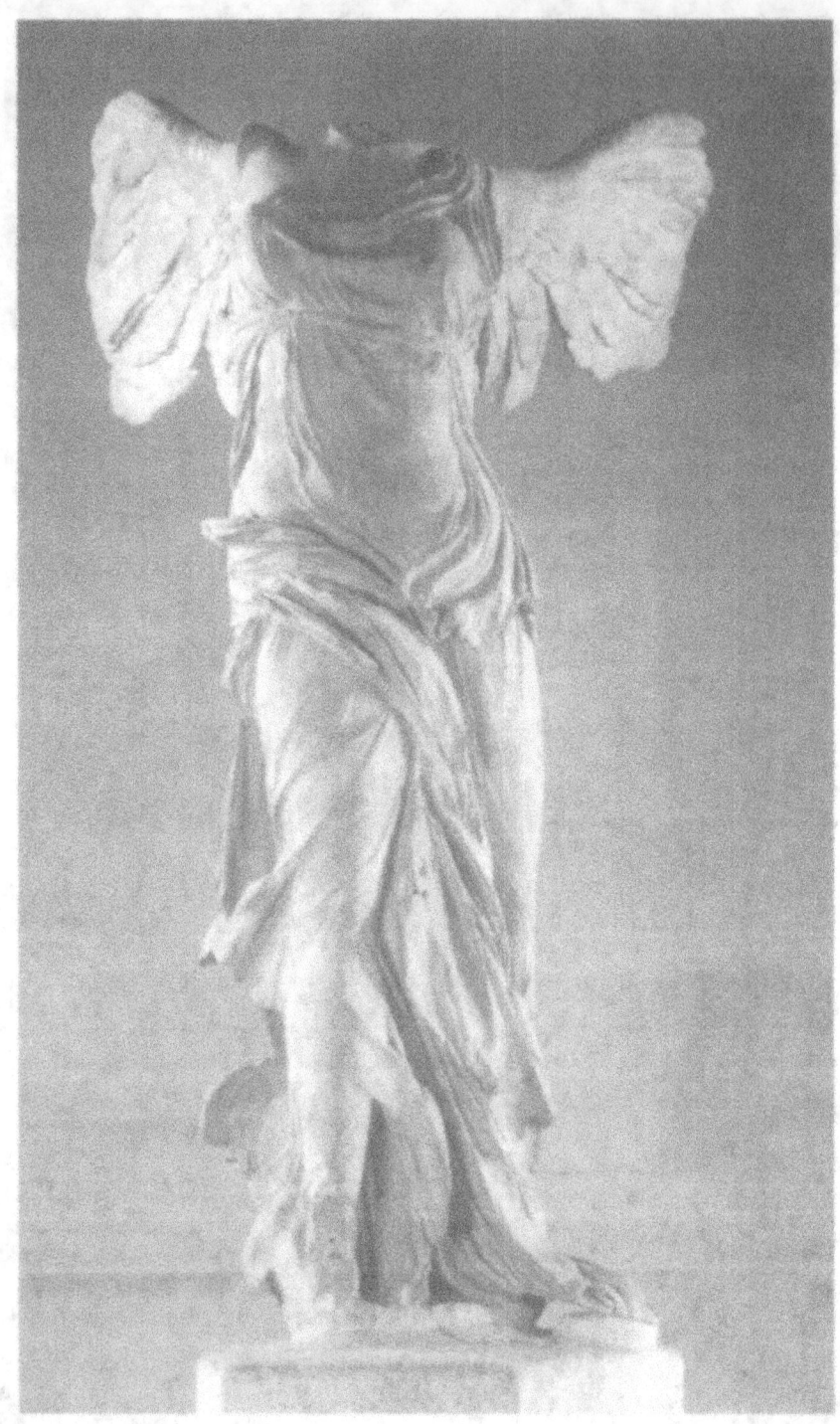

Plate 48. Paris, Louvre: Nike of Samothrake.

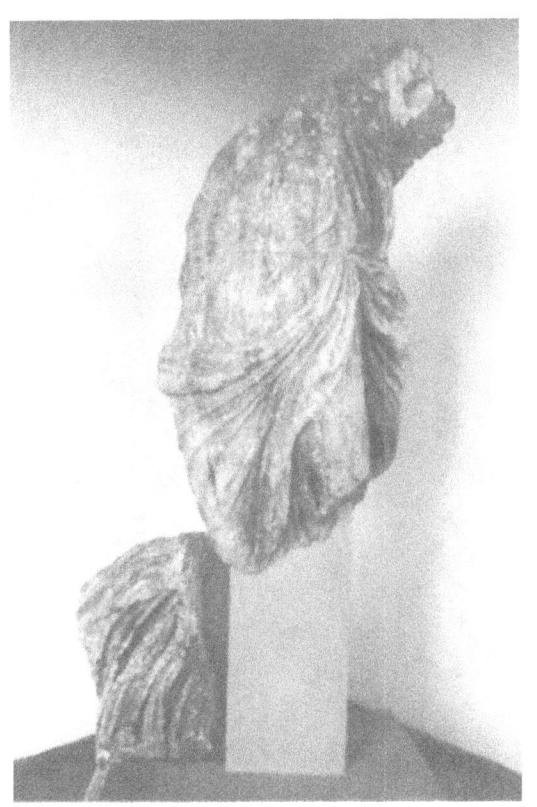

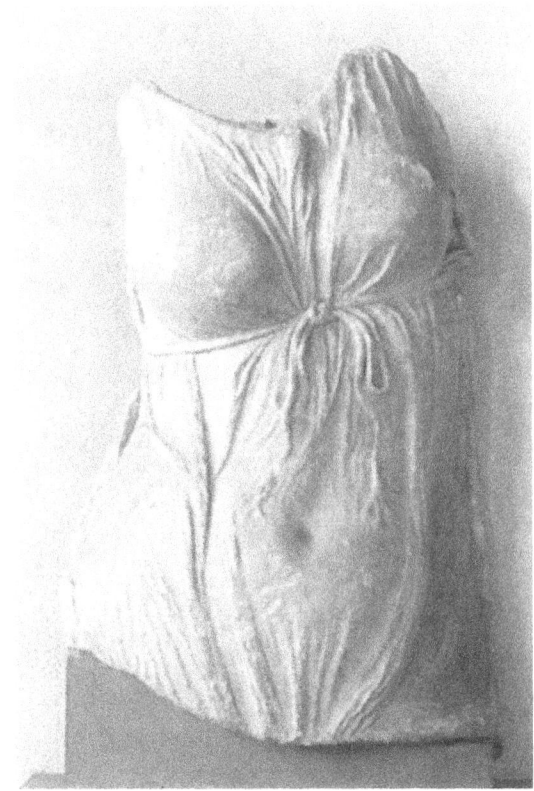

Plate 49. Palestrina Museum: black stone statue from Praeneste (Isis/Fortuna); cf. Ch. 5 n. 31.

Plate 50. Boston, Museum of Fine Arts no. 97.286: "Torso of a goddess," Catharine Page Fund.

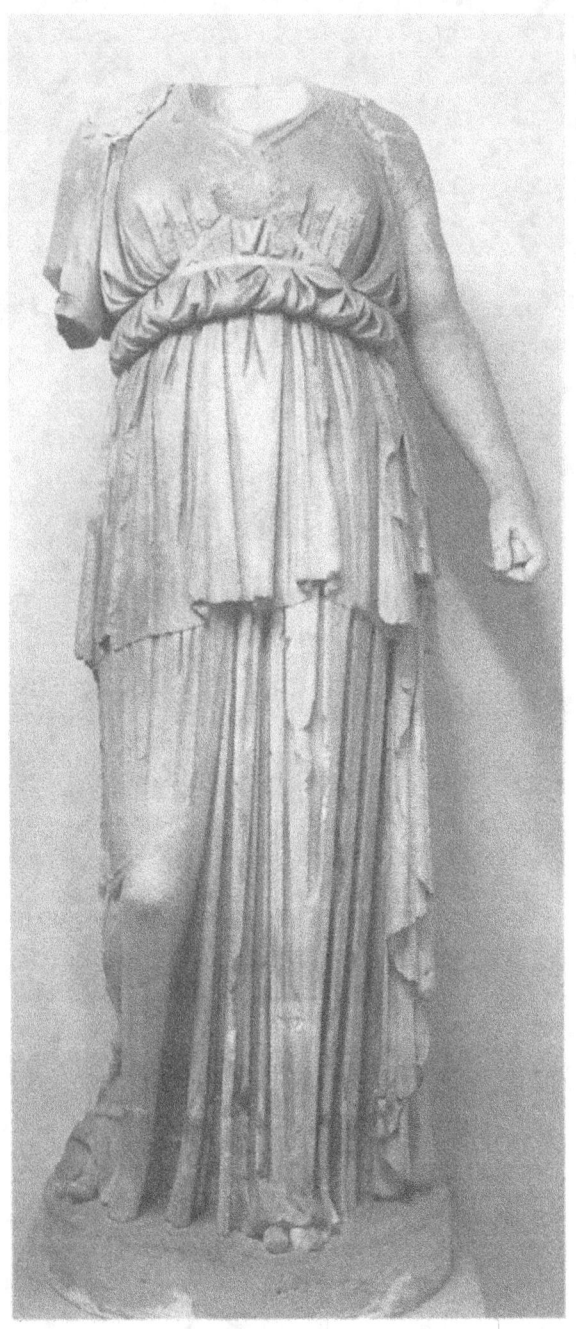

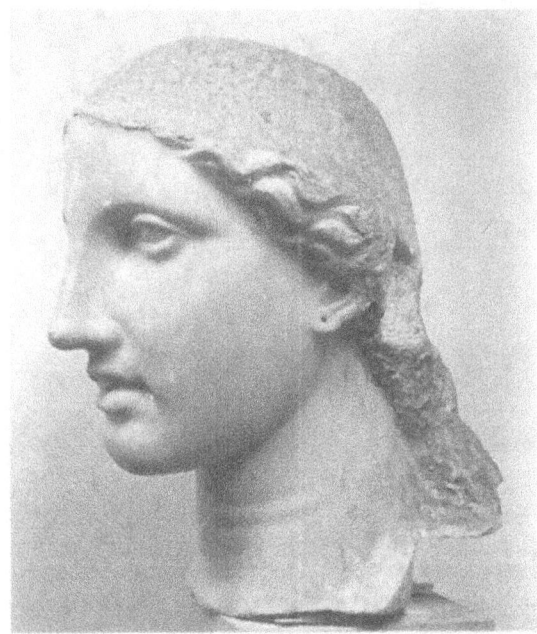

Plate 52. Venice, Archaeological Museum no. 264B: head of Athena from Hierapytna.

Plate 51. Venice, Archaeological Museum no. 264A: Nike from Hierapytna.

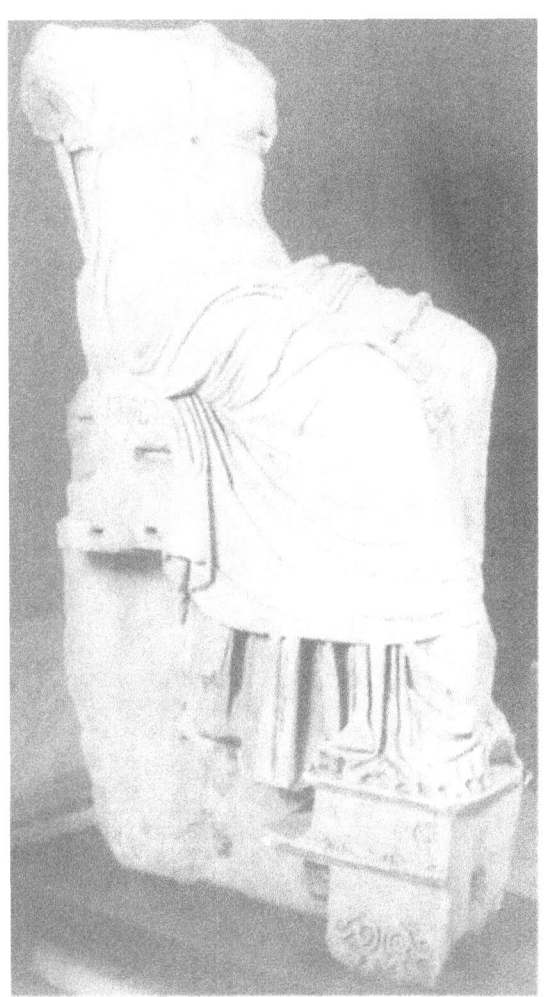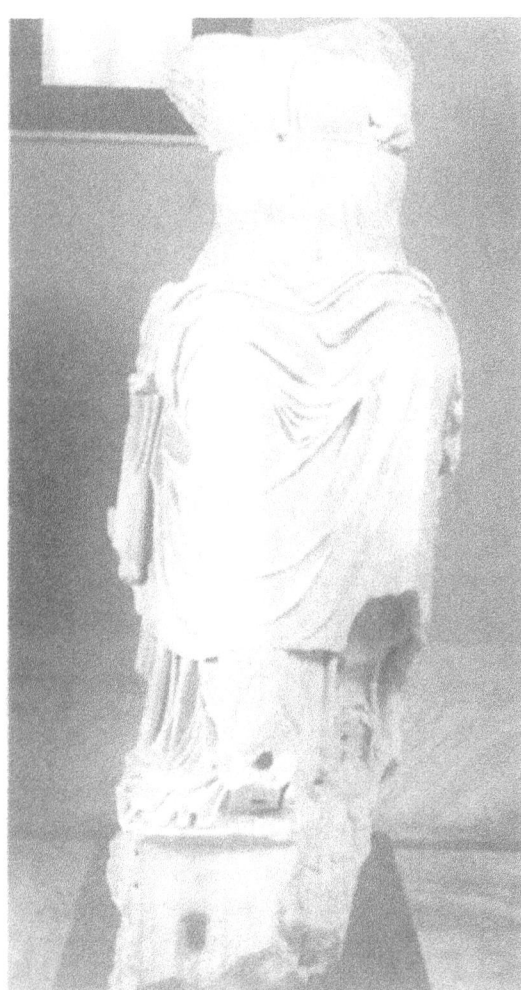

Plate 53a–b. Istanbul, Archaeological Museum no. 1356: seated figure from Kyzikos—
(a) three-quarter view, (b) front view.

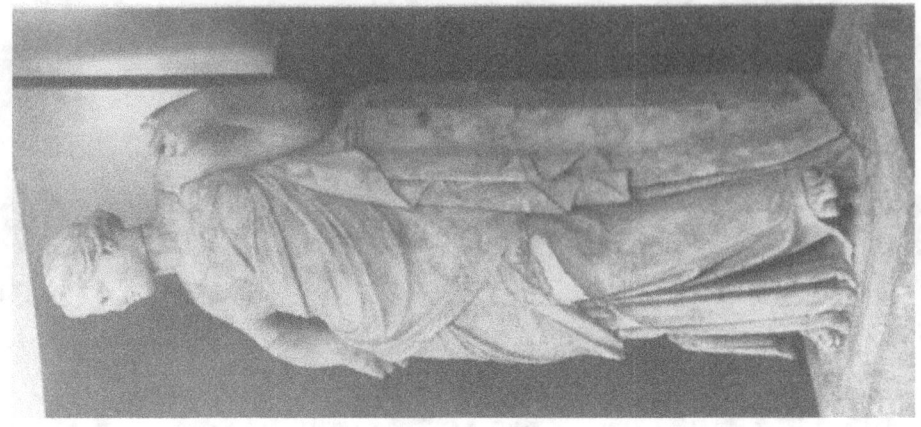

Plate 56. Soloeis (Solunto): female statuette.

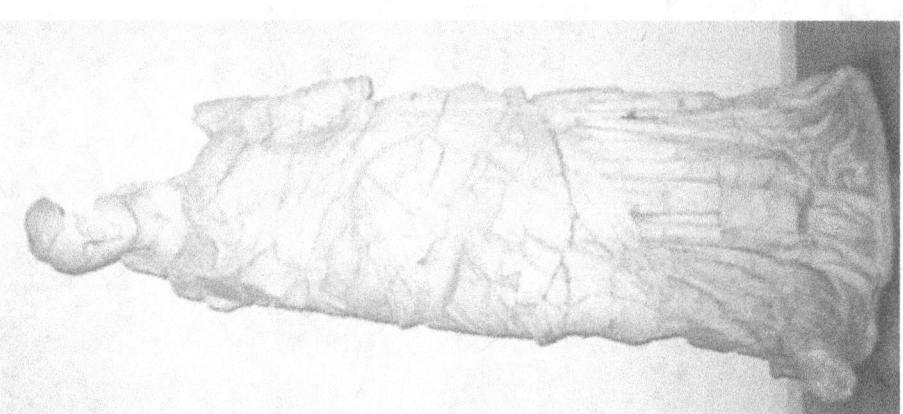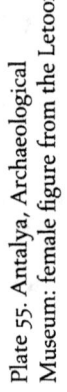

Plate 55. Antalya, Archaeological Museum: female figure from the Letoon.

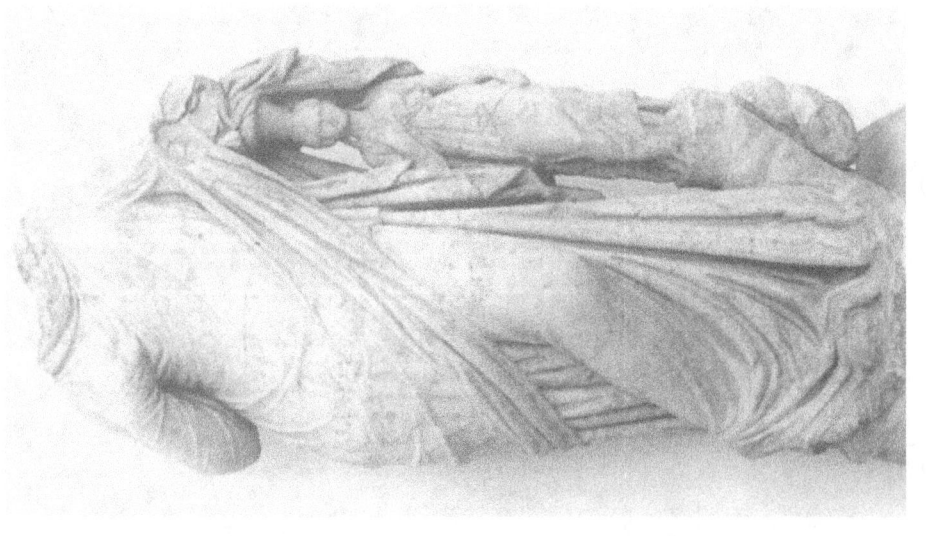

Plate 54. Athens, National Museum no. 238: statuette of Aphrodite leaning on Archaistic idol, from Melos.

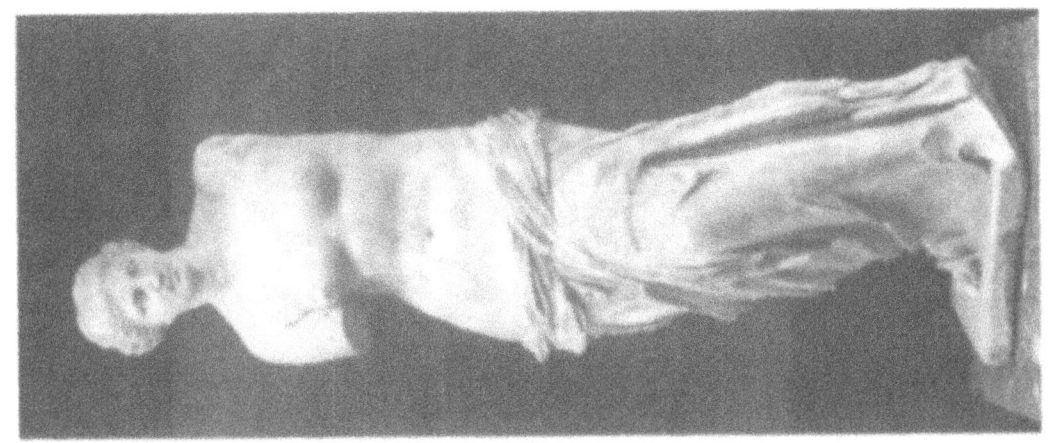

Plate 58. Paris, Louvre: Aphrodite from Melos.

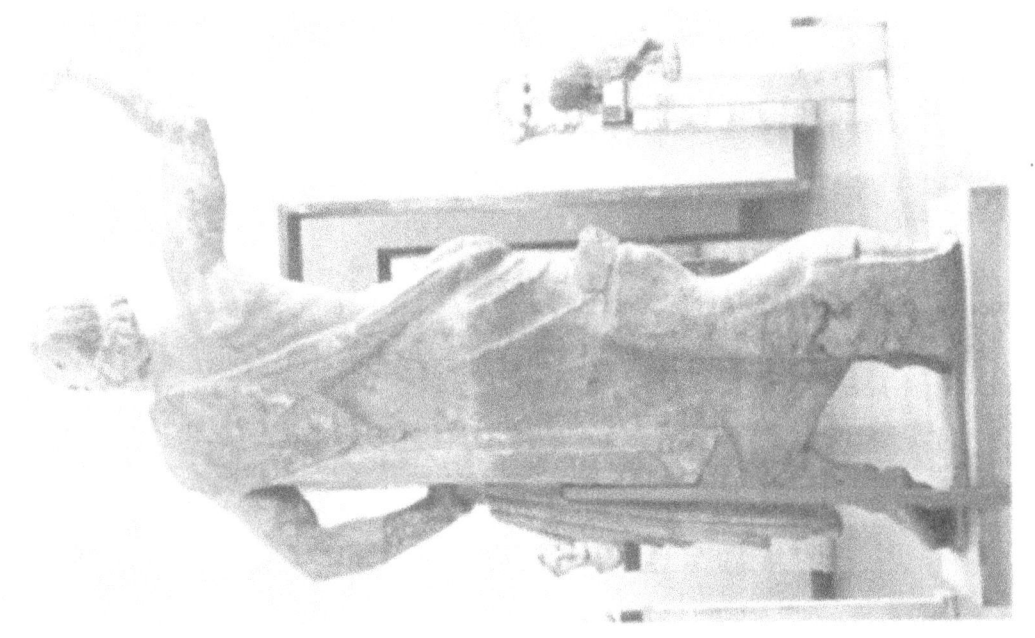

Plate 57. Athens, National Museum no. 235: Poseidon of Melos, rear view.

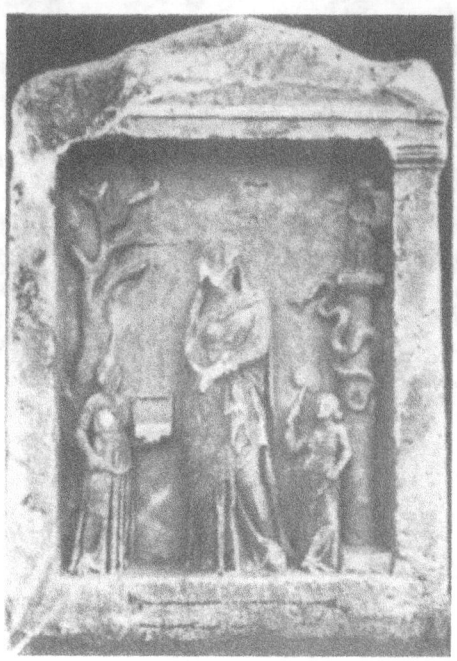

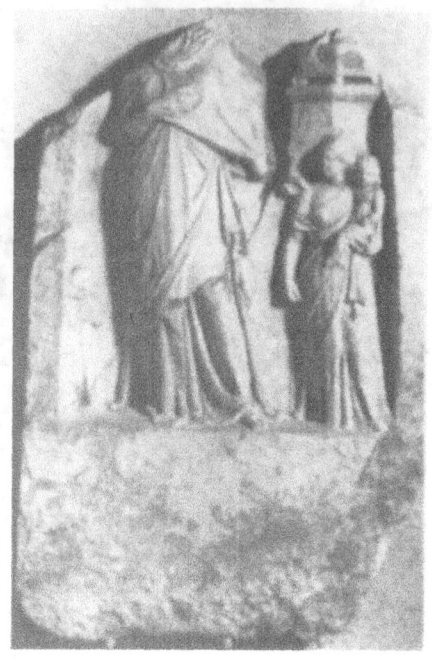

Plate 59. Izmir, Kültürpark inv. no. 31: stele from Notion. Note Psyche statuette on pier; cf. Ch. 6 ns. 9, 15.

Plate 60. Madrid, Museo Arqueologico Nacional: stele probably from Smyrna. Note woman in "Venice Muse" pose; cf. Ch. 6 n. 9.

Plate 61. London, British Museum: stele of Exakestes and Metreis, probably from Smyrna. Note the *dikerata* in the background, and the woman's costume (Priestess of Demeter?); cf. Ch. 6 n. 16.

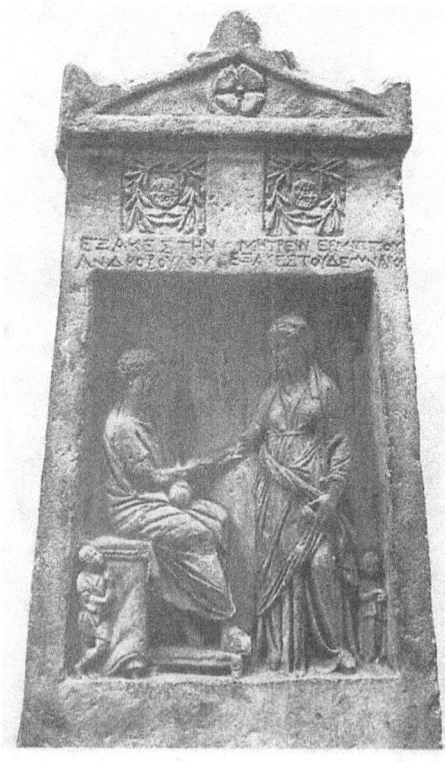

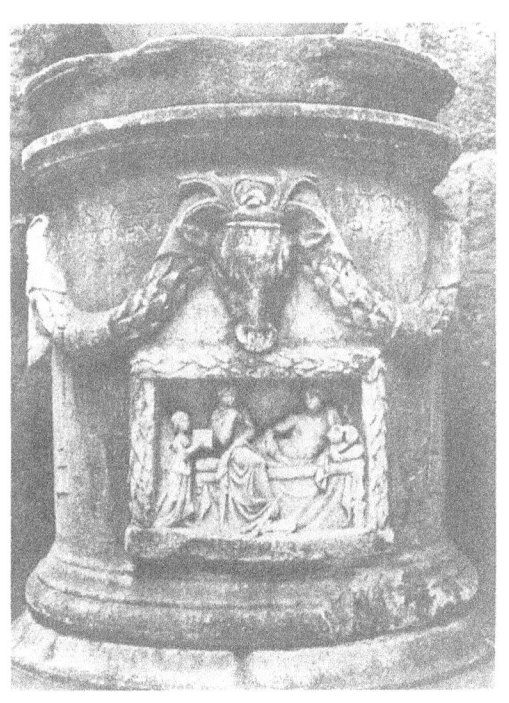

Plate 62. Rhodes, Archaeological Museum no. 13598: Altar of Archestrate (Funerary Banquet scene and deer's heads); cf. Ch. 6 n. 36.

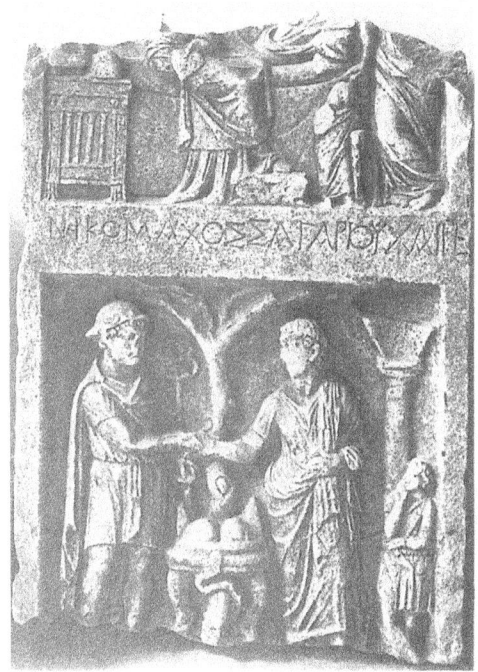

Plate 63. Izmit Museum, inv. no. 124: stele of Nikomachos (Funerary Banquet with *kylikeion*, over scene of *dexiosis* with Hermes, in front of sundial); cf. Ch. 6 ns. 20, 38.

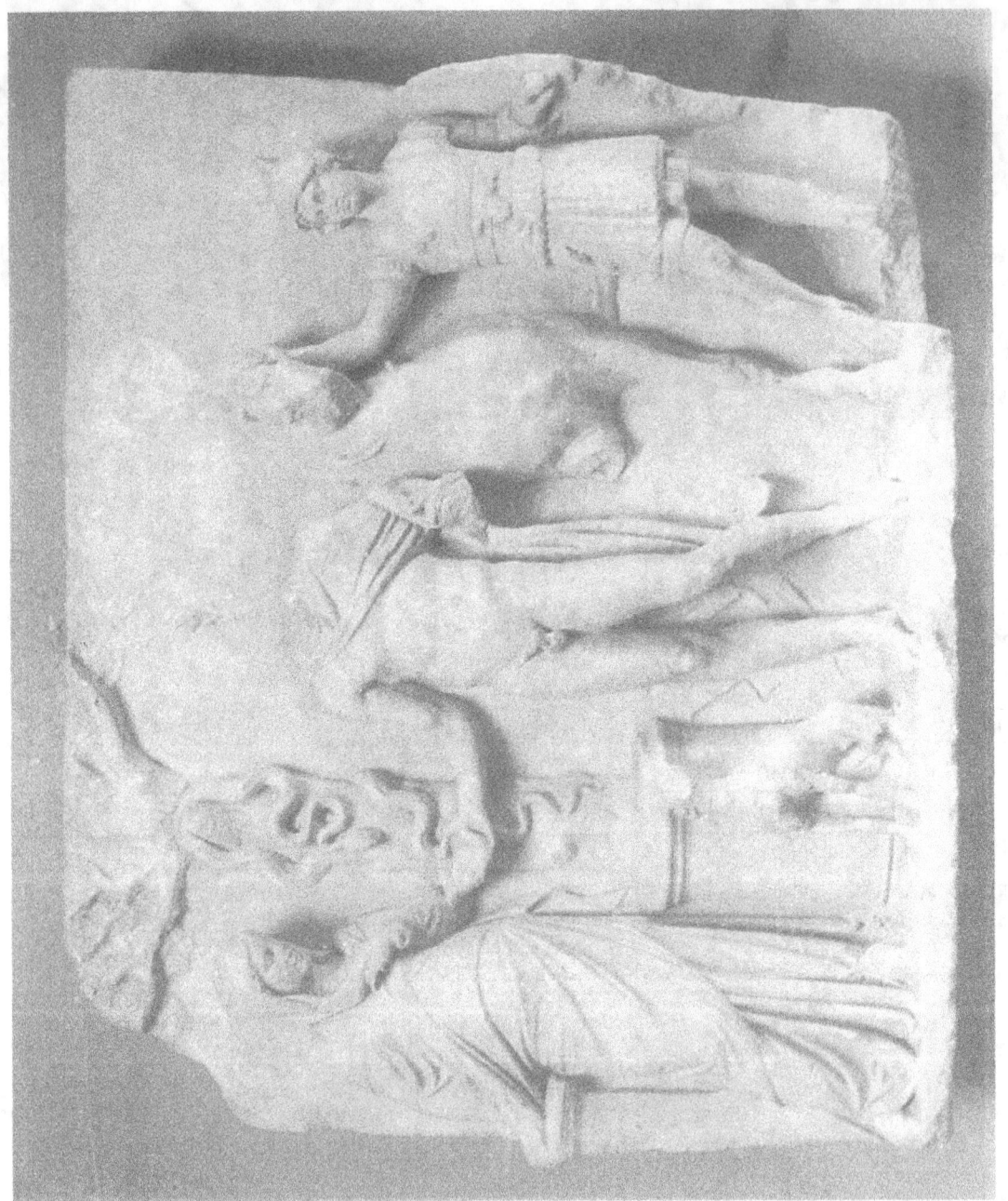

Plate 64. Istanbul, Archaeological Museum no. 362: Rider Relief from Pergamon. Note woman in "Venice Muse" pose and circular altar.

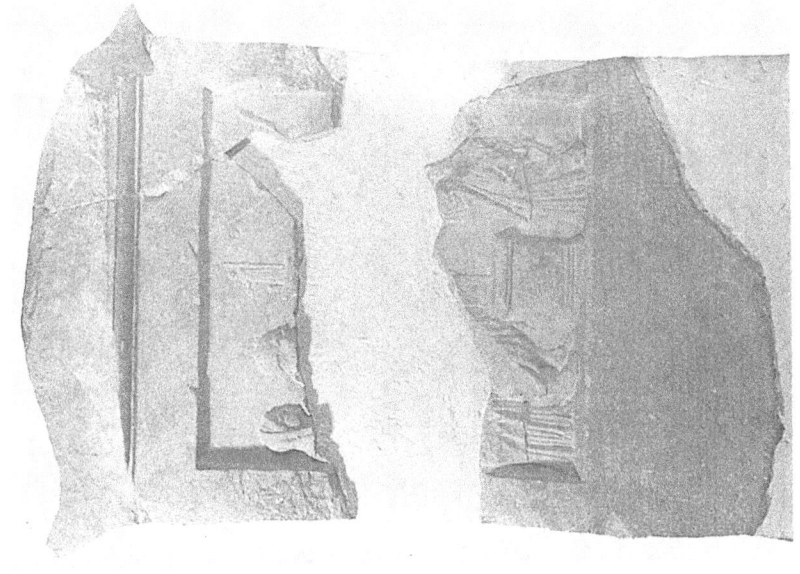

Plate 67. Athens, National Museum no. 3876: Document Relief in honor of Serapion of Herakleia.

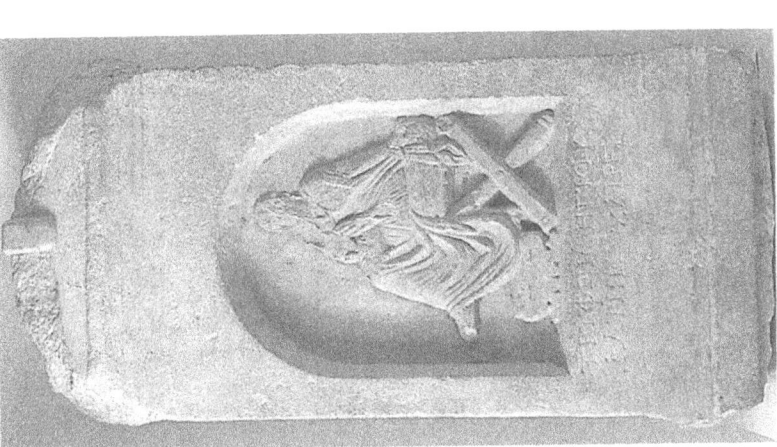

Plate 66. Princeton, The Art Museum, Princeton University, no. Antioch S 470: stele of Tryphe, from Seleukia. Note "Tyche of Antioch" pose and rounded frame; cf. Ch. 6 n. 34.

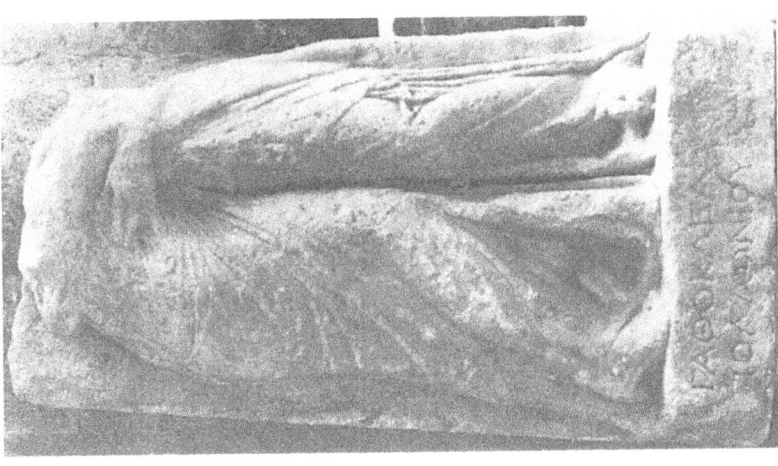

Plate 65. Rhodes, Archaeological Museum no. 189: stele of Agathoklea, from Tilos.

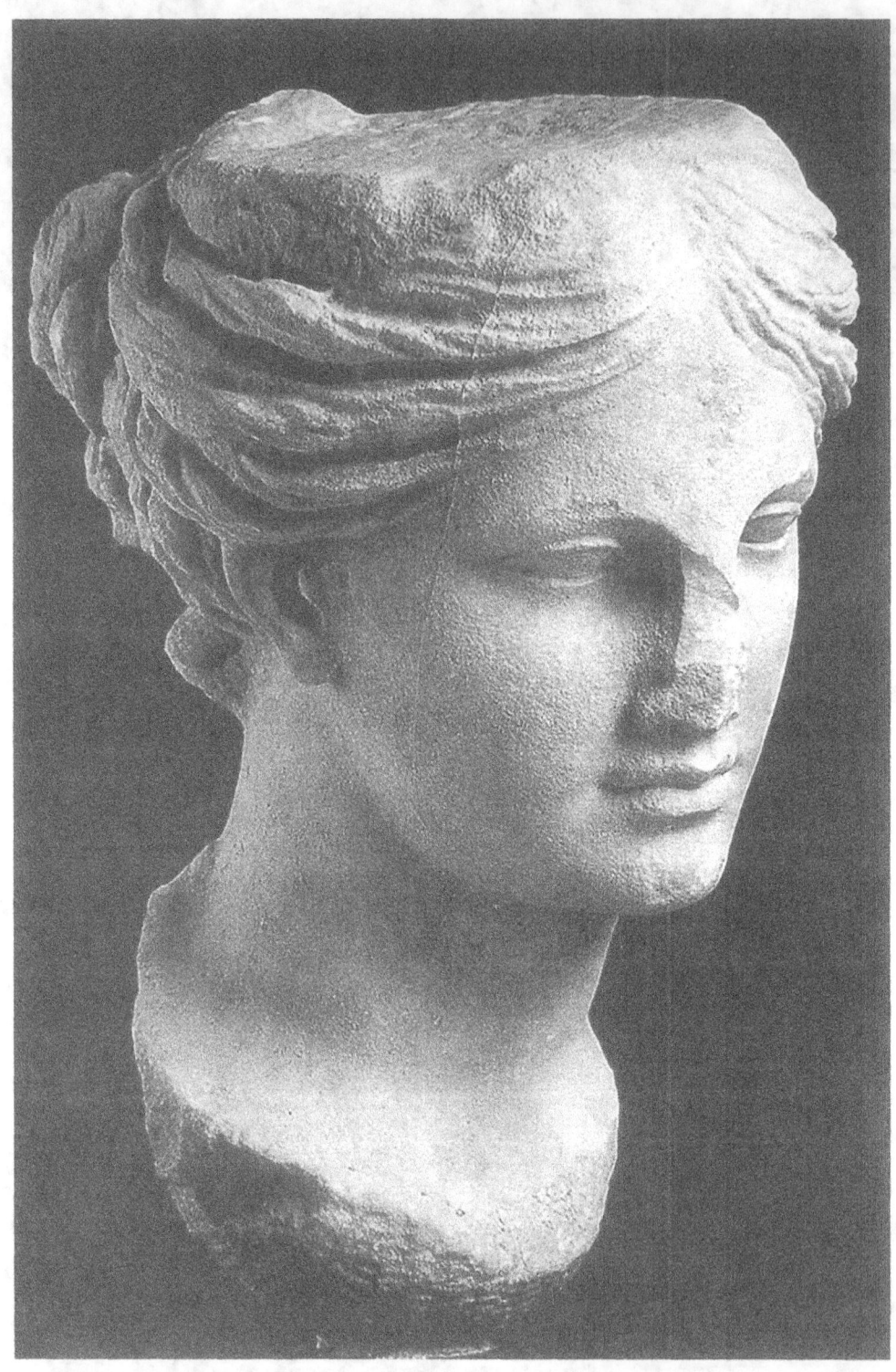

Plate 68. Antalia Museum no. 2.18.77: female head from the Letoon.

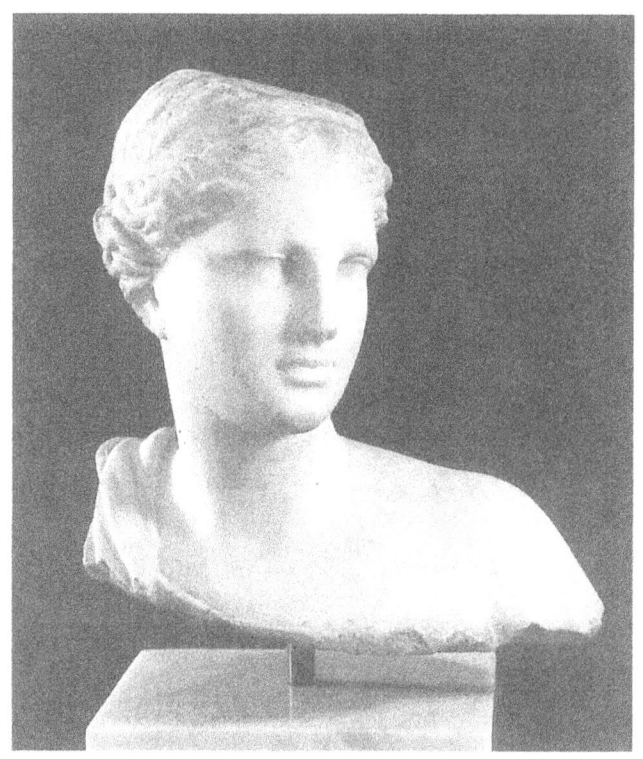

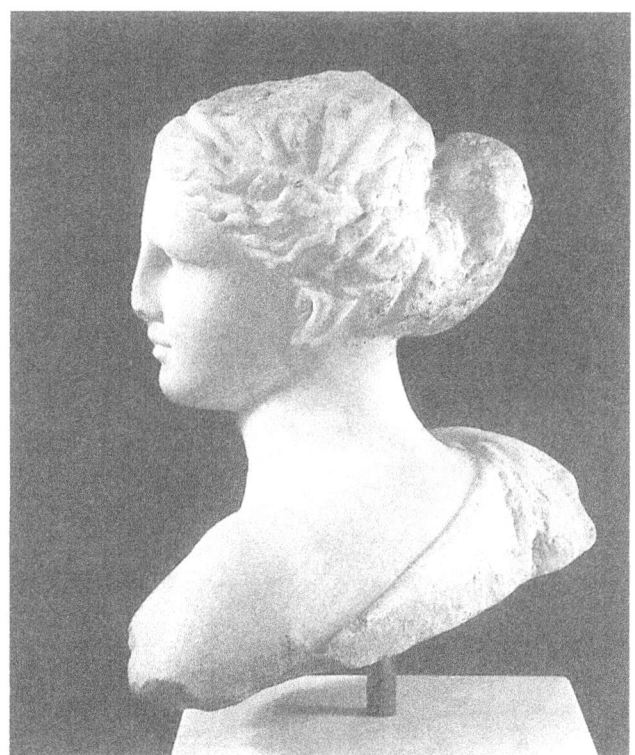

Plate 69a–b. Toledo, Museum of Art no. 37.5, Gift of Edward
Drummond Libbey: female bust—(a) front, (b) left profile;
cf. Ch. 7 n. 31.

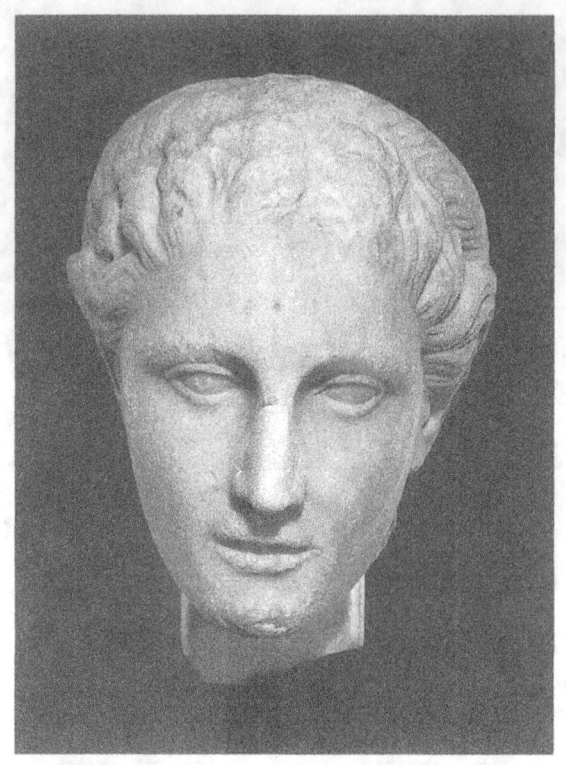

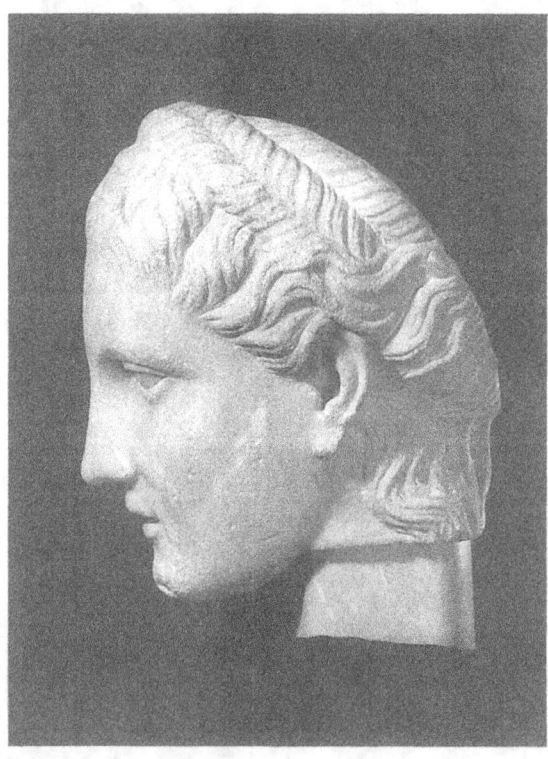

Plate 70a–b. Philadelphia, Museum of the University of
Pennsylvania no. 30.7.1: so-called Hope Goddess—
(a) front, (b) left profile.

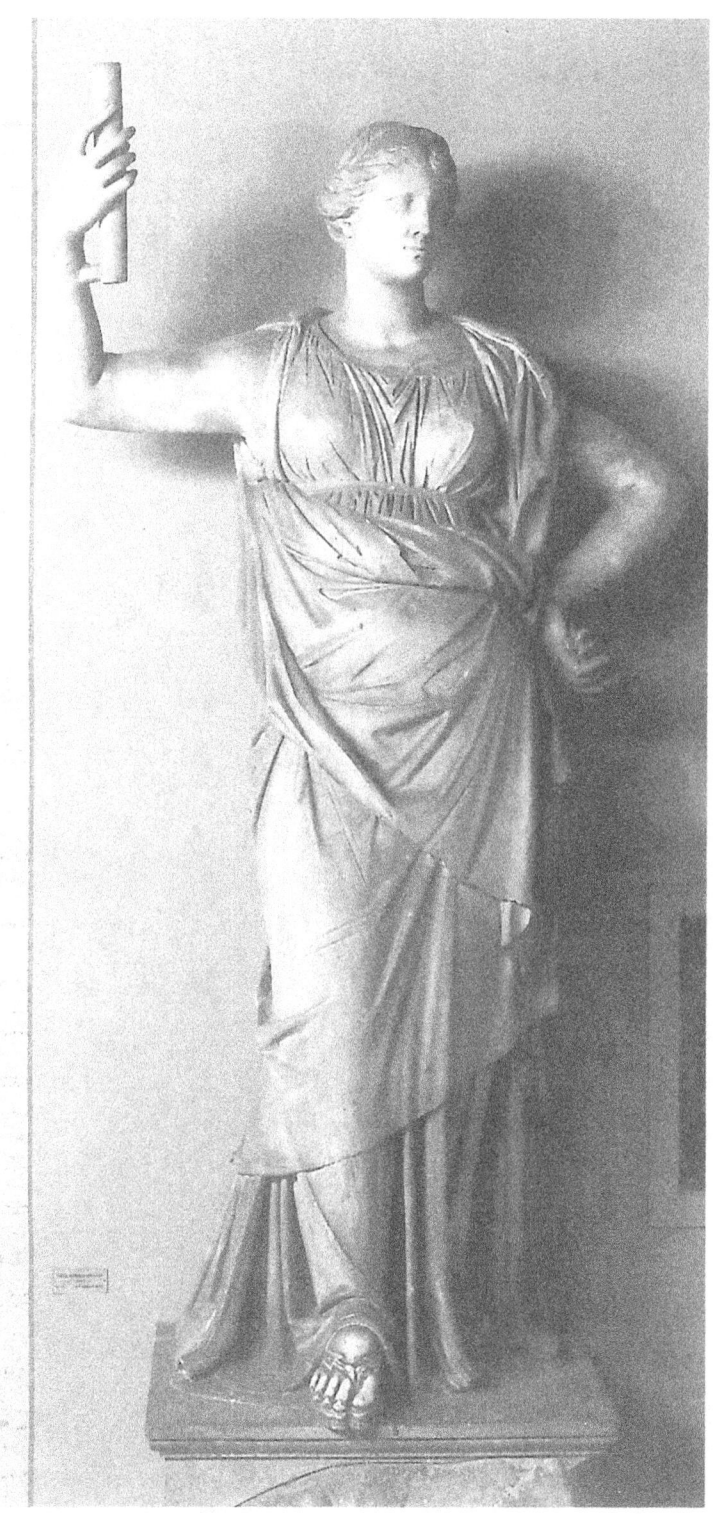

Plate 71. Rome, Capitoline Museum no. 731: so-called Juno Cesi.

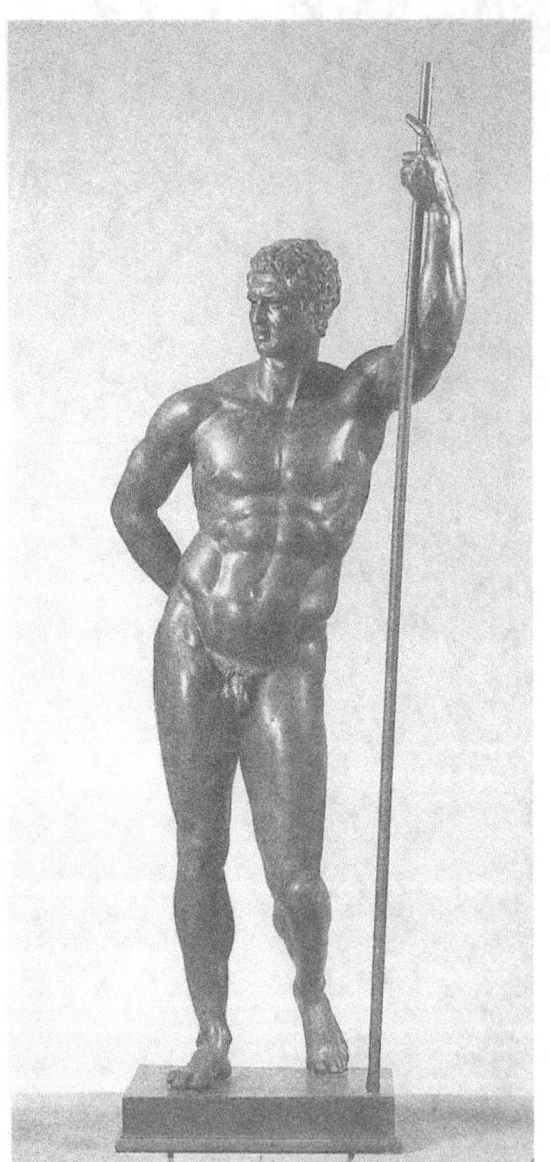
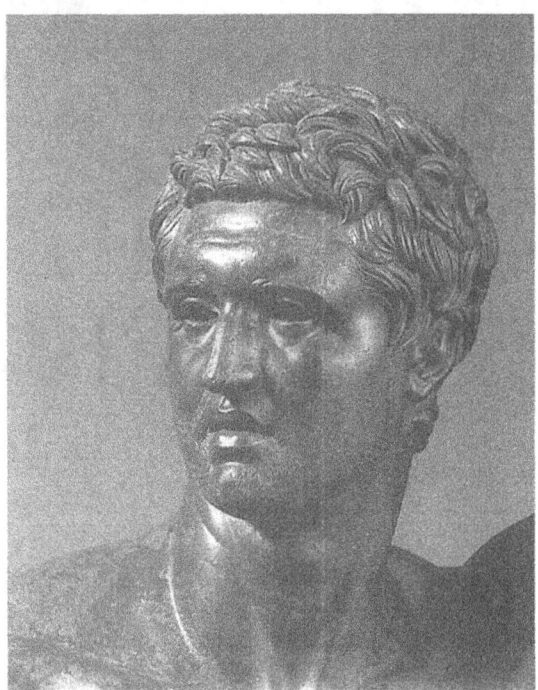

Plate 72a–b. Rome, National Museum (delle Terme) no. 1049: so-called Hellenistic Ruler—
(a) front, (b) three-quarter view of head.

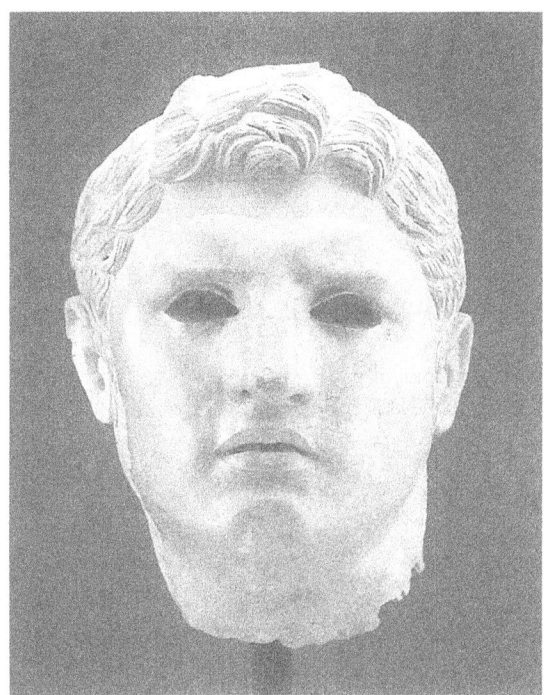
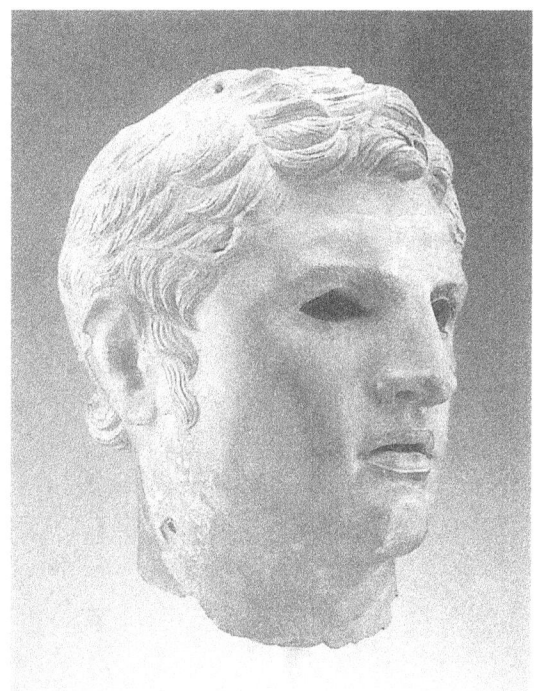

Plate 73a–b. Malibu, Calif., J. Paul Getty Museum no. 73.AB.8: bronze head of unknown man ("Sulla"?)—(a) front, (b) three-quarter right profile.

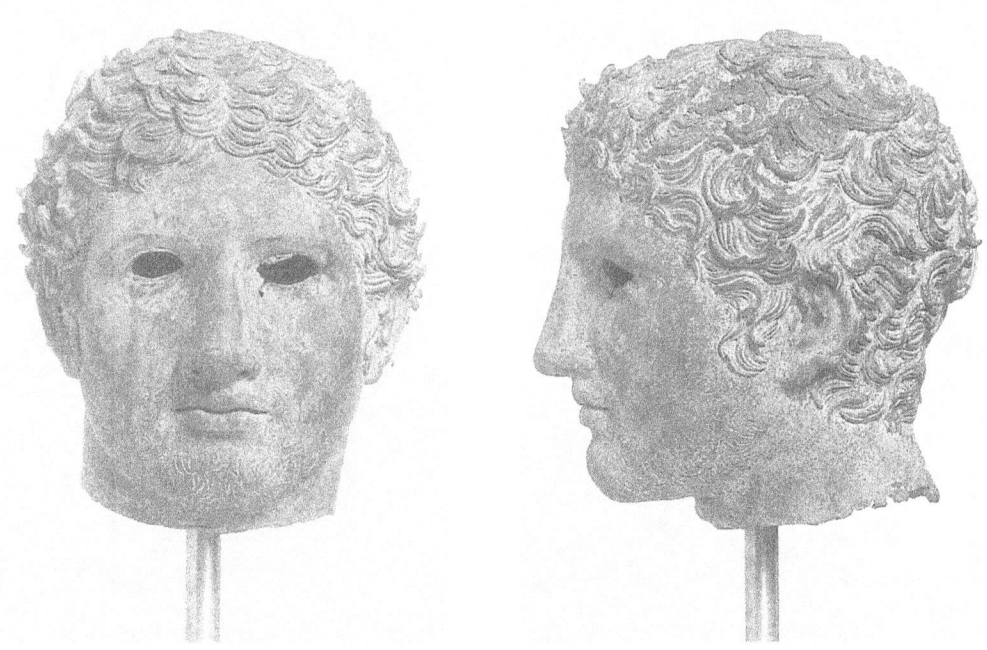

Plate 74a–b. Malibu, Calif., J. Paul Getty Museum no. 71.AB.458: bronze head of unknown youth—(a) front, (b) left profile. Note incised beard.

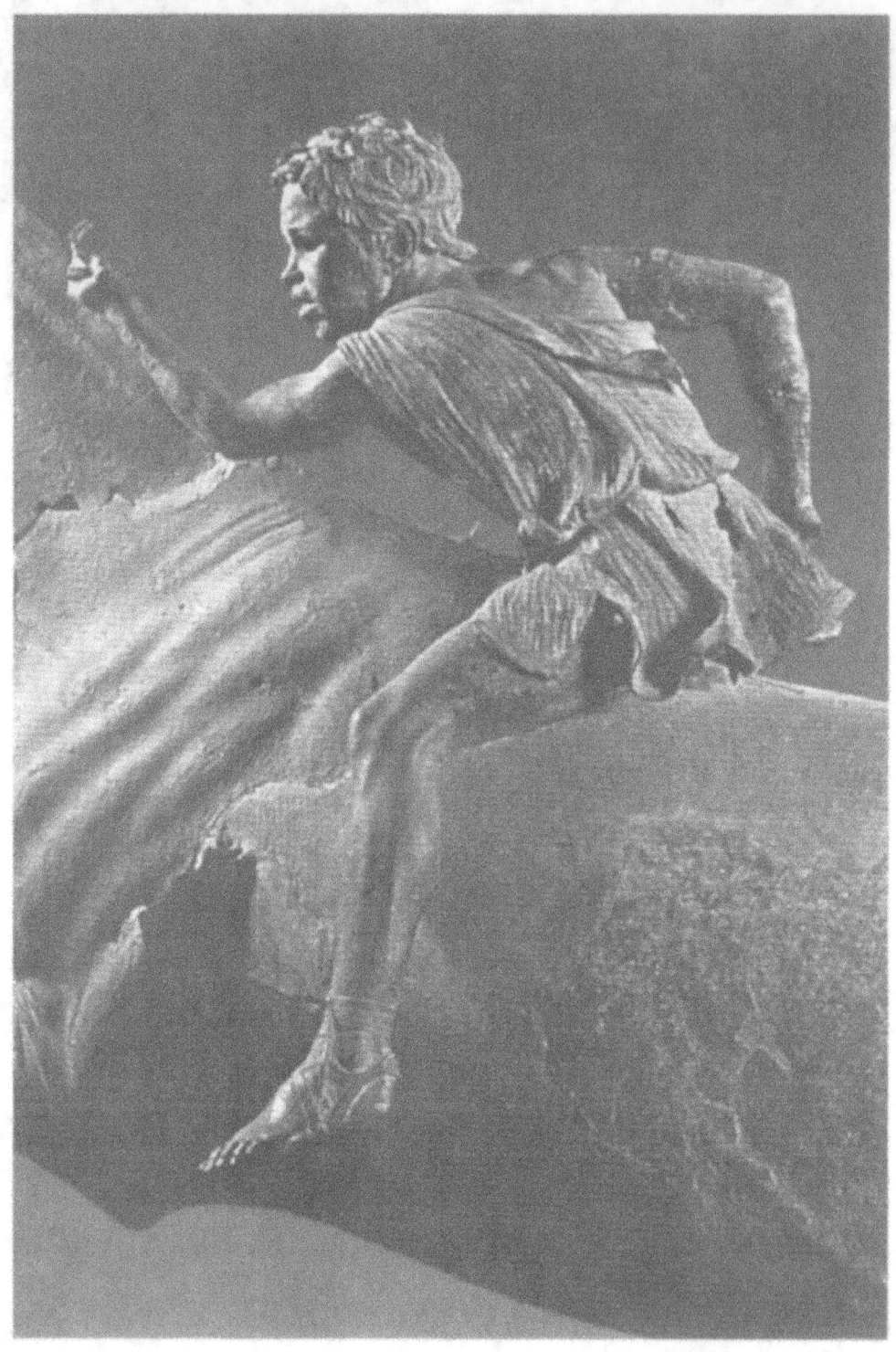

Plate 75. Athens, National Museum no. 15177: bronze Horse and Jockey from Cape Artemision, detail.

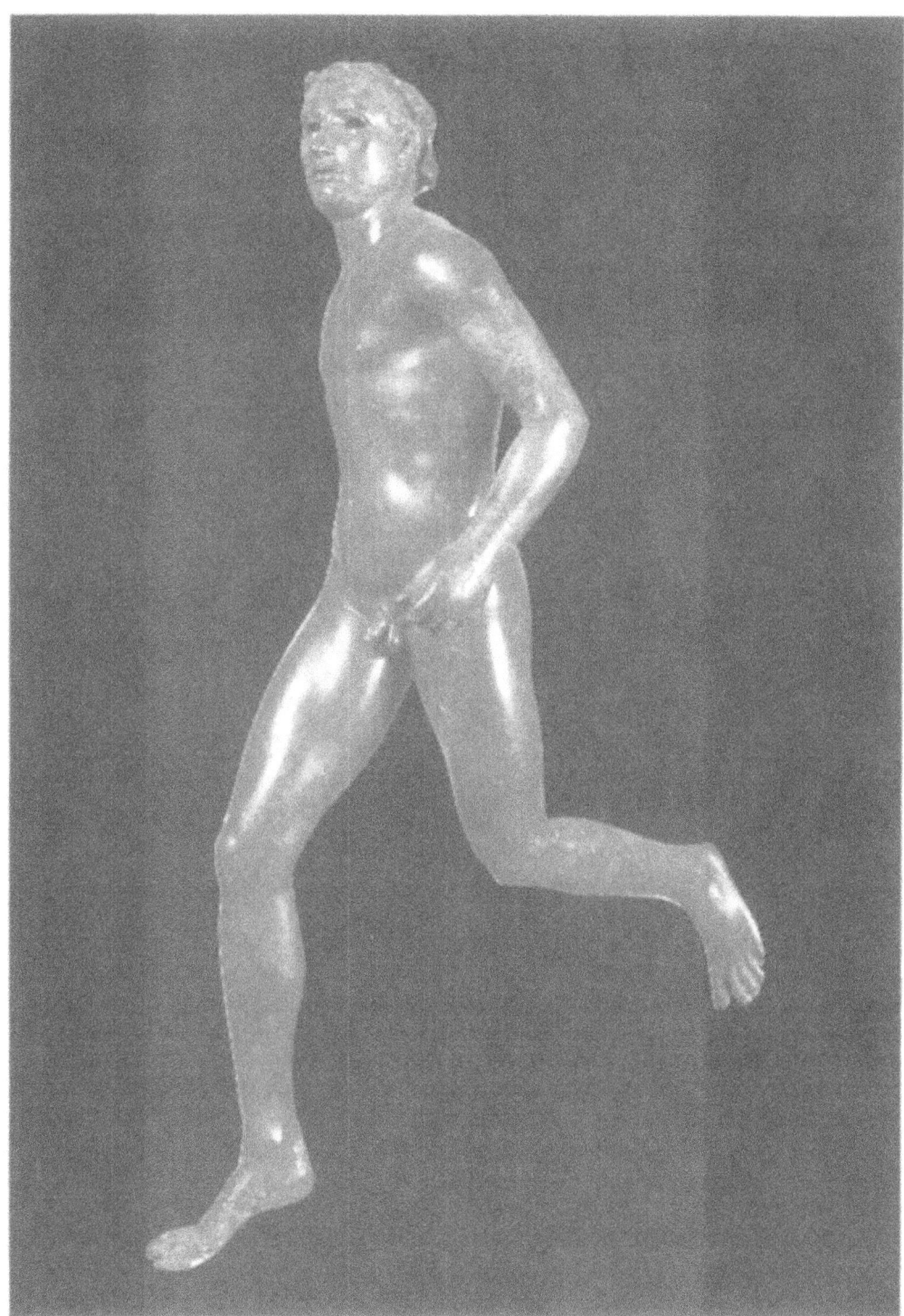

Plate 76. Izmir Museum no. 9363: bronze athlete from Kyme.

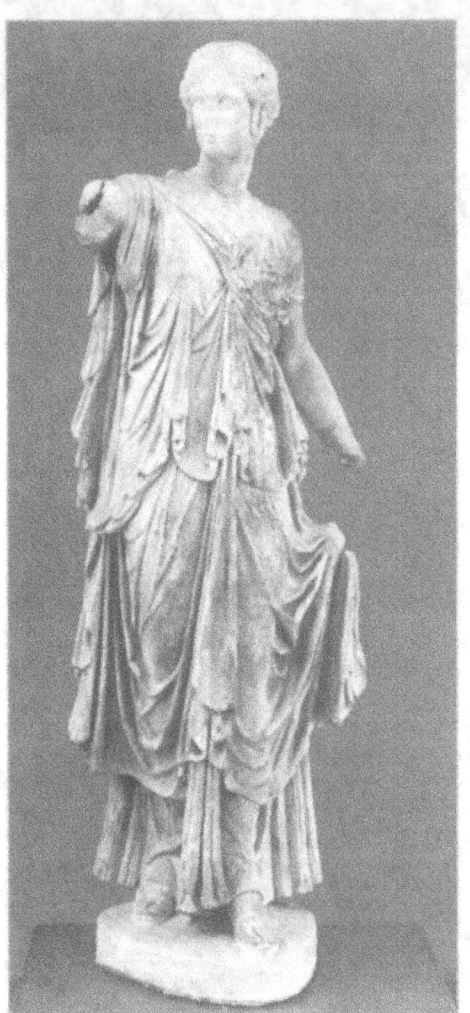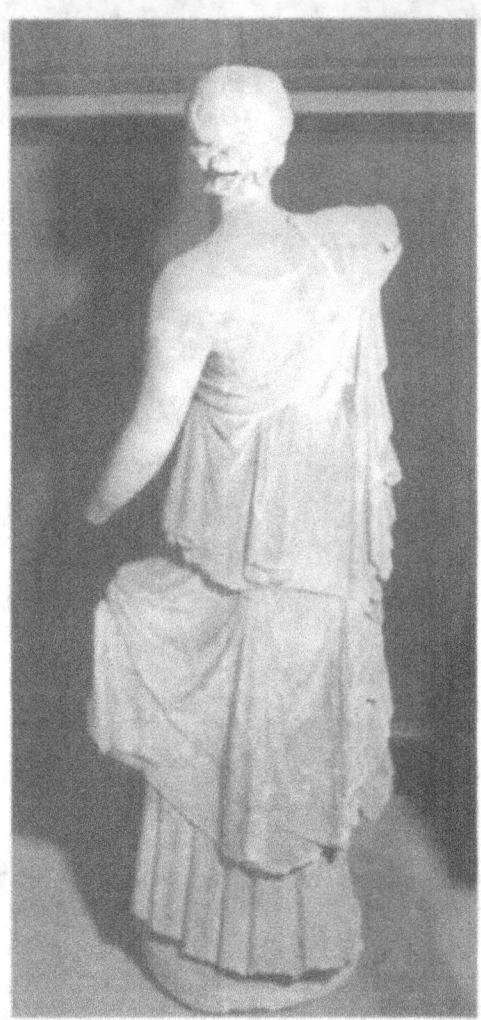

Plate 77a–b. Berlin Museum, no. PM 43: so-called Archaistic Dancer from Pergamon—(a) front, (b) back.

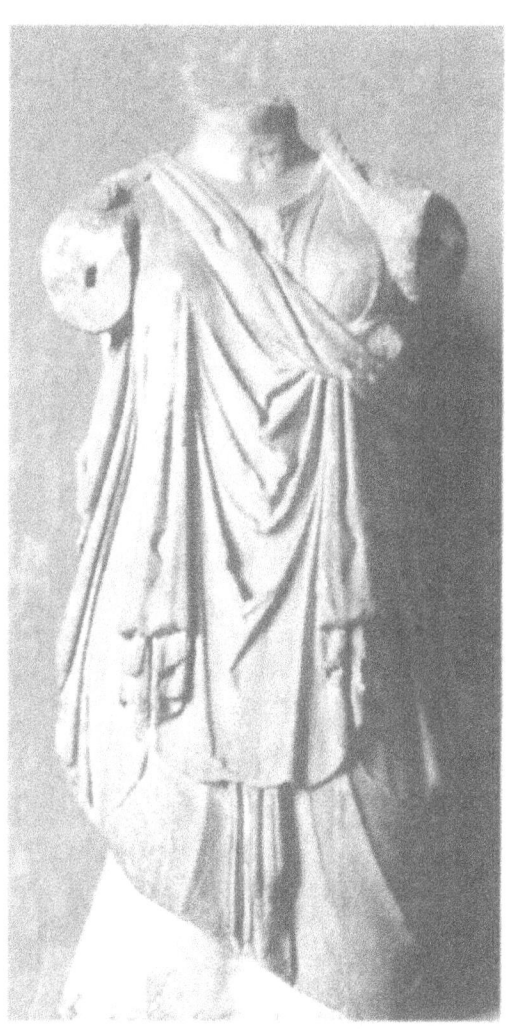

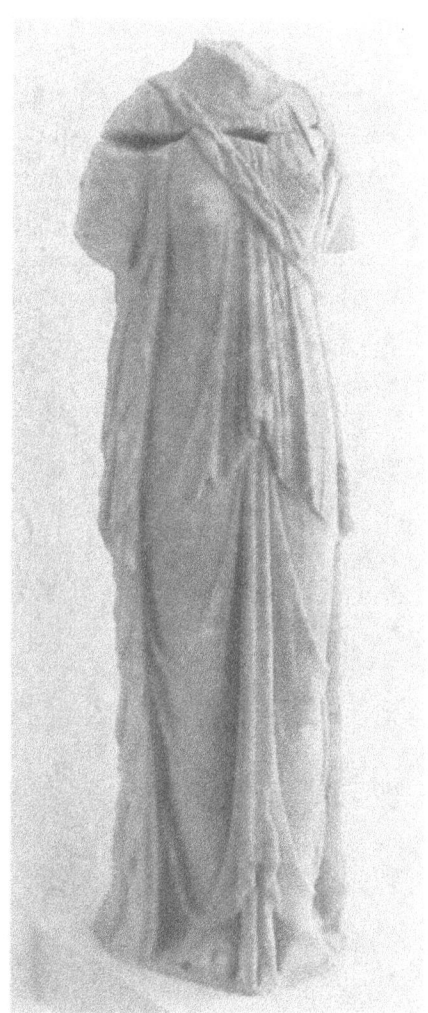

Plate 78. Istanbul, Archaeological Museum no. 481:
Archaistic torso from Pergamon (companion to
Dancer?)

Plate 79. Rhodes, Archaeological Museum
no. E 356: so-called Artemis-Hekate,
Archaistic.

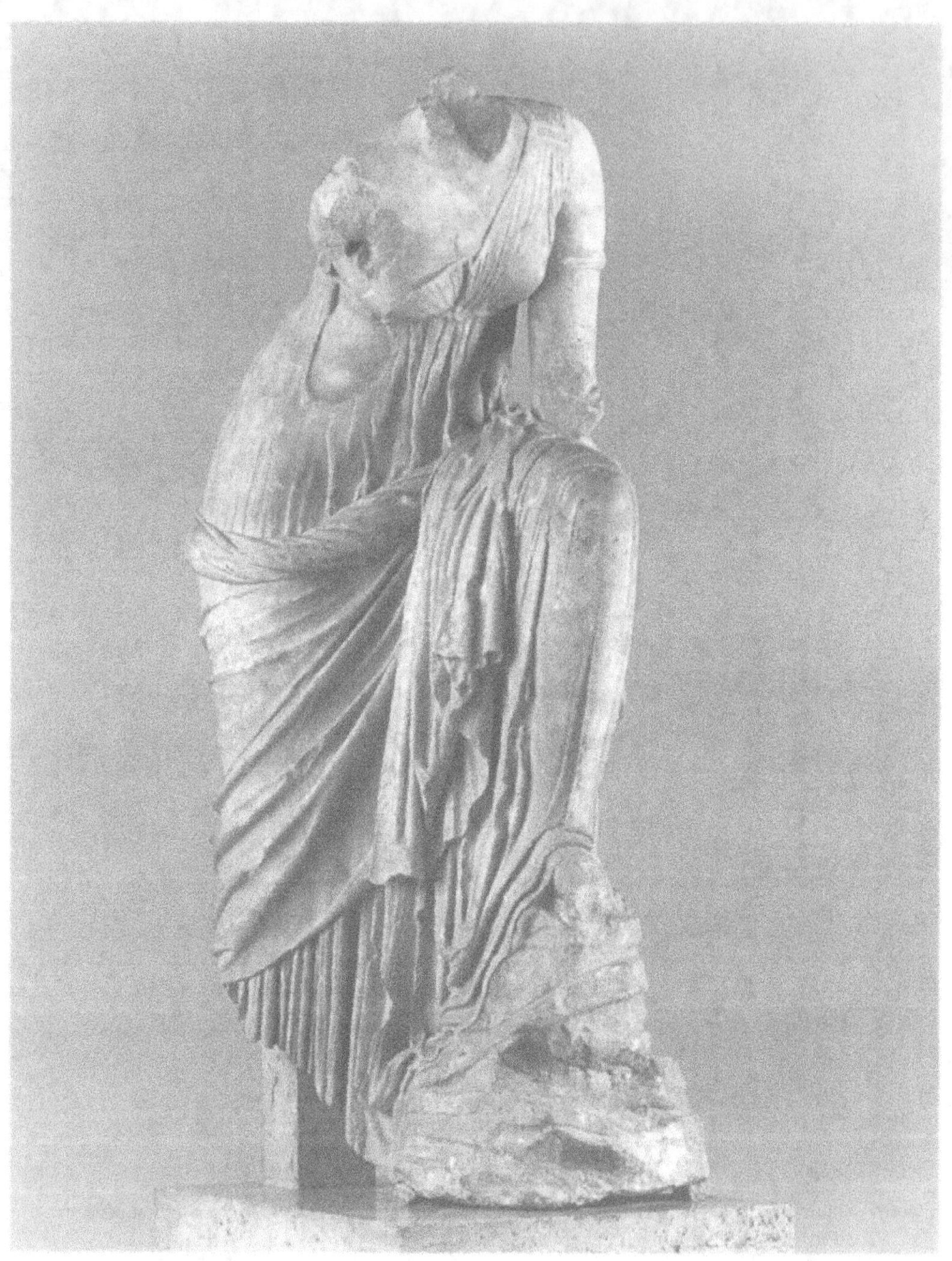

Plate 80a–b. Minneapolis, The Minneapolis Institute of Arts no. 56.12, John R. van Derlip Fund: so-called Tiber Muse, two views.

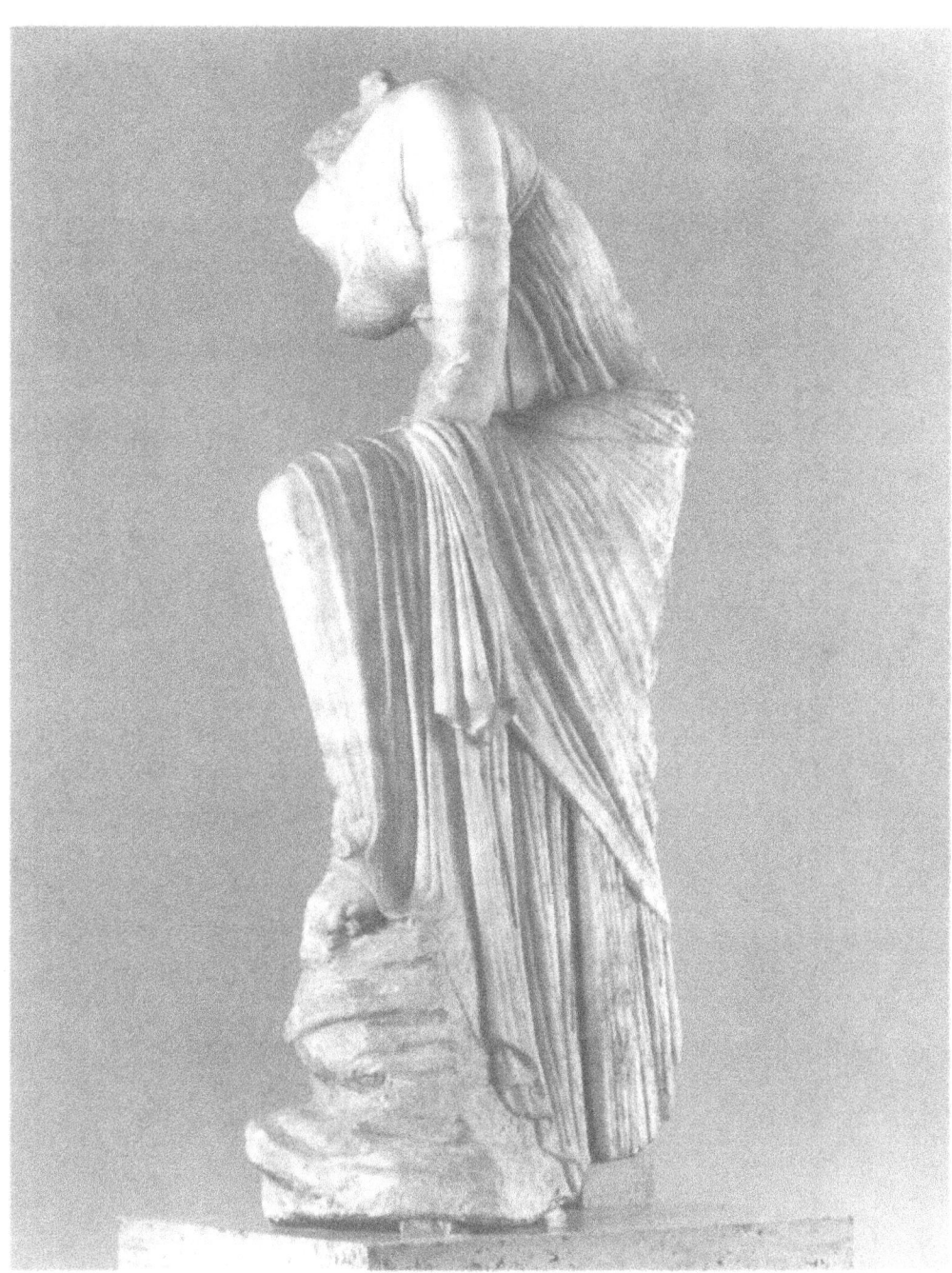

Plate 80b.

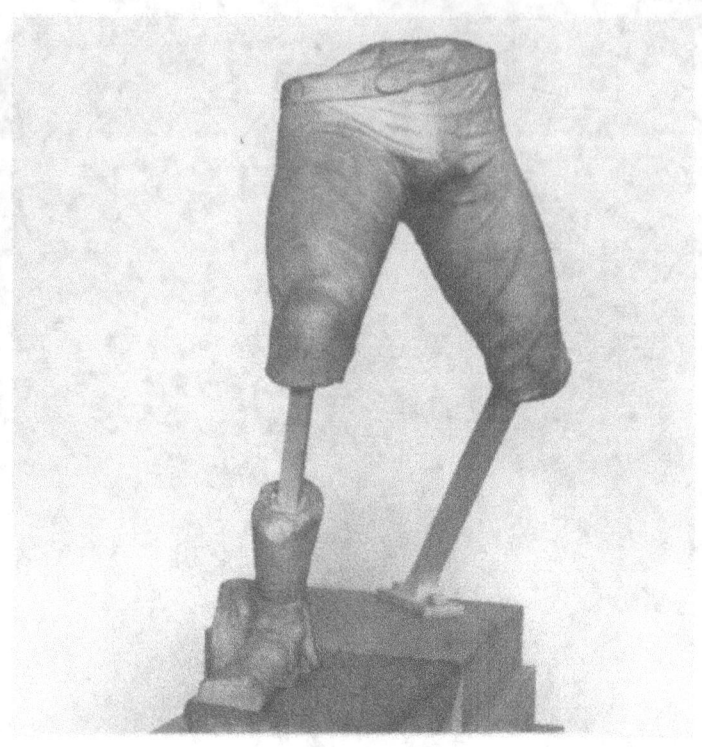

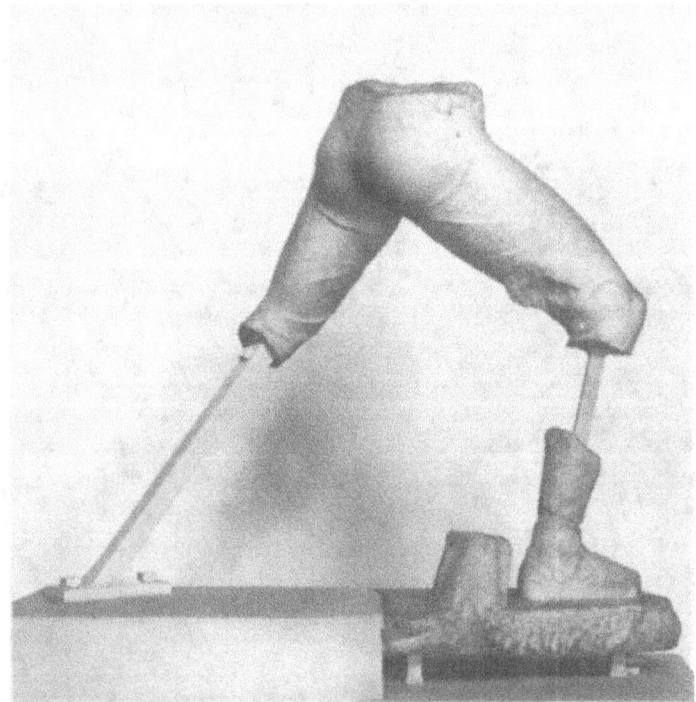

Plate 81a–b. New York, Metropolitan Museum of Art no. 08.258.48: Fighting Gaul from Cerveteri, two views.

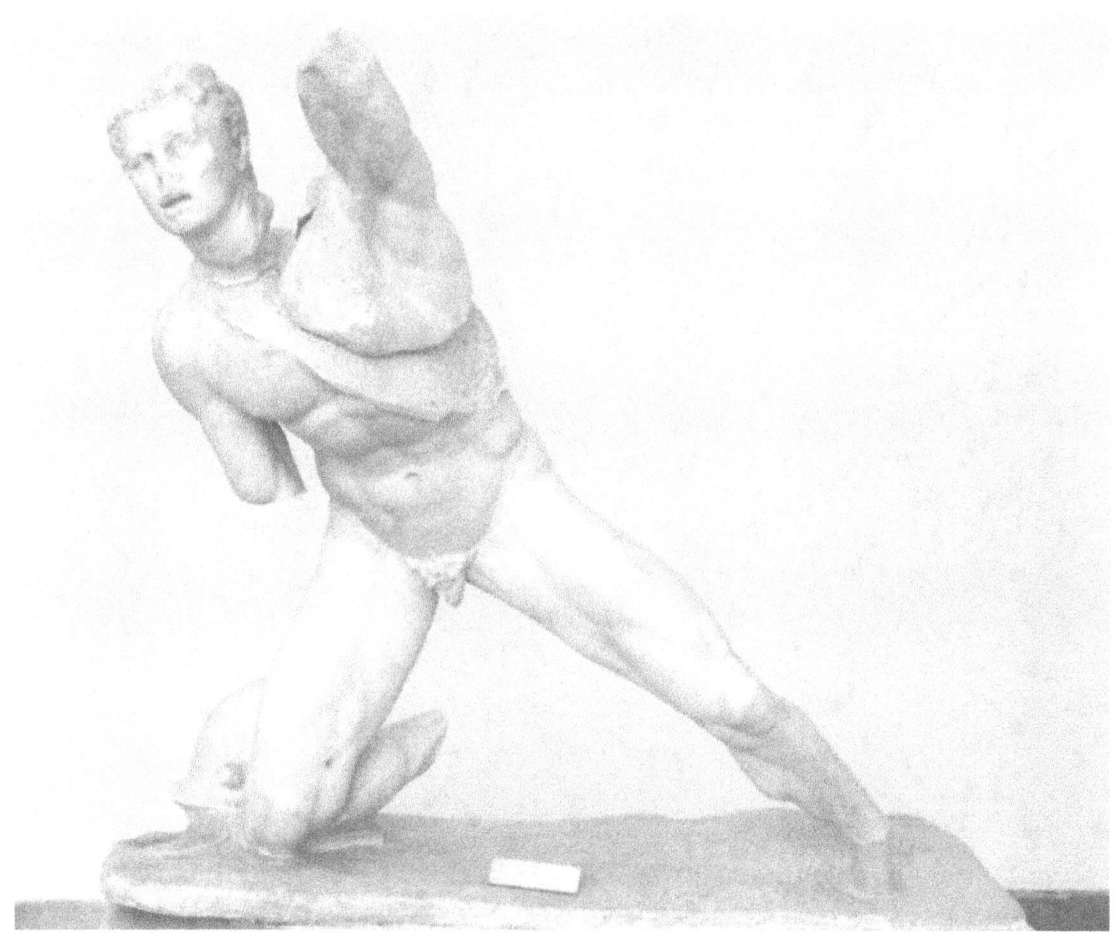

Plate 82. Athens, National Museum no. 247: Fighting Gaul from Delos, Agora of the Italians, niche J (cf. Ill. 24).

Wisconsin Studies in Classics

GENERAL EDITORS
Richard Daniel De Puma and Patricia A. Rosenmeyer

E. A. THOMPSON
Romans and Barbarians: The Decline of the Western Empire

JENNIFER TOLBERT ROBERTS
Accountability in Athenian Government

H. I. MARROU
A History of Education in Antiquity
Histoire de l'Education dans l'Antiquité, translated by GEORGE LAMB

ERIKA SIMON
Festivals of Attica: An Archaeological Commentary

G. MICHAEL WOLOCH
Roman Cities: Les villes romaines by Pierre Grimal,
translated and edited by G. Michael Woloch,
together with A Descriptive Catalogue of Roman Cities by G. Michael Woloch

WARREN G. MOON, editor
Ancient Greek Art and Iconography

KATHERINE DOHAN MORROW
Greek Footwear and the Dating of Sculpture

JOHN KEVIN NEWMAN
The Classical Epic Tradition

JEANNY VORYS CANBY, EDITH PORADA, BRUNILDE SISMONDO RIDGWAY,
and TAMARA STECH, editors
Ancient Anatolia: Aspects of Change and Cultural Development

ANN NORRIS MICHELINI
Euripides and the Tragic Tradition

WENDY J. RASCHKE, editor
The Archaeology of the Olympics: The Olympics and Other Festivals in Antiquity